MW00592382

International Business Acquisitions: Major Legal Issues and Due Diligence

Third Edition

WORLD LAW GROUP SERIES

Other titles in this series:

Karl-Eduard von der Heydt and Stanley Keller (eds), *International Securities Law Handbook*, 1995.
ISBN 1-85966-171-8

Michael Whalley and Thomas Heyman (eds), *International Business Acquisitions: Major Legal Issues and Due Diligence—1st Edition*, 1996.
ISBN 90-411-0893-9

Michael Whalley and Dr. Franz-Jörg Semler (eds), *International Business Acquisitions: Major Legal Issues and Due Diligence—2nd Edition*, 2000.
ISBN 90-411-9760-5

Mary K. Samsa and Kathleen S. Scheidt (eds), *International Employee Equity Plans: Participation Beyond Borders*, 2003.
ISBN 90-411-9919-5

Shelby R. Grubbs (ed), *International Civil Procedure*, 2003.
ISBN 90-411-2094-7

Jean-Luc Soulier and Marcus Best (eds), *International Securities Law Handbook—2nd Edition*, 2005.
ISBN 90-411-2291-5

Andrius R. Kontrimas and Mary K. Samsa (eds), *International Expatriate Employment Handbook*, 2006.
ISBN 90-411-2535-3

Michael Whalley and Dr. Franz-Jörg Semler (eds)
International Business Acquisitons: Major Legal Issues and Due Diligence-3rd Edition, 2007.
ISBN 97-890-4112-4838

International Business Acquisitions: Major Legal Issues and Due Diligence

Third Edition

Editors

Michael Whalley
Minter Ellison

Dr. Franz-Jörg Semler
CMS Hasche Sigle

Authored by
World Law Group
Member Firms

KLUWER LAW
INTERNATIONAL

Published by
Kluwer Law International
P.O. Box 316,
2400 AH Alphen aan den Rijn
The Netherlands
sales@kluwerlaw.com
http://www.kluwerlaw.com

Sold and distributed in the USA
and Canada by
Aspen Publishers, Inc.
7201 Mc Kinney Circle
Frederick, MD 21704
United States of America

Sold and distributed in all other countries by:
Turpin Distribution Services Ltd.
Stratton Business Park
Pegasus Drive, Biggleswade
Bedfordshire SG18 8TQ
United Kingdom

ISBN 97-890-4112-4838

© World Law Group 1996, 2007
First published in 1996
Third edition 2007

British Library Cataloguing in Publication Data

A catalogue record for this book is available from the British Library

Typeset in 10/12 pt Bembo by EXPO Holdings, Malaysia
Printed and bound in Great Britain by Antony Rowe Ltd., Chippenham, Wiltshire

CONTENTS

FOREWORD

Purpose

This third edition of *International Business Acquisitions* (the Handbook) is intended as an easily-accessed desk reference for lawyers, business executives and others concerned with the acquisition of the securities or business assets of a company located outside their own national jurisdiction. It is also directly relevant to those representing the sellers in such transactions, as they must anticipate and prepare for the foreign buyer's requirements and concerns.

The number and diversity of international acquisition transactions continues to increase, reflecting the need for every successful company to develop or acquire the resources to compete on an international scale. Many local business enterprises have discovered, often to their surprise and detriment, that this need to acquire or be acquired by foreign companies is no longer limited to large multinational groups. The World Trade Organisation, regional and bilateral trade agreements, instant world-wide communication, internationalisation of management, the reduction of language barriers and other factors have created a worldwide marketplace, where companies will compete primarily on the basis of economic efficiency. International acquisitions, to access foreign markets, to provide foreign production or marketing capacity, to obtain regulatory approvals, to acquire complementary product or service lines or simply to spread product, service or market risk and to reduce costs, have become the norm.

In addition, there has been an explosion in venture capital and private equity driven acquisitions, their aim generally being to identify and exploit underperforming assets or businesses (at the same time giving an outlet to companies wishing to divest themselves of such assets and businesses which are no longer central to their strategies, generally being described as 'non-core'). The high gearing (debt finance) of these acquisitions puts enormous pressure on management and investors to make assets and businesses perform quickly so as to realize value for investors through a subsequent trade sale or IPO (initial public offer), itself leading to further acquisition activity. This constant striving to achieve the most efficient return on assets and investments in business could be described as the virtuous circle of mergers and acquisitions activity.

Regrettably or fortunately, depending upon one's perspective, the legal practices, requirements and pitfalls relevant to cross-border transactions, despite significant harmonisation within the EU, continue to be aggressively and uniquely national in character. This reflects not only historical differences in the development of national systems, but also differences in cultural priorities and business practices which inevitably affect the negotiation, documentation and implementation of an international acquisition transaction. By way of example, it is interesting to note that substantial acquisition transactions in Italy are often completed with little or no written documentation—a situation beyond the comprehension of most lawyers from common law jurisdictions. Nevertheless, the influx of US and English law firms into most European jurisdictions has introduced increasingly common standards and documentation, and it could be argued that we are now seeing a much more global, and therefore consistent, approach in not only the process and procedures used to effect an acquisition in many different jurisdictions, but also in the documentation being used.

The need for a clear understanding of the major legal issues and careful, informed due diligence are even more important in international acquisitions than in domestic transactions, where both parties have a relatively good understanding of the legal environment. Consequently, legal practitioners and many others involved in cross-border acquisitions need a user-friendly source of information covering the most important jurisdictions. This Handbook is intended to meet this need.

Concept to Publication

This Handbook is the result of a World Law Group project which was conceived and implemented by the WLG International Corporate Transactions Practice Group. Special recognition must be given to those who recognized the value of this Handbook, shaped the content and assured its consistent high quality.

Initial encouragement and guidance came from Kingston Berlew, the first President of the World Law Group and a former Chairman of the International Corporate Transactions Practice Group.

Thomas Heymann, then a partner of the firm now known as Taylor Wessing (Germany), and Michael Whalley of the Australian firm Minter Ellison served as both authors and editors for the first edition, writing, in large part, both the introductory chapter and the due diligence chapter, on which the individual country annotations are based. They and Franz-Jörg Semler, Thomas Heymann's successor as editor for both the second and third editions, were also responsible for legal editing of the country annotations and the country-by-country analysis of major legal issues which appears in Chapter 2. Their respective backgrounds in civil and common law were instrumental in making it possible for the Handbook to cover international business acquisitions without having entirely separate sections for common law and civil law jurisdictions.

Leigh Brown of Minter Ellison was the first to recognize the need to cover major legal issues separately from due diligence, and was instrumental in producing the initial Australian version of the major legal issues section which, together with the German version, served as a model for other country contributions.

Individual international business lawyers in each of the member firms contributed to the preparation of the country-by-country analysis of major legal issues and to the refining and country annotations of the due diligence section. The time and effort required to complete this work, despite competing business and family demands, is recognized and greatly appreciated.

The World Law Group

The World Law Group decided to carry out this ambitious but practical project primarily because the lawyers involved believed that the Handbook would be a valuable tool for many of our own firms, enabling them to respond more effectively to client needs and to interact more easily with the other member firms. Often, in the international business acquisitions context, the need for speed and responsiveness is indispensable and the Handbook should greatly facilitate that capability. At the same time we, and our publisher Kluwer Law International, concluded that the Handbook would also be valuable to clients and others involved in cross-border acquisitions.

Since this Handbook is the result of a co-operative effort by most of the WLG member firms, a brief description of the Group is in order. Member firms are independent, and have not 'merged' or 'combined' by joining the WLG and each firm is solely responsible for its own work. There are currently 48 member firms with more than 10,000 lawyers in 37 countries and more than 100 international business centres.

The primary purpose of the World Law Group is to develop, maintain and co-ordinate the capabilities and resources required to provide high-quality, efficient legal services to international clients located throughout the world. We believe that bringing together in one group the legal knowledge, experience, resources and contacts of independent firms which represent the best in their communities and countries is the best way to accomplish this objective. The WLG is non-exclusive, which means that, while members are encouraged to refer matters to, and consult with, other WLG members, there is no policy that referrals go only to the WLG member in a given jurisdiction, nor are there any referral fees.

Practice Groups have been established in several areas including:

- Antitrust and Competition

- Banking and Finance

- Corporate Governance

- Corporate Restructuring and Bankruptcy

- Employee Benefits

- International Corporate Transactions

- International Taxation

- Internet and Intellectual Property

- Labour and Employment

- Litigation, Arbitration and Dispute Resolution

- Privacy Matters

These Practice Groups bring together lawyers with similar interests and clientele to share information and ideas, to work on projects such as this Handbook and to establish effective working relationships which are necessary for providing quality international legal services to our respective clients.

Legal counsel in the relevant jurisdiction(s) should be consulted both for the updating and application of applicable laws and regulations to specific matters.

Michael Whalley, WLG Handbook Series Editor

EDITORS' PREFACE TO
THE FIRST EDITION

The process of compiling and editing a handbook which brings together contributions from a number of jurisdictions throughout the world inevitably leaves the editors with some valuable insights and impressions. The common format of each of the country contributions, and the way in which each contributor has been forced, often some-what reluctantly, to summarize what are often complex legal issues, makes comparison easier.

At the same time, the need for simplicity and a common format has its dangers. Legal issues do not always fall happily into convenient pigeon holes and some issues have a habit of emerging in a number of different contexts. The rights of creditors and employees are obvious examples.

The editors have been struck by the surprising uniformity in the principles which underpin business laws throughout the world. Laws which on first glance appear very different often turn out to be very similar, differences only arising from the different use of language or expression. For example, a number of civil law jurisdictions use the term 'limited liability company' only in the context of a family or private company. This can sometimes leave the reader with the impression that a public company does not have limited liability but this is, clearly, not the case.

There have been inevitable difficulties in trying to render each contribution into a common grammatical style. The written and spoken English of each of the handbook's contributors is, without exception, excellent, but rules of grammatical construction differ enormously throughout the world and this is often reflected in the contributions. The editors hope that their attempts to give the text a common grammatical flow have not robbed each contribution completely of the style of its own author.

Readers will obviously draw their own conclusions from comparing the treatment of different issues by different jurisdictions. However, the editors have noted some interesting similarities or differences, some of which include:

- a number of civil codes provide that a seller of a business may not compete with the buyer after the sale, but no such restriction is generally imposed in common law jurisdictions;

- a purchaser of a business as a going concern (described in France, for example, as a *fonds de commerce*) can, in some jurisdictions, also inherit business liabilities even though these are not specifically dealt with in the agreement;

- the laws of different trading blocks are having an increasing influence over national laws: while other trading blocks do not have the same law-making powers as those enjoyed by the EU, the influence of international trade agreements over domestic business laws should not be underestimated;

- there has been almost universal abolition of exchange controls in the jurisdictions covered, which also largely welcome foreign investment (although still with a high level of government monitoring and, in some cases, interference, particularly in the case of 'sensitive' industries);

- civil jurisdictions appear to place an obligation on the parties to negotiate in good faith, but this is rare in common law jurisdictions;

- most jurisdictions seem to recognize and enforce non-competition covenants by both sellers and employees, provided they are reasonable;

- there is remarkable consistency in the principles which underlie competition laws throughout the world; and

- there is also surprising consistency in the issues which are relevant to a choice between buying shares or assets, the only notable exception being the issue as to whether the relevant jurisdiction requires the buyer of business assets to bear full responsibility for all of the employees of the business.

More extensive analysis may have to await a future edition. The catalyst for a new edition will, of course, be the response of readers, and the extent to which this handbook becomes a useful and continuing reference work.

Michael Whalley   *Thomas Heymann*
London   *Frankfurt am Main*

January 1996

EDITORS' PREFACE TO THE THIRD EDITION

Ten years after the publication of the successful first edition of the International Business Acquisitions Handbook, and six years after the second edition was published, the demand for an easily accessible source of information on cross-border acquisitions appears stronger than ever. We have therefore been persuaded to produce a third edition.

Like the second edition, the third benefits from both updating and substantial expansion of content. We are pleased to welcome additional contributors from China, Finland, Israel, Luxembourg, Austria and Argentina, making a total of 35 jurisdictions covered by this handbook.

The passage of time has not helped to simplify or harmonize the national legislation of different countries, and the need for this handbook is probably greater than ever.

We have noticed some significant developments impacting upon cross-border acquisitions in a number of jurisdictions. Some of note include:

- the increasing impact of European Union regulations and directives on corporate transactions, with the arrival particularly of the Prospectus, Takeovers and Transparency Directives;

- the introduction of tax grouping arrangements in Australia, which has significant implications for the de-accessioning of a company from a group as a result of a sale of that company out of the group;

- the liberalisation of exchange controls in Malaysia, particularly for the repatriation of profits and investment funds;

- in the Philippines, the introduction of legislation permitting foreign ownership of domestic banks;

- substantial changes to the companies laws in Japan which are intended to simplify the management of companies and to expedite their formation;

- new mergers and acquisitions legislation in Taiwan, and a new mergers act which has encouraged greater merger activity between Taiwanese companies;

- Taiwan has also modernized its pension laws, with employers now making a 6 per cent compulsory contribution to a defined contribution (money purchase) plan for each employee.

The South African chapter has also been expanded to include a description of the operation of the black empowment regime in that country.

We are also seeing increasing sophistication and often also some harmonisation in competition (anti-trust) laws, with new or revised laws being introduced in many jurisdictions, including Singapore, Ireland and the United Kingdom. 'Harmonisation' is occurring as worldwide competition laws seem increasingly to have as their basis the same fundamental aims, namely the prevention of:

- the abuse of a dominant position;
- the substantial lessening of competition;
- the restriction of competition through concerted practices or agreements.

Our chapter on due diligence has been revised and expanded, with the commentary recognising that due diligence now has many and varied purposes, and a different target audience for each. The spectacular growth of private equity investment vehicles as major players in the international mergers and acquisitions space is an example. Advisers now need to pay as much attention to their audience's aspirations and concerns as to the target itself.

This edition has been updated by each of our contributors to reflect the law in force in their respective jurisdictions as at 1 December 2006. As always, this Handbook is intended only as a guide, and proper legal advice should always be sought when any actual transaction is contemplated.

Michael Whalley   *Franz-Jörg Semler*
London   *Stuttgart*

December 2006

LIST OF CONTRIBUTIORS

ARGENTINA

Carlos Alfaro
Sebastian Rodrigo
Alfaro-Abogados
Av. del Libertador 498
(C1001ABR) Buenos Aires
Argentina
Telephone: (54-11)4393-3003
Fax: (54-11) 4393-3001
http://www.alfaro.law
Email: cealfaro@alfarolaw.com
Email: srodrigo@alfarolaw.com

AUSTRALIA

Michael Whalley
Minter Ellison
10 Dominion Street
London EC2M 2EE
United Kingdom
Telephone: +44 20 7448 4800
Fax: +44 20 7448 4848
http://www.minterellison.com
Email:
michael.whalley@minterellison.com

AUSTRIA

Peter Huber, LL.M.
CMS Reich-Rohrwig Hainz
Rechtsanwälte GmbH
Ebendorferstraße 3
A-1010 Vienna
Austria
Telephone: +43 (1)40443-165
Fax: +43 (1)40443-165
http://www.cms-rhh.com
Email: peter.huber@cms-rhh.com

BELGIUM

Cedric Guyot
CMS DeBacker
Ch. de la Hulpe 178
B-1170 Brussels
Belgium
Telephone: +32 2 743 69 64
Fax: +32 2 743 69 01
http://www.cms-db.com
Email: cedric.guyot@cms-db.com

BRAZIL

Renato Berger
Moira Huggard-Caine
Tozzini, Freire Advogados
R. Borges Lagoa 1328
04038-904 São Paulo SP
Brazil
Telephone: +55 11 5086-5000
Fax: +55 11 5086-5555
http://www.tozzinifreire.com.br
Email: rberger@tozzinifreire.com.br
Email:
mhuggardcaine@tozzinifreire.com.br

CANADA

Robert Vineberg
Davies Ward Phillips & Vineberg LLP
1501 McGill College Avenue
26th Floor
Montreal
Canada
H3A3N9
Telephone: +514 841 6444
Fax: +514 841 6499
http://www.dwpv.com
Email: rvineberg@dwpv.com

CHINA

Susan Ning
King & Wood
40th Floor
Office Tower A
Beijing Fortune Plaza 7
Dongsanhuan Zhonglu
Chaoyang District
Beijing 100022
Telephone: +86 10 58 78 55 88
Fax: +86 10 58 78 55 99
http://www.kingandwood.com
Email: nsusan@kingandwood.com

DENMARK

Morten Lau Smith, LL.M.
Jens Christian Hesse Rasmussen
Bech-Bruun
Langelinie Allé 35
DK-2100 Copenhage
Denmark
Telephone: +45 - 72 27 00 00
Fax: +45 - 72 27 00 27
http://www.bechbruun.com
Email: mls@bechbruun.com
Email: icr@bech-bruun.com

ENGLAND & WALES

Kuljit Ghata-Aura
Eversheds LLP
Senator House
85 Queen Victoria Street
London EC4V 4JL
United Kingdom
Telephone: +44 20 7497 9797
Fax: +44 20 7919 4919
http://www.eversheds.com
Email:
kuljitghata-aura@eversheds.com

EUROPEAN UNION – SOCIETAS EUROPAEA

Dr. Dirk Jannott
CMS Hasche Sigle
Bankstrasse 1
40476 Duesseldorf
Germany
Telephone: +49 - (0)211 4934-405
Fax: +49 - (0)211 4934-121
http://www.cms-hs.com
Email: dirk.jannott@cms-hs.com

EU – EUROPEAN MERGER CONTROL

Martijn van de Hel
CMS Derks Star Busmann
Louizalaan 20
B-1050 Brussels
Belgium
Telephone: +32 - (0)2 6262 217
Fax: +32 - (0)2 6262 309
http://www.cms-dsb.com
Email:
martijn.vandehel@cms-dsb.com

FINLAND

Johan Åkermarck
Castrén & Snellman Attorneys Ltd.
Erottajankatu 5 A
Fl-00131 Helsinki
Finland
Telephone: +358 (0)207 765 303
Fax: +358 (0)207 765 303
http://www.castren.fi
Email: johan.akermarck@castren.fi

FRANCE

Jean-Luc Soulier
Guillaume Pierson
Soulier
2, avenue Hoche
75008 Paris
France
Telephone: +33 - (0)1 40 54 29 29
Fax: +33 - (0)1 40 54 29 20
Visio: +33 - (0)1 43 18 00 75
http://www.soulier-avocats.com
Email: jl.soulier@soulier-avocats.com
Email: g.pierson@soulier-avocats.com

GERMANY

Dr. Franz-Joerg Semler
CMS Hasche Sigle
Schoettlestrasse 8
70597 Stuttgart
Germany
Telephone: +49 - (0)711 9764-333
Fax: +49 - (0)711 9764-931
http://www.cms-hs.com
Email:
franz-joerg.semler@cms-hs.com

HONG KONG

Tim Drew
Robert Wang Solicitors
Suite 2102
21st Floor
Nine Queen's Road
Central
Hong Kong
Telephone: +852 2843 7483
Fax: +852 2845 1222
http://www.robertwang.com
Email: timdrew@robertwang.com

INDIA

Satwinder Singh
Vaish Associates
Apts. 5-7
2nd Floor
10, Hailey Road
New Delhi 110001
India
Telephone: +91 11 42 49 2525
Fax: + 91 11 52 49 2600
Email: satwinder@vaishlaw.com

IRELAND

Suzanne McNulty
Mason Hayes+Curran Solicitors
6 Fitzwilliam Square
Dublin 2
Ireland
Telephone: +353 1 614 5041
Fax: +353 1 614 5001
http://www.mhc.ie
Email: smcnulty@mhc.ie

ISRAEL

Janet Levy-Pahima
Nick Cannon
Herzog, Fox & Neeman
Asia House
4 Weizmann Street
Tel Aviv 64239
Israel
Telephone: +972 3 692 2020
Fax: + 972 3 696 6464
http://www.hfn.co.il
Email: pahima@hfn.co.il
Email: cannon@hfn.co.il

ITALY

Francesco Gianni
Gianni, Origoni, Grippo & Partners
20, Via delle Quattro Fontane
00184 Rome
Italy
Telephone: +39 06 478 751
Fax: +39 06 487 1101
http://www.gop.it
Email: fgianni@gop.it

JAPAN

Tsuneo Sato
City-Yuwa Partners
Marunouchi Mitsui Building
2-2-2 Marunouchi
Chiyoda-ku
Tokyo
100-0005
Japan
Telephone: +03-6212-5502
Fax: +03-6212-5700
http://www.city-yuwa.com
Email: tsuneo.sato@city-yuwa.com

KOREA

Yong Suk Oh, Esq.
Keun Byung Lee, Esq.
Ri Bong Han, Esq.
Bae, Kim & Lee
Hankook Tire Building
647-15 Yoksam-dong
Kangnam-gu
Seoul 135-723
Korea
Telephone: +822-3404-0000
Fax: +822-3404-0001
http://www.BKL.co.kr
Email: yso@BKL.co.kr
Email: kbl@BKL.co.kr
Email: rbh@BKL.co.kr

LUXEMBOURG

Guy Harles
Eric Fort
Katia Gauzès
Arendt & Medernach
14, rue Erasme
B.P. 39
L-2010 Luxembourg
Telephone: +352 – (0)40 78 78 1
Fax: +352 – (0)40 78 04
http://www.arendt-medernach.com
Email:
guy.harles@arendt-medernach.com
Email:
eric.fort@arendt-medernach.com
Email:
katia.gauzes@arendt-medernach.com

MALAYSIA
Chen Lee Won
Shearn Delamore & Co.
7th Floor
Wisma Hamzah-Kwong Hing
No 1 Leboh Ampang
50100 Kuala Lumpur
Malaysia
Telephone: +603 20762835
Fax: +603 20785625
http://www.shearndelamore.com
Email: leewon@shearndelamore.com

MEXICO

Jorge León-Orantes B.
Santamarina y Steta, S.C.
Campos Eliseos 345, 2 and 3 floors
Col. Chapultepec Polanco
11560 México, D.F.
Telephone: +52 55 – 5279 5452
Fax: +52 55 – 5280 7614
http://www.s-s.com.mx
Email: jleon@s-s.com.mx

NETHERLANDS

Christian Delgado
Martika M. Jonk
CMS Derks Star Busmann
Mondrianantoren
Amstelplein 8 A
1090 GS Amsterdam
The Netherlands
Telephone: +31 20 3016 301
Fax: +31 20 3016 335
http://www.cms-dsb.com
Email:
christian.delgado@cms-dsb.com
Email: martika.jonk@cms-dsb.com

NORWAY

Thomas Aanmoen
Advokatfirmaet Schjødt DA
Dronning Maudsgt. 11
PO BOX 2444 Solli
NO-0201 Oslo
Norway
Telephone: +47 - 22 01 88 00
Fax: +47-22 83 17 12
http://www.schjodt.no
Email: thomas.aanmoen@schjodt.no

PERU

José Antonio Payet
Payet Rey Cauvi
Av. Victor Andrés Belaúnde 147
Centro Empresarial Real
Torre Real 3, Piso 12
San Isidro
Lima 27, Perú
Telephone: +511 -612-3202
Fax: +511 -222-1573
http://www.prc.com.pe
Email: jap@prc.com.pe

PHILIPPINES

Angelito C. Imperio
Jose Maria G. Hofileña
SyCip Salazar Hernandez & Gatmaitan
105 Paseo de Roxas
1226 Makati, Metro Manila
P.O. Box 4223
CPO 1002 Manila
Republic of the Philippines
Telephone: +632 817 9811
Fax: +632 817 3145
http://www.syciplaw.com
Email: acimperio@syciplaw.com
Email: jmghofilena@syciplaw.com

PORTUGAL

Manuel Barrocas
Albano Sarmento
Jorge Santiago Neves
Barrocas Sarmento Neves
Amoreiras Torre 2
16° floor
1070-274 Lisbon
Portugal
Telephone: +351 - 21 384 33 00
Fax: +351 - 21 387 02 65
http://www.barrocas.com.pt
Email: mpbarrocas@barrocas.com.pt
Email: asarmento@barrocas.com.pt
Email: jsneves@barrocas.com.pt

SCOTLAND

Kenneth Chrystie
McClure Naismith
292 St Vincent Street
Glasgow
G2 5TQ
Scotland
Telephone: +44 (0) 141 204 2700
Fax: +44 (0)141 248 3998
http://www.mcclurenaismith.com
Email:
kchrystie@mcclurenaismith.com

SINGAPORE

Gerald Singham
Rodyk & Davidson LLP
80 Raffles Place
#33-00 UOB Plaza 1
Singapore 048624
Telephone: +65 6225 2626
Fax: +65 6225 1838
http://www.rodyk.com
Email: gerald.singham@rodyk.com

SOUTH AFRICA

Hennie Bester
Mallinicks Inc
3rd Floor, Granger Bay Court
Beach Road
V&A Waterfront
Cape Town, 8001
South Africa
Telephone: +27 21 410 2209
Fax: +27 21 410 9000
http://www.mallinicks.co.za
Email: hbester@mallinicks.co.za

SPAIN

Raimon Segura
Cuatrecasas
Paseo de Gracia, 111
08008 Barcelona
Telephone: +34 - 93 290 55 00
Fax: +34 - 93 290 55 67
http://www.cuatrecasas.com
Email:
raimundo.segura@cuatrecasas.com

SWEDEN

Åke J. Fors
Håkan Fohlin
Setterwalls
Arsenalsgatan 6
SE-111 47 Stockholm
Sweden
Telephone: +46 8 598 890 00
Fax: +46 8 598 890 90
http://www.setterwalls.se
Email: ake.fors@setterwalls.se
Email: hakan.fohlin@setterwalls.se

SWITZERLAND

Dr. Max Albers
CMS von Erlach Henrici
Dreikoenigstrasse 7
8022 Zurich
Switzerland
Telephone: +41 44 285 11 11
Fax: +41 44 285 11 12
http://www.cms-veh.com
Email: max.albers@cms-veh.com

TAIWAN

Paiff Huang
Chunyih Cheng
Fengchun Yen
Formosa Transnational
15th Floor
136, Jen Ai Road
Section 3
Taipei 106
Taiwan
Telephone: +886 2 2755 7366
Fax: +886 2 2708 6035
http://www.taiwanlaw.com
Email: paiff.huang@taiwanlaw.com
Email:
chun-yih.cheng@taiwanlaw.com
Email:
feng-chun.yen@taiwanlaw.com

UNITED STATES

David Kay
DrinkerBiddleGardnerCarton
191 North Wacker Drive
Suite 3700
Chicago
Illinois 60606 – 1698
USA
Telephone: +312 569 1121
Fax: +312 569 3121
http://www.drinkerbiddle.com
Email: david.kay@dbr.com

Chapter 1

INTERNATIONAL ACQUISITIONS

Cross-border business is increasingly following a global pattern, with a largely common language (English), consistent accounting treatment and common principles of business regulation. But cross-border acquisitions inevitably involve different cultures, different laws and different business methods. Acquisitions often founder not on the failure of the target business to meet expectations, but simply on unknown local factors which are not discovered until too late.

One of the roles of a professional adviser is to ensure that the appropriate questions are asked so that all relevant issues can be identified early in the negotiations and dealt with properly. Failure to ask the right questions will result in important business, regulatory or cultural issues, which could be fundamental to the success of the transaction, being overlooked.

Acquisitions are generally initiated when a business determines that growth by acquisition is appropriate for the business and identifies the type of target most likely to be compatible with that aim, an investor or a group of investors identifying an appropriate target or simply by either responding to an information memorandum issued on behalf of the target's owner. In any case, it is important for appropriate, rational and skilled commercial judgment to be exercised at an early stage of the process to ensure that the target is the correct target, the intended benefits of the acquisition are likely to be achieved, and the likely price range is compatible with the intended and required returns.

A private equity investor may simply be interested in the internal rate of return (IRR) likely to be generated by the investment during its intended life through to disposal or ultimate listing via an IPO. Its analysis will therefore be almost exclusively quantitative. A company or trade acquirer, on the other hand, must make this assessment on both qualitative and quantitative factors, some of which cannot be measured or even predicted with certainty, which requires an even more impartial and dispassionate view of the wisdom of proceeding.

© World Law Group
International Business Acquisitions, M. Whalley, F.-J. Semler (eds.), Kluwer Law International, London, 2007; ISBN 9789041124838.

Once the commercial decision has been taken to proceed, there are five clear stages in most international acquisitions:

- initial identification of the target and negotiation of the broad terms of the deal, possibly leading to an exchange of heads of agreement or a letter of intent;

- either before or after the exchange of a formal agreement, a 'due diligence' examination of the target;

- negotiating and drafting formal agreements;

- obtaining third party and government consents or licences; and

- finalization of the transaction (referred to variously as closing, completion or settlement).

The first two stages are crucial to the buyer because a decision to complete the transaction should only be made once a proper assessment has been made of the target and its business. During the first stage, the buyer needs to decide on the structure of the deal, and identify any legal (including tax) issues associated with the acquisition. In the second stage, the buyer needs to satisfy itself that everything which it has been told about the target, or which it has assumed about it, is correct.

While this publication deals with these two stages separately, they are necessarily closely linked in the case of an international acquisition.

Major Legal Issues

The first stage requires the buyer or its advisers to look at a number of major legal issues which will be common to most jurisdictions throughout the world. Those issues will determine the structure of the acquisition and whether there are any major impediments to it. Using an economics analogy, the major legal issues list deals with macroeconomic questions. It looks at the environment surrounding the target business: foreign investment controls, other government regulation, taxation, contract law, competition law, employment law and employee rights, exchange controls and other issues relevant to any acquisition in that jurisdiction. The buyer's decision to acquire the target, and its assessment of the appropriate price to pay, must be based on a clear understanding of the environment in which the target operates.

Where the target operates in the same jurisdiction as the buyer, the buyer's enquiries will focus on the business itself, as the legal and regulatory environment in which the business operates is already familiar. The position is entirely different in a cross-border transaction. In that case, the buyer must be made aware of the inherent risks, both legal and commercial, which an unfamiliar jurisdiction involves. For that reason, the process for an international acquisition must also focus on the regulatory and business environment in which the target operates. The major legal issues identified in Chapter 2 provide a framework for, and answers to many of, these enquiries.

Because a familiarity with the legal and regulatory environment in which the target operates is essential, these threshold questions will always involve recourse to appropriate professional advice.

Due Diligence

The second stage involves what is commonly known as 'due diligence'—the detailed examination of the particular target's business or, to continue the analogy with economics, the micro-economic aspects of the acquisition.

While the object of the acquisition may be specific shares or assets, the target in a business sense is the enterprise as a whole. The target is not simply the sum of the individual assets or rights which are to be transferred, but a complex bundle of relationships (customers or clients, employees and management, and creditors and suppliers), goods and services, tangible and intangible assets, rights and obligations and business customs.

Effective due diligence requires the buyer's professional advisers to examine, and report on, each of these tangible and intangible assets and liabilities and the material business relationships which underpin the target's business. In an international acquisition, an understanding of the major legal issues identified in Chapter 2 enables the buyer and its decision-makers to view the results of the due diligence enquiries, which are the subject of the checklist in Chapter 3, in context.

Terminology

While the international business language tends to be English, there is, unfortunately, no common terminology of international business. Throughout this publication, the editors have attempted to use consistent terms, the most obvious of which, with their common international variations, being:

- closing: settlement, completion;
- seller: vendor, transferor;
- buyer: purchaser, transferee;
- company: corporation, legal entity;
- shares: stock, securities;
- officers: directors;
- shareholders: members, stockholders.

In addition, the word 'target' is generally used throughout to describe either the company being acquired (in the case of a share purchase) or the business as a whole (in the case of an acquisition of the goodwill of a business and its assets), depending on the context.

This guide does not deal with takeover offers for companies the shares of which are listed on a stock or securities exchange, but only with the buying and selling of shares or assets by private treaty or contract. Listed company takeovers involve compliance with stock exchange listing rules and the takeover laws or rules of the relevant jurisdiction (e.g. London's City Code on Take-overs and Mergers and the European Takeovers Directive). It must be remembered, however, that the acquisition of the shares of a non-listed company, or its assets, may still have implications under relevant stock exchange rules if the buyer is itself a listed company, the seller is a listed company, or if the target has a controlling interest in a listed company. In those cases, the acquisition timetable may be affected by the need to make regulatory filings or obtain shareholder or stockholder consents.

A buyer may also have to consider local securities laws if the buyer's own shares or debt securities are to be offered to the sellers as part of the purchase price. Again, these securities laws are outside the scope of this guide but are dealt with in *International Securities Law Handbook*, the first handbook in the World Law Group's series (Kluwer, 2nd Edition, 2005).

Finally, it is important to emphasize that this guide cannot take the place of proper professional advice in the relevant jurisdiction. The intention of the editors and contributors is to give lawyers, other professional advisers and business people an overview of the relevant issues in each of a number of the major business jurisdictions rather than to provide a substitute for proper professional advice.

This guide has been prepared on the basis of the laws in each relevant jurisdiction as at 1 December 2006.

Chapter 2

MAJOR LEGAL ISSUES

This chapter provides short explanations of the major legal issues that need to be considered when planning cross-border acquisitions of companies or business assets. The issues are examined by contributors from many jurisdictions, but each has provided a commentary under consistent headings. Each major issue has therefore been dealt with in the same way for each jurisdiction, so that the reader can find the approach taken in each place to the same issue.

The commentary:

- concentrates upon those issues that need to be considered before the participants strike their commercial bargain and prepare formal agreements;

- identifies issues which will help the buyer to decide whether the acquisition should be undertaken by the purchase of a company or the purchase of business assets;

- assists with questions relating to structuring and tax and duty minimization;

- identifies government regulatory issues that may have an impact on the ability of a foreign buyer to enter into the transaction, or on timing;

- identifies other issues that need to be resolved before an agreement can be signed, or which should form the basis of contract conditions.

What follows is not a due diligence checklist, which is used by a buyer to confirm the assumptions made by it in relation to the target itself when agreeing the price and to ensure that it will obtain good title to the shares or assets acquired. That checklist is the subject of Chapter 3. Rather, and as noted in Chapter 1, it is a summary, for each relevant jurisdiction, of the major legal and regulatory issues that will have an impact on an acquisition in that jurisdiction, and on the ability of a foreign buyer to consummate the transaction.

To use another analogy, a husband-to-be may be very satisfied with his future wife, but he may nevertheless need to persuade her parents that he is a fitting son-in-law and to determine whether social or religious rules and customs will allow the marriage. Companies wishing to combine their businesses often need to ask, and to have answered, very similar questions, not about themselves, but about the legal, regulatory and business environment in which they wish to operate together.

© World Law Group
International Business Acquisitions, M. Whalley, F.-J. Semler (eds.), Kluwer Law International, London, 2007; ISBN 9789041124838.

The major issues which are dealt with in this chapter by each of the separate country contributors are as follows:

1. Introductory Comments

2. Corporate Structures

3. Letters of Intent and Heads of Agreement

4. Taxes Affecting the Structure and Calculation of the Price

5. Extent of Seller's Warranties and Indemnities

6. Liability for Pre-contractual Representations

7. Liability for Pre-acquisition Trading and Contracts

8. Pre-completion Risks

9. Required Governmental Approvals

10. Anti-trust and Competition Laws

11. Required Offer Procedures

12. Continuation of Government Licences

13. Requirements for Transferring Shares

14. Requirements for Transferring Land and Property Leases

15. Requirements for Transferring Intellectual Property

16. Requirements for Transferring Business Contracts, Licences and Leases

17. Requirements for Transferring Other Assets

18. Encumbrances and Third Party Interests

19. Minimum Shareholder and Officer Requirements

20. Non-competition Clauses

21. Environmental Considerations

22. Employee Superannuation/Pension Plans

23. Employee Rights

24. Compulsory Transfer of Employees

25. Tax Deductibility of Acquisition Expenses

26. Levies on Acquisition Agreements and Collateral Documents

27. Financing Rules and Restrictions

28. Exchange Controls and Repatriation of Profits

29. Groups of Companies

30. Responsibility for Liabilities of an Acquired Subsidiary

31. Governing Law of the Contract

32. Dispute Resolution Options

33. Other Issues

Because Luxembourg companies are not generally a target for acquisitions of this nature, the Luxembourg chapter instead examines the use of Luxembourg companies and other vehicles for making acquisitions in Europe.

Separate sections then follow which deal with the competition laws of the EU which can have an impact on business acquisitions within the European Union and describe the European company–*Societas Europaea*.

1. ARGENTINA

Carlos Alfaro and Sebastian Rodrigo, Alfaro-Abogados

1.1 Introductory Comments

The Republic of Argentina is organized as a Federal Republic and is comprised of 23 provinces and the federal capital: the Autonomous City of Buenos Aires.

The procedural, administrative and tax laws are regulated by provincial legislation and the substantive laws (civil, corporate and commercial, criminal, labour, etc.) are regulated on a Federal level. Therefore, the laws applicable to the main aspects of an acquisition are federal rather than provincial.

The Argentine Constitution grants foreigners the same rights as it does to Argentine nationals. Foreign investments are also governed by Argentine Foreign Investments Law No. 21,382 that also states that foreigners investing in Argentina enjoy the same status and have the same rights that the Constitution affords to local investors.

Finally, foreign investments are also regulated by a framework of international bilateral treaties (BITs) that provide an additional protection to the party of the treaty investing in the country.

In principle, regulations on foreign investment do not impede and/or require any prior approval for the acquisition of assets or shares of Argentine companies by foreign investors, with some exceptions described below in this chapter.

1.2 Corporate Structures

The Argentine legal system provides several types of business structures, but foreign investors generally use a local corporation ('Sociedad Anónima' or 'SA') or a limited liability company ('Sociedad de Responsabilidad Limitada' or 'SRL') as their investment vehicle.

The SRL generally is used for small or medium size businesses and the number of members is limited to fifty (50). The SA structure is used for larger companies, either public or private.

Another valid investment vehicle generally used by foreign companies in Argentina is the branch. Pursuant to the Argentine Corporate Law, foreign companies that intent to conduct business activities in Argentina, on a regular basis, and are not incorporated as a local corporate entity, shall set up a branch or any other type of permanent representation that must be duly registered before the local Public Registry of Commerce.

Since 2003 several new rules have been issued in Argentina to maintain a close control on foreign shareholders of Argentine companies. The purpose of these regulations is to identify foreign entities that are registered in fraud to local legislation. In this sense, new regulations have provided that all foreign companies that participate as shareholders of

© World Law Group
International Business Acquisitions, M. Whalley, F.-J. Semler (eds.), Kluwer Law International, London, 2007; ISBN 9789041124838.

local companies shall submit evidence of assets and/or activities abroad and shall prove that these assets or activities represent the same or higher investment as the one carried out in Argentina. They have to demonstrate that the investment in Argentina is not the foreign company's main business.

Other regulations also require the foreign company to disclose information on the identity of its shareholders, with some exceptions for well-known foreign corporations or public companies, and companies considered 'vehicle companies' (companies used for the only purpose of investing in Argentina).

Registration of foreign off-shore companies in the City of Buenos Aires has also been restricted by the Inspeccion General de Justicia of the City of Buenos Aires ('IGJ').

1.3   Letters of Intent and Heads of Agreement

Since the acquisition of shares or assets usually require long negotiations, preliminary agreements on specific issues and topics are frequently concluded. Letters of intent and other forms of preliminary agreements are enforceable documents and in general are subject to the same regulations applicable to other types of contracts. They may consist of confidentiality agreements, conditions of the due diligence, and disclosure of information about the target company during the negotiations. They may also set out guidelines or the criteria for determining the price. Therefore, these covenants and stipulations are valid, unless it has been clearly stipulated by the parties on the contrary.

Preliminary agreements oblige the parties to conduct the negotiations on a loyal and good faith basis, and even to inform their respective partner about their intentions to conclude or to withdraw. Therefore, if one of the parties fails to fulfil the promises contained in such preliminary agreements, then the other party may request the specific performance of the obligations provided for in the agreement or otherwise claim for damages. For these reasons, a careful drafting is necessary when preliminary agreements are not intended to create any binding obligation upon the parties.

1.4   Taxes Affecting the Structure and Calculation of the Price

The capital gain obtained from the sale of shares of a local company by non-residents is exempt from income tax, even if the beneficiary transfers such gains abroad. The sales of shares (as well as other securities) are also exempted from VAT, and if the transaction takes place in the city of Buenos Aires it will also be exempted from turnover tax.

A purchase of shares will result in the purchasing company inheriting all of the tax and social security liabilities of the target company.

Dividends paid by the local company to the foreign investor are not subject to withholding tax in Argentina, regardless of whether paid to residents or non-residents, as long as the dividend does not exceed the local company accumulated taxable income; the excess amount is generally subject to a 35 per cent withholding tax.

If a taxable local company sells its business by selling its assets the transaction might be considered under certain circumstances as a 'transfer of a going concern' ('TGC'). The TGC is regulated by a special law in Argentina that sets forth special rules to protect the seller's non-tax creditors. The notice of the sale must be published in the Official Gazette of Argentina and in one or more local newspapers in order to cut off the assumption of the seller's non-tax liabilities to the buyer. The seller's non-tax creditors have 10 days to make objections to the sale of the assets.

A purchase of assets is, in principle, more costly than an acquisition of shares, from a tax point of view, principally due to the possibility of application of income tax, VAT and turnover tax on the sale of the assets. However, the investor might prefer to purchase assets instead of purchasing stocks, if does not want to assume the companies liability or if the stock purchase involves taking over tax attributes, such as the tax basis, net operating carry forwards, etc, since the acquisition of assets may, under certain restrictions, exclude the seller's tax liabilities.

1.5 Extent of Seller's Warranties and Indemnities

In general, the parties are free to determine the extent of the warranties and indemnities to be granted by the seller in order to enable the buyer to bring an action for damages caused by any breach or inaccuracy of a representation or warranty provided.

Regarding hidden defects, Argentine legislation provides that the seller is liable for those defects within the extent of his knowledge. Therefore, it is advisable to include a provision stating that the seller will be always liable for any hidden defects, as well as claims from a third party that reduce the value of the business or of any of the items sold, particularly it is advisable to specify those items which are considered to be essential for the business.

Warranties and indemnities may be backed by banking guaranties, collateral securities, or by the witholding of a portion of the purchase price by the buyer until termination of the limitation period agreed by the parties.

1.6 Liability for Pre-contractual Representations

The general principle stated by the Argentine Law is that all contracts shall be entered, construed and executed in good faith, according to what the parties understood or could have understood, acting with care and foresee ability. This principle also applies to the entire negotiation process.

Likewise, in cases of fraud, misrepresentation and negligence, the contract may be terminated and/or the seller may be held liable for damages. The purchase agreement can cover the seller's liability with warranties and indemnities.

1.7 Liability for Pre-acquisition Trading and Contracts

In the case of a transfer of shares, all contracts executed by the seller remain in full force and effect. Buyer will then assume liabilities and debts for which the seller is responsible. Notwithstanding this, it is possible that certain contracts entered by the company with third parties might required the consent of such party to any change in the control of the acquired company, or even provide for its termination in case the status of the control of the acquired company is modified.

If otherwise a transfer of business or assets is agreed, then the benefits and burdens of pre-acquisition trading and contracts will be subject to the terms and conditions agreed between the seller and buyer. The assignment of the contracts involving third parties could be possible, as long as the assignment was expressly provided in the contract. The third party will have to consent to the assignment to the buyer.

1.8 Pre-completion Risks

In an assets purchase agreement, the parties may determine which party would bear the risk of the loss of the assets as from the date of execution of the agreement until completion. In most of the cases the risk of loss is born by the seller until delivery of the assets to the buyer.

On a share acquisition, the matter is usually addressed through a warranty that no material adverse change has occurred since a specific date, and if such adverse change occurs, buyer may claim the termination of the agreement or a reduction in the purchase price, according to the amount of damage face by the buyer.

1.9 Required Governmental Approvals

In general, Argentine Law does not require any specific approval for the acquisition of shares and/or assets by foreign investors.

Notwithstanding the above, specific requirements and approvals may be requested by the Government for the completion of an acquisition of companies involved in certain businesses such as exploitation of natural resources, transportation, media, broadcasting activities, banking and insurance, as well as for the acquisition of land located in strategic places such as border zones.

1.10 Anti-trust and Competition Laws

Antitrust Law 25,156 enacted in 1999 (hereinafter the 'Law') prohibits acts that distort competition or constitute an abuse of a dominant market position. It also establishes that takeovers (defined in section 6 of the Law) shall be authorized by a governmental agency that should be created for the purpose of regulating the applicability of the Law in the cases mentioned below.

According to the Law, said governmental agency (not created yet) will be named 'Court of Defence of Competition'. The Law also provides that the current governmental agency, created by the previous Antitrust Law N° 22,262 ('Comisión Nacional de Defensa de la Competencia' or 'CNDC') will be in charge of enforcing the Law until the Court of Defence of Competition is finally created.

Pursuant to section 8 of the Law, takeovers shall be notified to the CNDC in order to obtain its approval, whenever the value of the business involved in the transaction exceeds AR$ 200M. However, section 10 provides for some exemptions to this rule in case the amount of the business is under the scope of section 8 but the amount of the transaction [that permitted the take over] and the value of the assets acquired, do not each one exceed the amount of AR$ 20M, unless (i) during the previous twelve (12) months there has been transactions between buyer and seller that together exceed the amount of AR$ 20M or (ii) during the previous thirty six (36) months there has been transactions between buyer and seller that together exceed the amount of AR$ 60M. In both cases, such transactions should have taken place in relation to the same relevant market.

Section 46 of the Law provides that individuals or entities that do not comply with the duty set forth in section 8 will be penalized with a daily fine applicable, jointly and severally, to directors, managers, auditors, and members of the surveillance committee, agents, and legal representatives that with their actions or omissions have allowed violations to the Law.

1.11 Required Offer Procedures

The 'Comisión Nacional de Valores' or 'CNV', governmental agency that administers the Securities Law in Argentina, issued regulations establishing that a listed company shall previously promote a biding public offers or a securities swap when an individual or entity intents to obtain the direct or indirect control of a company whose shares are listed. This offering shall be addressed to all security holders. This obligation will not apply in cases where the acquisition of the 'significant stake' does not entail the acquisition of the company's control, or in the cases where the change of control takes place as a consequence of the company's restructure, merger, or spin-off.

1.12 Continuation of Government Licenses

In an acquisition of assets where governmental licenses are involved, the buyer should verify whether the continuation of such licenses is impaired by the transaction since in some cases the change of control over the target company may cause the automatic revocation of fundamental licenses to operate. Consequently, during the negotiation it is advisable to ascertain which are the licenses required to conduct the business, and verify the governmental requirements to be met in order to obtain their re-issuance or continuation.

For example, in Argentina regulated activities that need the prior approval from the Federal, Provincial or Municipal authorities, are those related to, among others, banking, insurance, broadcasting and utilities.

1.13 Requirements for Transferring Shares

In general shares of a corporation are freely transferable by means of a book entry in the corporate share transfer book. Nevertheless restrictions such as first refusal rights may be established in the company by-laws or shareholder agreements.

The quotas of an SRL shall be transferred by public document authorized by a Public Notary and registered before the Public Registry of Commerce.

1.14 Requirements for Transferring Land and Property Leases

Argentina has a comprehensive system for title to land, and thus purchase of land requires compliance with certain formalities. In this sense, Argentine Civil Code foresees that the purchase agreement on real estate must be in writing, implemented through a public deed and registered at the Real Estate Registry of the corresponding jurisdiction in order to exclude third party claims against the transferred assets. Titles of land can be encumbered by mortgages or other charges and these encumbrances must be implemented in the same way as purchases.

In the city of Buenos Aires a Register of Isolated Acts has been created, in where the purchase of real estate by foreign companies shall be registered. If a foreign company conducts real estate activities on a regular basis within the country, it will be forced to register as a branch or as a local company.

1.15   Requirements for Transferring Intellectual Property

In case of transfer of shares all intellectual property rights owned by the target company remain in full force and effect. However, if the target company is not the owner of such rights but have them under a license agreement, a previous due diligence is advisable as the change of control may trigger the automatic termination of such license.

In an acquisition of assets, the transfer of any intellectual property right must be subject to specific assignments, either from the seller or the licensor as the case may be.

Agreements providing for the assignment of technology licenses, patents or trademarks must be registered before the Argentine Patent Office ('Instituto Nacional de Propiedad Industrial' or 'INPI') in order to be valid vis-à-vis third parties.

1.16   Requirements for Transferring Business Contracts, Licenses and Leases

Business contracts and licenses are, in principle, governed by what have been established by the parties in each particular agreement. Leases, in some cases, may have to be registered before the corresponding Public Registries.

Assignments of contracts where third parties are involved will require, in general, the express consent of the third party. If the third party happens to be a debtor of the seller, once it is informed of the transfer it cannot discharge its debts by paying to the seller. On the contrary, if the seller happens to be the debtor of the third party, it will be released completely from his obligations if his creditor agrees to the assignment.

Finally there are certain types of contracts like employment contracts that may be automatically assigned in order to preserve their continuity and the business organization.

1.17   Requirements for Transferring Other Assets

Assets not subject to registration do not need a public deed to be transferred and can be assigned by delivery, being sufficient that the transferred goods are placed at buyer's full disposal.

The acquisition of others assets such as real estate, ships and automobiles must be filed before the respective public Registries in order to become enforceable not only before the parties involved in the transaction but against third parties. In all these cases as well as in those where the transferred rights have been previously created through a public deed, such transfers must be instrumented through a public deed.

1.18   Encumbrances and Third Party Interests

Encumbrances and any other third party rights over the shares must be set up through a written document and notified to the company, which shall register the encumbrance in the company's appropriate book.

As a general principle, any purchase performed in good faith (that is, conducted without knowledge of the existence of an encumbrance of any kind over the acquired asset) is considered to be binding between the parties involved.

However, considering that certain assets may be subject to different kind of third party interests by virtue of private contracts, statutory provisions or laws, it is recommended that foreign investors seek for proper legal advice to perform a due diligence, before executing any given transaction.

Finally, to the extent that certain third party interests can exist without formal registration, in order to protect the purchaser, warranties from the seller regarding clear title and the absence of liens are of vital importance.

1.19   Minimum Shareholder and Officer Requirements

According to the Argentine Corporate Law, every company shall be formed by at least two (2) members. No restrictions based on the nationality are applied to become a member of a local company.

Until recently, foreign companies investing in Argentina complied with the two (2) minimum members' requirement by transferring only a very small percentage (i.e. 0.1 per cent) to another investor. In this way the company kept the control of its shares without mayor capital changes.

This has changed with a new regulation issued by the IGJ that now requires a 'significant' tenure by the minority shareholder of corporations incorporated in the City of Buenos Aires. In principle, holding around five (5) per cent of the corporate shares seems to satisfy this requirement, but is subject to the approval of the IGJ on a case by case basis. It is the interpretation of the IGJ that less than this 'significant' tenure will be a violation of the two (2) members' minimum requirement provided by the Argentine Corporate law.

To exercise management functions or become director or officer of a company, restrictions are applied not on the nationality but rather on the place of residence. That is the reason why a foreigner can be appointed as a member of a board or even as the president of a local company provided that the majority of the board has residency in the country. It is not necessary to be a shareholder or partner of a company to be appointed as officer.

1.20   Non-competition Clauses

Restraint of trade or non-competition covenants given by a seller within the sale of assets or shares is enforceable, provided that they are reasonable in scope and content. The reasonability will depend on the facts of each particular case, the effects on the seller, and the type of business involved.

Restraint of trade agreements may fall under the provisions of Argentina's anti-trust regulations which prohibit acts that affect or distort competition.

1.21 Environmental Considerations

In 1994, the articles 41 and 43 of the Argentine Constitution were amended strengthening the legal framework related to environmental matters. Said articles provide that all Argentine inhabitants have both the right to an undamaged environment and also an express duty to protect it. The primary obligation of any person held liable for environmental damage is to rectify such damage according to and within the scope of the applicable law. Pursuant to the Argentine legal regime, Federal Government sets forth the minimum standards for the protection of the environment, and Provinces and Municipalities establish specific standards and implement regulations. The amendment to the Constitution also prohibits the introduction of hazardous waste, including radioactive waste, into the country.

In the year 2002 an Environmental General Law was enacted, providing minimum standards for a sustainable environment management, setting out the objectives that the national environmental policy shall follow; and also the Integrated Management of Industrial and Service Industry Waste Law, and the Polychlorinated Biphenyls Law, among others.

This new legislation complements the already existing regulations on this matter, such as: Hazardous Waste Law (1992) which basically regulates production, handling, transportation, treatment and disposal of hazardous waste generated in federal jurisdiction or where the waste can affect more than one Provincial jurisdiction, and provides criminal sanctions for directors and other parties responsible for the damage; Criminal Code which determines that persons who commit crimes against public health might be subject to fines, imprisonment or both; General Rules of Tort Law according to Civil Code determines that an injured party may recover damages from the owner or custodian of an asset that produces environmental damage; in addition, it also provides that a transferor of an asset which has a hidden defect and later causes environmental damage might be liable after the transfer.

Representations and warranties concerning environmental liabilities are necessary in order to protect the buyer in a transaction and a full due diligence focused on the environmental matter is recommended.

1.22 Employee Superannuation/Pension Plans

The 'Administración Nacional de la Seguridad Social' or 'ANSES' is the governmental agency in Argentina in charge of social security matters. Basically social security contributions are:

Pension Fund: Employer and employee contributions to the pension fund are mandatory as a percentage of all monthly earnings in cash or in kind and amount to 11.7 per cent on behalf of the employer and 8 per cent on behalf of the employee.

Family Allowances: Employers contribute 4.44 per cent of all compensation to a family allowance fund. Employers may deduct family allowances paid to employees from contributions payable. The allowances consist of gradual amounts depending on the employees' salaries, paid for each child, for marriage and for the birth or adoption of a child. However, there is no family allowance for employees whose salaries exceed AR\$ 1,500—(except for maternity).

Unemployment Fund: Employers are required to contribute 0.89 per cent of all compensation to an unemployment fund.

Medical care benefits: Medical care is provided to workers with funding that comes from a 9 per cent payroll tax −6 per cent contributed by the employer and 3 per cent by the employee (plus an additional 0.5 per cent per dependent paid by the employee). The amounts paid are allocated to various organizations that provide medical assistance.

Therefore, employers pay in total 23 per cent of basic wages to social security and family allowance, while employees pay a minimum total of 11 per cent.

Not complying with the above mentioned social plans and basic wages will in principle give the right to the employee to terminate the employment, considering himself as 'dismissed' and entitling him to claim severance.

1.23   Employee Rights

Basic relations between the employer and individual employees are governed by a general Labour Contract Law, complemented by additional laws and statutes related to specific activities, and collective bargaining agreements between management and union representatives. For purposes of hiring employees, companies shall be registered employers before Ministry of Labour.

Work contracts are assumed to be of indeterminable length unless otherwise allowed by special legislation. The Law specifies a probation period of three (3) months that can be extended up to six (6) months through a duly authorized collective bargaining contract. For small and medium companies the probation period is six (6) months which can be extended to twelve (12) months through collective bargaining. During this period either party may terminate the labour relation without cause or need to give notice.

The Federal Council of Labour, Productivity and Minimum Wage establish a minimum monthly and hourly wage. The employer and the employee are free to agree on the amount of a wage, provided it is no less than the minimum wage or the one established in collective bargaining agreements or decisions reached through arbitration.

All regular workers receive a mandatory annual bonus ('aguinaldo') equal to one (1) month's salary, based on the average monthly amount paid to the worker during the last period.

Employees may be dismissed, without liability for the employer, based on a number of limited justifiable causes (committed an act of gross misconduct or a criminal offence for example). In case of unjustified dismissal, employees are automatically entitled to severance indemnities equal to one month's salary for each year of service. In case of termination for any reason whatsoever, the employee will be entitled to collect the mandated annual bonus and vacation accrued during the time concerned up to the date of firing the worker. It is important to mention that a recent modification of the Labour Law jurisprudence has raised a discussion on the legal cap of severances related to dismissals. Although said cap is now established by the Contract Labour Law, the Supreme Court has declared its unconstitutionality and consequently many chambers of the Labour Court of Appeals have followed this criteria by rejecting the validity of the legal cap.

1.24　Compulsory Transfer of Employees

Changes related to the employer or to employment conditions which adversely affects employees shall be consent by the employee. Otherwise the employee will be entitled to consider himself dismissed and claim the severance indemnification.

It is important to mention however that the change of the employer is not per se a circumstance that affects the status of the employee, and thus not always subject to severance. Even though the employee's consent is not required for the transfer, the new employer shall continue granting the same wages, salaries and benefits that were paid by the former employer and work will be carried out under the same conditions.

Finally, in the case of change of control over a company (and consequently the change of employer) the Law provides [for labour matters] a joint liability between buyer and seller regarding severance indemnification, if applicable.

1.25　Tax Deductibility of Acquisition Expenses

The Income Tax Law allows deductions for those expenses necessarily incurred for the purpose of obtaining income or ensuring its permanence. In addition, the Tax Law contains comprehensive rules for the treatment of particular expenses and specifically allows the deduction of certain items. Expenses incurred abroad are presumed to relate to foreign income and are not deductible unless the contrary can be proved. The expenses related to business income that is partially derived from a foreign source or is otherwise tax exempted, must be allocated between taxable and non-taxable income.

Expenditures are deductible only if they are properly supported by receipts. In addition, an expense disbursement that is not properly documented becomes subject to withholding tax at the maximum rate prescribed for individual income tax purposes. However, if evidence is available to support the disbursement as a necessary business expense, the deduction will be allowed and no withholding will be required. Provisions for contingencies and general reserves are not deductible.

Expenses incurred in the creation of all enterprises may be amortized by equal annual instalments over not more than five (5) years or, at the taxpayer's option, may be written off entirely in the first year. The same rules apply to certain direct exploration expenses of mining operations. Research and development expenses are deductible when incurred.

1.26 Levies on Acquisition Agreements and Collateral Documents

When considering the acquisition of companies or assets located in Argentina, the potential buyer should contemplate the possible application of stamp taxes according to the type of transaction and the Province where the company or assets are located.

This tax was largely suppressed in the city of Buenos Aires effective February 1, 1993. Since then it is only levied on deeds covering the transfer of title to real estate (at rates ranging from 0.75 per cent to 2.5 per cent of the price set for the transaction).

Stamp duty is levied by the Provinces on documents supporting legal transactions, such as deeds, mortgages, contracts, letters accepting proposals, etc. The rates and rules for assessment are determined in each jurisdiction.

Sample rates in the Province of Buenos Aires are 1 per cent for contracts, recognitions of liabilities, promissory notes, bills of exchange and 4 per cent for conveyance of real estate. There are exemptions for documents that instrument financial transactions and those connected with foreign trade, including pro forma bills of exchange.

There are rules designed to avoid double taxation in some cases involving instruments supporting transactions taking effect in other jurisdictions.

Other taxes that should be mentioned are the Land and Property Taxes which are levied by the Provinces and the Municipality of the city of Buenos Aires, based on the assessed valuation of the property. Rates vary from one jurisdiction to another.

Finally, the mandatory fees provided by several provincial laws regulating the participation of professionals should also be considered when pricing the transaction.

1.27 Financing Rules and Restrictions

Argentine Law makes no difference between a foreign-owned subsidiary or branch and local investors when requiring local or foreign sources of financing.

According to the new foreign money inflow rules, certain individuals and companies that inflows money to Argentina from a foreign country are required to constitute a reserve withholding, in foreign currency, equivalent to 30 per cent of the amount of the foreign money transferred. This reserve must be in a local financial entity for a three hundred and sixty five (365) day period.

There are several exemptions to this withholding, among them, the foreign direct investment in the country. This exception applies for example to (i) Non-Argentine resident's capital contribution to local companies and (ii) sales of shares of local companies to direct investors, provided that in the case of capital contributions, it should be capitalized in accordance with current legal requirements. In that case, evidence of the registration procedure must be filed before the Public Registry of Commerce.

1.28 Exchange Controls and Repatriation of Profits

Following the economic crisis of 2001, the Central Bank of the Argentine Republic imposed certain restrictions to the transfer of foreign currencies. After the termination of the convertibility regime and following a short period when the official exchange rate was combined with a free rate, the government established a Single Free Foreign Exchange Market. Since then the rate fluctuates freely based on market forces, but including as well the purchase and sale of currency by the Central Bank for purposes of maintaining certain stability on the exchange of the US Dollar vis-à-vis the Argentine Peso.

The Central Bank has subsequently reduced the exchange controls enacted as part of the 2002's restrictions, easing access to the Free Foreign Exchange Market and gradually regularizing both the acquisition and transfer abroad of foreign currency. In this sense, the Central Bank increased the maximum amount that companies may acquire in the Free Foreign Exchange Market without requiring its prior authorization.

The Central Bank prior consent is not required now for payments of principal on financial debts to non-residents from private sector (both non financial and financial institutions). Likewise, dividends and profits can also be remitted abroad without the Central Bank's prior authorization so far the corporate balance sheet has been audited and approved.

The Central Bank authorization is required for aggregate purchases of foreign currency for saving purposes in excess of U$ 2M (per month) in the case of individuals and companies who are residents, and of U$ 5,000.- (per month) for any purpose than those specifically exempted, in the case of individuals and companies who are not residents in Argentina.

Exchange controls also reinstated the obligation to repatriate foreign currency funds arising from exports of goods and services. Such funds shall be exchanged for pesos in the Free Foreign Exchange Market within a specific period of time, depending on the type of goods. Export proceeds that are applied to the repayment of export financing are exempted from repatriation, provided that the proceeds of such financing were originally transferred to Argentina and exchanged for pesos by the Central Bank.

Any failure to comply with Central Bank's regulations referred to the Single Free Foreign Exchange Market might imply a crime provided by the criminal legislation.

1.29 Groups of Companies

Argentine Corporate Law considers that a company has the control of another company if it holds more than 51 per cent of the voting rights in the latter or if it has the 'effective' dominant control over its decisions.

The city of Buenos Aires along with several Provinces have enacted new regulations regarding the 'group of companies' concept, mainly focused on the requirements to be filed by the comptroller company of a group or by the 'vehicle' companies used by the groups of companies for their investments in Argentina.

1.30 Responsibility for Liabilities of an Acquired Subsidiary

Parent companies are not subject to the liabilities incurred by their acquired subsidiaries. In the same sense, subsidiaries are not subject to liabilities of their parent companies.

However, labour and tax liabilities of the acquired company should be determined since social security and tax authorities have already made some attempts to reach the assets of controlling shareholders for the debts of their local subsidiaries. Also, the extension of bankruptcy claims to third parties is admitted by the Argentine Law by application of the 'disregard of legal entity' theory (similar to the piercing the veil doctrine). In this sense, the Bankruptcy Law extends the liability to the parent company of the debtor when the former improperly manipulated the interests of the latter for its own benefit or for the benefit of its economic group.

1.31   Governing Law of the Contract

The parties to an agreement are free to establish that the agreement will be governed by the laws of a country other than Argentina, and Argentine courts will honour such choice-of-law freely made between parties.

Limitations to such principle apply when the application of a foreign law may contravene Argentine public policy (in these cases the Argentine Court would substitute the applicable rule of Argentine law for the foreign rule) or if Argentine Law contains mandatory provisions which would apply to the transactions contemplated by such agreements irrespective of the law chosen by the parties (for example, exchange controls, bankruptcy laws, etc).

1.32   Dispute Resolution Options

The critical importance of judicial decisions affecting foreign investment, coupled with the traditional mistrust of foreign investors as to the independence and consistent enforcement of laws by host country judiciaries, has spurred a movement towards a supra nationalization of disputes regarding foreign investments, so as to place the procedure beyond the reach of the local judiciaries, therefore reducing uncertainty over erratic or unduly influenced decisions.

The techniques include agreements over foreign investment disputes in Bilateral Investment Treaties (BITs), arbitration clauses in individual contracts, international organizations such as the International Centre for the Settlement of Investment Disputes (ICSID). These techniques are widely employed in Argentine local tribunals, relieving the burden of settling investment disputes by means of decisions of potentially far-reaching economic, cross-border consequences.

Likewise, Argentina guarantees foreigners the same rights as local citizens, granting them full access to Argentine courts for the resolution of legal disputes. Foreigners may have access to Argentine courts provided that defendants are domiciled in Argentina, or that the place of performance of any obligation is located in Argentina.

Finally, Argentina is signatory to the New York Convention and international and Inter-American treaties, by virtue of which it recognizes judgments from courts sitting in foreign countries which are brought to Argentine courts for their enforcement.

2. AUSTRALIA

Michael Whalley, Gordon Williams & Victoria Absolon, Minter Ellison

2.1 Introductory Comments

Although Australia has, in the past, closely regulated acquisitions of Australian companies and assets by foreign interests, it now largely encourages foreign investment. There are, however, still a number of reporting requirements, and Australia's merger control and takeover laws can also restrict or prevent an acquisition in certain circumstances.

It must also be remembered that Australia is a federal system and that many of the laws which will be relevant to an acquisition are state, rather than federal, laws. While many of those laws, particularly in the business environment, tend to be largely uniform from state to state, regional variations mean that specific advice should be sought in each state in which the target may be carrying on business, or in which it holds assets.

Australia has a sophisticated business climate, and a complex regulatory environment to match it. Failure to comply properly with Australia's foreign acquisition, merger and takeover laws can have serious, and costly, repercussions. Early advice should always therefore be sought whenever an acquisition of an Australian company or assets, or of a group which includes Australian subsidiaries or assets, is contemplated.

2.2 Corporate Structures

The target of an acquisition of shares in Australia is likely to be a limited liability company, although Australia's corporations laws also permit no liability (NL) companies in connection with mining activities. A limited company can be either a private (proprietary or Pty) or a public company, and a public company may also have its shares listed on the Australian Stock Exchange (ASX).

Australia has a national corporations law (the Corporations Act 2001) which applies throughout all states and territories. Australia also has a national regulator, the Australian Securities and Investments Commission, which has responsibility for the supervision and enforcement of companies laws and the securities and financial services industries.

The shares of Australian limited liability companies do not have a par, or nominal, value, and there is no authorized share capital. An Australian company's share capital is simply the amount paid or payable on the shares actually issued by it.

It is possible to acquire shares or assets from anyone having legal personality and capacity, including private individuals, companies, statutory corporations or a state

© World Law Group
International Business Acquisitions, M. Whalley, F.-J. Semler (eds.), Kluwer Law International, London, 2007; ISBN 9789041124838.

or the federal government itself (acting as the Crown). While a partnership does not have a separate legal personality, it is possible to contract with a partnership, so as to bind each of the partners jointly and severally.

2.3   Letters of Intent and Heads of Agreement

An agreement (which can be either oral or written) is binding if it appears either from the document itself or from the circumstances that there is an intention to create legal relationships and if there is consideration given for any promises made or undertakings given by either party.

If it is intended that letters of intent or heads of agreement should not be binding on the parties until the exchange of more formal contracts, clear words should be used to that effect. The expression 'subject to contract' is often used in correspondence to achieve this, but agreements should have more specific provisions inserted to clarify whether, and to what extent, they are intended to be binding. This is particularly important in cases where certain parts of an otherwise non-binding heads of agreement are intended to be enforceable, for example, confidentiality or lock-out provisions.

2.4   Taxes Affecting the Structure and Calculation of the Price

A detailed examination of Australia's business taxes is beyond the scope of this guide. However, a purchase of shares will result in the buyer inheriting all of the target's taxation liabilities, whereas a purchase of assets will avoid this. Appropriate warranties or taxation indemnities can protect the buyer from any taxation liabilities of the target which should properly fall upon the vendor in the former case.

A new Australian income tax consolidation regime was introduced with effect from 1 July 2002 whereby wholly owned Australian groups can elect to be treated as a single entity for Australian income tax purposes. This effectively means that intra-group transactions will be ignored for income tax purposes.

For a consolidated group to exist there must be a head company and at least one subsidiary member. There are slightly different requirements for groups of companies that have the same foreign ultimate holding company. In determining whether an entity is part of a wholly-owned group, shares issued under employee share schemes in limited cases and certain finance shares may be disregarded.

While entering the consolidation regime is not mandatory, the previous grouping provisions (which allowed, for example, loss transfers, CGT roll-overs, and excess foreign tax credit transfers) ended for most corporate groups on 30 June 2003 (this date varying for those groups with substituted accounting periods). As a result, corporate groups are required to consolidate if they want any form of 'single entity' treatment. There is an exception for Australian branches of foreign banks. Generally, loss transfers are permitted between members of the same wholly-owned group where a party to the transfer is an Australian branch of a foreign bank, and the other is either the head company of a consolidated group or a non-member of a consolidated group.

If a group is consolidated, certain tax attributes (including tax losses, franking credits and foreign tax credits) will be transferred to the head company of the consolidated group. Some tax attributes will remain with the head company even when a group member leaves the consolidated group.

While an Australian company may hold assets which are exempt from capital gains tax (because they were acquired prior to 20 September 1985), anti-avoidance provisions remove this exemption where control of the company changes. Other assets will fall within the capital gains tax net in any event and there may be significant potential taxation liabilities in respect of appreciating assets, against which no provision may have been made by the company.

In addition, a change in control, unless the target is able to satisfy a continuity of business test or small business test (each test is available in certain circumstances only), will result in the loss of relief for past year losses which could otherwise have been carried forward against future profits. The continuity of business test is now limited to operations where income is less than AUD100 million. Otherwise, the capacity of companies to carry forward losses will be limited to the continuity of ownership test being satisfied.

The calculation of the price should always therefore take potential capital gains tax liabilities, and the potential loss of relief for carried forward losses, into account.

A non-resident acquiring business assets in Australia may be deemed to have established a branch or a permanent establishment in Australia, and its profits attributable to the Australian branch would then be subject to Australian taxation. An acquisition of shares, on the other hand, insulates the non-resident buyer from Australian taxation, other than taxation paid by the Australian target on its profits, any withholding taxes due on interest or dividends received by the buyer and taxation due on any gain on the subsequent disposal of shares.

A transfer of either shares or assets (including goodwill) may attract stamp duty in the state of Australia where the target is incorporated (in the case of shares) or in each state where assets are located (in the case of assets). Stamp duty rates vary, but asset transfers or assignments attract conveyancing duty at rates as high as 5.5 per cent, while the rate of duty on share transfers is 0.6 per cent. There is no transfer duty on shares in companies incorporated in Victoria, Tasmania and Western Australia unless they are 'land rich'.

A goods and services tax ('**GST**') has applied in Australia since 1 July 2000 to the supply of goods, real property, services and other supplies. GST is payable at the rate of 10 per cent.

2.5 Extent of Seller's Warranties and Indemnities

The nature and extent of warranties and indemnities depends on the size of the acquisition and the parties' relative bargaining strength. However, it is not unusual for sellers to give full warranties and indemnities relating to, for example, the accounts of the business or company to be acquired, title to the assets, taxation, litigation, employee issues etc.

It is always desirable to consider whether warranties and indemnities from a seller should be supported by a parent company guarantee, by a retention of part of the purchase price, or by warranty and indemnity insurance taken out by the vendor.

2.6 Liability for Pre-contractual Representations

Negligent and fraudulent misrepresentations may be actionable and can in certain cases allow rescission of the contract in addition to an action for damages. Australia also has legislation which prohibits misleading or deceptive conduct, which can provide a further basis for an action by a buyer who has been misled by a seller's pre-contractual representations or statements.

Acquisition agreements often attempt to preclude action for negligent misstatement or misrepresentation, leaving the buyer with a remedy only in damages for breach of warranty, but such exclusions often do not protect the seller in cases where a misrepresentation has induced the buyer to enter into the agreement.

Specific contractual provisions which exclude liability for representations made in pre-contractual negotiations, and which restrict rights of rescission to the period between exchange of contracts and completion, should cause the buyer to assume that it can only rely upon representations specifically repeated in the agreement, or facts and matters specifically warranted or in relation to which indemnities have been given.

2.7 Liability for Pre-acquisition Trading and Contracts

In a share acquisition, the benefit and burden of pre-acquisition trading and contracts remain with the target, and therefore pass to the buyer upon the acquisition of the target. Pre-acquisition profits may, however, be paid to the seller by way of dividend before the transfer of shares to the buyer is complete. All existing contracts and agreements entered into by the target company will remain with the company, and the benefit and burden of those contracts will therefore pass to the buyer indirectly.

In the case of a business (assets) purchase, on the other hand, the buyer's interest in the business's profits and its responsibility for the business's contracts depend upon the agreement made with the seller. If, for example, the purchase agreement includes a retrospective effective date, the buyer will, for accounting and taxation purposes, bear the loss or be entitled to the business's profits from the effective date.

After completion, the seller remains liable on contracts to which it was a party unless they are novated and a release given to the seller. While major contracts are sometimes novated, this is usually impracticable and it is common for contracts to be assigned. The buyer then undertakes to the seller to perform the contracts from completion and to indemnify the seller against any future claims under those contracts.

The seller also generally agrees to hold the benefit of contracts which are incapable of assignment on trust for the buyer, and to perform those contracts on behalf, and at the cost, of the buyer.

2.8 Pre-completion Risks

There is no clear rule in law which will determine when risk passes to a buyer under either a share purchase or an asset purchase, although sale of goods legislation generally raises the presumption that risk passes with title where goods are the subject of the contract. This is, however, a rebuttable presumption, and it is open to the buyer and seller to vary this rule by agreement.

It is therefore particularly important to clarify when risk is to pass. A buyer effectively is at risk as soon as contracts are exchanged, because it has an obligation to complete at the agreed price. This is notwithstanding a subsequent deterioration in the target's business or the assets, unless it can rely on a breach of warranty to rescind the agreement (or, alternatively, to claim damages in respect of any loss suffered).

A business acquisition agreement therefore typically contains a provision stating which party bears the risk of loss of assets between signing and completion. Risk usually remains with the seller so that it must maintain insurance until completion.

On a share acquisition, the matter is usually addressed by way of a warranty that there has been no material adverse change to the business since a warranted accounts date. The seller will usually resist any attempt to have such a warranty repeated at completion.

Alternatively, the price may be adjusted by reference to the value of the target's net assets at closing, as determined by accounts made up to the date of closing in an agreed form. By this method the seller effectively retains the benefit and burden of changes in the business up to completion.

2.9 Required Governmental Approvals

An acquisition of 15 per cent or more of the issued shares or voting power in an Australian company by a single foreign person and its associates must be notified to the Commonwealth Treasurer, unless the target company's total assets are valued at less than AUD100 million. The Treasurer is advised by the Foreign Investment Review Board.

Acquisitions with a total value of less than AUD100 million are not examined and are automatically approved, except in the media, urban real estate, civil aviation and uranium sectors.

These thresholds are increased where the acquirer is a US individual or entity, with the effect that acquisitions are only notifiable and subject to foreign investment review if the assets of the Australian target exceed AUD831 million (this is indexed annually).

The Treasurer must approve examinable acquisitions unless they are contrary to the national interest.

The Treasurer's powers also extend to the acquisition of shares where aggregate foreign interests in the target's shares exceed 40 per cent of the total voting shares and to the acquisition of control of an Australian business by, for example, acquiring an overseas holding company, purchasing assets, exercising control over the composition of a board of directors, or participation in management or profits. Advance notification of acquisitions having these results where the assets value thresholds are exceeded is, although not compulsory, recommended.

2.10   Anti-trust and Competition Laws

The Australian Competition and Consumer Commission (the ACCC) administers legislation which covers mergers, anti-competitive practices, consumer protection, and product liability. In the context of an acquisition, the most important aspect is merger control, but restrictive and non-competition clauses in an acquisition agreement can also fall foul of the law.

Australia's merger controls operate whenever an acquisition has, or is likely to have, the effect of substantially lessening competition in a market in Australia. An international acquisition may also be regulated if its results in a foreign person acquiring a controlling interest (either directly or indirectly) in an Australian company, if that acquisition may lead to a substantial lessening of competition and the acquisition is not in the public interest.

A proper and careful analysis of the relevant market(s) affected by the acquisition is always essential if substantial penalties for non-compliance with the merger provisions are to be avoided.

Merger guidelines published by the ACCC indicate that, in the absence of special circumstances, the ACCC is unlikely to examine mergers where:

- the four largest firms have less than 75 per cent market share and the merged firm has less than 40 per cent market share; or

- the four largest firms have more than 75 per cent market share, and the merged firm has less than 15 per cent market share.

2.11   Required Offer Procedures

Where the target company (whether public or private) has more than 50 members, the takeover provisions of Chapter 6 of the Corporations Law will apply.

Chapter 6 is complex and far-reaching (for example, it applies to options and informal agreements that precede a formal contract), but in broad terms a person cannot acquire an entitlement to more than 20 per cent of the voting shares of an Australian incorporated company other than by one of the permitted methods (which include a full takeover bid or prior shareholder approval).

The takeover provisions also apply to a 'downstream' acquisition where the buyer acquires more than 20 per cent of the voting shares in a non-Australian company which, in turn, holds or controls, directly or indirectly, more than 20 per cent of the voting shares in an Australian company to which the takeover rules apply.

Unsolicited offers to purchase the shares of a company which are made to shareholders in Australia must comply with certain procedural requirements imposed by Australian law. These include a requirement to make the offer in printed or electronic form to the offeree by name, to include certain information about the market value of the shares or a fair estimate of that value, to leave the offer open for acceptance for at least 30 days, and not to withdraw it other than by way of a formal withdrawal document addressed to the offeree.

These provisions will not usually apply to a private sale and purchase by way of a negotiated sale agreement, but care should be exercised if the target has other share-holders who are not involved in the negotiations and only receive final documents for signing once terms have been agreed.

If the buyer proposes to issue or transfer any form of security (shares or debentures) or interests in a managed or collective investment scheme (e.g. units in a unit trust) as payment for the shares or assets acquired, the offer of those securities or interests may only be made by way of a prospectus which complies with the Corporations Law. An offer of interests in a collective investment scheme may also only be made if the scheme has been registered in Australia.

2.12   Continuation of Government Licences

In certain industries it is necessary for the business's operator to have a licence. The relevant licence may be required under either federal or state legislation or both. Licences are required in, for example, banking, insurance, auctioneering, gaming and broadcasting. Various conditions may be attached to a licence and these need to be reviewed, particularly to determine whether the licence is revocable on a change of control of the licence holder.

Licences may also be required by local authorities in each place where the business is conducted, for example in relation to retail premises, the handling or treatment of hazardous or toxic waste, and general health and safety (e.g. fire certificates).

Licences are not normally transferable, so that a buyer of a business (as opposed to shares in a company) needs to obtain a new licence in its own name. The time taken to obtain the licence and the conditions which must be satisfied by the applicant are a relevant consideration.

2.13   Requirements for Transferring Shares

Restrictions on transfers of shares may be found in a company's constitution or, if there is one, in a shareholders' agreement. These documents should be reviewed. The Corporations Law does not, however, contain statutory pre-emption rights or other restrictions on the transfer of shares.

Subject to any special provisions in the constitution, shares are transferable by a simple written share transfer form. The form may have to be stamped (see **1.4**), must be approved for registration by the company's board of directors (if the company is a private company) and the buyer's name must be recorded in the company's register of members before the buyer can be said to have full legal title to the shares.

The acquisition of shares in companies which are listed on the ASX is beyond the scope of this handbook, but note that Australia has a system of electronic trading, settlement and registration which is now in widespread use and which has led to the dematerialization of share dealing and registration in the case of listed shares.

2.14   Requirements for Transferring Land and Property Leases

Australia has a comprehensive registration system for title to land (including leasehold interests). The purchase of any interest in real property requires execution of a pre-scribed transfer form and, subject to payment of the appropriate stamp duty, registration of that transfer in the land titles register in the state in which the land is situated.

Title to land can be specifically encumbered by mortgages or charges, or by caveats recording the interests of third parties in the land (such as easements or rights of way); in many cases title to land cannot pass and be registered in favour of the buyer until any prior encumbrances have been cleared or appropriate consents obtained.

2.15   Requirements for Transferring Intellectual Property

Title to all forms of intellectual property can be transferred by assignment.

The benefit of a licence to use a third party's intellectual property may also be assignable, but may require the licensor's consent.

Where the intellectual property is the subject of registration (which includes trade marks, registered designs and patents and domain names), notice of the assignment must be given to the appropriate registry, and specific forms may have to be used.

2.16   Requirements for Transferring Business Contracts, Licences and Leases

A business contract governed by the laws of an Australian state is only transferable or assignable in accordance with its terms. Assignment of the benefit of a contract does not release the transferor from the burden of the contract without a specific release from the other party to the contract. For this reason, many business acquisitions involve a formal novation of contracts (in which the buyer steps fully into the seller's place, the seller being released from all further liability) rather than a simple assignment.

Licences and business leases (finance leases, operating leases or hire purchase agreements) operate under the same rules.

In most cases, the consent of the other party to the contract (e.g. a lessor) is required before the contract can be assigned. It is not normally necessary to register or record an assignment of a business contract, although there may be stamp duty payable on the assignment document, and notice must be given to the other party that the contract has been assigned. The assignment of a debt may also require certain formalities in some Australian states.

2.17   Requirements for Transferring Other Assets

With the exception of real property and certain specific assets such as shares, goodwill, intellectual property, trading debtors and the benefit of contracts, assets generally can be transferred by delivery.

Assets that are the subject of a charge in favour of a bank or other creditor, or in which title has been retained by a trade supplier or a seller under a hire purchase or conditional sale agreement, continue to be encumbered by the third parties' rights following transfer to a buyer in most circumstances.

2.18   Encumbrances and Third Party Interests

Assets can be subject to many types of third party interests. Interests can arise under contract (e.g. a charge or a mortgage), by operation of law (e.g. a property right or a lien in favour of a statutory authority) or by virtue of specific registration on a public register (e.g. an encumbrance affecting land).

A buyer for full value (on open market terms) of an asset generally takes good title to it, unless it has actual or constructive notice of an encumbrance or the seller does not, in fact, have a clear title to that asset.

Certain title registers (particularly in the case of land) can be conclusive evidence of the title of the registered proprietor on which the buyer can rely, but other assets may be subject to an unregistered or unascertainable interest which a buyer will not be able to uncover. In such a case, warranties from the seller as to clear title are essential.

2.19   Minimum Shareholder and Officer Requirements

Private companies may now (as a result of recent simplification legislation for private companies) have only one director. At least one of the directors of an Australian company (and if there is only one, that person) must be resident in Australia. Public companies must have at least three directors' at least two of whom are residents.

There may not be more than 50 non-employee shareholders in a private company, which may now have a single shareholder. A public company may also have only one shareholder, but there is no upper limit. An Australian public company must, and a private company may, also have a secretary, who must ordinarily reside in Australia.

2.20   Non-competition Clauses

Restraint of trade or non-competition covenants given by a seller in the context of a sale of business are generally enforceable, provided that the extent and terms of the covenant are reasonable. What is reasonable depends upon the circumstances of the case, the nature of the business and the effect which competition could have on the buyer.

Restraint of trade or non-competition covenants given by employees, which apply after the termination of their employment, can also be enforceable if they are reasonable, but the test of reasonableness is stricter in the case of an employee than in the case of a seller. A non-competition restraint that has the effect of preventing an employee carrying on his or her actual occupation or exercising his or her skills may be difficult to enforce, particularly if it applies for more than a short period following termination of employment. More limited restraints, such as those preventing an employee soliciting their former employer's clients, are more likely to be enforceable (provided they are properly drafted).

Note that, in New South Wales, the courts have a discretion under the Restraints of Trade Act 1976 to 'rewrite' an unenforceable restraint clause to make it reasonable and enforceable. The courts are not limited, under the 1976 Act, to putting a line through particular words in the clause. However, the courts cannot enlarge the clause beyond its terms, but can only narrow it. There is some authority to suggest that the courts cannot rewrite a clause which is void for uncertainty.

Agreements in restraint of trade may also fall under the provisions of Australia's Trade Practices Act, which prohibits any agreement or understanding which has the purpose or effect of substantially lessening competition or which is an exclusionary provision (effectively, a collective boycott). The provisions of the Trade Practices Act are far-reaching and potentially apply in all acquisitions, particularly where the seller and buyer are, or would but for the acquisition be, in competition with each other.

2.21 Environmental Considerations

Australia has sophisticated laws for the protection of the environment, which are primarily administered by state government authorities. Substantial penalties can be imposed on businesses which damage the environment and a purchaser of a business or of a property can inherit responsibility for rectifying environmental damage. Directors and other people 'concerned in the management of a company' can also be found personally liable for environmental offences committed by their company.

Particularly in the case of the mining, manufacturing and chemical industries, appropriate environmental due diligence investigations are always advisable in the context of an acquisition of either shares or assets.

Warranties in relation to environmental damage and liability should also always be obtained from a seller, unless the buyer's own due diligence has extended to a full environmental audit.

2.22 Employee Superannuation/Pension Plans

Indirectly, the Australian government requires employers in Australia to contribute a minimum proportion of an employee's salary into an approved superannuation or retirement benefits scheme.

Larger companies sometimes operate final salary superannuation schemes (or defined benefit funds), under which employees' superannuation benefits are calculated by reference to their final salary (or final average salary) and years of service. However, these are relatively rare and, increasingly, employers are turning to defined contribution superannuation schemes under which the final benefits are determined by the investment return achieved by the superannuation fund on the contributions made to the fund.

Until 1 July 2007, strict taxation rules determine the maximum amount which (for the purposes of the company claiming a tax deduction) can be contributed in any year to a superannuation scheme. From 1 July 2007, these deduction limits will be replaced with limits on the amounts of contributions will receive favourable tax treatment.

Superannuation funds are always controlled by a separate 'responsible entity' but, by the nature of its agreement with its employees, a company may have an ongoing obligation to make contributions to the fund designed to ensure that it will always have sufficient assets available to meet its expected obligations to provide benefits for retiring employees. If, because of adverse market movements or other factors, the fund is under funded, there may be an obligation on the company to make a specific extraordinary payment or series of payments to the fund. A buyer must always therefore take steps to determine the nature and value of a fund established for employees of a target business where there is an obligation on the employer company's part to maintain the fund assets.

Where the target is a member of a group, or where the purchase is one of business assets, the employees who are transferred to the buyer with the business may need to withdraw from a group superannuation or employer sponsored scheme, in which case alternative superannuation arrangements must be provided for them.

2.23 Employee Rights

Australia's system of industrial relations results in employers being subject to four potential sources of laws and regulations (or any combination of them) in relation to their dealings with employees:

- the employee's specific contract of employment;

- collective or individual workplace agreements with employees or unions which are approved in accordance with legislation;

- industrial 'awards' which may prescribe terms and conditions of employment; and

- Federal or State legislation (including the Fair Pay Standard).

The work choices employment legislation in Australia introduced in March 2006 saw most corporate employers moving from the state to the federal system.

The terms of the contract, award, agreement or legislation may deal with many issues in addition to the basic terms of employment, such as the terms on which employees may be made redundant, and the payments which must be made to them in that event, and employee's long service leave and holiday entitlements.

In addition, industrial tribunals or courts have power to order the reinstatement of a dismissed employee, or to award compensation for unfair dismissal. However, as a result of the new legislation, many employers with less than 100 employees will be exempt from this unfair dismissal jurisdiction.

2.24   Compulsory Transfer of Employees

Australia does not yet have 'transfer of undertakings' legislation which would make a buyer of business assets responsible for the employees previously associated with that business following its transfer. It is therefore possible for the buyer of business assets to 'cherry pick' employees (providing it does not offend anti-discrimination or freedom of association legislation), leaving the seller to continue to have responsibility for any employees to whom offers are not made by the new owner of the business. Equally, though, employees of the seller are free to refuse an offer of employment from the buyer. In either case, the seller will then be liable for the costs associated with the termination of the employment of those employees if other jobs cannot be found for them

In many cases, where the buyer takes on the seller's employees, the buyer is obliged (at least commercially, even if not legally) to recognize the transferring employees' past service and accrued entitlements to annual and long service leave and often severance pay.

Employees of a company the shares of which are acquired by a buyer continue, however, to have all of the rights previously enjoyed, notwithstanding the change in the ultimate ownership of the company, and the company continues to be liable for employee pay and benefits both before and after the date of acquisition of its shares.

2.25   Tax Deductibility of Acquisition Expenses

Where the buyer is a company or individual not resident or taxable in Australia, the deductibility of its acquisitions expenses is determined by the laws of its home jurisdiction.

Where, however, the buyer is an Australian taxpayer, acquisition expenses are only deductible to the extent that they are an outgoing properly incurred in order to gain assessable income. Expenses incurred in the acquisition of capital or a capital asset, such as shares or business assets, are not deductible. Expenses of a capital nature may, however, be included in the cost base of an asset for the purpose of calculating any subsequent tax on capital gains payable on disposal of that asset where the proceeds of sale exceed its cost base.

2.26   Levies on Acquisition Agreements and Collateral Documents

Stamp duty in Australia is always relevant to business and share acquisitions. Stamp duty is a state tax generally levied in relation to shares of companies incorporated in, or assets situated in, the state. Duty is generally substantially higher on the transfer of assets (up to 5.5 per cent) than on a transfer of shares (0.6 per cent, or none on ASX-listed shares or shares in companies incorporated in Victoria, Tasmania and Western Australia). The transfer of shares in a land-rich company can attract the high rates of duty which would have been payable on a transfer of the property itself.

It is important to determine the purchasing vehicle's identity before exchange of contracts. Stamp duty exemptions for intra-group transfers are limited, although most states allow exemptions for duty on genuine corporate reconstruction transactions. It is therefore important to finalize the intended structure, and to identify the correct purchaser, before agreements are exchanged if further duty on a subsequent intra-group transaction or subsale is to be avoided.

2.27   Financing Rules and Restrictions

Australia's taxation laws include thin capitalization rules which have the effect of denying a deduction to an Australian company or business in respect of interest payments made to a non-resident controller if the Australian business's debt to asset ratio exceeds certain prescribed limits.

Dividends paid on preference shares can be treated, for tax purposes, as 'debt dividends' in certain cases, with the result that any franking credits otherwise attaching to those dividends as a result of company tax paid by the Australian company are disregarded, leading to a withholding tax liability on the dividend paid which would not otherwise have arisen.

Australia's Corporations Act prohibits a company giving financial assistance to purchase its own shares or the shares of its holding company if that assistance results or would result in 'material prejudice' to the company or its shareholders, or to the company's ability to pay its creditors. There are some exceptions to this rule, and a company can be authorized to give financial assistance by a special resolution of its shareholders or a resolution of all ordinary shareholders and, if it has an Australian holding company after the acquisition, by a special resolution of the members of that holding company.

2.28   Exchange Controls and Repatriation of Profits

There are no longer any exchange controls in Australia, except for transactions involving countries subject to UN sanctions. However, significant cash transactions, whether domestic or international, must be reported by financial institutions and other 'cash dealers' to a government agency.

Fully franked dividends (dividends paid out of company profits which have suffered full company tax in Australia) paid to non-resident investors in Australian resident companies are not subject to dividend withholding tax. Dividends, to the extent that they are unfranked, are subject to 30 per cent dividend withholding tax, which is generally reduced to 15 per cent if the investor is resident in a country with which Australia has a double taxation agreement.

The current Australian corporate tax rate is 30 per cent.

Franking credits attached to dividends are really only of advantage to resident shareholders and no refund is available to non-residents. Australian dividend withholding tax and underlying company tax may be allowed as a credit against the non-resident's tax liability in its home jurisdiction.

Australia imposes a 10 per cent withholding tax on interest paid to non-residents.

2.29   Groups of Companies

A company incorporated under Australia's Corporations Law is required to prepare consolidated accounts (a profit and loss account and a balance sheet) of the company and each of the entities it controls or has controlled from time to time during its financial year (apportioned if necessary).

A company incorporated under the Corporations Law must also ensure that its financial year and the financial years of each company or entity which it controls are synchronized. It is therefore not possible, without the specific consent of the Australian Securities and Investments Commission, for group companies in Australia to have different accounting balance dates. It is not, however, required that an Australian subsidiary of a foreign holding company has a common balance date with its parent, although accounting or company laws binding on the foreign parent in its home jurisdiction may require this.

2.30   Responsibility for Liabilities of an Acquired Subsidiary

Traditionally, shareholders in Australia have been insulated from liability for the debts of a company in which they hold shares, other than in circumstances where a specific guarantee, indemnity or other undertaking has been given in favour of a creditor.

Changes to Australia's Corporations Law, however, resulted in a parent company being potentially liable for a subsidiary's unsecured debt where the subsidiary incurs that debt at a time when it is insolvent, or if it becomes insolvent at that time as a result of incurring that and any other debts, and the holding company or one or more if its directors is aware at that time that there are reasonable grounds for suspecting that the subsidiary is or would become insolvent.

2.31   Governing Law of the Contract

Australian courts honour a choice of law freely made between parties to a contract. They do not insist on applying Australian law to a contract for the acquisition of shares or business assets in Australia, although a choice of law having no commercial or reasonable connection with the parties to the agreement may be disregarded on grounds of public policy in certain circumstances.

While a foreign law may govern both the agreement and the relationship between the parties, Australian state or federal law usually determines other questions such as the effect of a transfer of title to shares or other assets, or the rights of creditors and others.

2.32   Dispute Resolution Options

Australian laws, and the courts, recognize that parties to commercial contracts may wish to resolve disputes other than by litigation. The whole range of arbitration and mediation options is therefore available to resolve commercial disputes.

Australia is a signatory to the New York Convention and has adopted the UNCITRAL Model Law on International Commercial Arbitration. Australian courts therefore recognize and enforce international arbitration awards in certain cases.

Australia also has a sophisticated network of arbitration bodies which will appoint arbitrators to hear disputes, including the Australian Centre for International Commercial Arbitration in Melbourne.

Mediation has also been used successfully in many cases in Australia to resolve complex commercial disputes and is gaining in popularity as an effective way to avoid lengthy and costly litigation. A number of bodies provide mediators and mediation services in Australia.

Parties are free to adopt the arbitration or mediation rules of any Australian or international body in their contracts and the Australian courts will recognize and honour the wishes of the parties in this respect. It is not, however, possible to oust the jurisdiction of the Australian courts in a dispute over which they have jurisdiction, although a court may be bound by a determination of an expert or an arbitrator on questions of fact if the parties have so agreed.

Finally, Australia is also a signatory to a number of treaties giving recognition to the judgments of superior courts overseas, and it is possible in many cases to register a judgment obtained overseas for the purposes of enforcing it in Australia.

2.33 Other Issues

Further simplification of Australia's Corporations Act is expected. The simplification programme has already introduced straightforward rules for share buybacks, eased the regulatory burden on private companies and made radical changes to the share capital structure and constitution of Australian companies.

3. AUSTRIA

Peter Huber
CMS Reich-Rohrwig Hainz

3.1 Introductory Comments

Austria is a federal republic consisting of nine states (*Bundesländer*). Most regulations relevant to business acquisitions (in particular the law of contracts, accounting regulations and corporate law) are federal rather than state laws.

There are only few legislative restrictions on business acquisitions in Austria generally and on acquisitions by foreign investors in particular. Certain requirements regarding merger control and securities laws have to be observed at the national as well as European level. A recent amendment to the Austrian Takeover Act, which came into force on 9 June 2006, introduced certain regulations that go beyond the EU Directive 2004/25/EC on takeover bids and are specific to Austrian law. The regime of group taxation, introduced in 2005, provided rather unique tax incentives.

A member state of the European Union since 1995, Austria has become an attractive business location despite relatively high labour costs. Austria is used by many international investors as a hub for Central and Eastern Europe. The legal and economic environment is generally considered stable and favourable to foreign investment.

3.2 Corporate Structures

As in many other European jurisdictions, the most common form of corporation in Austria is the private limited company (*Gesellschaft mit beschränkter Haftung* or *GmbH*), followed by the joint-stock company (*Aktiengesellschaft* or *AG*). The shareholders of these two legal entities are generally subject to liability for the corporation's debts only to the extent of their capital contributions.

The following are non-corporate legal forms of business undertakings where the shareholders (except for the limited partner of a limited partnership) are personally liable for the debts of the business on an unlimited basis:

- sole proprietorship (*Einzelkaufmann*);

- civil law partnership (*Gesellschaft bürgerlichen Rechts* or *GesbR*);

- general partnership (*Offene Gesellschaft* or *OG*);

- limited partnership (*Kommanditgesellschaft* or *KG*).

© World Law Group
International Business Acquisitions, M. Whalley, F.-J. Semler (eds.), Kluwer Law International, London, 2007; ISBN 9789041124838.

As of 1 January 2007, an amendment to the Austrian Commercial Code (renamed '*Unternehmensgesetzbuch*' or *UGB*) entered into force whereby the general registered partnership (*Offene Erwerbsgesellschaft, OEG*) and the limited registered partnership (*Kommanditerwerbsgesellschaft, KEG*), two forms of partnership available for activities which have not traditionally been considered trading activities (*Handelsgewerbe*) such as the ownership of real estate, were abolished and absorbed by the general partnership and the limited partnership, respectively.

GmbH

The *GmbH* is a legal entity (*juristische Person*) whose shareholders are generally not personally liable for liabilities of the company. Their liability is limited to the obligation to fund the share capital, as stipulated in the articles of incorporation or a subscription certificate (*Übernahmserklärung*). The stated share capital (*Stammkapital*) is divided into quotas of subscribed capital (*Stammeinlagen*) towards which the shareholders make their contributions. In contrast to an *AG*, no share certificates may be issued and the listing of quotas in a *GmbH* on an Austrian stock exchange is not possible. Each shareholder may only hold one quota.

The minimum stated share capital of a GmbH is EUR 35,000, of which at least half must be raised in cash upon incorporation, except where an existing business is contributed by the founders or contributions in kind are made on the basis of an independent valuation.

The articles of incorporation may provide for further transfer restrictions like the approval by the company's shareholders.

Any natural person or legal entity can be a shareholder of a *GmbH*; neither Austrian citizenship nor Austrian residency is required. A *GmbH* must have one or more managing director(s) (*Geschäftsführer*) who represent the company both in and out of court and manage the business of the company. A managing director can only be an individual who is capable of entering into legal transactions; neither Austrian citizenship nor Austrian residency is required. They are appointed by the shareholders' meeting and may basically be recalled at any time without cause. The shareholders have a direct influence over the management, since they can issue binding instructions to the managing director(s). A supervisory board (*Aufsichtsrat*) which is independent of the board of directors (based on a two-tier management system) is compulsory only for a larger *GmbH* meeting certain statutory criteria.

AG

The liability of the shareholders of an *AG* is generally limited to the obligation to fund the share capital. The stated share capital (*Grundkapital*) is divided into shares with a par value of at least EUR 1 (*Nennbetragsaktien*) or into non-par value shares representing an equal part of the company's share capital (*Stückaktien*). Furthermore, the shares may be issued in the form of registered shares (*Namensaktien*) or bearer shares (*Inhaberaktien*).

The minimum stated share capital is EUR 70,000, of which at least one quarter must be raised in cash before the registration of the company. Shares are freely transferable (without a notarial deed).

An *AG* must also have one or more managing director(s) (*Vorstand*) who represent the company both in and out of court and manage the business of the company. Also an *AG* managing director can only be an individual who is capable of entering into legal transactions; neither Austrian citizenship nor Austrian residency is required. In contrast to the *GmbH*, however, a managing director of an AG is appointed for a maximum term of five years by the supervisory board and may be recalled only for cause. Neither the shareholders nor the supervisory board may give instructions to the managing director(s) in the course of day-to-day business. A supervisory board (*Aufsichtsrat*) is compulsory. The members of the supervisory board are appointed partly by the shareholders' meeting and as to one-third of its members by the workers' council.

General Partnership (Offene Gesellschaft, OG)

A general partnership consists of two or more partners with unlimited personal liability for the general partnership's debts. There is no prescribed minimum capital.

Limited Partnership (Kommanditgesellschaft, KG)

A limited partnership consists of at least one general partner (*Komplementär*) with unlimited liability and at least one limited partner (*Kommanditist*) whose liability is restricted to the amount of his contribution registered with the commercial register (*Firmenbuch*). The general partners represent the company and manage its business. There is no prescribed minimum capital.

In order to limit liability, while at the same time enjoy the tax benefits of a partnership structure, a limited partnership where the only general partner is a *GmbH* may be established. Such limited partnership is referred to as a *GmbH & Co KG*. Due to the corporation-like structure of such partnerships, certain rules governing corporations may apply by way of analogy (e.g. capital maintenance rules).

3.3   Letters of Intent and Heads of Agreement

When two or more parties enter into negotiations with the intent to acquire a business, a pre-contractual relationship is created which imposes on the parties *inter alia* the obligation to act in good faith. Such relationship may be created by way of oral communication, in writing or even by conclusive actions. In the context of proposed business acquisitions, Austrian legal practice has adopted the Anglo-American style 'Letter of Intent' for regulating the preliminary stages of a transaction, often outlining the envisaged transaction process and the proposed transaction's material terms and conditions. The legal value of a letter of intent depends upon its specific language. To avoid ambiguity, it is recommended that one expressly determines whether the letter of intent (and which provisions thereof) is (are) to be binding upon the parties.

Usually the letter of intent will be non-binding, with the exception of certain terms, e.g. confidentiality, exclusivity, break-up fees and access to information. Nevertheless, based on the general good faith principle, a party discontinuing negotiations without any cause, where the parties have relied *bona fide* on the continuation of the negotiations, may be liable for damages on the basis of *culpa in contrahendo*. A proviso in a procedure letter or similar document that reserves a party's right to discontinue the transaction at any time without cause will typically cover against this liability risk.

A binding letter of intent would be deemed a '*Punktation*' or a pre-agreement (*Vorvertrag*) depending on its specific wording. A '*Punktation*' is an agreement which contains only the essential terms of an agreement that are regarded as binding, so that the parties may demand direct specific performance of the agreement. A pre-agreement constitutes a binding agreement for the parties to conclude a certain agreement in future, thus giving the parties only the right to demand the execution of the specified agreement, but not to request direct specific performance of such agreement. A pre-agreement is still concluded under the condition of no change of circumstances. Nevertheless, a failure to execute the definitive agreement on the agreed date is considered a breach and may make the responsible party liable for damages.

3.4 Taxes Affecting the Structure and the Calculation of the Price

Under Austrian law, as in other jurisdictions, the treatment of asset deals and share deals differs significantly. The tax consequences of an acquisition also differ depending on the legal form and the tax domicile of the acquirer. The acquisition of an Austrian business by a foreign acquirer will typically be conducted through an Austrian vehicle.

Asset Deal

A step-up in the tax basis of the acquired assets is generally available. Goodwill originating from an asset deal may generally be amortized for tax purposes. The transfer of tax loss carry-forwards to the acquirer is restricted.

Generally, the transfer of assets is not subject to transfer taxes. This does not apply to real property where the transfer is subject to property transfer tax (*Grunderwerbsteuer*) at a rate of 3.5 per cent of the consideration. Registration of the buyer as owner of the real property with the Austrian land register (*Grundbuch*) triggers an additional registration fee of 1 per cent of the consideration (see **26.** below).

Subject to the structure of the deal, the assignment of claims and other rights in the course of an asset deal may be subject to a stamp duty of 0.8 per cent of the consideration, provided that a document within the meaning of the Austrian Stamp Duty Act (*Gebührengesetz 1957*) is executed (see **26.** below).

Share Deal

In a share deal, a step-up in the tax basis of the target company's assets is not generally available. Limited goodwill depreciation of up to 50 per cent of the allocated acquisition costs may be available to the buyer, if certain conditions are satisfied.

The transfer of shares is not subject to transfer taxes. However, the transfer of a 100 per cent participation triggers real property transfer tax amounting to 3.5 per cent of the double standard tax basis (*Einheitswert*) of the relevant property. The standard tax basis is usually significantly lower than the market value of such property. Property transfer tax can be avoided easily by transferring a nominal minority participation to another group company of the acquirer.

3.5 Extent of Seller's Warranties and Indemnities

The general provisions of the Austrian Civil Code (*ABGB*) on physical and legal defects applicable to the sale of assets apply to purchase agreements regarding shares or businesses unless contracted out by the parties.

As a matter of Austrian law, the implied representations made by a seller of shares in a corporation only relate to the rights represented by the shares and not to the value of the shares or the corporation's business. The Austrian Supreme Court (*OGH*) has, however, held that physical or legal defects of a business undertaking itself amount to a defect of the sale shares, if all shares in the corporation are being sold. It is likely that this rule would be extended to certain majority shareholdings. The scope of such implied warranties for the underlying business is not entirely clear. The seller is deemed liable for defects which influence the merchantability or the value of the enterprise as a whole and for the absence of characteristics of the business or of material assets which are generally assumed in a business of the type being sold.

It is therefore highly advisable to agree on a specific set of representations and warranties both in an asset deal and in a share deal governed by Austrian law.

In case there is no special stipulation as to the remedies in an Austrian business or share purchase agreement, the purchaser has a claim for the cure (*Naturalrestution*) of the defect (if practicable), a reduction of the purchase price (*Minderung*) or, in the event of a material defect or a breach of specific contractual representations and warrant, rescission (*Wandlung*) of the agreement. It is, however, customary to stipulate specific remedies in the acquisition agreements, particularly to avoid the rather broad rescission right under statutory law. The rescission remedy is usually excluded or restricted to extreme cases and the purchaser's rights in all other cases of a breach are limited to reduction of the purchase price and compensation. The two-year statute of limitations for warranty claims based on defects of movable assets and three years for defects of immovable assets is often shortened or extended. *De minimis* thresholds for warranty claims and/or liability caps are regularly stipulated in Austrian law agreements and generally do not present enforceability issues.

For a purchaser it is generally recommendable and not uncommon to ask the seller to support his representations and warranties through a guarantee from a parent company, a bank guarantee or by retention of part of the purchase price.

3.6 Liability for Pre-contractual Representations

The seller may be liable for any declarations about the target company or the transaction process made during the preparation or negotiation of an acquisition agreement, if the purchaser thereby acquires a false or misleading impression of the target company and on that basis enters into the agreement. In case the purchaser would not have acquired the target company, had he not been misled, the purchaser may rescind the agreement. Furthermore, the seller may be liable for the damages resulting from negligent or wilful misrepresentation.

Due to difficulties in practice to prove which declarations have been made and which information has been provided by the seller in the course of the negotiations, the seller will typically attempt to limit his liability to the representations expressly stated in the acquisition agreement, thus removing any liability for the correctness or completeness of any pre-contractual communication.

An exclusion of liability for wilful misconduct would, however, not be enforceable. The exclusion of liability for negligent conduct is basically permitted between entrepreneurs unless it relates to cases of wannton (*krasse*) negligence or to personal injury.

Based on the *bona fide* principle, the seller as a prudent businessman is obliged to inform the purchaser about all aspects regarding the transaction which the purchaser may in good faith expect to be revealed. The seller may be liable on the basis of *culpa in contrahendo* for damages resulting from the negligent failure to reveal such information. In a customary due diligence process where the seller responds to relevant inquiries of the purchaser regarding the target company, a potential liability of the seller should not materialize.

3.7 Liability for Pre-acquisition Trading and Contracts

In case of an acquisition of shares in a corporation (i.e. a private-limited company or joint-stock company) the purchaser as new shareholder, as a general rule, is not liable for the company's debts. The liability of a purchaser of shares in a corporation is limited to the liability for the contribution towards the subscribed capital which has not yet been paid out by the seller and its predecessors (former shareholders). A change in the shareholder structure has no influence on the company's rights and obligations, since it is a separate legal entity.

In case of an acquisition of an interest in a non-corporate company (i.e. a civil law partnership, general partnership or a limited partnership), the purchaser is liable for certain pre-acquisition obligations of the company as specified in the Austrian Civil Code and the Austrian Commercial Code.

In case of an asset deal, only the contractually stipulated obligations are transferred to the purchaser. According to statutory provisions, the purchaser is further liable in the following cases:

- Pursuant to Section 1409 of the Civil Code, the purchaser of a business is jointly and severally liable with the seller towards the business' creditors for any pre-acquisition debts connected with the business which he knew or should have known of at the time of the acquisition. The liability of the purchaser is, however, limited to the value of the acquired assets. This liability of the purchaser may not be excluded or limited by an agreement with the seller. The purchaser's liability is reduced by any amounts paid directly by the purchaser the business' creditors.

- Pursuant to Section 25 of the Commercial Code (*HGB*), the purchaser of a business who continues the business under the former company name (*Firma*) was liable for any pre-acquisition debts of the business on an unlimited basis. Section 38 of the new Commercial Code *(UGB)* provides for a transfer of contracts subject to the right of objection of the respective third parties irrespective of whether the company name is maintained.

- Pursuant to Section 67 of the General Social Security Act (*ASVG*), the purchaser of a business is jointly and severally liable with the seller for any unpaid employer's social security contributions which have become due during the last twelve months prior to the acquisition. The purchaser may ask the social security agency for a binding statement indicating any outstanding amounts and thereby limit his liability to such amount.

- Pursuant to Section 14 of the Federal Fiscal Code (*Bundesabgabenordnung*), the purchaser of a business is liable for taxes and charges which have arisen in connection with the acquired business since the beginning of the calendar year preceding the acquisition date and which the purchaser knew of or should have known of at the time of the purchase. Such liability of the purchaser is limited to the value of the acquired assets.

3.8   Pre-completion Risks

The risk of loss lies with the seller until the title has effectively been transferred to the purchaser, i.e. until the closing of the acquisition agreement. The parties are, however, free to agree on a different date of transfer of risk.

For the purchaser, it is therefore advisable to seek protection through a material adverse change clause relating to the period between the signing and closing of the acquisition agreement. Furthermore, provisions limiting the seller's freedom to dispose of material assets and requiring the maintenance of appropriate insurance until closing are customary.

3.9   Required Governmental Approvals

The purchase of Austrian real estate and the acquisition of a controlling shareholding of a company owning Austrian real estate by foreign individuals, foreign companies or Austrian companies controlled by foreign individuals may require an approval by or a notification of the local authorities in accordance to relevant legislation which differs significantly from state to state.

The acquisition of a material shareholding in a banking or insurance business requires advance notification to and possibly an approval by the relevant regulatory authority.

The acquisition of shares in an Austrian company and the acquisition of a business by foreign individuals or entities does not require any further specific governmental approvals, except for approvals or consents under EU and domestic merger control legislation (see **10.** below). It should be noted that in certain industries (like electricity generation and distribution) federal law requires a certain level of government or state shareholdings which may necessitate an amendment to the relevant law in order to implement a particular transaction.

3.10 Anti-trust and Competition Law

Austrian merger control regulations apply to concentrations (this term includes merger and acquisitions of interests of 25 per cent or more in an Austrian undertaking) which exceed all of the following turnover thresholds during the financial year preceding the concentration:

- EUR 300 million for the aggregate world-wide turnover of the undertakings concerned;

- EUR 30 million for the aggregate Austrian turnover of the undertakings concerned; and

- EUR 5 million for the world-wide turnover of each of at least two of the undertakings concerned.

The implementation of the concentration is not permissible prior to a clearance by the cartel authorities. Agreements providing for implementation in the absence of or prior to clearance are void and attract a fine of up to 10 per cent of the world-wide turnover of the relevant undertaking in the preceding business year.

A concentration implemented outside of Austria may still be subject to clearance by the Austrian cartel authorities, if the concentration has an effect on the Austrian market, due to the undertaking concerned selling goods or providing services in Austria or otherwise.

Austrian merger control regulations do not apply to concentrations falling within the European Commission's jurisdiction under the Council Regulation (EC) No 139/2004 (EC Merger Regulation).

The Austrian rules on restrictive agreements have been amended in 2005 to reflect EC Regulation No. 1/2003 on the interpretation of the rules of competition stipulated in Articles 81 and 82 of the EC Treaty. The Austrian regulations generally accord with the EC competition law regime prohibiting agreements which restrict, distort or prevent competition in Austria.

3.11 Required Offer Procedures

The Austrian Takeover Act (*Übernahmegesetz*) regulates both voluntary and mandatory public takeover bids for shares in a joint-stock company with its registered seat in Austria, provided that such shares are listed on the Vienna Stock Exchange for official trading (*amtlicher Handel*) or regulated unofficial market (*geregelter Freiverkehr*). The Austrian Takeover Code has been substantially revised as of 9 June 2006, in part to implement the EU Takeover Direct but also to address concerns about the clarity of the existing law.

The Takeover Act provides that the acquirer of a controlling shareholding in a target company has to make a public takeover bid to the remaining shareholders for all outstanding shares (mandatory takeover bid). Under the revised Act, control is constituted by a shareholding of more than 30 per cent. Certain restrictions and obligations, other than the obligation to make a public takeover bid, are triggered by the acquisition of a shareholding exceeding 26 per cent. Mandatory takeover bids (and voluntary tender offers by which the offeror is seeking control of a target company) have to be priced at the higher of (i) the average share price for the six month period preceding the offer, and (ii) the highest price paid by the bidder for target shares during the twelve month period preceding the offer.

Non-compliance by a (potential) bidder with certain material obligations under the Takeover Act leads to a suspension of voting rights and attracts monetary fines.

A new law (*Gesellschafterausschlussgesetz*) which entered into force concurrently with the revised Takeover Act facilitates squeeze-outs of minorities of up to 10 per cent, particularly following public tender offers.

3.12   Continuation of Government Licenses

Governmental licenses are generally issued to specific persons, and a transfer or assignment to a third party requires the consent of the competent authority or the re-issuance of the license.

In some cases, licenses are issued in respect of physical objects. Such licenses authorize and oblige the owner from time to time of such object, and therefore transfer automatically to the acquirer in the event of an asset deal. Such *in rem* licenses include permits for the operation of plants, building permits or water rights.

In the event of a share deal, licenses of the target company generally remain unaffected, and no approval by an authority is required unless the license contains a change of control provision.

3.13   Requirements for Transferring Shares

Shares in a private-limited company are freely transferable, unless a restriction is stipulated in the articles of association. The transfer may be subject to approval by the company, the shareholders' meeting or even by all shareholders. The sale and transfer of a quota in a private limited company as well as arrangements for a future transfer of a quota (including call- and put-options) require a notarial deed form. This formal requirement relates to the transfer itself. It is therefore possible to acquire a quota in an Austrian *GmbH* on the basis of a share purchase agreement which is not notarized and contains provisions regarding the determination of the purchase price, representations and warranties and a short-form notarial deed providing for the transfer of the quota. Certain Austrian notaries (qualified as court-sworn translators) may draw up Austrian notarial deeds in the English language without the requirement of a German translation. Deeds created by German notaries are generally recognized as equivalent to Austrian deeds. The situation regarding other foreign notaries is less clear.

Any change of shareholders of a GmbH has to be registered with the Commercial Register. Such registration is, however, only of a declaratory nature and a failure to notify does not affect the validity of the share transfer. On the other hand, one may not fully rely on the entries in the register when conducting a due diligence of the ownership of an Austrian private-limited company.

Bearer shares in an Austrian joint-stock company may be transferred without observing any particular form, by physical delivery or instruction to a depositary. Registered shares and interim certificates (*Zwischenscheine*) in a joint-stock company may be transferred by endorsement or assignment followed by the surrender of the share certificates to the acquirer. The transfer of registered shares and interim certificates has to be declared to the company that records the new shareholder in the shares register. Such registration is only of a declaratory nature. The sale and transfer of registered shares and interim certificates (unlike the transfer of bearer shares) may require the approval of the target company or its shareholders' meeting. If such approval is withheld without cause, the court may approve such transfer instead.

The transfer of a shareholding in a general or limited partnership is only permissible if the articles of association so provide or if all partners (including the limited partners) approve such transfer. There are no formal requirements for the transfer. The change of shareholders has to be declared to the Commercial Register.

3.14 Requirements for Transferring Land and Property Leases

In an asset deal including real property, a purchase agreement containing specific transfer and registration language, which has to be notarized, has to be created. The transfer must be registered with the Land Register (*Grundbuch*) in order to be effective towards third parties. The purchaser of real property may generally rely on the accuracy of the entries in the land register if the purchaser is acting in good faith. The purchaser may therefore even acquire the ownership from a seller lacking title to the real property.

The purchase of real estate by foreigners may require an approval by or a notification of local authorities under state legislation (see **9.** above). Under certain state laws, the acquisition of farm land and forests as well as land designated for development is also subject to approval by or notification of the local authorities.

Any mortgages and other encumbrances such as easements (*Servituten*) must be registered with the Land Register. When properly registered, they generally follow ownership of the real property.

Any purchaser of real estate should verify that the dedication (*Widmung*) of the property according to the zoning plan fits the intended purposes. The acquirer of a property may under certain circumstances be held liable for the costs of remediation of contaminations of the acquired property.

Under the Austrian Lease Act (*Mietrechtsgesetz*) a lessee of a business premises has the right to transfer the lease agreement to the purchaser of the business, if the same business undertaking is continued in the leased premises. In such a case, the lessor has to be informed immediately of the disposal of the business undertaking. The lessor may demand an increase of the rent to the fair market rent within six months, as further specified in the Lease Act. If the lessee of the business premises is a company, the lessor is entitled to increase the rent to the fair market rent upon change of control in the company. These provisions have to be taken into consideration, since in many cases the rent tends to be below the fair market value, in particular due to the conclusion of long-term lease agreements on favourable terms in the past.

If a target company has rented out property, the lease agreement is transferred to the purchaser of the business.

3.15   Requirements for Transferring Intellectual Property

Patents, trademarks, models and designs may be transferred by assignment. The copyright as such is not assignable, but specific rights of the copyright holder may be licensed. Trademarks, designs and patents and transfers thereof must be registered with public registers, even if an entire enterprise is acquired. The seller of a business undertaking may decide not to transfer the intellectual property but to merely grant a license to the acquirer.

Under the Austrian Trademark Protection Act (*Markenschutzgesetz*), the right to a trademark and related licenses held by a company will transfer to the new owner whenever the entire business undertaking is transferred, unless other arrangements are made. If only a part of a business undertaking is sold, the trademark rights will not transfer to the acquirer unless otherwise agreed. No consent of a third party is required. The Austrian Trademark Protection Act also provides for the partial transfer of trademark rights.

The Austrian Copyright Act (*Urheberrechtsgesetz*) states that if a business holding an exploitation right (i.e. the right to use a work exclusively) is being transferred in whole or in part to a third party, the author's consent is not required to assign the right to the acquirer, provided there have been no stipulations to the contrary.

The transfer of shares has no impact on intellectual property rights, unless a license contains a change-of-control clause.

3.16   Requirements for Transferring Business Contracts, Licenses and Leases

In share deals, the target company remains the bearer of any of its rights and obligations. Long-term contracts may contain change-of-control clauses which are generally enforceable under Austrian law. Even in the absence of an explicit change-of-control clause, a change in the shareholder structure of one contractual party may be deemed a fundamental change to the basis of the agreement (*Geschäftsgrundlage*), thereby entitling the other party to terminate or adjust the agreement, if it appears from the agreement itself or from the circumstances of its conclusion that the party invoking this remedy has relied on the maintenance of the shareholder structure.

The transfer of business by way of an asset deal is, from a legal point of view, not a single act but a bundle of individual transfers. Generally speaking, the transfer of contractual relationships as part of a business transfer can be achieved in one of three ways: (i) statutory transfer of contract (e.g., transfer of employment relationships, transfer of certain leases and certain insurance contracts, trademark rights), (ii) transfer without a requirement of consent of the party (e.g., patent license agreements, trademark license agreements), and (iii) transfer with the consent of a third party (most commercial agreements). Certain contractual rights are not assignable (e.g., rent receivables under protected residential leases)

Whenever a transfer of a contract appears undesirable or impracticable, the parties will agree that the seller of the business continues to remain a party to such contract in its own name, and that the economic benefit of the contract shall accrue to the purchaser of the business, with the seller acting as a trustee.

3.17 Requirements for Transferring Other Assets

The distinction under Austrian law between taking title and taking possession is important for the transfer of movable physical assets. A sale and purchase agreement represents legal title but its conclusion does not in itself transfer ownership of the relevant asset. The buyer acquires ownership only by physically taking over the assets or by instructing the seller (or a third party) to hold the assets for the benefit of the buyer.

The transfer of receivables is effected by the execution of a deed of assignment and by giving notice of the assignment to the debtor or as an entry in the books of the assignor. In the absence of notice to the debtor, the debtor may discharge his liability by payment to the assignor.

3.18 Encumbrances and Third Party Interests

A mortgage on Austrian real estate is only valid when registered with the Land Register. The rank of one of several mortgages over the same property generally depends on the chronological order (priority) of their entry into the Land Register.

Customary security interests over movables include pledge, transfer by way of security (*Sicherungsübereignung*) and retention of title (*Eigentumsvorbehalt*). The retention of title to secure the claims for the purchase price, unlike the pledge or the transfer of title, is generally not subject to strict publicity requirements.

For the acquirer of shares or of a business such security interests are not generally apparent. In an asset deal with title defects, the acquirer's good faith in the transferor's ownership is protected to a certain extent. Good faith of the transferee of the receivables or other claims or rights is generally not protected. The bona fide acquisition from an unauthorized seller is possible in respect of bearer shares of a joint-stock company, but not in respect of a quota in a private limited liability company.

3.19 Minimum Shareholder and Officer Requirements

An Austrian general or limited partnership must have at least two shareholders. The limited partnership and joint-stock company require only one shareholder. It should be noted that a joint-stock company has to be founded by at least two founders.

The maximum number of shareholders is unlimited for all types of partnerships and corporations. Companies require at least one managing director (*Geschäftsführer* or *Vorstand*) who does not have to be an Austrian resident and, where a supervisory board has to be established or is established voluntarily, at least three members of the supervisory board (*Aufsichtsrat*).

3.20   Non-competition Clauses

Non-competition clauses, entered between the seller and the purchaser of a business, are generally enforceable, provided that the duration and scope are reasonable. Non-competition undertakings of the seller are generally unenforceable for a period in excess of five years.

3.21   Environmental Considerations

A large number of environmental regulations under federal and state laws affect the operation of businesses in Austria. Many aspects of environmental protection are regulated in the Trade Act (*Gewerbeordnung*). The Trade Act requires a permit for the operation of plants and facilities (*Betriebsanlagen*), provides for waste-management plans and regulates clean-ups and remediation requirements upon the closure of plants. Other important provisions can be found in the Act on the Remediation of Old Waste Sites (*Altlastensanierungsgesetz*), the Water Act (*Wasserrechtsgesetz*), the Waste Management Act (*Abfallwirtschaftsgesetz 2002*), and the Forestry Act (*Forstgesetz 1975*). These laws, apart from clean-up obligations, provide for monetary fines for non-compliance. Pollution of the environment, under certain conditions, constitutes a criminal offence. The acquired owner of property may be held liable for the acts and omissions of its predecessor.

In view of potential risks, buyers should consider undertaking an environmental due diligence investigation of the property. It should be noted that Austrian civil engineers are under an obligation to notify the competent authorities of certain contaminations detected in the course of a due diligence investigation. Appropriate environmental presentations and warranties should be included in the acquisition agreement.

3.22   Employee Superannuation/Pension Plans

Upon retirement, employees are entitled to severance payments, and those who have contributed to social security for at least 15 years are generally entitled to a social security pension funded by the employee's and employer's past contributions.

Companies as employers are free to establish pension plans granting their employees additional income after retirement. However, the pension plan must be in accordance with the Company Pensions Act *(Betriebspensionsgesetz)*.

In principle, additional pension rights for employees can be introduced by way of collective agreement (*Kollektivvertrag*), works agreement (*Betriebsvereinbarung*), through individual stipulation by the employer or through contractual agreement with the employee.

3.23 Employee Rights

Industrial relations in Austria are determined by what is referred to as the 'Social Partnership' (*Sozialpartnerschaft*). This frequently used term denotes a principle rather than an institution: it is a mixture of a spirit of cooperation and compromise and high-level and centralized problem-solving within a loose organizational framework.

Sources of labour law in Austria are:

- employment contracts and generally established business practice (*Betriebsübung*)

- statutes (*Satzungen*)

- collective agreements *(Kollektivverträge)* between trade unions and statutory employer organizations, regulating issues like payment and working conditions; such agreements are applicable to all employees who fall within the scope of the respective agreement, not only to members of the trade union;

- works agreements *(Betriebsvereinbarungen)*: are agreed upon in writing between the company and the works council; the scope of such agreements is determined by law or by collective bargaining agreements;

- the Patent Act provides for special rules regarding employees' inventions.

3.24 Compulsory Transfer of Employees

In the transfer of a business or part of a business by way of an asset deal the employment relationships of the workforce employed will, as a general principle, be transferred to the new employer automatically and by operation of law the rights and obligations of employer and employee will be unaffected.

If the position of an employee is adversely affected by the transfer, in particular as regards severance payments, the employee is entitled to terminate the employment agreement, while enjoying the same claims as in the case of a termination without cause by the employer. A termination of the employment contract by the new employer in connection with the transfer of the business is generally void, subject to an exception for reorganizations.

The new employer is fully liable not only for all current obligations as of the date of transfer, but also for all accrued rights of the transferred employee. The old employer is jointly and severally liable with the new employer for all such accrued rights. The liability of the former employer for severance payments and for company pensions is limited to five years after the transfer of business.

The parties to an asset deal are well advised to regulate the allocation of burdens from the statutory transfer of employees in detail in the acquisition agreement.

A share purchase generally does not affect employees' individual rights or the applicability of collective agreements, company work agreements or the structure of the works council.

3.25   Tax Deductibility of Acquisition Expenses

If the acquirer is an Austrian taxpayer, as a general rule, the acquisition costs are deductible to the extent that they qualify as operating expenditures and reduce the acquirer's taxable income in Austria. If the take over is effected by way of an asset deal, the costs arising in connection with the financing of the purchase price are deductible as business expenses by the purchaser. In share deals interest on loan/credit facilities *(Fremdkapitalzinsen)* for the acquisition of domestic or foreign participations is generally tax deductible since 2005, irrespective of whether or not the companies are part of a tax group. However, other costs of financing are not deductible.

3.26   Levies on Acquisition Agreements and Collateral Documents

Land transfer tax (Grunderwerbsteuer)

The transfer of real estate by way of an asset deal is subject to a land transfer tax. The tax amounts to 3.5 per cent of the sale price. Furthermore a registration fee of 1 per cent is levied. Real estate transactions are generally exempt from VAT.

Land transfer tax is also levied, where 100 per cent of the shares of a corporation owning real property are transferred or where unification (by either an individual or a legal entity) of 100 per cent of the shares of a corporation holding real property occurs (the tax assessment base equals 300 per cent of the property's assessed value). Consequently, taxation can be easily avoided by retaining a minimum holding.

In 2000, the tax on the transfer of shares and quotas in a GmbH was abolished. However, tax at 1 per cent is levied on the issuance of shares and on any increase in capital stock or other capital contribution in a corporation (capital transfer tax, *Kapitalverkehrsteuer*).

Stamp Duties (Rechtsgeschäftsgebühren)

Stamp duties are levied on various types of legal transactions concluded in written form. Austria's stamp duties are often levied on the basis of transaction volumes (without caps), and therefore may be higher than stamp duties in other jurisdictions. It is generally not the legal transaction which triggers the stamp duty but—with a few exceptions—the written instrument executed to document such transaction. Unlike in other areas of Austrian tax law, the principle of substance over form does not apply to stamp duties. The avoidance of stamp duties, therefore, often determines transaction structures.

Transactions triggering stamp duties include: commercial and residential leases, assignment of receivables, credit agreements, settlements and bills of exchange.

Percentage rates frequently range between 0.8 per cent and 2 per cent of the relevant transaction value.

Fees for public notaries and the fees for registration of ownership and mortgages in the land register are also related to the values involved and may therefore be substantial.

3.27 Financing Rules and Restrictions

The minimum share capital for a private-limited company is EUR 35,000, and for a joint-stock company EUR 70,000. No specific thin capitalization rules are stated in Austrian tax law. However, case law has established criteria in which shareholder loans are treated as quasi-equity, and the interest payments on such loans are not tax deductible, but are treated as disguised dividends.

3.28 Exchange Controls and Repatriation of Profits

There are, as a general matter, no restrictions on payments from Austria to foreign countries, but for statistical purposes, notification is obligatory in various cases under Austrian National Bank regulations. The transactions to be reported include: foreign exchange transactions and holdings of securities, the maintenance of foreign bank accounts, certain money transfers and netting operations, transit transactions and balances held abroad.

Dividends distributed by an Austrian corporation are, at the shareholder's personal level, subject to capital yields tax (*Kapitalertragssteuer*) at a current rate of 25 per cent, which is withheld at source. On the basis of the 'affiliation privilege' (*Schachtelprivileg*), which is available both at the national and the international level, capital yields tax is not payable where an Austrian resident company directly holds a 25 per cent participation in the share capital of another resident company and dividends are paid by virtue of that holding. Dividends received by an Austrian corporation from another Austrian tax resident corporation are tax-exempt.

A similar rule applies when an Austrian resident corporation has held a holding of at least 10 per cent of a foreign corporation for a minimum period of one year. The affiliation privilege is also accorded to Austrian branch offices of foreign companies. If the dividends are paid to an EU resident parent company, withholding tax may be claimed back under the refund procedure (or relief at source is granted if additional criteria are fulfilled), provided that the parent company has held a shareholding of at least 10 per cent for a minimum period of one year. If none of the above mentioned tax exemptions apply, the capital yields tax may be reduced or even eliminated under applicable Double Taxation Treaties.

3.29 Groups of Companies

Accounting

Parent companies (private-limited companies and joint-stock corporations) with their corporate seat in Austria are required to prepare consolidated financial statements for all domestic and foreign subsidiaries (*Konzernabschluss*) and a consolidated report on the state of the group (*Konzernlagebericht*).

Parent companies are exempt from the obligation to prepare consolidated financial statements and a consolidated group report if they are themselves included as subsidiaries in consolidated financial statements and group reports that have been prepared and audited pursuant to Austrian or equivalent foreign standards. Austrian parent companies are also exempt from the requirement to prepare consolidated financial statements if the total group assets, the total sales or the total number of employees do not exceed certain materiality thresholds.

Corporate

Austrian corporate law, unlike German law, does not include a body of rules regarding corporate groups (*Konzernrecht*). The enforceability of certain types of group agreements, like domination agreements (*Beherrschungsverträge*), customary in other jurisdictions, is therefore doubtful.

Taxation

As of 1 January 2005, a new scheme of group taxation enabling the pooling of earnings within a group of companies was introduced in Austria. Members of such a tax group may be corporations or cooperative societies that are subject to unlimited taxation in Austria as well as foreign entities, which are comparable to Austrian corporations or Austrian cooperative societies and which are held by an Austrian group member or the Austrian group parent company. A corporation domiciled in a Member State of the European Union, which is subject to limited taxation in Austria and has an Austrian-registered branch (*Zweigniederlassung*) may also act as group parent company.

A direct or indirect participation of the group parent company of at least 50 per cent of the capital and the voting rights is required for the company to qualify as a group member.

Within the tax group, the depreciation of the participation of other group members is not tax-deductible. Upon acquisition of a participation in a corporation with an operating business being subject to unlimited taxation in Austria, the group parent or another group member may claim a tax-deductible depreciation of the goodwill of the target company limited to 50 per cent of the acquisition cost, provided that the target is not a member of the tax group. The goodwill may be depreciated over a period of 15 years.

To achieve recognition of the tax group, a written group application, signed by the Austrian group members, has to be filed. The application has to include an agreement between the group members concerning the intra-group compensation of tax effects of the pooling of earnings and losses.

The tax group has to remain in existence for at least three years. A premature withdrawal from a tax group triggers a re-calculation of profits for tax purposes.

3.30 Responsibility for Liabilities of an Acquired Subsidiary

Shareholders of an Austrian corporation are, as a general rule, not liable for the corporation's debts. A liability of shareholders may arise where a parent company has exercised its powers of direction continuously and intensively, has thereby acted as a *de facto* manager of the subsidiary and infringed upon the interests of the subsidiary. Co-mingling of the parent's and the subsidiary's funds may also justify piercing the corporate veil. Directors of an Austrian corporation may *inter alia* be personally liable for the corporation's obligations if they did not file for bankruptcy in a timely manner.

3.31 Governing Law of the Contract

The choice of law made by the parties in sale and purchase agreements is generally recognized by Austrian courts if the choice is expressed or demonstrated with reasonable certainty through the terms of the contract. The chosen law also prevails over all mandatory Austrian rules, unless it infringes upon community law, public policy (*ordre public*) or is contrary to mandatory provisions protecting Austrian consumers or employees. In the absence of a choice of law, the law of the jurisdiction with the closest connection applies. Freedom of choice is limited in the areas of property law and corporate law. The relevant rules are set forth in the Austrian Conflict of Laws Act (*IPRG*) as well as bi- and multilateral treaties.

3.32 Dispute Resolution Options

A choice-of-forum clause in a business acquisition agreement is generally recognized by Austrian courts if no exclusive jurisdiction exists. It is also common for parties to an agreement for the sale and transfer of an Austrian business to stipulate arbitration clauses. The Austrian Code of Civil Procedure contains regulations applicable to arbitration proceedings, but such provisions are usually contracted out by the parties to international transactions. The parties may agree on arbitral proceedings before the International Arbitral Centre of the Austrian Economic Chamber in Vienna if at least one of the parties has its seat outside of Austria.

Foreign arbitral awards may generally be enforced in Austria under the condition of reciprocity, as manifested in bi- or multilateral agreements to which Austria is a signatory state. Austria has ratified nearly all important enforcement conventions, such as the Geneva Protocol and the Geneva Convention, the New York Convention on the Enforcement of Foreign Judgments and Foreign Arbitral Awards of June 10, 1958, the Convention on jurisdiction and the enforcement of judgments in civil and commercial matters done at Lugano (88/592/EEC), the 1968 Brussels Convention on jurisdiction and the enforcement of judgments in civil and commercial matters and the Council Regulation (EC) No. 44/2001 on jurisdiction and the recognition and enforcement of judgments in civil and commercial matters.

4. BELGIUM

Cedric Guyot
CMS Derks Star Busmann Hanotiau

4.1 Introductory Comments

The term 'corporate acquisition' is hereinafter understood in a broad sense as the acquisition of a business. This transaction may include assets such as owned or leased real property, plant, machinery and equipment, inventories, accounts receivable, patents and trade marks, the customer base and other goodwill. It covers, in most cases, trade and financial liabilities, in addition to more complex contractual relationships with third parties such as employees, landlords, licensors, suppliers or distributors.

The transfer of business may be operated by way of sale and assignment of all the elements constituting the business (hereinafter referred to as 'asset transaction') or, if the business is incorporated, by transfer of all shares or, at least of a controlling interest in such company (hereinafter referred to as 'share transaction').

4.2 Corporate Structures

Nine different types of partnerships and corporations can be identified in Belgium:

- *société civile* (civil partnership);

- *association momentanée* (temporary association);

- *société en participation* (sleeping partnership);

- *société en nom collectif* (general partnership);

- *société en commandite simple* (limited partnership);

- *société en commandite par actions* (partnership limited by shares);

- *société coopérative* (co-operative partnership);

- *société anonyme* or SA (public company limited by shares); and

- *société privée à responsabilité limitée* or SPRL (private company limited by shares or closed corporation).

Except for the *société civile*, the legal rules concerning these corporations and partnerships can be found in the Federal Commercial Code, Book I, Title IX (*Lois Coordonnées sur les Sociétés Commerciales*, hereinafter referred to as 'LCSC').

However, a new Company Code has been created by the Law of 7 May 1999. This Code will come into force on 6 February 2001 at the latest. The new Company Code

© World Law Group
International Business Acquisitions, M. Whalley, F.-J. Semler (eds.), Kluwer Law International, London, 2007; ISBN 9789041124838.

does not substantially modify the existing legal provisions regarding commercial companies. The purpose of this code is to co-ordinate, harmonize and bring together in one single code all legal provisions applying to commercial companies. Some references are made hereinafter to this new Company Code.

This section is limited to the 'assets' and 'share' transaction of the SA, which is the most common type of company in Belgian business life.

4.3 Letters of Intent and Heads of Agreement

Before a sale of shares agreement is drafted, the buyer and the seller should set down a record of the commercial terms they have agreed upon in a letter of intent or heads of agreement.

The first point to consider in this regard is whether the provisions are to be nonbinding and subject to contract, or binding and meant to create a legal relationship between the buyer and the seller.

The course of action to be adopted depends on the nature of the particular transaction:

- If they are to be non-binding, the parties should state this clearly and, as long as no binding agreement has been concluded, each of the parties is free to interrupt the negotiations. The only limit to that freedom is to claim damages for abusive breach. Parties must take into consideration during the contract negotiation the doctrine of *culpa in contrahendo*. This doctrine implies that the parties must conduct their negotiation in good faith and that they can be held responsible in case of sudden and unjustified breach of the negotiation. A party which falls victim to the misconduct of the other party to the agreement can claim compensation for the incurred damage (sustained costs, waste of time, and loss of an opportunity to conclude a contract with a third party).

- If the letters of intent are to be binding, all the conditions which are necessary for the validity of a contract and which are laid down in Article 1108 of the Civil Code are to be fulfilled. Therefore, the object of the transaction must be clear and the price of it stipulated in, or at least determinable in function of elements laid down in, the letter of intent.

4.4 Taxes Affecting the Structure and Calculation of the Price

The choice between an 'assets' and a 'shares' transaction is often made on the basis of tax law considerations. Indeed, the two operations are subject to different tax law provisions. Under Article 90.9 of the Income Tax Code, the tax authority may impose a capital gains tax on the first seller if either:

- a controlling participation is sold to a non-Belgian resident; or

- the buyer resells the shares within 12 months to a company or physical person without residence in Belgium or to an organization named in Article 227.2° and 3° of the Income Tax Code.

4.5   Extent of Seller's Warranties and Indemnities

The legal obligations of a seller are governed by Articles 1602–1694 of the Civil Code. The following obligations are considered as implied warranties and therefore need no express provision in the agreement:

- obligation to deliver;

- warranty of peaceful possession; and

- warranty against hidden defects.

However, it is advisable that the parties expressly mention these warranties in the agreement. In practice these obligations may not always be clearly distinguished:

- In the case of a 'share transaction', the seller's warranties are strictly limited to the existence of the shares sold. There are no implied warranties as to the assets' good standing or the company's liabilities. In the event that the seller fails to deliver the shares, the buyer may request specific performance or rescission of the agreement and, in either case, damages for incurred expenses and loss of profits (Articles 1610 and 1611 of the Civil Code).

- In asset transactions, courts generally assume an implied obligation of the seller not to compete with the business sold. In most cases, however, this principle does not apply to 'share transactions'. It is therefore advisable to address this problem in an express specific contractual provision. In a case where the buyer has lost some of his or her clients following a breach by the seller of his or her obligations not to compete, he or she may seek injunctive relief and damages. In the event that, after the sale, the seller has created and sold a competing business, the buyer may even compel the closing of such business operated by a third party.

- The warranty against hidden defects in the case of a 'share transaction' has a limited effect, since it only applies to the defects affecting the shares themselves, but not to defects concerning the company's asset. Examples of defects of the shares are the nullity of the corporation, possibly restricted voting rights of the shares sold or the fact that the shares have not been fully paid up. In most instances, however, such defects are not regarded as hidden since the buyer could have discovered them by verifying the company's by-laws and corporate records. In case of breach of the warranty against hidden defects, the buyer may seek in court either the rescission of the agreement or a reduction of the purchase price.

Parties are free to insert express warranties in their agreement. Such warranties may cover all points listed in the due diligence checklist (see Chapter 3). The seller should expressly guarantee that it has transmitted all information and that the buyer's findings during the due diligence investigation are correct.

The seller may want to exclude certain information from any representation and warranty. This is usually done in a separate enclosure to the agreement known as the 'disclosure letter'. Parties should expressly agree upon the warranty period.

4.6 Liability for Pre-contractual Representations

A significant error about the business sold or a misrepresentation by the other party regarding such business would void the consent of both parties (Article 1109 of the Civil Code).

Where a business is sold by way of an 'asset transaction', the error must concern an essential element, (e.g. the very existence of clientele, the volume of business, licence or ownership of the business' main equipment), and the purchaser must show that, but for the error, he or she would not have bought the business. In share transactions, a rescission is available only where the error relates to the shares transferred and not to the company and/or to its business. In the event that one party has intentionally caused the error, the other party may request a rescission of the contract for misrepresentation.

The misrepresentation must be such that had the other party known about it, it would not have entered into the contract (Article 1116 of the Civil Code). A rescission may also be sought where the misrepresentation relates to the value of the thing sold.

4.7 Liability for Pre-acquisition Trading and Contracts See 4.3

4.8 Pre-completion Risks

Belgian law does not prescribe where the risk lies as between a seller and a buyer of assets or shares. An assets acquisition agreement should therefore address which party bears the risk of loss of assets between signing and completion. Usually the risk remains with the seller, so it is important that insurance cover is maintained until completion.

Any share acquisition agreement should contain a warranty which stipulates that there has been no material adverse change to the business since a specified date.

4.9 Required Governmental Approvals

Information to the Minister of Economic Affairs, the Minister of Finance and the Secretary of State of the Regional Economy

All acquisitions of at least one third of the capital of companies with activities in Belgian territory and with net assets of at least BEF 100 million must be notified to the Minister of Economic Affairs, the Minister of Finance and the Secretary of State of the Regional Economy.

Nevertheless, there is no sanction for a violation of this rule and none of the above-mentioned ministers has the power to prevent or delay the transaction pursuant to this Act. In practice, this obligation to inform is restricted to mailing a letter to the ministers, in which is given a general description of the proposed transaction.

Workers' council (conseil d'entreprise)

The establishment of a workers' council is obligatory in all companies with at least 100 workers.

The workers' council has to be consulted effectively and in advance about the effect such transactions can have on the employment situation (Royal Decree of 12 September 1972, Article 11).

4.10　Anti-trust and Competition Laws

Belgian anti-trust law (Law of 5 August 1991) regulates the acquisition of a so-called 'concentration'. A concentration takes place when:

- two or several enterprises merge; or

- one or several persons who already possess the control of an enterprise, or one or several enterprises, acquire, directly or indirectly, by means of an acquisition of shares or an acquisition of assets, the control of the entirety of or of a part of one or several enterprises.

Article 10 of this Act stipulates that such concentrations are subject to prior approval by the Competition Council, which decides whether or not concentration is admissible. Various thresholds are fixed by the legislation which means that only important acquisitions (shares or assets) must be notified.

4.11　Required Offer Procedures

Belgium has modified its legislation in accordance with the EU Disclosure Directive (Council Directive of 12 December 1988 on the information to be published when a major holding in a listed company is acquired or disposed of, OJ L 348, 17 December 1988, p. 62). The regulation is laid down in three basic texts:

- Law of 2 March 1989 pertaining to the publication of important shares in companies on the stock exchange and regulating public purchases, MB, 24 May 1989, p. 8913, hereinafter referred to as 'Disclosure Law';

- Royal Decree of 10 May 1989, MB, 24 May 1989, p. 8926, hereinafter referred to as 'Disclosure Decree';

- Royal Decree of 8 November 1989, MB, 11 November 1989, p. 18603, hereinafter referred to as 'Takeover Decree'. Two different, though somehow linked types of acquisitions are dealt with here: the public takeover bid and the underhand transferral of controlling holdings.

The public takeover bid (Chapter II of the Takeover Decree)

The public offer must extend to all voting securities in a company, unless the offeror wants to obtain no more than 10 per cent including the securities he or she already holds. The offeror may, however, make the offer conditional on a minimum level of acceptances.

Anyone intending to make a public offer must notify the Banking and Finance Commission 30 days in advance (Article 26 of the Royal Decree No. 185 of 9 July 1935, as modified by the Act of 22 March 1993, read in conjunction with Article 22 of the Act of 10 June 1964). The notification must be accompanied by information concerning the price, the conditions and other aspects of the offer as well as a draft prospectus, the contents of which are specified in the Takeover Decree.

The Banking and Finance Commission then checks the prospectus on possible disruptions to the capital market and on the correctness of the information. No evaluation by the Commission of the advisability or quality of the transaction is involved.

Following approval, the prospectus and an acceptance form are published as a free brochure, available through a financial institution indicated by the offeror. A counter-offer by a third party must be notified at least two days before closure of the offer and must be at least 5 per cent higher.

The underhand transferral of controlling holdings (Chapter III of the Takeover Decree)

According to the new regulation, an important distinction must be made between two situations, depending on whether the price paid for control is higher than the market price.

Articles 38–40 of the Takeover Decree, based on Article 15 §2.7° of the Disclosure Law, provide a mandatory prior disclosure of an intended change in control.

Articles 41–44, based on Article 15 §2.7° 8° of the Disclosure Law, apply in case of payment of a higher price than the market price (the payment of a so-called 'control premium'). These articles contain an obligation to give equal opportunities to the shareholders who did not transfer their shares.

Cross-border transactions of shares are normally governed by the *lex contractus*. However, to the extent that the transactions give rise to a change of control of a company under Belgian law and where the shares are spread among the Belgian public, the *lex societatis* (Chapter III of the Takeover Decree) is applicable.

Hostile takeover bids have recently led several Belgian companies to introduce defensive measures. Two of the most important and most widespread of these measures are the insertion of pre-emption rights (transfer blocking clauses which allow the board of directors to prevent the transfer of shares to a possible raider) in the company's articles of association, and the use of authorized capital which has the effect of diluting the existing shareholders' rights and increasing the target company's total value.

4.12   Continuation of Government Licences

In the case of an assets transaction, the transfer of a permit or authorization can cause particular problems. This is especially true when the permits and authorizations have been issued in the name of the company the assets of which have been transferred. It might be necessary for the competent authority expressly to approve the transfer of the permit or authorization to the purchaser.

The same problem arises concerning subsidies, which are always granted in the name of a company.

4.13   Requirements for Transferring Shares

Legal transfer restriction related to payment

Before the Act of 13 April 1995, a share in an SA could not be transferred if the legal minimum of one quarter had not been paid up. Consequently, it was impossible to transfer 'future' shares before the company had been established (Article 46 of LCSC). This prohibition was inspired by a concern to prevent speculation on non-existent shares.

The Act of 13 April 1995, however, has introduced a fundamental change. Shares in an SA may be transferred even though the minimum amount has not yet been paid. Therefore, the transfer of 'future' shares of a company which is not yet established is possible. If third parties have a claim against the company dating from before the publication of a transfer of partly paid shares, the seller is still liable for the unpaid part for five years following publication (Article 52 of LCSC). This issue should be dealt with carefully in the sale of share agreement.

Transfer restriction following from the will of the incorporators

In the SA, free transferability of shares is the rule, irrespective of whether these shares are registered ('*nominative*') or to bearer ('*au porteur*'). However, this transferability can be restricted by the articles of association. A transferability restriction in the articles in an SA usually takes the form of an acceptance clause combined with a preemption clause. These clauses only make sense if the articles of association also provide for the shares being registered: otherwise adherence to the clause could not be enforced:

- An acceptance clause means that a shareholder in an SA who wishes to transfer all or part of his or her shares can only do so if the prospective purchaser is accepted by the board of directors or the general meeting. Under Belgian law, if the board of directors or the general meeting refuses the candidate, it assumes the responsibility for finding a purchaser for the shares.

- A pre-emption clause means that the other shareholders may purchase the shares by priority if one shareholder decides to sell his or her own participation. If the shares in an SA are to bearer, shareholders' agreements can lead to a degree of control over the transfer of shares: the parties to the agreement give each other a pre-emption right. The question remains, however, whether a vote held or a transfer effected in breach of the agreement may be cancelled. As immediate relief, an injunction can be obtained from the court to suspend the voting or dividend rights. The courts generally cancel the sales of shares made in breach of pre-emption rights.

Since the new legislation, acceptance and pre-emption clauses can only restrict the transferability of shares for a maximum period of six months.

The Act of 13 April 1995 has moreover created two new types of shares:

- *Dematerialised shares*. Article 41 mentions, next to the nominative shares and the shares on bearer, the so-called 'dematerialised shares'. This type of share has the same value as the other two types, but is to be distinguished by the fact that it only appears through an inscription on a bank account. This inscription with an authorized institution gives the dematerialized share all its effects. No material support is needed for the existence of all rights attached to the dematerialized share.

- *Certification.* Since the Act of 15 July 1998, the certification of shares or convertible bonds in a public or private limited company has been made possible. This separate document (certificate) can be nominative, on bearer or dematerialized shares, and represents the shares or convertible bonds referred to in the certificate. Certificates are issued, after an 'exchange' with the company's shares, by a different legal entity (holding) which becomes owner of the shares and all the rights attached to it. The issuing company retains the ownership of the certificates, but commits itself to transfer all the capital gains or bonds to the certificate's beneficiary.

28 International Business Acquisitions

4.14   Requirements for Transferring Land and Property Leases

Belgium has a comprehensive registration system for title to land.

The transfer of land only has effect against third parties after it has been notified and registered in the Mortgage Office. In order to be registered, the transfer agreement needs to be drawn up in a notarial act.

However, when a company's shares are transferred, assuming that the company remains the owner of the land, no registration is required.

4.15   Requirements for Transferring Intellectual Property

'Intellectual property' is a generic term covering patents, trade marks, utility models and industrial designs and copyright.

Patents

Patent law in Belgium must be analysed in the light of EU law. However, note that national patents continue to exist side by side with Community Patents (Parliament Act of 28 March 1984). The European Patent Convention of 1973 enables applicants to obtain from the European Office in Munich a set of patents in respect of each of the states which have ratified the Convention. Each transfer of patents must be notified and registered by the European Patent Office.

Trade marks

The Convention regarding the Uniform Benelux Legislation in relation to trade marks was signed on 19 March 1962.

This Convention was adopted in Belgium by Parliament Act of 30 June 1969, which resulted in the abolition of the old Belgian legislation of 1879.

As in the case of patents, applications for trade mark registration can be filed with the Benelux Trade Mark Office in The Hague.

Every transfer of, or licensing agreement in respect of, a trade mark must be notified and registered in the Benelux Office to have effect *vis-à-vis* third parties.

Models and designs

The protection of models and designs is regulated in a Benelux Act (BTMW), which has been in force since 1 January 1975 in the three Benelux countries—Belgium, The Netherlands and Luxembourg.

Exclusive rights in respect of models and designs can be obtained by means of a deposit in the Benelux Office. The holder of a deposited model or design has the right, according to Article 13 of BTMW, to transfer its property rights or to license those rights.

The transfer or licence agreement must be in writing and only has effect against third parties after being registered in the Benelux Office.

On a European level, the Commission at the end of 1993 took the initiative to put in place common protection for models and designs throughout the European continent.

Copyright

Copyright in Belgium is regulated by the Parliament Act of 30 June 1994. According to Article 3 §1, only property rights and not moral rights can be transferred or be the subject of a licence agreement, whether or not exclusive.

4.16 Requirements for Transferring Business Contracts, Licences and Leases

In the case of an assets transaction, particular attention should be paid to the problem of the transfer of contracts. In the past, receivables could only be transferred after notification of the transfer to the debtor or after acceptance of the transfer by the debtor in an authentic act (old Article 1690 of the Civil Code).

Since the amendment to Article 1690 by the Act of 6 July 1994, receivables can be transferred by mere agreement between the parties involved without any formal notification of the transfer agreement. On the other hand, debts can only be transferred with the creditor's agreement.

4.17 Requirements for Transferring Other Assets

No specific rules exist under Belgian law. Each case has to be dealt with in the transfer agreement.

4.18 Encumbrances and Third-Party Interests

Privileges and guarantees in favour of third parties issued by the company are not modified in the case of a transfer of shares, except if linked with the shares themselves.

4.19 Minimum Shareholder and Officer Requirements

The general principle is that an SA must have at least three directors. However, since the Act of 13 April 1995 the board of directors can consist of only two directors if the company has been incorporated by two founders only or when the shareholders establish at a general meeting that the company has only two shareholders.

Under no circumstances may the directors be named in the articles of association. Normally, they are appointed during the first general meeting by a simple majority vote.

The length of time for which a director is appointed must be fixed and may not be more than six years (Articles 53 and 55 of LCSC). In principle, unlimited renewals of appointments for the same period are possible (Article 56 of LCSC). The revocable character of the mandate to act as a director means that a director, in that capacity only, may not be an employee because of the labour law protection against forced dismissal. However, a director may at the same time be an employee of the company: he or she must then hold a different position in the company, which is clearly distinct from the task of director, and in the exercise of which he or she is under the authority of another company organ.

4.20 Non-competition Clauses

The validity of non-competition provisions must be viewed in the light of EU law. Non-competition clauses imposed on the seller generally fall within the category of 'ancillary restraints' and therefore are not prohibited by Article 85 of the EC Treaty, because they guarantee the transfer to the buyer of the full value of the business assets transferred. However, such a restriction must be limited in its duration, its geographic scope and its subject-matter.

Duration

Normally, the duration of a non-competition clause imposed on the seller of a business should be of a fixed and predetermined period. The Ancillary Restriction Notice published by the European Commission states that a period of five years is appropriate if the sale includes goodwill and know-how, and two years if it only includes goodwill. However, special factors may enable non-competition provisions of potentially longer duration to be acceptable.

Geographic scope

Non-competition clauses should be limited to the area where the seller has established business with the products or services before the transfer.

Subject-matter

The scope of the non-competition clause should be limited to products or services which constitute the same economic activity as the business transferred.

4.21 Environmental Considerations

Responsibility for environmental matters has been transferred since the Acts of 8 and 9 August 1980 to the Regional Councils of Flanders, Wallonia and Brussels.

The Councils can enact decrees which have the same legal effect as an Act of Parliament. Most of these decrees are implementations of EU directives on environmental matters. Therefore, an overall view of the applicable legislation cannot be limited to Belgian legislation but must extend to European law.

4.22   Employee Superannuation/Pension Plans

This is not the subject of Belgian legislation. It must be dealt with on a case-by-case basis.

4.23   Employee Rights

Employers are subject to three sources of law and regulations in relation to their dealings with employees:

- the binding provisions of legislative Acts;

- Collective Employment Agreements; and

- the employee's specific contract of employment.

Each of these sources of law may set forth rules pursuant to which employees or workers may be made redundant and the extent to which indemnities must be paid to them.

4.24   Compulsory Transfer of Employees

The question of the transfer of employees in the event of an assets transaction must be considered in the light of the Collective Employment Agreement No. *32bis*, which is an application of EU law. This provides that in the event of a transfer of a business:

- the transferred employees' consent is not necessary; and

- the buyer is bound to take over all obligations under existing employment contracts, including acquired rights such as holiday pay, salary, bonus entitlements and seniority.

In other words, the employer cannot use the transfer of the business as a reason for dismissing employees. On the other hand, employees cannot treat the transfer as a breach of their employment contract by the employer.

Article 9 of the Agreement stipulates, however, that employees who are transferred can still be dismissed for economic, technical or reorganizational reasons, causing changes in their area of employment. In that case, the employer is liable to pay severance money.

A collective dismissal, which is a dismissal resulting, over a period of 60 days, in a reduction of 10 per cent of the number of employees with a minimum of six persons, is permissible for economic or technical reasons. In the event of a collective dismissal, the employer also has specific criteria to meet in addition to the payment of severance money and extra indemnities.

Pursuant to Article 8*bis* of the Collective Employment Agreement No. 32*bis*, the seller and the buyer are held responsible together for the payment of the debts existing at the moment of transfer and which arise from the existing employment agreements.

However, claims against the seller are restricted to a time limit of one year, which starts to run from the date of the transfer (Labour Court Brussels, 15 June 1981, JTT, 1982, 170).

4.25 Tax Deductibility of Acquisition Expenses

The costs and expenses linked to an acquisition can be deducted by the buyer.

4.26 Levies on Acquisition Agreements and Collateral Documents

No transfer tax is due on the transfer of existing shares, it being immaterial whether the shares are registered or in the form of bearer instruments. However, a simultaneous transfer of all shares in a real estate company may trigger the registration tax (12.5 per cent) due on transfers of Belgian real estate.

Value added tax might have to be paid if an asset transfer does not represent a branch or division of a company.

4.27 Financing Rules and Restrictions

A Belgian company (SA, SPRL and SC) cannot grant a loan, make an advance payment or issue guarantees supporting the acquisition of its shares by a third party.

An exception is provided when the acquisition is made pursuant to a management buy-out. However, in that case, a loan can be granted or a guarantee issued only if the amount concerned would not reduce the company's net assets below the amount of its paid-up capital.

4.28 Exchange Controls and Repatriation of Profits

Depending on the country of origin, some exchange controls can be imposed. There are no limits in Belgium on the repatriation of profits.

4.29 Groups of Companies

Parent companies incorporated under Belgian law should present consolidated accounts if they control one or more companies incorporated under Belgian or foreign law. However, the parent company may be exempted from doing so if various thresholds fixed by the Royal Decree of 6 March 1990 are not exceeded, which means that only important companies must present consolidated accounts.

A subsidiary can only be 'consolidated' when the parent company controls it—in other words has a decisive influence on the appointment of the majority of the subsidiary's directors or on the orientation of its policy (Article 2 of the Royal Decree of 6 March 1990).

Consolidated accounts must be audited by the statutory auditor and normally correspond to the parent company's financial year. They must be presented to the shareholders within the six-month period after the ending of that year and at least 15 days before the ordinary general meeting (Article 76 of the Royal Decree of 6 March 1990). The publication of consolidated accounts is subject to the same rules as the publication of annual accounts.

4.30 Responsibility for Liabilities of an Acquired Subsidiary

By acquiring a company, the purchaser is indirectly acquiring control of all of its subsidiaries.

An acquisition of shares does not change the liabilities toward third parties of the company acquired or of its subsidiaries. It should, however, be ascertained whether there are any provisions in important company contracts which would give a right of termination when a change of control takes place.

4.31 Governing Law of the Contract

The parties to the agreement are free to establish that the agreement will be governed by the laws of a country other than Belgium. However, a principle of Belgian international private law is that the Belgian judge must always apply his or her national 'mandatory rules'. The concept of mandatory rules is closely linked with 'public policy': it is a tradition for courts to insist upon applying principles of Belgian public policy, even when dealing with cases that are governed entirely by a foreign law.

4.32 Dispute Resolution Options

The parties are free to agree whether to submit any further dispute regarding the interpretation and execution of the agreement to a particular court or to an arbitral tribunal.

If the transaction has significant foreign elements (the buyer or the seller is a foreign resident or legal entity or if the Belgian transaction is only part of an international transaction), the parties may choose a foreign court.

If there is no agreement on jurisdiction, the rules that decide upon the possible jurisdiction of the Belgian courts are set forth by:

- the European Convention on Jurisdiction and the Enforcement of Judgments in Civil and Commercial Matters of 27 September 1968; and

- the Convention between Belgium and France (8 July 1899) and that between Belgium and The Netherlands (28 March 1925).

When no convention is applicable, the Belgian courts' jurisdiction can be based on Article 635 or on a combination of Articles 636–638 of the Judicial Code. However, Article 56 of the new Company Code states that Belgian laws apply to a company which has its effective corporate seat located in Belgium even if it is incorporated abroad.

Moreover, Article 15 of the Civil Code contains the general principle that a defendant who has Belgian nationality can always be sued before a Belgian court, which is only applicable if no other article provides grounds for justifying the jurisdiction of the Belgian courts.

4.33 Other Issues

Squeeze-out of minority shareholders

In the case of companies listed on a Belgian Stock Exchange (or in general, in companies which have made a public offer of their shares in Belgium), one or more shareholder(s) owning, together or alone, at least 95 per cent of the voting rights may acquire all of the shares issued by the company. The procedure is regulated by a Royal Decree of 11 June 1997 which has been modified by a Royal Decree of 21 April 1999. At the end of the procedure, any shares that have not been offered to the majority shareholder(s), whether or not the holder thereof appeared, shall be considered as fully transferred to this shareholder(s).

The same applies in companies which are not listed on a Belgian Stock Exchange (no public offer of its shares). However, in that case, the minority shareholder may refuse, in writing, to transfer its shares. The procedure is regulated by a Royal Decree of 3 May 1999 and applies to SPRLs and SAs.

In companies which are not listed on a Belgian Stock Exchange (no public offer of its shares), one or more shareholder(s) holding, together or alone, at least 30 per cent of the voting rights may initiate proceedings to squeeze out any shareholder for good reasons. Whether or not there are any 'good reasons' is left to the discretion of the Court. This applies to SPRLs and SAs.

Compulsory buy-out of shares

In companies which are not listed on a Belgian Stock Exchange (no public offer of its shares), any shareholder may initiate proceedings to force, for good reasons, the others shareholders, to which such good reasons relate, to purchase his shares. Whether or not there are any 'good reasons' is left to the discretion of the Court. The factual circumstances are very important. This applies to SPRLs and SAs.

Abuse of corporate goods

The Act of 8 August 1977 introduced a new Article 492*bis* in the Belgian Criminal Code on the abuse of corporate assets. This article applies to all types of companies. The use of corporate assets or credits, in conflict with the interests of the company, is an offence, insofar as an intention to defraud exists.

Insider trading

Belgium also introduced a new Article 509 into its Criminal Code to make certain forms of insider trading in companies listed on a Belgian Stock Exchange a criminal offence, in particular the misuse of inside information.

Criminal liabilities for companies

The Law of 4 May 1999 has introduced into Belgian Law the principle of criminal liability of legal entities. Every company is therefore criminally liable for offences closely linked to the realization of its corporate purpose or the defence of its interest, or when the circumstances show that the offences have been committed by it.

5. BRAZIL

José Luis de Salles Freire
(Tozzini, Freire, Teixeira e Silva Advogados)

5.1 Introductory Comments

Since the 1990s, Brazil has become much more stable both politically and economically. As a result, Brazil has been experiencing economic growth based on a stable currency and an open economy, and is currently a leading emerging market.

Various milestones contributed to this development, including measures taken by the Brazilian government to foster foreign investment and international trade. The implementation of MERCOSUL, one of the most relevant economic blocks in the world, with a population of more than 200 million, provides access to millions of potential consumers and countless business opportunities. At the domestic level and in response to demands from the new economic scenario, new regulations were enacted to provide a more liberal and welcoming environment to foreign investments. Some steps taken by the Brazilian government in order to accelerate economic development and attract foreign investment include: the privatization program initiated in 1990; constitutional changes that have opened to foreign investment sectors such as telecommunications, mining, electricity, oil and gas; extensive reforms in foreign exchange regulations; and the enactment of several statutes relating to concessions for public services, public-private partnerships (PPPs) and other mechanisms for the development of infra-structure.

5.2 Corporate Structures

The most common forms of business organization adopted by wholly owned subsidiaries of foreign corporations or joint venture companies receiving foreign investments are the limited liability company and the corporation. The selection of the most appropriate business form will take into account the desired ownership structure, legal flexibility, cost and confidentiality issues. For example, certain fundamental matters affecting the limited liability company must be approved by partners representing at least 75 per cent of its capital. Accordingly, the limited liability company may not be suited for a joint venture depending on the distribution of powers envisioned by the parties. On the other hand, if the company is a wholly owned subsidiary, this issue will not be relevant. In these circumstances, the use of a limited liability company will result in cost savings and confidentiality benefits, since publication of financial statements will not be required. On the other hand, only corporations may issues securities and, given the extensive regulations in the Corporation Law, a corporation may be the preferred form in more complex structures, especially with respect to minority shareholders and joint venture arrangements.

© World Law Group
International Business Acquisitions, M. Whalley, F.-J. Semler (eds.), Kluwer Law International, London, 2007; ISBN 9789041124838.

5.3 Letters of Intent and Heads of Agreement

Letters of intent and other forms of preliminary documents can be deemed enforceable documents if they contain all major aspects of a final agreement and the parties fail to specify that their terms are not binding. In this case, any party will be entitled to demand execution of a final agreement, including through a court order for specific performance if the factual circumstances so permit, or seek damages arising from the breach of the obligations contained in the preliminary document.

5.4 Taxes Affecting the Structure and Calculation of the Price

As far as an acquisition of shares is concerned, the parties must evaluate the impact of any capital gains tax on the transaction. If the seller is an individual or legal entity domiciled in Brazil, Brazilian capital gains tax will be applied at rates which may vary depending upon the individual's or legal entity's tax brackets. If the seller is a non-resident individual or legal entity, Brazilian capital gains tax will be applied at the rate of 15 per cent, unless the beneficiary is resident in a tax haven jurisdiction, in which case a 25 per cent rate will apply. Capital gains tax in the case of non-residents is assessed on the excess over the amount of the foreign investment registered with the Central Bank of Brazil.

In the event that the transaction is structured as a purchase and sale of assets, the acquisition of moveable assets may be subject to sales tax (ICMS) and in some instances to excise tax (IPI). In addition, the acquisition of real property will be subject to transfer tax (ITBI).

5.5 Extent of Seller's Warranties and Indemnities

Warranties and indemnities are becoming increasingly common in purchase and sale agreements even in contracts involving solely Brazilian parties because of the influence of US practices. Perhaps the main issue related to warranties and indemnities is the period during which they are to remain in force. This issue is normally subject to negotiations conducted according to the particularities of each case. The statute of limitations, which varies and may be fairly long in Brazilian law in certain situations, is also an important factor. The outcome of negotiations will be strongly influenced by the bargaining power of sellers. In most cases, contractual limitations will be based on the statute of limitations for tax claims, ranging from five to six years. Warranties and indemnities may be backed by banking guarantees, collateral securities (involving the seller's securities' portfolio), or by the retention of a portion of the purchase price by the buyer until the end of the limitation period.

5.6 Liability for Pre-contractual Representations

Brazilian law determines that the parties to an agreement must act in good faith at all times in their relationship, which includes information exchanged prior to, or as the basis for, the execution of the agreement. In cases of fraud and misrepresentation, the contract may be rescinded or damages may be sought. Warranties and indemnities provided in the purchase agreement can cover liability for pre-contractual misrepresentations or for misrepresentations contained in the purchase agreement itself.

5.7 Liability for Pre-acquisition Trading and Contracts

If the transaction is structured as a transfer of shares, all contracts executed by the company will remain in force according to their terms. However, it is likely that certain contracts will either require the consent of the other party to any change in control of the company or provide for the termination of the agreement upon a change in control.

If the transaction is structured as a transfer of assets, the transfer of the pre-acquisition trading and contracts depends on a formal assignment of the agreement from the seller to the buyer, in which case the other party usually has to acquiesce. In the event that the transaction is not categorized as a transfer of individual assets, but rather as a transfer of an entire operational unit, those contracts pertaining to the activities of such business unit will be automatically transferred to the buyer, provided, however, that the other party may terminate the agreement within 90 days if there is just cause for termination as a result of the transfer.

5.8 Pre-completion Risks

In a purchase of assets structure, the risk of loss remains with the seller until title is effectively transferred to the buyer. In the case of a sale of shares, the risk of loss remains with the company. The purchase and sale agreement in the latter case may make the transaction subject to any material adverse change in the assets or net worth of the company and in this case the risk of loss must be examined in the light of such a provision.

5.9 Required Governmental Approvals

Brazilian law does not usually require any special approvals for the acquisition of assets or shares by foreign individuals or entities.

Foreign investment, however, may be subject to some restrictions in a few sectors of the economy. Examples of restricted sectors include newspapers and broadcasting activities—where foreigners may not hold more than 30 percent of the relevant company—, nuclear energy, and domestic aviation.

5.10 Anti-trust and Competition Laws

In general terms, Brazilian law follows the US competition law model, but in Brazil there is no bar on closing and no mandatory waiting period, thereby allowing the parties to close the transaction at their own risk. It is important to note that, although transactions may be closed and implemented before clearance, CADE (the Brazilian anti-trust agency) has the discretionary power to impose whatever measures it deems necessary to remedy any anti-competitive impacts resulting from a given transaction.

The legal thresholds for notification requirements are either (i) a combined market share of 20 per cent or (ii) a turnover in Brazil by any of the parties in excess of BRL 400 million.

All kinds of mergers, acquisitions and associations, including joint ventures, are affected by the Competition Law, provided they produce effects in Brazil and either of the two thresholds established by the law are met.

5.11   Required Offer Procedures

Not applicable.

5.12   Continuation of Government Licences

Continuation of ordinary government licences is not usually affected by the transfer of shares of a company. However, if the company operates in regulated industries or renders public services according to concessions or authorizations from the government, any transfer of control would normally require the consent of the applicable regulatory authorities.

In the case of an acquisition of assets, if government licences are part of the transaction, the buyer should verify whether the continuation of any licences is impaired by the transaction since the seller may be holding precarious licences that cannot be assigned.

5.13   Requirements for Transferring Shares

Title to shares is evidenced in a registry book kept by the company, and transfers are effected by means of a book entry in the appropriate corporate share transfer book. Alternatively, shares may be registered in a special account held by a financial institution, in which case transfers are made through an entry in the records kept by the financial institution. Share transfers may be subject to rights of first refusal, which may be laid down either in the corporate bylaws or in shareholders' agreements.

The capital of a limited liability company is divided into units called quotas. Changes in capital ownership are effected by an amendment to the articles of association registered with the competent state registry. Quota transfers and assignments among the partners and/or to third parties are subject to the provisions of the articles of association, including any rights of first refusal. In the absence of specific provisions in the articles of association, quotas may be freely transferred among partners, and may also be transferred to third parties if there is no objection from partners representing at least one-fourth of the capital.

5.14   Requirements for Transferring Land and Property Leases

Pursuant to Brazilian law, a transfer of title to real estate must be made by means of an appropriate entry with the relevant Real Estate Registry Office, and the transfer must be executed pursuant to a public deed. The entries in the Registry are, generally speaking, quite reliable, and a title search can be conducted by the buyer. No title insurance is available.

Property leases are assignable with the prior written consent of the landlord, which may be already established in the lease agreement. The real estate may be sold during the contractual period, in which case the tenant will have a right of first refusal. If the agreement has been recorded in the relevant Real Estate Registry Office and the landlord does not observe the right of first refusal, the tenant will be entitled to deposit the purchase price and receive title to the real estate that has been wrongly transferred to a third party. If the tenant does not exercise the right of first refusal and the property is sold, the new owner must respect the lease agreement only to the extent that the agreement has been registered in the relevant Real Estate Registry Office and only if it contains a provision stipulating that the agreement will remain in force if the property is sold.

5.15 Requirements for Transferring Intellectual Property

In a share transaction, all intellectual property rights owned by the company remain in full force and effect. In the case of intellectual property licensed to the company, it is necessary to investigate whether the change of control will require the consent of the licensor or cause automatic termination of the applicable licence.

In an asset transaction, the transfer of any intellectual property must be subject to specific assignments, either from the seller or from the relevant licensor if these rights were only licensed to the seller.

Agreements providing for the assignment of intellectual property rights, including patents and trade marks, must be registered with the Brazilian Patent and Trademark Office (INPI).

5.16 Requirements for Transferring Business Contracts, Licences and Leases

Transfers of contracts in general, including business contracts and leases, are usually effected through a private instrument executed by the parties. The procedures for transferring government licences will vary depending on the specific requirements established by the applicable authorities.

5.17 Requirements for Transferring Other Assets

As a general rule, moveable assets are transferred through physical delivery from the seller to the buyer.

5.18 Encumbrances and Third Party Interests

Third party interests and encumbrances are protected only to the extent that such interests and encumbrances are perfected in accordance with the requirements provided for in the law. Such requirements, although normally based on filing documents with a Public Registry, may vary depending on whether the interests and encumbrances are related to real estate, moveable assets or shares.

5.19 Minimum Shareholder and Officer Requirements

The formation of limited liability companies or corporations requires the subscription for quotas or shares by at least two individuals or legal entities.

Management of a limited liability company must be vested in one or more Brazilian resident individuals. Managers may or may not be quotaholders, but in the latter case the articles of association must expressly authorize the appointment of non-quota-holder managers.

Management of a corporation is vested in a board of directors and executive officers. The board of directors is optional in the case of a privately held company, provided that its bylaws do not specify an authorized capital level. Each corporation must have at least two executive officers, who must be resident in Brazil. The board of directors must be comprised of at least three individual shareholders, who may or may not be resident in Brazil.

5.20   Non-competition Clauses

The acquisition agreement may provide for non-competition clauses. Although there are limited court precedents regarding their enforceability, non-competition provisions are in principle enforceable, provided that reasonable time limits are imposed.

5.21   Environmental Considerations

An analysis of the compliance by the company to be acquired with the applicable environmental rules and regulation is required, since Brazilian laws on the protection of the environment provide for potentially high clean-up expenses and other penalties if it is determined that the company's activities are harmful to the environment.

5.22   Employee Superannuation/Pension Funds

In Brazil, the National Institute for Social Security (INSS) is the governmental agency responsible for social security. It is responsible for a system that gives medical and retirement assistance to employees. A contribution to maintain this system is due every month to INSS, by both the employee and the employer. Employer contributions range between 23.7 and 28.8 per cent of the employee's overall salary, depending on the company's business.

Employers must also deposit monthly 8 per cent of an employee's salary in the name of that employee in a severance pay fund (FGTS) administered by a federal savings bank (CEF). The employee or his or her heirs may withdraw the funds deposited in their name in certain situations that include dismissal without cause (in such case the employee is also entitled to receive from the employer the equivalent of 40 per cent of the balance of the severance pay fund account, and the employer must pay an additional 10 per cent of such balance to the government), acquisition of residential real estate, retirement or death.

5.23   Employee Rights

The basic principles concerning labour relations in Brazil are consolidated in the Labour Code, enacted in 1943. Since then, however, scattered statutes have been passed covering wage increases, social security and pension funds, strikes, health and safety standards, and protection of certain specific classes of workers. The 1988

Constitution has also given certain rights to urban and rural workers, which overruled some of those set forth by the Labour Code.

Employers and employees may freely negotiate labour contracts provided, however, that the provisions of the law, the decisions of the competent authorities and the terms and conditions of the relevant collective agreement, if any, are observed.

Collective labour agreements are those executed between employers and the employees' unions, or between the employees' union and a specific company, in order to establish general and normative rules which govern the relationship between the employer and a given category of employees.

Payment of employees' remuneration must take place at least monthly. Employees are entitled to receive a 13th (Christmas) salary based on the average of their monthly remuneration. Workers are guaranteed a nationwide minimum wage established by law. Finally, for each period of 12 working months, an employee is entitled to a 30-day vacation. Compensation during vacation must be at least one third above the normal salary.

5.24 Compulsory Transfer of Employees

As indicated before, all contracts executed by the company, including labour contracts, remain in full force and effect in the case of a sale of shares.

A sale of assets often results in the buyer inheriting the seller's past liabilities. In certain circumstances, the buyer may mitigate this liability by requesting the seller to terminate all employment contracts of employees who are to continue to work for the buyer. The termination of employment contracts, however, can be costly and, to the extent that the buyer's due diligence indicates that the likelihood of employees filing claims for past liabilities is low, the buyer may choose to have the employment contracts simply assigned to it in order to negotiate better purchase terms with the seller.

5.25 Tax Deductibility of Acquisition Expenses

When the buyer is a non-resident individual or legal entity, the tax deductibility of acquisition expenses is governed by the buyer's home country tax laws.

When the buyer is a Brazilian taxpayer, the expenses incurred in the acquisition of shares are non-deductible, in principle. All assets subject to wastage by regular use, by natural causes, or by obsolescence can suffer depreciation, which must be based on a straight-line basis over the assets' useful life. Depreciation of property, plant, and equipment is an allowable deduction for income tax purposes, provided that such assets were directly used in the production or trade of goods or the rendering of services.

The depreciation deduction for income tax purposes must be utilized by the taxpayer who carries the economic burden of the wastage or obsolescence, in accordance with principles of property, possession and use of the asset.

In any case the accumulated value of depreciation instalments must not exceed the acquisition cost of the asset.

5.26 Levies on Acquisition Agreements and Collateral Documents

No stamp duty or other similar tax is levied on acquisition and collateral agreements under Brazilian tax law. Registration of acquisition and collateral documents before local authorities, such as the Commercial Registry and other Public Registries, is subject to the payment of fees.

5.27 Financing Rules and Restrictions

Not applicable.

5.28 Exchange Controls and Repatriation of Profits

Capital investments, repatriations and profit remittances related to foreign capital duly registered with the Central Bank of Brazil may be effected at any time without prior authorization, subject to compliance with applicable corporate and tax legislation. Registration of foreign investments is effected electronically through a special system administered by the Central Bank of Brazil.

The remittance of dividends is not subject to withholding tax. The repatriation of capital investments and reinvestments registered with the Central Bank of Brazil is tax exempt, but any remittances in excess of the registered amount are subject to a 15 per cent capital gains tax, unless the beneficiary is resident in a tax haven jurisdiction, in which case a 25 per cent rate will apply.

Payments of royalty and technical assistance fees are subject to withholding tax at the rate of 15 per cent, in the absence of any lower rate established by a double taxation treaty.

5.29 Groups of Companies

Brazilian law does not have a concept of groups of companies for accounting consolidation purposes. Rather, Brazilian companies are required to value their investment in affiliated companies and subsidiaries using the net equity accounting method in order to assess relevant investments in:

- affiliated companies (under Brazilian law, affiliation is characterized when a company owns at least 10 per cent of the capital of another company) over whose management the company has influence or in which it participates with 20 per cent or more of the capital; or

- controlled subsidiaries.

An investment is deemed relevant when:

- for each affiliated company or controlled subsidiary, the book value of the investment is equal to or greater than 10 per cent of the company's net worth; or

- taking all affiliated companies and controlled subsidiaries as a whole, the aggregate book value of the investments is equal to or greater than 15 per cent of the company's net worth.

5.30 Responsibility for Liabilities of an Acquired Subsidiary

As a general rule, corporations and limited liability companies under Brazilian law have limited liability, and therefore parent companies are not subject to the liabilities incurred by their subsidiaries and vice versa. However, Brazilian law recognizes the concept of disregarding the legal entity in certain circumstances. A general provision in the Brazilian Civil Code authorizes the court to apply the disregard doctrine in cases of fraud. In addition, specific statutes also allow the courts to extend liability to shareholders in relation to, for example, damages to the environment or to consumers. Labour courts have also developed a disregard doctrine that has been broadly applied whenever the company fails to pay its employees.

5.31 Governing Law of the Contract

Generally speaking, parties to an international agreement are free to choose the governing law of the contract. Nevertheless, acquisitions or other transactions involving real property located in Brazil are governed by Brazilian law.

5.32 Dispute Resolution Options

Enforcement of foreign judgments

Foreign judgments may be ratified and enforced in Brazil irrespective of reciprocity or the existence of a specific foreign judgment treaty or convention.

In establishing the rules for ratification and enforcement of foreign judgments, Brazil has adopted the system of limited review whereby judicial control is exercised without re-examination of the merits of the original action.

Any final judgment of a foreign court may be enforced in Brazil after being ratified by the Brazilian Superior Court of Justice.

In order to be ratified by the Brazilian Superior Court of Justice, a foreign judgment must meet the following conditions:

(i) it must comply with all formalities necessary for its enforcement under the laws of the place where it was rendered;

(ii) it must have been given by a competent court after the proper service of process on the parties, or after sufficient evidence of the parties' absence has been given as established pursuant to applicable law;

(iii) it must not be subject to appeal;

(iv) it must not offend Brazilian national sovereignty, public policy or good morals, and

(v)   it must be duly authenticated by a competent Brazilian consulate and be accompanied by a sworn translation thereof into Portuguese.

Enforcement of foreign arbitration awards

Brazil has ratified both the Geneva Protocol of 1923 on arbitration clauses and the United Nations Convention of New York of 10 June 1958 on the recognition and enforcement of foreign arbitration awards.

Any final arbitration award rendered outside Brazil would be enforceable in Brazil without any retrial or re-examination of the merits of the original arbitration proceedings after being ratified by the Brazilian Superior Court of Justice.

In order for a foreign arbitration award to be ratified by the Brazilian Superior Court of Justice, the following conditions must be verified:

(i)   the parties to the arbitration agreement must have legal capacity;

(ii)   the arbitration agreement must be valid under the laws of the jurisdiction chosen by the parties or, if the agreement is silent, under the laws of the jurisdiction where the award was rendered;

(iii) the defendant must have been given proper notice of the appointment of arbitrators or of the arbitration procedure, and the defendant must have been given full opportunity to defend its case;

(iv)   either the arbitration award must not have exceeded the terms of the arbitration agreement, or it shall be possible to divide the award so as to consider solely that portion within the limits of the arbitration agreement;

(v)   the commencement of the arbitration proceedings must have been in accordance with the arbitration agreement;

(vi)   the arbitration award must be binding upon the parties and its effects must not have been invalidated or suspended by a court in the jurisdiction in which it was rendered;

(vii) under Brazilian law, those matters submitted for arbitration must be eligible for dispute resolution through arbitration; and

(viii) the arbitration award must not offend Brazilian public policy, national sovereignty or good morals.

6. CANADA

Robert S. Vineberg, Davies Ward Phillips & Vineberg LLP

6.1 Introductory Comments

Canada is a federal state in which jurisdiction is constitutionally divided between two levels of government, federal and provincial. In some areas, either the federal government or the provincial government may have exclusive jurisdiction. In others, both levels of government may regulate different aspects of a particular activity.

All the provinces of Canada except Québec are common law jurisdictions, with strong historical ties to the British common law. Québec is a mixed common law/civil law jurisdiction in which private law matters, such as contract and property, are governed by a Civil Code. It may initially be somewhat puzzling to the observer to learn that each of Canada and its ten provinces has its own corporations statute and each province has its own securities act and laws governing such issues as labour, employment and the environment, that there are two levels of income tax (federal and provincial) and income and other taxes vary markedly in each of the ten provinces. The federal government and each of the provinces also have their own set of incentives designed to encourage business to locate in their respective jurisdictions and increase employment, research and development expenditures and other similar matters. There is real competition among the provinces to attract investment and, while that competition is principally in evidence in their taxation statutes and incentive programmes, there is some level of competition among the provinces reflected in certain of the provisions of their other statutes, as each tries, with varying degrees of success, to make its province a more hospitable place for business.

6.2 Corporate Structures

There are five types of business vehicles in Canada: sole proprietorships, partnerships, joint ventures, corporations and trusts.

Sole Proprietorship

A business owned by one person is called a sole proprietorship. The individual is responsible for all the business's obligations. Accordingly, his or her personal assets may be seized to meet these obligations. Since sole proprietorships are suitable for small enterprises, they are not targets of international mergers and acquisitions.

Partnerships

Partnerships are divided into general and limited partnerships. The main characteristic of a general partnership is the unlimited liability of each partner for the liabilities of the partnership. Each partner is jointly liable for all debts and obligations incurred by the

© World Law Group

International Business Acquisitions, M. Whalley, F.-J. Semler (eds.), Kluwer Law International, London, 2007; ISBN 9789041124838.

partnership. However, a partner is generally not liable for obligations incurred before it became or after it ceased to be a partner. All partners may take an active role in operating a general partnership. As each partner is an agent of the others, each partner may bind the others unless there are restrictions in the partnership agreement of which third parties have notice.

A limited partnership combines the advantages of limited liability and the ability to flow profit and losses for tax purposes through to passive investors. This form of business structure is often used for public financing and real estate syndication. A limited partnership is made up of one or more general partners, each of whom has the same rights and obligations as a partner in a general partnership, and one or more limited partners, whose powers and liabilities are limited. The general partner or partners manage the partnership. A limited partner may not take part in the partnership's management without jeopardising its limited liability, though in most circumstances it may act as an employee, agent or consultant. The primary advantage of a limited partnership over a general partnership is the limited liability of the limited partners. This enables passive investors to receive returns proportional to the amount of their contribution with minimal personal risk.

Joint Venture

A joint venture is an agreement entered into by two or more parties (individuals, partnerships or corporations) to pool capital and skills for the purpose of carrying out a specific undertaking. Since a joint venture is not a recognized entity for tax purposes, income and losses for tax purposes are computed separately by each joint venturer rather than at the joint venture level. A joint venture is thus a means to carry out a single operation using common resources, with each party retaining a substantial degree of independence and its own flexibility in tax matters. Joint venturers who do not want their joint venture to be a partnership should enter into a written agreement setting out their respective rights and obligations in detail. Otherwise, there is a risk that the joint venture may be characterized as a general partnership. If so, each partner would be fully liable for partnership obligations and subject to tax as a partner rather than as a joint venturer.

Corporations

The federal and provincial levels of government have each enacted legislation providing for the incorporation and regulation of corporations (or companies, which are indistinguishable from corporations) and the parties can choose which statute they wish to govern the corporation. A federal corporation has the right to carry on business under its corporate name in any province in Canada, while under the provincial corporate statutes there is no such entitlement. Although most of the corporate statutes are similar, they are not uniform. In terms of liability, with the exception of unlimited liability companies that may be incorporated in the provinces of Nova Scotia and Alberta (and forthcoming in British Columbia), all corporations have limited liability. Although this protects the shareholders, there is legislation, particularly with respect to tax, environment and criminal laws, which hold the directors personally liable for certain infringements of the corporation.

Trusts

The trust is derived from English common law but is subject to different rules in each province, particularly Québec. The trust is primarily used in certain tax-driven circumstances to achieve tax deferral. A unique feature of Canadian tax law regarding trusts is that the trust is deemed to dispose of all of its assets every 21 years at fair market value. This rule is subject to some exceptions.

6.3   Letters of Intent and Heads of Agreement

Letters of intent outline the 'business deal' of the transaction as they express the intent of the parties and the general principles, terms and conditions that will be the subject of further, more detailed, negotiation and documentation. Although these letters can be binding on the parties, language is most often used so that the letters are non-binding and solely express an intention to enter into a definitive agreement upon more formal terms at a later date. Despite this, some sections of letters of intent are often expressed as being binding regardless of the eventual outcome of the proposed transaction. For example, provisions respecting confidentiality provisions and 'break-up' fees will necessarily contain language expressing binding intent.

6.4   Taxes Affecting the Structure and Calculation of the Price

As in every jurisdiction, taxes have an important role to play in the assessment of the feasibility of a transaction and in the structure. The combined federal/provincial basic rate of tax for a corporation carrying on business in Ontario, including a non-resident corporation, is 36.12, per cent; but it may be reduced to 34.12 per cent in respect of profits from Canadian manufacturing or processing. In Québec, the basic rate is 32.02 per cent, but there is no reduction in respect of profits from Canadian manufacturing or processing.

In addition, many provincial tax statutes impose capital taxes. Effective 1 January 2006, the federal capital tax has been eliminated. Certain provinces have indicated that they will also abolish such tax.

A non-resident corporation that is a member of a partnership which carries on business in Canada is generally subject to tax in Canada on its share of the partnership profits as if it carried on the partnership business directly as a Canadian branch. A partnership with a non-resident partner is considered to be a non-resident for the purposes of determining whether the withholding tax must be deducted from certain passive income payments made to non-residents. In addition to liability for normal income tax on its Canadian source business income, a non-resident corporation that carries on business in Canada through an unincorporated branch is liable for a branch tax of 25 per cent of an amount approximately equal to the after-tax earnings of the branch not reinvested in Canada. The rate of branch tax may be significantly reduced by an applicable tax treaty.

6.5   Extent of Seller's Warranties and Indemnities

The type of seller's warranties and indemnities varies depending on the size of the transaction and the parties' relative bargaining strength. The seller almost always warrants as to the proper constitution of the company, title to assets, litigation, payment of taxes, compliance with environment standards and regulations, status of employees (unions and labour standards) and accounts receivable. While these warranties should be expected in most transactions in Canada, none of the warranties are required by law to be included in a transaction.

Normally, the acquisition agreement provides for an indemnity to cover any losses suffered as a result of a breach of a warranty, with a time limitation for making claims. In practice, a stipulation providing for an indemnity is sometimes qualified by a pre-determined threshold in order to minimize frivolous small claims and needless litigation. This threshold takes the form of either a deductible where only amounts in excess of the threshold amount will be indemnified or a first-dollar approach where all losses are indemnified once that threshold level is reached. In any type of indemnity situation, it is often appropriate to arrange for a parent company or bank guarantee to ensure the ability to realize on an indemnity subsists regardless of the seller's future fortunes or misfortunes. A guarantee can also be obtained by setting aside part of the purchase price in escrow, or delaying payment for a certain period of time.

6.6   Liability for Pre-contractual Representations

The parties may be liable for any representations or warranties, written or verbal, that they make in an invitation to offer, during the course of the negotiation, or any other event leading up to the final acquisition agreements. Negligent and fraudulent misrepresentations can be actionable and, depending on the severity of the breach, can result in an action in damages or rescission of the entire agreement. Furthermore, under the applicable securities legislation, any sales of securities of public companies carry with them the obligation on the seller not to make any misrepresentations or omissions of 'material facts'. Such liability is of public order and the parties to the sale of public securities cannot contract out of it.

In most acquisition agreements, the parties provide that the only representations and warranties that they have made are those found in writing within the acquisition agreements themselves. Although such clauses might not always stand up in a court of law, particularly if there is evidence of bad faith or fraud, standard practice and prudence suggests that such clauses are necessary components to any acquisition agreement.

6.7   Liability for Pre-acquisition Trading and Contracts

The liability for pre-acquisition trading and contracts is different depending on whether there is an asset or share sale. In a sale of shares, the buyer is liable for all pre-acquisition trading and contract obligations of the business. This is because the buyer acquires the business as a going concern. If the amount of liability is unclear at the time the transaction closes, it is advisable for the buyer to set aside a portion of the purchase price in order to cover potential surprises.

The situation is totally different in a sale of assets. Without legislation, the buyer would only be liable for those obligations arising after the closing date of the transaction because the buyer is not buying the business as a going concern but is only purchasing specified assets. To overcome the potential difficulty that would arise for unsecured creditors, certain provinces have enacted 'bulk sale' legislation which is subject to some judicial exemptions. Its effect is to ensure, when there is a sale of a business' assets, that the sale proceeds are first applied to the payment of the creditors of the business being sold. A preliminary issue that must often be dealt with is whether the sale of a division or of a portion of an operating business constitutes the sale of a business for bulk sale purposes. The test is generally that bulk sale legislation applies when one is selling all or substantially all of a business. It is possible in certain jurisdictions to obtain a court order prior to closing stating that a particular transaction will not be subject to the bulk sales legislation.

6.8 Pre-completion Risks

It is up to the parties to determine who is liable for risk of loss between the date that the acquisition agreements are signed and the closing date of the transaction. Generally, it is the seller who assumes liability for risk until the closing date because the seller usually operates the business until that time. Hence, the seller must maintain insurance on the business's assets until the closing date.

In share acquisitions, a buyer can be protected from any adverse changes in the business from the time of signing until the closing date by a representation provided by the seller in the acquisition agreement that there has been no material adverse change to the business during the relevant period. The buyer generally has the right to rescind the sale or adjust the sale price, depending on the severity of the change, if there has been any material change before closing.

6.9 Required Government Approvals

The Investment Canada Act (ICA) provides for the review by Investment Canada of the acquisition of certain businesses by non-Canadians, as follows:

- a direct acquisition of a Canadian business with assets of CAD5 million or more;

- an indirect acquisition of a Canadian business with assets of CAD50 million or more;

- an indirect acquisition of a Canadian business with assets of CAD5 million or more if the assets of the Canadian business represent more than 50 per cent of all of the assets acquired in the international transaction.

However, these thresholds have been significantly increased or eliminated for investors from World Trade Organization (WTO) countries. A direct acquisition by a WTO investor is reviewable only when the assets being acquired exceed CAD281 million (which amount varies annually according to a GDP-based formula), and indirect acquisitions are no longer reviewable. Anyone acquiring a Canadian business controlled by a WTO investor (other than a Canadian) also benefits from these increased thresholds. A WTO investor includes an entity the voting interests of which are ultimately controlled, directly or indirectly, in a WTO country. The ICA has detailed rules for determining the 'control' of an entity.

Direct control of a Canadian corporation may be acquired by purchasing the corporation's voting shares or all or substantially all of the assets used in carrying on the Canadian business. Indirect control of a Canadian corporation is acquired by purchasing voting shares in a non-Canadian corporation that controls a Canadian corporation or by acquiring voting interests in a non-Canadian, non-corporate entity that controls the Canadian corporation.

It is important to note that the acquisition of a business occurs not only where the majority of voting shares is acquired, but also where one third or more (but less than 50 per cent) of the shares are purchased, unless it can be shown that the acquired shares do not give control in fact to the investor.

If an acquisition is reviewable, the investor must file an application with Investment Canada. With limited exceptions, the application must be filed and approval granted before completing the transaction. The Minister of Industry has an initial period of 45 days to determine whether the investment will be of net benefit to Canada, which may be extended by a further 30 days.

The factors which the Minister will consider include:

- the investment's effect on the level and nature of economic activity in Canada;

- the degree of participation by Canadians in a Canadian business in particular and in the relevant industry in Canada in general;

- the investment's effect on productivity, industrial efficiency, technological development, product innovation and product variety in Canada;

- the investment's effect on competition in the relevant industry in Canada;

- the investment's compatibility with Canadian industrial, economic and cultural policies, taking into account the policy objectives of affected provinces; and

- the effect of the investment on Canada's ability to compete in world markets.

There are special provisions in the ICA for investments which may affect 'Canada's cultural heritage or national identity'. There are also other types of businesses which do not benefit from the higher WTO thresholds for reviewable transactions, including uranium industries and businesses providing financial and transportation services. See also **6.13** below in relation to other shareholding restrictions in certain industries.

Subject to the exceptions referred to above dealing with Canada's cultural heritage or national identity, other investments by non-Canadians in Canada are not reviewable. However, there is a requirement that a notice be filed with Investment Canada within 30 days after the acquisition by a non-Canadian of a business in Canada.

6.10   Anti-trust and Competition Laws

The Competition Act is the anti-trust statute in Canada which establishes a comprehensive legislative and regulatory framework for reviewing and controlling mergers and acquisitions. Transactions may be subject to review by an administrative tribunal and those which meet certain size thresholds may also be subject to pre-notification requirements and waiting periods. Any merger may be reviewed by the Competition Tribunal if an application is made by the Director of Investigation and Research under the Competition Act; such an application may be brought in connection with the proposed transaction or within three years of its completion. The Tribunal may issue a prohibition order with respect to all or any part of a proposed transaction, and may dissolve a completed transaction or order divestiture of assets or shares.

Before making an order, the Tribunal must determine that the transaction prevents or lessens or is likely to prevent or lessen competition substantially in the relevant market. In making this determination, the Tribunal generally applies economic and legal analyses similar to those employed by US courts in anti-trust matters. Among the factors which the Tribunal will always consider are the likelihood of foreign competition, whether the acquired business has failed or is likely to fail, the extent and availability of acceptable substitutes, barriers to entry and innovation in the market. The Tribunal may also consider whether the transaction will result in the removal of a vigorous competitor from the market and whether effective competition would remain in the market following the transaction.

Advance notification is required if the proposed combination, or if one of the parties to the transaction, exceeds certain size thresholds, and the parties are precluded from completing the transaction before the expiry of a review period.

In general, two size thresholds must be met for the pre-notification rules to apply. First, the parties to the transaction, together with their affiliates, must have total assets in Canada or total revenues from sales in, from or into Canada that exceed CAD400 million. Secondly, the transaction itself must be of a minimum size: for acquisitions of assets, the Canadian assets acquired or the annual gross revenues from sales in or from Canada from such assets must exceed CAD50 million (CAD70 million for a corporate amalgamation). Share transactions are subject to pre-notification where the value of the Canadian assets or sales derived from the corporation the shares of which are acquired and all other corporations controlled by that corporation would exceed CAD50 million (CAD70 million for a corporate amalgamation). Other types of non-corporate combinations may also be subject to the pre-notification rules in circumstances where a similar CAD50 million threshold as to assets that are the subject-matter of the combination or the sales generated therefrom is exceeded.

6.11   Required Offer Procedures

Securities regulation of public companies is a provincial jurisdiction. Each province has enacted rules with respect to 'takeovers' of public companies. Although time limits and exemptions vary from one province to another, the principles are the same. A takeover bid occurs when one party, and its associates, attempt to obtain control of

20 per cent or more of a target company's voting rights. Such bids are tightly regulated and require offering identical consideration to all registered shareholders. The bid must stay open for a minimum amount of time (generally 21 days) and the shareholders are entitled to deposit and withdraw their shares at any time prior to the expiry of the offer.

Takeover bids can be for less than all of the shares of the target company. In such cases, if the bid is over-subscribed, the shares are purchased by the acquirer on a pro-rata basis. Potential acquirers should be aware of 'shareholders' rights' plans or 'poison pills' that have been enacted by a number of public companies in order to, as some say, entrench management, buy time to find a more preferable suitor (a 'white knight'), or encourage a bidding war. Such plans can make a takeover bid much more costly in terms of share price or can lead to protracted litigation.

6.12   Continuation of Government Licences

In some industries, the government has made it necessary to have a licence in order to legally operate the business. Licences are required in the fields of broadcasting, insurance, securities, banking and telecommunications. The transferability of such licences depends on the specific industry and the licence terms. Many licences are not transferable and require formal re-applications with the government.

Subject to the discussion below, some industries are heavily protected by the government and there are restrictions on the maximum amount of foreign ownership that the government will allow. In such cases, a foreign acquirer is prohibited from obtaining the necessary licence on the grounds of preserving Canada's cultural autonomy and/or financial sovereignty.

6.13   Requirements for Transferring Shares

Under corporate and securities statutes, a private company's shares, by definition, are subject to a restriction on transfer. In order to transfer such shares, one must first obtain the board of directors' approval. Generally, the restrictions on share transfers are found in the company's articles of incorporation. However, additional restrictions and conditions may be found in shareholders' agreements.

Subject to the above requirements, shares can be transferred by endorsing the back of the share certificate and ensuring that the appropriate changes have been made in the company's share register. This share register is found in the company's minute book.

There are also limited restrictions with respect to the transfer of shares in public companies; primarily with respect to shares in cultural industries such as broadcasting. In order to preserve autonomy and sovereignty over these areas, the government limits the extent of foreign ownership of companies in these industries. In such cases, it is impossible for foreigners to acquire control of these Canadian companies. Moreover, in some regulated industries such as banks, the government has limited the maximum number of voting shares that can be owned by one person, Canadian or non-Canadian, to ensure that no one has control. In some areas of the banking industry, the maximum number of shares that can be owned by one shareholder and its associates is 10 per cent.

Where a non-resident transfers shares of a private corporation, there can be certain tax withholding requirements imposed on the purchaser.

6.14   Requirements for Transferring Land and Property Leases

Land is governed exclusively by the provinces. Each province has its own land registry; some are computerized, while others maintain a paper-based system. Each transfer of land must be registered with the appropriate provincial registry. Most provinces impose a land transfer tax based on the property's value. There are some limited exceptions to this tax for certain transfers between related parties.

All mortgages or other encumbrances on land can be found in the appropriate land registry. If the mortgage or other encumbrance is properly registered in the public registry, it generally follows the property into the hands of a third party acquirer in good faith.

In certain provinces, foreigners seeking to register ownership of land or any charge on land must disclose their citizenship.

Where a non-resident transfers real estate in Canada, there are tax withholding requirements imposed on the purchaser.

6.15   Requirements for Transferring Intellectual Property

Intellectual property is exclusively in the federal domain. The title to all types of intellectual property (copyright, patent, trademark and industrial design) can be transferred by assignment, with the exception of moral rights in copyright which an author can waive but cannot assign. Moral rights include the right of an author or creator to claim authorship of and the right of integrity of the work, i.e. the right to restrain or sue for damages in respect of any distortion or modification of one's work which prejudices the creator's integrity or reputation.

Not all types of intellectual property must be registered. However, any assignment of registered intellectual property should be accompanied with a notice to the appropriate federal registrar. For some types of intellectual property, such notice requires the payment of a fee.

6.16   Requirements for Transferring Business Contracts, Licences and Leases

The transferability or assignability of business contracts, licences and leases depends on the terms of the agreement. The transfer of a contract does not relieve the transferor of liability under the contract unless a specific release is obtained from the other contracting party. It is not generally necessary to register the assignment or transfer of a contract. However, notification to all interested parties is strongly advised, and in some cases (such as a lease) it may be required.

6.17   Requirements for Transferring Other Assets

Other tangible property can usually be transferred by simple delivery. However, if there is a perfected security interest on the property, it normally follows the property into the hands of the acquirer. In order to be enforceable against a third party acquirer, these security interests must appear in the public registry.

6.18   Encumbrances and Third Party Interests

Assets can be subject to many types of encumbrances and third party interests. Such interests may arise from contract, in the form of a mortgage or hypothec on the property; by operation of law (legal right of way in favour of a statutory authority or a lien arising under federal or provincial law covering such aspects as tax or construction balances outstanding); or by virtue of specific registration in a public registry (an easement or servitude on land).

A search of certain title registers (e.g. real property) reveals evidence of the title of the registered owner on which the buyer may rely. However, other assets (generally personal property) may be subject to unregistered or unascertainable interests which a buyer will not necessarily be able to uncover. In order to protect a buyer, it is recommended that specific warranties are obtained from the seller.

6.19   Minimum Shareholder and Officer Requirements

Private companies must have a minimum of one director, who must be a physical person. If the company is constituted under federal laws, or the law of certain provinces, a certain percentage of the directors must be 'Canadian residents' (or residents of that province) and no business can be carried on at a meeting of the board of directors if the requisite number of directors present are not residents of Canada or the province. However, in British Columbia, Québec, Nova Scotia, New Brunswick and Prince Edward Island there is no residency requirement for any directors. Thus, a company incorporated under the laws of these provinces can have foreign directors exclusively.

Public companies must have a minimum of three directors. They are generally subject to the foregoing Canadian resident requirements but are also subject to regulation by the stock exchange on which they are listed.

Every corporation must have a minimum of one shareholder. Under corporate and securities law, in order to be a private company, there must be a restriction on the transferability of the securities. In terms of officers, there must be a minimum of one officer to perform all necessary corporate functions. The positions of president and secretary can be occupied by the same person. If the company is private, this person can also be the company's sole shareholder and director.

Shareholder meetings of both private and public companies must be held, at a minimum, once a year in order to elect directors and appoint auditors. Under federal law, companies must have their shareholder meetings in Canada unless all shareholders agree otherwise; there are different requirements under the various provincial statutes. In the case of private companies, shareholder meetings do not have to actually take place; it is sufficient that all shareholders sign a resolution in lieu of an annual meeting.

6.20 Non-competition Clauses

The enforceability of non-competition covenants is a matter of provincial law. Generally, Canadian courts have been reluctant to enforce such covenants unless the geographic scope, time period involved and type of employment or activity are limited and reasonable and the grantor (employee or seller of a business) is considered to have received reasonable compensation for such covenant. The tax implications of non-competition payments must be considered in any such arrangement.

6.21 Environmental Considerations

Environmental issues in an acquisition are among the most difficult to assess, because the regulatory regime includes both statutory law and a variety of policy matters including guidelines, procedures and criteria which are applied on a case-by-case basis by regulators. There is often substantial discretionary power given to these regulators to establish the context and scope of the regulations which they enforce and, while there are courts and tribunals to adjudicate complaints, relatively few decisions have been rendered. The risk of environmental liability is broad, and may arise both from the operations of the business to be acquired (on existing and former sites) as well as from those of its predecessors which occupied the lands and buildings presently occupied by the target. Liability includes penal as well as civil remedies, and civil remedies encompass both remediation as well as the cessation of prohibited activities. Often a purchaser's due diligence includes at least a Phase I environmental study, with a view to determining whether there appears to be environmental risks which require further investigation.

6.22 Employee Superannuation/Pension Plans

The Canada Pension Plan (CPP) is compulsory. With the exception of employers and employees in Québec, all employers and employees in Canada are required to contribute to this Plan. Québec established a provincial pension scheme in the Québec Pension Plan (QPP), which provides benefits comparable to the CPP. The employee's contribution under the CPP or QPP is a percentage of earnings which is supplemented by the employer's contribution. Each of the employee's and employer's contributions for 2007 are 4.95 per cent of certain earnings, to a maximum contribution by each of the employee and employer of CAD1,989.90. The employer can deduct contributions under CPP or QPP for tax purposes as a business expense.

CPP provides several possible types of benefits for employees who have made a minimum contribution towards the Plan:

- retirement pensions to contributors who have reached age 65;

- benefits to a surviving spouse and/or surviving dependent child of the contributor; and

- disability benefits to a contributor who is no longer able to pursue a substantially gainful occupation.

All provinces also have pension benefits standards legislation governing the elements of a private pension plan.

6.23 Employee Rights

Each province, as well as the federal government, has employment standards legislation setting out minimum entitlements for employees. The minimum standards cannot be contracted out of nor waived.

The main topics covered by this type of legislation include wages, overtime, vacation and holidays, pregnancy and/or parental leaves of absence and termination pay. The provisions of these laws are minimums. Most employers provide more in the way of wages and other benefits than is prescribed by law.

The federal and all the provincial governments have adopted human rights legislation with a view to removing discrimination in the workplace. Prohibited are distinctions or preferences based on, among other factors, race, colour, sex, pregnancy, sexual orientation, age, civil status, religion, political convictions, language, ethnic or national origin, social condition or handicap. Moreover, it is illegal in every province in Canada to pay a woman less for doing the same job as a man.

6.24 Compulsory Transfer of Employees

Most employment legislation in Canada is provincial, and thus varies from province to province. There is no concept of 'termination at will' employment in Canada. In the absence of serious reason for termination, all employees, whether unionized or not, are entitled to notice of termination. The notice may be by way of 'working notice' or pay in lieu of such notice. The amount of notice is, at a minimum, the statutory requirements as set out in the relevant employment standards legislation. However, in addition to the statutory minimums, employees are generally entitled to claim for additional notice for a 'reasonable' period. Such notice period may range from an amount not substantially greater than the statutory minimum to up to 24 months for senior executives.

Generally, labour laws call for the compulsory transfer of unionized employees when a business is sold or transferred. These laws are quite rigorous. If the business is continued in any form, even in a different location, the union and the employees will follow. Although most of Canada's workforce is non-unionized, 'union busting' is not an easy task.

6.25 Tax Deductibility of Acquisition Expenses

Where the purchaser is not a resident of Canada under the Canadian Income Tax Act, the deductibility of acquisition expenses is subject to the fiscal laws of its home jurisdiction.

Where the purchaser is a Canadian resident, acquisition expenses are generally not deductible in the year that they are incurred. Subject to the exception to follow, acquisition expenses should be capitalized. Hence, the legal, accounting, expert, appraisal and other professional fees incurred in an acquisition are added to the cost of the asset purchased. When the asset is eventually sold, the acquisition expenses help offset the gain on the sale, if any. The only exception to the rule is with respect to certain financing expenses. These are deducted on a 20 per cent per year straight line basis over a period of five years.

6.26 Levies on Acquisition Agreements and Collateral Documents

Neither the federal government nor the provincial governments impose any significant type of levies on acquisition agreements or collateral documents.

6.27 Financing Rules and Restrictions

Subject to the thin capitalization rule discussed below, a Canadian subsidiary may, in accordance with the usual rules relating to interest deductibility, deduct interest paid by it to a non-resident in computing its income, provided that the amount of interest is reasonable in the circumstances and the borrowed money is used to gain or produce income from business or property.

The 'thin capitalization rule' is intended to prevent a Canadian incorporated subsidiary from underly reducing its taxable Canadian profits, and hence its liability for Canadian tax, by maximising its interest expense to related non-resident creditors. The rule denies the resident subsidiary's deduction of interest on that portion of its debt owed to non-arm's length non-resident shareholders (or other related persons) that exceeds two times the total shareholder's equity (being retained earnings, contributed surplus and the paid-up capital of shares) of the subsidiary.

Numerous other taxation-related issues arise, including those relating to transfer pricing, the benefits available under various tax treaties and conventions, and whether a business carried on in Canada is best carried on as a branch operation or as a Canadian subsidiary.

6.28 Exchange Controls and Repatriation of Profits

The Canadian dollar is traded freely on world markets.

A resident of Canada that makes a payment to a non-resident in respect of most forms of passive income (including interest, dividends, rent and royalties) is generally required to withhold tax equal to 25 per cent of the gross amount of the payment, which rate may be significantly lowered under an applicable tax treaty. However, the 2007 Federal Budget proposes to eliminate witholding tax on interest paid to a non-resident lender. With-holding tax is due whether the resident payer is a subsidiary of, or is unrelated to, the payee. Although the tax is imposed on the non-resident, the resident payer is required to deduct the tax and remit it to the Canadian authorities on the non-resident's behalf. There are certain exemptions from withholding tax, such as interest paid by a Canadian corporation on money borrowed from an arm's length lender where the borrower may not, under the terms of the loan, be required to repay more than 25 per cent of the principal of the loan within five years from the date on which the loan was made.

A Canadian incorporated subsidiary of a non-resident corporation is a Canadian resident for Canadian income tax purposes and is therefore subject to tax in Canada on its worldwide income at the above corporate tax rates.

Equity of a Canadian subsidiary of a non-resident corporation may, to the extent of paid-up capital, be returned tax free to the non-resident shareholder. However, any distribution of capital made to the non-resident shareholder in excess of paid-up capital is generally deemed to be a dividend and therefore subject to withholding tax. Repayment of principal loaned to a Canadian subsidiary by its non-resident parent is not subject to withholding tax but tax must be withheld in respect of interest paid on the loan.

6.29 Groups of Companies

There is no consolidation of financial statements of a group of companies for income tax reporting purposes. Each related company is a separate and distinct entity from its parent, sister or subsidiary company. Thus, each company must file its own tax return annually. The losses of one company are not available to offset income of a related entity.

Canada's corporate laws do, however, permit the reorganization of companies within a corporate group. Companies in the same jurisdiction can amalgamate or wind up into a related corporation. Although this ensures the offsetting of gains with losses incurred in future fiscal years, the tax laws are quite strict with respect to the use of losses incurred prior to the reorganization.

6.30 Responsibility for Liabilities of an Acquired Subsidiary

Since each company has its own distinct corporate entity, the general rule is that a shareholder is not liable for the debts of a corporation and a parent company is not responsible for the liabilities of any of its subsidiaries. This principle is subject to the exception of piercing the corporate veil. Generally, a court may disregard the principle of limited liability and lift the corporate veil where the corporation is essentially an agent or puppet of the shareholder and where the shareholder is acting fraudulently or in bad faith. Moreover, a shareholder or a company may be responsible for liabilities of another company if it has granted a guarantee, indemnity or other undertaking to a creditor on the company's behalf.

6.31 Governing Law of the Contract

Provincial conflict of law rules are quite liberal and generally allow for the application of any jurisdiction's laws so long as the contract was consented to freely and without fraud. However, regardless of the choice of law clause found in the agreement, it is important to note that while a foreign law may govern the agreement, Canadian law will govern the effect of transfer of title to shares or other assets and the rights of any third parties.

6.32 Dispute Resolution Options

Because of the substantial backlog of cases already in the judicial system, Canadian courts and Canadian legislators recognize and encourage the use of alternate dispute mechanisms including arbitration, mediation and conciliation. In some areas, such as labour and family law, alternative dispute resolution is a required step before proceeding to other, more formal, methods.

6.33 Other Issues

Despite the multi-tiered degree of legislation and regulation, Canada provides an attractive climate for foreign business. It has stable political and economic systems and is rich in both natural and human resources. As the largest trading partner of the USA, Canada may offer foreign businesses improved access to the vast US market. The North American Free Trade Agreement among Canada, the USA and Mexico provides a substantial degree of economic integration without barriers to trade and investment.

7. CHINA

Susan Ning, King & Wood

7.1 Introductory Comments

Ever since the People's Republic of China ('China' or 'PRC') successfully joined the World Trade Organization ('WTO') on 11 December 2001, China has been continuously performing its committed obligation to further open up the domestic market and improve the foreign investment environment. A large number of laws and regulations that prohibited or restricted overseas enterprises from investing in China have been revised or abolished, and new regulations including but not limited to those governing mergers and acquisitions of domestic enterprises by foreign investors have been promulgated and entered into force.

The dramatic growth of China's economy, the gradually opened-up industry sectors, and the plentiful and cheap labour resources have made China one of the most attractive places for foreign investors. The past few months have witnessed a surge in the number of merger and acquisition transactions in China, and more acquisition transactions are expected to take place in the foreseeable future.

It is important to note that the PRC law governing acquisition transactions by foreign investors is complicated and far from perfect. Continued state ownership and control of a significant part of the economy adds sophisticated political and social issues to many acquisition transactions, certain burdensome legal requirements continue to exist, local rules and policies must be fully understood and taken into consideration, etc.

This handbook aims at discussing those topics generally relevant to the potential purchasers under acquisition transactions only. As the laws and regulations of China governing acquisition transactions may differ, depending on various factors (including but not limited to the nature of the specific transaction, the industry sector involved, and the location where the relevant transaction is contemplated), potential purchasers or sellers should seek specific legal advice before conducting any acquisition transactions in China, rather than relying on the contents of this handbook.

Certain regions of China, including Hong Kong, Taiwan and Macau, are governed by legal systems differing from China. Any reference to 'China' herein shall therefore exclude those regions, and no legal issues in relation to those regions have been discussed below.

7.2 Corporate Structures

China adopts a uniform company law country-wide, which has been fundamentally amended and became effective on 1 January 2006. The material changes involve corporate governance, the capital contribution system, the rights and duties of directors etc., and, on the whole, grant greater autonomy to the companies.

A Chinese company shall be a company with the status of limited liability, in the form of either a limited liability company that has registered capital but issues no shares ('**LLC**') or a company limited by shares. A company limited by shares may, subject to qualification and approval requirements, list its shares on the relevant stock exchange in Shenzhen or Shanghai ('*Domestic Stock Exchanges*'), or on stock exchanges abroad. A Chinese resident or legal person is now allowed to establish a one-person company following the enforcement of the amended Company Law.

The acquisition transactions result in the establishment of relevant foreign-invested enterprises ('**FIE**'), which are governed by specific laws and regulations in addition to the amended Company Law. A *FIE* may take the form of an equity joint venture ('*EJV*'), a cooperative joint venture ('**CJV**'), a wholly foreign-owned enterprise ('**WFOE**'), or a foreign-invested joint stock limited company ('**FISC**'), subject to relevant legal restrictions on the form and ratio of foreign investment, among other things. A joint venture enterprise, whether an EJV or a CJV, is normally a *LLC* established by a foreign investor(s) and a Chinese entity(ies), though a **CJV** is permitted under the PRC law to have the legal status of a non-legal person. A *WFOE* is a limited liability company solely owned by a foreign investor(s), a form which is preferred by many foreign investors but may be subject to more stringent investment restrictions. A *FISC* is a limited liability company that may issue shares, which is extremely rare in practice.

7.3 Letters of Intent and Heads of Agreements

An agreement, whether in written, oral or other forms, shall be concluded with an offer and acceptance under the PRC law. The agreement is legally binding on the contractual parties upon the conclusion thereof, unless PRC law or the agreement *per se* provides otherwise. Unlike most countries subject to common law legal system, consideration is not necessarily required for the conclusion or enforcement of an agreement governed by PRC law.

No PRC law imposes requirements on the execution of a letter of intent for an acquisition transaction. However, due to the complexity of an acquisition transaction, the relevant parties usually reach a letter of intent to clarify certain crucial issues in the early stages of an acquisition. Though letters of intent are generally deemed as not binding in nature from a regulatory point of view, legal disputes on the enforceability of the relevant letters of intent are not rare in practice. As such, it is advisable for the parties to explicitly include provisions to that effect to avoid disputes, if the relevant letters of intent should not be legally binding. Where the parties decide that certain specific provisions of a non-binding letter of intent (such as the obligation of confidentiality, the resolution of disputes and the governing law) shall be abided by, additional and specific words (e.g. the expression 'this letter expresses the preliminary opinions of the parties on the relevant matters and does not constitute a legally binding agreement on the whole, except that Article [..] shall be binding on the parties') should be inserted in the letter of intent as well.

7.4 Taxes Affecting the Structure and Calculation of the Price

An acquisition can be achieved in many ways, including the wholly indirect offshore acquisition, direct onshore equity acquisition, direct onshore asset acquisition by foreign investors, and direct onshore asset acquisition by the *FIE* established for the acquisition purpose. Besides other factors to be taken into consideration, tax considerations play an important role in ascertaining what structure is to be adopted.

Except under certain circumstances, a wholly indirect offshore acquisition involving no sale or purchase of equity interests in Chinese companies or transactions in China is not subject to Chinese tax law.

The direct acquisition of equity interests in domestic Chinese companies by foreign investors would normally result in enterprise income tax levied on the seller and stamp tax levied on the seller and acquirer, but generally, no value-added tax or business tax, or deed tax will be imposed. If an unlisted domestic Chinese company is converted into an *FIE* upon the equity acquisition in which the foreign investor holds no less than 25 per cent of the registered capital, the *FIE* may enjoy applicable tax preferential treatment in normal circumstances. Losses arising from the previous period of the domestic Chinese company before conversion can be made up by the *FIE* after conversion on a continual basis during the remainder of the term using the method for making up losses as specified in the relevant PRC tax law.

Where a foreign investor of a *FIE* transfers its equity interests therein to another foreign individual or entity, enterprise income tax will normally be imposed on this foreign investor if the selling price exceeds the amount of its original capital contribution for the transferred equity interests.

Compared with equity acquisitions, asset acquisitions are subject to a variety of taxes. In addition to enterprise income tax levied on the seller, value-added tax, business tax, stamp tax, deed tax, and land appreciation tax, among others, may be applicable to the transfer of certain assets.

Considering the complexity of the taxation of acquisitions, a thorough understanding of acquisition-related tax laws and a careful consultation with local tax authorities are suggested for the purpose of arranging a suitable acquisition structure and ascertaining the acquisition price.

7.5 Extent of Seller's Warranties and Indemnities

The sellers of the equity interests or assets are usually required by the purchasers thereof to provide warranties and indemnities upon the occurrence of certain events. The extent of the warranties and indemnities by and large depends on the nature of each relevant transaction and the respective negotiation power of the parties.

Since an acquirer of equity interests shall generally bear the debts and liabilities of the target company upon acquisition under PRC law, it will be in the best interests of the acquirer if full and comprehensive warranties and representations regarding the entire business operation of the target company, including but not limited to the assets, debts, taxation, labour issues, social welfare, and any litigation of the target company, have been specified in the relevant equity transfer agreement. For an asset acquisition, the warranties and indemnities of the seller generally focus on the title to and the quality of the assets to be sold.

An indemnity clause relating to the warranties and representations is usually required by the purchaser. In some circumstances, the purchaser also requests the seller to provide guarantees to secure the performance of the Seller's obligations.

7.6   Liability for Pre-contractual Representations

According to PRC law, a party who causes losses to another party due to the deliberate provision of false information in concluding a contract or the performance of other acts violating the principle of good faith shall be liable for damages caused as a result of those indiscretions. Where a party enters into a contract as a result of serious misunderstanding or when the terms of the contract are obviously unfair at the time it is concluded, the party has the right to request a court or an arbitration commission to modify or revoke such contract. However, from a practical point of view, without detailed guidance on defining relevant terms (such as 'serious misunderstanding', 'obviously unfair', etc.), the court or arbitration commission is often reluctant to render a verdict in favour of a party who claims against the other party for the compensation or rescission of the contract based on the said grounds.

It is therefore advisable for an acquirer of equity interests or assets to specify the detailed pre-contractual representations and the indemnity for the violations thereof in relevant equity interests (or assets) agreements.

7.7   Liability for Pre-acquisition Trading and Contracts

Given that the target company still exists after an equity acquisition, the benefits and liabilities arising out of pre-acquisition trading conducted by the target company usually remains with the target company, and will be borne by the buyer in proportion to and to the extent of its capital contribution to the target company. In practice, the pre-acquisition contracts originally executed by the target company might nevertheless be updated to reflect the change in the legal status of the target company.

In a situation where the main business of a target company is acquired, the issue of whether or not the purchaser shall be liable for the pre-contractual trading and contracts largely depends on the agreement between the buyer and the seller, subject to certain mandatory legal requirements.

7.8   Pre-completion Risks

In an equity acquisition, the purchaser is likely to be in a more risky position than the seller due to the following reasons: first, there is no clear guidance on when the risk of losses or damages may pass to the buyer; second, the seller of an equity acquisition usually expects to receive a fixed price for transferring its equity interests based on the result of a valuation usually conducted before the execution of relevant transfer agreement, in which case the purchaser will be obliged to pay such price irrespective of whether the value of the target company has depreciated at the time the transaction is completed.

It is therefore advisable for the purchaser to conduct a thorough due diligence investigation into the business operation of the target company from both legal and financial perspectives in the early stage of the transaction. Moreover, the purchaser should refrain from conducting any activities that might cause a materially adverse impact on the target company upon the execution of the equity acquisition agreement, the violation of which might result in the rescission of the contract or damages to be paid by the seller. It is important to note that, in practice, due to the difficulty of revoking an equity transaction already approved by competent Chinese approval authorities, many foreign purchasers choose to claim against the sellers for damages, rather than rescinding an acquisition agreement that is already concluded and approved.

Relevant PRC law provides that the risk of damage to or loss of an object shall be borne by the seller before the delivery of the object and by the buyer after the delivery thereof, subject to the exception that the risk is on the buyer if the object cannot be delivered within the agreed period of time due to the fault of the buyer. This general rule may nevertheless be varied by the buyer and seller through negotiation.

7.9 Required Governmental Approvals

Where an acquisition transaction is conducted offshore, no PRC governmental approvals are required in general, except that an anti-monopoly review by the Ministry of Commerce ('*MOC*') and the State Administration for Industry and Commerce ('*SAIC*') and registration with the relevant foreign exchange bureau (as discussed below) may be required.

A direct onshore acquisition is usually subject to the approvals, verifications, and registrations of various competent Chinese authorities, including at least (i) the *MOC* and/or its local authorized agency responsible for approving the acquisition, the relevant acquisition contracts and joint venture contracts (if any) and articles of associations of the proposed *FIEs;* (ii) the National Development and Reform Commission ('*NDRC*') or its local authorized agency responsible for verifying or recording foreign investment projects (including acquisition projects) in most cases, and (iii) the *SAIC* or its local authorized agency responsible for registering the conversion or establishment of the *FIE*. In this regard, there are still a number of uncertainties about the verification and recording system adopted by the *NDRC*, such as whether non-fixed assets projects fall into the scope of this system and to what extent the system shall be implemented by local authorities.

It is important to note that the approvals of other specialized administrative agencies may also be required in particular cases, depending on the nature of the target enterprises, as well as the transactions *per se* and the targeted industry sectors. For example, approval of competent authorities in charge of certain industry sectors (such as advertising, telecommunications) may be required. Direct acquisitions of state-owned enterprises shall be approved by the relevant state-owned assets supervision authorities.

Direct acquisitions of the companies listed on the Domestic Stock Exchanges must be approved by the China Securities Regulatory Commission.

7.10   Anti-monopoly and Competition Laws

With the promulgation of the *Interim Provisions for Merger with and Acquisition of Domestic Enterprises by Foreign Investors* in 2003, the Chinese government began to evaluate potential adverse effects of certain acquisition activities on the domestic Chinese market, which covers not only onshore equity or asset acquisitions but also offshore acquisitions. The anti-monopoly review requirements are reiterated under the *Provisions for Merger with and Acquisition of Domestic Enterprises by Foreign Investors* ('M&A Regulations') promulgated on 8 August 2006 (effective as of 8 September 2006) in replacement of the 2003 Interim Provisions.

An anti-monopoly review may be required if a foreign acquirer or a foreign seller has a business turnover or a market share in China that exceeds certain limits prior to, or as a consequence of, the relevant acquisition at issue. An anti-monopoly review is normally initiated by the foreign acquirers, except that it can also be launched upon the request of any competing domestic enterprise, relevant functional department or industrial association in certain direct acquisitions.

The authorities in charge of anti-monopoly review include the *MOC* and the *SAIC*. They will review the application and related materials to explore whether such an acquisition will result in excessive concentration of the domestic Chinese market, impair fair competition, and/or damage consumers' interests, and then decide to approve or disapprove the acquisition. Parties to an acquisition may apply to the *MOC* and the *SAIC* for exemption from the anti-monopoly review under certain circumstances.

It is important to note that the effective enforcement of this review requirement remains problematic, due to the lack of detailed operational rules and clear definitions of certain crucial concepts such as 'market', 'relevant industries', etc.

7.11   Required Offer Procedures

For an acquisition of equity interests in a Chinese *LLC* (including the domestic Chinese company and the *FIE*), which is the most common form of onshore equity acquisition, consent to the acquisition and a waiver of pre-emptive rights must be obtained from all other investors of the Chinese *LLC*. In addition, resolutions of the board of directors of the target company approving the acquisition are also required.

In a situation where the target company is a state-owned (controlled) enterprise, the state-owned enterprise reform will be involved. The arrangement of the employees of the target company is one of the crucial issues. An employment resettlement arrangement must be passed by the labour union of the target company and submitted to relevant approval authorities.

Acquisitions of equity interests in the companies listed on the Domestic Stock Exchanges are subject to strict legal requirements under the amended PRC Securities Law and related regulations and circulars. An investor holding 5 per cent of the shares issued by a listed company through trading at a stock exchange must make relevant reports and notifications, and, if it intends to hold or control more than 30 per cent of the outstanding shares of the target company, must make a general offer to all the shareholders of the target company unless otherwise waived by competent Chinese authorities. Moreover, the transfer of state-owned shares and legal person shares are still limited, notwithstanding the fact that the Chinese government is taking measures to ease relevant restrictions.

7.12   Continuation of Government Licenses

In various industrial sectors in China, such as telecommunications, software, broad-casting and others, special government licenses are required. Under certain circum-stances, more than one government license is needed if a cross-industry operation is involved. It is therefore important to conduct due diligence investigation into whether all required licenses have been obtained by the target company.

In an equity acquisition conducted by foreign purchasers, certain government licenses may continue to be used upon the conversion of the target company, provided that its term of validity does not expire. Nevertheless, certain government licenses may not be continuously used by the *FIE* according to specific requirements of the competent Chinese authorities. It is important for the foreign acquirers to clarify this issue with competent Chinese authorities in each specific case.

Governmental licenses of the target company are not transferable in an asset acqui-sition. Where a new *FIE* is established for the operation of the transferred assets, the *FIE* must apply for relevant governmental licenses. Since certain industries are either prohibited or limited for foreign investors, it is important for foreign investors to evaluate the feasibility of obtaining appropriate and necessary licenses in the early stages of the transaction, and adjust their acquisition strategy accordingly.

7.13   Requirements for Transferring Shares

The successful transfer of equity interests of a target company normally requires the agreement of the relevant parties, consents and waivers from other shareholders of the target company, and board resolutions passed by the relevant parties. It is also important to check if the articles of association of the target company include any restrictive provisions regarding the transfer of the equity interests.

The equity interests to be purchased by foreign investors must be valued by a qualified valuation company, and the result of such valuation is the basis for determining the transfer price. It remains unclear to what extent flexible price adjustment provisions can be recognized by approval authorities in practice. For an equity acquisition targeting a state-owned or controlled enterprise, the transfer price must not be less than 90 per cent of the valuated net assets value subject to certain exceptions.

As mentioned above, equity and asset acquisitions are subject to approvals, verifications, and recording of various competent Chinese authorities. Registration with the relevant administration for industry and commerce is also required. Different industry sectors and total investment amounts usually result in the completion of the relevant procedures with different authorities and at different levels of the same authorities.

Upon the transfer of equity interests in an unlisted domestic *LLC*, the converted *LLC* must include the relevant information about the acquirer in the shareholder list, and must issue a capital contribution certificate to the acquirer. The transfer of equity interests in a listed company is subject to registration with the relevant stock exchange.

7.14   Requirements for Transferring Land and Property Leases

The transfer and lease of real property is one of the most complex and potentially problematic issues in acquisition transactions for foreign acquirers. It is important to note that, different to many western countries, land in the territory of China belongs to the State or to different levels of peasants' collectives. Any entities or individuals can only obtain the right to use land, instead of obtaining ownership thereto. Obtaining the right to use land usually requires a execution of relevant contract and filing of a land use application with the competent authority in charge of land administration for approval and/or registration. The registered contracts granting land use rights and a relevant land use right certificate issued by the competent land administrative authorities are usually effective proof for legitimizing land use rights in practice.

Though the right to use land is generally transferable under PRC law, the transfer would be nevertheless subject to encumbrances if the land use right has been mortgaged by the land user or the transferor fails to fulfil its legal obligations (such as fully paying the assignment consideration etc.). Registration of the relevant transfer agreement with the competent land administrative authority is also required. In the event that the right to use land is to be transferred, the title to real properties built on the land usually needs to be transferred as well, and *vice versa*.

In the event of the sale of real estate, the seller is required to notify the tenant three months in advance, and in such circumstances, the tenant is generally granted priority to purchase such real estate on the same conditions.

7.15   Requirements for Transferring Intellectual Property

With China's participation in the Agreement on Trade Related Aspects of Intellectual Property Rights (TRIPs) and the promulgation of relevant PRC laws and regulations regarding intellectual property rights, the protection of intellectual property in China has been improving progressively. Obtaining certain intellectual property rights, such as patents and registered trademarks, is now subject to approval or registration with competent Chinese authorities. Though obtaining a copyright for works requires no mandatory registration, a voluntary registration system is in place to better protect the works' authors. It is therefore important to review relevant certificates of registration to ensure that the transferors are the owners of relevant intellectual properties.

The assignment of certain intellectual property (including patents and registered trademarks) is subject to registration of the relevant assignment contracts with the original approval/registration authorities. If the transfer involves any intellectual property falling into the administration scope of technology import and/or export, separate approval/registration formalities will be required.

7.16 Requirements for Transferring Business Contracts, Licenses and Leases

A party to business contracts governed by the laws and regulations of the PRC may assign, wholly or in part, its rights there under to a third party, except that certain rights may not be transferred due to the nature of such contracts or the agreement between the parties, or mandatory legal requirements. A party transferring its rights under such business contracts is required to notify the other party of the transfer, and failing to do so may result in the ineffectiveness of the transfer to the other party. A party to a business contract governed by PRC law shall obtain the consent of the other party before transferring whole or part of its obligations to a third party. A party is also allowed to transfer its rights and obligations under a commercial contract to a third party, subject to the said restrictions and the relevant legal requirements. For example, advance approval and/or registration will be needed for transfer in certain cases.

The transferee would, in addition to principal rights/obligations transferred, obtain collateral rights and/or assume collateral obligations that are related to the principle rights and obligations, with the exception of those collateral rights and obligations exclusively belonging to the transferor.

The transfer of licenses and business leases is more complicated and must be analyzed on a case-by-case basis.

7.17 Requirements for Transferring Other Assets

Other tangible assets such as equipment, transportation vehicles, raw materials and stock in trade are generally transferable, subject to mandatory legal requirements and agreements reached between relevant parties. It remains arguable under law whether goodwill may be transferred separately as a type of intangible assets, though in certain cases, goodwill of target companies (in particular the state owned/controlled companies) have been appraised as a part of the assets thereof.

The transfer of any mortgaged assets usually requires the advance consent of the mortgagee and notification of the transferee. Failing to comply with such requirement may result in the invalidity of the transfer.

It is important to note that the assets to be transferred under an asset acquisition by foreign investors must be appraised by a qualified appraisal company, and the price for such assets shall be based on the results of the appraisal. As previously mentioned, it is unclear to what extent the parties may depart from the official valuation in determining the relevant sale price.

7.18   Encumbrances and Third Party Interests

The transfer of assets by the target company may be subject to various encumbrances or third party interests arising out of the agreements between relevant parties (e.g. a loan agreement supported by mortgage) or the provisions of law (e.g. the pre-emptive rights to purchase the leased buildings), or the nature of the assets *per se* (e.g. the state and legal person shares). Some encumbrances may prohibit the assets from being transferred, while others may require additional approvals, consents or other formalities prior to the change of the owner of the assets.

Particular attention should be paid to the above issues during the due diligence investigation period. Purchasers of real property, patents and registered trademarks usually conduct research at relevant competent authorities to discover whether these assets are subject to encumbrances or third party interests. For other unregistered assets, purchasers can only rely on the review of all materials provided by and relevant warranties and representations made by the seller.

7.19   Minimum Shareholder and Officer Requirements

A *LLC* (solely state-owned enterprise excluded) was required to have at least two shareholders, a requirement which has been recently abolished under the amended company law. Now a *LLC* can be established by a single natural person or legal person. A *LLC* is required to establish a board of directors consisting of three to thirteen members, except that a *LLC* with few shareholders or that is comparatively small in scale may have an executive director without establishing such board. A company limited by shares shall have a board of directors of five to nineteen members.

Both the *LLC* and the company limited by shares are generally required to establish a board of supervisors consisting of at least three members including representatives of the staff and workers of the company , except that a *LLC* with few shareholders or that is comparatively small in scale may have one or two supervisors without establishing such board. One particular issue to be noted is that, according to policies recently promulgated by the competent Chinese authorities, a foreign invested enterprise is now required to have a supervisor(s) or a board of supervisors.

7.20   Non-competition Clauses

It is not unusual for a purchaser of equity interests or assets of a Chinese company to require the seller thereof to undertake no-competition obligations. Non-competition clauses are generally deemed valid as long as they are reasonable and constitute no violation of laws and regulations of the PRC then in force. It is important to note that the Chinese government has paid particular attention to the restraints of the promotion and development of technologies, and certain non-competition covenants under technology agreements may be deemed invalid if they violate relevant regulations governing technology protection.

The managers of a company owe fiduciary obligations to the company and are generally prohibited from conducting certain activities that conflict with the interests of the company. For example, he/she shall not, without going through required consent and disclosure procedures, take advantage of the convenience of his/her position to seize the opportunities of the company or to operate the same type of business as that of his/her company.

Any restrictive clauses regarding the employees' capability to engage in the same or similar business as that conducted by the company upon the termination of the employment relationship must be carefully drafted, to fully comply with PRC law. The period of non-competition obligations generally may not exceed three years, and a certain amount of economic compensation should be paid to the employee so burdened. Consultation with local labour protection authorities is necessary to ensure the validity and enforceability of such clause.

7.21 Environmental Consideration

Though the PRC government has promulgated various laws and regulations during the past several years to demonstrate its determination to strengthen the protection of the environment, numerous Chinese companies have failed to strictly comply with such laws and regulations in order to save operational costs. Given that a serious violation of environmental protection law may jeopardize the future operation of the company and result in severe penalties, it is essential for a foreign acquirer to ascertain whether the target company has obtained all necessary approvals, certificates, and consents from the competent environmental protection administration and whether it has fully complied with the environmental protection requirements and to assess potential environmental risks and liabilities in relation to the acquisition.

For those industries that may produce serious pollution such as energy source fields and heavy industries, it is always advisable to entrust a qualified environmental assessment company to conduct a thorough environmental investigation in the early stages of an acquisition.

7.22 Employee Superannuation/Pension Plans

The Chinese government has developed a social insurance system including superannuation pension insurance. The superannuation/pension of employees is paid to employees in the form of insurance after they retire (or reach the specified age). The superannuation premium should be paid by both the employer (including *FIEs*) and employees in proportion to the employees' income, and the detailed ratio of such payment is determined by local administrative authorities. Specific social insurance institutions have been established in China to collect and monitor superannuation pension funds, and employers are normally required to pay the funds to specific accounts established by the institution. Other than this statutory and basic insurance, companies (including *FIEs*) may also carry out supplementary insurance.

It is not unusual that certain companies (particularly state-owned enterprises) have failed to fully pay the required employee superannuation funds in strict compliance with relevant PRC law and local policies, which may cause an increase in the acquisition cost. Therefore, it is advisable for the acquirers to conduct a due diligence investigation in this regard.

7.23 Employee Rights

The Chinese government has attached great importance to safeguarding the rights of employees and workers (including but not limited to equal access for employment, minimum wages, maximum working hours, rest and vacations, work safety and health protection, job training, social security and welfare, and labour union etc.) during the past several years via the promulgation of comprehensive labour laws and regulations at both the central or local levels. Relevant labour administration authorities and labour dispute resolution organizations have been established and play a significant role in the implementation of such laws and regulations and in the protection of the rights of employees.

All employers are obliged to enter into written labour contracts with their employees, and the execution of a collective labour contracts are required in certain circumstances. A labour contract must cover such aspects as required by PRC law and comply with other mandatory provisions of relevant laws and regulations. According to PRC law, the employees of any enterprise (including *FIEs*) also have the right to establish a labour union, and the enterprise shall provide assistance, including contributing a certain amount of funding, for the establishment and operation of such labour union.

In most acquisitions involving state-owned enterprises, employees have the right to determine their own fate by vetoing or approving the staff resettlement plan proposed by the foreign purchaser and the target company.

7.24 Compulsory Transfer of Employees

The M&A Regulations impose no mandatory requirement on the transfer of employees; instead, it only provides that a plan for resettlement of employees, together with other application documents and material, should be submitted to the competent authority for approval, for either equity acquisitions or asset acquisitions by foreign investors. A resettlement plan generally deals with specific issues concerning the resettlement of the employees of the target company, such as retaining the employees, the settlement of unpaid wages and outstanding social insurance premiums and payment of severance fees. It is important to review relevant local policies and consult local authorities to ascertain if any specific conditions must be satisfied.

Special requirements will apply to equity or asset acquisitions if the controlling equity interests in or main assets of a state-owned enterprise, are to be sold to a foreign investor for reorganization. A resettlement plan must be prepared by the foreign investor and the state-owned enterprise and approved by the staff and workers' congress of the state-owned enterprise, and submitted to the local labour administration authority for examination and subsequently to the competent state-owned assets supervision authority for approval. By voting for the resettlement plan at the staff and workers' congress, the staff and employees may exercise their actual veto power on an acquisition should they be unsatisfied with the staff resettlement plan.

Moreover, the state-owned enterprise must use its current assets to pay, *inter alia*, overdue employee salaries and overdue social insurance premiums. New or modified employment contracts must be signed by the retained employees, and a severance payment must be paid in full to employees who are not retained. Relevant social insurance fees must be fully prepaid in one lump sum for those employees who are not retained to insure their full coverage under the social insurance system. In practice, local governments might have different rules for staff arrangements and severance plans.

7.25   Tax Deductibility of Acquisition Expenses

Like most countries, tax deductibility of acquisition expenses and charges incurred by foreign acquirers during the process of the equity and asset acquisitions, whether onshore or offshore, are normally governed by the laws and regulations of their respective home jurisdictions.

In a situation where a *FIE* newly established by foreign investors acts as the purchaser of assets of the domestic Chinese enterprise, acquisition expenses incurred by the *FIE* might be deducted from the taxable revenue thereof depending on the nature of the taxes and local tax policies. Consulting with local tax authorities will be helpful in this regard.

7.26   Levies on Acquisition Agreement and Collateral Documents

Stamp tax is a state tax levied on most acquisition agreements executed or delivered in the territory of China, and its rate depends on the nature of specific transactions. An equity transaction is subject to stamp tax, the rate of which is usually 0.05 per cent of the transfer price except that the rate of 0.1 per cent applies to A and B Shares transfer agreements relating to listed companies.

Stamp tax is applicable to asset acquisitions only if the law lists, or fiscal authority determines, such assets as stamp-dutiable properties. Consequently, it is advisable to specify the value of each item to be transferred in the relevant asset transfer agreement to avoid the possible risk that the competent tax authority imposes stamp tax on the total transfer price or based on a higher rate. For most properties, such as real estate and intellectual property, stamp duty rate is 0.05 per cent of the transfer price. Certain asset transactions, such as the assignment of the right to use land and equipment, are exempted from stamp tax.

7.27   Financing Rules and Restrictions

The form of consideration in an acquisition depends on the type of acquisition transaction and is subject to the relevant laws and regulations governing the payment of consideration. In general, a foreign acquirer in an onshore equity or assets acquisition usually pays the consideration in cash or by means of stock issued by such foreign acquirer. Nevertheless, it is important to note that, according to the M&A

Regulations, the payment of consideration in stock must satisfy strict pre-conditions (such as the stock being issued by an overseas reputable company whose stock is traded on an overseas stock exchange, provided an acquisition report is issued by acquisition consultants) and will only be permitted by the competent Chinese authorities in exceptional circumstances. Also, the payment of consideration by means of RMB-denominated assets is restricted and must be approved by the competent foreign exchange bureau. Since the payment methods involve complicated approval processes which are scrutinized by the competent Chinese authorities, prior consultation with such authorities on the feasibility of such payment methods is suggested in the early stages of an acquisition.

Consideration for transferred assets or equity interests must be paid to a seller within the required period of time as specified in the approved acquisition contract; provided, however, that in all events the payment shall be paid within one year from the date of issuance of the relevant businesses license to the converted *FIE* by the competent administration for industry and commerce. Unless and until the consideration is fully paid, the purchaser can only enjoy the right of dividends from the converted *FIE* in proportion to the payment it has actually made. If a foreign purchaser acquires a domestic Chinese company by subscribing for new capital of such company, the purchaser must pay 20 per cent of the increased capital when applying for a business license of the converted *FIE* and must pay the remainder of the capital increase it has subscribed for within the period of time required by PRC law.

In a situation where the foreign purchaser conducts an onshore equity or assets acquisition via its foreign investment vehicle established in China (usually a WFOE), such foreign investment vehicle might finance the investment with funds from its parent company or otherwise. It is important to note that the maximum borrowing capability of the WFOE will be a balance between its total investment amount and registered capital, and that it must complete the relevant formalities for such borrowing with the competent foreign exchange administration authority.

7.28 Exchange Controls and Repatriation of Profits

Since the currency of Renminbi is not freely convertible on the international foreign exchange market, foreign purchasers of onshore equity interests or assets face foreign exchange issues if the purchase price is paid in foreign currency from outside of China by the foreign purchasers.

Foreign exchange accounts are divided into two types, current accounts dealing with daily operational funds, and capital accounts dealing with funds generated from the import and export of capital. The conversion of current account items has been liberalized and generally can be effected with the relevant foreign exchange banks specially designated by a competent foreign exchange bureau, while capital account items are still subject to much stricter supervision. The purchase price for an equity or asset acquisition is construed as a capital account item in nature.

The foreign purchaser in an equity acquisition usually remits the purchase price into a capital account established by the seller, while the foreign purchaser in an asset acquisition usually remits the purchase price into a capital account established by the target company. In both circumstances, the remitted purchase price shall be converted into RMB. Where a large amount of foreign currency is remitted into China in payment of the purchase price in an acquisition transaction, the seller may be required to obtain the approval of the competent foreign exchange bureau for the settlement and conversion thereof. Upon the remittance and conversion of the purchase price, the foreign purchasers or the target company authorized by the purchaser must carry out special foreign exchange registration at competent foreign exchange bureau and obtain a registration certificate.

The profits, dividends or bonuses arising out of the *FIEs* are allowed to be repatriated out of China in foreign currency to relevant foreign investors under PRC law, on the condition that the *FIEs* have paid all relevant taxes and levies and have submitted to the banks specially designated for the foreign exchange all required documents and materials for verification. The repatriating bank is required to report such payment to the local foreign exchange bureau for selective examination.

7.29 Groups of Companies

With the enforcement of the independent legal person system in China, every company within the same company group is responsible for its credits and debts independently, and the affiliated transactions among group companies must be at arm's length, and are subject to other legal requirements and restrictions.

On the other hand, PRC law generally requires the enterprise groups incorporated in China to prepare consolidated financial accounts, including a balance sheet, a profit and loss account, a profit distribution sheet and a business condition alteration sheet, which integrates the financial status of the parent enterprise and all the companies it directly or indirectly controls inside or outside of China. In this regard, specific rules promulgated by competent administration authorities require that state-owned enterprises, companies listed on the Domestic Stock Exchanges and foreign trade companies must maintain consolidated financial accounts.

In preparing consolidated financial accounts, the parent company must ensure that its financial year, balance date and fiscal policy are consistent with those of the companies which it controls. Where the parent company sells or purchases a subsidiary company in the financial year, the fiscal activities of the subsidiary company during its existence are generally required to be recorded in the consolidated accounts.

7.30 Responsibility for Liabilities of an Acquired Subsidiary

The foreign purchaser in an equity acquisition will generally acquire all of the existing or contingent obligations or liabilities of the target company, while any existing obligations or liabilities of the PRC target company will remain the sole responsibility of the target company in the case of an asset acquisition in normal circumstances. A special rule permits a foreign purchaser to release or limit its liability if a special agreement on the settlement of the obligations and liabilities of the target company has been otherwise reached by the foreign purchaser, the target company, the creditors and other relevant parties and has been approved by competent Chinese authority. Special settlement agreements are, nevertheless, seldom approved in practice.

The foreign purchaser, as the shareholder of the target company upon acquisition, is required to be liable for its acquired subsidiary only to the extent of its committed capital contribution in theory, unless a specific guarantee or undertaking in relation to the subsidiary has been provided. Notwithstanding the above, the foreign purchaser might be held liable for the debts of the subsidiary in exceptional circumstances where the principle of 'piercing the corporation veil' specified in the amended Company Law applies.

7.31   Governing Law of the Contract

Any onshore direct equity or asset acquisition agreement concerning a company established in China, irrespective of whether both the seller and the purchaser are foreign investors, shall be construed with and governed by PRC law, excluding any possible choice of the law which might be otherwise available for other transactions.

It is unclear under PRC law as to whether an indirect offshore acquisition agreement under which the target company is a foreign invested enterprise established in China must be governed by PRC law. However, in practice some authorities tend to think such agreement is governed by PRC law and refuse to approve an agreement if it is governed by the laws of other jurisdictions. It is advisable for the relevant parties to consult the competent approval authorities in advance before they decide which law is to be the governing law.

7.32   Dispute Resolution Options

The parties to an onshore direct equity or asset acquisition may choose either the court or the arbitration commission to settle their dispute. In the consideration of quality and effectiveness, arbitration is adopted in most equity and asset acquisitions. Mediation may be used in the arbitration proceeding and litigation. From a practical point of view, mediation is an effective way to resolve complex disputes for which arbitration and especially litigation are time-consuming. However, the smooth implementation of mediation will largely depend on the willingness and cooperation of the parties in dispute.

Although onshore direct equity and asset acquisitions are governed by the PRC law, relevant parties may choose either a Chinese arbitration organization (i.e. China International Economic and Trade Arbitration Commission and its branches in the relevant cities such as Beijing, Shanghai and Shenzhen) or arbitration organizations established in other countries or regions to handle the dispute. The arbitration rules may be freely chosen by the parties. If the China International Economic and Trade Arbitration Commission is chosen as the arbitration authority and no arbitration rule is specified in an acquisition agreement, the commission's arbitration rules then in force shall apply.

China is a signatory to the New York Convention giving recognition and enforcement to the arbitration awards rendered by arbitration bodies of the party countries. It is worthwhile to note that, though the arbitration clause in the acquisition contract will oust the jurisdiction of the Chinese court, the Chinese court has the right to formally verify the arbitration award and send it back to the arbitration commission under certain circumstances.

7.33 Other Issues

Notwithstanding the great efforts taken by the Chinese government to improve the foreign investment environment, there are unsettled legal obstacles and conflicting or vague policies with respect to acquisitions in China. Each proposed acquisition transaction must therefore be analyzed from both the regulatory and practical points of view, so as to make the arrangement legitimate and favourable.

8. DENMARK

J. C. Hesse Rasmussen and Morten Lau Smith, Bech-Bruun

8.1 Introductory Comments

On the whole there are only few legislative restrictions on business acquisitions in Denmark. The relevant restrictions are primarily to be found in the Danish Competition Act.

Note, however, that the trend is towards increasing legislation on important legal fields pertaining to undertakings, partly resulting from the implementation of the EU directives. The rules apply mainly to company, tax, environmental, employment and competition issues.

The account below concerns Danish regulations and Danish contractual principles only.

8.2 Corporate Structures

As a general rule there is freedom of choice as to the legal form of a business entity.

The most common forms of legal entities in Denmark are the public limited company in respect of large undertakings ('*aktieselskab*' (A/S)—minimum share capital DKK 500,000) and the private limited company ('*anpartsselskab*' (ApS)—minimum capital DKK 125,000). The A/S may be a listed company.

Within the agricultural and dairy sector it is common to choose other forms of business entities; these are, however, still entities with limited liability. The statutes regulating such companies are to some extent different from those regulating A/S's and ApS's.

In addition, business entities may be organized as foundations, general partnerships, limited partnerships, sole traders, etc to which special rules apply.

8.3 Letters of Intent and Heads of Agreement

Generally, a letter of intent or a similar instrument is a forerunner to an agreement on an acquisition. The heading indicates that there are no actual legal obligations associated with such document, but the substance of the document or other circumstances may indicate that a legal obligation is implied.

If the document is not meant to be legally binding, this should be expressly stated.

In Denmark, a number of cases have been decided by the courts concerning documents described as letters of intent, but where ambiguity existed about whether the documents were in fact legally binding according to their substance.

© World Law Group
International Business Acquisitions, M. Whalley, F.-J. Semler (eds.), Kluwer Law International, London, 2007; ISBN 9789041124838.

8.4 Taxes Affecting the Structure and Calculation of the Price

A purchase of shares in a Danish company generally does not have any implications as to the target's taxation liabilities. Such liabilities remain the same after the acquisition. However, if a majority of the shares in the Danish target is transferred, this may have certain consequences concerning existing tax loss carry forward in the target.

For tax purposes, a purchase of assets or of a division of an existing company is usually treated as a transfer of assets and liabilities, giving rise to a charge of capital gains tax on any taxable gain realized. However, if certain conditions are met, including that the remuneration to the seller solely consists of shares in the buying company, it may be possible to obtain the Danish tax authorities' acceptance that the acquisition be tax-exempt if the buyer and the target are companies incorporated within the EU.

Where a company sells shares which it has owned for less than three years, any capital gain is taxable at the normal corporate income tax rate of 28 per cent (2006). Losses are tax deductible subject to certain ring-fence restrictions. If a company sells shares which it has held for three years or more, any gain realized is free of capital gains tax. Losses are not tax deductible. As for individuals, the Danish capital gains tax is rather complex, but generally, the effective tax rate is between 28–43 per cent. It falls outside the scope of this guide to give a detailed description of the rules.

An acquisition of shares insulates a non-resident buyer from Danish taxation other than taxation paid by the Danish target on its profits and any withholding taxes due on dividends and royalties received by the buyer. With the exception of certain interest payments to group related (subject to definition) parties, there is no withholding tax on interest in Denmark. However, a non-resident acquiring business assets in Denmark may be deemed to have set up a permanent establishment there, and its profits attributable to the Danish permanent establishment would then be subject to Danish taxation.

8.5 Extent of Seller's Warranties and Indemnities

It is customary for the seller to give warranties and indemnities relating to the business's affairs with respect to the accounts, taxes, assets, claims of any third parties, employment matters, etc.

It is not uncommon for the seller's parent company to be asked to warrant the correctness and to guarantee the enforceability of such warranties.

There is also a tendency for sellers to attempt to limit the scope of such warranties. This limitation is often achieved by giving the buyer access to due diligence investigations in respect of the target in question and, for example, by limitation of claims to direct loss only.

8.6 Liability for Pre-contractual Representations

If the seller has provided incorrect details to the buyer or withheld details from the buyer, the buyer may raise a claim for damages against the seller. If, in addition, the seller is in bad faith in this regard, the buyer can raise such claim irrespective of any provisions contained in a contract to limit the buyer's right to raise such claims.

The liability for pre-contractual representations may, depending on the circumstances, be limited by due diligence investigations carried out by the buyer. Although not explicitly stated in statutory Danish law, the recent development in industry practice and case law lead to the conclusion that the buyer will effectively be required at law to perform due diligence, failing which the buyer's remedies will be limited in case of the seller's breach of its representations and warranties.

In the agreement or in annexes thereto it should, therefore, be stated as accurately as possible what particulars the buyer has received prior to the agreement and what surveys the buyer has conducted. Furthermore, the effect of any information that the buyer may subsequently receive of a more comprehensive nature should be described in detail in the agreement.

8.7 Liability for Pre-acquisition Trading and Contracts

Where shares are acquired, the buyer will (indirectly) assume all rights and obligations of the business taken over in their entirety.

Where assets are acquired, the buyer does not assume the risk of any transactions entered into by the seller prior to the agreement, but to the extent the buyer enters into agreements with third parties, an accurate description of all implications should be made. In addition, it is necessary to obtain the consent of the third party in question of the buyer's assumption of the seller's obligations under the agreement in order to release the seller from the seller's obligations. The acquisition agreement should specify the details of each contract and the procedures to be followed if the third party withholds his or her consent or gives it only on certain conditions.

8.8 Pre-completion Risks

Until closing takes place the seller bears the risk of all assets to be taken over. After closing, the buyer bears all risk.

However, as a certain period of time may normally elapse between the signing and the closing, detailed provisions should be included describing the seller's rights and obligations in the period until closing, including a requirement that the seller shall maintain insurance of the assets to be taken over. Furthermore, any consequences of the seller's non-compliance with the provisions agreed on for the interim period should be outlined: whether the buyer is entitled to cancellation on certain conditions or whether the purchase price should merely be adjusted.

8.9 Required Governmental Approvals

As a general rule, no governmental approval is required in connection with the acquisition of a business in Denmark.

8.10 Anti-trust and Competition Laws

Since 1 January 1998, the Danish rules on anti-trust and competition laws have been in conformity with the EU competition rules.

As a rule, all anti-competitive agreements or practices and the abuse of any dominant position are prohibited. However, an exemption may be available insofar as an agreement carries primarily positive effects.

Mergers and acquisitions, whether share acquisitions or asset acquisitions, of businesses must be approved by the Danish Competition Authorities if certain turnover thresholds are exceeded. However, a merger or acquisition subject to approval by the EU does not need to be approved by Danish authorities as well.

8.11 Required Offer Procedures

There are certain requirements in this respect. In particular there are provisions pertaining to listed undertakings. A variety of requirements about form have to be observed when acquiring shares in a listed company and, if a controlling shareholding is acquired or a controlling influence is otherwise gained, the buyer must offer to buy the shares of all other shareholders on identical terms.

In addition, if a parent company of an A/S or ApS owns 90 per cent of the company's share capital and voting rights, the minority shareholders may demand that their shares be acquired at an agreed market value of the shares or, if no such market value can be agreed upon, at a market value estimated by independent experts appointed by the court. Correspondingly, a parent company holding 90 per cent of the share capital has a right to purchase the minority shareholders' shares on the above mentioned terms.

A target company's articles of association may also contain restrictions or requirements relating to an acquisition of the company.

8.12 Continuation of Government Licences

A licence is required for certain fields of business. Licences are primarily required within the banking, insurance, auctioning, gaming, radio, subsoil exploration and production, and television industries. The licence may be subject to certain conditions, for example concerning duration, amendment of ownership structure, etc.

As a general rule, licences may not be assigned to a third party. Thus the buyer of an undertaking must obtain a new licence relating to the business in question.

8.13 Requirements for Transferring Shares

No special statutory requirements apply and no separate approval must be obtained from any public body. However, the articles of association or a shareholders' agreement normally contains certain restrictions on sale of shares or sale of the company's assets.

Unless otherwise stated in the articles of association, shares may be transferred without observing special requirements about form. The share transfer does not require the board of directors' approval, but the buyer must be registered as a new shareholder in the company's register of shares. The acquired shares should be delivered with an endorsement concerning the transfer.

8.14 Requirements for Transferring Real Property

All interests in real property must be registered in the Danish Land Register in order to obtain protection against any third party. When purchasing real property, a deed of conveyance must be drawn up and a registration duty of DKK 1,400 plus 0.6 per cent paid on the higher of the agreed purchase price and the official tax assessment of the property, whereupon the deed of conveyance is registered in the Land Register on that property.

As the purchase of real property is typically financed by mortgage credit institutions or banks which will register a mortgage on the property as security for the debt, the purchase price should not be released to the seller until such mortgages have either been formally taken over by the buyer as part of the agreement or have been redeemed by the seller. When taking out a mortgage on real property, a registration duty of DKK 1,400 plus 1.5 per cent of the amount secured is payable.

In addition, note that zoning regulations, restrictive covenants, easements, etc that may restrict the owner's disposal are often registered. It is also important to determine any risk of previous contamination of the soil as liability for any pollution may be imposed upon the property owner.

8.15 Requirements for Transferring Intellectual Property

Intellectual property rights may be disposed of by assignment. This also applies to licensed rights, but the assignment of a licence normally requires the licensor's consent.

Where registration of intellectual property is possible (e.g. trade marks, patterns, designs and patents), notification of the assignment should be made to the Danish Patent and Trademark Office.

8.16 Requirements for Transferring Business Contracts, Licences and Leases

A contract concluded with a third party and subject to Danish law may only be assigned in accordance with the terms of the contract. This normally implies that the third party must give his or her consent before an assignment can take place. The assignor of a contract is not released from his or her obligations until the third party has accepted the release and has accepted that the assignee assumes the obligations under the contract.

In order to eliminate any doubt, it should be expressly stated in the contract that the buyer assumes all the seller's rights and obligations only as from the takeover date, which ensures that the seller continues to be liable for matters of an earlier origin.

This principle applies to any kind of contract, including short- and long-term leases, construction contracts, etc.

Prior to the acquisition of an undertaking, the buyer should ensure that all major contracts, as described to the buyer, can be assigned.

Note that leases in respect of real property are regulated by several laws providing tenants with very extensive protection.

Rights under a lease of real property of an unusual or burdensome nature should be registered in the Land Register.

8.17 Requirements for Transferring Other Assets

The same principles apply to the transfer of other assets as indicated in **8.14–8.16**, i.e. the consent of any third party must be obtained, and the (e.g. mortgage) rights of any third party subsist until an agreement has been concluded with the buyer.

8.18 Encumbrances and Third Party Interests

Assets may, following from **8.14–8.16**, be subject to third party rights. Such rights may typically arise in connection with a contractual relationship, but may also be statutory rights.

When acquiring an asset, the buyer acquires absolute ownership, including the right of disposal, unless the contractual rights or statutory restrictions to which the seller is subject (e.g. relating to environmental matters) dictate otherwise.

As such rights may exist without registration, warranties by the seller are of paramount importance.

8.19 Minimum Shareholder and Officer Requirements

There are no requirements for the number of shareholders in a company.

An A/S must have at least three directors. There are no mandatory requirements in respect of the residence of directors. Furthermore, there must be at least one manager. No residence requirement applies to such manager.

The same applies in principle to an ApS, except that the management (both board of directors and managers) may consist of one person only.

If an A/S or ApS has 35 employees or more (on an average over the last three years), the employees are entitled to nominate a number of members to the board of directors, corresponding to one third of the total number of directors with a minimum of at least two employee directors.

8.20 Non-competition Clauses

Where a seller in the course of a commercial acquisition accepts a non-competition clause, such clause has legal force, subject to limitations set out in applicable EU legislation. Generally, a non-competition clause applies for a number of years and provides for both liquidated damages and compensation in case of violation. Only in special cases is the conforming non-competition clause restrictively construed by the courts.

It is also common for a parent company or other group companies of the seller to be subject to a non-competition clause.

According to the Danish Competition Act, anti-competitive agreements are prohibited. An agreement containing a non-competition clause is only allowed (i) on specific terms set out by the EU Commission, in accordance with which the Danish Competition Act is construed, or (ii) between companies with a total annual turnover of less than MDKK 1,000 and a total market share in Denmark of less than 10 per cent or with a total annual turnover of less than MDKK 150.

Non-competition clauses in employment contracts accepted by employees for the term of their office are valid. However, special rules have been laid down in the statutes to the effect that a non-competition clause may not be invoked in all cases, for example where the employee is dismissed without due cause or the clause is considered unduly to restrict the employee's ability to obtain other employment. It is also a condition for the validity of a non-competition clause that the employer pays the employee compensation corresponding to 50 per cent of the salary of the employee. Case law shows that a non-competition clause effective for more than a year after the resignation of the employee is exposed to challenge with regard to fairness.

8.21 Environmental Considerations

On acquisition of production facilities in Denmark it is important to carry out an environmental due diligence check, involving technical as well as legal assistance.

The reason for this requirement is a detailed and fairly restrictive legislation. The most essential points of the Danish Environmental Protection Act are:

- prevention of air, water, soil and subsoil pollution and vibration and noise nuisances;
- limitation of raw material waste; and
- promotion of recycling and limitation of problems relating to waste disposal.

The fulfilment of these objectives is based on an approval system to the effect that the authorities determine in detail the conditions for operation of production facilities if such operation involves risk of pollution, including threshold limit values of any acceptable influence of pollution on human beings and the surrounding natural environment.

Such due diligence should comprise all present and previous affairs concerning real and business property, including:

- all public planning and rules for utilising the real property and the company's production;
- the company's waste disposal;
- the real property's current condition in relation to pollution;
- the pollution risk in a continued unchanged operation; and
- evaluation of the risk of more rigorous environmental requirements at the expiry of the company's environmental approval.

8.22   Employee Superannuation/Pension Plans

There are no statutory requirements in relation to pension schemes. Collective agreements (see **8.23**) increasingly contain provisions relating to pension rights, but otherwise there are no requirements for the employer to offer a pension scheme to the employee, unless an individual agreement has been made with the employee to that effect.

8.23   Employee Rights

In Denmark it is common for the relationship between employer and employee to be regulated mainly by either collective or individual agreements. As trade unions and employers' organizations have a great impact on the labour market, general or local collective agreements apply, in particular to wage earners, but also to certain salaried employees. In addition, the Danish Employees Act governs the rights and obligations of salaried employees towards their employers.

The relevant collective agreements and the Employees Act cannot be deviated from to the employees' detriment.

Disputes relating to collective agreements are settled before the Labour Court or by arbitration, whereas disputes involving salaried employees who are not subject to collective agreements are settled before the ordinary courts.

8.24   Compulsory Transfer of Employees

As in the other EU Member States, Denmark has an act determining the legal position of wage and salary earners in the event of an acquisition. This implies that the buyer of an undertaking must respect the rights of the employees in full, including the right to wages or salaries, to seniority and to other benefits. In principle, it therefore makes no difference whether the buyer acquires shares or assets.

Dismissals should not be effected in connection with the acquisition. Furthermore, special statutory provisions, and *inter alia* collective bargaining agreements, if any, (concerning notification of employees and consulting of trade unions) must be observed before dismissals can be implemented. According to statutory law, as applicable, certain obligations to involve an independent body overseeing the interests of employees, and to negotiate with employees or their representatives, apply in the case of dismissal within a period of 30 days exceeding certain numbers of employees within different intervals of total individuals employed.

Conversely, employees must accept transfer to another undertaking if the buyer acquires shares.

8.25   Tax Deductibility of Acquisition Expenses

Where the buyer is a company or an individual not resident or taxable in Denmark, the deductibility of its acquisition expenses is determined by the laws of its home jurisdiction.

If the buyer is a Danish taxpayer, acquisition expenses are not normally deductible. Generally, expenses incurred in the acquisition of capital or fixed financial assets such as shares or business assets are not deductible. However, in case of a subsequent sale of the acquired capital or fixed financial assets, the acquisition expenses may be added to the acquisition price for the purpose of calculating any taxable gain on the transaction.

Interest on acquisition debt in a Danish corporate acquisition vehicle would as a main rule be tax deductible and may normally be set off against income in the acquired Danish target.

8.26 Levies on Acquisition Agreements and Collateral Documents

No stamp duty is payable on the transfer of assets or shares. A registration duty is, however, payable when purchasing real property or when taking out a mortgage on real property or ships (see **8.14**).

8.27 Financing Rules and Restrictions

Thin capitalization rules apply to certain controlled debt, and is normally deemed to exist when a Danish company has non-arm's length debt to a company, if the borrower and the lender are under common control (subject to definition) and the debt equity ratio exceeds 4:1. If the debt equity exceeds that ratio, tax deductibility of interest expenses and capital losses is reduced for tax purposes in respect of the excess part of the controlled debt.

The Danish Companies Act prohibits the provision of loans or the offering of funds or security by a Danish company in connection with an acquisition of shares in the said company or of shares in its parent company. Contravention of these prohibitions constitutes a criminal offence. A recent EU directive provides for certain voluntary relaxation—it remains to be seen to what extent it will be implemented in Danish law.

8.28 Exchange Controls and Repatriation of Profits

No Danish exchange control permission is required for conclusion of an acquisition in Denmark. However, the exchange control authorities must be notified of the transaction—only for statistical purposes—with details of any part of the purchase price paid from abroad and how it was settled. Furthermore, there are no exchange controls in Denmark over the flow of funds in and out of the country.

Dividends paid are subject to a 28 per cent withholding tax that under a double taxation treaty may be eligible for refund in whole or in part to shareholders resident abroad. No withholding tax is imposed on dividends paid to a parent company resident in another EU Member State, or a parent company eligible for reduction or elimination of Danish withholding tax on dividends, if the recipient has owned at least 20 per cent (for the years 2005–2006), reduced to 15 per cent (for the years 2007–2008) and to 10 per cent (as of 2009 and later) of the nominal share capital of the distributing company for a period of at least one year during which time the distribution takes place.

8.29 Groups of Companies

A Danish company exerting a controlling influence (typically by owning more than 50 per cent of the share capital or holding more than 50 per cent of the voting rights) on one or more companies (parent company), whether Danish or foreign, must prepare consolidated accounts. Danish group related entities would normally be subject to mandatory Danish tax consolidation.

In addition, the financial year of group companies must coincide, unless the Danish tax authorities have permitted otherwise. A Danish parent company which itself is a subsidiary of a foreign company does not have to prepare group accounts pursuant to Danish rules if the foreign parent company prepares consolidated accounts fulfilling the EU minimum standards for consolidated accounts.

8.30   Responsibility for Liability of an Acquired Subsidiary

In general, an individual legal entity is liable for its own obligations. In certain cases (e.g. in the case of guarantees or indemnities provided by a parent company), the parent company may be liable towards some or all of the relevant subsidiary's creditors.

By way of exception, a liability in damages may be imposed upon a parent company towards the creditors of the subsidiary in the event of a compulsory liquidation of the subsidiary. Such liability would primarily arise if the parent company had unlawfully stripped the subsidiary of its assets or liquid funds or if the liquidation is because of gross negligent mismanagement of the subsidiary with the parent company's knowledge or acceptance. Examples of this have been seen in Denmark.

8.31   Governing Law of the Contract

Under Danish private international law the parties may freely agree on the applicable law. Only in very special cases would such choice of law be set aside, for example according to the *ordre public* principles.

Rules pertaining to Danish public law (e.g. provisions relating to real property, environment, bankruptcy, etc) must in certain cases be applied by the Danish courts, especially if creditor interests or other public interests so dictate.

8.32   Dispute Resolution Options

It is up to the parties to choose settlement of disputes before the ordinary courts or by Danish or international arbitration.

In connection with acquisitions, arbitration is normally preferred as awards are not made public, and expert arbitrators may be appointed (although in matters submitted to the ordinary courts, expert judges can also, subject to application, be appointed to the Bench). In major contracts or contracts relating to a company or business with major activities abroad, it is more common to have any dispute settled by an international arbitration tribunal.

Mediation is also used in Denmark, however to a modest extent yet in business related disputes.

An arbitration award is normally enforceable by the Danish ordinary courts without the courts having to prove the correctness of the award.

9. ENGLAND AND WALES

Martin Issitt
Eversheds

9.1 Introductory Comments

The current regulatory regime in England and Wales largely encourages foreign investment. There are, however, a number of reporting requirements which a buyer must comply with and the complex merger control laws and takeover laws, both at national and European level, can also restrict or prevent an acquisition.

England and Wales have a sophisticated business climate and a complex regulatory environment to match it. Failure to comply properly with national and European acquisition, merger and takeover laws can have serious, and costly, repercussions. Early advice should always be sought whenever an acquisition involving an English or Welsh company, or a group which includes English or Welsh subsidiaries or assets, is contemplated.

9.2 Corporate Structures

The target of an acquisition of shares in England and Wales is likely to be a limited liability company which can be either a private or a public company. The liability of the members of a limited company is generally limited by shares but can, in the case of a private company, be limited by guarantee. Private companies whose members' liability is unlimited can also be established.

A public company may have its shares publicly traded on the London Stock Exchange or other recognized investment exchange or market, or may be a privately owned company structured as a public company for commercial reasons (the owners believing this will give it more prestige). Public companies are in some respects subject to more stringent controls than private companies, particularly as regards maintenance of share capital.

Most companies are incorporated and registered under, and in compliance with, the provisions of the Companies Acts. However, a few companies (particularly older trading companies) have been incorporated under an Act of Parliament (statutory companies) or by Royal Charter (charter companies).

It is possible for anyone having legal personality and capability to buy or sell shares or assets. As well as companies, this includes private individuals and the Crown. A partnership does not have a separate legal personality and buys, sells and holds shares and assets in the names of the individual partners. However, it is possible to contract with the partners so as to bind each of them jointly and severally.

© World Law Group
International Business Acquisitions, M. Whalley, F.-J. Semler (eds.), Kluwer Law International, London, 2007; ISBN 9789041124838.

9.3   Letters of Intent and Heads of Agreement

An agreement is binding if it appears either from the document or from the surrounding circumstances that there is an intention to create legal relationships and if either there is consideration given for any promises made, or undertakings given by any party to the agreement are in writing and executed as a deed.

If it is intended that letters of intent or heads of agreement should not be binding on the parties, clear words should be used to that effect. The expression 'subject to contract' is often used together with a specific statement that the letter of intent or agreement is not intended to have legal effect. Often only parts of such a document are intended to be legally binding—for example, a lock-out clause or a clause to protect confidential information being disclosed. If this is the case, the particular provisions intended to have legal effect should be clearly identified and, as indicated above, unless the document is executed as a deed, there must be consideration given for the promises made or undertakings given in the relevant clauses.

9.4   Tax Affecting the Structure and Calculation of the Price

A detailed examination of the UK's business taxes is beyond the scope of this guide. However, a purchase of shares results in the buyer inheriting all of the target's taxation liabilities, whereas a purchase of assets avoids this. Appropriate taxation warranties and indemnities and an accountant's report can help to protect the buyer from any unforeseen taxation liabilities of the target in the former case.

A non-resident acquiring business assets in the UK is deemed to have established a branch or a permanent establishment in the UK and if the non-resident carries on trading activities from the branch its profits attributable to the UK branch would then be subject to UK taxation. An acquisition of shares normally insulates the non-resident buyer from UK taxation, other than tax paid by the UK target on its profits and any withholding taxes due on interest or dividends received by the buyer.

The optimum structure for an acquisition will depend in part on an analysis of the tax treatment of the purchase price. The structure is often affected by the seller's and the buyer's tax planning. We comment briefly below on issues which typically arise for UK resident buyers and sellers. Where the buyer or the seller is not resident in the UK similar issues to those outlined below will need to be considered under the laws of the relevant country.

A UK resident corporate seller may benefit from an exemption which applies to a sale of a substantial shareholding (subject to certain conditions being satisfied); whereas a sale of assets by the target may generate tax liabilities in the target. UK resident individual sellers are likely to be subject to capital gains tax, at effective rates of between 10 per cent and 40 per cent; whereas the corporation tax rate payable by the target on a profit realised on a sale of assets may be at 30 per cent. A UK corporate purchaser will obtain no immediate tax relief in relation to the purchase price paid to acquire the shares in a target; whereas amounts paid to acquire assets may attract tax relief. Specific rules apply to provide 'capital allowances' (a form of depreciation relief) in respect of the acquisition price of certain types of assets (e.g. 25 per cent annual relief on the tax written down as expenditure incurred in acquiring plant and machinery). Tax relief may also be available in respect of the amortization of the cost of acquiring intangible assets (such as goodwill) in accordance with accounting treatment. A purchase of shares in the target will not result in any uplift in the cost for tax purposes of the assets of the target and a buyer may therefore wish to reflect the contingent tax liabilities of the target in its calculation of the purchase price. Factors of the above nature will have to be considered, and potentially competing interests of buyer and seller reconciled, when structuring a transaction.

Other tax planning strategies undertaken by a seller may involve a pre-sale dividend or part payment in loan notes in order to improve the seller's net receipt after tax, allowing greater flexibility on the price generally.

9.5 Extent of Seller's Warranties and Indemnities

The nature and extent of warranties and indemnities depends upon the size of the acquisition and the parties' relative bargaining strengths. However, it is not unusual for sellers to give full warranties and indemnities relating to, for example, the accounts of the business of the company to be acquired, title to the assets, taxation, litigation, employee issues, real estate, environmental matters and so on. Some sellers, such as trustees and institutional investors, may seek to limit severely the nature and extent of the warranties they provide.

It is always desirable to consider whether warranties and indemnities from a seller should be supported by a parent company guarantee, or by a retention of part of the purchase price.

Often the seller's liability under the warranties (and, depending upon the circumstances, sometimes also under the indemnities) is limited in various ways.

9.6 Liability for Pre-contractual Representations

Pre-contractual misrepresentations not forming part of any subsequent contract may be actionable and can in certain cases result in rescission/termination of the contract and/or a claim for damages.

The seller will usually wish to exclude actions based upon pre-contractual misrepresentations, leaving the buyer with a remedy only in damages for breach of warranty. This is usually effected by incorporating an 'entire agreement' clause into the acquisition agreement. Whilst in many instances such an exclusion is effective, in some cases the exclusion may be challenged, particularly if not carefully drafted so as not to apply in the event of fraud.

To clarify both parties' positions, specific contractual provisions should be considered which exclude liability for representations made in pre-contract negotiations and which restrict rights of rescission/termination to the period between exchange of contracts and completion. The result will normally be that the buyer can rely only upon statements specifically repeated in the agreement and matters specifically warranted or in relation to indemnities which have been given.

9.7   Liability for Pre-acquisition Trading and Contracts

On a sale of assets, the agreement itself invariably specifies an effective date of sale, prior to which trading is for the seller's account and following which trading is for the buyer's account. Often this is the date of completion of the sale, but if a retrospective effective date is included, the buyer, for accounting and taxation purposes, bears the loss or is entitled to the business's profits from that date.

Section **9.17** deals with the transfer of contracts under an asset acquisition. Following completion, the seller remains liable in relation to pre-acquisition contracts to which it was a party unless released from the contracts by the third party. In relation to contracts which could have a major effect on the business, it is recommended that the rights and obligations under these contracts be transferred to the buyer under a contract of novation to which the third party is a party. To the extent that contracts are not novated, the rights under them are agreed to be assigned under the assets sale agreement to the buyer who undertakes to the seller to perform the contracts following the sale and to indemnify the seller against any liability he or she might incur under them after that time.

In the case of a share acquisition, pre-acquisition profits and losses are for the target's account itself. However, pre-acquisition profits may be paid to the seller by way of dividend before the sale. If they are retained in the target, the buyer effectively inherits them. In addition, the consideration for the share acquisition might have been determined, or be adjusted following completion, to reflect the profits or losses in the target at completion.

Whilst the target itself remains liable on any contracts it has entered into before the sale, the seller might have guaranteed the target's obligations under the relevant contracts, in which case the buyer often undertakes to use reasonable endeavours to procure the release of the seller from the guarantee following completion and in the meantime to indemnify it against any liability it might incur thereunder.

9.8   Pre-completion Risks

If there is a gap between the exchange of the purchase agreement and completion, the question of who should bear the risk of anything adverse arising prior to completion which affects either the target, where shares which are being transferred, where or the assets which are being transferred is one which should be considered carefully by the parties and addressed in the purchase agreement.

There are no fixed rules in this regard, but often the buyer is given limited rights to terminate the purchase agreement. This right might arise, for example, if there has been a material breach of any of the warranties given by the seller which are, or are deemed to be, repeated at completion. Sometimes the agreement excludes the buyer's right to terminate the agreement, in which case the buyer must complete the acquisition and rely on any right to claim damages against the seller. A refinement of this might involve a provision under which there is no right to terminate the agreement but the price is adjusted by reference to the loss suffered by the target or the business being transferred.

It is sensible for the buyer, in the case of a business acquisition agreement, to insure the assets with effect from the signing of the agreement. The alternative is a provision enabling him or her to terminate in the event of significant loss or damage to the business assets before completion. In the case of a share acquisition, the buyer should ensure that the target has adequate and proper insurance cover.

9.9   Required Governmental Approvals

The acquisition of a business or company in the UK is subject to anti-trust and competition laws as described in Section **9.10** below. The Secretary of State for Trade & Industry (a Government Minister) also has the power to intervene in relation to certain cases relevant to the UK public interest, including mergers in the defence sector which may raise issues of national security.

In relation to certain sectors, such as regulated utilities and financial services, additional consents or modification of operating licences may also be required.

9.10   Anti-trust and Competition Laws

The legal basis for merger control in the UK is the Enterprise Act 2002 (the 'Act') which establishes an administrative procedure for the control of qualifying mergers. As a general rule, mergers that fall under the scope of the European Community Merger Regulation are excluded from review under the Act.

A merger qualifies for investigation under the Act if either:

- as a result of the merger a share of at least 25 per cent of the supply or purchase of goods or services of any description in the UK or a substantial part of it will be created or enhanced; or

- the value of the turnover in the United Kingdom of the enterprise taken over exceeds GBP 70million;

The Act provides that the Office of Fair Trading ('OFT') is responsible for monitoring merger activity generally and for the first stage of merger control. The OFT is under a duty to refer to the Competition Commission a qualifying merger which it believes has resulted or may be expected to result in a substantial lessening of competition.

In the event of a reference, the Competition Commission conducts a detailed second phase investigation and must reach a final determination on whether a merger results in a substantial lessening of competition. The Competition Commission can impose remedies in the event of an adverse finding, including the prohibition of a transaction or the divestment of a business.

Merging parties have the option to notify a qualifying merger to the OFT for clearance but are not under any obligation to do so and there are no sanctions for not notifying. The question of whether to notify a qualifying merger to the OFT is essentially one of commercial risk assessment. It is routine not to notify a merger which qualifies for investigation but raises no substantive competition concerns. However, even if no notification is made, the OFT may still investigate and make a reference to the Competition Commission which may impose remedies including prohibition or divestment.

9.11   Required Offer Procedures

If the target is a public company in the UK (whether or not its shares are quoted on any stock exchange), any takeover offer made in relation to its shares is regulated by the City Code on Takeovers and Mergers ('the Code'). The Code also regulates takeover offers in relation to limited classes of private companies.

The Code contains detailed provisions for the timing and nature of a takeover offer and also contains mandatory bid requirements. In general terms, in circumstances where:

- a person acquires, whether by a series of transactions over a period of time or not, interests in shares carrying 30 per cent or more of the voting rights of a target company regulated by the Code; or

- a person who is interested in shares carrying not less than 30 per cent but not more than 50 per cent of a relevant target company's voting rights acquires any additional shares that increase that person's percentage of the voting rights in the target company;

that person is obliged to make a full takeover bid for the target's equity shares (both voting and non-voting). A person and anyone acting in concert with him or her are treated as one for these purposes. Such an offer must be in cash or be accompanied by a cash alternative at not less than the highest price paid by the person or anyone acting in concert with him or her for such shares during the twelve months prior to the announcement of that offer, or if higher, the price paid by such persons during the period following the announcement of the mandatory offer and such offer closing for acceptance.

There are a number of refinements and exemptions from the rule and also the Take-over Panel can waive any obligation to make a takeover offer if a 'whitewash procedure' is followed.

9.12   Implications of Financial Services and Markets Act 2000 ('FSMA')

It will be important on any corporate transaction involving shares or securities to consider whether there is any potential conflict with the financial promotion restrictions set out in FSMA.

Under section 21 FSMA a person must not, in the course of business, 'communicate an invitation or inducement to engage in investment activity unless that person is an authorized person or the contents of the communication have been approved for the purposes of FSMA by an authorized person. For example, an information memorandum inviting recipients to enter into an agreement to purchase the shares of the target (i.e. engage in a controlled activity) would be a communication which needs to be issued or approved by an authorized person unless a relevant exemption applies (e.g. all recipients of the communication are certified high net worth individuals).

One of the main exemptions is in respect of any communication by or on behalf of a body corporate, a partnership, a single individual or a group of connected individuals which relates to an acquisition or disposal of 50 per cent, or more of the voting shares in a body corporate or a transaction, the object of which may reasonably be regarded as being the acquisition of day to day control of the affairs of a body corporate.

9.13 Continuation of Government Licences

In certain industries, it is necessary for the business operator to have a licence. Licences are required in, for example, banking, insurance, telecommunications and broadcasting. Various conditions may be attached to a licence and these need to be reviewed, including whether the licence is revocable on a change of control of the licence holder.

Licences are not normally transferable, so that a buyer of a business needs to obtain a new licence in its own name. The time taken to obtain the licence may be a relevant consideration.

9.14 Requirements for Transferring Shares

Restrictions on transfers of shares may be found in a company's articles of association or, if there is one, in a shareholders' agreement. These documents should be reviewed.

Subject to any special provisions in the articles of association, shares are transferable by a written stock transfer form. The form must be stamped, if appropriate, and must be signed by the seller. A buyer is only required to sign if the shares are partly paid. The transfer must be approved for registration by the company's board of directors; the buyer's name must be inserted in the company's register of members and (subject to exceptions) the company must provide the buyer with a share certificate within a prescribed period.

Stock Exchange dealings are transferred through the CREST system, a centralized electronic settlement system for UK and Irish securities.

9.15 Requirements for Transferring Land and Property Leases

England and Wales have a comprehensive registration system for title to land (including leasehold interests exceeding 21 years). Any property not already registered must be so registered following completion of a transfer. The purchase of any registrable interest in real property requires the execution of a prescribed transfer form and, subject to the payment of the appropriate stamp duty and registration fee, registration of that transfer at the Land Registry for the area in which the property is situated.

Title to the land can be specifically encumbered by mortgages or charges or by caveats recording the interests of third parties in the property (such as easements or rights of way). In many cases title to the property cannot pass and be registered in favour of the buyer until any prior encumbrances have been cleared or appropriate consents obtained.

9.16 Requirements for Transferring Intellectual Property

Title to all forms of intellectual property can be transferred by assignment.

The benefit of a licence to use the intellectual property of a third party may also be assignable, but may require the licensor's consent.

Where the intellectual property is the subject of registration (which includes trade marks, registered designs and patents), notice of the assignment should be given to the appropriate registry.

9.17 Requirements for Transferring Business Contracts, Licences and Leases

The benefit of a business contract governed by the laws of England and Wales is transferable or assignable without the other contracting party's consent unless the terms of the contract prohibit assignment or the contract is categorized as a personal contract. Assignment of the benefit of a contract does not release the transferor from the burden of the contract without a specific release from the other party to it. For this reason, many business acquisitions involve a formal novation of contracts or an agreement to novate contracts (in which the buyer steps fully into the seller's place, the seller being released from all further liability) rather than a simple assignment. Licences and business leases (finance leases, operating leases or hire purchase agreements) operate under the same rules.

Routine purchase and sale contracts are normally assignable without consent, and their performance is simply completed by the buyer after completion. In most other cases, the consent of the other party to the contract (e.g. a lessor) is required before the contract can be assigned or novated. It is not normally necessary to register or record an assignment of a business contract, although there may be stamp duty payable on the assignment document, and notice should be given to the other party that the contract has been assigned.

9.18 Requirements for Transferring Other Assets

With the exception of real property and certain specific assets such as shares, goodwill, intellectual property, trading debtors and the benefit of contracts, assets can generally be transferred by delivery, and a transfer by delivery rather than by formal document may have favourable stamp duty implications.

Assets that are the subject of a charge in favour of a bank or other creditor, or in which title has been retained by a trade supplier or a supplier under a hire purchase or conditional sale agreement, continue to be encumbered by the rights of the third parties following transfer to a buyer in most circumstances.

9.19 Encumbrances and Third Party Interests

Assets can be subject to many types of third party interest. Interests can, for example, arise under contract (e.g. a charge or a mortgage), or by operation of law (e.g. a property right or a lien in favour of an unpaid vendor).

Certain title registers (particularly in the case of land) can be conclusive evidence of the title of the registered proprietor on which the buyer can rely, but other assets may be subject to unregistered or unascertainable interests which a buyer may not be able to uncover.

Most mortgages and charges created by companies are registrable at the Companies Registry. The effect of a failure to register is that the charge is invalid as against any liquidator or creditor of the target or buyer of the charged assets. The company is still bound by any unregistered charge.

A buyer should always make a search against the charges register of a corporate seller or a target. Only in a small percentage of cases are registrable mortgages and charges not properly registered.

In addition, warranties from the seller as to good title to the shares or assets being sold and, in the case of a share purchase, warranties that the target's assets are unencumbered should always be sought.

9.20 Minimum Shareholder and Officer Requirements

In June 1998 the London Stock Exchange published the Principles of Good Governance and Code of Best Practice ('the Combined Code') which embraces the work of the Cadbury, Greenbury and Hample committees which had previously reported on government issues for publicly listed companies. The Combined Code (the latest updated version of which was published in June 2006) is maintained by the Financial Reporting Council (FRC) and sets out the main principles, supporting principles, and more detailed provisions of corporate governance. The Combined Code has been supplemented by the following related guidance and good practice suggestions: (i) guidance on internal controls (the Turnbull Guidance); (ii) guidance on audit committees (the Smith Guidance); and (iii) suggestions for good practice from the Higgs Report. The Combined Code, which is applicable to public companies listed on the Official List maintained by the Financial Services Authority, provides that the Board should include a balance of executive and non-executive directors such that no individual or small group of individuals can dominate the Board's decision taking. The Board should include non-executive directors of sufficient calibre and number for their views to carry significant weight in the Board's decisions. Except in the case of smaller companies, non-executive directors determined by the Board to be independent should comprise not less than one half of the Board.

Every company must have a secretary, who may also be a director, but not the sole director. However, under the Companies Bill, which received Royal Assent on 8 November 2006 and which is expected to come into force by October 2008 (the 'Companies Bill'), private companies will no longer require a secretary, although a public company will continue to require a secretary.

Single-member private companies are permitted, but a public company must maintain a minimum of two shareholders (although this will be changed to one shareholder, once the Companies Bill comes into force).

9.21 Non-competition Clauses

Restraint of trade or non-competition covenants given by a seller in the context of a sale of business are generally enforceable, provided that the extent and terms of the covenant are reasonable and do not exceed that which the buyer requires to protect its legitimate business interests. What is reasonable depends upon the circumstances of the case, the nature of the business and the effect which competition could have on the buyer.

Covenants given by employees in employment agreements can also be enforceable if they are reasonable, but the test of reasonableness is likely to be stricter in the case of an employee than of a seller. A blanket prohibition on an employee carrying on his or her actual occupation or exercising his or her skills is likely to be considered unreasonable, as is a restraint which goes beyond a short period following termination of employment.

Under the Competition Act 1998, which is based broadly on EU competition law, agreements which may affect trade within the UK or part of the UK and which have as their object or effect the prevention, restriction or distortion of competition within the UK are prohibited and void unless the agreement is of a type specifically excluded from the Act, or benefits from an exemption. Similarly, there are further general bans on abuses of a dominant position. The Office of Fair Trading has significant investigatory powers similar to those of the European Commission.

9.22 Environmental Considerations

England and Wales have sophisticated laws for the protection of the environment, ranging from criminal sanctions against polluting emissions to air, water and land to requirements for detailed authorizations and consents for industrial processes and waste disposal (including producer responsibility obligations in relation to waste products such as waste electrical and electronic equipment). Regulatory control is exercised both by central and local government agencies. Substantial penalties can be imposed where regulatory provisions have been breached. Although the basic principle behind many of these provisions is that 'the polluter pays' (including in relation to property previously occupied) ownership and occupation of land can carry liability for the remediation and rectification of environmental harm.

Directors and other officers of companies causing pollution can be made personally liable for certain breaches of environmental laws where the pollution incident arises from the deliberate or negligent acts or neglect of those persons.

In civil law, the law of negligence (and particularly nuisance) has been adapted to the protection of property and personal interests from pollution. Where liability is established, the courts can award damages and/or injunctions restraining the continuation of the polluting activity together with remediation of the contamination caused.

Warranties in relation to environmental damage and liability should be obtained from a seller unless the buyer's own due diligence has extended to a full environmental audit. Indemnities to cover specific areas of concern may also be appropriate.

9.23 Employee Superannuation/Pension Plans

Some employers operate occupational pension schemes under which their employees receive pension benefits. These occupational pension schemes usually take one of two forms. They will either be final salary (or 'defined benefit') pension schemes, under which the employee receives a pension which is calculated by reference to his or her final salary at the date of leaving or retirement and his or her years of service as a member of the pension scheme, or they will be money purchase (or 'defined contribution') pension schemes under which the final benefits are dependent upon the investment return achieved by the fund and annuity rates at the time of retirement.

It used to be the case that the Inland Revenue prescribed limits to contributions which could be paid into pension schemes and benefits which could be paid out. With effect from April 2006, this has been replaced by a lifetime allowance on the total value which a member can build up, and an annual allowance on contributions for defined contribution pension schemes. For defined benefit pension schemes, the annual allowance is based on how much the value of a member's benefits has increased during the year. These allowances are not absolute limits, but there are tax consequences when they are exceeded.

Although established by the sponsoring employer, the responsibility for running an occupational pension scheme is in the hands of the scheme trustees. The trustees are required to administer the scheme in accordance with trust law, their general duty to act in the best interests of the members and other beneficiaries under the scheme, and with their statutory duties prescribed by legislation. The employer, however, invariably retains the right to terminate its liability to make contributions to the scheme, often bringing the scheme to an end. Termination in this way has consequences in employment law terms in respect of the employer/employee relationship.

Where a defined benefit pension scheme is wound up and it is underfunded, any underfunding is a debt due from the employer. At the date of publication, most schemes are underfunded on the actuarial basis used to calculate the debt. Depending on the extent of underfunding, the level of the resulting debt can be very large and a significant cost for the employer.

Where a scheme is wound up in surplus, the destination of the surplus funding depends upon the precise rules of the scheme. The trustees may have the power to apply at least a proportion of the surplus to improve employee benefits payable, and the rules may also state that after benefit improvements have been granted to members, any surplus left over may be returned to the employer, subject to certain requirements.

Where the target company participates in a group wide pension scheme or where the purchase is one of business assets, the employees who are to move to the buyer with the business or the target will not be able to continue their membership of the seller's scheme. Subject to the terms of the agreement between the buyer and the seller, employees' accrued pension rights may be transferred as a group to the occupational pension scheme of their new employer, they may be retained in the pension scheme of their former employer, or they may be transferred to a personal arrangement of their choice. When the target company ceases to participate in the seller's scheme in these circumstances, the target is liable to pay for its share of any deficit as a debt. It can be possible to prevent the full debt from falling due, but to do so requires negotiation with the scheme's trustees and the Pensions Regulator (see below) and is not straightforward. Also, when employees are transferred to a buyer as a result of an asset purchase, there is a legal obligation on the buyer to meet certain pension commitments to these employees for the future. These commitments depend on the type of pension scheme the employee is a member of pre and post transfer.

Where the buyer is to acquire the target by way of share purchase and the target has its own scheme then, unless alternative arrangements are put in place, the target continues to be the sponsoring employer of the pension scheme and the buyer will have introduced the scheme into its own group of companies. In such circumstances the buyer needs to investigate the financial state of the pension scheme, taking account of any underfunding in the scheme in its negotiations as any deficit will remain the responsibility of the target and could be substantial.

In April 2005 a new Pensions Regulator with wide-ranging powers came into operation. These powers include powers to 'pierce the corporate veil'—that is, impose liabilities on companies in a group other than the employer (and, sometimes their directors)—if a defined benefit scheme is in deficit and other conditions apply. These conditions are, in brief, that the Regulator believes that there has been avoidance of a pensions debt or deliberate prevention of such a debt from falling due, or that the pension scheme's position has been prejudiced by a weakening of the employer's finances. This raises significant issues for underfunded pension schemes in corporate transactions. If a party is concerned that the Regulator will use its powers, it can apply for clearance which, if obtained, removes that risk.

Where there is no occupational pension scheme, employers frequently contribute to personal pension schemes. These are contract-based arrangements between the individual members and insurance companies. Personal pension schemes are always money purchase schemes.

9.24 Employee Rights (share transfers)

Employee rights and employer obligations on a share transfer may be affected by the following:

- Employees' individual contracts of employment (which may incorporate terms negotiated with trade unions at local, industry or national level), which will contain relevant notice provisions applicable to any terminations and may contain relevant procedural or 'change of control' clauses and restrictive covenants;

- Domestic legislation which confers various rights on employees and specifies minimum terms and conditions of employment and termination rights. Where the minimum terms and conditions are not met the statutory regime prevails over the contract terms. Employers may have duties to inform Government of mass redundancy proposals. Listed companies may also have duties to inform and consult employee representatives about aspects of the transaction following the UK's transposition into domestic law of the EU Takeover Directive;

- Establishment-wide, divisional or national information and consultation forums, established voluntarily or pursuant to regulation, which may need to be consulted, particularly over associated large-scale redundancies. If not already in existence, the employer may need to invite elections for the appropriate employee-representative body;

- International group-wide information and consultation mechanisms such as European Works Council agreements or European Company (Societas Europea) provisions, which typically affect cross border transfers involving major multinationals, may be triggered;

- Employees will have legislative protection against any associated dismissal being deemed 'unfair' either substantively or procedurally. Reinstatement, re-engagement or compensation up to statutory maximum amounts can be awarded. If dismissals surrounding the acquisition are discriminatory on grounds including sex, sexual orientation, race, ethnicity, religion, physical or mental disability, or age, unlimited compensation is potentially available. Part-time employees, atypical workers and fixed term contract staff are also protected.

Warranties and indemnities will be required in the acquisition agreement to ensure that the buyer is informed of and protected against accrued liabilities and exposures within the target company or group. Wording will be dictated by the results of due diligence on issues such as compliance with tax withholding obligations, health and safety matters, industrial unrest, employment litigation, regulatory investigations, grievances, collective agreements, unusual terms and conditions, efficacy of post-termination covenants (particularly in a people business), details of bonus plans, stock options and the like.

9.25 Compulsory Transfer of Employees (business transfers)

On an acquisition or disposal of assets by way of business transfer, where the assets comprise an identifiable and stable economic unit, the employer is at greater risk. EU-derived regulations require the seller to:

- inform and consult affected employees (through elected representatives), whether or not appropriate mechanisms yet exist, and in addition to any other provisions which might apply in a share transfer (see Section **9.24** above);

- seek information from the buyer as to measures it, the buyer, intends to adopt in relation to employees and to pass that information on to the seller's employee representatives; and

- assist the buyer by providing stipulated employee information at least 14 days in advance of the transfer.

The buyer must:

- likewise inform and consult elected representatives of any of its affected existing employees: if the representative body does not exist, the buyer may have to hold elections;

- assist the seller by responding to a request for information about any measure it, the buyer, proposes to take which may affect the workforce being acquired;

- take on all employees assigned to the business being acquired on existing terms and conditions and with all accrued service unless, either the employees object to the transfer, or their services are terminated for an economic, technical or organizational reason involving changes in the workforce ('ETO'), effectively meaning the dismissal must be for redundancy: the transfer of employment contracts happens automatically with no break in service and thus no offer of employment from the new employer; and

- adopt existing collective bargaining agreements.

The buyer and seller may be jointly and severably liable for any failure to consult and inform employee representatives. The seller may also be exposed to significant claims for any failure to provide the employee information to the buyer, referred to above. The buyer cannot validly harmonize terms and conditions with those of its existing workforce save in very limited circumstances. It automatically acquires most if not all liabilities of the seller in connection with employee contracts, including past actual and contingent liabilities. Having taken on the employees it cannot subsequently dismiss an employee for a reason connected with the transfer without that dismissal being automatically 'unfair'—unless the dismissal is for an ETO reason.

Over and above the considerations set out in Section **9.24** above therefore, additional due diligence, warranties and indemnities are required to ensure the equitable (e.g. time-apportioned) division of risk and liability as between buyer and seller. Particular emphasis will be placed upon identifying those employees assigned to the unit being transferred and the treatment of those who might have been overlooked.

9.26   Transaction Taxes

Stamp duty or stamp duty reserve tax is levied at 0.5 per cent on the transfer of shares in UK companies. It is normally possible to avoid such liabilities where shares in non-UK companies are sold.

Stamp duty land tax (SDLT) is payable in respect of transactions involving real estate (including transfers of real estate to and from partnerships and transfers of interests in partnerships which own real estate). SDLT is payable where the consideration for commercial property exceeds £150,000 at rates of between 1 per cent and 4 per cent (the 4 per cent rate applies where consideration exceeds £500,000 and applies to the total consideration, not the excess over £500,000). The grant of a lease also attracts SDLT, with the above rates applying to any premium payable and a charge at 1 per cent on the net present value in excess of £150,000 of rent payable under a lease of commercial property.

Generally, therefore, an acquisition of shares in a UK company attracts a 0.5 per cent duty and an acquisition of a business attracts duty of between 0–4 per cent on the consideration attributable to real estate interests.

Once acquired, assets can generally be moved within the acquiring group without payment of further duty.

Value added tax is not payable in relation to a purchase of shares. Where a business is sold value added tax will potentially be payable in relation to many categories of assets typically comprised within a business, but usually relief from the liability can be obtained under rules relating to the transfer of a business as a going concern. The specific conditions for securing this relief must be considered.

9.27 Financing Rules and Restrictions

The general rule is that a company giving financial assistance for the purchase of its own shares or the shares of its holding company or for reducing or discharging a liability incurred for the purpose of such an acquisition is prohibited. There are certain limited exceptions to this rule. In addition, a private company is permitted to provide financial assistance provided it complies with certain conditions, including the making by the directors of a statutory declaration of solvency. Under the Companies Bill, the prohibitions on giving financial assistance will no longer apply to private companies but will continue to do so for public companies.

The UK's thin capitalization rules treat certain interest payments to shareholders as dividends for tax purposes. These apply where a non-shareholder would not have made a loan on similar terms. There are no formal debt to equity ratio limits although a 1:1 ratio would normally be regarded as acceptable. Informal clearances can be obtained for greater debt ratios.

9.28 Exchange Controls and Repatriation of Profits

There are no exchange controls in the UK relating to the movement of goods or currency. However, the export of various classes of goods to certain countries is prohibited because of the adoption of various sanctions put in place by the United Nations. Dividends paid to non-resident investors in UK companies attract no withholding tax.

Resident shareholders are entitled to a tax credit such that basic rate individual taxpayers have no further personal income tax liability on the dividend and higher rate individual taxpayers have a further tax liability equal to 25 per cent of the dividend. UK resident corporate shareholders have no UK corporation tax liability on receipt of a dividend from a UK resident company.

A non-resident corporate shareholder which owns at least 10 per cent of the UK company's shares may be able to obtain credit for the underlying UK corporation tax on the profits out of which the dividend is paid against the non-resident's tax liability in its home jurisdiction.

Double taxation agreements often provide for part of the credit to which a UK resident individual would be entitled to be refunded to a non-resident shareholder. However, the amount of the credit available to a UK resident individual was reduced in 1999 and a consequence of this reduction is that the amount of any refund available to a non-resident shareholder is typically nil or minimal.

The UK imposes a 20 per cent withholding tax on interest paid to non-residents, but this is reduced or extinguished under the terms of most of the UK's double taxation agreements, subject to the appropriate claim for relief under the applicable agreement being made.

9.29   Groups of Companies

A parent company is required to prepare and publish consolidated accounts (profit and loss account and balance sheet) for itself and (with certain limited exceptions) all its subsidiary undertakings.

A subsidiary undertaking is defined as one where there is a parent company that:

- holds a majority of its voting rights;
- is a member and has a right to appoint and remove directors holding a majority of the voting rights at meetings of its board;
- has the right to exercise a dominant influence over it;
- is a member and controls a majority of its voting rights; or
- actually exercises a dominating influence over the undertaking or is managed on a unified basis with it.

With certain exceptions, individual accounts of each of the subsidiary undertakings must also be prepared and published and the parent company itself must prepare individual accounts but, subject to compliance with certain requirements, these need not be published.

Companies that fall into the categories of 'small' and 'medium-sized' under companies legislation (based on the number of employees and turnover) are granted exemptions from full compliance with the legislation relating to company accounts. There are detailed provisions in this legislation relating to the methods used to account for mergers and acquisitions during a company's financial year.

Companies legislation provides that, unless there are good reasons against it, the financial year of subsidiary undertakings should coincide with that of the parent company.

9.31   Responsibility for Liabilities of an Acquired Subsidiary

Shareholders are insulated from liability for the debts of a company in which they hold shares, other than in circumstances where a specific guarantee, indemnity or other undertaking has been given in favour of a creditor.

However, a parent company may become a 'shadow director' of its subsidiary if the subsidiary directors are accustomed to acting in accordance with its instructions. The parent company (in common with the subsidiary directors) might be liable to the subsidiary's creditors in the event of the insolvent liquidation of the subsidiary. This liability would arise if, before the liquidation, the parent knew, or ought to have concluded, that there was no reasonable prospect of avoiding the insolvency and it did not do all in its power to minimize the potential loss to creditors.

9.32 Governing Law of the Contract

English and Welsh courts will honour a choice of law freely made between parties to a contract. They will not insist on applying English law to a contract for the acquisition of shares or business assets in England and Wales. There are, however, certain limits imposed on such freedom of choice, which provide the English and Welsh courts with grounds to disregard a choice of law.

Jurisdiction may be determined by mandatory rules which override any decision freely arrived at by the parties. These include certain rules relating to:

- Consumer Protection;
- Competition Law;
- Financial Services;
- Employee Rights;
- Patents;
- Real Property;
- Commercial Agents (Council Directive) 1993;
- Electronic Commerce (EC Directive) Regulations 2002.

A court should not apply a foreign governing law to the extent that a rule of that law would be manifestly incompatible with the public policy of the forum.

While a foreign law may govern the agreement, and the relationship between the parties, English and Welsh law usually deals with other questions such as the effect of a transfer of title to the shares or other assets, or the rights of creditors and others.

9.33 Dispute Resolution Options

English and Welsh laws, and the courts, recognize that parties to commercial contracts may wish to resolve disputes other than by litigation. The whole range of arbitration and mediation options are therefore available to resolve commercial disputes.

The UK is a signatory to the New York Convention and has adopted the UNCITRAL Model Law on International Commercial Arbitration. English and Welsh courts therefore recognize and enforce international arbitration awards in certain cases. England and Wales also have a sophisticated network of arbitration bodies which appoint arbitrators to hear disputes.

Mediation is also gaining in popularity as an effective way to avoid lengthy and costly litigation. A number of bodies provide mediators and mediation services in England and Wales.

Parties are free to adopt the arbitration or mediation rules of any English or Welsh or international body in their contracts and the English and Welsh courts recognize and honour the wishes of the parties in this respect. It is not, however, possible to oust the jurisdiction of the English and Welsh courts in a dispute over which they have jurisdiction, although a court may be bound by a determination of any expert or an arbitrator on questions of fact if the parties have so agreed.

The Arbitration Act 1996 has a clear principle that the courts should support rather than displace arbitration and that there should be non-intervention by the courts other than in certain specific circumstances.

Finally, the UK is a signatory to a number of treaties giving recognition to the judgments of superior courts overseas, and it is possible in many cases to register a judgment obtained overseas for the purposes of enforcing it in England or Wales.

10. FINLAND

Johan Åkermarck

10.1 Introductory Comments

It has been noticed already a long time ago that the company legislation can be used as a tool to promote success of Finnish business. Functional and competitive company legislation has a positive impact on foreign investments into Finland. Finnish company regulation has undergone some fundamental changes during recent years and the new Companies Act was given on 1 September 2006, containing an extensive revision of the regulations compared to the old one.

The objectives behind the legislative proposal for the reform of the Companies Act were flexibility and competitiveness. The individual amendments and objectives of the reform aimed to modernize the regulations of the Companies Act. With the amendment of capital structure, the new Companies Act tries to achieve an easier and simpler procedure in mergers and acquisitions and in acquiring capital. The purpose is to increase opportunities for transactions. This together with the fact that Finland has been elected three times running as the most competitive country in the world by the World Economic Forum and with a well slim-lined administration makes the country an interesting playground for companies.

Finland is bilingual (Finnish and Swedish) and a member of the European Union since 1995. Finland is also a member of the European Economic and Monetary Union.

10.2 Corporate Structures

According to the Finnish Ministry of Trade and Industry, in relation to the population there are more companies than ever in Finland. The most popular corporate structure in Finland is the limited liability company. Limited liability companies are regulated by the Finnish Companies Act (*Osakeyhtiölaki* 624/2006). The act covers two types of limited liability companies: the private and the public limited liability companies. The private limited liability company (*osakeyhtiö, Oy*) has a minimum share capital of EUR 2,500 and the public limited liability company (*julkinen osakeyhtiö, Oyj*) has a minimum share capital of EUR 80,000.

Primarily, all the shares of the company produce the same rights. All the shares include among other things voting rights, and pre-emptive rights on the company's profit and assets. However, the company may have prescribed in its Articles of Association that the company has different series of shares, which carry different types of rights. In the limited liability companies the shares are usually assignable. The shareholder may sell the shares to a third party unless otherwise is agreed. The limited liability company may issue share certificates, but it is not obligatory.

© World Law Group
International Business Acquisitions, M. Whalley, F.-J. Semler (eds.), Kluwer Law International, London, 2007; ISBN 9789041124838.

The securities of the public limited liability companies may be admitted to the public trade on the Helsinki Stock Exchange regulated by the Finnish Securities Markets Act (*Arvopaperimarkkinalaki* 1989/495). The Helsinki Stock Exchange is nowadays a part of the Nordic Exchange. The Nordic Exchange is a combined list for the stock exchanges in Stockholm, Copenhagen, Iceland and Helsinki.

There are also other kinds of corporate structures such as partnership (*avoin yhtiö, Ay*), limited partnership (*kommandiittiyhtiö, Ky*), sole proprietor, cooperative society, association and foundation. However, these structures are not described later in this chapter.

10.3 Letters of Intent and Heads of Agreement

A typical M&A transaction involving one purchaser can start with the signing of a confidentiality agreement followed by a letter of intent. Letter of intent—documents are used especially in the international transactions. Even though the letter of intent is not binding under Finnish law, this must be clearly stated in it, making it only stating the intention of the parties to negotiate on the transaction.

Despite of drafting and signing the letter of intent the parties to a contract are free to decide not to enter into a final agreement. However, it is advisable to stipulate well which provisions of the letter of intent are not binding. Sometimes, even though the letter is not normally legally binding, the circumstances may constitute an obligation to enter into a final agreement. The negotiating party preventing the final agreement by negligence or intention may be liable to compensate the negotiation expenses of the other party.

10.4 Taxes Affecting the Structure and Calculation of the Price

Income of a limited liability company is taxed as business income of the company. The tax rate is flat 26 per cent and the business income includes e.g. profits of the share sales. A purchase of shares does not result in any changes of the taxation of a target group.

A foreign company may be deemed having a permanent establishment in Finland if the company has an office or a branch in Finland whose activities fulfil the criteria set forth in the double tax treaties or the relevant domestic tax law. In this case, the company pays in Finland an income tax on the income attributable to this permanent establishment with the tax rate of 26 per cent.

Non-residents e.g. foreign corporate bodies have a limited tax liability in Finland. If they receive dividends from Finland, the payer withholds a final source tax on the disbursement. The source tax rate is 28 per cent, but normally it is reduced to between zero and 15 per cent in various double tax treaties concluded by Finland with more than 60 countries.

Additionally, dividends paid to a shareholder holding at least 20 per cent of the voting rights or capital of the company distributing dividend is exempt from withholding tax in accordance with the EC Parent Subsidiary Directive. From the beginning of year 2007 the minimum shareholder holding entitling to this exemption from taxes is 15 per cent and 10 per cent from the beginning of year 2009.

Under certain circumstances, transactions between Finnish companies and companies located within the EU area may be carried out tax-free.

10.5 Extent of Seller's Warranties and Indemnities

Fairly wide warranties are as a general rule included in the acquisition agreements and they are similar to those used in other European jurisdictions. Naturally, warranties should be tailored to fit each transaction on a case-by-case basis. This means that the extent of seller's warranties varies and they are dependent on the size and the risks of the acquisition. A standard set of warranties includes those governing the corporate structure of the target company, share capital, authority to transfer title to the target, financial statements, title to assets, liabilities such as debts and guarantees, agreements remaining in force to despite the transaction, labour law, pension and competition law liabilities, such as non-existence of e.g. unlawful terminations of employment, pending or threatened litigation and threat of re-assessed taxes and environmental matters.

Primarily, the Finnish law provides for the freedom of contract. Therefore, the limitation of liability in agreement is allowed. Especially in contracts between companies it has been seen that there is no need to protect the parties by extensive mandatory legislation. However, if the contract provision is unfair or its application would lead to an unfair result when considering the transaction as a whole, the term may be adjusted or set aside according to the Finnish Contracts Act (*Laki varallisuusoikeudellisista oikeustoimista* 228/1929).

The parties to a contract have customarily agreed on the quality and other properties of the goods (in this context sold shares or the business assets). If the goods acquired do not correspond with the terms agreed in the contract they are defective. According to the Finnish Sale of Goods Act, (*Kauppalaki* 1987/355) even if the goods (shares or assets) are sold 'as is' they are deemed defective if e.g. they are in a substantially worse condition than what the purchaser justifiably had reason to expect taking into consideration the price and other circumstances. The purchasers duty to inspect is primary to the seller's duty to disclose when goods are sold 'as is', i.e. contrary to the general rule.

The purchaser cannot claim that the goods are defective if he can be assumed to have been aware of the defect at the time of entering into the contract. In addition to the warranties, it is therefore advisable for the purchaser to perform proper investigation relating to the goods. Provided that the purchaser has examined the goods, for example performed due diligence, or if he has without acceptable reasons disregarded the seller's proposal to examine the goods, it is generally difficult for the purchaser to claim that the goods are defective due to the fact that the purchaser should have noticed it while examining the goods.

10.6 Liability for Pre-contractual Representations

As mentioned above, the negotiating party preventing the final agreement by negligence or intention may be liable for the negotiation expenses of the other party. In addition the seller is under the Sale of Goods Act (*Kauppalaki* 1987/355) also liable if the goods do not correspond with the information relating to their properties or use that was given by the seller before the conclusion of the contract and this information can be considered to have had an effect on the contract.

As mentioned in chapter 10.5, the liability of the seller may be reduced by the due diligence examinations that the purchaser may perform before entering into a final agreement.

10.7 Liability for Pre-acquisition Trading and Contracts

In case of a share transaction the obligations and liabilities of the target company remain the same. As a general rule the pre-acquisition profits are retained in the target and hence received by the buyer, unless otherwise is agreed. The availability of the tax (e.g. losses carried forward) of the target is affected by the change of its shareholder.

In an asset deal, only those obligations that are transferred contractually are transferred to the buyer. See further 10.16.

Various representations and warranties, covenants and other such undertakings of the contract are used to protect the buyer of the target from losses or adverse changes in connection with events that occur after the signing but prior to closing of the acquisition.

10.8 Pre-completion Risks

The parties' freedom of contract concerning the provisions of passing of risks depends on the transaction. According to the Sale of Goods Act (*Kauppalaki* 1987/355), the provisions of the act are applied only secondarily. If the parties have not agreed otherwise or if no established practice between the parties or a common trade practice exists the provisions of the Sale of Goods Act (*Kauppalaki* 1987/355) shall apply.

According to the Sale of Goods Act (*Kauppalaki* 1987/355), the risk passes to the buyer when delivery of the goods takes place under the contract. When transferring real property the passing of the risk is regulated by the Finnish Land Law Code (*Maakaari* 1995/540).

10.9 Governmental Approval

The Financial Supervision Authority (FSA) has the power to supervise banks, investment firms, management companies, listed companies and their management, and the stock exchange as well as other financial institutions. The FSA and the Ministry of Finance have also issued a number of guidelines and recommendations on e.g. public tender offers and takeovers.

The acquisition of shares in a bank or other credit institution or an investment service firm is subject to prior notification to the FSA if the acquisition exceeds certain thresholds described in the Act on Activities of Credit Institutions (*Laki luottolaitostoiminnasta* 1607/1993) and the Act on Investment Service Firms (*Laki sijoituspalveluyrityksistä* 579/1996).

An investment in an insurance company exceeding certain thresholds must in advance be notified to the Ministry of Social Affairs and Health.

The authorities mentioned above must within three months from the filing of the notification decide whether they oppose the acquisition.

According to the Act on Monitoring of Foreign Acquisitions (*Laki ulkomaalaisten yritysostojen seurannasta* 1992/1612) acquisitions of large companies or businesses must be notified to the Ministry of Trade and Industry of Finland at the latest one month from the acquisition. The government may refuse to accept the acquisition if it endangers a vital national interest. Large companies are defined to have more than 1.000 employees or an annual turnover exceeding 168 million euros. EEA and OECD nationals are excluded from the monitoring by a degree (1343/1995) except in relation to companies within the defence industry.

As to competition law notifications see chapter 10.10 below.

10.10   Anti-trust and Competition Law

According to the Finnish Competition Act (*Laki kilpailunrajoituksista* 480/1992) a concentration shall be notified to the Finnish Competition Authority (FCA) if:

- The combined aggregate worldwide turnover of the parties exceeds EUR 350 million; and

- The aggregate turnover of at least two of the parties accrued from Finland exceeds EUR 20 million for both parties.

The seller is not seen as a party, but the object of sale is. The turnover figures are established in accordance with a decision of the Ministry of Trade and Industry and is necessarily not equal to the ones presented in the latest financial statement. Also transactions with the same seller group of companies must be added to the turnover, if that has taken place during the last two years. It can come as a surprise that a pure foreign to foreign transaction involving no companies in Finland can be caught by the notification requirements, if the turnover figures are met, concerning income originating from Finland. As to power companies there are certain special thresholds to consider.

A concentration must be notified to the FCA within one week of acquiring control of an undertaking or acquiring a business. However, if a public tender offer is presented to the public, the seven day period starts already from such presentation. The FCA investigates the concentration and will either clear it or request the Market Court (*markkinatuomioistuin*) to prohibit it if the acquisition creates or strengthens a dominant position or restrains competition. FCA can also clear the acquisition with conditions. Before the final decision the parties shall not implement the acquisition.

The primary way to find a solution is to impose conditions on the acquisition to reduce the harmful effects of the concentration. In 2006, the FCA made 39 merger decisions. Of these, 37 were cleared as such and two conditional decisions were made. No proposals to prohibit an acquisition were made in 2006. One concentration was sent by the FCA to the European Commission.

If the concentration has a so-called community dimension, the acquisition shall be notified to the European Commission, who has the sole right to examine the concentration.

10.11 Required Offer Procedures

An offer to purchase a non-listed company does not require any specific form, but it is binding unless stated that it is not or it is qualified.

According to the Securities Markets Act (*Arvopaperimarkkinalaki* 1989/495), the decision to launch a public tender offer to purchase shares in a listed company has to be published immediately through appropriate media as well as served upon the listed target company and to the relevant market place. The bid must indicate the volume of the shares that are bid on, the period the bid is valid, the consideration offered and the time and place of payment. The bid must also contain information about the procedure applied if the affirmative answers cover a greater volume of shares than is included in the bid.

According to the Securities Markets Act (*Arvopaperimarkkinalaki* 1989/495), shares may not be marketed or acquired by giving false information or by using a procedure that is unfair or otherwise contrary to good practice. The minimum offer period is two weeks and the maximum offer period three months. This period can be extended if there are certain obstacles to closing the offer, e.g. pending merger control clearance.

At the end of the offer period, the bidder must, without delay, publish the ownership and voting rights it will have in the target post-offer, including any shares acquired previously.

The bidder is, in principle, free to determine the terms of a public offer. The acceptability of conditions must however be assessed on an individual basis and the tender offer document must be approved by the Financial Supervision Authority. The Securities Markets Act (*Arvopaperimarkkinalaki* 1989/495) regulates the conditions attached to a voluntary public offer by:

- imposing a general obligation to act in accordance with good business practice;
- requiring equal treatment of the holders of all securities that are tendered for;
- introducing a threshold for voting rights that triggers the requirement to make a mandatory offer to acquire the remaining shares of the company.

According to the Securities Markets Act (*Arvopaperimarkkinalaki* 1989/495), a shareholder who holds directly or indirectly more than 3/10 of the voting rights in a listed company must make an offer to buy the remaining shares and the securities that give the holder the right to subscribe for such shares.

10.12 Continuation of Government Licenses

The operation of e.g. banking, credit institution or investment service businesses require a license from the Financial Supervision Authority. The acquisition of shares in such companies exceeding certain thresholds requires a prior notification to the Financial Supervision Authority, which must within three months from the filing of the notification decide whether they oppose the acquisition.

The operation of an insurance business requires a license from the Ministry of Social Affairs and Health. The acquisition of shares in insurance companies exceeding certain thresholds requires a prior notification to the Ministry of Social Affairs and Health, which must within three months from the filing of the notification decide whether they oppose the acquisition.

Licenses related to environmental matters are, as a rule, transferable with the business operation they are connected to. A new license may be required if the business operation changes in scope or character.

10.13   Requirements for Transferring Shares

There are no statutory requirements for transferring shares. Restrictions and requirements concerning the transfer of shares can be found in the target company's Articles of Association or in a shareholders' agreement.

As a general principle, the title to the shares is transferred by agreement between the parties either when a part of the purchase price has been paid or when all of it has been paid. The title to subscribed shares is valid and enforceable after the increase of the share capital has been registered with the Trade Register maintained by the National Board of Patents and Registration of Finland. The company will not register the transfer of title until the purchaser has presented evidence of ownership and, if applicable, of payment of transfer tax in the amount of 1.6 per cent (See further 10.26). All rights of a shareholder cannot be used until a person has been entered into the share register. The registration does not itself prove ownership of the shares—one who has sold its shares, but is not yet deregistered cannot vote. The share register is a document that anyone can request a copy of (against reimbursement of copy costs).

A private limited liability company may give share certificates to its shareholders. If the shares are transferred an endorsement shall be made on the certificates.

10.14   Requirements for Transferring Land and Property Leases

The assets are transferred in accordance with the agreement made between the parties. Real property must be transferred in a form prescribed by Land Law Code (*Maakaari* 1995/540) i.e. by written agreement certified by a public notary. The acquisition of real property is subject to transfer tax of 4 per cent, and the transfer of title has to be registered with authorities at the location of the real property within six months of acquisition. Title is transferred between the parties on agreement but in relation to third parties the registration of transfer of title should be filed without delay. Consequently, real property is normally transferred under a separate agreement from the acquisition agreement.

Agreements in general are transferable only if stated so in the agreement (see 10.16 below).

Other property leases than renting a plot of land and renting a plantation are transferable, unless otherwise is agreed in the relevant agreement. The renting of a plot of land and the renting of a plantation are not transferable, unless otherwise is agreed by the owner and the tenant. Tenancy agreements must be transferred in the form prescribed by the Tenancy Act (*Maanvuokralaki* 258/1966), i.e. by written agreement signed by both parties.

If real property is owned by a company and the shares in the company are sold, no separate agreements regarding the land needs to be drafted.

10.15   Requirements for Transfer of Intellectual Property

The National Board of Patents and Registration (*Patentti- ja rekisterihallitus*) is the registration authority for patents, trademarks and designs in Finland.

Registrable intellectual property rights, such as trademarks, may be protected by applying for registration. Registration gives an exclusive right to use e.g. a trademark as a symbol for goods and services. Only the registration holder may use the trademark in his business, and he may also, when necessary, prohibit others from using his trademark or another mark likely to be confused with it.

The seller can normally assign any intellectual property right in his possession. The intellectual property rights are transferred in accordance with the agreement made between the parties.

10.16   Requirements for Transferring Business Contracts, Licenses and Leases

In case of transfer of the shares in the target company, ultimate beneficial ownership to the business contracts, licenses and leases is transferred with the company, since the parties to the underlying agreement remain the same.

An asset transaction is not considered a general succession under Finnish law. Consequently, if a contract does not contain a right of transfer clause it cannot be transferred to the purchaser without the explicit consent of the contracting party. In the relation between the seller and buyer the transfer is valid but in relation to the contracting party it is not until consent has been obtained. The contracting party is not obliged to agree to the transfer. The contracting party may decide to terminate the agreement without giving reasons for doing so other than the transfer i.e. generally no reasonability valuation will take place. The clauses concerning the transferability of the agreement may vary i.e. general prohibition of transfer, prohibition except within the same group of companies, prohibition of transfer without consent or without written consent etc. The contracting party may, if the consent is not sought, terminate the agreement within a reasonable time period after having found out about the transfer.

Various permits e.g. to conduct specific business or to store hazardous waste are not automatically transferred to the purchaser of the assets even if obtaining of new permits may be considered a mere formality.

10.17 Requirements for Transferring Other Assets

There are relatively few requirements regarding the transfer of assets under Finnish law. See further 10.16.

10.18 Encumbrances and Third Party Interests

M&A transaction may include e.g. a transfer of a real estate. The real estates may be encumbered by easements. Under a general rule, it is possible to transfer the rights in the contract and the assignee of such rights acquires the same position that the original contractor had. Specific property law provisions shall resolve a double sale of an asset or other situation connected with a third party interest.

10.19 Minimum Shareholder and Officer Requirements

There exists no requirement for the number of shareholders in a Finnish limited liability company.

A company shall have a Board of Directors consisting of one to five members. In case the Board of Directors has less than three members it shall also have at least one deputy member.

At least one of the members of the Board of Directors and the Managing Director shall have a permanent place of residence in the EEA unless the National Board of Patents and Registration of Finland grants the company an exception from this. Same applies also to the deputy members of the Board of Directors.

Other requirements concerning the members of the Board of Directors, Managing Director or corresponding executives can be stipulated in the Articles of Association of the company.

If neither the Board Members nor the deputies, the Managing Director, the persons authorized to sign the company name or holders of procuration rights have their permanent domicile in Finland, also a representative with a permanent domicile in Finland shall be elected.

According to Employee Representation Act (*Laki henkilöstön edustuksesta yritysten hallinnossa* 725/1990), a company's employees shall have employee representation in the Board of Directors, or in the Supervisory Board. However, the aforesaid act applies only if the company has at least 150 employees.

10.20 Non-competition Clauses

The purpose of non-competition clauses in share purchase agreements is to protect the acquirer against competitive acts of the vendor. Such a clause may be justified when the duration, the geographical field of application, its subject matter and the persons subject to it do not exceed what is necessary to the implementation of the concentration and it relates to the business of the company as it was when it was sold. They must also be economically effective and the benefits for competition must outweigh the damage.

The Finnish Competition Authority has approved these prohibitions on competition usually as supplementary conditions to the acquisition, but such review must be requested in connection to a notification of a concentration. According to the Commission Notice on restrictions directly related and necessary to concentrations (2005/C 56/03), non-competition clauses are justified for periods of up to three years, when the transfer of undertaking includes the transfer of customer loyalty in the form of both goodwill and know-how. When only goodwill is included they are justified for periods up to two years. Generally, a case by case examination is needed and good guidance for what is acceptable can be sought from the Commission Notice mentioned above.

10.21   Environmental Considerations

Liability for environmental damages in Finland is based both on public and private law regulations. Liability relating to public law regards the liability to remedy contaminated areas. Liability relating to private law regards the liability to compensate the environmental damages to a third party.

In general the principle relating to liability of environmental damages is *the polluter pays principle*. However, according to the Act on Environmental Damage (*Laki ympäristövahinkojen korvaamisesta* 737/1994) both the entity engaged in the activity and the acquiring party are liable for the caused damage provided that the acquiring party at the time of transfer knew or should have known about the damage or threat of damage.

Furthermore, the owner (or the holder) of the land is secondarily liable for the remediation by virtue of the Environmental Protection Act (*Ympäristönsuojelulaki* 86/2000). This liability requires that the acquirer of land knew or should have known of the contamination. If the liable person does not exist anymore or has become insolvent, the municipality where the land is located may be held liable to remedy the soil.

It should be noted that the buyer of a real estate has an obligation to investigate the possible environmental problems, especially when industrial activities have been carried out on the site. In practice, a mere doubt of contamination transfers the liability to the buyer.

Regardless of the awareness of the potential environmental problems or damage of the acquiring party, the said party may be held liable for the remediation costs and for damage in relation to third parties in case he continues the same activity (i.e., the liability is strict).

In an asset transfer the entity engaging in the activity changes and the liability inter parties may be agreed upon. Under certain circumstances it is advisable to perform an environmental due diligence (both technical and legal) e.g. to make sure that the representations, warranties and special indemnity clauses of the seller regarding the environmental issues are defined properly in the acquisition agreement.

10.22 Employee Superannuation/Pension Plans

The Finnish system of pension rights is divided into three different pension schemes; the national pension system and the statutory earnings-related pension system, the collective voluntary pension insurance and the personal (additional) pension insurance.

The national pension is paid only to persons who do not receive an earnings-related pension or whose earnings-related pension is inadequate, e.g., due to interruptions in the work history. The earnings-related pension accrues from the earnings for each year by an age-related accrual rate.

There are two types of collective voluntary pension insurance in Finland. One is the so-called 'registered supplementary pension', which is based on the earnings related pension legislation, and the other is the so-called 'non-registered supplementary pension', which is based on the Insurance Contracts Act (*Vakuutussopimuslaki* 543/1994). Both these pensions are arranged as group pensions, and groups must be formed using objective criteria, such as 'all employees', 'the office personnel', etc. The voluntary pension insurance is a supporting pillar to the statutory pension schemes.

In a transfer of business it is important to assess the payment requirements and what liabilities could be transferred with the employees.

The statutory age of retirement in Finland is currently 65, but the actual average retirement age is closer to 59.

10.23 Employee Rights

The Finnish employment and occupational safety legislation is applied to all employees working in Finland regardless of their nationality. The Employment Contracts Act (*Työsopimuslaki* 55/2001) is a general law concerning employment contracts. In addition, the employer's unions and workers trade unions agree upon payment and other terms of employment in collective agreements, which are regulated by the Collective Agreements Act (*Työehtosopimuslaki* 436/1946). Generally the terms of the collective agreement are in favour of the employee in comparison to the common legislation. In several working branches, there is a collective agreement, which binds all employers in the applicable sector (a generally applicable collective agreement) and it can be applicable even when the employer has not signed it. In addition, a collective agreement binds the employer if the employer is a member of a union which is a part of a collective agreement (normally binding). Under certain circumstances the collective agreement can be applicable even when the employer is not a member of the respective union (generally binding).

Any agreement, which diminishes the rights and interests secured for employees in the employment legislation and/or the collective agreement (if applicable), is void.

10.24 Compulsory Transfer of Employees

According to the Employment Contracts Act (*Työsopimuslaki* 55/2001), the employer (the transferor or the acquiring party) is not entitled to terminate employment contracts solely on the basis of the transfer of business.

The concept of transfer of business is harmonized to comply with the EU directives 77/187/EEC and 98/50/EU. According to the Employment Contracts Act (*Työsopimuslaki* 55/2001), the rights and obligations of the employer deriving from the employment contracts in force at the time of transfer are automatically transferred to the acquiring party. Further, it should be noted that a resumption obligation of nine months imposed on the acquiring party applies also to the employees whose employment contracts were no longer in force at the time of transfer i.e. when the acquiring party assumed control of the business.

If only a part of a business is being transferred the employees being affected are determined based on the organizational structure of the business, i.e. by divisions, departments or entities formally employing each employee.

10.25   Tax deductibility of Acquisition Expenses

Under Finnish tax legislation the general rule is that the costs and expenses deriving directly from an acquisition (for instance due diligence investigations and market analyses) must be capitalized as acquisition costs.

If the buyer is a company that is not taxable in Finland, then this question is determined by the regulations in his or her home jurisdiction.

10.26   Levies on Acquisition Agreements and Collateral Documents

No transfer tax is paid on share transfers on the Helsinki Stock Exchange. On share transfers outside the Helsinki Stock Exchange, a transfer tax of 1.6 per cent of the relevant purchase price is payable by the purchaser. If the purchaser is a non-resident, the seller must collect the transfer tax from the purchaser, because the tax authorities will hold the resident party responsible for the tax. This is only a rule in relation to the tax authority, which means that it is free to agree *inter partes* who shall pay the tax. The transfer of shares is exempted from property transfer tax if both the seller and the purchaser are non-residents.

10.27   Financing Rules and Restrictions

Financing of an acquisition with the funds of the target is generally prohibited in the Finnish Companies Act (*Osakeyhtiölaki* 624/2006). On one hand, a company is not allowed to grant loans or give security to enable the recipient or someone in the inner circle of the recipient to acquire shares in the company or in another company belonging to the same group of companies. On the other hand, the Companies Act (*Osakeyhtiölaki* 624/2006) expressly allows loans between companies within the same group.

In the light of the above described, there is no correct answer to the question whether acquisition financing can be replaced by a loan from the target, that has become a new subsidiary as a result of the acquisition. The general advice is that the purchaser must be able to show that it had raised funds for the acquisition separately from the funds of the target, and that such financing could have been maintained for a period of time, which is considered normal for such financing. If under those circumstances the purchaser, after the transaction, borrows money from the new subsidiary, and repays some of the loans taken in conjunction with the acquisition, then this inter-group borrowing and prepayment of loans would most likely be considered to accord with the provisions of the Finnish Companies Act (*Osakeyhtiölaki* 624/2006).

Finnish private limited liability companies are not allowed to purchase all of their own shares and public limited liability companies are not allowed to own more than 10 per cent of their own shares.

The distribution of a company's assets or profits to its shareholders may not exceed the company's unrestricted reserves. This applies both to dividends and other forms of repatriation of profits from the company.

There are no separate regulations concerning thin capitalization in Finland. There is a theoretical possibility to deny tax deductibility of interests in a situation of thin capitalization or to the extent the paid interest deviates from the market price principle, but this has not yet been done in practice.

A limited liability company must voluntarily enter into liquidation, if its capital is less than half of its registered share capital.

10.28 Exchange Controls and Repatriation of Profits

There are no general restrictions concerning the transfer of funds from Finland to foreign countries.

Dividends from a Finnish branch are subject to the source tax rate of 28 per cent. However, the Finnish tax treaties normally reduce this per centage (see 10.4). Note that even though the fact is that an interim dividend from a Finnish subsidiary is not permitted under Finnish law, it can be issued under special circumstances when the outcome of the profit can be safely estimated. It is also possible during the same fiscal year to decide to pay more dividend than is agreed on the annual shareholders' meeting, if there are established profits and free distributable equity left.

10.29 Groups of Companies

Even if the concept of a group of companies is not directly defined in the Finnish legislation, it is acknowledged, that a group of companies exists where a company holds control in another company. Control in another company exists where a company holds the majority of votes in another corporation or the right to appoint the majority of the members of the governing body of another corporation.

A parent company must prepare consolidated accounts consisting of a consolidated income statement and consolidated balance statement each financial year.

The different companies in the group should have the same fiscal year.

If a parent company (or any shareholder) holds more than 90 per cent of the shares of a company and the shares attaching to all the shares, it has the right to redeem the shares held by other shareholders at a market price. On a reciprocal basis, a shareholder, whose share can be redeemed, also has the right to demand redemption of his share.

10.30   Responsibility for Liabilities of an Acquired Subsidiary

Subsidiaries are under Finnish law separate legal entities, which are liable for their own obligations. The Companies Act (*Osakeyhtiölaki* 624/2006) does not contain any regulations on a parent company's liability for its subsidiaries.

According to the Companies Act (*Osakeyhtiölaki* 624/2006), the parent company is, however, liable to compensate damage it has caused to the company, a shareholder or a third person in its capacity as a shareholder wilfully or through a grossly negligent act or through infringement of the Companies Act or the Articles of Association.

Special legislation such as competition law or environmental law can in special circumstances lead to liability for a parent company for certain actions of the subsidiary.

10.31   Governing Law of the Contract

The parties of a contract are under Finnish international private law generally free to decide which country's law is applicable to the contract. Normally it is required that there is some relation to the country, which laws are referred to, but it could be possible to use a third country's legislation in a share purchase transaction, especially when that country or its system is not too far from either party's geographical position or its legal system. Even in that situation naturally there will be compulsory legislation that must be considered and cannot be escaped.

If the agreement does not contain a provision on the choice of law the general rule is that the law of the place of business of the seller at the time of entering into the agreement is applicable.

10.32   Dispute Resolution Options

Generally, the disputes are handled in the court of first instance at the domicile of the defendant, but disputes can also be settled in arbitration according to the arbitration rules of the Board of Arbitration of the Central Chamber of Commerce of Finland, ICC rules or the rules of another arbitration tribunal. An agreement may include a clause that specifies the forum. The forum can, for instance, be determined based on the interest of the dispute i.e. if the interest falls below a defined limit the dispute is handled in the court of first instance and if it exceeds the determined limit the dispute is taken to arbitration and solved by one or three arbitrators.

Finland is a party to and obligated by the New York Convention on the Recognition and Enforcement of Foreign Arbitral Awards (10 June 1958).

10.33   Additional information

Bankruptcy of a company can give the bankruptcy estate the right to decide whether it will continue the contracts of the company or not. There are several aspects that deviate from general practice in case of bankruptcy.

11. FRANCE

Jean-Luc Soulier and Guillaume Pierson Soulier

11.1 Introductory Comments

During the past two years foreign investments in France have increased significantly due in part to the simplification and streamlining of the foreign investment procedures so as to remove barriers to foreign investments. Generally, foreign investments are made either through the acquisition of shares of a company or the acquisition of the going concern (*fonds de commerce*) or a branch of activity of a company. Of course, the acquisition of certain assets only of a company is also possible.

Investments in France are regulated by the French Code of Commerce, directives and regulations of the European Union (EU), international treaties ratified by France as well as general principles applicable to international acquisitions. In addition, in France specific rules and regulations apply to investments made in public companies or where the shares of a company are admitted to a regulated market. Investments in France are also subject to specific labour laws.

11.2 Corporate Structures

Corporate structures are determined by traditional French concepts and largely through the development of EU law.

The French Code of Commerce sets forth the rules applicable to most of the corporate structures which may be of interest to a foreign investor.

Commercial companies regardless of their business purpose fall into one of the following three categories:

- Partnerships in which the partners have unlimited liability for the company's debts/ liabilities. The two companies falling into this category are (i) general partnership (*sociétés en nom collectif*), and (ii) limited partnership (*sociétés en commandite simple*);

- Joint stock company, a company in which the liability of a shareholder is limited to the value of his/her capital investment in the company. The joint stock companies used in France are (i) corporation (*société anonyme* or SA), (ii) limited partnership with shares (*société en commandite par actions*), (iii) simplified joint stock company (*société par actions simplifiée* or SAS), and (iv) European company (*société européenne*);

- Limited liability companies in which the liability of a shareholder is also limited to the value of his/her capital investment in the company. The two limited liability companies used in France are (i) limited liability company (*société à responsabilité*

© World Law Group
International Business Acquisitions, M. Whalley, F.-J. Semler (eds.), Kluwer Law International, London, 2007; ISBN 9789041124838.

limitée or SARL), and (ii) limited liability company with sole ownership (*entreprise unipersonnelle à responsabilité limitée* or EURL).

As the SA, SAS and SARL are the most common investment vehicles for foreigners, we have set forth below the main characteristics of them.

Société anonyme (SA)

An SA, the closest French equivalent to an American corporation, is a joint stock corporation with a minimum of seven shareholders and a minimum capital of € 37,000 or € 225,000 in the event the shares are offered for sale by way of a public offering. Under French laws only one half of the capital must be paid in at incorporation. The liability of the shareholders of an SA is limited to the value of his/her capital investment in the company.

The shares of an SA are freely transferable unless the by-laws of the company or a separate agreement provide otherwise (e.g. transfers to non-shareholders are subject to prior approval by the board of directors or shareholders).

Under French laws, two types of management structures are available for an SA. An SA may be run by either a board of directors (*conseil d'administration*) or by a management committee (*directoire*) and a supervisory board (*conseil de surveillance*). Although both forms are available, a majority of SAs are run by a board of directors.

An SA may be managed in one of the following ways:

1. In an SA with a board of directors, the general management (*direction générale*) of the SA may, upon the decision of the board of directors, be organized as:

    i.   Concurrent mandates (*cumul des fonctions*): the same individual is appointed as chairman of the board of directors and general manager (*directeur général*) of the SA. The general manager may be assisted by one or several assistant general managers (*directeurs généraux délégués*); or

    ii. Separate mandates (*séparation des fonctions*): the chairman of the board of directors and the general manager of the SA are two different individuals. The general manager may be assisted by one or several assistant general managers.

    In both cases, the SA is managed by a board of directors, a governing body consisting of three to 18 directors (either an individual or a legal entity), each of which must be a shareholder of the SA and elected by the shareholders of the SA for a maximum term of three years in a newly incorporated SA or six years in all other cases. The directors may be re-elected and removed at any time by the shareholders.

    The board of directors determines the main orientation of the activities of the company and supervises their implementation.

    The general management (*direction générale*) of the SA is carried out by the chairman of the board of directors when the SA is one of concurrent mandates (*cumul des fonctions*) or by the general manager (*directeur général*) when the SA is one of separate mandates (*séparation des fonctions*).

2. In an SA with a management committee (*directoire*) and a supervisory board (*conseil de surveillance*), the model of which is based on the German model of the *Aktiengesellschaft*, the company is managed by the management committee, a collegiate body which is controlled by the supervisory board.

    The supervisory board is composed of at least three but no more than 18 members (either an individual or a legal entity), each of which must be a shareholder of the SA and elected by the shareholders of the SA for a maximum term of three years in a newly incorporated SA or six years in all other cases. The members of the supervisory board may be re-elected.

    The management committee (*directoire*), which consists of no more than five members (or seven in the event the shares of the SA are publicly traded), manages the company. The members of the management committee, which must be individuals and are not required to be shareholders of the company, are appointed by the supervisory board for a term between two and six years and may be re-elected.

    Again, this type of SA is not commonly used in France.

The shareholders of the SA hold (i) ordinary meetings to approve the annual accounts, to appoint directors or members of the supervisory board, and (ii) extraordinary meetings to amend the by-laws of the company.

At extraordinary meetings of shareholders, resolutions are adopted by two-thirds of the shareholder votes present or represented at the meeting. At ordinary meetings of shareholders, resolutions are passed with a majority of the shareholder votes present or represented at the meeting.

An SA must have at least one independent statutory auditor and an alternate independent statutory auditor. Such auditors must verify the accuracy of the company's financial statements as well as the information submitted to the company's shareholders. The role of the French statutory auditor is far more supervisory than the role of an American certified public accountant as, in France, the statutory auditor does not prepare the company's financial statements, but rather verifies their accuracy.

Société par actions simplifiée (SAS)

The SAS is a simplified joint stock company which is used mainly by large industrial companies as the corporate vehicle for holding companies and joint ventures both on a national and international level. Technically, an SAS is a significantly modified form of an SA.

An SAS may have one or several shareholders, either individuals or legal entities. As with an SA, the minimum registered capital of an SAS is € 37,500, and only one half of the capital must be paid in at incorporation. Unlike an SA, however, an SAS may not sell its shares by way of a public offering or list its shares on a regulated market.

Compared to an SA, an SAS offers a flexible management structure as French laws only require that a president be appointed to represent the company in its dealings with third parties. Apart from the appointment of the president, the management of an SAS is determined by the shareholders and set forth in the by-laws. An SAS, like an SA, must have at least one independent statutory auditor and an independent alternate statutory auditor.

As a result of its flexible management structure, the SAS is used more and more frequently in France.

Société à responsabilité limitée (SARL)

The SARL is a limited liability company similar to the SA in many respects. The members of an SARL or an SA are liable for the company's liabilities only to the extent of their capital contributions. In addition, an SA and an SARL receive similar tax treatment in France.

There are, however, significant differences between an SA and an SARL. Unlike an SA, an SARL may not sell its shares by way of a public offering and it only requires a minimum of two shareholders (or one shareholder if it is an EURL—see below) and a minimum share capital of € 1,00. In addition, the SARL does not have a board of directors and only requires a statutory auditor if two of the following criteria are met at the end of a fiscal year:

• the sum of the net value of the SARL's assets exceeds € 1,550,000;

• the SARL has a pre-tax turnover greater than € 3,100,000;

• the SARL employed an average of at least 50 employees during the relevant fiscal year.

An SARL is managed by one or more individuals referred to as managers (*gérant*), who are not required to be shareholders.

The shareholders of an SARL must meet at least once a year to approve the annual accounts. Although ordinary decisions of the SARL are passed with a majority of the votes present or represented, the amendment of the by-laws, depending on the date of incorporation of the SARL, requires either a two-thirds or three-quarters majority of the votes present or represented.

An EURL (*entreprise unipersonnelle à responsabilité limitée*) is a special type of SARL requiring only one shareholder and as a result is often attractive to foreign investors.

Société Européenne (SE)

A European Company (*Societas Europaea*) is a joint stock limited liability company with a minimum required capital of € 120,000.00. An SE is governed by the EU Regulation 2157/2001, the EU Directive 2001/86 and the national laws of the country where the registered office of the SE is located. Although the EU Directive was implemented in France by the Law of 26 July 2005.

The SE has the following principal characteristics: (i) the SE does not have the nationality of the EU Member State in which it has its registered office, (ii) the registered office of the SE may be freely transferred within the EU, and (iii) the SE is managed by a single or two-tier board just like an SA—either managed by a board of directors or by a supervisory board (*conseil de surveillance*) and a management committee (*directoire*).

An SE may be formed in one of the **four** following ways:

1. By merging of two or more public limited liability companies, such as an SA in France, incorporated under the laws of at least two different EU Member States and with registered and principal offices in the EU;

2. By creating a holding company by having the shareholders of two or more public or private limited companies (such as an SA or SARL) from at least two different EU Member States and with their registered offices in the EU, exchange their shares for shares of the SE;

3. By creating a joint subsidiary of two or more corporate bodies governed by the laws of at least two different EU Member States; or

4. By transforming into an SE a public limited liability company, such as an SA, incorporated under the laws of an EU Member State and having its registered and principal offices in the EU, and having had at least one subsidiary in another EU Member State during the preceding two years.

The shares of an SE are freely transferable unless the by-laws provide limitations on transferability, such as pre-emption rights or requiring the approval of the other shareholders prior to transferring any shares.

11.3 Letters of Intent and Heads of Agreement

As negotiations for the acquisition of a business entity or company often require a great deal of time, it is common practice for the negotiating parties to enter into preliminary agreements, such as confidentiality agreements, letters of intent, to address specific issues, including the conditions under which due diligence should be carried out, the criteria for determining the purchase price and the confidentiality of information about the target company during the negotiations. Preliminary agreements referred to as a 'letter of intent', 'memorandum of understanding' 'agreement in principle' or 'heads of agreement' are frequently used by the negotiating parties to set forth the agreement in principle that they have reached at that stage of the negotiations.

Although a preliminary agreement does not require the parties to enter into a subsequent final and binding agreement, it does oblige the parties to conduct the negotiations in good faith and to inform the other party about its intentions to conclude or to withdraw from the negotiations. In addition, if a party breaches one of its obligations under the preliminary agreement, such as the obligation to negotiate in good faith, such breach may be the basis for a claim for damages by the non-breaching party. Pursuant to French case law, damages may not be awarded on the earnings (*gains*) that the purchaser might have realized if the transaction had been completed, or on the lost opportunity to realize such earnings. Only the costs and expenses incurred during the negotiation may be taken into account to determine the damages to be awarded, if any, to the non-breaching party. To determine potential liability in the event the negotiations are terminated, a French judge will focus on the common intention of the parties and as a result will carefully review the preliminary agreements. It is therefore very important to carefully draft preliminary agreements.

French law requires that the purchase price be either determined or determinable by objective criteria. For example, a proposed range of purchase prices or a preliminary assessment of a purchase price is not sufficiently precise and a unilateral price assessment by one party is legally invalid. The parties may, however, provide that the price be determined by a jointly appointed expert and set forth guidelines/rules pursuant to which such expert shall assess the purchase price. It is important to note that a letter of intent which fails to expressly stipulate a purchase price does not constitute a valid sales contract and as a result may not form the basis of a claim for specific performance.

11.4 Tax Affecting the Structure and Calculation of the Purchase Price

In France, the transfer of the shares of an SARL or a partnership is subject to a registration tax equal to 5 per cent of the purchase price. The transfer of the shares of an unlisted SA or an SAS, however, is subject to a registration tax of 1.10 per cent of the purchase price per transfer and is capped at € 4,000.00. In order to simplify the organization of the SARL and to benefit, at the same time, from a lower registration tax, it is often contemplated to transform such company into an SAS prior to the transfer of any shares. The transfer of the publicly listed shares of an SA is not subject to any registration tax unless the transfer is provided for in a written agreement.

The sale of a going concern (*fonds de commerce*) is subject to a registration tax, which is calculated based on the purchase price of the value of the assets constituting the going concern, such as intellectual property rights, clients, leases, and equipment. Currently, the registration tax is calculated as follows:

1.   If the purchase price of the going concern is less than € 23,000.00, the registration tax is equal to € 25.00; and

2.   If the purchase price of the going concern is greater than € 23,000.00, the registration tax is equal to 5 per cent of the difference between the purchase price and € 23,000.00.

Any additional assets that are purchased together with the going concern (e.g. merchandise inventory, raw materials) are subject to value added tax (VAT) at the ordinary rate of 19.6 per cent.

The geographic location of the going concern may exempt the sale of such going concern from a registration tax. In addition, specific laws apply to going concerns which focus on community services (*fonds de commerce dits de proximité*).

The registration tax, whether for the transfer of a going concern or shares, is paid by the purchaser unless the parties agree contractually that the seller shall pay such tax. In the event the registration tax is borne by the seller, such a payment is considered as an additional portion of the purchase price for purposes of calculating the registration tax.

The tax treatment of the proceeds from the sale of a going concern depends on whether the purchaser is an individual and thus subject to individual income tax, or a company and thus subject to corporate income tax. With respect to small and medium sized businesses (*petite et moyenne entreprise*) the capital gains realized may, in whole and in part and regardless of whether the purchaser is an individual or a company, be exempt from the capital gains tax provided that certain conditions are met, including but not limited to the condition that the business has been run for a minimum of five years prior to the sale and that the market value of the assets transferred is less than € 500,000.00. Other exemptions may apply with respect to companies subject to individual income tax.

11.5 Extent of Seller's Warranties and Indemnities

Sale of company shares

In all sales, the seller must warrant to the purchaser the right to the peaceful enjoyment (*la jouissance paisible*) of the shares transferred. Unless otherwise provided, the seller must only warrant to the purchaser the existence of the shares transferred and not the value or the composition of the assets of the company (*consistance du patrimoine de la société*).

As the purchaser thus takes on inherent risks by assuming the target company's liabilities, French businesses traditionally require a contractual warranty from the seller allowing the purchaser to be indemnified in the event such liabilities are greater than the seller warranted. This distinct contractual warranty is known as an asset-liability warranty (*garantie d'actif et de passif*). There are several different types of asset-liability warranties. It is advisable to avoid relying on certain types of warranties, such as the 'net asset' warranty. As the net asset warranty aims to guarantee the target company's net asset value, disputes may easily arise over the exact net asset value of the company. Recourse would then have to be made to one or several experts to assess the net asset value of the company, which will likely be a lengthy and time-consuming process.

A 'reconstitution' warranty provides an acquiring company with more protection as under such warranty the seller typically agrees to indemnify the target company against any of the following changes in the financial condition of the target company which appears after the acquisition, but originates prior to the acquisition:

- increase in the target company's liabilities;

- decrease in the target company's asset value;

- a combination of the above two elements;

- negative variation of the net value.

Under this type of warranty, French case law has held that the seller's indemnification liability is not limited to the purchase price. In practice, however, it is extremely rare for the seller not to limit his liability and generally the purchase price is the cap on the seller's liability

Another type of warranty referred to as the 'value' warranty, offers similar coverage, but typically indemnifies the purchaser of the target company rather than the target company itself.

Regardless of the type of warranty given by the seller, the seller often secures the warranty by providing a first demand bank guarantee or parent company guarantee, if possible.

The tax consequences of a warranty depend on the type of warranty given and on the parties involved in the transaction. For instance, a reconstitution warranty is generally favourable for the seller subject to corporate income tax as any indemnification made under the warranty may be qualified as damages, which, in principle, are tax deductible in France.

Regardless of the type of asset-liability warranty the seller provides to the purchaser, such warranty alone is unlikely to be sufficient. It is advisable for the purchaser to require the seller to make certain representations on any number of issues ('representation warranty'). For instance, the purchaser may request that the seller represent that there are no (i) government regulations that may adversely affect the target company's profitability, or (ii) golden parachute provisions granted to current management. As misrepresentations made by the seller may not directly affect the target company's state of accounts, the purchaser would not be indemnified by the seller under an asset-liability warranty. As a result, it is advisable for the purchaser to rely only on a comprehensive composite warranty containing both an asset-liability warranty and a representation warranty.

In order for the purchaser to be in a solid negotiating position when discussing the contents of the seller's warranty, it is strongly advisable for the purchaser to carry out a thorough audit of the target company. A thorough audit will allow the purchaser to identify precisely the representations needed in connection with the sale and to carefully draft such representations. Such audit should cover the financial, tax and legal aspects of the transaction and also include a review of the target company's commercial contracts to determine, among other things, whether such contracts are assignable and the extent of any guarantees.

Sale of a going concern

The sale of a going concern, which is regulated by the French Code of Commerce, must be set forth in writing. The seller must, pursuant to mandatory public policy rules, include in the sales agreement certain information listed in said Code, such as ownership title (*origine de propriété*) and the revenue and profits realized during the last 3 years of operation. Failure to provide this information may result in the sale being null and void. Certain legal formalities must also be carried out, such as registration, publicity of the sale and filing with the register of commerce, in connection with each sale. As the creditors of the seller have the right to object to the sale within a legally required time period, it is advisable to place the purchase price in escrow until the end of such period.

11.6 Liability for Pre-contractual Representations

Negligent and fraudulent misrepresentations may render the contract null and void and may give rise to claims for damages. A contract may be held null and void due to an error or fraudulent misrepresentation. Additionally, there is long-standing French case law requiring the seller to disclose to the purchaser all aspects of the transaction as well as all aspects of the company to be acquired, which the purchaser would in good faith expect to be disclosed. Negligently withholding such information may give rise to a claim for damages by the purchaser.

All claims for negligent or fraudulent misrepresentation, as well as for negligent withholding of information, are actions in tort. Consequently, they are not subject to any limitation of liability clauses. Frequently, contracts in the United States provide that representations made prior to the execution of the contract have no legal force or effect. Such stipulations have no legal force or effect under French law.

Pre-contractual documents, agreements and past practices are of great importance, not only with respect to the above-mentioned legal actions, but also in interpreting the contract. For more information, see section 11.3 above.

11.7 Liability for Pre-acquisition Trading and Contracts

In principle, the transfer of shares does not affect the selling company's legal and contractual obligations. The company's legal status remains unchanged and consequently all its pre-acquisition activities and contracts remain unaffected. The purchaser should, however, be aware of the risk arising from *intuitu personae* agreements, which contain a 'change of control' clause entitling the contract partner to terminate such contract if the controlling shareholder of the target company changes.

Generally, no liabilities or contracts are transferred to the purchaser in connection with the acquisition of a going concern. As an exception to such rule, specific contracts which are essential for operating the business, in particular commercial lease contracts, are transferred by law to the purchaser. Special rules apply to employment contracts which are transferred to the purchaser by virtue of Article L 122-12 of the French Labour Code. Some insurance contracts are also transferred by force of law. All other contracts must be assigned explicitly to the purchaser and thereby require the contracting party's consent.

As a result, in connection with the sale of shares or a going concern, it is important to conduct a thorough audit so as to ensure that the contracts required to operate the business are transferred to the purchaser. The contracts entered into by companies with the public institutions, state-owned companies and administrative authorities (*établissements publics*) or municipalities/government services (*l'administration*) (e.g. hospitals and town halls) may, in principle, only be transferred with the prior written consent of the contracting party, which in practice is very difficult to obtain.

11.8   Pre-completion Risks

By law, the risk is transferred from the seller to the purchaser upon the transfer of title, which often occurs on the date the contract is executed. The parties, however, are free to mutually agree that the transfer of risk shall take place on a different date and may even agree that such transfer shall not occur until certain conditions precedent are satisfied. Generally, the transfer of risk takes place on the closing date.

11.9   Required Governmental Approvals

French Regulations regarding foreign investments were modified by a law, dated 9 December 2004, and more recently by a Decree, dated 30 December 2005. As a general rule, foreign investments in France are unrestricted and are only subject to a simple administrative declaration. Foreign investments in sensitive industries, however, are subject to specific authorizations or controls.

Articles L. 151-1 to L. 151-4 of the French Monetary and Financial Code regulate foreign investment and set forth the following notification and/or authorization procedures:

Notification Obligations

Any and all foreign investment in France must, in principle, be subject to an administrative declaration. Administrative declarations must be filed with the competent administrative agency at the time the investment is made. Failure to declare such investment will result in a fine of € 750.00.

Declarations must be filed with the Minister of the Economy in the event a foreign company or a non-resident individual makes one of the following types of direct investments:

- creation of a new company;

- acquisition, in whole or in part, of the branch of activity of a French company;

- any and all operations resulting in the investor holding more than 33.33 per cent of the capital or voting rights.

When the investment is made by a French company, declarations must also be filed if a foreign company hold more than 33.33 per cent of the capital or voting rights of such French company.

The following are classified as foreign investments and are therefore subject to notification: (i) granting of loans or substantial guarantees, (ii) purchase of patents or licenses, and (iii) acquisition of a commercial contract which results in a take-over of a French company by a foreign company or by a non-resident individual.

The following operations are exempt from notification:

- commencement or extension of the activity of an existing French company controlled, directly or indirectly, by a foreign company or by a non-resident individual;

- increase in ownership shares in a French company controlled, directly or indirectly, by a foreign company or a non-resident individual by an investor already holding more than 50 per cent of the capital or voting rights;

- subscription to a capital increase in a French company controlled, directly or indirectly, by a foreign company or by a non-resident individual, provided that such company or individual does not increase shares or the percentage of ownership interest;

- direct investments made among companies of the same group, in other words, companies in which more than 50 per cent of the shares are held, directly or indirectly, by the same shareholders;

- loans, advances, guarantees, debt consolidation or forgiveness, subsidies or branch funding granted to a French company controlled, directly or indirectly, by a foreign company or by a non-resident individual;

- direct investments, in the amount of up to € 1.5 million, in French companies in certain industries, such as crafts, retail sales, hotel, restaurant and community services *(services de proximité)*.

Authorization Procedure

Certain economic sectors are considered sensitive because they affect vital public interests. Foreign investments in such sensitive areas require the authorization of the Minister of the Economy. The Decree, dated 30 December 2005, distinguishes between foreign investments from EU Member States and foreign investments from countries outside the EU; investments made by investors from EU Member States benefit from favourable treatment.

The following industries are notably deemed sensitive: (i) lottery games/gambling sector *(jeux d'argent)*, (ii) encryption, (iii) business activities of companies holding classified defence secrets, (iv) activities relating to research, production or sale of weapons and ammunitions, and (v) any activities involving equipment used for remote detection and interception of communications and conversations.

The authorization of the Minister of the Economy may be subject to certain conditions to ensure that the foreign investment will not jeopardize national interests.

Failure to comply with such procedure will result in heavy fines and may even render the investment null and void.

Regulation of foreign managers

In principle, foreigners may not occupy the following positions without first obtaining registration as a foreign businessperson *(carte de commerçant étranger)*: (i) manager of an SARL *(société à responsabilité limitée)*, (ii) chairman of the board of directors or general manager of an SA *(société anonyme)*, or (iii) president or chief executive officer of an SAS *(société par actions simplifiée)*. Any foreigner, on the other hand, may be a board member of an SA. A decree should be published in the near future eliminating the requirement of the *carte de commerçant étranger* and replacing it with an administrative authorization (*autorization préfectorale*).

Nationals of the European Economic Area (the EU, Iceland, Lichtenstein and Norway) as well as nationals of countries which have signed a treaty with France (e.g. Andorra, Monaco and Algeria) are exempt from obtaining a *carte de commerçant étranger*. As soon as the aforementioned decree is published, nationals of the following countries will also be exempt from obtaining an *autorization préfectorale:* member countries of the OECD, and in particular Australia, Canada, Japan, Mexico, New Zealand, Switzerland, Turkey and the United States.

11.10   Anti-trust and Competition Law

It is important to keep in mind that European anti-trust and competition law supersedes national laws when anti-competitive practices take on a European dimension.

Article L. 410-2 of the French Code of Commerce sets forth the principle of the free exercise of competition, specifically with regard to the pricing of goods, products and services. Breach of this provision may result in criminal, civil or administrative sanctions. The Competition Council (*Conseil de la concurrence*) is the government agency authorized to implement applicable regulations as well as to decide on the appropriate sanction relating to anti-competitive practices.

Article L. 420-1 prohibits any practices which has as its object or effect the prevention, restriction or distortion of competition. Consequently, the effects that an acquisition or an investment may have on a relevant market must be taken into consideration.

Anti-competitive agreements

French law prohibits any explicit or implicit agreement which has the aim or effect of restraining or altering the competition in a market by:

• limiting the access of other companies to the market, or limiting competition between companies in that market;

• facilitating the artificial rise or fall of prices;

• limiting or controlling production, investments or technical progress; or

• dividing the market or supply sources.

Abuse of dominant market position

It is possible for a company or a group of companies which have a dominant position in the market (or even just a significant market share) to exploit such a position to restrain or alter the competition in such a market.

Although under French law being in a dominant market position is not illegal, the abuse of a dominant market position by a company or a group of companies in all or a significant part of the domestic market for the purpose of restraining or altering competition therein is prohibited.

Pursuant to French case law, a dominant position implies the power to prevent effective competition. In order to be deemed to be in a dominant market position, a company must be in a position of economic strength as a result of its market share. To determine whether a dominant market position exists, three elements must be met: (i) capacity to be in a dominant position, (ii) existence of a market that may be dominated, and (iii) actual market domination.

Abuse of an existing state of economic dependence

French law also prohibits the abuse of a dominant market position by a company or group of companies in its relationship with a client or supplier by virtue of the latter's state of economic dependence. The analysis focuses on whether, vis-à-vis the client or supplier, the company or group of companies is in a position of dominance so as to exploit the latter's state of economic dependence.

Examples of abusive practices include refusal to sell, tie-in clauses, applying discriminatory conditions to sales and termination of established business relationships for failure to accept unjustified commercial obligations or conditions. Moreover, abuse of a state of economic dependence of a client or supplier by a company or group of companies which results in a distortion of competition in the relevant market is also prohibited.

Concentrations

Articles L. 430-1 *et seq.* of the French Code of Commerce govern concentrations and strive to preclude the economic dominance of one company from distorting competition. Concentrations may arise through a merger of independent undertakings or an acquisition of controlling interest, in whole or in part, of another undertaking through an asset purchase, a contract or by any other means.

Concentrations are regulated by the French Code of Commerce and specifically require prior authorization from the Minister of the Economy and the French Competition Board (*Conseil de la concurrence),* if the following conditions are met:

- the total worldwide turnover, exclusive of taxes, of the parties to the concentration is greater than € 150 million; and

- the total turnover, exclusive of taxes, in France of two or more parties to the concentration is greater than € 50 million.

Once the proposed concentrations fall within the scope of EU regulations, French law is no longer applicable.

11.11 Required Offer Procedures

The Financial Market Regulatory Authority (*Autorité de Marchés Financiers* or AMF) is an independent public body in charge of controlling dealings on the stock exchange.

When a person, acting alone or in concert, acquires more than 33.33 per cent of a French listed company's share capital or voting rights, he or she must (i) immediately notify the AMF, and (ii) make an offer for 100 per cent of the shares and securities of the company concerned. The same obligation arises in relation to the acquisition of control of a company which itself holds, directly or indirectly, more than 33.33 per cent of the share capital or voting rights of a listed company, provided the shares or securities concerned represent a significant part of the assets of the company of which control is taken. The AMF, however, provides a limited number of exceptions to the obligation to make a mandatory offer. As part of its control, the AMF verifies whether or not there has been an actual change in control of the target company. For example, the AMF may rule that the shareholder reaching the relevant threshold is exempt from filing a mandatory offer when the target company was already in fact controlled by the investor, acting alone or in concert, prior to the triggering event.

11.12   Continuation of Government Licences

Some professions and commercial activities may only be carried out if the person or corporate entity doing business in France obtains prior authorization from the appropriate authorities or procures a permit, licence or registration. It is strongly advised that before proceeding with an investment in France, the foreign investor ascertains whether its targeted activity is subject to specific regulations. For example, banking, insurance and the manufacturing of pharmaceutical products are subject to authorization from the relevant Ministry.

11.13   Requirements for Transferring Shares

SARL

With respect to an SARL, the transfer of any shares to a third party that is not a shareholder requires the prior consent of a majority of the shareholders representing at least one half of the company's share capital, unless the by-laws provide for a larger majority. Each share transfer must be set forth in a written agreement between the purchaser and the seller and such agreement must be notified to the company. See section 10.4 above for information regarding the registration tax.

SA or SAS

With respect to an SA or an SAS, the by-laws may require the approval of the company in the event of a share transfer, but such a clause is not mandatory. The company's approval may be given by its board or be made subject to the approval of the shareholders.

As a result, the share of an unlisted SA or an SAS is transferred by signing a transfer order form (*ordre de mouvement*). This is a form signed by the purchaser and countersigned by the company. The *ordre de mouvement* is notified by the purchaser to the company and the transfer of the shares is recorded in the share register thereby making the purchaser a new shareholder of the company. See section 10.4 above for information regarding the registration tax.

11.14   Requirements for Transferring Land and Property Leases

Under French law, the direct transfer of real property must be made pursuant to a formal deed of sale in an authentic act, prepared by a French notary (*notaire*) who is a public official and legal professional with a monopoly in conveyancing, matrimonial and testamentary matters.

With regard to the sale of real property, it is important to determine whether the local authorities have a pre-emption right (*droit de préemption urbain*). Such right is limited to certain geographical zones. If the real property is located in such a zone, then a pre-emptive right exists granting a district or municipality the priority to purchase the real property. Prior to the closing of the sale, the seller must notify the holder of this right (generally the mayor) of its intention to sell and provide such holder with information on the sales price and general conditions. The holder may exercise its pre-emptive right during the two months following such notification. If the holder fails to respond within such two month period, the pre-emptive right is deemed to have been waived and the sale may be completed. For information, the district or municipality rarely exercises its right of pre-emption.

In order to be enforceable against third parties, all direct transfers of real property must be recorded in the Land Registry of the place in which the real property is located. The acquisition of commercial real estate is currently subject to transfer taxes (*droits de mutation*) of approximately 5.09 per cent of the sale price, unless the sale is subject to VAT. This tax rate may vary slightly depending on the location of the real property. *Notaire's* fees, which are based on a sliding scale in conjunction with the sale price, are also due and payable by the purchaser.

This registration requirement concerns only direct transactions involving real estate. The transfer of shares of a company, which holds or owns real estate, is not generally subject to this right of pre-emption.

11.15   Requirements for Transferring Intellectual Property

Intellectual property rights referred to under French law as 'industrial property rights,' such as trademarks and patents, are generally protected by an entry in an official register.

Registered intellectual property rights may only be validly transferred pursuant to a written agreement. In order for such transfer to be enforceable against third parties, the transfer must be registered with the central registry of industrial property rights (*Institut National de la Propriété Industrielle* or the INPI). Failing such registration, the new owner may not assert his or her rights against third parties (e.g. in the context of a patent law suit based on infringement by a third party).

The transfer of shares of a company has no direct impact on these property rights, unless the target company only holds a licence and the licence agreement provides for termination in the event of a change in ownership.

When the seller of a going concern is a licensee, the licensor must consent to the transfer of the licence.

11.16   Transferring Business Contracts, Licences and Leases

Business contracts

The following rules apply to the assignment of contracts:

- If the contract contains an assignment clause, such contract may be assigned. The assignment clause may set forth the conditions of the transfer, e.g. upon notification or prior authorization;

- In the event the contract does not include an assignment clause, it is necessary to obtain the prior authorization of the contracting party;

- Moreover, if the contract is deemed *intuitu personae,* an assignment may not occur without the prior authorization of the contracting party;

- The aforementioned rules apply to the transfer of a going concern *(fonds de commerce)* with the following two exceptions: if employment agreements and commercial leases are included in the going concern, they are automatically transferred to the purchaser;

- In the event of a share transfer, the contracts already entered into by the company shall continue to have full force and effect, unless such contracts contain notification and/or prior consultation clauses in the event of a change in shareholders.

Licences and leases

Licences and leases may also be transferred in accordance with their terms and the consent of the contracting party.

The transfer of commercial leases is always permitted when it occurs simultaneously with the sale of the going concern operating on the leased premises. Any stipulation to the contrary is null and void.

If the transfer does not occur with the sale of the going concern and if the commercial lease agreement does not prohibit the transfer of the lease, the lessee must notify the lessor of the main conditions surrounding the assignment. Once the assignment has been completed, the assignee has all the rights and obligations of the former lessee, including his or her rights to renewal of the lease.

11.17   Requirements for Transferring Other Assets

The transfer of property and title of assets is done pursuant to an agreement between the parties, unless otherwise provided by law (e.g. real estate, shares, going concern). The parties may also stipulate that the transfer of title occurs upon delivery or upon full payment.

11.18   Encumbrances and Third Party Interests

Encumbrances and third party interests may result from third party guarantees, pledges of property and title retention clauses *(clause de réserve de propriété)*.

A pledge is valid and enforceable when the pledged property has been placed and remains in possession of the pledgee, unless French law provides that the pledge be registered.

A title retention clause defers the transfer of ownership of an asset until payment in full. For real property, pledges of property are recorded in the Land Registry.

11.19 Minimum Shareholder and Officer Requirements

With regard to minimum shareholder and officer requirements, please refer to section 11.2 above.

With regard to management of an SA and SAS, please refer to section 11.2 above.

11.20 Non-competition Clauses

French law distinguishes between non-competition clauses contained in employment agreements and those agreed upon by sellers in business transfer or share transfer agreements.

Non-competition clauses in employment agreements:

During the term of the employment agreement, the employee is bound by general obligations of professionalism, confidentiality, respect of company rules, regulations and hierarchical structure, and loyalty. The duty of loyalty prohibits the employee from exercising or engaging in any activity which competes with that of the employer. Failure to comply with these obligations may lead to sanctions, including dismissal.

Upon termination of the employment agreement, the employee is generally free to work in any activity, even a competing one, unless the employment agreement contains a non-competition clause. For such clause to be enforceable, the following conditions must be met:

• it must be necessary to protect the legitimate interests of the company;

• it must be limited in time and geographical scope;

• it must take into consideration the specificities of the employee's duties; and

• it must be accompanied by a financial counterpart paid by the employer, generally determined by the applicable national collective bargaining agreement (*convention collective nationale ou régionale* or NCBA).

Non-competition clauses in the transfer of a going concern:

Article 1625 of the French Civil Code requires that the seller guarantee peaceful enjoyment (*possession paisible*) of the thing sold, warrant against the latent defects of such thing and against any redhibitory defects.

Pursuant to French case law, the seller also warrants that it will abstain from any and all acts which could divert the clientele from the assets transferred, regardless of whether such a clause is included in the transfer agreement.

It is common practice and advisable to broaden the scope of such warrant by including a specific and narrowly defined non-competition clause with a limited duration.

Non-competition clauses in share transfer agreements:

In any share transfer agreement resulting in a change in control, it is common practice and advisable to include a non-competition clause. For such clause to be enforceable, it must not be disproportionate to the protection of the commercial interests in question. Specifically, the clause may not prevent the assignor from exercising any activity in management or from working as an employee. Generally, such clause contains an indemnification clause pursuant to which the assignor will indemnify the assignee in the event of breach of such clause.

11.21   Environmental Considerations

Environmental risks have gained considerable importance in connection with the acquisition of French companies. Generally, every investor considering the purchase of an existing commercial property must inquire into whether the property is a classified installation (*installation classée*) and, if so, whether the proper authorization has been received or the proper notification has been filed concerning the site. The purchaser should also review, among other things, any particular operating conditions that may have been required by the competent administrative authority. If the property is a classified installation and assuming the necessary administrative requirements have been fulfilled, the purchaser is protected to a limited extent due to the regular inspections conducted at the site by the governmental authorities.

Relying on such limited protection is not necessarily advisable. The purchaser may be liable, however, for any latent or hidden pollution that is discovered and that is caused by the business' activity. If, for instance, an unforeseen contamination of ground water is discovered, the authorities will require the new owner of the facility to carry out the necessary reparations regardless of whether the ultimate cause lies with the previous owner's activity.

In response to this type of risk, it may be advisable to conduct an extensive pre-purchase environmental audit of the site. Based on the results of such audit, the environmental issues of potential environmental liability should be addressed in the appropriate sale warranties granted by the seller.

11.22   Employee Superannuation/Pension Plans

Employees may receive pensions upon their retirement, the amounts of which will vary depending on the length of employee contributions to the retirement system. Generally, the employee may exercise his/her rights to request his/her pension and receive the full amount of his/her retirement benefits if (i) he/she reaches the age of 60 (in a few rare cases, an employee may exercise such rights before 60), and (ii) he/she has contributed to the retirement system for the requisite contributed period. If, however, the second condition is not met, the employee may still retire at 60, but he/she will only receive a percentage of his/her retirement benefits, the amount of which will vary depending on the number of quarters actually worked. Even if both conditions are met, the employee may also decide to continue working in order to obtain higher retirement benefits.

The applicable NCBA may set forth different retirement provisions which are more favourable to the employee.

Many companies offer supplementary retirement benefits through capitalization, often giving the priority to directors or managers *(dirigeants)* and executives *(cadres)*. Different benefits may be granted, depending on (i) the objectives sought and, (ii) the tax and social contribution regimes to be applied.

11.23   Employee Rights

French Labour law is based on a large set of compulsory legal rules, general NCBAs, inter-company agreements and the individual labour contracts. The purchaser of a French company with employees should examine in particular:

- the applicable NCBA;
- the employment agreements;
- any existing enterprise-specific collective bargaining agreement *(accord collectif d'entreprise)*;
- the number of employees;
- their annual salaries;
- the seniority of the employees in the company;
- any litigation in progress; and
- any additional benefits which have been granted under the individual contract over and above the enterprise-specific collective bargaining agreement, NCBA or unilateral agreements.

French Labour law requires that employee representative institutions (e.g. Works Council) be created within certain companies, with varying functions and authority, depending on the number of employees in the company.

For example, in companies with at least 11 employees, elections for employee representatives *(délégués du personnel)* must be organized. The main duties of the employee representatives include presenting individual or collective demands of employees relating to salaries and ensuring the application of the provisions of the French Labour Code.

In companies with at least 50 employees, a Works Council must be created to ensure collective representation of employees. Such representation guarantees that employee interests are taken into consideration when decisions are made concerning the management and economic and financial development of the company.

The Works Council has significant power. For example, if the company is to be sold to a third party, the Works Council must, prior to the sale, be informed and consulted and the purchaser must be introduced to the Works Council.

11.24 Compulsory Transfer of Employees

In the event the legal situation of an employer changes due to an acquisition or a transfer of activity, Article L. 122-12 of the French Labour Code requires that all employment agreements in effect between the former employer and its employees at the time of the transfer be transferred to the new employer. The purchaser thus effectively substitutes and takes the place of the seller in each individual employment agreement.

The transfer applies in respect of every aspect of the employment agreement, including seniority, salary, payment of vacation indemnities, bonuses and use of a company car. Further, the transfer of employment agreements is a matter of public policy. As such, and pursuant to current case law currently in force, the seller, the purchaser and even the employees may not refuse such transfer.

In addition to the transfer of individual contractual obligations, the investor acquiring the business should be aware of the transfer of possible employer obligations stemming from an applicable NCBA. This may occur in two forms. First, employees in France generally enjoy certain rights granted under the respective NCBA applying to all businesses operating within a designated economic sector of activity (e.g. metallurgy and retailing) as defined in such agreement. The relevant NCBA applying to the seller's business will thus automatically remain in effect following the transfer in ownership of the business (though, under certain conditions, it is possible for the new owner to move the business out of the scope of a given NCBA regime and into another).

Secondly, in addition to their entitlements under the applicable NCBA, employees may also benefit from enterprise-specific collective bargaining agreements (*accord collectif d'entreprise* or ESCBA) which stipulate additional entitlements granted exclusively by the individual employer. Any existing ESCBA continues to have effect 15 months following the acquisition or until a new agreement is executed. Where a new agreement is executed, it takes the place of the former agreement and cancels all the benefits previously provided for. If, at the end of this 15 month period, the new employer and employees fail to sign a new agreement, all the legally defined 'collective' benefits enumerated in the former agreement cease to apply. In this case, the 'individual' benefits are deemed to be incorporated into the individual employment contracts of all of the employees, subject to the former agreement. Determination of whether a particular employee benefit is 'individual' or 'collective' is a matter of case law and determined on a case-by-case basis.

Finally, any customary practices (*usages*) in force within the acquired business are also transferred and the purchaser must comply with such practices until the purchaser formally denounces them by following the necessary procedures (informing the employee representatives, if any, then informing each employee individually, complying with the appropriate notice period, and maintaining any vested advantages and/ or benefits).

11.25   Tax Deductibility of Acquisition Expenses

Where the purchaser is a company or an individual not subject to taxation in France, the deductibility of its acquisition expenses is determined by the law of its home jurisdiction.

When the purchaser is subject to French taxation, as of 1 January 2005, transfer taxes, legal fees, commissions or costs associated with an acquisition may, at the purchaser's option, be attributed to the cost of acquiring capital assets or they may be registered as expenses. When the aforementioned costs and expenses are entered as an asset, they become part of the cost of acquiring capital assets and do not appear on a deferred expenditure account. The depreciation period corresponds to the period of time the good is used. If the aforementioned costs and expenses are attributed to non-depreciable assets (such as *fonds de commerce* or going concern, titles, etc.), no deduction may be taken.

Deducting VAT due on acquisition expenses requires the existence of a direct and immediate link between such expenses and the performance of business operations subject to VAT.

The cost of acquiring a going concern is generally subject to VAT. As such, VAT may, in principle, be deducted from such acquisition cost.

With regard to VAT due on expenses incurred in the acquisition of equity participations, the tax administration has adopted the position of the European Court of Justice and admitted that there were grounds to consider such expenses as general expenses of the company, which constitute, in principle, the costs of its taxable business operations. As such, these expenses may be deducted under the following conditions:

- If all taxable business operations of the company are entitled to a VAT deduction, the total VAT amount is deductible. As per the tax administration, it is particularly necessary that the cost of the expenses be passed along and included in the cost of doing business;

- If none of the taxable business operations are entitled to a VAT deduction, the company cannot deduct the VAT due on these expenses (this is the case of a 'pure holding');

- Finally, if some of the taxable business operations are entitled to a VAT deduction, the VAT due on the applicable expenses are, in principle, partly deductible on a prorata basis. A total deduction, however, may be taken if the company demonstrates that these expenses are part of the cost of business operations which are entitled to a VAT deduction.

11.26   Levies on Acquisition Agreements and Collateral Documents

With the exception of registration taxes, addressed in section 10.4 above, no further stamp duty or levies are due on acquisition agreements or on collateral documents.

11.27   Financing Rules and Restrictions

A general manager (*directeur général*) or board member of an SA is prohibited from (i) borrowing, in any manner whatsoever, from the company, (ii) having the company grant him/her a bank overdraft, or (iii) having the bank act as a guarantor or surety for any obligations he/she owes towards third parties.

If, however, the board member is a legal entity, the aforementioned restrictions do not apply.

On the other hand, it is legal for the company to receive fixed-term advances or loans (called *avances en compte-courant* or overdrafts) from its shareholders or board members. Depending on the interest rate on these *avances en compte—courant,* prior authorization from the board of directors may be necessary.

From a tax standpoint, the interest on these *avances en compte-courant* may be deducted from the company's taxable results under two conditions: (i) the interest does not exceed a certain percentage set forth each year by the Minister of Finance, and (ii) the total amount of the *avances en compte-courant* does not exceed 1.5 times the amount of the company's capital.

11.28   Exchange Controls and Repatriation of Profits

As of 1990, international money transfers are no longer restricted. This is also true with respect to the repatriation of profits.

The repatriation of profits (e.g. dividends), however, may be subject to a withholding tax in France by virtue of the applicable treaties against double taxation.

11.29   Groups of Companies

Under French law, corporate groups have more of an economic purpose than a legal purpose. Each company belonging to a group is incorporated and has a legal existence of its own; companies form a group for various economic reasons. As such, the economic reality of corporate groups is significant. Certain specific rules have been enacted to address legal issues relating to corporate groups.

Several legal entities falling under the effective control of one parent company are deemed to be a corporate group. The consequences for the legal entities and for the parent company are mainly the following:

- Subsidiaries which own the shares of the holding company have no voting rights, so as to limit what is called the 'self control' of the holding company;

- The group must publish the financial statements of each company of the group as well as consolidated accounts if certain conditions, specifically staff size, amount on the balance sheet and the amount of the turnover, are met;

- If one of the subsidiaries is a listed company in France, the parent company must file a declaration with the AMF when the ownership threshold levels of 5 per cent,

10 per cent, 15 per cent, 20 per cent, 33.3 per cent, 50 per cent, 66.6 per cent, 90 per cent or 95 per cent (in capital and voting rights) are crossed;

- The agreements entered into between a subsidiary and its parent company, or a company in which one of its directors is a board member, must be first approved by the board of directors, and the statutory auditor must prepare a special report on such agreements; prior approval is not necessary for agreements concerning on-going operations if such agreements were entered into under normal business conditions and do not significantly affect any of the parties;

- In the case of the sale of a subsidiary, prior consultation of the parent company's Works Council, if any, is required.

11.30 Responsibility for Liabilities of an Acquired Subsidiary

The existence of a corporate group may affect the treatment of the debts and liabilities of companies belonging to such group. Creditors of one company may demand payment of the debt owed by another company belonging to the same group if the creditors reasonably believe that both companies are one unified corporate entity, or an amalgamation of companies' unified by common economic interests.

The same analysis applies in bankruptcies. The courts have, in certain cases, held companies of the corporate group (e.g. parent company) liable for the debts of the bankrupt company if they actively and regularly managed the bankrupt company. The courts have even extended the scope of the bankruptcy proceedings to include such 'managing' companies of the corporate group.

In other cases, if the conduct of an individual or corporate shareholder of a bankrupt company leads the creditors to reasonably believe that such company and its controlling shareholder(s) constitute one entity, the bankruptcy proceedings may also be extended to include such controlling shareholder(s).

11.31 Governing Law of the Contract

In principle, French law allows the parties to choose the governing law of their agreement when such agreement is international and commercial in scope. Under French law, an agreement is deemed international in nature when the parties, the performance obligations, the *situs* of the object, or the place of performance has a legal connection with a foreign jurisdiction.

This freedom to choose the governing law is, however, restricted. For example, the possibility of a choice of law is limited in labour law, and for tax and administrative matters, French law must be applied. French law must also govern chattels, immovable property as well as sureties (except personal sureties).

Finally, French corporate law sets forth a large number of mandatory rules pertaining to the choice of law provisions.

11.32 Dispute Resolution Options

Parties to a contract may agree to resolve any contractual differences through national courts and legal systems or through arbitration.

Arbitration is frequently provided for as a means of dispute resolution, in particular in cross-border acquisitions as the issues normally at stake are arbitrable. For example, the acquisition of shares often raises the problem of multi-party arbitration.

France enacted an arbitration law in 1980 and ratified the Convention on the Recognition and Enforcement of Foreign Arbitral Awards (the New York Convention of 1958). Additionally, the International Chamber of Commerce, which is the seat of the International Court of Arbitration, is located in Paris.

Arbitration may be conducted pursuant to French law or pursuant to any other set of institutional rules which the parties have agreed upon (e.g. UNCITRAL). French case law, however, sets forth strict rules regarding equality of the parties when appointing arbitrators.

Alternative dispute resolution (ADR) mechanisms such as conciliation and mediation have been growing since the late 1980's. Parties may, outside court proceedings, establish their own rules to be applied in respect of conciliation or mediation. They may also follow the rules set forth by institutional bodies such as the ICC or the French Arbitration Association (*Association Française de l'Arbitrage*). The French Code of Civil Procedure allows the judge to appoint a mediator with the agreement of the parties.

12. GERMANY

Dr. Franz-Jörg Semler
CMS Hasche Sigle

12.1 Introductory Comments

The acquisition of businesses has become a standard procedure in Germany. There are no particular regulations for the acquisition of businesses by foreign purchasers. General civil law and merger control law provide the legal framework; the latter is relevant both at national and at EU level.

One peculiarity of the German legal system which often surprises the foreign investor comes from German employment law. Employees have, by virtue of numerous legal regulations regarding co-determination, considerable influence on strategic business decisions such as the purchase or the sale of a business. In addition, employees in Germany enjoy, corresponding to the applicable law in other EU Member States, particular protection against dismissal in the context of the sale of the business in which they are employed.

12.2 Corporate Structures

The target company is often organized in the legal form of a limited liability company ('*Gesellschaft mit beschränkter Haftung*' (GmbH)). In Germany there are, in December 2006, roughly one million GmbH. Less often, the investor has dealings with a stock corporation ('*Aktiengesellschaft*' (AG)). Only about 16,000 companies, comprising however a large number of the biggest ones, are organized in this form. Both of these company forms are characterized as 'Capital Companies' in German legal terminology. In Germany, more often than in other states, businesses are run in partnerships, for which there are principally two legal forms: the general partnership ('*Offene Handelsgesellschaft*' (OHG)) and the limited partnership ('*Kommanditgesellschaft*' (KG)).

These company forms are characterized by the following features:

Gesellschaft mit beschränkter Haftung (GmbH)

The company's share capital must amount to at least EUR 25,000. However, a reduction to EUR 10,000 is discussed and will probably be introduced during the year 2007. The shareholders' liability is limited basically to the obligation to fund the share capital. The directors (*Geschäftsführer*), who may or may not be shareholders themselves, manage the business of the company. The shareholders have direct influence on the management in that the shareholders' meeting can issue instructions of any kind to the management. The GmbH must have a supervisory board, separate from the management board and structured very similar to the supervisory board of the AG (see below), if the company including its subsidiaries has more than 500 employees.

International Business Acquisitions, M. Whalley, F.-J. Semler (eds.), Kluwer Law International, London, 2007; ISBN 9789041124838.

Aktiengesellschaft (AG)

The share capital must amount to at least EUR 50,000. Also in the AG the share-holders' liability is limited to funding the share capital. The corporate governance in the AG is characterized by a two-tier system: The board (*Vorstand*) manages the AG's business. The supervisory board (*Aufsichtsrat*) appoints the board and supervises it. With some minor exceptions the supervisory board is elected partly in the general share-holders' meeting (*Hauptversammlung*) and partly under the rules of co-determination directly or indirectly by the employees and the trade unions. The supervisory board has a strong position in the company, not only because it appoints the board but also because many decisions of the board require the consent of the supervisory board. The general shareholders' meeting does not as a rule have the authority to issue instructions to the board or to the supervisory board. A rare and particular form of the stock corporation is the limited partnership on shares ('*Kommanditgesellschaft auf Aktien*' (KGaA)). In this form, apart from the limited shareholders, who are liable only for providing the share capital, there is at least one shareholder who has unlimited liability for the company's obligations. Only *Aktiengesellschaften* (AG) and *Kommandit-gesellschaften auf Aktien* (KGaA) are listed on the stock exchange. In total on 31 December 2006 there were slightly less than 1,000 German companies listed on the various German stock markets.

Offene Handelsgesellschaft (OHG)

The general partnership is characterized by the shareholders having unlimited liability for the company's obligations. There is no prescribed minimum share capital. In practice OHG are rare.

Kommanditgesellschaft (KG)

In the limited partnership at least one shareholder must have unlimited liability for the company's obligations. He is characterized as 'the fully liable partner'. The remaining shareholders ('*Kommanditisten*') are liable only for providing the investment to which they have subscribed. There is no prescribed minimum share capital. Practice has developed the particular form of the 'GmbH & Co. KG'. In this, the owners of the business form a GmbH which assumes the role of the fully liable partner in the limited partnership. The owners as shareholders of the GmbH are only liable for funding the share capital of the GmbH but they have no personal liability for the obligations of the GmbH. The owners (shareholders of the GmbH) are at the same time the limited partners of the limited partnership. The GmbH as the only fully liable partner is normally provided with the minimum share capital of, at present, EUR 25,000 (pos-sibly to be reduced to EUR 10,000). This structure fulfils the formal legal requirement that at least one partner of the limited partnership, i.e. the GmbH, has unlimited liability for the partnership's obligations and, at the same time, protects all of the owners from being liable for obligations of the KG. Thus in a limited partnership a limitation on liability is *de facto* achieved for all owners. The GmbH & Co. KG enjoyed particular popularity in the past as it combined the limitation on liability of capital companies with the particular tax advantages of partnerships. Many of these tax advantages have been reduced in the meantime and thus the number and significance of GmbH & Co.

KG has receded. Nevertheless there are still many companies of this type and they still offer certain tax advantages, also for foreign investors who purchase a business in Germany. The legal form of GmbH & Co. KG is thus used sometimes in setting up a vehicle for the acquisition of businesses in Germany.

12.3 Structure of the Acquisition Agreement; Letters of Intent and Heads of Agreement

German law conceptually distinguishes between the sale and purchase agreement (SPA), which governs the parties' rights and obligations, in particular containing provisions on the purchase price and the vendor's guarantees; and the act by which the business is transferred to the purchaser in fulfilment of the sale and purchase agreement (assignment of title to the assets of the target in an asset deal or assignment of the target's shares). Both acts, i. e. the sale and purchase agreement and the assignment of the assets or the shares which are the object of the transaction are necessary parts of a business acquisition. In an asset deal, the SPA and the assignment of the acquired assets usually take place in two separate legal acts. In a share deal, however, the sale and purchase of the shares and their assignment, though conceptually distinct are regularly executed in a single deed.

Fundamentally, each party may break off negotiations at any time, without owing the other side any justification or indemnity. Legal obligations generally arise only once an agreement has materialized in the legally prescribed form. Nevertheless, even before the conclusion of the SPA, certain legal obligations may arise for the parties. This is, of course, the case, when preparatory agreements such as confidentiality or exclusivity agreements or agreements on pre-emption rights are concluded. In addition German legal practice has adopted the legal institute 'letter of intent' (LoI) from the Anglo—American practice and derives certain rights and obligations from it. Except for very special cases under German law the letter of intent does not give rise to an obligation of a party to conclude a contract according to the expressed intention. But it does oblige the parties to go on with the negotiations according to the expressed intent until one party informs the other that it has changed its intention. If a party does not comply with this obligation it may be liable to the other party for damages which this other party suffers from being left in the belief that the first party sticks to its expressed intention. Heads of agreement are uncommon in German legal practice as an autonomous legal institution, although the parties are of course free to establish lists of items which they consider essential or to submit non-binding draft agreements. In summary it may be underscored that entering into negotiations does not create an obligation for a party to conclude the agreement. However, the parties are bound to negotiate in good faith which implies the obligation not to enter into or to continue negotiations, if the respective party does not have the intention to conclude an agreement.

12.4 Taxes Affecting the Structure and the Calculation of the Price

The tax structure of an acquisition may have considerable significance for the purchase price. The vendor will often accept a lower purchase price if the tax liability on his capital gain can be kept low. The purchaser can pay a correspondingly higher purchase price, according to how favourable the transaction is structured for him from a tax perspective. At times the parties' tax interests collide and it can so happen that the tax structure which is perfect for one party is disadvantageous for the other. The purchaser as a rule strives for a tax structure which:

- provides for high depreciation possibilities for the purchase price;

- keeps the total tax of the future operations low, taking into account the applicable double taxation treaties. For the fulfilment of this goal it can be necessary to transform the acquired German business into another legal form. The details of this cannot be dealt with here.

It is to be emphasized that in a share deal the acquired shares are to be entered on the balance sheet at acquisition cost. Under the German Fiseal accounting rules normally no depreciation takes place. In the past certain ways of structuring the acquisition of shares in a way which would lead to taxation as if it were an asset deal (so-called 'step up') were possible. They have been radically limited by the legislator in the last years. The acquisition of real property in an asset deal is subject to property acquisition tax of 3.5 per cent whereas fundamentally no tax is levied on the acquisition of shares. However, real property acquisition tax arises if 95 per cent or more of the shares are acquired in a company which owns real property. Losses of the target company may be carried forward also under new ownership if the target company's business operations are continued essentially in the same way as before.

12.5   Extent of Sellers' Warranties and Indemnities

Purchase agreements over a business are subject to the general provisions of civil law applicable to the sale of defective property as laid down in the German Civil Code (*Bürgerliches Gesetzbuch* [*BGB*]). That applies for both asset and share deals, if the purchaser acquires all or nearly all of the shares. The general laws are, however, too little geared to the purchase of a business and very often do not provide proper solutions for disputes in M & A transactions.

It is therefore customary for the seller to give a wide range of guarantees. In this respect sale and purchase agreements in Germany increasingly make use of the drafting techniques developed in the Anglo-American practice. That aside, contracts in Germany are as a rule considerably shorter than is customary in the UK and the USA. Guarantees regarding the legal existence of the seller and the target company or regarding the authority of the persons representing the seller are most often superfluous, because these matters can easily be ascertained by checking the commercial register. Guarantees on particular legal and economic circumstances of the target business, in particular with reference to the accuracy of the seller's accounts for the last business years, are however both relevant and usual. According to the circumstances the purchaser will ask for and the seller will usually give guarantees against specific risks which the purchaser sees in the company such as relations with customers or suppliers and employment matters. More and more environment matters have become an area of particular concern for the purchaser.

The legal consequences when a guarantee case arises are not easily derived from statutory provisions. The M & A practice, normally excludes claims for rescission of the SPA or limits rescission to extreme cases. The purchaser's rights are usually restricted to claims for reduction of the purchase price or for compensation of the difference between the value which the acquired business had if the guarantees were true compared to its actual value where the guarantees are not true. There is sometimes an overlap between these two claims. The seller normally tries to restrict the maximum amount of claims for reduction of the purchase price or for compensation, for example to a certain percentage of the purchase price. In practice one finds often percentages between 10 per cent and 100 per cent of the purchase price, depending on the relative bargaining strength of the parties. By law claims based on non—compliance with guaranties are subject to a statutory period of limitation of three years. Very often this period is contractually limited to two years.

By law the seller is not liable for defects which are 'known' to the purchaser on conclusion of the sale and purchase agreement. The parties often derogate from this statutory rule or draft specific clauses which define under which conditions 'knowledge' of the purchaser can be assumed. In most transactions a considerable number of people tend to be involved and it is often difficult to establish exactly which circumstances were known by which person and to what extent that knowledge can be attributed to the 'purchaser'. In practice it is often agreed that only those circumstances which have been notified to the purchaser by the seller in a disclosure letter are considered as 'known' to the purchaser. Often the seller's declarations with reference to specific circumstances of the target company are supplemented with a general declaration that the seller is not aware of any circumstances which have a materially negative effect on the value of the target. Should this declaration be wrong then, according to case law and drafting practice, the purchaser is entitled to reduce the purchase price to the amount which the parties would have convened upon had the purchaser known of the circumstances hidden by the seller.

12.6 Liability for Pre-contractual Representations

During the negotiations the seller often makes declarations about the target, which are not taken up in the form of express guarantees in the sale and purchase agreement. If the buyer thereby gains a false impression of the target the seller can be legally obliged to pay compensation if he intentionally or negligently gave false or misleading information. In practice it may be difficult to establish which information in detail the seller gave during the negotiations. Because of this uncertainty, the seller's liability is often contractually limited to the express guarantees, as outlined above. This does not affect the seller's liability for fraudulent misrepresentation, for which he is always liable.

12.7 Liability for Pre-acquisition Trading and Contracts

In a share deal the purchaser takes over the target with all its rights and obligations existing at the time of the transfer of the shares. The change in title of the shares does not influence the company's rights and obligations. The purchaser of shares in a limited company, in a stock corporation or in a limited partnership is, however, liable for the contribution which the seller has subscribed but not yet made. In addition, on the acquisition of shares in a limited partnership the buyer can to a certain extent be liable for obligations of the company. The German Commercial Code (*Handelsgesetzbuch* [*HGB*]) regulates the details.

In an asset deal, basically only those rights and obligations are transferred to the purchaser which he takes over contractually. However, further liability applies by law in the following cases:

- all employment contracts are automatically transferred to the purchaser; he may not terminate an employment contract because of the transfer of the business;

- the purchaser is liable for taxes which have arisen in connection with the acquired business from the start of the calendar year in which the acquisition takes place; and

- the purchaser is liable for all obligations which have arisen in the acquired business if he continues the business under the same name.

Doubts may arise over how far either the vendor or purchaser is entitled to the target's profits of the current fiscal year. By law, the buyer has a claim to profit only from the time of transfer of the shares. However, it is often agreed that the buyer will receive the profit of the current fiscal year in total.

12.8   Pre-completion Risks

By law, the risk is transferred with the transfer of the object of the purchase to the purchaser. Thus in an asset deal the risk attached to the target and its assets are transferred at the moment when the individual assets are assigned to the buyer. In a share deal the buyer acquires shares. Risks of the target company are not transferred but stay with the target.

This legal situation does not provide, in many cases, an adequately clear and economically appropriate solution: The parties tend to negotiate on the basis of certain financial statements of the target, which were set up for a specific point of time in the past. More or less important changes will necessarily have occurred by the time at which the SPA is completed and further changes may occur by the time, when the title passes to the purchaser. To take account of this situation, the parties will often define a preliminary purchase price in the SPA, which is subject to adjustments according to the financial status of the target at the transfer of the title to the shares or, in an asset deal, to the assets (closing accounts). In addition the seller will often guarantee that since the end of the last fiscal year no fundamental circumstances have arisen which would negatively affect the target's business. These negative circumstances can be physical (e.g. a fire), legal (e.g. insolvency of a debtor), or commercial (e.g. loss of important customers). A particular situation may arise when the SPA is completed subject to certain conditions which may take some time to materialize (e.g. clearance by antitrust authorities) or when, for other reasons, the transfer of the target is to take place only some time after completion of the SPA. The purchaser may require, in such cases, additional protection against material adverse changes in the target's business, including the right to rescind the SPA. Usual clauses relating to material adverse changes may be found in public take over bids, which are accessible via the website of the Federal Financial Supervisory Authority (*Bundesanstalt für Finanzdienstleistungsaufsicht* [*BaFin*]).

12.9 Required Governmental Approvals

The acquisition of shares in a German company requires, as a rule, no governmental approval (with the exception of merger control, dealt with infra in 12.10 and in Chapter [36]). Some exceptions exist in the banking and insurance sectors. The same applies for the acquisition of a business in an asset deal. Note, however, that local communities often have a pre-emptive right to purchase real property. It should be further noted that certain businesses require licences or concessions under German law and that these might expire with a change in the ownership (see 12.12 infra).

12.10 Anti-trust and Competition Law

The acquisition of a business can be subject to the German control of concentrations regime (merger control) under the Act against Restraints of Competition (*Gesetz gegen Wettbewerbsbeschränkungen* [*GWB*]). Concentrations (mergers) include in particular the acquisition of all or a substantial part of the assets of an undertaking (asset deal). Mergers also include cases where the shareholding of the purchaser reaches, after the acquisition, 25 per cent or 50 per cent of a company's capital or voting rights and a number of other transactions, by which an undertaking achieves control over another. The regulations on merger control generally apply when the participating undertakings achieve a combined aggregate worldwide turnover of more than EUR 500 million and when, in addition, the domestic (German) turnover of at least one undertaking concerned exceeds EUR 25 million. Special provisions apply for mergers with small independent undertakings, in narrow markets and when a merger restricts competition in the field of publishing or producing or distributing newspapers or magazines.

If the turnover thresholds are reached, the merger must be notified to the Federal Cartel Office (*Bundeskartellamt* [BKartA]) prior to being put into effect (pre-merger notification). The Federal Cartel Office will prohibit the merger if it is to be expected that the merger creates or strengthens a dominant position unless the undertakings concerned prove that the concentration will also lead to improvements of the conditions of competition and that these improvements will outweigh the disadvantage of dominance.

European merger control law applies to certain large transactions (see Chapter [36] below. To the extent that European merger control applies, it displaces German law.

12.11 Required Offer Procedures

Specific disclosure requirements apply for the purchaser of shares in stock corporations. Whoever acquires more than 25 per cent of the voting rights must inform the affected company. A further notification is required if altogether more than 50 per cent of the shares have been acquired. The acquisition of shareholdings in listed companies is to be notified to the Federal Financial Supervisory Authority (*Bundesanstalt für Finanzdienstleistungsaufsicht* [*BaFin*]), when the shareholding reaches or exceeds the thresholds of

3 per cent, 5 per cent, 10 per cent, 25 per cent, 50 per cent or 75 per cent of the voting rights. In addition, shareholders whose shareholding falls below these thresholds must also notify this.

Whoever acquires control over a listed stock corporation is to notify this to the Federal Financial Supervisory Authority and has to make a public takeover offer for the rest of the shares. Acquisition of control is, inter alia, assumed when at least 30 per cent of the voting rights of a stock corporation are acquired.

12.12   Continuation of Government Licences

For many business activities in Germany some kind of licence is required. If the transaction is carried out as an asset deal, the acquirer must ensure that the licence is transferred to him; this takes place as a rule only with the agreement of the competent authority. In the case of a share deal, the licence issued to the company remains in force, but can be cancelled by the competent authority in some cases on change of ownership. If state aid has been granted, there may be a provision that it must be paid back in the case of a change of ownership.

12.13   Requirements for Transferring Shares

Different regulations for the transfer of shares apply to the different types of companies. The sale and the transfer of shares in a limited liability company must be certified in due legal form by a notary. The notarial costs for this can be considerable (see no 11.26 infra). Case law accepts that certain foreign notaries may also notarize the transfer. Note that there are no share certificates for the shares in a limited liability company. The transfer of the shares is to be notified to the management of the company. In stock corporations bearers shares can be transferred without keeping to a particular form, but written form is customary; it is further necessary that the share certificates be transferred to the acquirer. For the transfer of registered shares to be effective it is necessary to notify the change of ownership in the company's share register. The transfer of shares in a general partnership or in a limited partnership requires no particular form. It is to be notified to the Commercial Register.

Third parties with an option to buy may oppose the acquisition in some circumstances. It could also be that the statutes of a limited liability company make the transfer of shares dependent on the agreement of the shareholders in general meeting or even of the agreement of all or of individual shareholders. The transfer of registered shares in a stock corporation can be linked in the statutes to the corporation's agreement. Shares in partnerships can be transferred only with the other shareholders' consent. This consent can be granted generally in the statutes of the partnership or *ad hoc*.

12.14   Requirements for Transferring Land and Property Leases

For the sales agreement and for the transfer of ownership in land it is necessary to have the contract notarized as a deed and to have the transfer of ownership registered in the Land Register. Practically all properties which can be affected by the purchase of a business are entered in local Land Registers. These also identify the owners. The registers are nearly always correct. In any case the good faith of the purchaser in the owner registered in the Land Register is protected. The purchaser thus becomes the owner of a property also if the person disposing of the property, registered as owner in the Land Register, did not in reality own it. In Germany, therefore, 'title insurance' is superfluous. If the target company has rented out property, the lease agreement is transferred to the acquirer of the target business. If the target business has leased property, the lease agreement is transferred to the buyer only if the landlord consents.

All these questions come into play only in asset deals. If shares have been acquired in a company which owns real property, this does not change the ownership in that property. The same is true of lease agreements.

12.15 Requirements for Transferring Intellectual Property

If the target business owns intellectual property, then care should be taken in an asset deal that this is also transferred to the acquirer. Patents, trade marks, utility models and designs can be transferred. The transfer of patents, trade marks and utility models must be notified to the Federal Patent Office (*Bundespatentamt*). From time to time it may also be that the seller of the business does not transfer the intellectual property rights but merely grants a licence to the acquirer. This may be adequate for the acquirer in some cases only. Copyright is not as such transferable, but the right to exercise the copyright can be transferred.

12.16 Requirements for Transferring Business Contracts, Licences and Leases

German law as a rule allows the assignment of individual rights resulting from contracts, but not the transfer of the contract as a whole without the other party's consent. It is evident that a party to a contract cannot transfer its contractual obligations to another person without the consent of the creditor. The assignment of individual rights can be contractually excluded. Such exclusions are frequent and do not need to be registered in a publicly accessible register. It is difficult for the purchaser to ascertain, whether the seller is entitled to assign such rights and he will often require a formal guarantee from the seller. Of course, these questions have direct significance only in asset deals. In share deals the target company remains the bearer of rights and obligations.

Note, however, that many contracts contain change-of-ownership clauses. That applies for many licence, distribution and co-operation agreements as well as for many joint venture agreements.

12.17 Requirements for Transferring Other Assets

The transfer of movable assets takes place by the vendor and the purchaser agreeing on transfer of ownership and the vendor transferring possession to the purchaser. The transfer of possession does not necessarily need to take place by physical handover. Alternatively the claim for return of an asset which is in the possession of a third party may be assigned, or an agreement that the disposer continues to possess the object (e.g. as a lessee having transferred title to the object), may be concluded and are equivalent to physical handover.

12.18 Encumbrances and Third Party Interests

Movable objects which are used in the target business often do not belong to the owner of that business. In Germany the supplier of machines or of other supplies often retains ownership in the delivered object until complete payment of the purchase price. Once the purchase price has been paid, the goods are often transferred by the owner to a bank for security on credit. For the acquirer of the business in an asset deal or of the shares in a share deal, these third party entitlements are not as a rule apparent. They do not need to be registered in a public register to be legally valid and enforceable. In the case of an asset deal the acquirer's good faith in the disposer's ownership is protected to a certain extent. There is, however, no protection of good faith that the disposer is the owner of claims or rights which he has sold. In summary a degree of uncertainty as to the title of moveable assets and rights has to be reckoned with. Even so title insurance is not common in Germany.

Different rules apply to real property. Ownership in real property and encumbrances are apparent from the Land Register. The acquirer in good faith is protected.

It is important in practice that it cannot be established with complete certainty whether shares in a limited liability company belong to the seller and whether they are charged with a security in favour of a third party. Since shares in a limited liability company are very often the object of a share deal, the acquirer has at present considerable legal uncertainty. The limited company keeps a list revealing its shareholders and the directors must inform the Commercial Register of each change of shareholding. It is customary that the acquirer checks these lists and the Commercial Register. They offer, however, only limited protection. The acquirer's good faith in the accuracy of this information is not protected at present. It is possible that in the context of the envisaged reform of the law on companies with limited liability (see no 12.2 supra) some protection of purchasers in good faith will be introduced.

12.19 Minimum Shareholder and Officer Requirements

The partnership (general or limited) must have at least two shareholders (partners). The limited liability company and the stock corporation need only one shareholder. The maximum number of shareholders is unlimited for all types of companies. Partnerships and limited liability companies rarely have more than 50 shareholders. Companies with more shareholders are in virtually all cases organized as stock corporations. Companies need at least one director (limited liability company) or one member of the board (stock corporation). This person is the legal representative of the company. He does not need not be a German citizen or have a place of residence in Germany nor does he need to have a shareholding in the company.

However, the legal representative of a partnership may only be a shareholder who as a rule is personally liable. If the personally liable shareholder is a limited company, in particular in the case of the GmbH & Co. KG (see **12.2** above), the partnership is managed by the GmbH which for its part acts through its directors. Directors of a GmbH and members of the board of a stock corporation may only be natural persons.

12.20 Non-competition Clauses

The following non-competition obligations may be of significance in the context of the acquisition of an undertaking in Germany.

The vendor of an undertaking is subject to an implied obligation to abstain from doing business in the same branch for a certain time after the sale of his undertaking. This non-competition obligation is considered necessary in order to transfer to the purchaser the full value of the target and it applies regardless of whether the target is acquired by an asset deal or by a share deal. The exact scope and duration of the vendor's non-competition obligation is often regulated in the SPA. In accordance with the opinions of the European Commission and the German Federal Cartel Office non-competition-obligations are in practice often agreed upon for a period of up to three years.

Managing directors (in a limited liability company) and members of the board (in a stock corporation) are subject to non-competition obligations during the term of their appointment. However, when the appointment has ended, non-competition obligations exist only to the extent that they have been expressly agreed upon by the director (member of the board) and the company. The same applies to employees. According to statutory labour law post-contractual non-competition agreements with respect to employees are only enforceable if the non-competition obligation does not exceed two years and if the employee is entitled to a compensation at a rate of at least half of his contractual salary. These rules are not directly applicable to managing directors and board members as these are not deemed to be employees of the company and their relations with the company are not governed by labour law. However, it has become increasingly common that similar provisions are agreed upon contractually with respect to managing directors and members of the board. The purchaser of a business should therefore check in all cases, whether the post-contractual obligations of the managing directors (members of the board) are in line with what he requires.

Additionally, the statutes of limited liability companies or limited partnerships may contain non-competition clauses at the expense of shareholders. The purchaser of shares is bound by such provisions as he acquires the shares with all rights and obligations attached to them by the statutes of the company. This is relevant for the purchaser mainly if he does not acquire a majority of the voting rights sufficient to modify the statutes. It should be noted, however, that the scope of non-competition clauses imposed on shareholders is limited by the general laws against restraints of competition. Whether such clauses are enforceable or not must therefore be examined under these laws.

12.21 Environmental Considerations

There are a large number of environmental protection regulations which affect businesses. They relate in particular to the emission of gases and noise, the disposal of waste water in canals, rivers and lakes, the removal of waste and the avoidance of ground pollution. Many businesses do not completely fulfil these requirements. In particular there are many properties which have been polluted with oil or other chemicals.

The clean-up of such polluted property can be expensive and it may be appropriate for the purchaser to thoroughly enquire the potential costs. Regularly purchasers require guarantees that the requirements of environmental protection have been fulfilled. Occasionally local authorities have in the past quietly tolerated an illegal situation but there is no guarantee that this practice will continue once the business has been sold.

12.22   Employee Superannuation/Pension Plans

Many businesses have pension commitments; these are often covered by insurance. In many cases, however, businesses have made accruals only for their future pension obligations. The accruals are a balance sheet item; normally there is no specific funding of these accruals. Instead they are balanced by the totality of assets and thus are not necessarily readily available. Furthermore, the accruals are not always adequate. The buyer must check this matter with particular care in the due diligence and in many cases it is appropriate to obtain an actuary's opinion. According to the Company Pensions Act pension promises are regularly non-forfeitable if the employee from the granting of the promise has been active in the business for ten and more years. The details are regulated by law. The non-forfeitability has an effect for the purchaser even in asset deals, because the employment contracts are automatically transferred to him with all rights and obligations.

12.23   Employee Rights

The rights of the employee are to be found:

- in employment contracts and generally established business practice;

- in agreements between the business and the works council (works agreements);

- in contracts concluded between the business and a trade union, or between an employers' union to which the business belongs and a trade union (collective bargaining agreements); and

- in statutory law.

Some foreign purchasers of businesses are surprised by the extent of employee rights in Germany and the difficulties which arise in terminating employment contracts. Employment contracts can, as a rule, be terminated only if there are particular reasons relating to the individual employee or if the termination is necessary for operational reasons. The burden of proof lies with the employer. Note also that businesses with more than 500 employees must, as a rule, have a supervisory board in which the employees are represented. If the business has more than 2,000 employees, the supervisory board must have the same number of employee-elected members as shareholder-elected ones. The supervisory board plays an important role. In particular it has competence over the formation and supervision of the management board of the GmbH and the AG. A wide range of significant business operations requires the supervisory board's consent. In addition, the management board must supply the supervisory board with numerous reports on the business's economic situation.

The rights under the law governing employee inventions also belong to the legal rights of employees. Employees, who, in carrying out their obligations under their employment contract, have collaborated in an invention, in particular one which leads to a patent or a utility model, have a claim to special remuneration, comparable to a licence fee. That may have considerable economic consequences for businesses conducting intensive research.

12.24   Compulsory Transfer of Employees

In the case of a share deal, the transaction does not change the legal relationship between the target business and its employees. The changes at the shareholder level have basically no influence on the legal relations of the company to third parties. In an asset deal, however, the contractual rights and obligations of the seller are transferred to the buyer, only by virtue of specific agreements or of specific legal regulations. Such a specific regulation is contained in the German Civil Code (*Bürgerliches Gesetzbuch* [BGB]) under which in the case of the transfer of a business or of an entire separate part of a business all employment contracts are transferred to the buyer, including all those employee rights arising out of works agreements and collective bargaining agreements. Employees can, however, oppose the transfer of their employment contracts. Neither the purchaser nor the vendor can validly terminate employment contracts on the ground of the transfer of the business. In practice the vendor sometimes tries to reduce the personnel of the target business at an early stage of the intended transaction when the context with the transfer of the business is not yet apparent. In any event the continuance of labour contracts may constitute a considerable burden and the SPA should deal with attribution of this risk.

12.25   Tax Deductibility of Acquisition Expenses

The costs of acquisition of a business consist of financing and other costs. Financing costs are, for example, interest for a loan taken out for financing the purchase price or the discount which the loan creditor retains. Other costs are, for example, costs of carrying out the due diligence, advisors' costs and the costs of concluding the sale and purchase agreement and the winding-up of contracts. The financing costs are treated as operational expenses by the German tax authorities. If the purchaser is subject to German taxation, these costs accordingly reduce the taxable income of the purchaser in Germany. According to the consequences for the foreign purchaser under a double taxation treaty between Germany and the purchaser's home state, it can be in his interest to set up a German holding company as acquisition vehicle to acquire the German business. The other costs must be differentiated: according to the circumstances of the individual case they may have to be considered as ancillary acquisition costs which have to be capitalized by the purchaser. They may, however, be treated in other cases as immediately deductible operating expenses. The latter applies in particular for advisors' costs and due diligence costs. To the extent that the costs are not operating expenses, they are in the case of an asset deal to be allocated to the acquired assets and increase the depreciation volume.

12.26   Levies on Acquisition Agreements and Collateral Documents

The acquisition of businesses is not as such subject to tax. However, property acquisition tax at the rate of 3.5 per cent of the property value applies if:

- real property has been acquired in an asset deal; or

- at least 95 per cent of the shares have been acquired in a company or partnership which is the owner of real property.

The sale and purchase of shares in a GmbH requires certification in due legal form by a notary (notarization as a deed). The same is true for an asset deal when the assets comprise real property. The notarial fees depend on the value of the transaction and can be considerable. The maximum notarial fees for notarising a share deal with a value of EUR 60 million or more amount to EUR 52,274.00 plus Value Added Tax (VAT). If certain ancillary acts are notarized, too, additional notarial costs may arise.

If real property belongs to a business which is being sold in an asset deal, the form requirement extends not only to the real property of the business. Instead, all other transactions which are economically inseparably connected with the sale of the real property are also to be notarized as a deed. In most cases the whole acquisition therefore requires notarization as a deed. A separation of the transaction into real property purchase agreements which are to be notarized as deeds on the one hand, and in contracts for other assets which would not, as such, require notarization on the other, does as a rule not work.

12.27   Financing Rules and Restrictions

A GmbH must have a share capital of at least EUR 25,000 (reduction to EUR 10,000 under discussion and likely to be implemented in 2007); an AG must have a share capital of at least EUR 50,000. Fundamentally there is nothing to stop further financing requirements of the company being covered by a loan. Loans can be provided by credit institutions and by other third parties, including shareholders. If the shareholders grant a loan to the company when an ordinary prudent businessman would have contributed capital, this loan is treated fundamentally as owners' equity and cannot be asserted as a creditor's claim in bankruptcy of the company.

The thin capitalization rules of corporation tax law require that the debt-to-equity ratio in any company, operative or not, does not exceed 1.5:1. The German treasury does not otherwise recognize interest payments on company loans as operational costs, but treats them as concealed dividend payments which do not reduce the taxable profit of the German company.

12.28   Exchange Controls and Repatriation of Profits

There are no restrictions on payments from Germany to other countries. Dividends and liquidation proceeds can be freely transferred. The payments must be declared, however, to the *Deutsche Bundesbank*.

Dividend payments of a German GmbH or AG to a foreign shareholder are subject to tax deduction at source. This amounts as a rule to between 10 per cent and 25 per cent. The details are to be found in the double taxation treaties which Germany has concluded with most countries.

12.29 Groups of Companies

Germany has created detailed statutory rules relating to groups of companies ('*Konzern*'). A 'Konzern' is understood to be a number of legally independent companies which are run under the common direction of a controlling company (also called 'parent company'). The law relating to groups of companies was developed first for stock corporations. It covers, however, in the meantime limited companies and even applies to a certain extent to partnerships (see **12.2** above).

If groups of companies are under the direction of a capital company which has its seat in Germany, the parent company must prepare group accounts and a group report. This does not apply if the German parent company is itself a subsidiary of a parent company which has its seat in another Member State of the EU or the EEA and if this parent company itself prepares group accounts and a group report in the German language. The details are regulated by the German Commercial Code (*Handelsgesetzbuch* [*HGB*]).

In certain circumstances, according to case law parent companies can be obliged to assume the subsidiaries' liabilities. Essentially, this applies if the parent company exercises its power of direction continuously and extensively and, in addition, takes no reasonable consideration of the subsidiary's interests.

12.30 Responsibility for Liabilities of an Acquired Subsidiary

Shareholders of a limited partnership are liable to a certain extent for obligations of the partnership. Shareholders of a capital company are not liable for the obligations of the acquired business as a rule (see **12.2** above). That also applies in case of bankruptcy of the acquired company.

Directors can be personally liable for the company's obligations if they did not, contrary to the provisions of insolvency law, file a petition in bankruptcy when the company becomes unable to pay its debts. If they refrained from this following an instruction from the parent company then the parent company may be liable. Neglecting the duty of filing a petition in bankruptcy is in addition a criminal offence. These rules are, to a certain extent, the equivalent to the concept of wrongful trading applicable in other jurisdictions.

12.31 Governing Law of the Contract

German law distinguishes between the obligations created by the sale and purchase agreement and the fulfilment of these obligations (see **12.3** above). This applies to both share and asset deals. The act of fulfilment is subject, according to German International Private Law, to German substantive law as the law where the property is located. As opposed to that, the parties are free to choose the applicable law which is to govern the sale and purchase obligations under the law of obligations. If no express or implied choice is made then the law of that state applies which has the closest connection with the performance. In selling and purchasing a German business, as a rule this will be German law. It can be otherwise, for example if the German business is sold in the context of a transaction which extends to businesses in several states.

It can therefore so happen that in the acquisition of a German business, by virtue of the parties' choice of law, a different substantive law can apply to the agreement under the law of obligations as it can to the acts of performance.

12.32 Dispute Resolution Options

The choice of law has nothing to do with the question of who decides a dispute arising from the transaction.

In business acquisitions the parties often conclude an arbitration agreement; in the absence of such the state courts are competent. The general jurisdiction over a party lies with the court competent for its registered office or place of residence. The parties can also agree, additionally or exclusively, on other fora in or outside Germany.

If the parties wish to have disputes resolved by arbitration they may choose *ad hoc* arbitration where they are free to decide on the procedure in the context of the applicable legislation on arbitration. Since 1998 Germany has a new and modern arbitration law which largely follows the UNCITRAL model law. The parties can instead submit their dispute to arbitration institutions ('institutional arbitration') such as the International Court of Arbitration of the International Chamber of Commerce (ICC), the London Court of Arbitration (LCIA) or the American Arbitration Association (AAA). Increasingly the German Institution of Arbitration (*Deutsche Institution für Schiedsgerichtsbarkeit (DIS)*) is also chosen as the body which is to administer the arbitral proceedings. Germany is a party to the UN convention on the Recognition and Enforcement of Foreign Arbitral Awards of 10 June 1958 ('New York Convention'). Thus foreign arbitral awards are enforceable in Germany subject only to very minor restrictions such as the requirement that the arbitral award is not contrary to the German *ordre public*.

13. HONG KONG

Michael Dalton and Tim Drew, Robert Wang Solicitors

13.1 Introductory Comments

On 1 July 1997, sovereignty over Hong Kong transferred to the People's Republic of China with Hong Kong designated the Hong Kong Special Administrative Region of the PRC. Upon resumption of sovereignty to China, Hong Kong became subject to the Basic Law, which is a mini–constitution applicable to Hong Kong for a period of 50 years following the handover date (i.e. until 30 June 2047). The Basic Law provides that during such time, Hong Kong's capitalist system and way of life will remain unchanged and Hong Kong will have a high degree of autonomy in its internal affairs. Since the handover, it is evident that the change of sovereignty has had little practical effect upon its business community, there being no significant changes in law or otherwise to adversely affect private contractual arrangements.

On the whole, the acquisition of Hong Kong companies and assets by foreign interests is not heavily regulated. There are only a few exceptions (e.g. the acquisition of a broadcasting corporation, a bank or insurance company).

In transactions involving a public company, however, regard must be had to the provisions of the Hong Kong Stock Exchange Listing Rules and the Hong Kong Code on Takeovers and Mergers, which are beyond the scope of this overview.

Hong Kong has a sophisticated business climate and an equally sophisticated regulatory environment to match it. Failure to comply properly with Hong Kong's relevant laws and regulations can have serious, and costly, repercussions. Early advice should therefore be sought whenever an acquisition involving a Hong Kong company or business, or a group which includes Hong Kong subsidiaries or Hong Kong assets, is contemplated.

13.2 Corporate Structures

The target of an acquisition of shares in Hong Kong is likely to be a limited liability company. A limited liability company can be either a private or a public company, and a public company may also have its shares listed on the Hong Kong Stock Exchange.

It is possible to acquire shares or assets from anyone having legal personality and capacity, including private individuals, companies, statutory corporations or the Hong Kong government itself. While a partnership does not have a separate legal personality, it is possible to contract with a partnership so as to bind each of the partners jointly and severally.

© World Law Group
International Business Acquisitions, M. Whalley, F.-J. Semler (eds.), Kluwer Law International, London, 2007; ISBN 9789041124838.

13.3   Letters of Intent and Heads of Agreement

Generally speaking, an agreement can be either oral or written and is binding if it appears either from the document or the circumstances that there is an intention to create a legal relationship and there is consideration given for any promise made or undertaking given by either party. Exceptions for agreements requiring writing include those relating to land.

If it is intended that letters of intent or heads of agreement should not be binding on the parties until the exchange of a more formal contract, clear words should be used to that effect. The expression 'subject to contract' is often used in correspondence to achieve this, but agreements should have more specific provisions inserted to clarify whether, and to what extent, they are intended to be binding.

13.4   Taxes Affecting the Structure and Calculation of the Price

A detailed examination of Hong Kong's business taxes is beyond the scope of this overview. However, a purchase of shares usually results in the buyer potentially inheriting all of the target company's taxation liabilities, whereas a properly structured purchase of assets can avoid this. Appropriate warranties and/or taxation indemnities seek to protect the buyer from unforeseen taxation liabilities of the target in the former case.

In Hong Kong, there is generally no capital gains tax nor is there any withholding tax on interest or dividends received by the buyer.

13.5   Extent of Seller's Warranties and Indemnities

The nature and extent of warranties and indemnities depends on the size of the acquisition and the parties' relative bargaining strengths. However, it is not unusual for sellers to give full warranties and indemnities relating, for example, to the accounts of the business or company to be acquired, title to the assets, taxation, litigation, employee issues etc.

Frequently, the seller seeks to limit the life of the warranties to a specified period. He or she may also seek to limit the maximum amount recoverable under the warranties to the total purchase price or otherwise.

A seller is unlikely to be able to offer unqualified warranties and normally seeks to limit the extent of warranties and representations in the form of a disclosure letter. Matters such as disputed accounts, claims, adverse factors affecting sales, staff problems and debts due where there is the likelihood of non-payment should be set out in the disclosure letter.

It is always desirable to consider whether warranties and indemnities from a seller should be supported by an appropriate guarantee, or by retention of part of the purchase price.

The Limitation Ordinance provides that the limitation of action period is six years from the date of cause of action for breach of the share purchase agreement and 12 years from the date of cause of action for breach of the deed of indemnity.

13.6 Liability for Pre-contractual Representations

Misrepresentations may be actionable and can in certain cases allow rescission of the contract in addition to an action for damages.

Acquisition agreements may attempt to preclude action for negligent misstatement or misrepresentation, leaving the buyer with a remedy only in damages for breach of warranty, but such exclusions often do not protect the seller in cases where the misrepresentation has induced the buyer to enter into the agreement.

Specific contractual provisions which exclude liability for representations made in pre-contract negotiations, and which restrict rights of rescission to the period between exchange of contracts and completion, should cause the buyer to assume that it can only rely upon representations specifically repeated in the agreement, or facts and matters specifically warranted or the subject of indemnities.

13.7 Liability for Pre-acquisition Trading and Contracts

If the agreement includes a retrospective effective date for the purchase, the buyer, for accounting and taxation purposes, bears the loss or is entitled to the business's profits from the effective date.

After completion of a business acquisition (as opposed to a share acquisition), the seller remains liable on contracts to which it was a party unless they are novated and a release given to the seller. Sometimes major contracts are novated, but for many contracts this may not be so practicable. Frequently contracts are assigned with the buyer undertaking to the seller to perform the contracts from completion and to indemnify the seller.

In order to protect the buyer of a business against liability for the business's pre-completion debts and liabilities, it is essential that the provisions of the Transfer of Businesses (Protection of Creditors) Ordinance (requiring among other things the publication of a prescribed notice of transfer) be satisfied.

13.8 Pre-completion Risks

A business acquisition agreement typically contains a provision stating which party bears the risk of loss of assets between signing and completion. Usually, risk remains with the seller so that it must maintain insurance until completion.

On a share acquisition, the matter is usually addressed by way of a warranty that there has been no material adverse change to the business since a warranted accounts date and, if there is, the buyer has a right to rescind.

A refinement of this might involve a provision under which the price is adjusted by reference to the proportion which the lost assets bear to the purchase price.

13.9 Required Governmental Approvals

Governmental approval to acquisitions is generally not required except in certain, more regulated areas such as broadcasting, banking and insurance.

13.10   Anti-trust and Competition Laws

At present, Hong Kong does not have legislation governing anti-competitive practices, though it does have an active Consumer Council which is increasingly drawing attention to restrictive practices and the like.

13.11   Required Offer Procedures

Where the target company is a public company in Hong Kong, the provisions of the Hong Kong Code on Takeovers and Mergers applies.

13.12   Continuation of Government Licences

In certain industries it is necessary for the business operator to have a licence. Licences are required, for example, for the banking, insurance, travel services, gaming and broadcasting businesses. Conditions may be attached to a licence. These need to be reviewed on a change of control of the licence holder and consideration given, for example, over whether this could cause the licence to be revoked.

Licences are not normally transferable so that a buyer of a business (and sometimes even a buyer of shares in a company) must obtain a new licence in its own name. The time taken to obtain the licence may be a relevant consideration.

13.13   Requirements for Transferring Shares

Restrictions on transfers of shares may be found in a company's articles of association or, for example, in a shareholders' agreement. These documents should be reviewed.

Subject to any special provisions in the articles of association, shares are transferable by a simple written share transfer form and contract note. The transfer form and contract note must be stamped (see **13.26**) and approved for registration by the board of directors. Legal title in the shares does not pass until the buyer's name is inserted in the company's register of members.

13.14   Requirements for Transferring Land and Property Leases

In Hong Kong, only leasehold title to land is granted. At present, there is a system of registration of documents affecting interests in land which provides a record of the holders of estates and other interests subsisting in a parcel of land. All contracts for the sale of land must be in writing or evidenced in writing by a memorandum or note and, subject to the payment of the appropriate stamp duty, the contract, together with the conveyance, is registered with the Land Registry.

Title to land can be specifically encumbered by mortgages or charges, or by caveats recording the interests of third parties in the land (such as easements or rights of way), and in many cases title to the land cannot pass and be registered in favour of the buyer until prior encumbrances have been cleared or appropriate consents obtained.

13.15   Requirements for Transferring Intellectual Property

Title to all forms of intellectual property can generally be transferred by assignment.

Where the intellectual property is the subject of registration (which includes trade marks, registered designs and patents), notice of the assignment must be given to the appropriate registry.

13.16 Requirements for Transferring Business Contracts, Licences and Leases

A business contract governed by the laws of Hong Kong is transferable or assignable unless prohibited, for example, by its terms or by necessary implication (such as for a personal contract) or by a provision of law applying specifically to the type of contract in question (e.g. pre-completion assignments of land or companies owning land). Assignment of the benefit of a contract does not release the transferor from the burden of the contract without a specific release from the other party. For this reason, many business acquisitions involve a formal novation of contracts (in which the buyer steps fully into the seller's place and the seller is released from further liability), rather than a simple assignment.

Licences and business leases (e.g. operating leases and hire purchase agreements) should be considered with the above in mind. In most cases, the consent of the other party to the contract (e.g. a lessor) is required before the contract can be assigned. Except for real and intellectual property, it is not normally necessary to register an assignment of a business contract, although notice must be given to the other party that the contract has been assigned.

13.17 Requirements for Transferring Other Assets

With the exception of real property and specific property such as shares, goodwill, intellectual property, trading debtors, the benefit of contracts and those covered by the Bills of Sale Ordinance, assets can generally be transferred by delivery.

Assets that are the subject of a charge in favour of a bank or other creditor, or in which title has been retained by a trade supplier or a seller under a hire purchase or conditional sale agreement, continues to be encumbered in most circumstances by the right of the third parties following transfer to a buyer.

13.18 Encumbrances and Third Party Interests

Assets can be subject to many types of third party interest. Interests can arise under contract (e.g. by a charge or mortgage), by operation of law (e.g. under insolvency) or by virtue of specific registration on a public register (e.g. an encumbrance affecting land).

A buyer for full value (on open market terms) of an asset generally takes good title, unless he or she has actual or constructive notice of an encumbrance or unless the seller does not, in fact, have title to the asset.

Certain title registers can be conclusive evidence of the title of the registered proprietor, but other assets may be subject to unregistered or unascertainable interests which a buyer is not able to discover. In such a case, warranties from the seller as to clear title are essential.

13.19   Minimum Shareholder and Officer Requirements

Every company, whether private or public, must have at least one director. A private corporate body can act as a director, but not if it is a member of a group of companies which includes a company listed on the Hong Kong Stock Exchange.

A company may also be incorporated with just one shareholder. There must not be more than 50 shareholders in a private company, but there is no upper limit for a public company. Every company must have a secretary who must be resident in Hong Kong if an individual or which must have its registered office or a place of business in Hong Kong if a body corporate. From the day on which a company begins to carry on business, or 14 days after its incorporation, whichever is earlier, a company must have a registered office in Hong Kong.

A company incorporated outside Hong Kong which establishes a place of business in Hong Kong is governed by Part XI of the Companies Ordinance. Such company must have at least one person resident in Hong Kong who is authorized to accept service of documents on behalf of the company.

13.20   Non-competition Clauses

Restraint of trade or non-competition provisions given by a seller in the context of a sale of business is generally enforceable, provided that the extent and terms of the restrictions are reasonable. What is reasonable depends upon the circumstances of the case, the nature of the business and the effect which competition could have on the buyer.

Restrictions on employees in employment agreements can also be enforceable if they are reasonable, but the test of reasonableness is likely to be more difficult to satisfy in the case of an employee than of a seller. A blanket prohibition on an employee carrying on his or her occupation or exercising his or her skills is likely to be considered unreasonable, as is a restraint going beyond a short period following termination of employment.

13.21   Environmental Considerations

Hong Kong does not currently have a comprehensive framework of environmental legislation, but this is an area under review by the government. At present, there is legislation relating to air pollution control, waste disposal, water pollution control and noise control administered by the Environmental Protection Department. There are numerous other pieces of legislation which, although not under the authority of that department, also relate to the environment. Substantial penalties can be imposed on businesses which damage the environment and a buyer of a business or of a property can inherit responsibility for rectifying environmental damage.

Certain international treaties can be applicable. They include the Vienna Convention for the Protection of the Ozone Layer and the Montreal Protocol on Substances that Deplete the Ozone Layer, among others.

Appropriate environmental due diligence investigations are always advisable in the context of an acquisition of either shares or assets, particularly in the case of manufacturing and chemical industries.

Warranties in relation to environmental damage and liability should be obtained from a seller, unless the buyer's own due diligence has extended to a full and satisfactory environmental audit.

13.22 Employee Superannuation/Pension Plans

At present, employers are not obligated by law to provide any form of superannuation or pension fund for the benefit of their employees. However, if such a fund is operated, it must comply with the terms of the Occupational Retirement Schemes Ordinance. Tax benefits are granted to such of these retirement schemes as are approved by the Inland Revenue Department. The Mandatory Provident Fund Ordinance obligates almost all employers to provide minimum retirement benefits to their employees.

Superannuation funds are generally controlled by independent trustees but, by the nature of its agreement with its employees, a company may have an ongoing obligation to make contributions to the superannuation fund so as to ensure that the fund will have sufficient assets available to meet its expected obligations for benefits for retiring employees. If, because of adverse market movements or other factors, the fund is underfunded, there may be an obligation on the company to make a specific extraordinary payment to the fund. A buyer must take steps to determine the value of a fund established for employees of a target business where there is an ongoing obligation on the part of the employer company to maintain the fund's assets.

Where the purchase is one of business assets and the employees are to be transferred with the business, special transfer arrangements may be necessary in relation to any provident fund or retirement scheme. Not all retirement schemes provide a mechanism for transfer, and it may be that unless special arrangements can be made, the effect of the transfer of the business will be to require the payment of termination benefits under the scheme.

13.23 Employee Rights

On dismissal by his or her employer by reason of redundancy or lay-off, an employee may be entitled to a severance or long service payment. 'Lay-off' occurs when an employee is not given work on at least half of the normal working days in any period of four consecutive weeks, or one third of the normal working days in any period of 26 consecutive weeks, and the employee is not contractually entitled to be paid for those days without work. 'Redundancy' is dismissal because of the closure or moving of the business, or surplus labour.

The Employment Ordinance provides for a severance payment to be paid to an employee who has been employed under a continuous contract of not less than 24 months and who is dismissed by reason of redundancy or lay-off.

Where the employer is not liable to pay his or her employee a severance payment, an employee with the prescribed minimum length of continuous service may be entitled to a long service payment. The prescribed minimum length of continuous service ranges from five to ten years, depending on the employee's age.

The amount of any gratuity or retirement scheme payment received by an employee is taken into account in the calculation of a severance or long service payment.

Where there is a transfer of business and the previous owner (i.e. the seller) has given notice of termination or paid wages in lieu of notice to an employee, that employee is not considered dismissed if he or she unreasonably refuses an offer of employment by the new owner (i.e. the buyer) on the same terms or on terms that are no less favourable. Such offer must be made not less than seven days before the date on which the contract of employment terminates. Where ownership in a business has been transferred, the continuity of service accrued by an employee is not broken by the entering into of a contract of employment with the new employer.

13.24 Compulsory Transfer of Employees

It is possible for the buyer of business assets to 'cherry pick' employees, leaving the seller to continue to have responsibility for any employees to whom offers are not made.

Employees of a company where the shares are acquired by a buyer, however, continue to have rights previously enjoyed, notwithstanding the change in the ultimate ownership of the company, and the company continues to be liable for employee pay and benefits both before and after the date of acquisition of its shares.

13.25 Tax Deductibility of Acquisition Expenses

Acquisition expenses are only deductible to the extent that they are incurred in the production of assessable profits. Expenses incurred in the acquisition of capital or a capital asset, such as shares or business assets, are not deductible. Hong Kong has no capital gains tax, and profit arising from the sale of capital assets is generally not chargeable to profits tax.

13.26 Levies on Acquisition Agreements and Collateral Documents

Stamp duty in Hong Kong is always relevant to business and share acquisitions. Stamp duty is levied in relation to Hong Kong shares (at the rate of 0.2 per cent, plus HKD5.00 for each instrument of transfer) or immovable property situated in Hong Kong (at variable rates of duty up to a maximum of 3.75 per cent). Nevertheless, provided certain requirements are satisfied, stamp duty is not chargeable on the transfer of Hong Kong shares or immovable property from one associated body corporate to another. Therefore, it is important to finalize the intended structure before the acquisition.

On a sale of a company, value shifting, such as the 'deferred share trick', is still practised from time to time in Hong Kong. This is a stamp duty avoidance scheme originally developed in the UK. Under this scheme, the existing shares in the subject company are converted into commercially valueless deferred shares. New common shares (with the normal rights and privileges attached) are then issued to the intended buyer and an option is granted to the buyer to purchase the deferred shares for a nominal consideration. Little or no stamp duty is paid on the transfer of the valueless deferred shares. Although not specifically covered by the Stamp Duty Ordinance, it is possible that value shifting may, in the future, be held by the courts to be inappropriate tax avoidance, and therefore such schemes are not generally recommended (especially for purchasers) unless certain other circumstances exist.

13.27 Financing Rules and Restrictions

Hong Kong's tax laws provide deductions for relevant interest on money borrowed for the purpose of producing assessable profits and expenses connected with such borrowing.

Dividends received from a corporation chargeable to profits tax are generally not taxable in the hands of the shareholders. Dividends from sources outside Hong Kong are not subject to profits tax.

Subject to certain exceptions, Hong Kong's Companies Ordinance prohibits giving a company financial assistance for the acquisition of its own shares or the shares of its holding company. Most financial arrangements (including the novation or assignment of debt or the giving of guarantees) constitute financial assistance for this purpose.

In the case of an unlisted company, there is a relaxation procedure specifically available which permits such a company to give financial assistance for the acquisition of its own shares or shares in an unlisted holding company provided certain conditions are met. The rules are complex. In brief, the net assets must not be reduced by the financial assistance or, to the extent that they are reduced, the amount of the reduction must not exceed the amount of the company's distributable profits as defined. The transaction requires the approval by the shareholders of the company proposing to give the financial assistance and, where the acquisition is of shares in a holding company, also the approval of the shareholders of the holding company and of each intermediate holding company. Statutory declarations from a majority of the directors of each of the companies are also required.

13.28 Exchange Controls and Repatriation of Profits

There are no exchange controls in Hong Kong.

13.29 Groups of Companies

A company incorporated under Hong Kong's Companies Ordinance is required to prepare annual consolidated accounts (profit and loss account and balance sheet) for itself and its subsidiaries. For these purposes, a company is a subsidiary of another (the holding company) where the amount of shares held by the holding company is more than 50 per cent of the subsidiary's issued share capital, or is such as to entitle the holding company to more than 50 per cent of the voting power in the subsidiary, or the holding company has power directly or indirectly to appoint the majority of the subsidiary's directors.

A company incorporated under the Companies Ordinance must ensure that its financial year and the financial years of its subsidiaries are synchronized and it is therefore not possible, without the specific consent of the Registrar of Companies, for group companies in Hong Kong to have different balance sheet dates. It is not, however, required that a Hong Kong subsidiary of a foreign holding company should have a common balance sheet date with its parent, although accounting or company laws binding on the foreign parent in its home jurisdiction may require this.

13.30 Responsibility for Liabilities of an Acquired Subsidiary

Shareholders in Hong Kong are generally insulated from liability for the debts of a company in which they hold shares, other than in circumstances where a specific guarantee, indemnity or other undertaking has been given in favour of a creditor. As a general rule, the only liability upon shareholders is the payment of uncalled capital on shares held by them in the subject company.

13.31 Governing Law of the Contract

Hong Kong courts generally honour a choice of law freely made between parties to a contract. They do not insist on applying Hong Kong law to a contract for the acquisition of shares or business assets in Hong Kong, although a choice of law having no commercial or reasonable connection with the parties or the agreement may be disregarded on grounds of public policy in certain circumstances.

While a foreign law may govern the agreement and the relationship between the parties, Hong Kong law usually deals with other questions such as the effect of a transfer of title to shares or other assets, or the rights of creditors and others.

13.32 Dispute Resolution Options

The Labour Relations Ordinance lays down formal procedures for solving industrial disputes, and the Labour Relations Division of the Labour Department offers a conciliation service for settlement. The Labour Tribunal has jurisdiction to adjudicate monetary claims.

14. INDIA

Satwinder Singh
Vaish Associates

14.1 Introductory Comments

Increasing integration with the global economy, a surge in cross border activity both by Indian companies expanding abroad and multinational companies looking at India, and renewed business confidence with ample availability of funds has made India one of the hottest spots in the area of mergers and acquisitions. India, reportedly, has had the highest growth rate in mergers and acquisition activity across the globe.

The terms 'merger', 'amalgamation', 'takeover' and 'acquisition' used in relation to business combinations carry generally synonymous connotations and can be used interchangeably. In India, however, the law distinguishes between takeover and acquisition by way of merger, demerger or reconstruction.

'Acquisition' in a business sense means purchase by one company of a controlling interest in the share capital of another existing company. A 'takeover' is an acquisition and both terms are used interchangeably. 'Merger' is defined as a combination of two or more companies into a single company where one survives and others lose their existence. 'Demerger' is defined as a process by which one company disposes of one or more of its undertakings to another existing company or a new company formed for the purpose.

Corporate acquisition attracts public interest by involving different parties-shareholders, employees, consumers and creditors. Therefore, in order to safeguard the public interest in economic activities, mergers and acquisitions are regulated by the provisions of various enactments/regulations in India. These are the Companies Act 1956 (the Companies Act), the Industries (Development & Regulation) Act 1951 (IDRA), the Foreign Exchange Management Act 1999 (FEMA), the Sick Industrial Companies (Special Provisions) Act 1985 (SICA), the Income Tax Act 1961 (ITA), the Securities Contracts (Regulation) Act 1956, the Securities and Exchange Board of India Act 1992 (SEBI Act), and the Securities and Exchange Board of India (Substantial Acquisition of Shares and Takeovers) Regulations 1997 ('Takeover Regulations').

14.2 Corporate Structures

The most common form of legal entities in India are private limited companies and public limited companies. The public limited company can be a closely held company or may be a listed company, the shares of which are listed on any of the recognized stock exchanges and have at least 25 per cent public shareholding (10 per cent in case of infrastructure companies). The company is a separate legal entity in the eyes of the law

International Business Acquisitions, M. Whalley, F.-J. Semler (eds.), Kluwer Law International, London, 2007; ISBN 9789041124838.

and is governed by the provisions of the Companies Act. It can enter into contracts, and buy and sell shares and assets in its own name. The target of an acquisition of shares in India is likely to be a limited liability company.

The major distinction between public limited and private limited companies is that, in the case of a private limited company, the number of members is limited to a maximum of 50 and there is a restriction on the rights of its shareholders to transfer its shares. Further, a private company prohibits any invitation to the public to subscribe for any shares in, or debentures of, the company or to invitation or acceptance of deposits. However, a private company can accept deposits from its members (that is, registered shareholders) and/or directors subject to provisions in the articles of association of the company. There are no such restrictions in the case of a public limited company

In addition to amalgamation of companies incorporated in India (Indian companies), the Companies Act also envisages an amalgamation between a foreign company or a branch of a foreign company, as a transferor company, with a company incorporated under the Companies Act, being a transferee company. Mergers between branches of foreign companies in India with Indian companies have been sanctioned in the past, pursuant to the Companies Act.

14.3 Letters of Intent and Heads of Agreement

Letters of intent and other forms of preliminary documents like term sheet or memorandum of understanding are entered into, after the basic terms are settled between the parties which set the ground rules for detailed negotiations.

It is open to the parties specifically to exclude enforceability of the heads of agreement, letter of intent/term sheet/memoranda of understanding by an express clause stating that where such a document does not materialize into an acquisition contract as intended, the parties shall not be liable to each other for any specific performance of the obligations stated in it.

After signing of such preliminary document like term sheet/letter of intent, the parties formulate the scope of the due diligence exercise to be conducted. But before the signing of such preliminary document, a buyer conducts an informal and preliminary due diligence of the company in question to make a decision to take the deal to the next stage of discussions. The need to carryout a due diligence exercise stems from the legal concept 'caveat emptor'—let the buyer beware.

The present law does not recognize contractual mergers. The mergers have to be sanctioned by the High Courts of the respective States in which the companies being merged/amalgamated are registered. There is a proposal to amend the Companies Act to allow contractual mergers, which will legitimize mergers among group companies as well as closely held companies, without the approval of High Courts as required currently.

14.4 Taxes Affecting the Structure and Calculation of the Price

A crucial part of any merger and acquisition transaction is the tax incidence on the shareholders and the companies. The tax incidence is mainly on account of capital gains taxes (income tax), sales tax/value added tax and stamp duty.

In India, there are no state level income taxes and the ITA is the central income tax legislation. An Indian company presently is liable to tax on its net profits at applicable rates as specified in the annual Finance Act (there is a temporary surcharge and additional surcharge also at present). Certain specific heads of income such as long term capital gains, royalties/technical know how fees in case of non-residents etc. are taxed on a stand alone basis at different rates. The tax incidence varies in the various modes adopted for the restructuring exercise and could be a crucial factor in deciding on a particular mode of restructuring.

The various modes and the tax incidence are briefly discussed below:

Mergers/demergers requiring High Court approval

Transfer of assets by one company to another in an amalgamation or demerger that fulfils the specific requirements set forth in the ITA do not attract capital gains tax if the transferee company is an Indian company. The shareholders of the transferor company are also not liable to capital gains tax on the exchange of their shares with shares in transferee company. The transaction is practically income tax neutral. There is also no levy of sales tax/value added tax in such cases. However, in certain cases stamp duty may be payable to the concerned State Government as explained hereinafter in para 14.26.

Piecemeal asset acquisitions

In an asset acquisition, where only certain assets are purchased from the transferor company, the gains realized by the transferor company from a sale of assets will be subject to tax in India. The incidence will depend upon several factors like period of holding of the asset, its entitlement for depreciation and nature, and whether it is movable or immovable. Such sale may also attract sales tax/value added tax as well as stamp duties.

Slump sale

When an entire unit or undertaking is sold on a going concern basis for a lump sum consideration, without values being assigned to the individual assets and liabilities, the sale is described as slump sale as opposed to piecemeal sale or acquisition of assets. Capital gains tax is levied on the difference between the sale consideration and net worth of the undertaking as of the date of the transfer.

As opposed to sales of individual assets, a slump sale is more tax efficient because it does not attract sales tax/value added tax, which is otherwise levied on sale of individual assets. Stamp duty may, however, be payable on the transfer of assets involved in the slump sale.

Share acquisitions

When the shares of a company are acquired by an entity from its existing shareholder, the seller will be subject to capital gains tax on gains realized by it from such transfer.

Long term capital gains arising from transfer of shares held for a period of more than 12 months from the date of acquisition are taxed at rates lower than short-term capital gains. However, sale of long term listed securities on a recognized stock exchange in India is not subject to capital gains tax, and a nominal rate of securities transaction tax on the transaction value is payable each by the transferor and the transferee. Short-term capital gains are taxed as part of the total taxable income of the entity at normal rates. However, short-term capital gains of listed securities transacted through a stock exchange attract a concessional rate of capital gains tax. Further, securities transaction tax would be payable each by the transferor and the transferee.

Cross-border taxation issues

India has entered into Double Taxation Avoidance Agreement (**DTAA**) with various countries which eliminates/minimizes dual tax levy in international transactions between residents of India and the relevant country and extends certain beneficial rates of taxation. Income arising from an international transaction between two associated enterprises, one or both of whom are non-residents, is computed in accordance with the arm's length price as per the transfer pricing regulations incorporated in the ITA.

Depreciation and Carry forward and set off

In an amalgamation/demerger, aggregate depreciation is calculated at the prescribed rates as if the amalgamation/demerger had not taken place. The depreciation is then apportioned between the transferor and transferee companies in the ratio of the number of day's usage during the year.

In the case of a slump sale or of acquisition of identifiable assets, only the transferee company is entitled to the benefit of depreciation on the assets transferred during the year on the acquisition cost.

In an amalgamation, it is possible for the transferee company to carry forward and set off the unabsorbed depreciation and losses of the transferor company for a specified number of years if it fulfils certain conditions stipulated in the ITA. In a demerger, where losses carried forward or unabsorbed depreciation are directly relatable to the undertaking being transferred, then the same are allowed to be carried forward and set off in the hands of the transferee or the resulting company. Where such loss or depreciation is not relatable to the undertaking being transferred, it is allocated in the ratio of assets transferred to assets retained. Unabsorbed depreciation and losses cannot be transferred to the transferee company in the case of a slump sale or share acquisition.

Deductions

In the case of amalgamations/demergers which fulfil the conditions set out in the ITA, certain special deductions with regard to amortization of cost of patents & copyrights, technical know-how, licenses to operate telecommunication services, certain preliminary expenses etc. which were initially available to the transferor company, can be utilized by the transferee company for the residuary period for which the benefit was originally available.

14.5 Extent of Seller's Warranties and Indemnities

The acquisition agreement usually contains detailed warranties and representations by the seller. The purchaser has relied on the same and no investigation or analysis shall absolve the seller from or detract from the validity or enforceability of the sellers' representations and warranties. Such representation and warranties are based on the result of the due diligence exercise and other disclosures made by the transferor company. The warranties and indemnities normally relate to the accounts of the business of the company to be acquired, proper authorizations, compliance with applicable laws, title to the assets, taxation, litigation, employee issues etc. It is advisable to define clearly the consequences of a breach of warranty, including the invocation of indemnity. Generally the seller seeks to limit the life of the warranties to a specified period, usually one to two years, and the maximum amount recoverable under the warranties to the total purchase price or otherwise. The seller's warranties and indemnities can be secured by third party guarantees or retention of part of the purchase price. The issuance of guarantees by an Indian entity in favour of a foreign entity, except in certain circumstances and repatriation of indemnity amount to a foreign entity require prior approval of Reserve Bank of India (RBI).

14.6 Liability for Pre-contractual Representations

Any agreement the object of which is immoral or contrary to public policy or which involves or implies injury to the person or property of another is unlawful. Every agreement the object of which is unlawful is void. An exclusion of liability for any inaccuracy or misleading statement in the information provided to the buyer in an agreement which is void will not be enforceable.

Normally, in acquisition agreements, a responsibility statement is included wherein the directors of the seller company confirm, and accept responsibility for, the information contained in the agreement, that the information contained therein is in accordance with the facts, and no material fact has been omitted. Such a responsibility statement/representation survives the termination of such acquisition agreement.

14.7 Liability for Pre acquisition Trading and Contracts

The distinction between the transfer date (also called the appointed day) and the effective date in the case of a share acquisition or merger is very important. The transfer date is the date on which assets and liabilities of the transferor company/undertaking vest in or are deemed to vest in the transferee company. The effective date is the date on which the last of the approvals shall have been obtained. Generally, as from the transfer date, the transferor company is deemed to have carried on and to be carrying on all business and activities and to stand possessed of the properties to be transferred on behalf of and for the account of the transferee company until such time as the acquisition becomes effective on receipt of the last of the approvals. The profits accruing to the transferor company or losses arising or incurred by it, on and after the transfer date, are treated as the profits or losses of the transferee company.

In a merger, the contractual and other obligations and liabilities (subject to certain limited exceptions) of the transferor-company are vested in the transferee company pursuant to the scheme of merger, upon being sanctioned by the court. The court order has the effect of vesting such contractual and other obligations and liabilities in the transferee company.

The Securities and Exchange Board of India (Prohibition of Insider Trading) Regulations ('Insiders Trading Regulations') prohibits, among other things, any dealings in securities of a listed company by person who are in possession of unpublished price sensitive information. Mergers and acquisitions are deemed to be price sensitive information under the Insiders Trading Regulations.

14.8 Pre-completion Risks

The question of bearing the risk of loss of assets during the period between signing the acquisition agreement and its completion should be considered by the parties and addressed in the agreement.

There are no fixed rules in this regard, but often the seller is given limited rights to terminate the purchase agreement in the event of a loss of assets. Sometimes, the agreement excludes the buyer's right to rescind the agreement, in which case the buyer must complete the acquisition. The prevailing practice in India is to make provision in the purchase agreement itself, where there is no right to rescind the agreement, for adjustment of the price by reference to the loss suffered by the buyer.

In any event, it is advisable for the buyer, in the case of a business acquisition agreement, to insure the assets with effect from the signing of the agreement. The acquisition agreement often imposes an obligation on it to do so.

14.9 Required Government Approvals

Foreign investment in India is governed by the 'FEMA' which replaced the Foreign Exchange Regulation Act, 1973 (FERA) effective 1 June 2000. Erstwhile FERA was a criminal law while FEMA is a civil law. The major difference under FERA and FEMA is that there was a presumption of *mens rea* under FERA i.e. culpable mental state. The power of arrest and detention has been taken away under FEMA and contravention shall result only in imposition of a monetary penalty and not arrest. Civil imprisonment will be imposed in case of failure to pay the penalty.

Industrial Policy issued by the Government of India and regulations made under FEMA regulate foreign direct investment ('FDI') in India. FDI means investment by way of subscription and/or purchase of securities of an Indian company by a non-resident investor. FDI up to 100 per cent is permitted in Indian companies engaged in almost all industries, except for certain select industries / sectors, under the automatic route (i.e. without requiring prior approval of either RBI or Foreign Investment Promotion Board (FIPB)). In certain sectors however, FDI is permitted under the automatic route subject to prescribed ceilings (called sectoral caps), which are generally in the range of 26 per cent, 49 per cent, 51 per cent and 74 per cent. There may be certain restrictions and/or conditions for some sectors even under the automatic route. Approval of the FIPB is required for investment in certain notified sectors. In addition, the following investments require the prior approval of the FIPB:

- Investments in excess of specified sectoral caps or where FDI is not permitted under the automatic route;

- Investments by any person who has an existing joint venture or technology trans-fer/trademark agreement in the same field as that of the company in which the investment is proposed to be made. However, no prior approval is required if: (a) the investor is a venture capital fund registered with the SEBI, or (b) in the existing joint venture, investment by either of the parties is less than 3 per cent, or (c) the existing joint venture or collaboration is defunct or sick;

- Investment being more than 24 per cent in the equity capital of units manufacturing items reserved for small scale industries;

- Proposals where manufacturing activities requiring a license under the Industries (Development and Regulation) Act, 1951 are proposed to be located outside a radius of 25 km of the standard urban limits.

A person resident outside India may transfer the shares held by him in Indian companies in accordance with the applicable regulations. Recently, general permission is granted for the transfer of shares by way of sale or gift by a person resident outside India to a person resident in India and by way of sale by a person resident in India to a person resident outside India, subject to compliance with certain terms and conditions includ-ing pricing norms and reporting requirements.

Foreign Institutional Investors (FIIs) and venture capital funds are also permitted to invest in shares of Indian companies subject to restrictions and compliances as mentioned under applicable regulations.

In the case of merger or amalgamation of Indian companies or a reconstruction by way of de-merger or otherwise of an Indian company, the RBI has granted a general permission to a merged/transferee company or the new company, to issue shares to its foreign investors subject to the foreign shareholding in the merged/transferee entity not exceeding a percentage specified in the approval granted by the Central Government or the RBI, or prescribed sectoral caps. Where the percentage is likely to exceed the percentage specified in the approval or the prescribed sectoral caps, the transferor company or the transferee or new company may, after obtaining an approval from the Central Government, apply to the RBI for its approval under the regulations. Further, the transferor company or the transferee or new company may not engage in agriculture, plantation or real estate business or trading in TDRs

(Transfer Development Rights); and must comply with the specified reporting requirements.

A business acquisition by way of merger/demerger/amalgamation requires the sanction of the relevant High Courts which have jurisdiction in the state where the transferor company's and transferee company's registered offices are situated. The scheme of amalgamation provides for the transferor company's undertaking, property, assets and liabilities to be transferred to the transferee-company and for the dissolution of the transferor-company.

14.10 Anti-trust and Competition Laws

The existing Monopolies and Restrictive Trade Practices Act, 1969 (**MRTP Act**) which governs anti-trust and competition in India is to be replaced by the Competition Act, 2002 (**Competition Act**). Though the Competition Act has been passed in 2002, only some sections pertaining to constitution of the Competition Commission have been made effective. The relevant provisions pertaining to regulations of combinations are not yet in force. The MRTP Act frowns upon dominance and has laid down an arithmetical test. The Competition Act does not consider a firm's dominance per se inimical to competition, and frowns only upon abuse of dominance. It seeks to regulate agreements that inter-alia control production, supply, markets, technical developments or investment in provision of services. All such agreements are considered anti-competitive and a penalty can be levied.

The Competition Act as and when it comes into force will *inter alia* regulate, through the Commission all anti competitive agreements, or combinations including mergers, amalgamations and acquisitions that may give rise to anti-trust issues, and the abuse of dominant position by an enterprise.

A combination will be regulated beyond a threshold limit. There is also a prohibition on combinations which would cause an appreciable adverse effect on competition within the relevant market in India and such a combination would be deemed to be void. Any person or enterprise which proposes to enter into a combination can approach the Commission for approval of the combination within a period of seven days after the approval of the board of directors of the concerned enterprises for the combination or after the execution of any agreement or other document for acquisition. If the Commission is of the opinion that the combination has, or is likely to have, an appreciable adverse effect on competition within India then the Commission could direct that such combination shall not take effect. If pre-acquisition approval is not given, the Commission has one year to look into the matter on its instigation own or on an application made to it by a third party and, if it so decides, to unravel the transaction.

Under the MRTP Act, however there is no requirement for advance clearance of an amalgamation on the ground of potential monopolistic or restrictive trade practices. If the company's working practices are found to be prejudicial to the public interest or lead to monopolistic or restrictive trade practices, central government is entitled to act according to the law.

14.11   Required Offer Procedures

The provisions of the Takeover Regulations apply in the case of a takeover or substantial acquisition of shares of a listed company. Takeover of a listed company is usually in the form of either direct acquisition of shares from the promoters having a controlling interest or from the public or by a preferential allotment of shares. The regulations prescribe the detailed offer procedure to be adopted and specify instances where the acquirer has to make a public announcement offering to acquire a minimum of 20 per cent of the shares of the company. In addition, regardless of whether there has been any acquisition of shares or voting rights in a company, an acquirer cannot directly or indirectly acquire control over a company (for example, by way of acquiring the right to appoint a majority of the directors or to control the management or the policy decisions of the company) unless such acquirer makes such a public announcement.

The regulations are not applicable in case of an acquisition of shares in a company the shares of which are not listed on any stock exchange. However this exemption is not applicable if, by virtue of an acquisition or change of control of any company, whether in India or abroad, the acquirer acquires control over a listed company.

In the case of a business acquisition by way of merger/amalgamation, there is no requirement of making an open offer. However, the detailed procedure for scheme approval from the High Court must be complied with

14.12   Continuation of Government Licences

Industrial licensing is governed by the IDRA. Pursuant to the New Industrial Policy 1991, industrial licensing has been abolished for almost all industries, irrespective of the level of investment. Businesses which operate in areas involving state security and defence products or which manufacture products of a hazardous nature or luxury goods, or industries which involve significant safety or environmental protection issues, are all subject to compulsory licensing under the provisions of IDRA.

Certain industries are reserved for the small business sector, and will continue to be so reserved. Industries where security and strategic concerns predominate continue to be reserved for the public sector. The industries in respect of which industrial licensing is compulsory are defined on the basis of the Indian Trade Classification, which follows the harmonized commodity description and coding system.

A change in the control of a company as a result of a change in share holding would not lead to the company losing or having to renew or reapply for its existing licences. However, a change in control through the acquisition of a unit or undertaking will require renewing or applying for fresh licences as licences are company specific and not asset specific.

The sanction of the High Court for any business acquisition involving a scheme of amalgamation normally provides for the transfer of all approvals and consents, licences, registrations etc, without any further act or deed, to the transferee-company.

14.13   Requirements for Transferring Shares

Following the introduction of the Depositories Act, 1996 and the repeal of Section 22A of the Securities Contracts (Regulation) Act, which enabled companies to refuse to register transfers of shares in some circumstances, the equity shares of a public company are now freely transferable.

Shares held through depositories are transferred in the form of book entries or in electronic form in accordance with the regulations laid down by the SEBI. Transfers of beneficial ownership of shares held through a depository are exempt from stamp duty.

Pursuant to the listing agreement with the stock exchange/s, in the event that a listed company does not effect a transfer of shares within one month or where it fails to communicate to the transferee any valid objection to the transfer within the stipulated time period of one month, the company is required to compensate the aggrieved party for the opportunity loss caused during the period of the delay.

In the case of companies where the trading of their shares are in compulsory demat/ electronic mode, a shareholder has the right to hold the shares in either physical or electronic form. However, transfer of such shares held in physical form can only take place through the stock exchanges after the shares are converted into electronic form.

In the case of transfer of shares in physical form, a proper instrument of transfer in a prescribed form duly stamped and executed by or on behalf of the transferor and by or on behalf of the transferee and specifying the name, address and occupation, if any, of the transferee along with the certificate relating to the shares is required to be delivered to the company to effect the transfer of shares.

14.14   Requirements for Transferring Land and Property Leases

There is a special law concerning the registration of documents. The object and purpose of the Registration Act, among other things, is to provide a method of public registration of documents so as to give information to people regarding legal rights and obligations arising or affecting a particular property, to preserve documents which may afterwards be of legal importance and to prevent fraud. The instruments for which registration is compulsory include instruments of gift of immovable property; other non-testamentary instruments which purport or operate to create, declare, assign, limit or extinguish, whether in the present or in future, any right, title or interest, whether vested or contingent, of the value of INR100 and upwards, to or in immovable property; leases of immovable property from year to year, or for any term exceeding one year or reserving a yearly rent; and any non testamentary instruments transferring or assigning any decree or order of a court of any award when such decree or order or award purports or operates to create, declare, assign, limit or extinguish, whether in the present or in future, any right, title or interest, whether vested or contingent, of the value of INR100 and upwards, to or in immovable property.

Although the transfer cannot be effected except by registered instrument, as soon as the instrument of transfer is registered it operates from the time from which it would have commenced operating if no registration was necessary. Accordingly the transfer takes effect, retrospectively upon registration, from the date of its execution.

14.15   Requirements for Transferring Intellectual Property

Title to all forms of intellectual property can be transferred by assignment. Apart from assignment, it is also possible to grant a license. A registered trademark as well as an unregistered trade mark can be assigned, whether with or without the goodwill of the business. A trademark can be allowed to be used on a licensed basis for any or all of the goods and services in respect of which it is registered.

A trade mark is a property which can be transferred by a document for consideration, subject to certain provisions in the relevant Act. However, only the person for the time being entered in the Register at the office of the Registrar of Trade Marks as proprietor of a trade mark has power to assign it. When an assignment of a trademark is made, the assignee must apply to the Registrar of Trade Marks to register his or her title.

An assignment in a patent or a share in a patent or a mortgage, license or the creation of any other interest in a patent is permissible. In the case of patents, assignment is valid only when it is in writing and the agreement is reduced to the form of a document embodying all the terms and conditions governing the rights and obligations of the parties to the agreement. The agreement must be filed for registration within a period of six months from its execution or within such further time not exceeding six months as the controller may allow. The application for registration is required to be made by the transferee in the prescribed form.

14.16   Requirements for Transferring Business Contracts, Licences and Leases

Under the Indian Contract Act, as a rule, the benefit of a contract is assignable in the absence of a contrary intention, express or implied, unless the contract does not qualify as a personal services contract. However, the duties under a contract, in the absence of a contrary term, are not assignable under any circumstances without the prior approval of the other party/parties.

In a merger/amalgamation, the contractual and other obligations and liabilities (subject to certain limited exceptions) of the transferor company are vested in the transferee or the surviving company pursuant to the scheme of merger, which is sanctioned by the court. A court order has the effect of vesting such contractual and other obligations and liabilities in the transferee/surviving entity.

In other forms of business acquisitions, it is important to include a provision or agreement for novation of contracts. Novation in the context of Indian laws of contract means the extinguishment of the terms of an earlier contract and the creation of another between new persons, at least one of whom was a stranger to the original contract. It is essential for the principle of novation to apply that there must be mutual consent of all parties concerned.

14.17   Requirements for Transferring Other Assets

Other than immovable property which is incapable of transfer by physical delivery, and certain specific assets like patents, trade names, trade marks or other industrial rights, capital work in progress, investments etc, assets which are movable in nature or otherwise capable of transfer by physical delivery or by endorsement and delivery can be transferred without any deed or instrument of conveyance and become the property of the transferee company once the acquisition is approved by the competent authority.

Assets that are the subject of a charge in favour of a bank or other creditor or in which title has been retained by the seller continue to be encumbered by the rights of third parties following transfer to a buyer in most circumstances.

14.18   Encumbrances and Third Party Interests

The Companies Act requires the registration of certain charges with the Registrar of Companies. Registration identifies the assets which are the subject of the charge, and operates as constructive notice and as a protection to all classes of persons interested in knowing the asset position of the company. It makes the said charges effective against all, including a liquidator. The method of registration under the Companies Act is the filing of particulars of the charge in a prescribed form with the Registrar within the period prescribed. The register of charges is maintained both by the company and by the Registrar of Companies.

The company may satisfy the charge and free its assets. The memorandum of satisfaction is also required to be registered so that the register of charges at all times reflects the true position of the company's assets. Pursuant to the provisions of the Companies Act, 'charge' includes a mortgage. An equitable mortgage or charge created by deposit of title deeds also requires registration under the Act.

If a mortgage or charge which requires registration is not registered, it does not mean that the transaction is altogether void or the debt is not recoverable. The only consequence is that the security created by the mortgage or charge becomes void as against a liquidator and other creditors.

14.19   Minimum Shareholder and Officer Requirements

In the case of public limited companies, there must be at least three directors and seven members (i.e. registered shareholders). Private limited companies must have a minimum number of two directors and two members. For private limited companies, the maximum number of members is restricted to 50.

14.20   Non-competition Clauses

The law in relation to non-competition clauses is primarily based on the common law. The Constitution of India guarantees to all citizens the right to practice any profession or to carry on any occupation, trade or business. The Indian Contract Act expressly provides that every agreement by which any person is restrained from exercising a lawful profession, trade or business of any kind is to that extent void. However, one who sells the goodwill of a business may agree with the buyer to refrain from carrying on a similar business, within the specified local limits, so long as the buyer, or any person deriving title to the goodwill from him or her, carries on a like business within those limits provided such limits appear to the court to be reasonable, having regard to the nature of the business.

Contracts which can impose lawful constraints, if reasonable, can be divided into three classes:

- Contracts of employment, in which an employee agrees that he or she will not, during employment and after his or her employment with the current employer, compete against his or her employer either by entering the service of a competitor or by setting up a rival business on his or her own account. The courts in India, though have upheld non-compete clauses during the course of employment, have not generally approved any such clause after the employment, whether or not such restraint is reasonable;

- Contracts imposing restraints on a vendor of the goodwill of a business who agrees that in future he or she will not carry on a similar business in competition with that of the purchaser; and

- Combinations for the regulation of trade, where the manufacturer or merchant forms a combination to regulate trade relations.

The above statutory principles, which are based on public policy, apply to each of the above cases but not to the same degree.

For all non-compete clauses there should be a time limit prescribed during which the non-compete clause will be effective. Any such clause without any time limit would be against the constitutional right of the parties.

14.21 Environmental Considerations

Environmental laws play crucial preventive and remedial roles and are a prime catalyst for promoting environmentally responsible behaviour. The current environmental laws are complex in nature and put numerous obligations on industries which establish and operate an industrial unit. There are also specific obligations, responsibilities and rights which a business is required to know and comply with while setting up or operating an industrial unit. The main legislation in India protecting the environment are the Water (Prevention and Control of Pollution) Act 1974, the Air (Prevention and Control of Pollution) Act 1981, the Environment (Protection) Act 1986, the Public Liability Insurance Act 1961 and rules made under the said legislation.

The company and its officers are liable to be prosecuted for any violation of these environmental laws.

14.22 Employee Superannuation/Pension Plans

The Employee's Provident Fund and Miscellaneous Provisions Act 1952 provides for the institution of provident funds, employee deposit linked insurance and pensions for workers and their families in factories and other establishments. The Act applies to every establishment employing 20 or more persons and to employees with a wage ceiling of Rs. 6,500 per month.

The Act and the employees' provident fund scheme provided for in the Act are a self-contained code which fixes on the employer the responsibility to deduct contributions from the employee's salary, to contribute an employer's share in equal proportion, and to deposit both contributions to the employee's provident fund account within the time specified in the Act and the scheme. Mandatory compliance with the Act is required and violation attracts criminal penalties.

The Act prescribes the rates of contribution payable by the employer and the employee. The normal employer contribution under the Act is 12 per cent of the basic wages, cost of living allowance and retaining allowance, if any, for the time being payable to the employee, whether he or she is employed by the employer directly or through a contractor. The employee's contribution is equal to the contribution payable by the employer in respect of the employee. If an employee so wishes, he or she may make contributions exceeding 12 per cent of his or her basic wages, cost of living allowance and retaining allowance.

The payment of contributions is mandatory and the Act provides for no exception under which an employer can avoid mandatory liability.

The Act also prescribes the Employee's Pension Scheme for the purpose of providing for:

- superannuation pension, retiring pension or permanent total disablement pension to the employees of any establishment or class of establishment to which the Act applies; and

- widow or widower's, children's or orphan's pension payable to the beneficiaries of such employees.

No separate contribution is payable additionally by the member for the Pension Scheme benefits. The Pension Scheme derives its financial resource by partial diversion from the Provident Fund contribution, the rate being 8.33 per cent. The Central Government contributes at the rate of 1.16 per cent on the wages at the end of the year.

The court is to take into account the employees' interests, and ensure that they are not adversely affected by the scheme and that adequate provision is made for them. In view of this, when reaching agreement for a business acquisition, a clause is generally included so that as far as the provident fund, gratuity fund, superannuation fund or any other special fund created for the employees' benefit of the transferor company are concerned, upon the acquisition becoming finally effective, the transferee company shall stand substituted for the transferor company for all purposes whatsoever in relation to the administration or operation of such schemes or funds or in relation to the obligation to make contributions in accordance with the terms provided in the respective trust deeds. All the rights, duties, powers and obligations of the transferor company in relation to such funds then become those of the transferee company.

14.23　Employee Rights

The Constitution of India guarantees the fundamental rights of persons and citizens. The Directive Principles of State Policy ensure social and economic justice. To achieve industrial harmony and peace, the Industrial Employment (Standing Orders) Act 1946 was enacted to require employers in industrial establishments to define formally the conditions of employment with sufficient precision and to make them known to the workers. The payment of cost of living allowance, enhanced wages and employee's right to reinstatement in cases of illegal and wrongful discharge and dismissal are examples of the obligations created by industrial adjudication through the machinery of the Industrial Disputes Act 1947 or analogous state statutes. Employee rights are also governed by the provisions of the Factories Act, Workmen's Compensation Act, Payment of Minimum Wages Act, Payment of Gratuity Act, Payment of Bonus Act, Provident Fund Act, Maternity Benefit Act and other related labour legislation.

14.24　Compulsory Transfer of Employees

A business acquisition by way of merger and amalgamation is subject to the approval of the court. One of the principles laid down by the Supreme Court of India is that any scheme of merger and amalgamation should not be contrary to public policy. As a general principle, the court must take into consideration the interests of the employees of the two companies so as to ensure that they are not adversely affected by the acquisition and that adequate provision is made so that the workers and employees are not prejudiced by it.

As such there is no specific provision for compulsory transfer of employees in the case of a business acquisition, but adequate compensation as a matter of public policy should be given to non-transferring employees. The employee treatment in case of an acquisition shall depend on the terms of the transaction.

14.25　Tax Deductibility of Acquisition Expenses

Any expenditure incurred by an Indian company on or after 1 April 1999 for the purposes of amalgamation or demerger is allowed as a deduction in five successive years beginning with the year in which the amalgamation/demerger takes place.

14.26　Levies on Acquisition Agreements and Collateral Documents

The rates of stamp duty on instruments (i.e. bills of exchange, promissory notes, bills of lading, letters of credit, policies of insurance, transfer of shares, debentures, proxies and receipts) are specified in entry 91 of the Union List of the Constitution of India. The rates on other instruments are the subject of State legislation. As the revenue from stamp duties is assigned to the States in which they are collected, each State Government has dictated that stamps purchased in that State alone should be used for instruments executed in it. The different rates in different States for sale deeds, mortgage deeds and agreements relating to deposit of title deeds have tempted parties to resort to carrying out their transactions in the State where the rates are low even though the properties may be situated in another State. A company having offices in different States can execute documents creating a charge over its assets in the State where the rate is low and have the copy thereof registered with the Registrar of Companies in the State where its registered office is located. All transfers of movable or immovable property by sale or otherwise and not otherwise specifically provided for under the provisions of the Stamp Act are chargeable as 'conveyances'. Any agreement or conveyance under which any movable or immovable property is transferred to or vested in any other person by a lifetime transfer is required to be stamped as such. Immovable property and intellectual property rights can only be sold by a written instrument and the States generally levy stamp duty thereon as a specific percentage of the market value of the said property. The assignment of copyright does not attract duty as a conveyance in many States. Plant and machinery permanently fastened to the earth constitutes immovable property for stamp duty purposes.

Under the Bombay Stamp Act, a conveyance includes an order made by the High Court under Section 394 of the Companies Act 1956 in respect of the amalgamation of companies. It is liable to stamp duty at 10 per cent of the aggregate of market value of shares issued or allotted in exchange or otherwise and the amount of consideration paid for such amalgamation; provided that it shall not exceed (a) 5 per cent of the true market value of the immovable property of the transferor company located in Maharashtra or (b) 0.7 per cent of the market value of shares issued by the transferee company to shareholders of the transferor company and the amount of consideration paid by transferee company for amalgamation, whichever is higher. Similar amendment has been made by certain other States whereby the definition of 'conveyance' includes an order of the High Court under Section 394 of the Companies Act in respect of amalgamation of companies. In view of the recent judicial pronouncement by the Supreme Court, exemption from levy of stamp duty in amalgamations of companies in other States, where no such similar amendment has taken so far, may become contentious.

The rate of stamp duty is different in different States. Except for some States which have separate Stamp Acts, the Indian Stamp Act applies subject to modification by each State. Stamp duty is normally levied at 0.25 per cent of the value of the shares transferred in a physical mode in India. The transfer of shares in electronic mode does not attract stamp duty. The share purchase agreement generally carries a nominal duty.

14.27   Financing Rules and Restrictions

Recently, companies in India are allowed to buy back their own shares subject to compliance with the regulations made by the SEBI in the case of shares or other securities listed on any recognized stock exchange and in other cases, subject to compliance with the guidelines prescribed by the Central Government. The purchase consideration for the buy back shall only be out of its free reserves, securities premium account or the proceeds of any shares or other specified securities. At present, a company may not buy back more than 25 per cent of its total paid-up capital and free reserves provided that in any financial year, the buy-back should not be more than

25 per cent of its paid-up equity. Further, the ratio of the debt owed by the company should not be more than twice the capital and its free reserves after the buy-back.

No company is permitted, directly or indirectly, to purchase its own shares through any subsidiary company; or through any investment company or group of investment companies

In addition, no public company and no private company which is a subsidiary of a public company are permitted, whether directly or indirectly and whether by means of loan or guarantee, the provision of security or otherwise, to give any financial assistance for the purpose of, or in connection with, a purchase or subscription made or to be made by any person of or for any shares in the company or in its holding company.

However, certain exceptions have been provided under the law for a company to finance the purchase or subscription of its shares of the company for the benefit of its employees. The prohibition on share buy-back does not apply to a buy-back of debentures as the Companies Act gives authority to the company to purchase its own debentures and to keep them alive in the name of a nominee of the company.

However, in exercise of this power, the company may buy any debentures which are convertible into shares. The law also prohibits, without obtaining authorization from the shareholders in general meeting by special resolution and the Central Government's prior approval, the making of any loan, or the giving of any guarantee or security in connection with a loan made by any other person, to or to any other person by any body corporate and acquisition by way of subscription, purchase, or otherwise, the securities of any other body corporate where the aggregate of the loans & investments so far made, the amounts for which the security or guarantee so far provided to or in all other bodies corporate along with the investment, loan, guarantee or security proposed to be made or given by the Board exceeds sixty percent of its paid-up share capital and free reserves or one hundred percent of its free reserves, whichever is more.

14.28 Exchange Controls and Repatriation of Profits

All foreign investments are freely repatriable except for cases where non resident Indians (NRIs) choose to invest specifically under non-repatriable schemes. Dividends declared on foreign investments can be remitted freely through an authorized dealer.

An authorized dealer can allow the remittance of sale proceeds of a security (net of applicable taxes) to the seller of shares resident outside India, provided the security has been held on repatriation basis, the sale of security has been made in accordance with the prescribed guidelines and a no-objection/tax clearance certificate has been produced. Income tax payment clearance is required, but there are generally no delays beyond 60 days. RBI has recently granted general permission for the transfer of shares by way of sale or gift by a person resident outside India to a person resident in India, subject to compliance with certain terms, conditions and reporting requirements.

There are generally no restrictions on remittances for debt service or payments for imported inputs.

The condition of dividend balancing (which requires that foreign exchange needed for dividend payments be matched by equivalent export earnings) is applicable in case of 22 specified industries in the consumer goods sector and in other activity as stipulated by Secretarial for Industrial Assistance in terms of Industrial Policy and Procedures. There is no restriction as to the rate of dividend on equity shares under the foreign exchange regulations. However, the rate of dividend on preference shares or convertible preference shares under foreign direct investment should not exceed 300 basis points over the State Bank of India's prime lending rate, prevailing on the date of the meeting of the board of directors in which the issue of such shares is recommended.

The Indian rupee is fully convertible for current account transactions. Capital account transactions are open for foreign investors, subject to various clearances. With growing foreign exchange reserves, the Indian government took additional steps to relax foreign exchange and capital account controls for Indian companies and individuals. For example, individuals are now permitted to transfer abroad for any purpose up to USD 25,000 (expected to increase to USD 50,000) without approval for any capital account transaction.

14.29 Groups of Companies

The Companies Act prescribes certain restrictions for inter-corporate loans, investments and guarantees. However, certain exceptions have been provided where the loan is made or the guarantee is given or security is provided by a private company (unless it is a subsidiary of a public company); where a loan is made by a holding company to its wholly owned subsidiary; or a guarantee is given or security provided by a holding company in respect of any loan made to its wholly owned subsidiary; where the principal business of the company is the acquisition of shares, stock, debentures or other securities or where it is a banking company or insurance company; or a housing finance company or a company established with the object of financing industrial enterprises or providing infrastructure facilities.

The law also places an obligation on a holding company to attach to its balance sheet a copy of the profit and loss account and balance sheet of each subsidiary along with a copy of the report of its auditor and board of directors and a statement of the holding company's interest in the subsidiary. The Companies Act also prescribes the manner and content of the documents to be attached where the financial year of the holding company and subsidiary do not coincide.

14.30 Responsibility for Liabilities of an Acquired Subsidiary

One of the characteristics of a company is that it is a distinct and independent person in law and is empowered with special rights and privileges. The liability of the shareholders of limited liability companies is limited to the extent of capital unpaid on their shares or limited to the amount of any amount remaining unpaid towards the guarantee in respect of a company limited by guarantee. The shareholders cannot be made liable under a decree against a company; it is only the company's assets which can be proceeded against. However, the Companies Act as well as various judicial decisions provide for the circumstances in which corporate veil may be lifted and the individual members/directors may be made liable for certain transactions.

These circumstances include when:

- there is a reduction in the number of members below the statutory minimum; or

- an officer of a company signs any bill of exchange, hundi, promissory note or cheque on which the company's name is not mentioned in the prescribed manner (such officer can be held personally liable unless it is duly paid by the company); or

- it appears that any company's business has been carried on with intent to defraud its creditors or any other person or for any fraudulent purpose (the persons who were knowingly parties to the carrying on of the business shall be personally responsible without any limitation of liability for all or any of the debts or other liabilities of the company as the court may direct).

The independence of a subsidiary from its holding company may be pierced if the corporate veil is used by the holding company to violate the law or for any illegitimate purposes.

14.31 Governing Law of the Contract

Common contract terms are found in almost all contracts and tenders with government, local bodies and the private sector in India. These clauses have received judicial interpretation from various courts in India and abroad from time to time and have also stood the test of time. One of these clauses is that the contract is to be governed by the laws of India for the time being in force. In many cases, a standard condition is attached to approvals for foreign collaborations in India providing that the foreign collaboration shall be subject to Indian laws.

14.32 Dispute Resolution Options

With the enactment of the Arbitration and Conciliation Act 1996, the law in India relating to arbitration and conciliation has come of age. The said Act embodies the mature vision of a modern nation and is the product of conceptual thinking and of much debate and consultation. It provides not only for domestic arbitration, but extends to international commercial arbitration. It also consolidates and modernizes the Indian law relating to the enforcement of foreign arbitral awards. It provides for greater autonomy in the arbitral process, and limits judicial intervention to a narrower circumference than under the previous law. Conciliation has been specially included in this legislation, which recognizes the important function of persuading disputing parties to settle their disputes amicably. The Act has taken into account the Model Law and Rules as adopted by UNCITRAL, making a significant contribution to the establishment of a unified legal framework for the fair and efficient settlement of disputes arising in international commercial relations.

15. IRELAND

David O'Donnell & Liam Brazil Mason Hayes + Curran

15.1 Introductory Comments

Ireland is an open economy in the EU and actively encourages overseas investment. Apart from certain sensitive areas such as agricultural farm land, the press and broadcasting, Ireland does not discourage foreign acquisitions.

Ireland has merger control laws which require certain mergers, acquisitions and joint ventures to be notified to the Competition Authority. A transaction may be prohibited from going ahead or may be deemed void if clearance is not sought where it is required.

15.2 Corporate Structures[1]

The vast majority of business entities in Ireland are private limited companies, of which over 138,215 were active as at 31 December 2004. There are fewer than 1,200 public limited companies with only 63 of those at any one time having a quote of sorts (full list, unlisted securities market, mineral exploration market, smaller companies market) on the Irish Stock Exchange.

In addition to Irish registered companies, there is a significant number of registered branches or places of business of overseas corporations (approximately 3,500 as at 31 December 2004). The popularity of such structures sometimes derived from the historically less extensive accounts filing requirements imposed on such corporations, but this has recently been changed.

Unlimited companies are usually used for the purpose of property investments or financial engineering.

Under Irish law, partnerships do not have a separate legal personality.

It is also worth mentioning that co-operative societies (of which there were 1,100 as at 31 December 2004) constitute a significant proportion of the Irish economy, especially in agri-business and fisheries.

15.3 Letters of Intent and Heads of Agreement

Agreements in Irish law may be oral or written, save in the case of real estate where the contract must be evidenced in writing. An agreement is legally enforceable if undertakings are given by either party, consideration is given by the party to whom an undertaking is given (whether by way of cash or kind or mutual undertaking) and there is an intention to create legal relations.

---

1. Information taken from the Companies Report 2004.

International Business Acquisitions, M. Whalley, F.-J. Semler (eds.), Kluwer Law International, London, 2007; ISBN 9789041124838.

It is important, where letters of intent or heads of agreement are not to be binding on parties until execution of a formal contract, that words should be used to that effect. It is also important that in the formal contract there is an express withdrawal of all former letters of intent and heads of agreement. Case law suggests that such provisions in the formal contract may be ineffective to prevent an action for misrepresentation where a misrepresentation has induced a party to enter into an agreement.

The expression 'subject to contract—contract denied' together with an explanatory paragraph is usually placed in the opening correspondence of lawyers involved in the transaction. It is frequently repeated in correspondence and placed on the draft agreements that are put in circulation.

15.4   Taxes Affecting the Structure and Calculation of the Price

This guide does not extend to a full examination of Ireland's taxation system.

A buyer of shares takes over all the target's taxation liabilities, whereas a buyer of assets avoids this (except in the case of stamp duty arising on the acquisition, where liability is likely to attach to the buyer). It is usual for taxation warranties and a tax deed of indemnity to be given by the seller of shares with a view to protecting the buyer from any unforeseen taxation liabilities of the target.

It is worth mentioning that where a target is leaving a group, this may trigger capital gains tax liabilities in the target which otherwise would not have arisen. An indemnity against this taxation liability is usual.

If a non-Irish company acquires business assets in Ireland then, depending on the circumstances, it may find that it must pay Irish taxation on profits attributable to these assets. An acquisition of shares protects a non-resident buyer from Irish taxation, other than that payable by the target on its profits and withholding taxes that may be due on interest, dividends and royalty income received by the buyer.

Stamp duty (ie a document tax) is paid on documents transferring ownership of assets such as shares, real estate, debts receivable, certain intangible assets and certain other items. Stamp duty applies to the higher of the consideration paid and the market value of the assets transferred. Different rates of duty apply depending on the nature of the assets transferred. The rate is 1 per cent in the case of shares and 9 per cent for most other assets. Lower stamp duty rates apply where the market value or consideration paid for assets is less than EUR 150,000. Different stamp duty rates may apply to residential property. This can be an incentive to a buyer to structure an acquisition as a share purchase rather than an asset purchase. Stamp duty in Ireland is a compulsory tax.

The buyer of Irish real estate, business goodwill or mineral exploration rights or shares in a company deriving the greater part of their value from real estate or mineral exploration rights needs to obtain from the seller a certificate of clearance from Irish capital gains tax where the consideration exceeds EUR 500,000. If such clearance is not obtained, then the buyer becomes liable to withhold 15 per cent of the purchase price and pay this directly to the Irish tax authorities.

15.5 Extent of Seller's Warranties and Indemnities

The nature of warranties and indemnities depends on the nature of the business being acquired, the consideration and the parties' relative bargaining power. It is usual for sellers to warrant accounts, title to assets and taxation compliance. Depending on the industry involved environmental warranties may also be given.

It is usual for the seller to seek to limit the amount it is liable for under warranties and indemnities in terms of amount and the time during which claims may be made under them. It is not unusual for warranties and indemnities to be secured by a parent company guarantee or retention of a portion of the purchase consideration.

15.6 Liability for Pre-contractual Representations

Negligent and fraudulent misrepresentations may be actionable. In certain cases, they permit both rescission of the contract and an action for damages. Acquisition agreements frequently seek to exclude all prior representations, heads of agreements or understandings with a view to precluding any action for a negligent misstatement or misrepresentation, and with a view to leaving the buyer with a remedy only in damages for breach of warranty under the acquisition agreement. Recent case law suggests that such exclusions do not protect the seller where the misrepresentation has induced the buyer to enter into the agreement.

15.7 Liability for Pre-acquisition Trading and Contracts

In a share acquisition, pre-acquisition profits may either be paid to the seller by way of dividend or retained in the company, in which case the buyer inherits those profits. For the purposes of Irish capital gains tax and stamp duty liability, the distribution of pre-acquisition profits to a seller may in certain circumstances be treated as consideration upon which capital gains tax or stamp duty should be paid. There are rules restricting the distributability of pre-acquisition profits.

In the case of an asset purchase agreement, the buyer bears the loss or is entitled to the profits from closing or, if the agreement includes a retrospective or prospective effective date, the buyer bears the loss or is entitled to the profits from this date.

In an asset purchase, after closing the seller remains liable under contracts to which it was a party unless they are entered into afresh or are novated and a release given to the seller. Certain contracts may be capable of assignment without the requirement for novation. Usually, major contracts are novated and contracts are undertaken by the buyer with the buyer indemnifying the seller against any liability under the contracts.

15.8 Pre-completion Risks

Irish law does not prescribe where risk lies as between a seller and a buyer of shares. Under the Sale of Goods Acts, risk in 'goods' passes to a buyer of such assets once the agreement comes into effect, although the parties can agree otherwise.

A business acquisition agreement usually contains provisions specifying which party bears the risk of loss of assets between signing and closing. Risk usually remains with the seller so that it needs to maintain insurance until closing. Frequently, a buyer seeks to take over such insurance and a seller seeks to remain a co-insured on the buyer's policy for third party liability after closing.

On share acquisitions there can be a warranty that there has been no adverse change to the business between signing and closing. It is possible to specify that the buyer has a right to rescind. Alternatively, there may well be closing accounts upon the basis of which a price variation may be agreed.

It is usual in Ireland, however, for business acquisitions and share acquisitions to be by way of contract which is signed immediately before closing; therefore, the question of pre-closing risks does not usually arise. Where there is an interval between signing the agreement and closing the transaction, it is usually because of a regulatory requirement, for example clearance under the Irish Competition Act or, in the case of a listed company, approval of the transaction by the company in general meeting, so as to satisfy Stock Exchange regulations.

15.9 Required Governmental Approvals

Since 1 January 2003, Ireland has been subject to a new mergers regime pursuant to the Competition Act, 2002. Under this new regime, the Irish Competition Authority rather than the Minister for Enterprise, Trade and Employment (as was formerly the case) has the power to approve, amend or veto mergers. The Competition Act includes thresholds in respect of the turnover of the parties involved which when exceeded render a merger compulsorily notifiable to the Competition Authority for assessment. The test against which the Competition Authority will assess mergers notified to it is whether the notified merger will result in substantial lessening of competition in the markets for the relevant goods or services within the Republic of Ireland. Public interest criteria are no longer applied (with the exception of media mergers). Where a merger is not compulsorily notifiable, the Competition Act allows parties to notify a merger which does not exceed the thresholds where the parties feel that the merger may give rise to competition issues. This has the effect of throwing a good deal of uncertainty into Irish mergers law as it will necessitate a thorough analysis of a proposed merger in order for the parties to satisfy themselves that a competition issue does not arise even where the thresholds are not met. A merger which is voluntarily notified by the parties is subject to the same procedures as a compulsorily notifiable merger and may not be put into effect until it has been approved by the Competition Authority.

If a compulsorily notifiable merger is not notified, it is void and an offence is committed. Once a merger has been approved by the Competition Authority, it is immune from attack on the basis of non-compliance with Irish Competition law. Where a merger does not exceed the thresholds and is not notified voluntarily, it could be open to attack for breaches of Irish competition law from both the Competition Authority and third parties. There are special provisions dealing with media mergers and the final decision on media mergers rests with the Minister for Enterprise Trade and Employment who must consider public interest issues in dealing with such mergers.

Separately, special clearances are required for the acquisition of 10 per cent or more of a bank and for the acquisition of an insurer, and pre-clearance with the Broadcasting Commission of Ireland is encouraged in the case of acquisitions of any material interest in a broadcasting company to ensure that the licence held by the broadcaster is not revoked.

The purchase of agricultural land in Ireland by a person other than an Irish citizen requires the Irish Land Commission's consent. Where the land is to be used for industry, the consent is always given.

The nationality, residence or domicile of an intending buyer is not especially relevant.

15.10   Anti-trust and Competition Laws

The Irish Competition Authority administers the Competition Act, in addition to dealing with mergers and acquisitions, prohibits anti-competitive agreements and abuse of a dominant position. An anti-competitive agreement is one which has as its object or effect the restriction or limitation of competition in Ireland.

Whilst it is not possible to obtain a formal clearance from the Competition Authority for breaches of the Competition Act, the Competition Authority has the power to issue a declaration that a particular category of agreements complies with certain 'efficiency' conditions listed in the Competition Act and, as such, is exempt from the prohibition on anti-competitive arrangements. The agreements must contribute to the improvement of the production or distribution of goods and services or promote technical or economic progress and may not impose restrictive terms on undertakings which may lead to an elimination of competition. Each declaration sets out specific conditions for its application. The Competition Authority also has the power to issue 'Notices' under the Act and has used such Notices to give an opinion that certain categories of agreement are exempt. A Notice offers slightly less legal certainty than a declaration.

The Competition Authority has, since its institution in 1991, given several decisions concerning acquisitions. It is always useful to refer to its previous decisions in a particular industry when making a filing. The mere taking out of a competitor by a buyer does not of itself transgress the Competition Act. However, matters are looked at carefully if the effect of the transaction is to reduce the number of players in a particular market so that four or fewer parties will control 40 per cent or more of that market.

A proper and careful definition and analysis of the relevant markets affected by an acquisition is essential.

15.11   Required Offer Procedures

Where a corporation agrees to acquire 80 per cent or more of an Irish target company (whether public or private), any holder of the remainder of the shares involved may require the buyer to buy its shares. In the same way the buyer may compulsorily acquire the shares of all such holders.

Under the statutory mechanism of the Irish Take-over Rules, acquisitions of 30 per cent or more of the shares of a listed company trigger the requirement to make a mandatory bid for the remainder of the company's share capital.

15.12 Continuation of Government Licences

In certain industries in Ireland the operator must have a licence. Licences are required for banking, insurance, auctioneering, gaming, broadcasting, milling, investment intermediaries, sale of alcohol, sale of precious metals, slaughter of animals, smelting of ores and stockbroking.

It is important that conditions attached to a licence be reviewed, including whether the licence is automatically revoked or is subject to revocation on the change of control of the licence holder.

Such licences are not transferable; thus, the buyer of a business must obtain a new licence in its name. The timing for obtaining a new licence may be an important point to consider.

15.13 Requirements for Transferring Shares

Restrictions on transfers of shares must exist in the case of a private company in order for it to have private company status. These will be found in the company's articles of association. If there is a shareholders' agreement, it will be important to review it in case there are contractual restrictions on the transfer of shares.

Shares in a limited company may be transferred by a simple stock transfer form executed by the seller. In the case of a transfer of shares in an unlimited company, a deed of transfer executed by the transferor and transferee must be executed. The form must be stamped (stamp duty at a rate of 1 per cent of the higher of the consideration or market value is due on the transfer of shares in limited or unlimited companies) and approved for registration by the board of directors of the company, and the name of the buyer must be inserted in the register of members of the company as the holder of those shares.

15.14 Requirements for Transferring Land and Property Leases

Ireland has two different systems for proving title to land. There is a Land Registry in which title to nearly all agricultural land in the country is registered. There is also a system of proof of title by reference to title deeds (confusingly referred to as the Registry of Deeds system) where one looks at the chain of title proved by various deeds. In the case of registered land, a transfer is executed; in the case of unregistered land, a conveyance (for freehold land) or an assignment (for leasehold land) is executed. Such documents must be stamped with the appropriate stamp duty which will usually be 9 per cent of the higher of the consideration and the market value (save where the consideration or the market value is less than EUR 150,000 in which case lower rates apply). The transfer, conveyance or assignment must be registered at the Land Registry or Registry of Deeds as appropriate. In the case of residential property, different rates of stamp duty may apply. Value Added Tax ('VAT'), Capital Gains Tax ('CGT') and other tax issues may arise depending on the facts.

Title to land may be encumbered by mortgages or charges one the rights of third parties in the land such as easements or rights of way.

15.15 Requirements for Transferring Intellectual Property

Title to all forms of intellectual property can be transferred by assignment. The benefit of a licence to use the intellectual property of a third party may be assignable, but may require the licensor's consent. In the case of a trade mark where there is a registered user agreement or a certification trade mark where there are regulations, such arrangements may need to be novated.

Where the intellectual property is the subject of registration (which includes trade marks, patents and registered industrial designs) notification to the Registrar of Patents and Trade Marks and other formalities may be required.

Stamp duty should not arise on most transfers or licenses of intellectual property. However, VAT, CGT and other taxes may apply depending on the facts.

15.16 Requirements for Transferring Business Contracts, Licences and Leases

Business contracts in Ireland are transferable only in accordance with their terms. The transfer or assignment of the benefit of a contract does not release the seller from the burden of the contract without a specific release from the other party to it. Therefore, many business acquisitions involve a formal renewal or novation of contracts in which the buyer steps fully into the seller's place and the seller is released from further liability, as opposed to a simple assignment. Licences and financial leases, operating leases and hire purchase agreements operate under the same rules.

It is worth noting, however, that leases of real estate are assignable and a lessor may not unreasonably withhold consent to assignment. Once an assignment of such a lease has taken place, the seller is exonerated from further liability under the lease after the next rent payment day.

Typically, the approval of a lessor is needed before the relevant leasing agreement can be assigned. There is no registry of transfers of business agreements, although stamp duty may be payable.

Irish stamp duty and other tax issues may arise on such transfers or assignments depending on the facts in each case.

15.17 Requirements for Transferring Other Assets

Assets can be transferred by delivery save for real estate, shares, goodwill, intellectual property, debts receivable and the benefit of contracts. Assets which are subject to a charge in favour of a creditor (eg a bank) or in which title has been retained by a supplier continue to be encumbered by the rights of such third parties following transfer to a buyer.

Irish stamp duty and other tax issues may arise on such transfers depending on the facts in each case.

15.18 Encumbrances and Third Party Interests

Assets may be subject to many types of third party interests, for example under contract (eg a charge or mortgage), by the operation of law (eg a property right), or by virtue of a specific registration on a public register (eg at the Land Registry).

A bona fide buyer for value, without notice, of an asset generally takes good title to it unless the buyer knows or is deemed by law to know of any encumbrance and unless the seller does not in fact have good title to the relevant asset.

The Land Registry is conclusive evidence of the title of the registered owner. There is no comparable register for any other asset. Therefore, warranties of the seller as to good title are essential. Under contracts for the sale of 'goods' there is an implied warranty in every agreement that the seller has good title and this implied warranty cannot be excluded from the terms of any agreement.

15.19 Minimum Shareholder and Officer Requirements

Private companies must have at least two directors and one or more shareholders. Public companies must have at least two directors and at least seven shareholders. There are no residence or nationality requirements for shareholders. With regard to directors, every company must have at least one Irish resident director unless the company holds a bond in the prescribed form with the Registrar of Companies to the value of EUR 25,395 which can be called upon if the company fails to pay any sums due under either the tax code or the company law code. An alternate director resident in Ireland does not satisfy the requirement to have one resident Irish director.

A private company may not have more than 50 shareholders (save for employees and former employees).

15.20 Non-competition Clauses

Non-compete, non-deal, non-solicit, non-poach and other similar covenants given by a seller in the context of the sale of a business or a company are generally enforceable provided that their terms and extent are reasonable. They also must comply with the rules of the Competition Act so as not to constitute a prohibited restriction or limitation on competition. Generally, the Competition Authority has imposed a limitation of two years on non-compete covenants etc, save where the business involved is high tech when a period of five years can be obtained, for example in the case of the sale of a software company where the seller is the originator of source code. In addition to compliance with the Competition Act, the common law principles of restraint of trade and principles under the written Constitution of Ireland need to be considered. Generally, it is assumed that if the Competition Act is complied with, those principles are also complied with.

Restrictive covenants given by employees in employment agreements are enforceable only to the extent that they are reasonable. A prohibition of an employee carrying out his or her actual occupation or exercising his or her skills is likely to be considered unreasonable as is any restraint going beyond a short period following termination of employment.

15.21   Environmental Considerations

Ireland has in the last 20 years introduced steadily more complex law for the protection of the environment. An Environmental Protection Agency has been established to draw together environmental protection legislation generally.

Businesses are liable to substantial penalties where unauthorized pollution or contamination of the environment results from their activities.

In the case of mining, manufacturing and the chemical and pharmaceutical industries, appropriate environmental due diligence investigations are advisable in the context of the acquisition of either shares or assets. It is not unusual for buyers to obtain copies of press coverage of targets involved in environmentally sensitive industries. This is to gauge the possibility or likelihood of local objections to the continuation or expansion of facilities.

Warranties and in some cases indemnities in relation to environmental damage will be sought, save where the buyer's own due diligence has extended to a full environmental audit.

15.22   Employee Superannuation/Pension Plans

Employee pension schemes tend to be either money purchase schemes, defined contribution schemes or defined benefit schemes. In the case of defined contribution schemes, the enquiry into the fund extends to its proper constitution and the payments required having been made. If the scheme is a defined benefit scheme, then it is important to see that the value of the assets in the pension fund is adequate and that compliance with the Pensions Act's requirement for periodic actuarial reviews has been achieved.

Since 15 September 2005, employers are obliged to provide access for employees (including, for example, part-time, fixed-term contract and seasonal employees) to a new form of pension arrangement known as Personal Retirement Savings Accounts (PRSA) including, for example, where the employer is not operating a pension scheme, eligibility to an existing scheme is limited or where employees have to wait more than six months from the date of joining employment to be included in the existing pension scheme. The employer is only obliged to facilitate access to the PRSA and to facilitate the deduction of employee contributions. The employer is not obliged to make any contribution.

15.23   Employee Rights

As well as an employee's contract of employment, the state can add to the terms of employment of an employee where the employer is involved in certain industries. Joint labour committees established under the Department of Enterprise, Trade and

Employment set minimum wages and other standards of employment, usually in low-paid sectors.

The Employment Appeals Tribunal deals with claims for unfair dismissal. An employee may be reinstated or re-engaged, or awarded damages for unfair dismissal.

In the case of employees who hold an office in the company (eg director or secretary), proceedings for wrongful dismissal can be taken in the event of their being dismissed as such officers (whether or not in conjunction with the termination of their employment).

15.24 Compulsory Transfer of Employees

Ireland has implemented EU Directive EEC 77/187 through the European Communities (Protection of Employees' Rights on Transfer of Undertakings) Regulations 2003 (the 'Regulations') which replace the previous regulations of 1980 and 2000. The Regulations operate in order to safeguard the rights of employees when there is a change in ownership in the business in which they are employed. The effect of the Regulations where they apply to a business transfer is that the employees of the business being transferred will transfer automatically to the buyer along with all rights and liabilities arising out of their employment and on the same terms and conditions of employment in place before the transfer.

The dismissal of an employee is deemed to be automatically unfair if the grounds are the transfer of the business, unless the dismissal can be justified on the grounds of economic, technical or organizational reasons which entail a change in the work force.

The Regulations impose specific obligations on both the seller and the buyer to inform their respective employee representatives affected by the proposed transfer, and where 'measures' are envisaged, a consultation process must also take place within a specified time frame.

The company continues to be liable for employee pay and benefits arising both before and after closing. A buyer may be held liable for a seller's failure to comply with its obligations under the Regulations. It would be usual to seek comprehensive warranties and indemnities from the seller in respect of employees and related matters including the seller's compliance with the Regulations.

15.25 Tax Deductibility of Acquisition Expenses

Where the buyer is not resident or taxable in Ireland, the deductibility of acquisition expenses is decided by the laws of its home jurisdiction.

Where the buyer is Irish resident, acquisition expenses (including stamp duty) are generally not deductible from trading income for the purpose of Irish corporation tax. The availability of an input credit for VAT paid on professional fees incurred in relation to the acquisition will depend on the facts in each case.

15.26 Levies on Acquisition Agreements and Collateral Documents

Stamp duty is always relevant to business and share acquisitions. Stamp duty is at a flat rate of 1 per cent for transfers of shares in companies, whether limited or unlimited, private or public. The rate for transfers of non-residential property and other assets is 9 per cent. Where the consideration or market value, as relevant, is less than EUR 150,000 lower stamp duty rates apply. In the case of residential property, different rates may apply.

There are exemptions and reliefs from stamp duty for certain intra-group transfers and on certain qualifying reconstructions or amalgamations but there are important time limits, restrictions and formalities to be observed.

15.27 Financing Rules and Restrictions

Ireland's companies legislation prohibits a company giving financial assistance for the purpose of or in connection with purchasing its own shares or those of its parent company. Whilst the definition of financial assistance is wide, it is prohibited in connection with purchases or sales of shares but does not apply to an exchange of shares. Private companies that comply with a procedure involving the passing of a special resolution and the directors making a statutory declaration of solvency are able to give such financial assistance. Public companies cannot give such financial assistance.

15.28 Exchange Controls and Repatriation of Profits

There are no exchange controls in Ireland but there are, in line with other EU states, financial sanctions adopted under under the Common Foreign and Security Policy and related EC implementing measures.

Dividend withholding tax was introduced by the Finance Act 1999. The rate of withholding tax is currently 20 per cent, unless an exemption applies. There are a number of exemptions from the withholding tax. An exception from this tax applies to individual persons who are neither resident nor ordinarily resident in Ireland but who are resident in a country with which Ireland has concluded a double tax treaty or an EU Member State (other than Ireland). The exception also applies to companies that are resident in an EU Member State (including Ireland) or with which Ireland has implemented a double taxation treaty. There is also an exemption for companies not resident in Ireland which are ultimately controlled by residents of a tax treaty country or an EU Member State (other than Ireland). Companies whose principal class of shares or the shares of its 75 per cent parent are substantially and regularly traded on a stock exchange in a tax treaty country or an EU Member State (other than Ireland) or such other stock exchange as may be approved by the Minister of Finance, may also avail of the exemption.

To claim the exemption the relevant declaration must be made to the Irish Revenue Commissioners. There is a 20 per cent withholding tax on interest, rents and patent royalties paid to non-residents, subject to certain exemptions and any relevant relief available under double taxation treaties. Ireland has an extensive network of double taxation treaties in place. As at 1 January 2005 there were 44 such agreements in operation and nine new treaties being negotiated.

15.29   Groups of Companies

A group consisting of a parent company and one or more subsidiaries must prepare consolidated accounts (profit and loss account and balance sheet), save in the case of certain groups of private companies with low turnover. Members of the same group of companies must have the same financial year end, although an Irish subsidiary of an overseas company is not bound by this rule.

For tax purposes, it is usually possible to surrender certain tax losses around an Irish group. It should also be possible to transfer assets within the group without crystallizing an immediate capital gains tax liability. From a stamp duty perspective, assets can be transferred between qualifying group companies without giving rise to Irish stamp duty, provided that a number of conditions are met. For VAT purposes it is possible for a group of companies to register as a VAT group in certain circumstances, which results in cashflow benefits and enables the group to make one VAT filing, as opposed to a VAT filing for each company.

15.30   Responsibility for Liabilities of an Acquired Subsidiary

A parent company can be liable for a debt or liability of a subsidiary where that debt or liability is incurred at a time when the company is insolvent or where, in its administration of the subsidiary, the parent company has blurred the distinction between it and the subsidiary. This might occur if the parent company participates in the management of the subsidiary or represents the group to creditors generally, without making clear with which company the creditors are dealing. A failure to convene board meetings in a subsidiary, with decisions being made at parent board level, would be indicative of a situation where liability might be imposed.

15.31   Governing Law of the Contract

Irish courts enforce a choice of law made by parties to a contract and do not insist on applying Irish domestic law to an acquisition in Ireland. However, when a dispute to which the non-Irish law is to be applied comes before an Irish court, logistical issues present themselves such as to how this law is to be proved to an Irish court.

15.32   Dispute Resolution Options

The choice for dispute resolution in Ireland is to go to the courts, or to go through arbitration or some other alternative dispute resolution method. Arbitration is frequently preferred to going to court by reason of its comparative speed. Arbitrations can also be conducted for a longer period of time during a day, whereas judges tend to sit only for two periods of two hours per day. Arbitration is also confidential, whereas most court proceedings are held in open court with no reporting restrictions. It can take over a year before a commercial dispute comes into the Irish High Court lists, whereas it is easier for arbitrations to be set up quickly. However, in January 2004 a new Commercial Court was set up to deal with a wide variety of business related transactions where the value of the claim is in excess of EUR 1,000,000. Issues such as intellectual property cases and commercial 'passing off' claims will also be dealt with. It is expected that the establishment of the new Commercial Court will provide a fast and effective means of resolving commercial disputes.

Ireland is a signatory to the New York Convention. Irish courts enforce and recognize international arbitration awards in certain instances. Parties to a contract are free to adopt the arbitration or mediation rules of any Irish or international body in their contracts. Generally, the courts do not entertain a dispute until the arbitration option has been exhausted. Ireland is a party to the Brussels Convention on the Enforcement of Judgments.

Mediation is also gaining in popularity as a means of avoiding lengthy and costly litigation.

15.33   Other Issues

Ireland has an extensive structure of grant support to industry. The main agency is the IDA. It has satellites for certain areas such as the Shannon Free Area Development Company (otherwise known as SFADCo) and Udarás na Gaeltachta for the Irish or Gaelic speaking areas, most of which are on the western seaboard. There are always change of control provisions in the grant agreements. Therefore, if an acquisition proceeds without pre-clearance from the relevant agency, the amount of the grant may need to be repaid in full or in part. Generally speaking the clawback period for grants is ten years. The seller of a target may be a guarantor of its liabilities under the grant agreements and therefore will seek to be released from the guarantee. It is thus important that consultation with IDA Ireland and the other agencies proceeds at an early stage.

16. ISRAEL

Janet Pahima, Nick Cannon Herzog, Fox & Neeman

16.1 Introductory Comments

The State of Israel is a parliamentary democracy whose political system is based upon the principle of parliamentary supremacy. Israel's parliament, known as The Knesset, is the primary authority for both the enactment and repeal of legislation.

Israel does not yet have a comprehensive constitution though the enactment of a full constitution is under discussion. However, Basic Laws set out specific fundamental laws, analogous in some respects to a written constitution. These 'Basic Laws' concern The Knesset, Israel Lands, the President of the State, the Government, the State Economy, the Army, Jerusalem Capital of Israel, the Judiciary, the State Comptroller, Human Dignity and Freedom, and Freedom of Occupation. Despite being considered fundamental laws, the Basic Laws are nevertheless, subject to amendment by The Knesset and interpretation by the Supreme Court.

The Israeli judiciary is apolitical, and follows specific and customary juridical principles: the power to create case law via the exercise of judicial discretion; the binding effect of decisions by the Supreme Court on lower courts; and the supremacy of the highest court, the Supreme Court which is not bound by its own decisions.

There is no single law that regulates the conduct of business in Israel. Instead, there are a number of substantive laws which impact either directly or indirectly upon the conduct and regulation of business. Amongst the more important and relevant laws are: the Companies Law 5759-1999 (the 'Companies Law'), the Securities Act 5728-1968, the Restrictive Trade Practices Law 1988, the Encouragement of Industrial Research and Development Law 1984, the Income Tax Ordinance [New Version] 1961 (the 'Tax Ordinance'), various labour laws (including the Collective Agreements Law 1957 and the Severance Pay Law 1963), and regulations promulgated under several of such laws.

Israel has an attractive business climate for investment, based upon a speedily developing infrastructure, well educated work force, advanced industrial base (particularly in the high-technology and biotechnology areas), tax incentive programs, and a mature legal system, incorporating progressive business, investment and tax laws.

Successive governments have facilitated investment in Israel through a number of measures including the significant liberalization of foreign exchange controls, specific tax and investment incentives, government grants and loan guarantees. A substantial part of the investment in Israel by non-residents is made through purchases of securities of Israeli companies traded on foreign stock exchanges, while other investment by non-residents is through holdings of Israeli listed and non-listed securities, real estate and equity holders' loans.

© World Law Group
International Business Acquisitions, M. Whalley, F.-J. Semler (eds.), Kluwer Law International, London, 2007; ISBN 9789041124838.

16.2   Corporate Structures

A business can establish a presence in Israel in a number of ways.

One of the most common ways for a foreign company to operate a business in Israel is through a subsidiary company. There is no particular difficulty in registering a subsidiary which is accomplished in days and the cost is relatively low. Capital may be minimal and shareholders and directors are not required to reside in Israel—except in the case of so-called 'independent directors' of public companies, where such directors are required to be residents of Israel. The company can be either a public or a private company.

Under the Companies Law, a private company is defined as any company that is not a public one. A public company is defined as a company whose shares are listed for trading on a stock exchange or which were offered to the public by prospectus, and are held by the public. A company may have a single shareholder. The Articles of Association (or by-laws) of a company must include the name of the company, the company's objectives, particulars of the company's registered share capital and particulars of the limitation of liability. Recently, the Companies Registry has begun insisting that new companies are incorporated with Hebrew language Articles of Association. The Companies Registry has not required existing companies with English Articles of Association to translate them into Hebrew nor has the Registry objected to companies (including new companies) adopting restated and amended Articles of Association in English.

The Companies Law imposes a duty on shareholders to exercise their shareholder rights and duties, both towards the company and towards other shareholders, in good faith and in an accepted manner and to refrain from the exploitation of their power in the company for harmful purposes, including with respect to voting in the general meeting of shareholders regarding changes in the Articles of Association, increasing the share capital of the company, a merger of the company and the approval of related party transactions. In addition, a shareholder is required by the law to refrain from unfairly prejudicing the rights of other shareholders. The duty to act in good faith and in an accepted manner will be examined in the light of particular circumstances. The principles of unfair prejudice to minority shareholders are broadly similar to English law rules. The court has discretion to intervene not only where the company's affairs have been conducted in an unfairly prejudicial manner but also where there is material suspicion that they are being conducted in an unfairly prejudicial manner.

In addition, a 'controlling shareholder' has an obligation of 'fairness' towards the company. 'Control' is where a party has the ability to direct the operations of the company.

The Companies Law imposes upon directors the duties of care and loyalty as well as fiduciary duties (including the duty to act in good faith and in the interests of the company and to refrain from any activity involving a conflict of interest).

Partnerships are either general or limited. In a general partnership the partners are jointly and severally liable for partnership debts. A limited partnership must have one or more general partners who are liable for all partnership debts. Limited partners are not liable beyond their capital commitment. A partnership is a separate legal entity, and must be registered with the Registrar of Partnerships.

Israeli partnership law is restricted by the rule that no partnership may be registered with more than twenty partners, although a partnership of lawyers or accountants established for the purposes of professional practice may have more than twenty partners, but in no case more than fifty.

Other forms of association are available. It is possible to form an entity called an Association but such an entity, although flexible, is only suitable for a non-profit organization. Israel also has cooperative associations but those too are not normally well adapted for foreign business involvement.

16.3 Letters of Intent and Heads of Agreement

The creation of a contract in Israeli law is conditional upon the fulfilment of four basic elements: offer, acceptance, certainty and the intention to create a legal relationship. There is no need for consideration for the completion of a contract. The question as to whether a letter of intent or heads of agreement can be considered as legally binding on the parties, ultimately depends on the intention of the parties as evidenced by the wording of the letter of intent or heads of agreement.

The Israeli courts do not give decisive weight to using the format of a preliminary agreement in order to negate its binding force. The present approach is essentially a pragmatic one, whereby the court will seek to deduce the parties' intention from both the wording and their conduct before, during, and after the preliminary agreement. However, the performance of obligations pursuant to a memorandum of agreement is strong evidence of intention.

Even where there is a document which is clearly not binding, such as a comfort letter or letter of intent, a party can still be exposed to a claim for compensation if that party acted without good faith during the negotiations. The duty to act in a customary manner and in good faith, or briefly 'the duty of good faith', which is set out in the Contracts Law (General Part), 5733-1973, is a fundamental and significant pre-requisite of Israeli contract law and applies both in negotiating a contract (i.e. the pre-contractual process) as well as in fulfilling or exercising an obligation or right arising out of a contract. It also extends, mutatis mutandis, to legal acts which do not amount to a contract and to obligations which do not arise out of a contract.

The principle of good faith permits the injured party to relief equivalent to compensation for the expectation or performance of the contract.

Certain types of conduct in negotiations may be construed as lacking good faith. Examples include concealing details, retiring from negotiations, negotiating with no intention to enter into a contract, failure to disclose negotiations with a third party, and raising demands at late stages, especially illegal demands. In every case, the question of whether good faith is lacking is examined in accordance with the particular circumstances surrounding the case.

As regards the breach of the duty of good faith in the performance of a contract (and other obligations), the courts have jurisdiction to award any relief, including declaring that certain acts were undertaken without good faith, modifying contractual obligations or making them subject to conditions.

As contracts are interpreted by the intent of the parties, in order to ascertain whether any letter of intent or heads of agreement is likely to be legally binding, the court will also have recourse to examining the circumstances surrounding the transaction.

Also, where a party to a contract undertakes to perform an act in favour of a third party who is not a signatory to the contract, Israeli law provides that the third party will be entitled to require performance of the act (in addition to the right of the party to the agreement to do so), provided the intention to grant such right may be deduced from the contract.

16.4   Taxes Affecting the Structure and Calculation of Price

Capital gains of a foreign resident are subject to Israeli tax if they derive from the disposal of assets situated in Israel or assets outside Israel which represent a right, direct or indirect, to assets in Israel. In general, the tax rate in respect of capital gains tax made by foreign entities is 20 per cent or 25 per cent. It follows that, in general, gains deriving from a sale of shares in an Israeli company and also gains deriving from a sale of shares in a non-Israeli company, a substantial part of whose assets are in Israel, are subject to Israeli capital gains tax. However, specific income exemptions have recently been enacted to provide relief from tax on capital gains to foreign residents in the following circumstances:

(i)   The sale of securities traded on the Tel Aviv Stock Exchange or a foreign stock exchange provided the securities were acquired after the registration for trade, if not attributable to the Israeli 'permanent establishment' of the foreign resident.

(ii) The sale of shares, acquired upon issuance, in an Israeli 'research and development intensive company' as defined in income tax regulations. The regulations essentially specify the minimum period during which a company's assets must have been used for research and development and the minimum level of expenditure incurred for that purpose.

(iii) The sale of the securities of an Israeli company by an individual or company which is resident in a country which has a double taxation treaty with Israel where the securities were acquired between 1 July 2005 and 31 December 2008, if not attributable to the Israeli 'permanent establishment' of the foreign resident. Seventy five per cent (75 per cent) of the means of control of the company selling the shares must have been held by individuals who were residents of a country with which Israel has a double taxation treaty for the ten years preceding the sale and the sale must have been reported to the Israeli and foreign tax authorities.

The registration of shares for trade on the Tel Aviv Stock Exchange is deemed to be a disposition of the shares in certain cases until 2005. A shareholder may elect to defer the payment of the tax to the date of actual disposition, and pay the lesser of the tax on the gain realized or the tax due upon registration supplemented in the latter case by an interest charge.

Any capital gain is subject to any relief available under an applicable double taxation treaty.

Under the Tax Ordinance, the income of a foreign resident is subject to tax in Israel if it accrues in or is derived from Israel. Section 4A of the Tax Ordinance sets out source rules for income and provides, inter alia, that interest, linkage differentials (described below) and dividends paid by an Israeli resident are deemed to have an Israeli source. Dividend and interest income paid by an Israeli resident to a foreign resident is subject to withholding tax at the rate of 25 per cent or such lower rate as is specified under an applicable double taxation treaty. The term 'linkage differentials' means the linkage of a stated amount in a contract or document to the Israeli Price Consumer Index. The basis of the index is the year 1993 (100). The linkage is a mechanism, inter alia, to protect a lender against inflation. Accordingly, linkage differentials means any amount added to a base amount as a result of the linkage of that base amount to the Index

Section 302 of the Companies Law states that a company distribution must satisfy the 'profits test' (namely, the distribution must be out of profits) and the 'solvency test' (namely that there must not be reasonable grounds for suspecting that the distribution will prevent the company from being able to satisfy its existing and anticipated debts as they fall due). The definition of 'profits' for these purposes is the higher of: (i) the company's surplus balances; and (ii) the company's surpluses which have accumulated over the last two years, after taking into account previous distributions.

Section 303 of the Companies Law authorizes the court, on application by the company, to permit a distribution which does not satisfy the 'profits test' so long as it satisfies the 'solvency test'. The company must inform its creditors that it has applied to the court, and the creditors have the opportunity to submit objections although the court has the authority to approve the distribution notwithstanding such objections.

16.5   Extent of Seller's Warranties and Indemnities

It is the invariable practice for the seller in any asset purchase agreement or share purchase agreement under Israeli law, to give a number of representations and warranties that will be negotiated. Conventionally these include: the organization and qualification of the seller and its subsidiaries; the authorization for the seller to enter into the asset purchase agreement ('APA') or the share purchase agreement ('SPA') and its effect on other obligations of the seller and its subsidiaries; financial statements; the absence of undisclosed liabilities; the binding effect of contracts entered into by the seller; the seller's suppliers and customers; the title to property including leased property; the filing of tax returns and taxes paid; intellectual property; litigation; environmental matters; compliance with applicable laws and permits; employment matters; product warranties; relationships with related persons; grants and subsidies; receivables and bank accounts, absence of brokers, and disclosure of all material information.

Subject to any restrictions set out in the APA or SPA concerning, for example, materiality and disclosures, any breach of a representation or warranty gives the buyer various remedies. These include damages, both actual and consequential, provided that in the case of consequential loss, the buyer must demonstrate foreseeability and have taken steps to mitigate the damages. Israeli law also grants the buyer the right to rescind the contract and receive restitution or to demand specific performance, depending on whether the breach can be considered as being fundamental.

Although penalty clauses are invalid and unenforceable, liquidated damages are permissible and widely used in contracts.

It should also be mentioned that the duty to act in a customary manner and in good faith is of direct relevance where a court considers an application for damages based upon a breach of a representation or warranty.

16.6   Liability for Pre-contractual Representations

Pre-contractual representations may be relied upon by the buyer and form the basis of legal action against the seller. However, to overcome liability, the seller would turn to a number of factors, including: the contract itself and the presumed intention of the parties as appearing from the contract; the circumstances in which the contract was made (note that the Supreme Court of Israel has taken the position that the language of the contract is to be interpreted in light of the circumstances in which the contract was made and accordingly, the 'circumstances' enjoy a considerable degree of significance); the practice which is customary in contracts of that kind; and statutory supplementation, namely the importation of provisions and particulars existing in applicable law into the relevant contract.

In this regard, Israeli law gives considerable regard to the intention of the parties, particularly with regard to any preliminary agreements, including memoranda of understanding and agreements to make a contract, applying an essentially pragmatic approach such that the court will seek to deduce the parties' intention from both the wording of the contract and the conduct of the parties before, during, and after the preliminary agreement.

Even where there is a document which may not be obviously binding on the parties (for example a 'letter of intent'), a party may still be exposed to a claim for compensation if that party acted without good faith during the negotiations. It should be emphasized that Section 12 of the Contracts (General Part) Law (the duty to act in good faith and in a customary manner), applies from the parties' first encounter through to either the making of the contract or the termination of negotiations. Hence, Section 12 applies regardless of whether or not a contract is made at the conclusion of the pre-contractual negotiations and regardless of whether or not additional causes of action exist.

16.7   Liability for Pre-acquisition Trading and Contracts

Israeli law recognizes the fundamental distinction and consequences which arise between an asset purchase agreement (APA) and a share purchase agreement (SPA): under an SPA the liabilities of a company remain the liabilities of the company before, during and after the closing of the transaction for the sale and purchase of the shares in the company. In the case of the sale and purchase of a business (an APA), the buyer may be entirely selective as to which assets it acquires and liabilities it assumes in connection with the seller's business, including the acquisition of contractual benefits and assumption of obligations. Accordingly, the APA will conventionally list the contracts which are being transferred or assigned to the buyer. In this regard, and in order to perfect a valid legal form of assignment, notice of the assignment has to be given to the other contracting party and if required under the terms of a contract, consent of the other contracting party may be required.

Israeli law requires that in the case of the transfer of obligations, the other contracting party must consent.

Subject to the duty of the parties to the acquisition agreement to act in good faith, the courts will uphold the express intention of the parties regarding the assumption of pre-acquisition liabilities. The discussion of 'the duty of good faith' in Section 16.3 above should be noted, as it is relevant both in negotiating a contract and in fulfilling or exercising an obligation or right arising out of a contract.

16.8   Pre-completion Risks

The courts will respect the express intention of the parties to the acquisition agreement and accordingly, if closing is subject to certain conditions and those conditions are not complied with, the buyer will be released from any obligation to proceed with the acquisition. However, this will again be subject to the duty of both parties to act in good faith (see Sections 16.3 and 16.6 above).

With regard to the transfer of risk, in accordance with the principle of freedom of contract, Israeli law applies the basic rule that the parties are at liberty to decide upon the terms regarding the transfer of the goods and when risk shall pass to the buyer, for example, the parties can stipulate that risk passes upon delivery of goods, when payment has been made (i.e. transfer of goods under reservation of title), or upon the occurrence of any other event stipulated in the contract.

If the parties have not agreed on the transfer of risk, the Sale Law 1968 provides that risk shall pass to the buyer when the buyer takes possession of the goods directly from the seller. If the parties have agreed that the goods will be delivered by the seller to the buyer, then under the Sale Law, risk transfers to the buyer when the goods are delivered by the seller to the carrier.

16.9   Required Government Approvals

Under Israeli law, there is a need to obtain or file various approvals, consents, or notifications and to make the necessary preparations at an early stage of the acquisition process. These approvals, consents and notifications may include board and shareholder approvals; notifications and approvals from the Antitrust Commissioner (with reference to antitrust and restrictive trade practices legislation under the Restrictive Trade Practices Act 1988, as amended, and the Restraint of Trade Regulations 1989) encompassing mandatory pre-notification of mergers and acquisitions which fall within the specified threshold; notifications to and filings with the Tel Aviv Stock Exchange and the Israel Securities Authority applicable to public companies; and approvals with regard to certain industry sectors (e.g. telecommunications, broadcasting, and defence) and two special approvals described in the next paragraph.

Government Companies—that is, companies in which the State of Israel holds more than 50 percent of the issued shares or voting rights—are subject to certain constraints under both the Companies Law and the provisions of the Government Companies Law 1975. The acquisition of shares in a government company, modification of such a company's structure, or any merger concerning such a company will invariably require the approval of the government acting through the relevant ministry.

Particular attention needs to be paid to restrictions and conditions imposed with respect to Israeli companies that have received funding from the Office of the Chief Scientist of the Ministry of Labour, Industry and Trade under the Encouragement of Industrial Research and Development Law, with regard to the company's technology. Specific conditions and restrictions apply to the transfer of technology outside of Israel. In addition, conditions and restrictions apply to Israeli companies that have been granted a beneficial tax status referred to as an 'Approved Enterprise' by the Investment Centre of the Ministry of Labour, Industry and Trade encompassing changes in shareholdings, sale of assets, and transfer of operations or activities outside of Israel.

16.10   Antitrust and Competition Laws

Under Israel's Restrictive Trade Practices Law 1988, as amended (the 'RTP Law'), and the Restrictive Trade Practices (Register, Publication and Reporting of Transactions) Regulations, 2004, detailed provisions are set out for mandatory pre-notification of mergers (broadly defined) that fall within the specified threshold.

A merger of companies to which the RTP Law applies is defined as including the acquisition by one company of 'most of the assets' of another company or a purchase leading to (1) ownership of more than 25 percent of the capital or voting rights of a company, (2) the right to elect more than 25 percent of the directors, or (3) the right to participate in more than 25 percent of earnings. This definition has been very broadly interpreted.

The phrase 'most of the assets' pursuant to the above definition has not yet been analyzed by Israeli courts, but has nonetheless been interpreted by the Restrictive Trade Practices Commissioner (the 'Commissioner') as also applying to an acquisition of part of a company's assets, if these constitute a defined unit of the company's entire activities.

Principally, the RTP Law is a territorial law, applying solely to Israeli entities. However, in the event of a merger between an Israeli entity and a foreign entity which is itself either owned by an Israeli entity, has a subsidiary in Israel ('a subsidiary' under the RTP Law is defined a company under the control of another company. 'Control' is regarded as the holding of more than half of either the voting rights or the right to appoint the board of directors), or has a 'place of business' in Israel, the RTP law may apply.

The Commissioner takes the view that if a foreign company has no presence in Israel (including sales 'in' Israel but not including sales 'to' Israel, for example through an independent distributor), its first merger with an Israeli company will not require pre-notification, but its additional mergers may require notification, because the company is then deemed to have a presence in Israel by virtue of the first merger.

The RTP Law defines three situations, any of which, if applicable to a merger of companies, will subject the merger to the determination of the Commissioner, as follows:

1. When the combined or joint market share of the merging companies (including affiliates) is in excess of 50 percent of a relevant product market in Israel, or less than 50 percent if the Minister of Trade & Industry so decides regarding a special kind of asset or service. This will be a question of fact based upon available data.

2. When the joint annual turnover of the merged companies (based upon data from the last fiscal year for each company and its affiliates) exceeds NIS 150 million (the amount is periodically updated), and at least two of the merging parties (together with their respective affiliates) have annual turnover of at least NIS 10 million.

It should be noted that in the case of a merger with a company that conducts business both in Israel and outside of Israel, the above provisions apply only to the company's volume of sales, or market share, in Israel.

3. When one of the merging companies is a monopoly, so defined if its market share exceeds 50 percent.

According to the RTP Law, a monopoly occurs when a concentration of more than half of the total supply of assets or their acquisition or more than half of total services or their total acquisition is or will be held by one party. For the purposes of the RTP Law, such a party will include a company and its subsidiaries, the subsidiaries of one company, and also an entity that is controlled by that party.

It should be noted that there is no difference, for the purpose of this provision, if the company's monopoly is in a market which has no connection to the markets influenced by the proposed merger.

The merging companies must notify the Commissioner prior to the merger agreement being implemented and accordingly, the merger agreement should not be consummated until the merger notice is filed and the merger approved. An execution of a merger prior to its approval by the Commissioner is a breach of the RTP Law and the parties and their respective officers may be subject to criminal, administrative or civil sanctions.

The full merger agreement with all exhibits must be submitted with the application to the Antitrust Authority.

Within 30 days of receiving the merger notice, the Commissioner must notify the merging companies of his or her decision whether or not to approve the merger. Should the Commissioner request additional information to inspect the merger—whether from the companies or from third parties—the time that passes between the day the information is requested until the day it is received is not counted in the 30 day period. The Restrictive Trade Practices Tribunal (the 'Tribunal') may in certain circumstances extend the period of 30 days. The Commissioner is obliged to transfer a copy of the merger notification to the governmental ministry which is responsible for the activities of the merging companies.

The Commissioner may—after consulting the Exemptions and Mergers Committee—approve the merger, with or without subjecting it to specified conditions; and may alternatively object to the merger or stipulate that the merger should be subjected to specified conditions if, in his or her opinion, there is a reasonable suspicion that, as result of the merger as proposed, the competition in that particular industry will be significantly harmed or that the public will be harmed with respect to any one of the following: (1) the level of prices of an asset or service, (2) the quality of an asset or service, or (3) the quantity supplied of the asset or the scale of the service, or regularity and conditions of the supply.

The Commissioner is obliged to publish a notice in the Reshumot (the government's official publication concerning companies) and in two daily newspapers regarding his or her decision in a merger case.

In addition to the filing of a merger notice, in the event that the acquisition or merger agreement includes restrictions on any of the parties' future activities—for example, non-competition undertakings—such provisions may constitute a restrictive arrangement according to the RTP Law. Restrictive arrangements are prima facie prohibited by the RTP Law unless (1) they fall within one of the exceptions set forth in the RTP Law, (2) the Tribunal approves the restrictive arrangement, (3) the Commissioner exempts the parties from the need to obtain the Tribunal's approval of the arrangement, or (4) the Tribunal grants the parties a temporary permit to act according to the arrangement (the granting of a temporary permit is subject to the submission, to the Tribunal, of a request to approve the restrictive arrangement).

In February 2004, the Restrictive Trade Practices Rules (Block Exemption for Restrictive Arrangements Ancillary to Mergers) 2004 (the 'Block Exemption') were issued. In essence, the Block Exemption exempts merging parties from the requirement to file an application to the Commissioner to approve certain restrictive arrangements ancillary to the merger transaction.

The Block Exemption defines three specific restraints that do not need to be approved in a separate procedure, subject to the fulfilment of certain conditions:

(1) Non-competition restraint on the seller's part, including approaching customers or employees; (2) Continued supply restraint—that is to say, the obligation of a party to the merger to continue to supply goods or services to the other party, on the same conditions as existed prior to the merger, and (3) Obligation to protect trade secrets and information.

In addition, the Block Exemption also exempts a restraint 'that is necessary to protect the economic value of the business that was sold in the merger, as long as it is limited to a reasonable period of time'. This section provides the merging parties with the flexibility required to address the varying circumstances of each transaction, as long as the restraint is compatible with the purposes of the Block Exemption.

In order to receive an exemption from the Commissioner for restraints that do not meet the conditions specified in the Block Exemption, the parties are required to file an application for exemption with the Commissioner. The Commissioner is required to respond to such an application within 90 days of the date the application was submitted. Nevertheless, he or she is entitled to lengthen the period for an additional 60 days. However, this authority is rarely used. Should the Commissioner request additional information to inspect the application, the time that passes between the day the information is requested until the day it is received is not included in this time limit.

16.11 Required Offer Procedures

Mergers and acquisitions in Israel are governed primarily by Parts 8 and 9 of the Companies Law and the Companies Regulations (Mergers) 2000, together with other legislation which includes the Securities Regulations (Tender Offer) 2000, the Securities Law, the Restrictive Trade Practices Law described above, the Restrictive Trade Practices Regulations 1989, the Encouragement of Industrial Research and Development Law 1984, and the Tax Ordinance.

The Companies Law provides for the concepts of statutory mergers and forced sale provisions with respect to private companies and 'squeeze-out' mechanisms for public companies, including rules and restrictions applicable to tender offers.

The Companies Regulations (Mergers) 2000 is applicable to both private and public companies, setting out detailed procedures required to give legal effect to a merger.

Under Israeli law, takeovers of public companies are governed by extensive laws and regulations concerning tender offers. With respect to private companies (companies whose shares are not listed on a stock exchange and whose shares were not offered to the public by prospectus, or are held by the public), the Companies Law provides for a forced sale procedure. Under this procedure, a bidder acquiring at least 80 percent (or 90 percent if the company was incorporated before 1 February 2000), of the shares or classes of shares of a private company can require that the remaining shareholders sell their shares at the same conditions, unless otherwise decided by an authorized court, in accordance with a claim filed by one of the remaining shareholders. The threshold of 80 percent (or 90 percent, as applicable) may be changed (raised or lowered) under the company's Articles of Association.

Another structure which is used at times for an acquisition of both private and public companies, is based on section 350 of the Companies Law that allows for the filing of an application to the Israeli courts to approve an 'arrangement' between a company and its shareholders or creditors. Historically this mechanism was intended to address reorganizations aimed at implementing measures required to avoid the insolvency of the company in question. However, until the enactment of the Companies Law in 1999, in the absence of a statutory merger procedure, this mechanism was also used for mergers. Following the Companies Law and the introduction of the statutory merger procedure discussed above, the question has arisen as to whether the mechanism is still available for solvent transactions. There is some case law that supports the position that the mechanism may still be used for transactions and not solely in the case of insolvency and it in fact continues to be used occasionally.

Section 350 allows a company or any shareholder or creditor of the company to apply to the court to approve the proposed scheme of arrangement. The scheme of arrangement would typically involve the merger of the company in question with one or more other entities, although it is possible to propose a straightforward share purchase as a scheme of arrangement.

Under the procedure in Section 350, the court will first call meetings of the shareholders and creditors to consider whether to approve the scheme of arrangement. For these purposes, the court may—either at its own initiative or on application—order separate meetings of different classes of shareholders and creditors. The term 'class' of shares or debt does not refer solely to formal classes of shares (ordinary, preferred and so on) but also differentiates between groups of shareholders and creditors with 'different interests'.

The court will not usually consider the merits of the scheme at this initial stage.

At each such meeting, the approval of a majority of those present who must hold at least 75 per cent of the 'value' represented at such meeting (i.e. 75 per cent of the shares or 75 per cent of the aggregate debt present) is required for the arrangement to be approved. Where the interests at each meeting are divided into different classes, the approval of each class is required.

If the necessary approvals of creditors and shareholders have been obtained, the scheme is then submitted to the court for its approval. It should be noted that the court does not consider itself a 'rubber stamp' to the approval of the shareholders and creditors although in practice it would be rare for a scheme to be totally rejected by the court.

Once approved by the court, the scheme of arrangement becomes binding and effective.

16.12   Continuation of Government Licenses

In certain industries, it is necessary for the business operator to have a license. Licenses are required in, for example, banking, insurance, telecommunications and broadcasting in addition to a general business license. The field of manufacture of military defence equipment is another regulated industry.

Various conditions may be attached to a license and these need to be thoroughly reviewed, including with respect to provisions governing the need to obtain approval for a change of control or transfer of shares in the license holder. Typically, licenses may not be freely transferred and are subject to prior approval by the appropriate governmental agency.

A buyer of a business which is subject to licensing requirements may need to obtain a new license or otherwise obtain approval from the government to acquire control or shares in the business. The time taken to obtain a new license or receive approval to acquire control or shares in a business may be a relevant consideration.

16.13 Requirements for Transferring Shares

The requirements for transferring shares will ultimately depend upon the procedures set out in the Articles of Association of the company whose shares are being transferred and any other document which is binding upon the transferor and the transferee.

In many private companies, the board of directors of the company whose shares are being transferred must approve the transfer.

To transfer title to shares, the transferor and the transferee will sign a transfer deed setting out the details of the shares being transferred. The consideration need not be included in the share transfer deed.

The transfer will have to be recorded in the company's register of shareholders and notification will be made to the Israeli Companies Registry (the details of the transfer will then be available to the public).

Stamp duty has recently been cancelled and is no longer applicable.

16.14 Requirements for Transferring Land and Property Leases

Land which is privately owned as well as land that belongs to the State and leased to third parties for a long period is registered in the local land registry. Upon the execution of a contract for the sale of land, it is possible to register a 'cautionary' note in the land registry which usually grants the purchaser preference over a subsequent conflicting transaction by the seller, and also protects the buyer against the seller's creditors.

The registration is computerized and it is possible to obtain an extract of the registration of any particular property. The extract will show the present ownership and encumbrances on the property including mortgages, easements, details of the area of the parcel, etc. Information relating to past transactions can also be obtained from the Israel Land Registry Office. Israel's land laws trace back to the Ottoman Empire, and while most of the land has been updated and recorded, there still exists some land which is not yet 'settled' and not properly recorded, making transactions in these properties quite complicated and requiring many extra precautions.

The vendor of land may be liable for Betterment Appreciation Tax, Betterment Tax and Sales Tax.

In the case of state owned land, any transfer of rights is usually subject to the approval of the Israel Land Administration.

16.15   Requirements for Transferring Intellectual Property

Conventionally, rights in intellectual property may be assigned. Although in theory, an assignment of an intellectual property right could be effected verbally, the practice is usually to do so by a written deed of assignment.

With regard to patents, the legal requirement is to record the assignment in the Patents Register. There is no Register for copyright. The law requires copyright assignment to be made in writing, although the courts have interpreted this requirement as evidentiary rather than substantive. With regard to the assignment of a trade mark, the better practice is to record such assignment in the trade mark register.

The Registrar may refuse to record an assignment of a registered trademark if he or she is of the opinion that the use of the mark by the assignee is likely to deceive the public or if he or she is of the opinion that the assignment is contrary to public policy.

The owner of a registered trademark may authorize another person to use the trademark. There is a provision in the law for the recordal of a trademark license and in one case, the absence of such a recordal led to judicial revocation of the trade mark license and the cancellation of trademark registration. However, the particular circumstances of that case call into question whether such a result is required when a trademark license is not recorded.

Similarly, a registered design may be assigned and licensed to exploit such design.

A copyright may be licensed. Whilst the law appears to require the license be in writing, at least one decision of the Supreme Court of Israel found a valid license in the absence of writing, based on the conduct of parties.

16.16   Requirements for Transferring Business Contracts, Licenses and Leases

Under Israeli law, the assignment of any rights under a business contract (which will include third party licenses or leases) is subject to the provisions of the relevant contract. Accordingly, two possibilities exist: (i) assignment which is subject to the consent of the other contracting party (in some cases, the contract may state that 'such consent is not to be unreasonably withheld'); or (ii) where the contract is silent as to assignment.

In the first case, the assignment is only possible once the consent of the other contracting party is obtained. In the case where the contract is silent as to assignment, then assignment can occur without obtaining the consent of the other party to the contract, although notice of the assignment should be given. Assignment is commonly effected through an assignment agreement.

Under Israeli law, assignment of a contract will not discharge the assignor from any obligations entered into under the contract. For this to occur, a novation agreement is required, or the consent of the other contracting party must be obtained. Therefore the consent of the contracting party is required, if a contract is assigned in full, unless expressly permitted by the terms of the contract, if the contract contains any obligations of the assignor—including requirements of performance.

Licenses or permits granted by governmental authorities will generally require the consent of the issuing authority, which may impose conditions, require extensive information, or require a new application before consenting to the assignment.

16.17 Requirements for Transferring Other Assets

Aside from real property, intellectual property and shares, assets can be transferred by way of delivery, unless otherwise agreed between the parties to the transaction. A bill of sale is not necessary although commonly used.

Vehicles will require effecting and recording the transfer at the Ministry of Transportation.

Assets subject to a creditor's lien or pledge, or in which title is retained by a third party under reservation of title, will in principle continue to be encumbered by the rights of the third party subsequent to the transfer to the purchaser.

It is important to note that under Israeli law, retention of title provision may be enforced but subject to the vendor (typically a supplier) demonstrating that:

(i)   it has kept records concerning the products sold to the distributor which would indicate its continuing interest in identifying its title to the products;

(ii) it has received regular reports regarding sales of the products;

(iii) other means or conduct or actions were carried out by the vendor in order to enable the vendor to know the position regarding its title to the products (e.g. insurance); and

(iv) it had established policies and actions regarding any risks or problems with the products to which it had title.

Accordingly, it will be important for the vendor to demonstrate that these grounds not only will exist but that active steps have been taken by the supplier regarding the products sold (based on the above grounds) and, particularly, asserting its title to the relevant products.

16.18 Encumbrances and Third Party Interests

The principal legislation concerning encumbrances of company assets is the Pledges Law 1967. In addition, the Companies Ordinance [New Version] 1983 contains provisions which regulate this issue. These provisions were retained under the Companies Law 1999 and apply to the grant and registration of charges, both floating and fixed, over the assets of an Israeli company or an Israeli branch of a foreign company.

In order to effect a charge over a company's assets and to protect the assets charged from third party interests in the event of default, a charge must be registered in accordance with Israeli law. The charge must be registered with the Companies Registrar within 21 days of its creation and will be effective as of the date of its creation, with the exception of charges over real estate located in Israel that must be registered with the Companies Registrar within 21 days following the registration of a mortgage with the Land Registrar.

Charges over assets of individuals and partnerships require different registrations.

Under Israeli law there are three types of charges over company assets:

(i)   The Floating charge. Israeli law recognizes the concept of a floating charge, which covers all the assets of a company, both current and future assets, including physical and intangible assets, as well as contractual rights. The floating charge enables a company to continue making commercial use of its assets as long as any such usage can be regarded as 'in the ordinary course of business.' If and when there is cause for realization, the floating charge crystallizes and 'catches' all company assets which exist at that point in time, and forbids any further commercial use of the assets. A debenture creating a floating charge may include a provision restricting the company from creating any further charges over the assets of the company, and if such a provision forms part of the charge instrument that was registered with the Companies Registrar, such a floating charge shall have priority over all future charges that are registered in breach of this provision.

(ii) The Specific charge. As opposed to the floating charge, a specific charge can be placed on a specific asset, thereby preventing the company that granted the charge from being able to sell or license the charged asset without the permission of the chargee. Unless the charge agreement states otherwise, the company may create additional charges over the pledged assets but the chargor of the first charge shall have priority over all subsequent charges.

(iii) Purchase-money security interest (PMSI). Notwithstanding section (i) above, where a specific charge is created to secure the financing of an asset, it shall have priority in respect of the charged asset over a previous floating charge even if the floating charge includes a restriction as described in section (i) above.

It should be noted that a charge over shares of an Israeli company that are held by a non-Israeli shareholder can also be registered in Israel through the Israeli Pledges Registrar.

In general, realization of all charges can be accomplished through the Execution Office of the Israeli courts, with the exception of pledges over shares and other securities registered for the benefit of banks and other financial institutions. Therefore, it is common practice for banks, when receiving a pledge of shares or other securities, to actually transfer the shares into the name of the banks' trust companies and register the trust companies as the holder of the shares.

It also should be noted that charges over specific kinds of assets may require registration with specific governmental offices in addition to registration with the Companies

Registrar. For example, charges over real estate located in Israel must be registered with the Land Registrar, charges over Israeli patents must be registered with the Israel Patent Office and charges over aircrafts must be registered with the Aircraft Registrar.

16.19 Minimum Shareholder and Officer Requirements

The Companies Law states that a company may have a single shareholder. Prior to the adoption of the Companies Law in 1999, a minimum of two shareholders was required, and thus it was common practice for wholly-owned companies to have either one share or 1 per cent of the shares held by a trustee or nominee.

The board of directors of a private company may be comprised of only one director.

A director may appoint a substitute director. There is no restriction on the appointment of a corporate entity as a director. A public company must have two 'outside directors' (according to Section 239 of the Companies Law) who are appointed by the general meeting. The 'outside directors' must be Israeli residents and are subject to additional qualifications.

There are no requirements that shareholders or directors be resident in or citizens of Israel (Suljict, in the case of directors, to the requirement applicable to public companies); directors need not hold qualification shares.

In addition, public companies are required to appoint an individual as a general manager who shall be responsible for the operation of the company's affairs within the policy determined by the board of directors and subject to its instructions. The compulsory requirement to appoint a general manager does not apply to private companies.

16.20 Non-competition Clauses

Non-compete obligations of employees or consultants are infrequently enforced in Israel. In general, Israeli law gives precedence to the employee's freedom of occupation over the employer's right that a former employee will not compete. When specific consideration is given for a non-compete obligation, there is a better chance of enforcement.

The court's approach, in this regard, is that it is prohibited for an employee to breach confidentiality obligations towards a former employer by working with a competitor. However, only in rare circumstances will a breach of a confidentiality obligation result in an employee being prohibited in working elsewhere. Accordingly, an employee is prohibited from competing with a former employer, but only if such competition may harm a legitimate interest of the employer (such as the breach of a trade secret). The fact that during the employment period, the employee developed certain skills or qualifications does not necessarily justify the enforcing of a non-compete undertaking. Therefore, non-compete obligations of employees will not be enforced, unless there are specific circumstances that justify it.

Even if the Labour Court decides to enforce a non-compete undertaking, the enforcement will only be with respect to an obligation which can be considered reasonable and not too broad. The Court also has the power to re-draft the non-compete obligation in order to make it more reasonable, usually in respect of the scope of the employee's occupation, the restricted territory to which the clause applies and the non-compete period.

Protection of confidential or trade secret information is also subject to legislation under the provisions of the Commercial Torts Law, 5759-1999. This Law defines a 'Trade Secret' as being business information, of any kind, which is not public knowledge and cannot easily be disclosed by others, the confidentiality of which provides its owner with a business advantage over its competitors, provided that its owner took reasonable steps in order to keep its confidentiality.

The Law determines when the disclosure of a Trade Secret constitutes a tort/conversion. The Law also empowers the Labour Courts to adjudicate in a claim between an employee and an employer regarding a Trade Secret.

Protection of confidential or trade secret information based on the specific contractual terms entered into between the employee and the employer and confidentiality undertakings along with non-competition and ownership of intellectual property undertakings are standard practice in most technology industries in Israel.

Note that non-compete obligations of a seller of a business, if reasonable in time and scope, are enforced.

16.21   Environmental Considerations

Israel has a significant number of environmental laws and regulations which impose obligations of businesses and which are relevant to transactions, especially mergers and acquisitions. The subject is dynamic, and additional legislation, as well as tightening enforcement and increasing criminal penalties are anticipated, particularly due to increased public awareness and pressure concerning environmental issues. Noteworthy developments in the field include the promulgation of a securities regulation relating to environmental disclosure obligations of publicly-traded companies and issuance of restrictions on government grants to corporations in non-compliance with environmental laws.

Environmental law and regulation in Israel includes rules of civil liability, primarily relating to nuisances, and criminal liability provisions (including personal liability of corporate officers), which can be found in specific statutes on such issues as water and ground contamination, hazardous substances, air pollution and radiation.

Israeli law also provides for specific civil wrongs, such as nuisance. In the case of dangerous articles, case law has imposed a higher standard of care than would normally be required of a reasonable person. Where a civil wrong has been committed in respect of an individual, such an individual will be entitled to compensation for damage suffered and also, in general, to an order requiring the cessation and removal of the wrong.

In addition to a claim based on a civil wrong of a nuisance to an individual, a person who was harmed, or is likely to be harmed by an environmental disturbance may apply for an order of the court. The court has the authority to grant diverse orders, including an order to prevent environmental disturbance, to terminate its occurrence, and to repair the breach by restoring the situation to its condition prior to the breach.

16.22 Employee Superannuation/Pension Plans

At the present time there is no legislation which expressly provides for pension rights, however, such arrangements do exist in collective agreements and in many sectoral extension orders; in addition pension funds are common in companies which have no statutory obligation to provide for such rights.

In this context, the National Insurance Institute, similar in some respects to US Social Security, is noteworthy. Each employer, on a monthly basis, sets aside an amount equal to a certain percentage of the employee's salary, while at the same time making a deduction from the employee's wage. The payments to the National Insurance Institute form the basis by which the rights of all workers are insured for pension upon retirement, work accident insurance, maternity payments, compensation for armed forces reserve duty, and so forth. The health insurance of workers in Israel is also provided for in the National Health Insurance Law, this too by virtue of a monthly payment made by the employer based on a percentage of the employee's salary.

In addition, independently of the insurance provided by the National Insurance Institute, it is common for employers to insure their staff with various provident funds, although there is no statutory duty to do so.

In Israel, it is common for the employer to fund a Managers Insurance Policy or a Pension Fund for the employee. In such a case the employer's payments to such funds are partially on account of severance pay. Accordingly, in the event that the employee is dismissed, the sum accrued in the severance fund is paid to the employee on account of the employer's severance pay obligations. In such a case the employer transfers the funds accrued in the Managers Insurance Policy or the Pension Fund to the employee; sometimes the employer must also pay any shortfall between the amounts accrued in the Fund and the severance pay obligation.

The Law provides that an arrangement whereby amounts accumulated in a Managers Insurance Policy or a Pension Fund will be paid in full satisfaction of the employer's severance pay obligation (rather than merely on account of it) will be valid if it has been approved by the Minister of Labour or has been agreed upon within the framework of a collective agreement applying to the employer and employee. In such cases and only such cases, the employer will not be obliged to make up any shortfall in the fund.

16.23 Employee Rights

Labour legislation is well developed in Israel and a series of labour related statutes and regulations apply to all employees. Any employee's agreement with the employer which impose conditions on the employee inferior to those prescribed under labour law legislation is ineffective, unless such possibility to contract out of such legislative rules is specifically included in the relevant legislation.

Some of the major employment rights that are enshrined in legislation include:

The Hours of Work and Rest Law, 5711-1951. This Law has established the maximum number of hours' work permitted per day and per week.

It also prescribes payment of overtime and which employees can be employed without the requirement of paying overtime (generally their position much involve a fiduciary duty to the company).

This Law also requires all employees to be given a weekly day of rest corresponding to their religious day of rest.

The Severance Pay Law, 5723-1963. This Law provides that whoever has worked for an employer or at the same place of employment for at least one year and been dismissed is entitled to severance pay from the employer in an amount equal to one month's salary per year of employment, based upon the last month's salary. The Law prescribes several cases in which the employee, although not dismissed, will be entitled to severance pay.

The Annual Leave Law, 5711-1951. This Law prescribes a duty to grant employees a minimum annual vacation which increases with seniority.

The Sick Pay Law, 5736-1976. Under this Law, an employee who is sick and cannot work is entitled to sick leave, up to a maximum of one and a half days per month's employment, but not more than a total of 90 days in any year. The sick pay due to the employee is 75 per cent of the employee's salary, although the employee is not entitled to any remuneration for the first day's absence and only 37.5 per cent of salary on the second and third day of absence.

Discrimination laws also cover sex discrimination (including protection for pregnancy), equal pay, sexual harassment, disability, discharged soldiers and foreign workers.

The Minimum Wage Law, 5747-1987. The Minimum Wage Law prescribes a duty to pay a full time employee a minimum wage, which is defined as 47.5 per cent of the average salary in the economy, but subject to change.

The Wage Protection Law, 5718-1958. This Law provides that a salary not paid on time is subject to the addition of wage delay compensation of 5 per cent for the first week of delay and then 10 per cent for every additional week, or full linkage (see the meaning of the term 'linkage' in Section 1.4) plus 20 per cent interest, whichever is greater.

The Notice Period for Termination Law, 5761-2001. A full time employee is entitled to one day's written notice for each month during the first six months of employment and two and a half days for every additional month. A full time employee who has worked for a year or more is entitled to not less than one month's prior notice.

Collective agreements applicable to employees are not uncommon in Israel. Where there is a personal contract of employment with an employee who is also subject to a collective agreement, it is necessary to examine each single provision in order to ascertain whether the personal contract or the collective agreement is more favourable to the employee; the employee is always entitled to the benefit of the more favourable provision.

Similarly, if an employee is subject to two collective agreements—for instance a special agreement governing the enterprise in which he or she works and a general agreement with regard to his or her trade, the provision most favourable to the employee will apply.

16.24 Compulsory Transfer of Employees

The accepted view in Israel is that the employment contract is a personal contract: the employee is entitled to decide who will be his or her employer and the employer is entitled to the performance of the job, by the employee, on a personal basis. Accordingly, it is not possible to transfer an employee to another employer without the employee's consent. If the employee agrees to the transfer, the employment contract between the employee and the new employer is considered a new contract, even when the employee has been hired by the new employer on terms identical to those which were in effect with the previous employer.

A distinction should be made between an asset transaction or merger, which result in a change of employer, and accordingly, give rise to certain protection provided to employees regarding their rights in the workplace, and a share purchase, which is not considered a change in the legal identity of the employer, and therefore, all of the obligations and rights of employees are preserved exactly as they existed before the sale. Recently, however, this distinction between assets and shares transactions has been blurred in National Labour Court decisions.

According to Israeli employment law, the general rule is that asset transactions (including mergers) result in a change of employer and, consequently, the transfer of an employee to another employer is subject to the employee's consent. Therefore, if an employee does not give his or her consent to the transfer, the seller would need to either continue to employ the employee or terminate the employment of such employee (with all the implications of such termination, i.e., the applicable notice period must be given and severance pay must be paid).

In practice, there are two methods of transferring employees from the seller to the new employer in an asset sale. The first method involves the seller terminating the employees' employment and the new employer re-hiring such employees. The second method involves maintaining the employees' continuity of employment and seniority—i.e. the new employer steps into the seller's position as the employer for all intents and purposes.

In the last few years, the Labour Courts have set out three main obligations on an employer undergoing structural changes in its business , including following a change of employers: the obligation to provide information concerning the change being effected; the obligation to consult with the employees regarding the aspects of the change of employers; and the obligation to conduct negotiations with the employees' organization, allowing for a proper hearing and discussion of the union's demands. It should be noted that although these obligations apply, in general, to all employers, where there is no active workers' organization or committee, the implementation of these obligations is usually not practical.

In the case of fire and re-hire, although the employment contract between the employee and the new employer is considered a new contract, a number of legislative enactments in Israel created a linkage between the worker and the workplace. As such, there are a number of employee rights, the existence and increase of which are dependent on seniority in the same workplace. The most important examples of such legislation concern severance pay payable by the employer who dismissed an employee after continuous employment of at least one year by the same employer or at the same place of employment, and sick pay and vacation, which are calculated according to the seniority of the employee with the same employer or at the same place of employment.

In addition, there are certain specific contractual rights that will apply to the new employer, in light of the fact that the seller's employees had been transferred to the new employer (even under the fire re-hire method). For example, under Section 30 of the Wage Protection Law, 5718-1958, when a place of business has changed hands or been divided or been merged with another entity, the new employer will also be liable for any payment of wages and for payments to a provident fund, due from the previous employer.

Another example is Section 18 of the Collective Agreements Law, where a place of business has changed hands or been divided or merged in respect of which a collective agreement had been in force; the new employer will continue to be bound by such collective agreement even though it is not expressly assumed by the new employer.

Notwithstanding, the labour laws do not provide as a general matter that a change of employers in a given workplace amounts to a replacement of the previous employer by the new employer as a party to the existing employment contract. Such a condition can be included in an agreement between the new and previous employer, whereby the new employer accepts legal responsibility for all future claims and lawsuits initiated by employees based on the period prior to the change in employer, although an express exclusion of such liability for the period leading to the change of employers is the more common method.

Since a change in the composition of the company's shareholders, in and of itself, does not generally affect the legal personality of the company from the perspective of the employment relationship, this is not to be viewed as a change of employers. Consequently, it is not necessary to follow the provisions of statutes that deal with a change of employers, given that the rights of the workers are preserved.

However, should the changes caused by a shift in the control of the company prejudice a specific employee's status, by reducing his or her salary or moving his or her workplace a significant distance, the employee will almost certainly be entitled to resign and receive severance pay on the basis of one of the two alternate grounds of constructive dismissal enumerated in section 11(a) of the Severance Pay Law.

16.25 Tax Deductibility of Acquisition Expenses

Foreign taxable investors can usually obtain a foreign tax credit for taxes paid in Israel, which will be determined according to the rules of the individual investor's tax jurisdiction.

There are no explicit rules regarding this question under Israeli tax law. Generally, the acquisition expenses should be treated as a capital expense, that is, it will be regarded as increasing the amount of the investment (i.e., the tax basis/cost base) and will not be allowable as a trading expense. Many commentators on this subject believe that the tax treatment will follow the accounting treatment.

Under Israel's Value Added Tax Law, any supply of services to an Israeli resident is deemed to take place in Israel, and is therefore subject to VAT (currently at 17.5 per cent). Where the supplier is a non-resident, a 'reverse charge rule' applies and the obligation to pay the VAT falls on the recipient. This generally does not result in a net tax liability for the recipient since it is entitled to reclaim the VAT as input tax. However, input tax on expenses for acquiring an investment is not attributable to income which is subject to VAT and consequently, the party which has incurred the expenses will not be entitled to obtain the VAT refund.

Where an Israeli company receives services from a non-resident, and the services are provided entirely outside of Israel, the VAT charge is often not enforced.

16.26 Levies on Acquisition Agreements and Collateral Documents

Effective 1 January 2006, Israeli stamp duty was cancelled and documents signed after 1 January 2006 are no longer subject to payment of stamp duty.

16.27 Financing Rules and Restrictions

Under Israeli company law there is no outright prohibition on financial assistance. Rather, where a company (the 'Company')—or a subsidiary of the Company or a company controlled by the Company—provides, or undertakes to provide, directly or indirectly, funding for the purchase of shares in the Company, this is deemed to be a distribution by the Company, which must comply with the 'distributable profits' test and the 'solvency' test for distributions under the Companies Law.

Under the 'profits test' the distribution must be made out of 'profits', which for this purpose are defined as the higher of the company's profit balance and the company's profits accumulated over the preceding two years, as shown in the company's last adjusted audited or inspected accounts, provided these accounts were not drawn up more than six months before the date of the distribution. Under the 'solvency test', there must not be reasonable grounds for suspecting that the distribution will prevent the company from being asked to meet its existing and anticipated profits.

There are currently no thin capitalization rules under Israeli law.

16.28   Exchange Controls and Repatriation of Profits

Since 1998, the Israeli government's extensive system of controls for foreign currency have undergone a series of significant liberalizations, and as from 1 January 2003, all remaining exchange control restrictions have been lifted. The New Israel Shekel is convertible for all business purposes and is widely traded.

There is no banking or foreign exchange restriction in Israel on the funding of investments or the repatriation of earnings and gains.

In order to keep track of capital flows and thus effectively manage monetary policy, various reporting requirements apply to the carrying out of transactions in foreign currency.

As mentioned in Section 16.4 above, under the Tax Ordinance, income of a foreign resident is subject to tax in Israel if it accrues in or is derived from Israel. Section 4A of the Tax Ordinance sets out source rules for income and provides, inter alia, that interest, linkage differentials (described in Section 16.4) and dividends paid by an Israeli resident are deemed to have an Israeli source.

Generally, Israeli withholding tax applies to payments of interest, dividends, and outbound remittances, including payments under a guarantee, made by an Israeli resident to persons who are not resident in Israel. This rate of tax, which as a general rule would be 25 per cent, may, in certain cases, be subject to reduction by virtue of a prevailing treaty for the prevention of double taxation.

An application to the Israel Tax Authorities would be required, if exemptions were requested from liability to withholding tax. An exemption would generally apply if the payment of interest was either not considered to be from an Israeli source or if the exemption applied pursuant to and in accordance with the provisions of the applicable double taxation treaty.

16.29   Group Companies

Under Israeli tax law, there is no consolidation for tax purposes except for industrial companies. An industrial company can consolidate its income for tax purposes subject to a number of conditions.

16.30   Responsibility for Liabilities of an Acquired Subsidiary

The Companies Law sets out the basic principle that a company is a separate legal entity. However, Section 6 of the Companies Law expressly authorizes the court to 'lift the corporate veil'—namely to attribute rights and liabilities of the company to its shareholders or vice versa—in the following circumstances:

Section 6(a) states that the court may attribute a debt of the company to the shareholder if it considers it just and proper to do so, in the exceptional circumstances where the company's legal identity has been used (a) so as to mislead any person, or to prejudice the rights of a creditor of the company, or (b) in a manner prejudicial to the company's objectives, while taking an unreasonable risk in connection with the company's ability to pays it debts and provided the shareholder was aware of such use of the company's separate legal identity, and taking into account the shareholder's holding in the company, its compliance with its shareholder duties towards the company, and the company's ability to pay its debts. For these purposes, a person is regarded as being aware of the use of the company for these purposes if he or she suspected such use but failed make the necessary enquires (other than merely by reason of negligence).

Section 6(b) states that the court is entitled to attribute any right or debt of a shareholder to the company, or any right of the company to the shareholder, if it considers it just and proper in the circumstance.

Section 6(c) states that the court is in entitled to defer a shareholder's right to repayment of a debt by the company until the company has repaid its debts in full to all its other creditors, in circumstances where the court has determined that it may attribute the company's debt to the shareholders in accordance with Section (a).

As mentioned in Section 16.2, the Companies Law imposes a duty on shareholders to exercise their shareholder rights and duties, both towards the company and towards other shareholders, in good faith and in an accepted manner and to refrain from the exploitation of their power in the company for harmful purposes. Accordingly, any acts of the shareholders will be subject to this duty.

16.31   Governing Law of the Contract

The choice of law made by the parties to govern the relevant agreement—assuming it is a law of an acknowledged and well developed jurisdiction—will normally be recognized and upheld by the Courts of Israel and the submission by each of the parties to the jurisdiction of the Courts of the jurisdiction by which the agreement is governed, will be treated by the Courts of Israel as valid and binding on each of the parties.

16.32   Dispute Resolution Options

Mediation is governed by law and is growing more and more popular. With consent of the parties a court may refer the parties to mediation. Israeli courts refer litigants more and more to non-binding mediation before proceeding to trial, in response to the burdened docket of the courts. Usually such process will not affect trial dates. If a settlement agreement is reached through mediation, the court may give it the force of a judgment. Mediation can take place even prior to the initiation of court proceedings. Some courts have standing orders directing parties in cases of a given description to participate in mediation. However, the courts cannot enforce mediation on the parties.

The Arbitration Law 1968 governs arbitral proceedings. Parties may submit disputes arising out of existing relationships to arbitration, provided that the dispute concerns matters in respect of which the parties can reach an agreement. The courts will recognize a valid arbitration agreement and stay proceedings brought before it, provided that the party seeking such stay has been willing to take any necessary steps to conduct arbitration. In the event that the Convention on the Recognition and Enforcement of Foreign Arbitral Awards of 1958 (customarily known as the 'New York Convention') applies to a given arbitration agreement, the rules prescribed in this Convention will apply whenever a party seeks to stay court proceedings due to an arbitration agreement, as Israel is a party to the New York Convention.

The parties to an arbitration agreement may stipulate the governing rules of the agreement. If no rules are specified then the standardized rules provided for in a schedule to the Arbitration Law will apply.

The arbitration agreement must be in writing.

A party seeking confirmation of an arbitral award submits a motion with the district court of proper jurisdiction. Upon submittal of such motion, the court issues an order confirming the award unless the court finds grounds to deny its recognition or enforcement.

Courts will confirm arbitration awards unless certain extreme grounds pursuant to the Arbitration Law would prevent such enforcement. Grounds for rejection include arbitration awards rendered contrary to public policy; without authority of the arbitrator; or without having given all parties thereto a fair opportunity to argue their case. Generally speaking, unless found to be severely erroneous, the court will not see a reason to intervene with an arbitral award, as long as the arbitrator has acted within the scope of his or her authority. The fact that the court is convinced that the arbitrator committed a serious error does not suffice to overturn the decision.

Israeli courts recognize foreign arbitration awards subject to the New York Convention and in accordance therewith.

17. ITALY

Francesco Gianni Gianni, Origoni & Partners

17.1 Introductory Comments

The Italian legal system does not provide, in general, any restrictions on foreign investments in Italy carried out by means of an acquisition of shares, assets or going concern. Exchange control and foreign investment regulations have been progressively abolished by the Italian Government as a result of EU legislation on the freedom of movement of capital. Minor regulatory requirements are still in place, primarily for statistical purposes. Repatriation of profits is unrestricted. However, the anti-trust and takeover laws, as well as specific regulations set forth for strategic sectors (such as banking, insurance, publishing companies and television networks) may prevent or restrict an acquisition.

Italian law has been through a process of 'decodification'. A large number of specific statutes now regulate key areas that were, previously, virtually unregulated by the Civil Code, which has thus lost, to some extent, its centrality as a regulatory source. In such respects, it is worth mentioning that on 1 July 1998 the new Financial and Securities Act (hereinafter 'the Securities Act') came into force, introducing a coherent set of rules regulating financial intermediaries and listed companies. Although the main body of contract, corporate and labour rules are still contained in the Civil Code, an acquisition is always affected by special laws which may render more complex the negotiations and the drafting of the relevant agreements. In this respect, early advice may be helpful to address and solve in advance specific issues related to the acquisition.

Italy (as a civil law country) has a legal framework that substantially differs from those of common law countries. The main consequence of this is that, usually, Italian agreements appear to be less detailed than those drafted in common law jurisdictions. In addition, domestic mandatory rules (such as tax, corporate, contract, real property and labour) may affect, even indirectly, international acquisitions each time they have contact with Italy.

17.2 Corporate Structures

An acquisition in Italy usually concerns shares (if the target is a joint stock company or a partnership limited by shares) or quotas (if the target is a limited liability company). Joint stock companies may have their shares or other financial instruments listed on the Italian Stock Exchange. In addition, an acquisition may affect assets as well as part of or an entire going concern, if the scope of the acquisition is a group of assets co-ordinated to carry out a business.

© World Law Group
International Business Acquisitions, M. Whalley, F.-J. Semler (eds.), Kluwer Law International, London, 2007; ISBN 9789041124838.

The rules applicable to an acquisition of a going concern are substantially different from those applicable to an acquisition of shares or quotas. The main differences are briefly outlined in the following paragraphs.

The shares, assets or going concern may be acquired from individuals, entities with a legal personality and from partnerships.

17.3   Letters of Intent and Heads of Agreement

The negotiations of an acquisition in Italy are usually conducted, at least at the early stage, by business executives and not by professional advisers. In recent years letters of intent and memoranda of understanding have been considered as the main instruments for regulating the preliminary stages of negotiations.

Under Italian law, an agreement is deemed binding if either it is so stated in the document signed or the factual circumstances lead to the conclusion that the parties intended to enter into a binding agreement which contains the four elements of validity—subject-matter, consideration, consent and, if so required by law, a particular form. In order to avoid any ambiguity, it is always advisable to specify in a letter of intent or a memorandum of understanding whether an agreement is to be binding. A binding letter of intent is usually deemed as a preliminary agreement which must be followed by a final agreement. In case of breach of the preliminary agreement, the agreement may be enforced in court and the court's decision will allow the parties to obtain the same result that would have been reached by the final agreement.

When a non-binding letter of intent has been signed, it is worth noting that Italian law provides for pre-contractual liability if the negotiations are not carried out in good faith.

17.4   Taxes Affecting the Structure and Calculation of the Price

The tax implications for an acquisition of shares or quotas are different from those for an acquisition of assets or of a going concern. In the first case:

- the buyer inherits all the target's tax liabilities;

- the seller realises a capital gain or a capital loss, depending on whether the sale price is higher or lower than the book value of the shares or quotas sold; and

- stamp duties are due in relation to transfer of shares, except for intra-group transferor transactions. In the second case:

- the seller realises a capital gain or loss, depending on whether the sale price is greater than the book value of the assets included in the going concern;

- registration tax should be paid on the asset's commercial value at different rates, which vary depending on the nature of the relevant asset (including the goodwill);

- a special tax on the increased value, based on the value of real property, may apply, depending on the specific circumstances; and

- a non-resident acquiring a going concern in Italy may be deemed to have established a permanent establishment and, consequently, the profits are subject to Italian taxes.

A sale of assets is, in principle, subject to value added tax, unless the transaction is interpreted as a sale of a going concern. In that case the rules indicated above would apply.

17.5   Extent of Seller's Warranties and Indemnities

Although the extent of the representations and warranties made by a seller depends on the size of the acquisition, it is usual for the seller to give, in addition to statutory warranties, full representations and warranties (relating to title on the shares, employees, assets, corporate and environmental aspects, etc.). Italian representations and warranties may sometimes differ from the standard clauses usually adopted in international acquisitions. In addition, a transfer of a going concern generally requires some specific representations and warranties. As a general rule, the validity of representations and warranties is limited in time (for tax purposes the term is usually six years).

The indemnities granted are normally secured by a guarantee issued by the seller or by its parent company or, as an alternative, by a bank guarantee, or by depositing part of the purchase price into an escrow account.

17.6   Liability for Pre-contractual Representations

Italian law provides for pre-contractual liability. As a general principle, the parties are under an obligation to conduct the negotiations in good faith, disclosing, to the extent possible information which is relevant for the agreement. Any breach of this duty of disclosure during the pre-contractual phase may trigger the obligation to compensate the other party within the limit of the damages incurred.

Normally, the agreement provides for an indemnity in case of breach of representations and warranties. However, where such a clause is not set forth under the relevant agreement, the party who has suffered damages because of pre-contractual misrepresentations or behaviour in bad faith may also bring an action to recover damages incurred.

17.7   Liability for Pre-acquisition Trading and Contracts

Representations and warranties, and the related indemnities, are aimed at protecting the buyer or the target from losses in connection with events that occur prior to execution or closing of the acquisition.

In the case of share or quota acquisitions, the target will continue to perform any existing contracts unless the termination of those contracts constitutes a condition precedent of completion. Pre-acquisition profits may be paid to the seller by way of dividends or by way of a price adjustment. Similarly, losses deriving from events which occurred prior to, but arising subsequently to the closing of, the acquisition can be reimbursed to the buyer through price adjustment mechanisms.

In the acquisition of a going concern, unless otherwise agreed, the buyer succeeds to the agreements entered into by the seller relating to the going concern transferred. (Note that a third party is always entitled to terminate, within three months from the transfer, the assigned agreements for cause.) In addition, the buyer is jointly liable with the seller for all obligations relating to the going concern. In this respect, an indemnification clause to protect the buyer is usually provided.

17.8 Pre-completion Risks

Until the transfer of shares (or quotas), going concern or assets has actually occurred, the risks of loss remain with the seller. Transfer occurs at completion, but the parties usually sign an agreement which contains all the terms and conditions, with the formalities for the transfer postponed to a subsequent date. Such practice is usually adopted for acquisitions of shares, quotas and going concerns.

The agreements typically provide a clause that would terminate the agreement in case of a material adverse change in the business between signing and completion and state that the seller and seller's counsel must deliver to the buyer, on the completion date and as a condition precedent of completion, a certificate to confirm that all the representations and warranties given at the time of the signing are still valid and effective.

A price adjustment clause may also be inserted in relation to losses incurred between signing and completion.

17.9 Required Governmental Approvals

Governmental approvals are required, in some areas, for the implementation of an acquisition. Governmental controls are delegated to relevant public agencies such as the Bank of Italy, the supervisory authority for private insurance companies (ISVAP), the supervisory authority in the broadcasting and newspaper industry and the supervisory authority for the securities market.

In the case of acquisitions of companies involved in a specific business (such as banking, insurance, telecommunications and television), the approval of or communication to the relevant public agency may constitute a prerequisite for the completion of the acquisition. The procedure for gaining approval may, depending on the circumstances and the complexity of the acquisition, require some time to be completed (the average is usually one month). Such a requirement may be extremely important when determining the structure and the time frame of the acquisition.

17.10 Anti-trust and Competition Laws

The Italian Anti-trust Act, virtually reproducing the EU competition rules, is aimed at controlling horizontal and vertical agreements, as well as acquisitions of shares, quotas or going concerns, and mergers and joint ventures ('concentrations') affecting the Italian market. In particular, concentrations constituting or strengthening a dominant position of an undertaking in the national market may be prohibited by the Italian Anti-trust Authority.

The parties to a concentration must file a notification with the Italian Anti-trust Authority prior to its implementation when either one of the following thresholds is met: the aggregate Italian turnover of all the undertakings involved in the concentration is in excess of ITL 689 billion, or the aggregate Italian turnover of the undertaking to be acquired is in excess of ITL 69 billion. These thresholds are updated annually.

The Italian Anti-trust Authority has also extended the applicability of the Anti-trust Act to include concentrations among foreign undertakings, in the event that they control Italian companies or have sales in Italy that would exceed the relevant thresholds. Fines can be levied by the Italian Anti-trust Authority for any breach of the provisions governing concentrations.

17.11   Required Offer Procedures

The Securities Act provides for the regime concerning acquisition of a listed company's securities through a tender offer. A tender offer may be voluntary or mandatory. Voluntary tender offers may be launched to take over listed companies by means of acquiring a controlling participation on the market. Mandatory offers must be launched under specific circumstances to have the buyer of a certain participation in a listed company share the so-called majority premium among the minority shareholders. In particular, a public tender offer must be launched in the voting stock of a listed company if there is an acquisition:

* of direct or indirect control of a company which owns a participation higher than 30 per cent of the voting stock of a listed company; or

* of a participation higher than 30 per cent of the voting stock of a listed company.

Administrative sanctions are provided for acquisitions of shares carried out in violation of the provisions governing mandatory offers. In addition, if the voting rights relating to the shares acquired in violation of such rules are exercised, the validity of the resolutions taken by the shareholders' meeting may be challenged as being null and void.

17.12   Continuation of Government Licences

Special licences may be required under Italian law to carry on a business. Sometimes, the change of control may trigger the revocation of licences (see e.g. the telecommunications sector). Consequently, it is advisable, during the negotiation phase, to ascertain which licences are required to conduct the business and to verify the requirements to be met if applications for re-issuance of licences must be filed.

For the acquisition of a going concern, the licences must be transferred (subject to the approval of the relevant public agency) to the buyer and must satisfy the requirements provided by law.

17.13   Requirements for Transferring Shares

As a general principle, shares are freely transferable. However, certain restrictions (such as pre-emptive rights and call and put options) may be found in the company's by-laws or in shareholders' agreements. Certain restrictions on the transfer of shares or quotas are deemed null and void. On the other hand, the by-laws of companies formerly controlled by the state and which operate in certain strategic sectors (such as telecommunications, defence, energy, etc.) may grant a veto power to the Ministry of Treasury with respect to the transfer of shares.

The transfer of shares must be formalized either by means of the endorsement of the share certificate duly authenticated by a notary public or by a bank officer, or by means of a notarized purchase agreement. In either case, the transfer of shares must be registered in the company's ledger by one of the directors. For a transfer of quotas, a notarized copy of the acquisition agreement should be filed with the competent Register of Companies kept by the relevant Chamber of Commerce. Upon fulfilment of such requirement, the transfer can be registered in the company's ledger and deemed effective.

In the case of the acquisition of a going concern, a notarized agreement must be filed with the Register of Companies kept by the relevant Chamber of Commerce.

17.14   Requirements for Transferring Land and Property Leases

Italy has a comprehensive system for title to land, and thus the purchase of land requires compliance with certain formalities. A purchase agreement of real property must be in writing and, in order to be registered with the Real Estate Register, it should take the form of a public deed or, alternatively, have the parties' signatures duly notarized. A registration tax must be paid.

The same provisions are applicable to property lease agreements where the property is leased for a period of at least nine years.

17.15   Requirements for Transferring Intellectual Property

The sale of going concerns or assets raises issues relating to the transfer of intellectual property rights.

Title to trade marks may be freely transferred. Trade marks may also be licensed. The Italian Trade Mark Act provides that any transfer of trade mark rights should be registered by means of filing the relevant agreement with the Italian Trade Mark Office. The requesting party must file the agreement in the form of a notarial deed, or after having obtained the notarization of the parties' signatures. A registration tax must also be paid. Although the lack of registration does not affect the validity of the transfer between the parties concerned, registration grants the transferee (or the licensee) a priority right in case of claims raised by third parties.

With respect to copyright and patent law, a potential purchaser may only be entitled to exploit the economic rights related to the relevant patent and trade mark, while the so-called 'moral right', which is the right of the author to claim authorship of the work and to challenge any modifications or alterations introduced to it by third parties, is not transferable.

17.16   Requirements for Transferring Business Contracts, Licences and Leases

With respect to business contracts, the general rule is that each party may assign the agreement to third parties, provided that the obligations of the agreement have not yet been fulfilled and provided that the other party gives consent. Consent to assignment may be given in the agreement.

Lease agreements are subject to the same rules. However, in the case of the transfer of a going concern, lease agreements are usually automatically assigned to the buyer.

In addition, in the acquisition of a going concern, unless otherwise agreed, the buyer succeeds to the agreements, entered into by the seller, relating to the going concern being transferred. (Note that a third party is always entitled to terminate an agreement within three months of the assignment of the agreement for cause.)

17.17   Requirements for Transferring Other Assets

As a general rule, the transfer of movable assets does not require any specific formality. Title to movable assets is transferred by delivery, provided that the purchase is carried out in good faith. In other words, the title to movable assets is vested in the buyer through possession.

However, movable assets registered with special registers (such as cars) may only be transferred by means of an agreement in writing and the transfer must be registered. Registration grants to the buyer a priority right as against third parties.

17.18   Encumbrances and Third Party Interests

Movable assets may be pledged. Under the Civil Code, the pledge is created by delivery of the assets or the document representing them. The pledgee is given a preferential right on the asset with respect to the obligations secured. However, if the debt exceeds ITL 5,000 (USD 350), the preferential right is granted only if evidence of the pledge is given in writing.

Shares and quotas may be subject to a pledge. The pledge is usually created by an annotation and, as far as shares are concerned, by the delivery of the share certificates duly endorsed to the pledgee or to a third party jointly designated by the pledgee and the pledgor. The annotation must be registered both on the share certificate and in the issuer's ledger. For a pledge of quotas, only annotation on the issuer's ledger is required. The parties may decide, in addition to these compulsory formalities, to regulate the pledge by means of an agreement.

Immovable and registered movable assets may be made subject to a mortgage created by registering the mortgage with the Real Estate Register kept by the competent office. The mortgage grants to the creditor a preferential right on the relevant asset with respect to the obligations secured.

17.19   Minimum Shareholder and Officer Requirements

Joint stock companies must be incorporated by at least two shareholders. If one of the shareholders becomes a sole shareholder, he or she is deemed liable for the obligations undertaken by the company during the period in which he or she has been sole shareholder if the company becomes insolvent. As a general rule, a joint stock company can be listed if the floating capital is at least 25 per cent of the total capital in issue and a foreseeable market capitalization equal to at least ITL 10 billion. However, this rule, under certain circumstances, may be waived upon consultation with the Italian Stock Exchange.

A limited liability company may be incorporated by a sole quotaholder, provided that, *inter alia*, he or she is an individual. If certain requirements are met, the same regime indicated above with respect to the sole shareholder applies to the sole quotaholder for the obligations undertaken by the company, in the event of the company's insolvency.

A company can be managed by a board of directors or by a sole director appointed by the shareholders or quotaholders. Although no provisions prevent non-Italian residents from being appointed as directors, for practical purposes at least one Italian resident is usually appointed as a member of the board in order to carry out the day-to-day activities.

17.20   Non-competition Clauses

With regard to the transfer of a going concern, the seller must refrain from starting a new business which is likely to interfere with the business activity that was transferred for a period of five years from the transfer.

Clauses that limit competition must be evidenced in writing and are valid if confined to a specific territory or a specific business activity. The non-competition clause cannot exceed five years. If a longer term is indicated in the agreement the restriction is only effective for a period of five years from the transfer. A similar rule applies to non-competition clauses concerning employees.

Agreements that have the effect of preventing, restricting or distorting, in a consistent manner, competition within the Italian market or in a relevant part of it are deemed null and void. However, if certain conditions are met, the Anti-trust Authority has the power to exempt agreements potentially restrictive of competition for a certain period. As a general practice, non-competition agreements are usually filed with the Anti-trust Authority if they might have an impact on competition.

17.21   Environmental Considerations

A massive flow of special legislation has been enacted in Italy as a consequence of EU directives in this field. Special legislation and regulations are currently in force to regulate air, water and noise pollution and to regulate the waste management sector, as well as in the fields of landscape protection and environmental impact assessment.

All the administrative functions are attributed to the Environment Minister who exercises a general surveillance power. On a local basis, the competence of the state has been granted to the regions, provinces and municipalities, which have functions regarding the structure and the utilization of the territory, the protection of land, air and water, and control over noise pollution.

17.22 Employee Superannuation/Pension Plans

In all cases of dismissal, employees are entitled to receive a severance indemnity (TFR), which is calculated on the basis of the employee's salary, computing not only his or her base salary, but also any other compensation paid to him or her on a continuous basis (e.g. commissions, regular bonuses, etc.), but with the exclusion of the reimbursement of expenses and extraordinary (*una tantum*) compensation. The salary also includes compensation in kind and, therefore, the equivalent amount of all fringe benefits granted to the employee. The severance indemnity is equal to the amount resulting from totalling for each year of service the salary paid during such year, divided by 13.5. During each year of service, that amount is accrued by the employer on the books of the company and on 31 December of each year revalued by an interest rate equal to 1.5 per cent plus 75 per cent of the cost of living index variation for the relevant year. In practice, the employee is entitled to approximately one month's salary for each year of service.

Private pension schemes are permitted by Italian law in addition to the general state social security system, which is compulsory. Private pensions, recently introduced in the Italian legal system, are significantly developed in sectors such as insurance, banking and by large corporations, mostly for the benefit of managers.

Private pension funds are funded with a portion of the severance compensation and with voluntary contributions which are deductible both from the income of the employee and of the employer up to a maximum of ITL 2.5 million per year. In addition, such private pension funds are subject to income taxation on a fixed amount ranging from ITL 5 million to ITL 10 million.

The tax regime concerning private pension funds is in the process of being reformed by the Italian legislature at the time of writing.

Private pension funds can be set up bilaterally through collective labour agreements (CLAs), or unilaterally through arrangements among workers or according to rules set forth by the employer. The private pension funds' assets must be totally separate from all other corporate assets.

Private pension funds can have different legal structures and, in any case, must have prior authorization from the Labour Ministry. Before granting the authorization, the Ministry verifies the funds' financial solvency and also checks that it meets the minimum economic requirements in order to operate investments and to achieve the proposed targets.

17.23 Employee Rights

Entering into an employment agreement is not subject to any formal requirement, except for certain special provisions or agreements that must be in writing, such as non-competition clauses, employment contracts for a definite period, trial contracts and part-time contracts. Most of the wages and other labour conditions are contained in CLAs which cover virtually all sectors. The contents and provisions of a CLA may vary according to the sector concerned. Normally, the CLA sets the wages and other benefits payable to employees of different rank and category. Generally, the working week is 40 hours and employees are entitled to paid leave of absence and vacations. A CLA may also apply, under certain circumstances, to employees and employers who are not members of the signatory unions and associations and also, to some extent, to employees of foreign companies working in Italy. A CLA cannot be derogated from by individual agreements unless such agreements are more favourable to employees. Social security contributions are normally equal to 40–50 per cent of the compensation and are paid, in large part, by the employer.

Dismissal is subject to stringent restrictions. Employers cannot dismiss employees at will and mere labour-saving dismissals are not permissible. Generally speaking, a dismissal must be grounded on an adequate cause and an employee, if improperly dismissed, is entitled to be reinstated and to receive compensation. Less stringent rules apply to executive employees ('*dirigenti*') and companies having up to 15 employees in the same business unit.

Collective dismissals are subject to specific provisions.

17.24 Compulsory Transfer of Employees

When a transfer of a going concern with more than 15 employees is planned, the seller and the buyer must give a 25 day's advance notice in writing to their respective internal union representatives as well as to their respective trade associations, in order to start a consultation with them concerning the planned transfer of the going concern. The consultation requirement can be considered exhausted ten days from the start of the consultation whether an agreement is reached or not. Any violation by the seller or the buyer of the obligation to consult the unions entitles the unions to obtain temporary relief measures for 'anti-union' conduct.

In the case of a transfer of a going concern, the employment relationship continues with the buyer and the employee maintains all the rights deriving from it. The seller and the buyer are jointly and severally liable with respect to all the employees' vested claims and rights at the time of the transfer. The buyer must apply the contractual conditions provided for by the CLAs, including internal agreements, in force at the date of the transfer, unless such agreements are replaced by other CLAs applicable to the buyer's business. As a result, employees who are dismissed in connection with the transfer of a going concern (in the absence of other justifying reasons) can bring an action before the Labour Courts to obtain a judgment confirming the continuation of the employment relationship with the buyer and declaring the dismissal null and void. In addition, the employee is entitled to damages for an amount not lower than five times the monthly salary. As an alternative to reinstatement and in addition to the above damages, the employee can request payment of an indemnity equal to 15 times the monthly salary.

According to certain CLAs (e.g. in the industry sector), executives are entitled to resign and receive a special indemnity in the event of a transfer of a going concern by the company-employer or in the event of a change of control of the employer.

17.25 Tax Deductibility of Acquisition Expenses

Where the buyer is a company or individual not resident or taxable in Italy, the deductibility of its acquisition expenses is determined by the laws of its home jurisdiction.

Where, however, the buyer is an Italian taxpayer, acquisition expenses are deductible only to the extent that they are expenses incurred in connection with activities that generate taxable income. The price paid for the acquisition of shares or quotas is not deductible, but represents the cost base for calculating the taxable capital gain on disposal of such shares or quotas. The price paid for the acquisition of business assets can be depreciated over a certain number of years according to the depreciation rates.

17.26 Levies on Acquisition Agreements and Collateral Documents

The transfer of shares is subject to a limited stamp duty of 0.14 per cent of the sale price. However, intra-group transfers are exempt from such stamp duty.

The transfer of a business as a going concern is subject to registration tax at an average rate of 3 per cent, although different rates may apply with respect to the single assets included in the going concern, depending on their nature.

17.27 Financing Rules and Restrictions

There are no thin capitalization rules which have the effect of denying a deduction to an Italian company in respect of interest payments made to a non-resident shareholder.

Interest expenses arising on debt used to finance a transfer of assets between related companies are generally deductible for national corporate tax purposes, but not for local tax purposes.

The Civil Code prohibits a company from providing financial assistance to purchase its own shares or the shares of its holding company, and most financial arrangements (including the early repayment of debt or the giving of guarantees) may constitute financial assistance for this purpose.

17.28 Exchange Controls and Repatriation of Profits

There are no exchange controls in Italy. However, cash transactions exceeding certain fixed amounts, whether domestic or international, must be reported to a government agency by financial institutions and other cash dealers for statistical purposes.

Dividends paid to non-resident investors by Italian resident companies are subject to a dividend withholding tax of 27 per cent, reduced to 10 per cent or 5 per cent if the investor is resident in a country with which Italy has a double taxation treaty.

Moreover, Italy has enforced the Parent—Subsidiary EU Directive and, therefore, dividends paid to a qualified EU parent are usually exempt from the dividend withholding tax. Resident shareholders are normally entitled to tax credits attached to dividends. No refund is available to non-residents, except for qualified shareholders who are residents of certain countries (e.g. France or the UK). Italian dividend withholding tax and underlying company tax may be allowed as a credit against the non-resident's tax liability in its home jurisdiction.

Italy imposes a 12.5 per cent withholding tax on interest paid to non-residents. This tax may be reduced to 10 per cent if the recipient is resident in a country with which Italy has a double taxation treaty.

17.29   Groups of Companies

No definition of a group of companies (except in the banking industry) exists under the Civil Code, while various concepts of control are contained in a number of special laws currently in force.

Under the Civil Code, a controlling stake is held in a company where a company:

- owns the majority of the voting rights exercisable in a meeting of shareholders;

- may exercise a dominant influence over the shareholders' meeting by virtue of its holding of shares or quotas; or

- may exercise a dominant influence by virtue of special contractual relationships with the controlled company.

An Italian holding company is required to prepare consolidated accounts of the company and each of the subsidiaries controlled.

In the event that certain requirements are met, a holding company and its subsidiaries may be made subject to a special insolvency procedure called extraordinary administration.

17.30   Responsibility for Liabilities of an Acquired Subsidiary

As a general rule, a shareholder or a quotaholder is not liable for the company's debts. However, as indicated in **17.19**, a sole shareholder and (under certain circumstances) a sole quotaholder may, in the case of company insolvency, be deemed liable for the obligations undertaken by the company for the period in which he or she has been the sole shareholder or quotaholder of the company. In a partnership limited by shares, a special category of shareholders ('*soci accomandatari*') is liable for the obligations undertaken by the company without limit.

Except as indicated above, the parent company is not deemed liable for the obligations undertaken by the subsidiary, since the group of companies, according to the prevailing case law, is not deemed to be a legal entity, and each company is considered as an independent entity. However, a few scholars have argued that, under certain circumstances, the parent company may be potentially liable for the debts incurred by the subsidiary.

Where the acquisition is of a going concern, the purchaser is jointly liable with the seller for all the obligations registered in the mandatory accounting books relating to the going concern transferred.

17.31   Governing Law of the Contract

The Conflict of Laws Statute has been recently amended. The new Conflict of Laws Statute provides that contractual obligations are governed by the 1980 Rome Convention on the Law Applicable to Contractual Obligations.

According to the 1980 Convention, the parties are free to choose the law applicable to a contract. In the event the parties do not make any choice of law, the law applicable shall be that of the state which has the 'closest contacts' with the contract; that is, in general, the law of the state where the party which has to perform the characteristic obligation provided for by the contract (i.e. the non-monetary obligation) has its domicile (individual) or its main or registered office (companies and other entities). However, note that in spite of any choice of law made by the parties, an Italian court would nevertheless apply those provisions of Italian law that are deemed to be the 'rules of law of mandatory application' and would not accept any provision of foreign law that is contrary to public policy.

Finally, the 1980 Convention does not apply, *inter alia*, to contractual obligations arising from:

• negotiable instruments which are regulated either by the 1930 Geneva Convention (promissory notes, bills of exchange and cheques) or by the law of the state where the negotiable instrument has been issued (any other negotiable instrument); and

• rules governing the set-up, incorporation, management, liquidation and winding-up of companies or other unincorporated entities.

17.32   Dispute Resolution Options

Arbitration is the favoured alternative to litigation for settling disputes in international acquisitions. In particular, the Italian Parliament has enacted a specific set of rules concerning international arbitration, which are applicable to the extent that one party of the agreement has fixed his or her residence or business establishment in a foreign state or most of the obligations related to the relationship under dispute are to be fulfilled abroad.

Arbitration proceedings may be also carried out either under the rules of an arbitral institution or by establishing an *ad hoc* procedure. A foreign award rendered in connection with an international arbitration is enforceable in Italy subject to an *exequatur* procedure before the Court of Appeals of the district where the Italian party has its registered office, provided that certain requirements are met.

Alternative dispute resolution systems (such as negotiation, mediation, mini-trials, etc.) are rarely used in Italy, although lawyers and business people have started to pay more attention to such remedies.

17.33 Other Issues

Shareholders' agreements are contractual arrangements usually aimed at creating:

- understandings in connection with the exercise of votes in shareholders' meetings;

- arrangements providing for the formalities for the transfer of shares to third parties; or

- agreement as to the management of the company.

Shareholders' agreements are not enforceable *vis-à-vis* the company. Although shareholders' agreements are widely used in practice and are permitted by special legislation (see e.g. the Securities Act), the courts have sometimes held that certain provisions restricting the exercise of fundamental shareholders' rights are null and void to the extent they infringe fundamental principles of corporate law. In particular, case law has ruled that shareholders' agreements entered into for an indefinite term are null and void. Consequently, it is advisable to verify on a case-by-case basis in advance whether the terms of a shareholders' agreement will be deemed effective under Italian law.

18. JAPAN

Tsuneo Sato City-Yuwa Partners

18.1 Introductory Comments

Foreign investment in Japan has been increasing recently following long years of decline after the economic 'bubble' period came to an end. The Japanese Government is actively encouraging direct foreign investment in the country. On 10 March 2006, the Japanese Government officially decided to take measures to make the inbound investment by foreign companies double within four years.

Effective as from 1 May 2006, the law governing corporate entities, the Company Law Chapter of the Commercial Code (the 'Commercial Code') and the relevant laws and regulations were abolished and replaced with the new Company Law (Law No. 86, 2005) (the 'Company Law'). The Company Law will dramatically affect the law regarding the formation and management of companies in Japan. The detailed regulations of the Company Law were promulgated by the Ministry of Justice and became effective at the same time the Company Law became effective. The Company Law and the detailed regulations are intended to make the formation of companies faster and management of companies easier.

18.2 Corporate Structures

The Company Law will make incorporating in Japan much faster and cheaper than it was under the Commercial Code. There were three corporate entities, the Kabushiki Kaisha (K.K.), the Goshi Kaisha and the Gomei Kaisha entities under the Commercial Code. In addition, the Yugen Kaisha (Y.K.) was also available under a special law. The Y.K. is a limited liability company intended to be used by small or medium enterprises. The Goshi Kaisha is similar to a partnership and the Gomei Kaisha is similar to a limited liability partnership, though they are corporate entities separate from their shareholders. Nowadays, the Goshi Kaisha and the Gomei Kaisha are rarely adopted, and those that do exist are generally restricted to small enterprises with a very limited role in the business world in Japan.

Under the Company Law, the Y.K. was abolished and all existing Y.K.s became K.K.s while Goshi Kaisha and Gomei Kaisha may remain unchanged. After the Company Law became effective, the following corporate entities exist in Japan:

a) the K.K.;

b) the Godo Kaisha, which is similar to an LLC in the United States;

c) the Goshi Kaisha; and

d) the Gomei Kaisha.

International Business Acquisitions, M. Whalley, F.-J. Semler (eds.), Kluwer Law International, London, 2007; ISBN 9789041124838.

Before the Company Law became effective, K.K.s were required to have a capitalization of at least 10 million yen and Y.K.s were required to have a capitalization of at least 3 million yen. Under the Company Law the onerous capitalization requirements have been abolished and companies can be capitalized with as little as one yen. However, the Company Law will restrict when dividends can be paid to shareholders. Companies will not be permitted to pay dividends to any shareholders if the company's existing net assets, at the time the dividend is to be paid, is less than 3 million yen.

After the Company Law become effective, it is likely that most merger and acquisition targets will be K.K.s. and subsidiaries of foreign companies established in Japan will be likely incorporated as K.K.s.

18.3   Letters of Intent and Heads of Agreement

Japanese companies do not often execute letters of intent or heads of agreement when negotiating a domestic deal. However, Japanese companies that commonly engage in international business transactions will be familiar with such agreements and they are commonly used in international transactions in Japan.

Letters of intent and heads of agreement will be binding on the parties if it can be demonstrated that the parties intended to create a binding agreement when the documents were executed. If the parties do not intend to be bound by such documents a specific provision stating that the documents are not binding should be included and most letters of intent and heads of agreement include such a provision as a matter of course. The parties usually carve out exceptions to the non-binding provision to ensure that provisions related to things such as confidentiality or choice of law are binding should there be a dispute regarding the documents or transactions contemplated thereby.

18.4   Taxes Affecting the Structure and Calculation of the Price

If the transaction is the purchase of the target's shares, the target's tax liabilities and obligations will remain unchanged and the buyer will be responsible for causing the target to comply with such obligations unless the parties specifically make other provisions in their agreement.

If the buyer purchases the assets of the target company, the tax liabilities and obligations of the target will remain with the seller. The purchase of the assets will be subject to consumption tax liability of 5 per cent on the price for the assets. Generally, in Japan, the buyer pays the consumption tax.

A stamp tax will be imposed on agreements for certain kinds of transactions specified by the Stamp Duty Law, which are executed within Japan. Such transactions include among others the sale of real estate, intellectual property or a business. The stamp tax must be paid with respect to each original copy of the transaction documents. Generally, each party will bear the stamp tax associated with their original copy of the transaction documents. The amounts of stamp tax varies depending on the value of the assets being purchased, for example, if the price of the assets is 1 billion yen, the stamp tax is 200,000 yen per original copy of the sales and purchase agreement.

Further, if the transaction involves the transfer of real estate, a transfer tax must be paid. Generally, the purchaser pays the transfer tax for a real property transaction. The tax rate is currently 3 per cent of the value of real estate as evaluated by the municipalities.

18.5   Extent of Seller's Warranties and Indemnities

The types and extent of warranties or representations that are made by the parties are often some of the most heavily negotiated parts of a merger or acquisition deal in Japan. The bargaining power of the parties will play a significant role in what representations and warranties are finally included in the contract and whether any security (for example, holding back part of the purchase price in an escrow account) for the representations and warranties is required.

Typically the seller will warrant that there are no legal or regulatory prohibitions in Japan that would make the deal illegal. The seller will also warrant that it has authority to enter into the transaction and has good title to the assets or shares that are to be transferred. The buyer will generally make similar standard representations and warranties regarding the legality of the deal and the buyer's authority to enter into the deal. Beyond that, the representations and warranties vary widely as does the length of time the representations and warranties are valid after the closing.

Similar to the representations and warranties, the indemnities provided by the parties are also a major point of negotiations. Parties often choose to cap the indemnity at an amount equal to or below the purchase price of the assets or shares being sold and often include a floor or minimum damage amount that must be reached before the indemnity obligation is triggered.

It is not common for the buyer to demand that a percentage of the purchase price be placed in escrow as security. Whether an escrow arrangement will be utilized depends in part on the negotiating power of the buyer, the type of assets involved, the risk of a breach and the size of the deal. However, it should be noted that Japanese law does not have any provisions regarding an escrow system or escrow agents and finding a third party to hold funds in escrow is difficult in Japan. In domestic M&A deals between domestic companies, escrow is generally not adopted.

18.6   Liability for Pre-contractual Representations

In Japan a party may be liable for negligent or fraudulent pre-contractual representations if such representations induced the other party to enter into the contract. If a party learns that a pre-contractual representation or warranty made by the other party is false, that party would have grounds to bring an action for damages or, possibly, to rescind the contract.

Parties often attempt to limit their liability for all pre-contractual representations and warranties by including limiting provisions in the final contract that explicitly state that only the representations in the contract are binding on the parties. Such a provision may provide a party that made a false representation or warranty some protection if the representation or warranty was made without malice or an intention to induce the other party to execute the agreement. A limiting provision would not protect a party if the party made a representation knowing that it was wrong.

18.7 Liability for Pre-acquisition Trading Contracts

If the transaction is a stock purchase transaction, the pre-acquisition contracts of the target will generally remain effective without any changes to the obligations and rights thereto. Of course, all such contracts must be reviewed during due diligence in order to determine whether there are clauses that address a change of control of the target or whether any detrimental clauses may become effective upon the change of control of the target. The parties must address liabilities for claims related to such things as products liability actions or breach of contract claims that occurred prior to the transaction or they will be assumed by the buyer.

In an asset purchase deal, all pre-acquisition trading contract obligations will remain with the seller unless otherwise agreed by the parties. The contracts will generally not be transferred to the buyer without the express consent of the other contracting party.

18.8 Pre-completion Risks

If the transaction does not have a simultaneous execution and closing, the parties will generally address pre-closing risks by including closing conditions that set forth specific events that will excuse a party from completing the transaction. In addition, a seller will generally be required to warrant that all the significant representations and warranties regarding the condition of the assets or business are true at the signing and at the closing so that risks to assets and the overall condition of the business will generally remain with the seller until the closing. Unless otherwise agreed by the parties, the pre-completion risk will remain with the seller until the delivery of the assets and it will shift to the buyer only upon the delivery of the assets.

18.9 Required Governmental Approvals

A foreign buyer of a Japanese entity is generally not required to obtain any specific governmental approvals when acquiring a Japanese target entity. However, foreign entities that will acquire a share of a Japanese entity are required to file a report of acquisition with the competent Government agencies through the Bank of Japan within 15 days of the acquisition. Prior notice is required with respect to some specific industries such as weapons, airplanes, space, atomic energy and so on. If the transaction could imperil Japan's national security or adversely affect the smooth management of the national economy, the transaction may be disallowed or restricted.

Investments in certain regulated industries, such as banking or securities dealers, are subject to the approval of the government. However, this is true regardless of the nationality of the investor.

18.10 Anti-trust and Competition Laws

Japan's Antimonopoly and Fair Trade Maintenance Act (the 'Antimonopoly Act') was originally enacted in 1947 and has been amended substantially since that time.

It prohibits private monopolization in business, trade restraint and unfair business practices. The law makes no distinction between Japanese entities and foreign entities and no special regulations or reporting requirements apply only to foreign entities doing business in Japan. The Fair Trade Commission oversees enforcement of Japan's Antimonopoly Act. It is an independent administrative agency with the power to enact its own internal regulations as well as implement hearing procedures to enforce the Antimonopoly Act.

The Antimonopoly Act specifically prohibits businesses or individuals from engaging in, individually or in concert with others, activities that cause a substantial restraint on competition or engaging in unfair trade practices, such as dealing at artificially low prices. A merger or acquisition will be prohibited when it would cause a substantial restraint of competition in any particular trade. Factors that the Fair Trade Commission will take into account include the types of goods and/or services involved, the geographic extent in which the goods and/or services are traded and other factors. The Fair Trade Commission will find a substantial restraint of competition when the merger or acquisition will result in a change in the market structure that allows specific companies to control the market by unduly influencing the price, quality or quantity of goods.

Parties engaging in certain mergers or acquisitions in Japan must make filings in certain situations pursuant to the Antimonopoly Act. The Antimonopoly Act requires that the Fair Trade Commission be notified in advance when a company will acquire all of another company's business if one party has assets that exceed 10 billion yen, including the assets of any parent or subsidiaries thereof in Japan, and the other party has assets exceeding 1 billion yen. If the deal involves only the transfer of a substantial part of a company's business or business assets, the sales of which exceed 10 billion yen, the Fair Trade Commission must be notified in advance as well. Reports to the Fair Trade Commission must also be made in case of the acquisitions of shares in similar situations as those noted above each time that the shareholding ratio exceeds 10 per cent, 25 per cent or 50 per cent, provided that no reporting is required when a company is newly established and all of the new shares are acquired by a company. Failure to abide by the reporting requirements can result in criminal penalties being levied against the offending entity.

18.11 Required Offer Procedures

If the target is a publicly traded entity strict tender offer rules apply. If more than 5 per cent of the shares of the target are to be acquired other than at or through the stock market, the purchaser must comply with the procedures of a tender offer as stipulated in the Security Exchange Law, and certain information regarding the acquisition, such as the purpose, the price, the number of shares to be acquired, the period of acquisition, etc. must be publicly disclosed by publication in an approved newspaper and such disclosure is accompanied by an offer to purchase shares. At the same time as such disclosure and offer, the acquisition must be reported to the appropriate authority. The public offer for the purchase of shares shall take place for a period between 20 days and 60 days after the publication as determined by the purchaser. After the public disclosure and offer period has lapsed, the purchase of shares can be closed pursuant to the terms disclosed in the publication.

If the target is a private entity a potential purchaser of the shares may directly contact the shareholders and make offers to all or any of them for the purchase of their shares.

18.12   Continuation of Government Licenses

If the deal is a stock purchase of the target, it is likely that the existing government licenses and permits will continue to be effective after the closing. However, each license and permit must be reviewed to ensure that it will continue, and if not, the seller should agree to cooperate with the buyer in obtaining a new license or permit when necessary.

If the transaction is an asset purchase, governmental licenses and permits will almost certainly not be transferable to the buyer and all such licenses and permits will have to be newly obtained. The seller may agree to assist the buyer in obtaining such new licenses and permits between the execution and the closing but the seller generally cannot make any promise that the buyer will obtain the necessary licenses and permits by the closing date.

18.13   Requirements for Transferring Shares

In order to transfer the shares from the shareholders to the purchaser, the target must record the transfer in its registry of shareholders and the shareholders must deliver the physical share certificates to the buyer in cases where share certificates have been issued.

Shares are generally freely transferable. However, the company's articles of incorporation may subject the transfer of shares to the approval of the company.

18.14   Requirements for Transferring Land and Property Leases

Transferring land is accomplished by transferring the 'title deed' of the property from the seller to the purchaser. An entry of the transfer of the title is made in the register of land and/or building registration. The 'title deed' is an original copy of the application for registration receipted by the registrar, which shows that the relevant registration has been completed in favour of the applicant. A purchaser of real property should review the 'title deed' of the seller to ensure that title was properly obtained and confirm the registration of title in the name of the seller before purchasing the real property.

Real property may be encumbered by mortgages, certain easements or liens on the property. Under Japanese law, a building is deemed property that is independent from the land on which it is built. Generally, mortgages, liens and easements must be registered or they will not be enforced after a transfer of title to the land is properly registered.

Transferring a lease requires the approval of the lessor. The lessor has the right to accept or refuse any request to transfer a lease. If a request is made, the lessor may demand that the lease be amended in its favour before approving the transfer.

18.15   Requirements for Transferring Intellectual Property

The requirements for transferring intellectual property depend on the type of intellectual property being transferred. Transferring patents or patent applications requires that the registered owner execute the proper transfer form and the buyer file the form with the Japan Patent Office. Trademarks are also transferable in a similar manner. If the transfer is not properly registered with the Patent Office it will be ineffective. It must be noted that if a patent is jointly owned with a third party, that third party's approval must be obtained prior to the transfer. If the third party's authorization is not obtained, the transfer will be void. The third party's approval is also required for any licenses to be granted.

18.16   Requirements for Transferring Business Contracts, Licences and Leases

Business contracts may be assigned subject to the consent of the non-assigning party or as otherwise provided for under the contract. The assignment of the contract will generally not release the assigning party from liabilities incurred prior to the assignment.

Licenses may be assigned in the same manner as other business contracts. The assignment of intellectual property rights should be registered with the appropriate office as noted above.

Leases can be assigned only with the permission of the lessor at the lessor's discretion. It should be noted here that lessees of real property in Japan often enjoy substantial rights with respect to renewing the lease. Generally, a landlord cannot refuse to renew a lease at the end of the term unless the landlord has a justifiable reason to do so, such as when the landlord intends to use the real property itself. A lessor of a building can avoid this situation by executing a specific term lease without renewal and following certain procedural steps, such as providing the tenant with a separate written explanation stating that the lease will not be renewed at expiration.

18.17   Requirements for Transferring Other Assets

Accounts receivable may be transferred to the buyer, provided that a notice of transfer must be delivered to the debtor in a notary form or other special form in order to assert the transfer of debt against the debtor and any third party. There is no legal requirement that the seller deliver a bill of sale evidencing such sale to the buyer. If the asset is encumbered and registered, such encumbrance continues after the transfer of the asset unless it is waived by the encumbrance holder.

18.18   Encumbrances and Third Party Interests

Many different types of liens may encumber assets of a seller. Encumbrances must be registered in order to assert them against third parties. Security interests in things such as equipment or personal property are secured through the use of a pledge of the property to the secured party or transferring title to the property to the lien-holder and physically marking the property as being owned by the secured party.

18.19 Minimum Shareholder and Officer Requirements

There are no limits on the number of shareholders for a K.K. Under the Company Law, there are various kinds of classifications of K.K.s. First, as explained above, a K.K. may require that the transfer of its shares be subject to the approval of the company. Such K.K.s are defined as a 'Non-Public Companies', and the other K.Ks are defined as 'Public Companies'. Secondly, if a company has capital of 500 million yen or more or whose liabilities are 20 billion or more it is defined as a 'Large Company'. A K.K. must have one or more directors, but there are no residency or nationality requirements for the directors. However, a Public Company must have the board of directors which consists of at least three directors. A Public Company must also have a statutory auditor who audits the execution of the administration of the company by the directors. A Non-Public Company may have a board of directors, provided that it has a statutory auditor or accountant. In this context, the statutory auditor and accountant are officers of the company and different from outside auditors. However, an accountant, who is an officer of the company, must be appointed from among a CPA, a certified tax advisor or their professional firms.

Goshi Kaisha, Gomei Kaisha and Godo Kaisha can have an unlimited number of members and there are no restrictions that require members to be residents of Japan.

18.20 Non-competition Clauses

Non-competition clauses are generally enforceable in Japan for both employees and for businesses.

Non-competition agreements are valid to the extent they are reasonable. Courts in Japan consider among other things, issues such as the field of business, period and geographic area covered by the agreement, whether the restraint is necessary to protect a legitimate business interest and (in the case of employees) whether compensation was given to the employee in order to secure the agreement not to compete.

Courts examine non-compete clauses that restrain employees severely and are likely to find the clause unreasonable if the employer makes any attempt to over-reach.

18.21 Environmental Considerations

Environmental considerations will be a significant issue in any deal that involves real property such as a deal involving land, a factory, a warehouse or a laboratory in Japan. Sellers are likely to strongly resist making any representations or warranties regarding the environmental status of real property, and it is recommended that buyers conduct an environmental study prior to the closing of any deal involving real estate. Buyers may be responsible for the cost of clean up of any environmental damage even if they recently purchased the real property and were not responsible for the pollution. Remediation of real property can be very expensive, time consuming and render the real property useless for significant periods of time.

18.22 Employee Superannuation/Pension Plans

If a company adopts an employee pension plan the details of the plan must be set out in the company's work rules. Usually, pension plans are based on the employee's salary at the time of retirement and generally are certain multiples of the monthly salary. It is not common, but it is becoming popular in Japan to make defined contributions pension plans. Most companies have a plan for retirement allowance, which generally is a lump sum payment made at the time of retirement. However, recently, companies have begun to adopt pension plans that combine a lump sum payment with monthly pension payments. Often these new plans allow employees to choose to take a lump sum payment or combine a lump sum payment with a monthly payment.

If the deal involves a sale of assets and employees will transfer to the purchaser, they usually must be paid any retirement allowance that has accrued prior to transfer. This is generally the responsibility of the seller. The buyer will need to provide such employees with a new pension plan or a plan of retirement allowance that is similar to that of their former employer's plan.

18.23 Employee Rights

Employees in Japan enjoy substantial right with respect to employment. There is no concept of at-will employment in Japan. Employers with 10 or more employees are required to promulgate work rules that set forth the important terms of employment such as working hours, pay and how pay raises are determined, vacation time, retirement allowance, pension plan (if the company has one), etc. The employer is required to hear from the employee union (and if there is no union, the employer must hear from employee representatives chosen by the employees) before promulgating the work rules. The employer is not required to accept recommendations made by the union or employee representatives, however, it is required to at least hear them.

If the acquisition is a share purchase, the employees will continue as employees of the target and no substantive changes will occur with respect to their employment.

If the acquisition is the acquisition of a business or the assets of the target, employees may choose whether to be employed by the new owner or remain with the seller. This can become a contentious issue in asset deals. Employees may not wish to go to the new owner if conditions of their employment will change and they have the right to refuse such a transfer. However, when the assets are sold, the employees often have little or no work at the seller and the seller will not wish to keep them. Terminating the employees may be difficult. Therefore, in asset deals where the seller wishes to have the employees transferred, the purchaser usually agrees to make employment offers that are substantially the same as the employees' current work conditions and to adopt work rules that are the same as the existing work rules. If the buyer does not wish to employ the employees, the parties must come to some agreement regarding the employees and such an agreement will usually require severance payments to the employees.

18.24 Compulsory Transfer of Employees

As noted above, there is no compulsory transfer of employees in an asset sale and the seller cannot easily terminate the employees if they refuse to be employed by the purchaser.

In a stock sale, the employees will generally continue their employment without any substantial changes.

18.25 Tax Deductibility of Acquisition Expenses

If the purchaser is not a resident of Japan, tax treatment of acquisition expenses will be determined by the purchaser's home jurisdiction.

If a party is a resident of Japan or subject to Japanese laws, most acquisition expenses incurred by that party will be expenses that can be deducted from its tax liability.

18.26 Levies on Acquisition Agreements and Collateral Documents

Stamp duties are applicable in Japan on agreements for the sales of assets as discussed in Section 18.4. No stamp duty is imposed with respect to agreements for the sales of shares.

18.27 Financing Rules and Restrictions

Japanese tax law includes a thin capitalization rule for certain business entities. The rule applies to subsidiaries, affiliated companies, or other companies that are substantially controlled by a foreign company. According to this rule, if the average balance of any debt of the controlled company bearing interest to the foreign controlling company is three times (or more) greater than the share capital of the latter in the controlled company with respect to the relevant business year, any interest on debt that is in excess of three times the share capital of the controlled company will not be treated as a tax deductible expense. However, the rule will not apply if the average balance of the total debts bearing interest that are assumed by the controlled company is three times or less of the equity or share capital, whichever is bigger, of the controlled company with respect to the relevant business year.

18.28 Exchange Control and Repatriation of Profits

Generally, there exist no restrictions and no reporting is required with respect to repatriation profits from Japan. Japan does impose withholding taxes on dividends paid to non-residents and the tax rate generally varies from 5 per cent to 15 per cent as provided under the tax treaty between Japan and each country.

18.29 Groups of Companies

K.K.s may prepare consolidated accounts of the company and its subsidiaries. A company cannot file consolidated returns that include affiliates or associated companies that are less than wholly owned.

18.30 Responsibility for Liabilities of an Acquired Subsidiary

A shareholder in Japan will not be responsible for an acquired subsidiary's obligations and liabilities. Therefore, if the deal is a share transfer, the purchasing entity, as a shareholder, will not be responsible for the liabilities of the acquired subsidiary.

18.31 Governing Law of the Contract

The parties are free to choose the governing law of the contract but generally, the law of the buyer's home or Japanese law will be agreed upon by the parties. If the parties choose a governing law that has no relationship to the parties or the transaction, there is a risk that the court will not recognize the choice of law and will apply Japanese law to the contract.

18.32 Dispute Resolution Options

The parties are free to adopt a wide range of dispute resolution options and such choices will be binding on the parties. If the parties wish to avoid litigation, it is fairly common for them to agree on arbitration subject to rules of an established arbitration association.

Agreements also often include a provision that requires the parties to negotiate disputes in good faith prior to seeking any formal dispute resolution. The effectiveness of these good faith negotiation provisions is unclear, but the parties are bound to negotiate if the contract does contain such a provision.

Mediation by a third party organization or courts is available in Japan, but it is not widely utilized and a Japanese party is more likely to prefer litigation in Japan or arbitration over a requirement to mediate disputes. However, even if a suit is selected, Japanese courts strongly try to settle cases by agreement of the parties prior to the case proceeding to a final judgment.

19. SOUTH KOREA

Yong Suk Oh Bae, Kim & Lee

19.1 Introductory Comments

In the past, foreign investors faced numerous legal barriers when attempting the acquisition of Korean companies and business assets. However, the legal and business climate relating to foreign investment in Korea has in recent years undergone a transformation, and Korea embarked several years ago upon a sweeping liberalization plan of laws and administrative practices relating to foreign investment. Having received added impetus as a result of the ongoing financial recovery package that the IMF brokered with the Korean Government in December 1997, the Government has adopted measures designed to stimulate merger and acquisition activities of domestic companies by foreigners. Indeed, the Korean National Assembly passed a number of new laws relating to foreign investment, such as the Foreign Investment Promotion Act (FIPA), which replaced the Foreign Investment and Foreign Capital Inducement Act effective as of November 1998, and the Foreign Exchange Transaction Act (FETA), which replaced the Foreign Exchange Management Act (FEMA) effective as of April 1999, and amended other laws governing foreign investment, such as the Securities & Exchange Act (SEA) and the Monopoly Regulation and Fair Trade Act (MRFTA), for the purpose of dramatically liberalising the government restrictions.

While it is true that Korea has a central government system and that all laws passed by the central legislature are uniformly applied throughout the country, there are several individual local government entities situated in Korea's provinces and major cities. Foreign investors are therefore also advised to review local laws when contemplating a corporate acquisition.

As foreign investment and international corporate transactions increase, the regulatory infrastructure in Korea is rapidly becoming more sophisticated and complex, and, in given circumstances, sometimes provides for stiff penalties for violations of applicable law. Accordingly, it is essential for any foreign investor to seek legal advice early on before attempting to acquire either an individual Korean company or a group which includes Korean subsidiaries or Korean assets.

19.2 Corporate Structures

The Korean Commercial Code (KCC), FIPA and SEA, among others, comprise the principal sources of law in Korea pertaining to international corporate acquisitions.

Korean law provides for four types of corporations, comprising two classes of limited liability companies and two classes of unlimited liability companies. Most Korean limited liability companies take the form of joint stock companies, which are the most common target of acquisitions in Korea. Joint stock companies can be listed

International Business Acquisitions, M. Whalley, F.-J. Semler (eds.), Kluwer Law International, London, 2007; ISBN 9789041124838.

on the Korea Exchange (KRX)[1] provided that they meet certain criteria set forth in the SEA.

It is possible to acquire shares or assets from anyone having legal personality and capacity, including private individuals, companies, statutory corporations, local government entities or even central government. While partnerships do not have a separate legal personality, a buyer may contract with a partnership so as to bind each of the partners jointly and severally.

19.3   Letters of Intent and Heads of Agreement

An agreement, whether oral or written, is binding if it appears from the document itself or from the surrounding circumstances that the parties intended to create a legal relationship. Consideration is not necessary to show a binding and fully enforceable agreement. If the parties do not wish to be bound by a letter of intent until the exchange of formal contracts (if any), clear language unambiguously expressing this intention should be used. There is, however, no set formula, so long as the parties' intention in this regard is evident. Note, however, that expressions such as 'subject to contract' are generally insufficient for this purpose.

19.4   Taxes Affecting the Structure and Calculation of the Price

For real properties and certain kinds of assets (e.g. automobiles) that require registration, the local government imposes acquisition and registration taxes. If title to certain real properties or registered assets are transferred to the buyer in a bulk business transfer or asset transfer deal, acquisition and registration taxes are imposed on the buyer. If 51 per cent or more of the shares of the targeted Korean company are acquired, deemed acquisition taxes (in proportion to the shareholding in the acquired company) are imposed on the buyer as if such assets of the targeted company had been acquired.

An acquisition tax of 2 per cent (plus a 10 per cent surtax on the acquisition tax amount) is levied on transferred real estate. Such acquisition tax is increased three times if the real estate is located in certain metropolitan areas, such as Seoul. The mayor or governor having jurisdiction over the metropolitan area may adjust the tax rate within a 50 per cent range. In addition, a registration tax of 2 per cent (plus a 20 per cent surtax on the registration tax amount) is levied on transferred real estate. Such registration tax is increased three times if the real estate is located in above-mentioned metropolitan areas.

The tax base on which the acquisition and registration taxes are levied is the price reported by the taxpayer to the tax office as the acquisition price agreed between the parties. If such reported acquisition price is less than the 'current base value' (as defined under the pertinent tax regulations), then the current base value is the tax base.

---

1. The Korea Stock Exchange, the KOSDAQ (Korea OTC market) and the Korea Futures Exchange were merged and the new official name of the merged exchange is the Korea Exchange, which now consists of the Securities Market, the KOSDAQ and the Futures Market.

In the case of the acquisition of shares in the targeted Korean company, there are no carry-over tax liabilities, other than the payment of the target company's corporate tax. In the case of a bulk business transfer, however, the buyer may have carry-over tax liabilities if:

- the seller is unable to pay national taxes (such as corporate tax, VAT etc) assessed on the seller's business prior to the transfer date; and

- the value of the assets remaining with the seller after the transfer is insufficient to cover such taxes.

The buyer's liability is limited to the amount of the assets acquired from the seller.

19.5   Extent of Seller's Warranties and Indemnities

The nature and extent of warranties and indemnities largely depend on the size of the acquisition and the parties' relative bargaining power. However, it is not unusual for sellers to give full warranties and indemnities covering the accounts of the business or company to be acquired, title to the assets, taxation, litigation, employee issues, etc.

It is always advisable to consider whether warranties and indemnities from a seller should be supported by a parent company guarantee, or by a partial retention of the purchase price.

19.6   Liability for Pre-contractual Representations

Negligent and fraudulent misrepresentations may give rise to both criminal and civil liability. In certain cases they can furnish grounds for rescission of the contract, as well as an action for damages, matters covered by relevant provisions of the Korean Civil Code. Furthermore, various criminal statutes establish penalties (fines, imprisonment) for sellers who engage in fraudulent conduct. Acquisition agreements often attempt to preclude actions for negligent misstatement or misrepresentation, leaving the buyer with a remedy only in damages for breach of warranty.

However, such protective clauses are deemed null and void where it is established that the seller intentionally defrauded the buyer or intentionally withheld material information from the buyer.

Since sellers frequently use contractual provisions shielding them from liability for representations made during pre-contractual negotiations, and restricting rights of rescission to the period between the exchange of contracts and completion, buyers are well advised to rely only upon representations specifically repeated in the agreement, or facts and matters specifically warranted or related to indemnities that have been given.

19.7   Liability for Pre-acquisition Trading and Contracts

If the purchase agreement contains a retrospective effective date the buyer, for accounting purposes, bears the loss or is entitled to the business profits from the effective date.

After completion, the seller remains liable for contracts to which it was a party unless they are novated and a release is given to the seller. Occasionally large contracts are novated (where the buyer fully steps into the seller's place, the seller being released from all further liability); however, more often contracts are assigned with the buyer promising to the seller to perform the contract from completion and indemnify the seller.

In a share acquisition, pre-acquisition profits are generally retained in the company and hence ultimately received by the buyer. Therefore, such profits should be taken into consideration when calculating the purchase price.

19.8 Pre-completion Risks

No legislation in Korea specifically addresses the question of who bears the risk between a seller and a buyer of assets or shares. However, an acquisition agreement typically contains a provision identifying which party will bear the risk of loss of, or damage to, the assets occurring between signing and completion.

In a share acquisition, the matter is usually addressed by a warranty to the effect that there has been no material adverse change to the business since a warranted accounts date and declaring that if indeed there has been any such material adverse change, the buyer has a right to terminate.

Occasionally, provisions allowing for a price adjustment in proportion to any loss or damage to assets are included.

19.9 Required Governmental Approvals

In general, all foreign investment into Korea (whether subscribing for new shares or acquiring existing shares in an existing company or establishing a new company) is governed by the FIPA and FETA.

The first issue is whether the FIPA and its related regulations restrict or prohibit foreign investment in the target's business activities. As part of the restructuring of the Korean foreign investment system, almost all activities have become fully open to foreign investment, although certain business areas (classified according to the Korean Standard Industry Classification System) are still partially or completely closed to foreign investment. If foreign investment in a given business activity is restricted, then such restrictions may require that the potential foreign buyer obtain additional governmental approvals and may affect the investment amount, among other factors. In this regard, the Korean Government has significantly reduced the number of business areas that are partially or completely closed to foreign investment and has accelerated its schedule for further liberalization of foreign investment, including investment in the capital market.

For acquisitions of existing shares by foreigners, a buyer is only required to report its acquisition to a foreign exchange bank pursuant to the FIPA or FETA unless the targeted Korean company falls into the category of the defence industry, in which case the acquisition of shares in such industry requires the approval of the Ministry of Commerce, Industry and Energy (MOCIE).

For acquisitions of newly issued shares by foreigners, a buyer is only required to report its acquisition to a foreign exchange bank pursuant to the FIPA or FETA.

Since 25 May 1998, general foreign portfolio investment ceilings under the SEA on the acquisition of beneficial ownership of any class of shares in a company listed on the KRX have been wholly lifted for both single foreign investors and foreign investors in the aggregate.

A foreign buyer may also consider establishing or using an existing subsidiary in Korea to acquire the targeted Korean company. The FIPA regulates only direct equity or quasi-equity investment by foreign entities in Korean companies. The acquisition of assets is subject to a number of specific laws, such as the Alien Land Acquisition Act (ALAA) and FETA.

Under the ALAA, foreigners wishing to acquire land in Korea are required to report to the local government authorities within 60 days after the execution of the relevant contract, unless the land falls into certain categories which are specially designated for national purposes such as defence, environment or cultural preservation.

19.10   Anti-trust and Competition Laws

The MRFTA and the regulations promulgated thereunder are the Korean version of anti-trust and competition laws. The MRFTA governs anti-competitive and unfair trade practices, including mergers and acquisitions.

Certain business combinations, including both stock deals and asset deals, are required to be reported to the Fair Trade Commission (FTC), the governmental authority charged with overseeing the implementation of the MRFTA, either prior to and/ or immediately after the closing, depending on the total assets or gross annual revenues of the buyer and the target company.

Under Article 12 of the MRFTA, if the total assets or gross revenues of either the buyer or the target company (in each case including its worldwide affiliates on a consolidated basis before and after the transaction) are KRW 100 billion or more and the total assets or gross revenues of the other company (including its worldwide affiliates on a con-solidated basis before and after the transaction) are KRW 3 billion or more, the buyer must file a business combination report with the FTC within 30 days after any of the following events:

a.   If it acquires at least 20 per cent (15 per cent in the case of outstanding listed shares) of the voting shares or outstanding equity (including units of contribution) of another company;

b.   If it acquires more of the voting shares or outstanding equity in another company after the filing of a business combination report pursuant to paragraph a. above, and becomes the largest holder of such shares or equity in such company;

c.   If it subscribes for at least 20 per cent of the total issued shares or equity (including units of contribution) of a newly established company;

d.   If it merges with another company or acquires all, or a principal portion, of the business of another company (in case of business acquisitions, the total assets or gross revenues of worldwide affiliates are not included in assessing the amount of total assets or gross revenues of the seller); or

e.   If any of its officers or employees concurrently become an officer of another company (excluding its affiliated companies worldwide).

Notwithstanding the foregoing and also pursuant to the MRFTA, if the total assets or gross revenues of either the buyer or the target company (in each case including its worldwide affiliates on a consolidated basis before and after the transaction; provided, however, that in case of business acquisitions, the total assets or gross revenues of worldwide affiliates are not included in assessing the amount of total assets or gross revenues of the seller) are KRW 2 trillion or more, the buyer must file a business combination report with the FTC within 30 days from the execution date of the share transfer or acquisition agreement in the case of paragraph a. or b. above, within 30 days from the date of the decision (e.g. date of approval by the board of directors or share-holders) to subscribe for shares in the case of paragraph c. above or within 30 days from the execution date of the merger or business transfer agreement in the case of paragraph d. above. Such a pre-closing notification generally requires a standstill period of up to 30 days (which may be extended for another 90 days by the FTC), during which time no merger, transfer of business or acquisition of shares may be conducted. The report-ing company may, however, request that the FTC conduct a prior examination of the contemplated transaction in advance, in which case the 30 day period of no activity after the submission of the business combination report may be reduced. The reporting company must also notify the FTC within 30 days after the completion of the pertinent transaction.

In the past, the FTC has rarely investigated mergers and acquisitions of domestic companies by foreigners. The FTC's current policy, however, is that mergers and acquisitions of domestic companies by foreigners are subject to the requirements of the MRFTA. The MRFTA prohibits any business combination that will have an anti-competitive effect on the relevant market.

19.11   Required Offer Procedures

Under the Financial Supervisory Commission (FSC) rules, any foreign investor who seeks to invest in the Korean securities market is required to register with the Securities Supervisory Services to receive investment registration certificates which must be presented each time the foreign investor opens an account with a securities company or other financial institution in Korea. The application to register can be made either directly or through a standing proxy.

Although foreigners are not required by Korean law to designate a standing proxy, non-resident foreigners are recommended to have a standing proxy to ensure that their investment-related activities are carried out in a timely manner. Korean securities companies, banks and the Korean Securities Depository are eligible to be a standing proxy for foreign investors. The major services of standing proxies are investment registration, account opening, order placing, settlement and collection of dividends or interest.

Under the SEA, any shareholder who acquires in excess of 5 per cent of the shares of a listed company must file a report with the KRX and the FSC. Thereafter, any change involving 1 per cent or more of shares in the company must be reported.

The above 5 per cent reporting requirement is calculated by aggregating the listed shares (including convertible securities, such as convertible bonds and bonds with warrants) held by all affiliated groups (which include parties holding special interest and any group 'acting in concert', as defined in the SEA).

The above procedures and requirements only apply to foreign investors who seek to make an equity investment in companies that are listed on the KRX.

Under the FETA, other than in case of direct investments, such a foreign investor would normally designate a single foreign exchange bank where it would open a foreign currency account and a KRW account that is to be exclusively used for securities investments. No governmental authorization is required for inward remittance into Korea and deposits of foreign currency funds into such foreign currency account. No restrictions exist on outward remittances to a foreign country of any principal or interest in connection with securities investments.

Upon confirmation from a designated foreign exchange bank, such foreign currency funds may be transferred from the foreign currency bank account to a KRW account at a securities company or other financial institution for purposes of placing a deposit for, or setting the purchase price of, a securities transaction.

19.12   Continuation of Government Licences

With respect to certain industries, the business operator is required to hold a licence, a requirement which may be imposed under either central or local government law, or both. Examples of businesses requiring licences are banking, insurance, gaming and broadcasting. Various conditions may be attached to a licence and in any acquisition these require close scrutiny; for example, the licence may be revocable upon a change of control of the licence holder. Licences are in fact normally non-transferable so that a buyer of a business (as opposed to e.g., a buyer acquiring the shares of a corporation) must obtain a licence in its own name. In Korea, the waiting period for the review of licence applications and the granting thereof can be relatively lengthy, and thus may become an important factor to consider in an acquisition.

19.13   Requirements for Transferring Shares

Restrictions on transfers of shares may be located in shareholders' agreements. Hence, all shareholders' agreements should be closely reviewed. Note, however, that the only share transfer restriction permitted under the KCC is to require the approval by the board of directors of the company if the articles of incorporation so provide and further that a share transfer restriction for an extended period of time which does not allow for any practical possibility of exit by a shareholder and therefore blocks the fundamental right of the shareholder to freely transfer its shares is likely to be invalid.

Shares are normally transferable by mere written share transfer form or by simply conveying the share certificates in question. If a form is used, the form must be submitted to the company's board of directors and the buyer's name must be inserted in the register of company shareholders.

Under the KCC, the board of directors of the target Korean company has authority to issue new shares up to the authorized share capital amount, as stipulated in its articles of incorporation. If the authorized share capital amount needs to be increased, the articles must be amended by special resolution of the shareholders. In order to do so, under the KCC, such amendment must be adopted by affirmative votes representing at least two-thirds of the shares present and at least one third of the total issued and outstanding shares, unless a higher voting requirement is provided for in the articles.

Under the KCC, the existing shareholders of a Korean company have pre-emptive rights to newly issued shares, subject to any special provisions in its articles of incorporation. Therefore, if newly issued shares are to be allocated to the foreign buyer, the existing shareholders of the target company must waive their pre-emptive rights to such shares, unless the articles provide the new shares may, by a board resolution, be issued to parties other than shareholders.

19.14   Requirements for Transferring Land and Property Leases

Korea maintains a comprehensive registration system of title to land (including lease-hold interests). The purchase of any interest in real property requires the execution of a prescribed transfer form, and is subject to payment of stamp duty and registration with the Court Registry Office of the locality in which the land is situated. It is also advisable to register leasehold interests in land and buildings since unregistered lease-hold rights are unenforceable in the event such land or building is transferred to a third party.

Title to land can be specifically encumbered by mortgages or charges and other interests of third parties in the land (such as easements and rights of way). However, the buyer may rely on the recording system and assume that all encumbrances pertaining to the land have already been registered with the Real Estate Registry. Therefore, in principle, good title to the land may still pass to the buyer and be registered in favour of the buyer.

19.15   Requirements for Transferring Intellectual Property

Title to all forms of intellectual property can be transferred by assignment.

Patents, designs, utility models, service marks and trade marks must be registered with the Korean Industry Property Office (the KIPO) in order to benefit from protection. Thus all transfers involving such intellectual property rights must be registered with the KIPO, failing which the assignment is not enforceable by an assignee. In the case of copyrights, registration with the KIPO is not always necessary.

A licence to use the intellectual property of a third party as well as an assignment of the benefit of a licence must be registered with the KIPO in order to benefit from protection. Furthermore, the assignment of the benefit of a licence almost always requires the licensor's consent.

19.16 Requirements for Transferring Business Contracts, Licences and Leases

A business contract governed by the laws of Korea is only transferable or assignable in accordance with its terms. An assignment of the benefit of a contract does not release the transferor from the burden of the contract without a specific release from the other party. As a result, some business acquisitions involve a formal novation of contracts rather than a simple assignment. Licences and business leases (finance leases, operating leases or hire purchase agreements) are governed by the same rules.

In most cases, the consent of the other party to the contract (e.g., a lessor) is required before the contract can be assigned. Leaving aside registration with the KIPO (see **14.15**), it is not normally necessary to register or record an assignment of a business contract, although stamp duty on the assignment document may be required in some instances. Furthermore, notice must be given to the other party to the effect that the contract has been assigned.

19.17 Requirements for Transferring Other Assets

Personal property can usually be transferred by delivery. However, real estate, intellectual property, or substantial personal property (e.g. aircraft, automobiles, boats, etc) which is subject to registration requirements under local law, may be transferred by registration with the appropriate government agency or office.

19.18 Encumbrances and Third Party Interests

Assets can be subject to several types of third party interests. Interests can arise under contract (e.g. a charge or a mortgage) or by operation of law (e.g. a property right or a lien in favour of a statutorily protected interest).

A buyer for full value of an asset generally takes good title to it, unless the buyer has actual notice of an encumbrance. However, if the asset involved is real estate (land or building) or an item of personal property that may be registered (aircraft, boat, automobile, etc), a buyer for full value obtains good title provided that it has not received actual or constructive notice of an encumbrance. Furthermore, the buyer for full value of any asset cannot acquire good title if the seller does not, in fact, have clear title to such asset.

Certain title registers (particularly in the case of land) can constitute prima facie evidence of the title of the registered proprietor, on which the buyer can rely. However, other assets may be subject to unregistered or unascertainable interests which a buyer will not be able to identify. In such cases, warranties from the seller as to clear title are essential.

19.19 Minimum Shareholder and Officer Requirements

Joint stock corporations must have a minimum of three directors, one representative director (i.e. a director authorized to represent or act on behalf of the corporation) and one statutory auditor, provided that in case of a company the total capital of which is less than KRW 500 million, the number of directors may be less than three. Certain companies are required to have outside directors and/or an audit committee in place of the statutory auditor. A limited liability company must have at least one director. None of the above is required to be a Korean citizen or even a resident of Korea.

A joint stock corporation requires a minimum of one promoter at the time of incorporation. There is no maximum number of shareholders for a joint stock corporation.

19.20 Non-competition Clauses

Restraint of trade clauses and non-competition covenants given by a seller in the context of a sale of a business will generally be enforceable, provided that they are reasonable in scope and content. What is reasonable will depend upon the facts and circumstances, including the nature of the business in question and the effect that competition might have on the buyer.

Covenants furnished by an employee in employment agreements can likewise be enforceable, provided they are reasonable. However, the test of reasonableness is likely to be stricter in the case of an employee than in the case of a seller. A blanket prohibition on an employee engaging in his actual occupation or exercising his skills is likely to be considered unreasonable, as is a restraint of excessive duration following termination of the employment relationship.

Agreements involving restraint of trade may also fall under the sweep of the MRFTA, which prohibits any agreement or understanding the purpose or effect of which is to lessen substantially competition or which is an exclusionary provision (essentially, a collective boycott). The provisions of the MRFTA are comprehensive and far-reaching and can potentially surface in virtually any acquisition.

19.21 Environmental Considerations

Korea has enacted several laws aimed at protecting the environment, which are administered and enforced by both local governments and the Ministry of the Environment. Substantial penalties can be imposed on businesses that cause environmental damage. A purchaser of a business or property can inherit responsibility for rectifying environmental damage caused by the previous owner.

Korea is a signatory to two international environmental treaties: the Vienna Treaty for the Protection of the Ozone Layer and the Treaty on the Prevention of Ocean Pollution in Relation to Waste Material and Disposal of Dye Materials. In the case of mining, manufacturing and chemical industries, notably, appropriate environmental due diligence investigations are always advisable in the context of an acquisition of either shares or assets.

Warranties covering environmental damage and liability should always be obtained from a seller, unless the buyer's due diligence investigation has extended to a full environmental audit.

19.22 Employee Superannuation/Pension Plans

Pursuant to the Korean Employee's Retirement Payment Guarantee Act, employers are required by law to pay their employees a retirement allowance, which may be paid directly by employers in lump-sum or indirectly through retirement pension plans.

In addition to receiving a retirement allowance, employees receive other benefits from the National Pension Fund. The National Pension Act requires all employers and all employees to pay 4.5 per cent of their monthly wages into the national fund. The Fund is supervised and managed (independently from the company) by the National Pension Management Organization, which is operated under government control.

19.23   Employee Rights

The Labour Standards Act (LSA) prescribes the minimum terms and conditions of employee agreements such as working hours, holidays and the method of paying salaries, and also prohibits unfair dismissal. If an individual agreement violates the prescribed minimum terms and conditions set forth in the LSA, the offending provisions of such agreement are deemed null and void and the statutory minimum terms and conditions of the LSA replace such provisions.

The government periodically revises the minimum salary for employees, and any employer violating such minimum is, in theory, subject to criminal sanctions. The minimum salary is, nonetheless, relatively low compared to the prevailing salary levels in the Korean labour market. Employees in Korea have the right to organize labour unions as well as collective bargaining organizations and procedures.

19.24   Compulsory Transfer of Employees

In the case of an acquisition through share purchase, the buyer may not demand the dismissal of employees as a condition for completing such transaction.

In the case of a bulk transfer, the buyer usually acquires the labour force in addition to the seller's business assets. The parties may decide to enter into an agreement to transfer only a portion of the labour force to the buyer. Such agreement, however, would result in the dismissal of certain employees, in which case the seller is subject to the applicable laws, namely the LSA, that restrict the dismissal of employees. The buyer is subject to such restrictions under the LSA if it chooses to reduce the labour force.

Under the LSA, an employer may not terminate an employee's employment without valid cause. Further under the LSA, an employer may downsize its labour force only under the following conditions:

- the company must prove that management is in a state of crisis (which includes mergers and acquisitions);

- the company must exert its best efforts to avoid the dismissal of its employees;

- the company must select employees for dismissal using fair and reasonable criteria; and

- with regard to the possible methods for avoiding dismissal and the criteria for dismissal referred to above, the employer must, in good faith, consult with the employees or their representative (although no precise method for nominating such representative is mentioned by the court, leaving aside unionized companies)

60 days in advance. Note, however, that in practice 'consult' does not as such require the employees' actual permission or agreement.

With respect to the labour force acquired by the buyer from the seller through the bulk transfer, the existing employment agreements (and the rules of employment that are deemed to be part of such agreements) which set forth the working conditions of such labour force are transferred unless otherwise agreed with the employees. In this respect, the buyer is obligated to pay wages, to set the working hours, etc according to such agreements as the employer of the acquired labour force.

In the case of a simple transfer of certain assets of a company, the buyer may selectively acquire the seller's employees.

19.25 Tax Deductibility of Acquisition Expenses

Where a buyer is a company or individual neither residing nor otherwise taxable in Korea, the laws of its home country govern the deductibility of its acquisition expenses.

Pursuant to the Korean Corporate Tax Act, expenses incurred in the acquisition of shares or assets are generally deductible, provided that such expenses are incurred in making a new business investment (i.e. an investment which expands the industrial scope of the acquiring entity's business).

19.26 Levies on Acquisition Agreements and Collateral Documents

No stamp duties are payable in the case of a share transfer, but a securities transaction tax is applicable.

On the other hand, stamp duties are applied in the case of a business transfer involving a transfer of real property, intellectual property or other property subject to registration requirements under Korean law.

Any transfer of property requiring registration under Korean law is subject to registration tax and education tax.

19.27 Financing Rules and Restrictions

In general, expenses incurred in the normal course of business operations of the corporation are deductible, provided, however, that they are adequately supported by documentary evidence; expenses not supported by documentation may be disallowed. Depreciation, rentals, selling expenses, etc are the principal allowable expenses, with additional depreciation and provision for reserves deductible under certain conditions. Depreciation expenses, interest expenses and maintenance expenses relating to land not used for business purposes are not tax deductible.

Any common general administrative expenses incurred by an enterprise as a whole or its related office controlling the Korean branch and which are reasonably connected with the generation of domestic source income of the Korean branch are allocated on a reasonable basis for the computation of domestic source taxable income of the Korean branch.

Loans between related companies (e.g. a loan between a parent company and its subsidiary) for tax purposes may incur a statutorily prescribed interest rate.

Effective as of 1 January 2006, businesses are free to borrow foreign currency under loans regardless of the maturity thereof. In order to expedite the compilation of statistics on foreign borrowings, however, borrowers must report to the Ministry of Finance and Economy (MOFE) if the amount is USD30 million or more or to their correspondent foreign exchange banks when the amount is less than USD30 million.

Under the International Tax Coordination Act of Korea, if the amount of a loan extended to a Korean company by, or under the guarantee of, its foreign controlling shareholder (owning directly or indirectly 50 per cent or more of the total voting shares of, or otherwise having a substantial control over, the Korean company) exceeds 300 per cent (600 per cent, in case of financial institutions) of the amount of the equity capital contributed by such foreign controlling shareholder, then interest payments made on such excess portion of the loan will not be treated as deductible expenses of the Korean company for tax purposes.

19.28   Exchange Controls and Repatriation of Profits

The Korean Government unveiled a foreign exchange liberalization plan in June 1998 which introduced a comprehensive deregulation of foreign exchange transactions starting in April 1999. As a first stage liberalization measure, the FETA was enacted in September 1998 to replace the existing FEMA. The existing Act was aimed at regulating and managing foreign exchange transactions. However, the purpose of the new Act is to liberalize foreign exchange or other transactions with foreigners and minimize any regulations or restrictions on such transactions. As part of the government's reform of corporate borrowing, trading and foreign investment, the FETA is also intended to induce more foreign capital by improving the environment for investment in Korea by foreigners. The FETA came into effect on 1 April 1999.

Pursuant to the FIPA, the repatriation of profits earned from investment under the FIPA can be effected without restriction, with the exception of a withholding tax levied on dividends. Such withholding tax on dividends for a foreigner who does not have a 'permanent establishment' in Korea is 27.5 per cent. However, bilateral double taxation treaties in force between Korea and various countries can generally lower this to 5–15 per cent.

19.29   Groups of Companies

A company incorporated under the KCC is required to prepare financial statements (profit and loss account and balance sheet) for the company.

Joint stock companies with total assets exceeding KRW 7 billion (KRW 1 billion in case of listed companies) must be audited annually by independent certified public accountants, and an annual auditor's report must be prepared.

A company incorporated under the KCC is required to synchronize its financial year with that of each company or entity which it controls. Namely, a parent company with controlling interests in other companies should prepare consolidated financial statements which bring together the accounts of its own and its subsidiaries. In addition, business groups the total assets of which exceed KRW 2 trillion should prepare combined financial statements to bring together the accounts of companies that belong to the group.

19.30 Responsibility for Liabilities of an Acquired Subsidiary

In principle, shareholders in Korea are shielded from liability for the debts of a company in which they hold shares, except where a specific guarantee, indemnity or other undertaking has been given in favour of a creditor. Note, however, that if 51 per cent or more shares of a Korean company (which is not listed) are owned by a shareholder and its related parties, such controlling shareholders would have a secondary liability for payment of the national taxes assessed on the company. Such secondary tax liability arises only if the tax authorities are unable to collect on the primary tax liability.

19.31 Governing Law of the Contract

Korean courts honour a choice of law freely entered into between parties to a contract. They do not insist on applying Korean law to a contract for the acquisition of shares or business assets in Korea. However, a choice of law that has no commercial or reasonable connection with the parties and even the agreement itself runs the risk of being disregarded on grounds of public policy, in certain situations.

While the law of a foreign jurisdiction may govern the agreement and the relationship between the parties, Korean law usually governs collateral issues such as the effect of a transfer of title to shares or other assets, or the rights of creditors and others.

19.32 Dispute Resolution Options

Korean law acknowledges that parties to commercial contracts may wish to settle any disputes that occur by means other than litigation, and a range of arbitration and mediation options are available to them.

Korea is a signatory to the Convention on the Recognition and Enforcement of Foreign Arbitral Awards of 1958, commonly referred to as the New York Convention. Korean courts will thus in general recognize and enforce international arbitration awards, although it should be noted that Korea opted under the Convention to apply its terms only to awards rendered in another signatory state, and to differences arising out of legal relationships which are considered commercial under Korean law.

The Korean Commercial Arbitration Board maintains a list of potential arbitrators (including foreigners' resident in Korea) available to hear commercial disputes between parties, and oversees arbitrations conducted pursuant to its rules of arbitration.

Mediation has also been a successful dispute resolution process for commercial disputes in Korea, and is increasing in popularity due to its relative effectiveness in resolving disputes while at the same time avoiding lengthy and expensive litigation. In the course of litigation of a commercial dispute, a Korean court has the power in certain circumstances to halt proceedings so as to conduct a mediation session.

Parties are free to incorporate into their contracts the arbitration or mediation rules of any Korean or international body, and Korean courts will honour such choice. Further, pursuant to the Korean Arbitration Act, if the parties have agreed to resolve their dispute through arbitration, the courts will refuse to intervene unless the court deems the arbitration agreement to be null and void.

With respect to the enforcement in Korea of judgments rendered by a foreign court, the Korean Code of Civil Procedure enumerates the conditions that must be satisfied before a Korean court will enforce such a judgment:

- the jurisdiction of the foreign court is not disputed in any Korean laws and ordinances or in a treaty;

- proper service of a summons or other process necessary for the commencement of the suit was effected upon the defendant, other than by public notice, or else the defendant voluntary responded to the suit without having been served;

- the judgment of the foreign court is compatible with the 'public morals and social order' of Korea; and

- there is reciprocity for enforcement between Korea and the foreign jurisdiction in question.

It is therefore wise to investigate whether the courts of a given jurisdiction have previously enforced any Korean judgments, when one is faced with the possibility of seeking enforcement, in Korea, of a judgment rendered in such foreign jurisdiction.

20. LUXEMBOURG

Arendt & Medernach

INTRODUCTION

Special purpose vehicles incorporated in the Grand Duchy of Luxembourg are frequently used in major transnational deals. Why is it so? The reputation of Luxembourg as an international financial centre necessitates little commentary. With over 150 banks, it is one of the major financial centres in Europe, as well as internationally. The activities are numerous: private equity, private banking, money and securities markets, investment funds, pension funds, insurance and reinsurance activities.

The Grand Duchy's role as host to major European institutions, combined with the rapid growth of the international banking business, has reinforced the country's international character which links French and German cultures and traditions. The influence of Luxembourg's neighbours also extends to the legal system which is based on French civil law, Belgium corporate law and German tax law.

Transactions are structured so as to use Luxembourg entities because of the attractiveness and the flexibility offered not only by Luxembourg tax law, but also by the corporate, financial and investment funds regulations. This generally favourable environment is undoubtedly a major reason for the success of Luxembourg in attracting foreign investors.

In particular, Luxembourg is a well established jurisdiction for holding companies. Due to the participation exemption regime, fully taxable companies may operate as holding companies without a tax cost: this is the so-called **'SOPARFI'** regime *(SOciété de PARticipation FInanciére)*. One should note that the word SOPARFI is used by practitioners, but has no legal meaning.

Because of its incompatibility with European state aide rules, the well-known tax exempt 1929 holding regime was abolished on from 1 January 2007. Yet, grandfathering provisions will remain applicable during a transitional period.

Following this abolition, the Luxembourg government has proposed to create a new Luxembourg entity aiming at family property management (the **'SPF'** or *'Société de gestion de Patrimoine Familial'*). The law implement's this new vehicle was adopted on 11 May 2007.

The investment fund industry has also shown remarkable progress since the early 1980's. In 2005, Luxembourg had 2,060 funds with net assets of around EUR 1,525 billion[1], setting Luxembourg second in rank after the United States regarding assets under management.

---

1. Based on the annual report 2005 of the Commission for the supervision of the financial sector (CSSF), page 225.

© World Law Group
International Business Acquisitions, M. Whalley, F.-J. Semler (eds.), Kluwer Law International, London, 2007; ISBN 9789041124838.

Aside from this, Luxembourg has many advantages to offer to foreign investors:

- the government strongly encourages investments from all sources, whether Luxembourg or foreign. Prospective investors may obtain assistance of several kinds for projects offering good opportunities for growth and employment;

- Luxembourg offers fiscal incentives to promoters investing in the audio-visual sector or in venture capital;

- captive reinsurance companies created under Luxembourg law offer highly valuable risk management possibilities and tax planning opportunities;

- the Luxembourg maritime flag;

- the Luxembourg stock exchange has emerged as one of the major jurisdictions for bond registrations.

The scope of this article is not to address all the legal and fiscal aspects in relation with the above-mentioned regimes and incentives. It is only to provide a brief overview of certain types of Luxembourg entities which are used in most major transactions.

I. THE VEHICLES: SOPARFI, INVESTMENT FUNDS AND SICAR

In this section, we have chosen to focus on the general characteristics of three types of Luxembourg vehicles: the SOPARFI, the investment funds and the new private equity investment company in risk capital *(société d'investissement à capital risque* or **'SICAR')**.

A/INTRODUCTION TO THE SOPARFI

1. General information

The SOPARFI is a limited company[2] subject to the ordinary tax regime. Its taxable base can be reduced or even eliminated in pursuance of the parent-subsidiary regime (hereinafter referred to as the 'regime')[3] aimed at avoiding economic double or multiple taxation of the same income. The regime provides an exemption at three levels i.e. (a) the exemption of dividends or liquidation profits received by the SOPARFI from its subsidiaries, (b) the exemption of capital gains realized on the transfer of participations and finally (c) the withholding tax exemption on dividends paid by the SOPARFI to its shareholders. Furthermore, participations whose revenues could benefit from the regime are exempt for net worth tax purposes. The regime only applies to income derived from substantial participations that comply with certain conditions. Any other income is, as a rule, taxable at the ordinary rate (e.g. income derived from bonds, non-eligible participations and units of non-taxable investment funds).

---

2. *sociétés de capitaux* (hereinafter, 'companies').
3. This regime relies, among others, on the implementation of EU Council Directive 90/435/EC of 23 July 1990 on the common system applicable in the case of parent companies and subsidiaries of different Member States (the 'Parent-Subsidiary Directive'). This regime is also referred to as the participation exemption regime or *Schachtelprivileg*.

The SOPARFI is an ideal vehicle only when the investment policy targets substantial participations in fully-taxable companies.

The SOPARFI benefits from the application of tax treaties.

2. *Corporate Forms*

The SOPARFI can take the form of either a joint-stock company (the *société anonyme* or 'SA'), a private limited company (the *société à responsabilite limitee* or **'Sàrl'**) or a partnership limited by shares (the *société en commandite par actions* or **'SCA'**). These companies are governed by the provisions of the law dated 10 August 1915 concerning commercial companies, as amended (the **'Company Law').** The following paragraphs underline the major differences between these types of companies from a corporate law perspective.

a. Differences relating to the incorporation of each type of company

Capital

The minimum capital is EUR 31,000 for the SA and the SCA, and EUR 12,500 for the Sàrl. The use of the authorized capital is only possible for the SA and SCA and excluded for the Sàrl. In a Sàrl, the capital must be totally paid up, whereas in a SA and a SCA, shares may be partially paid up.

The number of partners of a Sàrl shall be comprised between 1 and 40. A SA may be incorporated with 1 shareholder without upper limit. It must be at least 2 for a SCA, without upper limit.

The SCA has two categories of shareholders, i.e. general partners being indefinitely (and jointly and severally) liable for the company's obligations and limited partners with limited liability.

The report of an independent auditor required in connection with the contribution in kind to a SA or SCA is not necessary for the contribution in kind to a Sàrl. Nevertheless, in practice some notaries require such a report.

The Sarl is not authorized to issue non-voting shares or bearer shares.

Bodies

In a SA the management body may be a one tier or two tier system. In a one tier system, the board of directors normally includes three directors, but under certain conditions a single director may be appointed. In a two tier system, the management is divided between the management board (at least two members, save for particular cases where one member is sufficient) and the supervisory board (at least three members, save for particular cases where one member is sufficient). The Sàrl and the SCA may be managed by a sole manager.

The manager(s) of a SCA must be selected from among the general partners of the company whereas a director/manager of a SA or a Sàrl can be any shareholder or a third party.

No statutory auditor is required for a Sàrl of less than 25 shareholders; the supervisory board of a SCA is composed of at least three statutory auditors.

The manager(s) of a SCA may in principle not be dismissed by the shareholders save by a court order for gross negligence on their behalf or if the articles of incorporation provide for such case.

The general partner(s) of a SCA may veto resolutions taken in the general meetings of shareholders if the articles of incorporation do not exclude such a possibility.

Majority level

For the SA and SCA, most of the important decisions shall be taken by the general meeting representing at least two-thirds of the shareholders present or represented. However concerning the SCA and as a matter of principle with regards thereto, any such resolution is subject to the approval of the general partner(s).

For a Sarl, most of the changes to the articles of incorporation shall be resolved upon by a majority of members representing three quarters of the corporate capital.

b.   Differences relating to the functioning of each type of company

Contrary to the free transfer of shares of a SA and a SCA, the transfer of shares of a Sàrl to third parties must be approved by the partners at a three-quarters majority and notified to the company.

In a Sàrl, no loan may be obtained by the public issue of bonds, nor may shares be the object of a public issue.

B/INTRODUCTION TO LUXEMBOURG INVESTMENT FUNDS

Luxembourg permits the creation of funds of the contractual type *(fonds communs de placement* or **'FCP'**) and of the corporate type (investment companies). The latter may either be established as companies with variable capital *(sociétés d'investissement à capital variable* or **'SICAV'**) or as companies with fixed capital *(sociétés d'investissement à capital fixe* or **'SICAF'**).

1.   Legal forms of investment funds

a.   FCPs

An FCP is a contractual vehicle, which is in certain respects similar to the unit trust in the UK and the mutual fund in the US. Investors subscribe for units of the fund, which entitles them to a proportional share of the net assets of the fund.

An FCP is managed by a management company domiciled in Luxembourg. This management company decides on the investment policies and strategies and generally manages the fund on behalf of its joint owners. Similarly to the shareholders of a public limited company, the liability of the unitholders of an FCP is limited to the amount contributed by them. This type of vehicle is very flexible, as it is not subject to the requirements of Luxembourg company law or a specific statutory regime.

As investors in this vehicle usually do not have any voting rights, the fund can be protected from hostile takeovers. However, if investor participation is seen as important, voting rights may be granted in respect of certain matters, or a committee of investors may be established.

This vehicle may issue several classes of units, permitting the fund to create classes with features which are attractive to different investors.

The FCP is not a legal entity and in most jurisdictions is considered as being transparent for taxation purposes. Income of the FCP is attributed proportionately to its investors, and an investor in a state which has a treaty with Luxembourg may be able to take advantage of treaty benefits, for example by offsetting his tax liability in his own jurisdiction against the withholding taxes incurred by the FCP in territories where the FCP has made its investments.

As a general rule, management companies may be incorporated in the form of a SA, Sàrl, SCA or cooperative company *(société coopérative)*.

The management company may manage one or more FCPs. If the corporate object of a management company is limited to the management of one single FCP, the management company is tax exempt.

With respect to the safekeeping of the assets of a mutual investment fund, a custodian bank must be appointed which will have similar duties to the custodian bank of an investment company.

The contractual rights and obligations of the unitholders, management company and custodian bank are set forth in the management regulations, which are signed by the management company and the custodian bank. Amendments to the management regulations may be decided by the management company, with the approval of the custodian bank.

b. SICAVs

A SICAV is an investment company with a variable capital which is always equal to its net assets. This frequently-used form offers the possibility to increase or reduce the share capital without formalities (approval of shareholders' meeting, notarization, publication).

Pursuant to a new law relating to undertakings for collective investment dated 20 December 2002 (the **'UCI Law'**), a SICAV must be set up as a SA. Except as otherwise determined by the UCI Law, the provisions of the Company Law are applicable. In accordance with the Company Law, important decisions concerning the company, such as amendments to the articles of incorporation, have to be made at a general meeting of shareholders (i.e. the investors). In practice, the shareholders of a SICAV do not use their voting rights very often, however, it should not be assumed that a general meeting of shareholders will never exercise an influence over the management of the SICAV or its investment policy.

c.   SICAFs

A SICAF is a fixed capital investment company. Changes to a SICAF capital, which may be made within the limits of its authorized capital, require periodic notarization and publication. It is often used for funds which do not offer shares continuously, but which have one or more offering periods. It is usually established as a SA, but within the scope provided by Luxembourg law, it may be established as a different type of company, such as a SCA, where a general partner manages the fund and the investors act as limited partners.

d.   Provisions applying to SICAVs and SICAFs

The incorporation of any investment company (SICAV or SICAF), must take place before a public notary. The amount of the initial share capital of an investment company, differs depending on the type of investment company concerned.

SICAVs subject to the provisions of Part I of the UCI Law (i.e. UCI in transferable securities or **'UCITS'** with European passport regulated by the UCITS Directive n°85/611/EEC, as amended) which have designated a management company, SICAVs subject to the provisions of Part II of the UCI Law (i.e. UCIs other than UCITS subject to the UCITS Directive) and SICAFs must have an initial capital of EUR 31,000.

SICAVs which have not designated a management company must have a minimum capital of EUR 300,000 at the moment of their admission on the official list of under-takings for collective investment (**'UCI'**) (and thus may be constituted with the minimum share capital as required by law for a SA, i.e. EUR 31,000).

Investment companies of any type must reach a minimum capital of EUR 1,250,000 within a period of six months following their authorization.

Self-managed investment companies governed by Part I of the UCI Law are subject to additional conditions for starting up business and operating conditions.

The disadvantage of a fund established as an investment company, as opposed to an FCP, lies (i) in the obligation to convene an annual general meeting of shareholders and (ii) in the fact that amendments to the articles of incorporation may only be passed by a decision of an extraordinary general meeting of shareholders. Moreover, the liquidation of an investment company may only be decided by an extraordinary general meeting of shareholders.

Other legal forms are not excluded insofar the UCI Law provides that the Luxembourg investment fund legislation is generally applicable to funds whose exclusive object is the collective investment of their assets according to the principle of risk-spreading, provided that they canvass the public for the subscription of their units by means of a public or a private offer.

2.   Main characteristics of investment funds

a.   Supervision

The law dated 23 December 1998 which established a Commission for the Supervision of the Financial Sector (the *Commission de Surveillance du Secteur Financier* or 'CSSF') has continued and integrated the prudential supervision competence guaranteed by the previous regulatory authority.

The CSSF is entrusted with the supervision of the Luxembourg financial sector in general and with the supervision of investment funds in particular. No Luxembourg investment fund may be registered and no foreign investment fund may be publicly marketed in Luxembourg without the approval of—or, with respect to foreign UCITS, notification to—the CSSF.

b.   Approval procedure

In order to set up a Luxembourg investment fund, a written application must be filed with the CSSF. The CSSF carries out a number of preliminary investigations in connection with any application regarding the identity of the promoter, the professional experience of the managers, and may ask for specific documentation concerning the promoter itself. In addition, constitutional, sales and ancillary documents must be approved by the CSSF.

The approval of an investment fund is announced by its inscription on the official list of Luxembourg funds. This list is published in the *Mémorial* (the Luxembourg official gazette) and is intended to inform the public. The marketing of units or shares is authorized from the day of such inscription.

The CSSF supervises funds on a continuous basis. The CSSF carries out the legal supervision of the fund which must always comply with the legal, regulatory and conventional provisions. The CSSF also monitors the operating conditions of funds.

c.   Management and administration

The management of an FCP is carried out by a management company, while an investment company may be managed by its board of directors (in such case, the investment company is self-managed) or by a management company.

The asset management of any investment fund may be carried out by an advisor from outside Luxembourg, either through individuals (general managers) or through legal entities (investment managers and advisers). The CSSF will, however, review the reputation and professional expertise of all persons involved in the management of a Luxembourg investment fund. There is a requirement that a number of administrative duties (duties of the so-called 'central administration') must be carried out in Luxembourg.

d.   Umbrella collective investment scheme

Collective investment schemes may take the form of a single collective investment scheme or of an umbrella collective investment scheme (also known as multi compartments collective investment scheme), which is a single entity comprising two or more compartments.

The UCI Law recognizes the multi compartments collective investment scheme provided the constitutional documents expressly permit it and the prospectus specifies the investment policy of each compartment.

By way of derogation to the Civil Code, the assets of a compartment are only subject to the liabilities of that compartment, unless the constitutional documents stipulate the contrary.

Classes of shares may also be created within each compartment and they may differ in terms of fees, reference currency, hedging policy, distribution policy or the type of investors they are dedicated to.

e. Allowable investments

The principle of risk spreading in terms of allowable investments applies to both UCITS and UCIs.

UCITS subject to Part I of the UCI Law

These collective investment schemes may invest in listed transferable securities, listed money market instruments, cash deposits, UCITS and other UCIs and financial derivatives as principal objective.

UCITS subject to Part I of the UCI Law are benefiting from an European passport which means that they are freely marketable throughout the EU.

UCIs subject to Part II of the UCI Law

Part II of the UCI Law contains no provisions regarding investment rules. Such rules are specified in CSSF circulars or determined on a case by case basis by the CSSF. The CSSF has to date issued rules or guidelines for Part II UCIs investing in the following activities:

— transferable securities;

— alternative investments;

— venture capital;

— futures contracts and options;

— real estate.

Institutional UCIs

Besides UCITS with European passport subject to Part I of the UCI Law and UCIs subject to Part II of the UCI Law, there is a third category of UCIs which are institutional UCIs which securities are not intended to be marketed to the public.

These UCIs were until now governed by a law of 19 July 1991 (the **'1991 Law'**)—and Part II of the UCI Law, where appropriate. The Luxembourg Parliament adopted on 13 February 2007 a law on specialized investment funds (the **'SIF Law'**) which replaces it.

Existing UCIs created according to the 1991 Law will *ipso jure* be subject to the SIF Law and will be able to take advantage of the extended flexibility provided by the latter, without being required to make any significant changes other than formal amendments to the documentation of the SIF.

The purpose of the SIF Law is *inter alia* to extend the definition of institutional investor and to provide more flexibility than before in terms of requirement of promotership, valuation of investments, investment restrictions permitting to correspond exactly to the need of investors and to offer a lighter framework to accommodate various types of funds such as hedge funds, real estate funds and private equity funds.

The SIF Law will provide a more adequate legal framework for specialized funds in the European context and thereby will help to strengthen the competitiveness of Luxembourg as a financial centre. Although procuring more flexibility, the SIF Law will offer a regulated vehicle subject to regulatory supervision guaranteeing thereby an appropriate protection of investors.

f. Custodian bank

As a general rule, all Luxembourg investment funds must appoint a custodian bank, which must be a bank established either as a Luxembourg corporation or as a Luxembourg branch of a foreign bank.

The custodian bank must be entrusted with the custody of the assets of the fund. The term 'custody' must be understood in the sense of 'supervision'. As a result, the custodian bank must know at all times where the assets of the fund have been invested and where and when the assets are available.

In addition, the custodian bank has various supervisory functions, the scope of which depends on the type of investment fund concerned.

g. Auditor

Any Luxembourg investment fund is required to have its books audited at least once a year by an authorized independent auditor *(réviseur d'entreprises)* designated by the fund with the approval of the CSSF. The UCI Law also imposes on management companies the obligation to have their annual accounts audited by an authorized independent auditor.

C/INTRODUCTION TO THE SICAR

1. General Information

Investments in venture capital and private equity have long been structured through various types of vehicles, mainly limited partnerships, corporate vehicles and investment funds. Such vehicles are generally subject to regulatory supervision when their securities are offered to the public. In Luxembourg, these vehicles were traditionally created under the form of either non-regulated ordinary companies such as SCAs governed by the Company Law, or as regulated UCIs governed by the UCI Law.

The need for an additional regime was felt by participants of the financial sector who proposed the creation of the SICAR. The response to this need is the new Luxembourg law on Risk Capital Investment Companies dated 15 June 2004 (the **'SICAR Law').** The SICAR Law introduces a new form of vehicle which is to be used for investments in risk capital.

SICARS are not intended to replace existing vehicles, but rather to offer an alternative to investors. They are supervised by the CSSF but are subject to a much more liberal regime than that governing UCIs.

As a key element of the regime, no specific risk-diversification requirements have been introduced. This clearly contrasts with UCIs which may never invest more than 20 per cent of their net assets in securities of the same issuer (for special funds as defined in circular 91/75 of the CSSF).

2. Characteristics

a. Regulatory Aspects

Due to their risky nature, investments in SICARs are reserved for sophisticated investors *(investisseurs avertis)* which can either be institutional investors, professional investors or other sophisticated investors.

The SICAR must be authorized by the CSSF in order to carry out its activities. It will only be authorized if the CSSF has approved its constitutional documents, its directors and the choice of depositary. The SICAR must further demonstrate that its head office *(administration centrale)* is situated in Luxembourg.

Unlike UCIs, promoters or investment managers of a SICAR are not subject to an approval from the CSSF.

As soon as the SICAR is approved by the CSSF, it is registered on an official list.

After the initial approval of the SICAR, any modification related to the constitutional documents, the depositary or the management of the SICAR is subject to approval by the CSSF.

The directors of a SICAR must be of sufficiently good repute and have sufficient experience for performing their functions.

The custody of the assets of a SICAR must be entrusted to a depositary. The depositary must be a credit institution and approved by the CSSF. The depositary must have its registered office in Luxembourg or be established in Luxembourg if it has its registered office in another State.

b. Eligible Investments

SICARs are not subject to investment restrictions (risk-diversification requirement), nor are they supposed to communicate their investments to the CSSF before or after acquisition. Such an investment may, of course, be primarily represented by shares or bonds issued by a target company. However, the absence of investment restrictions will further allow SICARs to pursue activities or to enter into transactions which are usually forbidden or restricted in the hands of UCI such as the granting of credits of any nature e.g. mezzanine loans.

The concept of indirect contribution referred to in the SICAR Law should include the investment in risk capital through a UCI or any other investment vehicle or via the use of derivatives. Similarly, nothing should prohibit a SICAR from acquiring securities issued by a Luxembourg securitization entity or by any similar foreign entity.

c. Corporate Aspects

SICARs must exist as corporate entities. The possibility of creating contractual arrangements (i.e. pools of assets without legal personality, like UCIs existing under the form of FCPs) has not been used by the legislator. The use of limited partnerships and partnerships limited by shares allows structuring SICARs on the basis of a model closely resembling private equity funds.

The articles of incorporation of a SICAR must expressly indicate that the company is subject to the provisions of the SICAR Law.

The share capital of a SICAR must amount to at least EUR 1,000,000. This amount must be reached within the twelve months following the approval of the SICAR.

The articles of incorporation may provide a variability of the share capital, i.e. that the amount of the share capital is equal at all times to its net asset value.

A minimum amount equal to 5 per cent of the par value of each subscribed share must be immediately paid-up.

The SICAR does not have to allocate 5 per cent of its annual profit to a legal reserve, which is a compulsory principle for ordinary companies until the legal reserve reaches 10 per cent of the share capital.

A great deal of flexibility is provided in relation to distributions and payments to investors. SICARs are not subject to any rules in relation to redemptions of own shares, distributions and payments of interim dividends other than those set forth in their articles of incorporation.

A SICAR must publish a prospectus and an annual report for each financial year.

SICARs must have the accounting information provided in their annual report audited by an authorized independent auditor *(réviseur d'entreprises)*. The auditor must have been authorized to audit SICARs by the CSSF. The auditor has, among other duties, the obligation to promptly notify the CSSF of any fact or decision of which he has become aware while carrying out the audit which is liable to constitute a material breach of the SICAR Law or the regulations adopted for its execution, or affect the continuous functioning of the SICAR, or lead to a refusal to certify the accounts or to the expression of reservations thereon.

II. GENERAL LUXEMBOURG TAX CONSIDERATIONS

In this second part, the focus will be concentrated on the general tax considerations relating to SOPARFIs, investment funds and SICARs.

A/SOPARFI

1. Corporate income tax and municipal business tax

Taxable profits of a Luxembourg company are as a general rule, subject to corporate income tax *(impôt sur le revenu des collectivités*—**'CIT'**) and municipal business tax *(impôt commercial communal*—**'MBT'**). CIT is levied at an effective maximum rate of 22 per cent in 2006 (22.88 per cent including the 4 per cent surcharge for the employment fund); lower rates apply if the taxable profits do not exceed EUR 15,000. MBT is levied at a variable rate according to the municipality in which the company is located, but generally MBT amounts to 6.75 per cent, for Luxembourg-city. The maximum aggregate CIT and MBT rate consequently amounts to 29.63 per cent.

Dividends received by a Luxembourg company are generally taxable and are consequently included in the taxable base. A tax credit is available for Luxembourg or foreign withholding tax retained by the distributing company. The same is true for liquidation proceeds.

Capital gains are taxable only upon realization. They are generally regarded as ordinary business income and are consequently included in the taxable base for corporate income tax. No special lower taxation rates apply to capital gains.

Dividends, liquidation proceeds and capital gains may however be tax exempt under the participation exemption regime. Dividends, which do not qualify for the participation exemption, can be exempt up to 50 per cent in certain cases.

2. Participation exemption on dividends and liquidation proceeds

In order to qualify for the participation exemption on dividends and liquidation proceeds, the following conditions must be met according to the Income Tax Law—'ITL'[4]):

a. the parent company must be a fully taxable Luxembourg resident company;

b. the parent company must hold a direct participation in the share capital of an eligible subsidiary (hereafter an **'Eligible Subsidiary'**), i.e.

- a fully-taxable resident capital company;

- a non-resident capital company liable to a tax corresponding to Luxembourg corporate income tax[5]; or

- a company resident in a European Union Member State and covered by article 2 of the EU Parent Subsidiary Directive[6].

Holding a participation through a tax transparent entity is deemed to be a direct participation in the proportion of the net assets held in this entity;

c. at the time the income is made available, the parent company must have held or must commit itself to hold the participation for an uninterrupted period of at least twelve months and during this whole period, either the level of participation must

---

4. *Loi de l'impôt sur le revenu* (Income Tax Law) dated 4 December 1967, as amended.
5. According to the administrative interpretation, this condition is met when the company is mandatorily subject to a tax at an effective rate of at least 11 per cent, calculated on a taxable base similar to the one applicable in Luxembourg.
6. EC Directive 90/43 5/EEC of 23 July 1990 on the common system applicable in the case of parent companies and subsidiaries of different Member States.

not fall below the threshold of 10 per cent or the acquisition price must not fall below EUR 1,200,000.

Anti-abuse measures deny the exemption in some circumstances, among others when a non-eligible participation is exchanged for an eligible participation in a tax-free manner.

Further, the participation exemption regime contains some rules intended to avoid a double benefit (exemption of income and deduction of expenses). If the acquisition of a participation is financed through an interest-bearing debt, such interest has an implication for the application of the participation exemption. Pursuant to the ITL, to the extent that received dividends or liquidation proceeds are exempt, the following expenses are not deductible: (1) business expenses in direct economic relationship with the income and (2) a value adjustment booked on the participation as a consequence of the distribution (the deductibility denial having to be determined in this order). If in a given year, related expenses exceed the income derived from the participation, the excess is deductible.

If the conditions of the participation exemption are not satisfied, dividends are as a rule taxable at the ordinary rate. As an exception, dividends deriving from participations in companies examined under a., b.[7] or c. above are generally exempt up to 50 per cent.

In addition to the domestic participation, almost all of the double tax treaties concluded by Luxembourg grant an international participation exemption.

3. Participation exemption on capital gains

Capital gains realized on the transfer of participations are exempt under the following conditions:

– The Luxembourg company must have held or commit itself to hold a direct participation in the share capital of the subsidiary for an uninterrupted period of at least twelve months and during this whole period, either the level of participation must not fall below the threshold of 10 per cent or the acquisition price below EUR 6,000,000.

– holding a participation through a tax transparent entity is deemed to be a direct participation in the proportion of the net assets held in this entity;

– the subsidiary must satisfy the same conditions as those applicable for the exemption of dividends (please refer hereabove).

If the above-mentioned conditions are not met, capital gains are, as a rule, taxable at the ordinary rate.

Further, when a participation is disposed of, the capital gain exemption does not apply to the extent of the algebraic sum of related expenses and value adjustments that have decreased the tax result of the current or preceding years. This rule is referred to as the recapture of previous deductions.

---

7. For companies mentioned under b., they must furthermore be resident in countries having concluded a tax treaty with Luxembourg.

4. Outbound dividend payments

Dividends paid to shareholders are as a rule subject to a 20 per cent withholding tax[8]. However, a withholding exemption applies under the following conditions:

- the parent company must have a direct participation in the share capital of the Luxembourg company. Holding a participation through a tax transparent entity is deemed to be a direct participation in the proportion of the net assets held in this entity;

- the parent company must be:

  - a fully-taxable resident company;

  - a company resident in a European Union Member State and covered by article 2 of the Parent Subsidiary Directive;

  - a Luxembourg permanent establishment of a company examined under the aforementioned point; or

  - a Luxembourg permanent establishment of a company resident in a country having a tax treaty with Luxembourg;

  - a Swiss capital corporation[9] which is effectively subject to corporate income tax in Switzerland without benefiting from an exemption;

- at the time the income is made available, the parent company must have held or must commit itself to hold directly for an uninterrupted period of at least twelve months a participation of at least 10 per cent or with an acquisition price of at least EUR 1,200,000 in the share capital of the Luxembourg company.

If the above-mentioned conditions are not satisfied, distributions made to treaty country resident shareholders benefit as a rule from reduced rates provided by tax treaties.

5. Outbound interest payments

Under Luxembourg tax law currently in effect, and subject to the exceptions mentioned here-below there is generally no withholding tax on payments of interest (including accrued but unpaid interest) made to Luxembourg residents and non-residents.

As an exception, the following kinds of interest payments may be subject to a withholding tax:

- profit allocations paid to a silent partner investing in a business and remunerated in proportion to the business profit;

---

8. According to a current bill, the withholding tax rate on outbound dividend payments will be lowered to 15 per cent.
9. i.e. a Swiss corporation organized under the form of either a SA, Sàrl or SCA.

– interest paid on profit-sharing bonds or notes (i.e. those bearing a fixed interest and an interest varying according to the profit distributed by the borrower, unless the variable interest simultaneously causes a decrease of the fixed interest without the total interest exceeding the interest initially set) are subject to a 20 per cent withholding tax;

– under the Luxembourg laws dated 21 June 2005 (the **'Laws'**) implementing the EC Directive 2003/48/EC on the taxation of savings income (the **'EU Savings Directive'**) and several agreements concluded between Luxembourg and certain dependant territories of the European Union, a Luxembourg based paying agent (within the meaning of the EU Savings Directive) is required since 1 July 2005 to withhold tax on interest and other similar income paid by it to (or under certain circumstances, to the benefit of) an individual or a residual entity in the sense of Article 4.2. of the EU Savings Directive[10] (**'Residual Entity'**) resident or established in another Member State of the European Union, unless the beneficiary of the interest payments elects for an exchange of information. The same regime applies to payments to individuals or Residual Entities resident in any of the following territories: Aruba, the British Virgin Islands, Guernsey, the Isle of Man, Jersey, Montserrat and the Netherlands Antilles (the **'Associated Territories'**). The withholding tax rate is initially 15 per cent, increasing steadily to 20 per cent and 35 per cent. The withholding tax system will only apply during a transitional period, the ending of which depends on the conclusion of certain agreements relating to information exchange with certain other countries (the transitional period may therefore never end).

– under the Luxembourg law of 23 December 2005, payments of interest or similar income made since 1 January 2006 (but accrued since 1 July 2005) by a paying agent established in Luxembourg to or for the immediate benefit of an individual beneficial owner who is resident of Luxembourg may be subject to a withholding tax of 10 per cent. Such withholding tax will be in full discharge of income tax if the beneficial owner is an individual acting in the course of the management or his/her private wealth.

Further, a withholding tax may be levied on excessive interest payments that are re-characterized as dividends.

6. Debt/equity ratio

According to the general practice adopted by the tax authorities, the debt/equity ratio applicable to a fully-taxable Luxembourg capital company is 15 for equity to 85 for all liabilities combined (shareholder and third party debt, represented or not by an instrument). It is understood that these liabilities finance the acquisition of participations and bear a market interest rate.

In case of non-compliance with said ratio, interest in relation to the excess of liabilities can be considered as dividends for tax purposes. The consequence is that such excess

---

10. A Residual Entity means an entity without legal personality whose profits are not taxed under the general arrangements for the business taxation and that is not, or has not opted to be considered as, a UCITS recognized in accordance with EC Directive 85/611/EEC.

interest is not deductible and is potentially subject to a withholding tax under the same conditions as distributed dividends (please refer hereabove).

Debt instruments may bear a fixed yield, a floating yield or no yield. In case they are non-interest bearing, they are considered as equity for the purpose of the applicable debt/equity ratio.

In cases where a Luxembourg company borrows money in order to lend it to companies belonging to the same group, no debt/equity ratio is applicable. The activities must however be structured in order to avoid any exposure to a credit or foreign exchange risk at the level of the Luxembourg company.

7. Capital duty

a. Principle

According to the Luxembourg Capital Duty Law[11] ('**CDL**'), any contribution, whether in cash or in kind, to a Luxembourg company is as a rule subject to a 1 per cent capital duty *(droit d'apport)*. In the event of contributions in kind, the 1 per cent capital duty is levied on the market value of the assets contributed. Capital duty applies to nominal value or accounting par value of the shares, as well as to share premium accounts.

Under some circumstances capital duty can be avoided by contributing either a shareholding of an EU company to a Luxembourg company or by contributing all of the assets and liabilities of an EU company to a Luxembourg company. Corporate reorganizations are generally exempt under the rules outlined in B1. and B2. below.

b. Exemption regarding contribution of all the assets and liabilities or a branch of activity of a company

Article 4-1 CDL provides that an exemption from capital duty applies to contributions by one or more companies of all their assets and liabilities, or of one or more branches of their activity, to one or more existing or newly-created companies. A branch of activity is defined as all of the elements invested in a business division and constituting, from a technical viewpoint, an independent enterprise, i.e. a business capable of functioning by its own means. The exemption applies if the following conditions are satisfied:

- the contributions are exclusively remunerated by the issue of shares of the receiving company. The remuneration may include a cash payment not exceeding 10 per cent of the nominal value or, in the absence of a nominal value, of the accounting par value of the issued; and

- the companies involved in the transaction must have either their registered office or their place of effective management in an EU Member State.

---

11. *Loi concernant l'impôt frappant les rassemblements de capitaux,* dated 29 December 1971, as amended. The law on capital duty has implemented the EC Directive 69/335/EEC of 17 July 1969.

c. Exemption regarding contribution of shares

According to Article 4-2 CDL, contributions of shares are not subject to the capital duty if:

– further to such contribution, the receiving company holds a participation of at least 65 per cent in the share capital of the company whose shares are contributed;

– the contribution is exclusively remunerated by the issue of shares of the receiving company (the remuneration may also include a cash payment not exceeding 10 per cent of the nominal value or, in the absence of a nominal value, of the accounting par value of the issued shares); and

– the receiving company as well as the company whose shares are contributed have either their registered office or their place of effective management in an EU Member State.

A clawback measure applies if, within a 5-year period, the receiving company disposes of the shares which were contributed in the context of the exempt contribution, or if the participation in the company whose shares were contributed falls below 65 per cent. However, there is no recapture if the disposal occurs in the framework of a reorganization which is exempt pursuant to arts. 4-1 or 4-2 CDL, or as a result of the liquidation of either the receiving company or the company whose shares were contributed.

8. Net worth tax

Luxembourg imposes net worth tax *(impôt sur la fortune—*'**NWT**') on resident companies at the rate of 0.5 per cent applied on net assets as determined for NWT purposes. Net worth is referred to as the unitary value *(valeur unitaire),* as determined at 1st January of each year. The unitary value is basically calculated as the difference between (a) assets estimated at their fair market value *(valeur estimée de réalisation* or *Gemeiner Wert)* and (b) liabilities vis-à-vis third parties. The NWT charge for a given year can be avoided or reduced under specific conditions.

The participation held in the share capital of an eligible subsidiary is an exempt asset for NWT purposes, if the conditions of the participation exemption for NWT are satisfied. Foreign assets held in treaty countries (e.g. real properties or assets invested in foreign permanent establishments) are generally exempt in Luxembourg based on double tax treaty provisions.

9. Advanced confirmations

The Luxembourg tax laws do not formally provide for an advanced confirmation procedure and no formal procedure is currently in place for obtaining advanced confirmations. However, tax authorities are generally willing to answer enquiries made by taxpayers or their advisers orally or in writing.

While the procedure is completely informal, it is generally acknowledged by legal scholars that answers given by the authorities will bind them if certain conditions are met, i.e. the advanced confirmation was issued by a competent civil servant, the advanced confirmation applies to a given combination of facts, the taxpayer made a fair and complete description of the facts and the answer given by the authorities does not contravene the law.

In practice, the procedure begins with a presentation of the structure to the tax inspector during a meeting. At the end of the meeting, the tax inspector orally confirms the applicable tax treatment of the structure. A written confirmation request may then be sent to the tax inspector for execution. The execution of said written confirmation may take up to several months.

B/INVESTMENT FUNDS

1.   Costs and fiscal provisions

The registration fee payable to the CSSF for the registration of a Luxembourg or foreign fund is presently EUR 2,650 for a single fund and EUR 5,000 for a fund with an umbrella structure. In addition, an annual supervision fee of the same amount is payable to the CSSF.

In relation to Luxembourg self-managed investment companies governed by Part I of the UCI Law, the registration fee is EUR 5,000, regardless of whether the investment company is set up as a single fund or as an umbrella fund.

A fund established in a corporate form must also pay a one-time capital duty of EUR 1,250. An annual registration fee of EUR 5,000 is due for each management company subject to Chapter 13 of the UCI Law (harmonized management company), except if the management company carries out portfolio management activities, where the registration fee then amounts to EUR 12,000. An additional annual registration fee of EUR 2,000 is due in respect to harmonized management companies for each branch established abroad.

Pursuant to the UCI Law, Luxembourg investment funds are subject to an annual subscription tax. The subscription tax is equal to 0.05 per cent of the aggregate net asset value of the investment fund as valued on the last day of each quarter.

2.   Taxation of investors

Shareholders are not subject to any capital gains, income or withholding tax in Luxembourg, except for:

- those domiciled, residing or having a permanent establishment in Luxembourg, or
- non-residents of Luxembourg who hold more than 10 per cent of the shares of a fund of the corporate type and who dispose of all or part of their holdings within six months from the date of acquisition, or
- in some limited cases, some former residents of Luxembourg who hold more than 10 per cent of the shares of such corporate-type fund.

a.   FCPs

The FCP is not a legal entity and is therefore transparent for taxation purposes. Income of the FCP should be attributed proportionately to its investors, and an investor in a state having a treaty with the jurisdiction of the investments may therefore, to the extent practicable, be able to take advantage of treaty benefits, for example by offsetting his tax liability in his own jurisdiction against the withholding taxes incurred by the FCP in territories where the FCP has made its investments.

b. SICAVs and SICAFs

In theory, the separate legal personality of a SICAV or SICAF in Luxembourg should entitle it to the benefit of any treaty that Luxembourg has in force with another state. In practice, however, this has often been denied to Luxembourg corporate funds, on the basis that their very low rates of domestic taxation lead them to be treated as though they were not companies residing in Luxembourg for the purposes of many treaties.

C/SICARs

In defining the fiscal regime of the SICAR and its investors, the legislator had three objectives in mind.

The first objective was to offer investors the choice between transparent and opaque entities. A transparent entity can be found with the use of a limited partnership *(société en commandite simple* or 'SCS') which does not have fiscal personality under Luxembourg law. The SCS is, thus, not personally subject to direct taxes on income and net worth existing in Luxembourg. No double level of taxation exists as each partner is directly taxed on his share of income and net worth in the SCS. Opaque entities encompass all other forms of corporate entities available to SICARs, i.e. the SCA, the SA, the Sàrl and the cooperative in the form of a public limited company *(société cooperative organisée sous forme de société anonyme* or SCOSA).

The second objective was to allow the vehicle to be as tax neutral as possible for the investor. For transparent SICARs, this implied an absence of taxation in Luxembourg in the hands of nonresident investors (to the extent the SICAR does not receive Luxembourg-source income).

The third objective was to ensure access to double tax treaties for opaque SICARs.

CONCLUSION

Luxembourg has many tools at its disposal and may easily be used as an international investment hub capable of ensuring tax optimization on an income basis or repatriation of profits to investors. Depending on the investor's choice, the Luxembourg vehicle may be regulated or non regulated or a combination of regulated and non regulated vehicles. Above all, the choice of a vehicle will depend on the type of anticipated investment, the tax regime of the shareholder and the income repatriation method.

The Luxembourg legislation is currently facing many important changes, which have recently occurred or which are about to be implemented. As described hereabove, the Holding 1929 regime will soon disappear. The SPF and the SIF are operational since early 2007. Other changes will be carried out in the upcoming months and the advice of qualified professionals in structuring the deals will be crucial.

ANNEX: List of tax treaties

Luxembourg has currently concluded tax treaties with the following States:

Austria	Israel	Singapore
Belgium	Italy	Slovak Republic
Brazil	Japan	Slovenia
Bulgaria	Latvia	South Africa
Canada	Lithuania	South Korea
China	Malaysia	Spain
Czech Republic	Malta	Sweden
Denmark	Morocco	Switzerland
Finland	Mauritius	Thailand
France	Mexico	Trinidad and Tobago
Germany	Mongolia	Tunisia
Greece	Netherlands	Turkey
Hungary	Norway	United Kingdom
Iceland	Poland	USA
Indonesia	Portugal	Uzbekistan
Ireland	Romania	Vietnam
	Russia	

Luxembourg is currently negotiating tax treaties with the following States:

Argentina	India	San Marino
Azerbaijan	Lebanon	Serbia and Montenegro
Estonia	United Arab Emirates	Ukraine

21. MALAYSIA

Michael Lim Hee Kiang & Chen Lee Won, Shearn Delamore & Co

21.1 Introductory Comments

The business laws of Malaysia, like the majority of its other laws, are based on what is generally known as the common law system. This is because Malaysia was administered by the British Government and inherited much of British laws.

Although Malaysia is a federation of 13 states, its business laws are largely federal laws; the business laws thus apply throughout the 13 states and the Federal Territory of Kuala Lumpur, Putrajaya and Labuan. Hence, a potential investor need not be unduly concerned about individual state laws.

21.2 Corporate Structures

The most common vehicle used for businesses is the company limited by shares incorporated under the Companies Act 1965. Other vehicles used are partnerships and sole proprietorships. Some businesses are conducted in the name of statutory corporations but these are generally government or quasi-government owned.

Companies limited by shares are separate legal entities following the common law principle of *Salomon v. Salomon* [1897] AC 22.

21.3 Letters of Intent and Heads of Agreement

Letters of intent and heads of agreements are used in Malaysia, but not frequently. The problem with letters of intent and heads of agreement is always to do with to what extent the parties intend the document to be binding on each other. By their very own terminology, they are not meant to be binding. But it is not uncommon for some clients to request to 'tighten' some words on exclusivity or confidentiality.

Letters of intent and heads of agreement are useful for those persons who do not have full authority to commit on behalf of the companies they represent. Those persons can return to head office with something in writing for their board of directors to consider.

Some heads of agreement allow for due diligence to be conducted and, as such, are also useful for such purposes.

Conditional agreements are commonly used in Malaysia because of the peculiarities of local conditions. Hence, many agreements are conditional upon various governmental approvals, board approval and shareholders' approval. There will be a clause requiring the parties to seek approval within a 'cut-off' date after which the agreement lapses.

© World Law Group
International Business Acquisitions, M. Whalley, F.-J. Semler (eds.), Kluwer Law International, London, 2007; ISBN 9789041124838.

21.4   Taxes Affecting the Structure and Calculation of the Price

Malaysia does not have a full-blown system of capital gains tax. The Real Property Gains Tax Act 1976 taxes gains arising from the sale of real property or from the sale of shares of real property companies which are companies which have real properties as their substantial assets. There is a technical formula to determine what a real property company is.

The rate of tax on the gains from a disposal is on a graduated formula depending on the year of disposal. For instance, on a sale within the first two years of acquisition of the chargeable asset, the tax is 30 per cent. The rate reduces as the years go by. Clearly then, the Real Property Gains Tax Act was enacted to discourage land speculation.

Stamp duties are payable on instruments of transfers. In a sale of shares, the instrument of transfer is the share transfer forms. In the case of an asset sale, the instrument of transfer is the National Land Code 1965 Form 14A for real property or, in the case of choses in action, the assignment itself. Stamp duties are levied on an ad valorem basis. The rates vary. For instance, duty on share transfers would be 0.3 per cent of the total consideration whereas the duty on land transfers may be as high as 3 per cent. In the 2005 Budget, the Malaysian Government had proposed to introduce goods and services tax in Malaysia to replace sales tax and service tax. At the time of writing, we are unable to comment on how the introduction of this tax will affect transfers of assets.

21.5   Extent of Seller's Warranties and Indemnities

The fashionable thing to do nowadays is to do a due diligence on the company to be acquired. This takes place usually upon the parties indicating seriousness in proceeding further with their negotiations. The parties may or may not have entered into a letter of intent at this stage. Sometimes, the buyer carrying out the investigation is required to enter into a secrecy agreement with the seller or the target company. The covenant would be that all information obtained during the course of the due diligence would be used only for the purpose of progressing the negotiations further and shall not at all instances be disclosed to any party not involved in the negotiations.

A due diligence exercise should not preclude a buyer from still seeking the 'boilerplate' warranties and indemnities from the seller. Sometimes, a difficult seller may argue that since a due diligence investigation has been performed by the buyer's accountants and lawyers, the buyer should purchase the company or business on an 'as is where is' basis. This argument should not be accepted by the buyer because a due diligence does not necessarily disclose everything. In fact, if a cunning seller wishes to, he can quite easily hide whatever he wants to hide from the investigators. Therefore, it is always advisable for the buyer to obtain the appropriate warranties so that he has a remedy after completion but prior to the expiry of the warranty.

In the case of an asset sale, the question of having a list of warranties and indemnities is not so appropriate, as assets are more easily verifiable and liabilities attaching to assets are cleared prior to completion.

21.6   Liability for Pre-contractual Representations

When a formal written agreement is entered between the parties, it is difficult for one party to allege that there are other oral terms and conditions not contained in the written document. The courts will not necessarily reject a plea that there are other terms and conditions not in the written document, but the plaintiff will have an uphill climb to convince the courts to accept extra documentary evidence. Therefore, it is important for the parties to capture all their terms and conditions as exhaustively as possible in the written agreement.

21.7   Liability for Pre-acquisition Trading and Contracts

In an asset sale, there is no liability for pre-acquisition contracts. This is particularly so in the case of an acquisition of land. Malaysia adopts the Torrens system of land titles. Hence, in a purchase of land, if a search at the Land Office reveals there are no encumbrances or other interests registered against the land, the buyer can be said to purchase the land free from encumbrances notwithstanding, say, the seller having sold the land to another party. This is because the system of registration of title assures indefeasibility of title. As for purchase of equipment and machinery, again a buyer without notice of other claims would also be able to obtain a clean title to the equipment or machinery. Sometimes, the buyer may wish to inherit some existing contract or liability; this may be achieved by novation or assignment. In the case of transferring of liability, the method to go by is by novation of the liability whereby a third party assumes the liability of an earlier party with the consent of the party to whom the obligation is owed. In the case of a chose in action which is an asset and not a liability, the chose in action is transferred by way of an assignment and notice is served upon the party to whom the obligation is owed. Sometimes there may a clause restricting assignments. In such a case, the debtor's consent must be obtained.

21.8   Pre-completion Risks

There is no common law principle which states that a party shall assume the risks of a business prior to completion. This is a matter of contract to be agreed between the contracting parties and it is common to have negative and affirmative covenants pending completion. In the absence of express agreement, the courts must determine what the parties' intentions were. This is a difficult task as the decision will be based strictly on evidence. Generally, it can be argued that prior to completion, the seller assumes the risk of the business, particularly where only a deposit is paid upon signing the agreement. However, there may be situations where the buyer may wish to run the business prior to completion. In such an instance the courts will probably transfer the risk to the buyer. In the case of the purchase of shares, the risk of the business rests with the company. In such a case, the question of risks is addressed by the appropriate warranties in the sale and purchase agreement, as for instance a warranty to say that the company's net tangible assets shall not be less than a certain amount on completion.

In Malaysia, it is common to have the agreement of sale conditional upon the approvals of various governmental authorities. These approvals can take up to six or nine months to process. Hence, it is often necessary to control the direction or business of the company during this period of waiting for approvals. The issue of risks prior to completion is then most relevant.

21.9   Required Governmental Approvals

There are two governmental approvals that are almost always required. The first is the Foreign Investment Committee (FIC) which is a committee set up by the Prime Minister's Department. The FIC has no statutory backing. It is merely a committee whose members consist of largely departmental heads of the government. The FIC has proclaimed a set of rules for investing in Malaysia called 'Guidelines for the Regulation of Acquisition of Assets, Mergers and Take-Overs'. Although the edicts are not laws and are described as 'Guidelines', they are almost always respected and followed by investors. This is because being issued by the Prime Minister's Department, they command an air of respectability and authority.

A breach of the Guidelines does not result in a fine or imprisonment. If a breach has occurred which comes to the FIC's knowledge, the FIC can make life miserable for the defaulter by instructing all relevant government departments to withdraw assistance or cooperation with the defaulter. The main tenets of the Guidelines are that the FIC's approval is required in, inter alia, the following cases:

- any proposed acquisition of interest in a local company or business in Malaysia which is MYR10 million or more by local or foreign interests;

- any proposed acquisition of interest of a local company or business in Malaysia by any means, which results in the transfer of ownership or control to foreign interest;

- any proposed acquisition of interest by any foreign interest of 15 per cent or more of the voting right of any local company or business in Malaysia or by any associated or non-associated group of foreign interests, in aggregate of 30 per cent or more of the voting rights of any local company or business in Malaysia regardless of whether the value in less than MYR10 million with the exception of open market acquisitions on Bursa Malaysia meant for short term holdings;

- any proposed merger or take-over of any local company or business in Malaysia by local or foreign interests; and

- any charging of shares in a local company to any foreign interest where the value of loan or the market value of the shares is MYR10 million or more.

At first glance, the Guidelines appear to be all encompassing and as such may be described as anti-foreign investment. However, in practice, they have not been found to be discouraging to foreign investment. The Guidelines were even relaxed in May 2003. In addition, FIC approval is not required for companies that have been granted special status, such as Multimedia Super Corridor (MSC) status, International Procurement Centres, Operational Headquarters, Representative Offices and Regional Office.

The origin of these Guidelines can be traced to the 13 May 1969 racial riots. A study of the reasons for the riots concluded that a major cause was the big disparity in wealth of the Malays and the non-Malays, particularly the Chinese. Hence, there was a need to restructure Malaysian society. Generally, the FIC in its approval would impose a condition that the company in which the foreign investor is intending to invest would be required to have a certain percentage of local shareholders, particularly Bumiputeras, the indigenous people of Malaysia. A common percentage used is 30 per cent ownership by Bumiputeras. Some businesses require a higher percentage (eg operating taxis or freight forwarding where foreign expertise is not necessary).

Generally, foreign investors understand the Malaysian policy of local content. Some foreign investors have attempted to circumvent the local content rule by various devices, such as trust deeds, blank transfers, proxies or powers of attorney. In essence, such devices make the local shareholder a mere agent or trustee of the foreign share-holder. In local parlance, such businesses are called 'Ali Baba' businesses. There is a serious issue over whether those devices are enforceable in a court of law. The correct view is that such devices are not enforceable because they are colourable instruments used to deceive governmental authorities and as such are against public policy.

The next relevant authority's approval required is the Ministry of International Trade and Industry (MITI)'s approval. Basically, under the Industrial Co-Ordination Act 1975 (ICA), all manufacturing activities require licences save for some small busi-nesses. Such licences are issued by MITI. The rationale behind the ICA is again to enable local equity participation. In the issue of the licences, conditions are almost always imposed on the manufacturer to have local participation. Manufacturing activity is widely defined as 'with its grammatical variations and cognate expression [to] mean the making, altering, ornamenting, finishing or otherwise treating or adapting any article or substance with a view to its use, sale, transport, delivery or disposal and includes the assembly of parts and ship repairing but shall not include any activity normally associated with retail or wholesale trade'. Previously, when issuing licenses, MITI may impose equity conditions, and they are based on the level of exports of the local company. Equity and export conditions which were previously imposed continue to apply. The requirements have, since 1998, been relaxed in order to further enhance Malaysia's investment climate. Foreign investors may now hold 100 per cent of the equity in all investment in new profits, as well as investments in expansion/diversification projects by existing companies, irrespective of the level of exports.

Again, most foreign investors accept the necessity of the ICA's requirements. It is also not uncommon for some foreigners to employ the 'Ali Baba' devices here. The same public policy laws apply and such devices are not enforceable.

21.10 Anti-trust and Competition Laws

There are no formal anti-trust and competition laws in Malaysia except in specific legislation such as the Communications and Multimedia Act 1993. Mergers and acqui-sitions almost always require the FIC's approval, the Securities Commission or MITI. But these bodies are not concerned with whether the merged entity is good or bad for consumers. Theoretically, it is legal for businesses to fix prices at the expense of consumers.

Certain consumer items like rice, bread, eggs and other essential items have maximum prices fixed by the government under the Price Control Act 1946. That appears to be the only extent of Malaysian competition laws.

21.11   Required Offer Procedures

Under the Malaysian Code on Takeovers and Mergers 1998, any person who acquires control of a public company whether listed or not is required to make a mandatory general offer for the remaining shares not owned by him or her. Control is defined in the Securities Commission Act 1993 as the acquisition of more than 33 per cent of a company's voting shares. A person also triggers the obligation if he holds between 33 per cent and 50 per cent and acquires 2 per cent more of the voting rights in any period of six months.

The offer price must not be less than the price paid by the acquirer in the last six months.

The Code also applies to 'downstream' companies where if there is an acquisition of the 'upstream' parent company, that acquisition gives rise to a change of control of the downstream company.

The Code represents a minefield of technicalities and a prospective buyer is well advised to consult lawyers and merchant bankers.

21.12   Continuation of Government Licences

As discussed in **21.9**, all manufacturing activities require a licence under the ICA. The exceptions are where the manufacturing activity employs less than 75 people and its paid-up capital is less than MYR2.5 million. Most licences are granted permanently in that they do not have to be renewed on a yearly basis. It is common to find a term in these licenses that the prior written approval of MITI is required for any transfer of shares to foreign investors.

21.13   Requirements for Transferring Shares

In a private company, shares are not freely transferable. Normally, there are preemption clauses in the articles of association or in the joint-venture or shareholders' agreement ensuring that existing shareholders are offered the shares of the selling shareholder before they are offered to strangers. The approval of the board of directors of the target company is also required for the transfer of shares. Bumiputera shares should be transferred only to Bumiputeras unless there are valid reasons for those shares to be warehoused prior to the finding of another suitable partner.

21.14   Requirements for Transferring Land and Property Leases

Malaysia has adopted the Australian system of land law, the Torrens system. This means basically that title to land and real property depends strictly on the registration of the title with the Land Office. Indefeasibility of title is practically guaranteed on registration. There are limited instances in which titles can be challenged. These would relate to fraud, forgery and illegality.

The system of title by registration offers good comfort to foreign investors when purchasing lands with titles issued. A search at the Land Registry confirms whether the seller is the landowner.

In many instances, foreigners purchase lands from state-owned entities. These are bodies which are set up specifically by the various states to own and develop industrial lands. As a consequence, there may not yet be separate titles issued for the various land pieces. This is not something to be unduly alarmed about as suitable covenants can be sought from the state entity to ensure the issue of the title.

21.15 Requirements for Transferring Intellectual Property

Malaysia has a system of registration of intellectual property as in the Trade Marks Act 1976, the Patents Act 1983, the Industrial Designs Act 1996, the Geographical Indications Act 2000 and the Integrated Circuits Act 2000. There is no system of registration for copyright in Malaysia, as eligible works are automatically protected under the Copyright Act. Malaysia is a signatory to the Paris and Berne Conventions as well as the Trade Related Intellectual Property Rights (TRIPS) agreement.

The transfer of intellectual property rights takes place by way of assignment as in common law. When the intellectual property right is registrable, the assignment will have to be registered at the relevant registry. The owner of an intellectual property can licence it out for a fee.

21.16 Requirements for Transferring Business Contracts, Licences and Leases

The transfer of business takes place in various steps. First, there is a sale and purchase agreement setting the various items of the business to be sold. The saleable items are the stock-in-trade, furniture and fittings, book debts, goodwill, patents and trademarks and any other assets as appearing in the balance sheet. Usually, the purchase of a business does not involve the automatic transfer of the bank loans like overdraft and trading facilities. Such liabilities can only be novated to the new buyer with the banks' consent.

21.17 Requirements for Transferring Other Assets

Individual assets to be transferred (eg items such as stock-in-trade) can be transferred by way of delivery to avoid payment of stamp duty. Book debts can be transferred by way of assignment with notice formally given to the debtor. Transfers involving instruments of transfer would incur ad valorem stamp duty ranging from 1 per cent to 3 per cent.

21.18 Encumbrances and Third Party Interests

A company's assets may be subject to third party interest. Interests can be created by agreement (eg a charge, mortgage or an option to purchase), by operation of law (eg an unpaid seller's lien) or by registration in a public registry (eg an encumbrance affecting title to real property). The assets employed in the business may also be subject to hire purchase or leasing agreements.

A buyer for good consideration of an asset generally takes good title to the property, save where it has notice of the prior interest or where the seller does not have title to the asset.

Where the asset purchased is real property, the buyer should conduct a search at the land registry, and interests such as caveats, charges or liens may be determined. As certain charges created by companies need to be registered with the Companies Commission of Malaysia (CCM), a buyer may conduct a search at the CCM to determine whether a charge has been created over the asset.

As there are other interests which may not be registered or ascertainable, it is essential that appropriate and extensive warranties are obtained from the seller.

21.19 Minimum Shareholder and Officer Requirements

Every company incorporated in Malaysia must have at least two directors who each have a principal or only place of residence within Malaysia (Companies Act 1965, Section 122(1)).

The number of shareholders must not be less than two. There can only be one shareholder if the sole shareholder is a company. A private company cannot have more than 50 shareholders, counting joint holders as one shareholder and not counting any employee of the company or of its subsidiaries (Companies Act 1965, Section 15(1)).

21.20 Non-competition Clauses

In general, restraint of trade or non-competition covenants made by sellers are unenforceable (Contracts Act 1950, Section 28). Under this section, any agreement whereby a person is restrained from exercising a lawful profession, trade or business is to that extent void. Such covenants are often included only as a deterrent.

There are three exemptions to this prohibition. First, where a person sells the goodwill of his or her business, he may agree to refrain from carrying on a similar business within specified local limits, provided that the limits are reasonable. Secondly, in a partnership, the partners may, upon or in anticipation of a dissolution, agree that some or all of them will not carry on a business similar to that partnership within local limits which must be reasonable. Thirdly, the partners may agree that some or all of them will not carry on any business other than that of the partnership during the continuance of that partnership.

21.21 Environmental Considerations

Malaysia has a legal framework for the protection of the environment. Penalties are imposed on companies causing damage to the environment. Directors of such companies may also be personally liable. This is usually an area for concern where the business or company acquired is engaged in the business of manufacturing.

Warranties in relation to compliance with environmental laws and directives issued by the Department of Environment, environmental damage and liability should always be obtained to minimize the buyer's risks.

21.22 Employee Superannuation/Pension Plans

It is compulsory for employees and employers to contribute towards the Employees Provident Fund (EPF) established under the Employment Provident Fund Act 1951. The new employer must continue to pay the minimum rate of contribution or such higher rate paid to the employees prior to the acquisition.

Some companies establish a trust or retirement scheme in addition to the EPF. When a company within a group or where assets are acquired, the employees may no longer be eligible under the scheme. As this may amount to a variation of the employees' terms of employment, provisions must be made for the seller to compensate the employees.

The alternative to contributing towards the EPF is to contribute towards a fund approved pursuant to Section 52 of the EPF Act 1991. There are only a few such funds in Malaysia. The approval of the Director-General of Inland Revenue is necessary so as to enjoy the benefits of tax relief for the contribution by the employer.

21.23 Employees' Rights

Employees' rights are primarily governed by the Employment Act 1955 or by contract, in the case of employees falling outside the scope of the Act. Employment relationships are also regulated by collective agreements, awards of the Industrial Court, common law and legislation (eg. the Trade Unions Act 1959, the Industrial Relations Act 1967 and the Employees Social Security Act 1969).

Employees may pursuant to the Employment Act 1955 or the terms of any collective agreement be entitled to termination and lay-off benefits. The Industrial Courts have powers to order reinstatement or compensation in lieu of reinstatement and back wages.

21.24 Compulsory Transfer of Employees

There is no statutory requirement for the compulsory transfer of employees. In an acquisition of a business, the buyer may choose to offer employment on terms no less favourable to the employees. If the buyer does not wish to do so, the liability to pay termination and lay-off benefits rests with the seller.

In an acquisition of a company, the buyer should obtain an indemnity from the seller indemnifying the buyer from and against any outstanding claims or payments, including termination claims.

21.25 Tax Deductibility of Acquisition Expenses

Where the buyer is not taxable in Malaysia, the deductibility of its acquisition expenses is determined in accordance with the laws of its home country.

Acquisition expenses are deductible from the income of a Malaysian taxpayer only and to the extent that the expense was incurred in the production of income. Expenses incurred in connection with the acquisition of a capital asset are not deductible.

21.26   Levies on Acquisition Agreements and Collateral Documents

Stamp duty is payable for the conveyance of assets and shares. Stamp duty of 0.3 per cent of the purchase consideration is payable on the transfer of Malaysian shares, whereas ad valorem stamp duty ranging from 1 per cent to 3 per cent is payable on an asset purchase agreement. Transfers of shares listed on Bursa Malaysia Securities Berhad, the stock exchange, are made by way of book entries and stamp duty is payable only on the broker's contract notes at the rate of 0.1 per cent up to a maximum of MYR200, and a clearance fee of 0.04 per cent is payable, up a maximum of MYR500.

21.27   Financing Rules and Restriction

A Malaysian company obtaining credit facilities from a non-resident requires exchange permission if such credit facilities exceed the prescribed thresholds (presently, the equivalent of MYR 50 million for resident companies on a corporate group basis and MYR10 million in aggregate for resident individuals). For the purpose of exchange control, credit facilities include redeemable preference shares and as such, there is an additional approval to be obtained if a foreign buyer chooses to subscribe for redeemable preference shares exceeding the thresholds.

There are no peculiar financing rules and restrictions. Each bank has its own rules for lending but they are generally quite similar to rules practised internationally by other bankers. If a project is commercially viable, many banks would willingly finance it.

The target company is not permitted to finance the acquisition of its own shares, and as such, the buyer must look for its own funding. This is not an issue in an asset purchase.

21.28   Exchange Control and Repatriation of Profits

Owing to the financial crises in 1997 and 1998, the government imposed strict exchange control rules to protect the Malaysian ringgit on 1 September 1998. The exchange control requirements have, over the years, been gradually liberalized, with the latest amendments in March 2005. In addition, in 2005, the currency peg was lifted and the Central Bank now adopts a managed float.

There is no restriction for a non-resident investor to repatriate funds out of Malaysia arising from proceeds of sale of MYR assets, profits, and dividends.

21.29   Group of Companies

For income tax purposes, group companies are generally not taxed as a group. Each individual group member is treated in law as a separate legal entity. It is always a moot point whether the courts would lift the corporate veils of group companies to regard them as one single entity. Generally, the courts have approached this matter cautiously, following the common law closely. However, it is envisaged that if a holding company persistently trades by way of a pattern of 'MYR 2' companies, the courts would be tempted to uplift corporate veils.

There is currently only limited group relief available in Malaysia introduced by the Finance Act 2005 with effect from the year of assessment 2006. The group relief is provided to all locally incorporated resident companies under the Income Tax Act 1967 and allows 50 per cent of a company's current year losses to be offset against the income of other companies in the same group. The relief only applies to companies with a paid-up capital exceeding MYR 2.5 million and companies within a group must have a minimum of 70 per cent ownership between them.

21.30   Responsibility for Liabilities of an Acquired Subsidiary

The liabilities of an acquired subsidiary stays with the subsidiary in line with the concept of corporate separate entity. In some instances, the previous holding company or shareholder could have executed corporate guarantees for the subsidiary. Care should be taken by the sellers of these subsidiaries to require the buyer to release the sellers of these guarantees prior to or on completion or on any other suitable protection.

21.31   Governing Law of the Contract

As the Malaysian system of law is the common law system, most foreign investors are quite contented to have their contracts governed by Malaysian law as they are familiar with the concepts. For companies which have licences controlled by the Ministry of Trade and Industry, the Ministry normally requires any technical assistance agreement, royalty and related agreements to be governed by Malaysian law as a condition of the licence.

Occasionally, foreign laws can be agreed between the contracting parties as the governing law of the agreement. The Malaysian courts do recognize the parties' choice of foreign laws, if the choice is not made mala fide or to avoid the operation of Malaysian law or public policy.

21.32   Dispute Resolution Options

A common form of dispute resolution in Malaysia is arbitration, which is regulated by the Arbitration Act 1952. There is a formal arbitration centre called 'The Kuala Lumpur Regional Centre for Arbitration'. This Centre was set up under the auspices of the Asian–African Legal Consultative Committee of the United Nations. The rules for arbitration are UNCITRAL with certain modifications and adaptations. Recently, there has been an increasing use of the process of mediation in industries such as insurance and banking set-up; mediation bureaux have been set up.

22. MEXICO

Jorge A. León-Orantes B. Santamarina y Steta S. C.

22.1 Introductory Comments

Foreign investment is allowed in most activities. There are, however, a limited number of activities in which foreign participation is excluded or limited.

Mexico is a federal system and most of the laws which are relevant to an acquisition are federal, rather than state.

Early advice should always be sought whenever an acquisition involving a Mexican company, or a group which includes Mexican subsidiaries or Mexican assets, is contemplated.

22.2 Corporate Structures

The target of an acquisition of shares in Mexico is typically a stock company (*sociedad anónima* or SA). The capital of an SA is represented by shares, which are registered, negotiable credit instruments, evidencing the capacity and rights as shareholder of a company.

An SA can be either a private or a public company, in the latter case with its shares listed on the Mexican Stock Exchange.

Mexico's corporation laws also provide for other types of companies, such as a limited liability company, in which the capital is represented by capital participations and not by shares. These type of companies may afford tax advantages in certain foreign jurisdictions, notably the United States, so it has been extensively used lately. In Mexico they are treated exactly the same as an SA. The capital of these types of companies may also be subject to acquisition.

Mexico's corporation laws are of a federal nature and must be observed by all Mexican states.

It is of course possible to acquire shares or assets by anyone with legal personality and capacity according to Mexican law, including private individuals and private or public companies.

22.3 Letters of Intent and Heads of Agreement

An agreement (which can be either oral or written) is binding if it appears either from the document itself or from the circumstances that there is an intention to create legal relationships. Consideration is not required in Mexico to be given for any promises made or undertakings given by either party.

International Business Acquisitions, M. Whalley, F.-J. Semler (eds.), Kluwer Law International, London, 2007; ISBN 9789041124838.

If it is intended that letters of intent or heads of agreement not be binding on the parties until the exchange of more formal contracts, clear words should be used to that effect.

22.4   Taxes Affecting the Structure and Calculation of the Price

A detailed examination of Mexico's business taxes is beyond the scope of this guide. However, a purchase of shares results in the buyer inheriting all of the target's taxation liabilities, whereas a purchase of part of the assets avoids this. Appropriate warranties or taxation indemnities can protect the buyer from any unforeseen taxation liabilities of the target in the former case.

A non-resident acquiring business assets in Mexico may be deemed to have a permanent establishment in Mexico and its profits attributable to the Mexican establishment would then be subject to Mexican taxation. An acquisition of shares, on the other hand, insulates the non-resident buyer from Mexican taxation, other than taxation paid by the Mexican target on its profits or other taxable events and withholding taxes due on interest or other taxable payments.

The tax effects for the parties deriving from the sale of shares may be significantly different from the tax effects deriving from the sale of assets. This aspect may become one of the most critical aspects of the transaction and should be analysed early in the negotiating process.

22.5   Extent of Seller's Warranties and Indemnities

The nature and extent of warranties and indemnities depends on the size of the acquisition and the parties' relative bargaining strength. However, it is not unusual for sellers to give full warranties and indemnities relating to, for example, the accounts of the business or company to be acquired, title to the assets, taxation, litigation, employee issues, etc.

It is always desirable to consider whether warranties and indemnities from a seller should be supported by a parent company guarantee, or by a retention of part of the purchase price.

22.6   Liability for Pre-contractual Representations

Negligent and fraudulent misrepresentations may be actionable and can in certain cases allow rescission of the contract in addition to an action for damages. Mexico has legislation that prohibits misleading or deceptive conduct, which can provide a further basis for an action by a buyer who has been misled by a seller's pre-contractual representations or statements.

Acquisition agreements often attempt to preclude action for negligent misrepresentation, leaving the buyer with a remedy only in damages for breach of warranty, but such exclusions often do not protect the seller in cases where the misrepresentation has induced the buyer to enter into the agreement.

Specific contractual provisions which exclude liability for representations made in pre-contract negotiations, and which restrict rights of rescission to the period between exchange of contracts and completion, should cause the buyer to assume that it can only rely upon representations specifically repeated in the agreement, or facts and matters specifically warranted or in relation to which indemnities have been given.

22.7   Liability for Pre-acquisition Trading and Contracts

If the purchase agreement includes a retrospective effective date and so has been agreed by the parties, the buyer, for accounting and taxation purposes, bears the loss or is entitled to the business's profits from the effective date.

After completion of an asset transaction, the seller remains liable on contracts to which it was a party unless they are novated and a release given to the seller. Sometimes major contracts are novated but, as this is usually impracticable, more frequently contracts are assigned and the buyer undertakes to the seller to perform the contracts from completion and to indemnify the seller.

In a share acquisition, pre-acquisition profits may be paid to the seller by way of dividend or retained in the company, in which case the buyer inherits those profits.

22.8   Pre-completion Risks

Mexican law prescribes that pre-completion risks remain with the owner of the assets or shares.

However, a business acquisition agreement typically contains a provision stating which party bears the risk of loss of assets between signing and completion. Usually, risk remains with the seller so that it must maintain insurance until completion.

On a share acquisition, the matter is usually addressed by way of a warranty that there has been no material adverse change to the business since a warranted accounts date and, if there is, the buyer has a right to rescind.

22.9   Required Governmental Approvals

The Mexican Foreign Investment Law (the Law) provides that foreign investors may participate in any proportion in the capital stock of Mexican corporations, acquire fixed assets, participate in new economic activities or the manufacture of new product lines, open and operate facilities, and expand or relocate those already existing, except for certain restricted economic activities classified in the Law as:

- Those exclusively reserved for the Mexican state, such as: oil and other hydrocarbons; basic petrochemicals; electricity; generation of nuclear energy; radioactive minerals; telegraphs; radio telegraphy; postal service; issuance of bills; minting of coins; control, supervision and surveillance of ports, airports and heliports; and the others expressly provided for by the applicable legal provisions;

- Those exclusively reserved to Mexicans or Mexican corporations with clauses excluding foreign participation, such as: domestic ground passenger transportation, tourism transportation and cargo transportation, not including courier and packaged goods services; retail trade of gasoline and distribution of liquid petroleum gas; radio broadcasting services and other radio and television services, other than cable television;

credit unions; development banking institutions; and the rendering of professional and technical services expressly set forth by the applicable legal provisions. In these cases, foreign investors cannot participate directly in the activities and corporations mentioned above, either through trusts, agreements, partnerships or corporate agreements, pyramiding structures or other mechanisms granting control or participation, except through 'neutral investment', in the terms defined in the Law;

- Those economic activities and corporations, where foreign investment may participate up to the following percentages:

- Up to 10 per cent in co-operative production corporations;

- Up to 25 per cent in domestic air transportation; air taxi transportation; and specialized air transportation;

- Up to 49 per cent in insurance companies, bonding companies, money exchange companies, general deposit warehouses, companies referred to in article 12 bis of the Stock Market Law, retirement funds administration, manufacturing and commercialization of explosives, fire weapons, cartridges, ammunitions and fireworks, without including the acquisition and use of explosives for industrial and extractive activities, nor the elaboration of explosive compounds for consumption in said activities; printing and publication of newspapers for exclusive circulation in the national territory; series 'T' shares of corporations owning agricultural, cattle and forest lands; fresh water fishing, coastal fishing and fishing in the exclusive economic zone, without including aqua culture; integral ports administration; port pilot services for ships for interior navigation in terms of the law on the matter; shipping corporations engaged in the commercial exploitation of ships for interior navigation and coastal sailing, with the exception of tourist cruises and the exploitation of dredges and naval devices for port construction, maintenance and operation supply of fuels and lubricants for ships, aircrafts and railroad equipment; and companies holding a concession under the terms of articles 11 and 12 of the Law on Telecommunications. In these cases, the limits for the participation of foreign investment provided must not be directly exceeded, either through trusts, agreements, partnerships or corporate agreements, or any other mechanism granting control or a participation higher than the one established, except through 'neutral investment', in the terms defined in the Law;

- Those economic activities and corporations where the National Commission of Foreign Investments' consent is required for foreign investors to participate in a majority percentage, such as: port services to ships to carry out interior navigation operations, such as towing, rope grip and lighterage; shipping corporations dedicated to the exploitation of ships exclusively in foreign commerce; administration of airline terminals; private services of pre-school, elementary, junior high, high school, college and combined education; legal services; credit information corporations; securities rating institutions; insurance agents; cellular telephony; construction of pipelines for the transportation of oil and derivative products; and drilling of oil and gas wells; and construction, operation and exploitation of railroads that are general means of communication, and public service of railroad transportation.

In summary, except for the activities mentioned above, foreign investors may freely participate in any proportion in the capital stock of Mexican corporations.

The USA, Canada and Mexico executed in 1993 the North America Free Trade Agreement (NAFTA), which entered into effect as of 1 January 1994. Under the NAFTA provisions, there are investment advantages for US and Canada residents, particularly in the area of financial services.

In the case of acquisition of shares of established Mexican corporations, the Law provides that the National Commission of Foreign Investments' consent is required in order that foreign investors may acquire, directly or indirectly, more than 49 per cent of a corporation's capital stock, if the total value of the assets of the corporation, at the time of filing the corresponding application for the acquisition, exceeds the sum to be annually determined by this Commission, which amount at present is of MXN 2,185.9 million. No restriction is provided on the acquisition of assets of established corporations.

The Law provides that Mexican corporations with clauses admitting participation of foreigners may acquire real estate properties located in the restricted zone, for non-residential activities, with the obligation to record such acquisitions with the Ministry of Foreign Affairs. Foreign individuals and corporations and Mexican corporations with clauses admitting participation of foreigners may acquire real estate properties in the restricted zone, for residential purposes, only through trusts.

According to the Law 'neutral investment' is an investment in Mexican corporations or in trusts authorized under the different alternatives and conditions provided for in Section 5 of the Law, which do not grant, or which significantly limit, voting rights. Neutral investment is not taken into account when determining the percentage of foreign investment in the capital stock of a Mexican corporation.

22.10 Anti-trust and Competition Laws

Mexican anti-trust laws must be carefully observed in an acquisition.

The Mexican Federal Economic Competition Law very broadly defines concentrations as any concentration of companies, associations, shares, trusts or assets carried out among economic agents. It also provides that the Federal Competition Commission will oppose and penalize those concentrations the purpose or effect of which is to reduce, affect or impair competition and the free flow of goods or services.

It further provides that concentrations must be notified in advance in the following cases:

- if the value of the transaction exceeds 18 million times the minimum wage for the Federal District (currently MXN 876 million);

- if the transaction implies the acquisition of 35 per cent or more of the assets or shares of a company the assets or sales of which exceed 18 million times the minimum wage for the Federal District (currently MXN 876 million); or

- if two or more economic agents participate in the transaction the assets or annual sales of which, considered on a global world basis, individually or jointly, exceed

48 million times the minimum wage for the Federal District (MXN 2,336 million) and such transaction implies the additional accumulation of assets or corporate capital in excess of 8.4 million times the minimum wage for the Federal District (currently MXN 408.830 million), this latter aspect considering only the maxican assets or corporate value.

It is advisable to review each transaction and the pertinent financial information, to determine whether a proposed transaction falls within any of the above three categories and whether it is necessary to notify the Commission.

22.11   Required Offer Procedures

There are no takeover provisions in Mexican corporation law, except in the case of public companies.

22.12   Continuation of Government Licences

In certain activities the business operator must have a licence under federal legislation. Licences are required, for example, in banking, insurance and broadcasting. Various conditions may be attached to a licence and these must be reviewed, including whether the licence is revocable on a change of control of the licence holder.

Licences are not normally transferable so that a buyer of assets (as opposed to shares) may need to obtain a new licence in its own name. The possibility and the time taken to obtain the licence may be a relevant consideration.

22.13   Requirements for Transferring Shares

Restrictions on the transfer of shares may be found in a company's articles of incorporation or by-laws or, if there is one, in a shareholders' agreement. These documents should be reviewed.

Subject to any special provisions in the articles of incorporation or by-laws, shares are transferable by endorsement of the corresponding share certificates. The buyer's name, nationality and domicile must be inserted in the company's stock registry book.

22.14   Requirements for Transferring Land and Property Leases

Mexico has a very formal registration system for title to land (sometimes including leasehold interests) and the purchase of any interest in real property requires the execution of a public deed granted before a notary public and, subject to the payment of the appropriate transfer taxes and registration duties, registration of that transfer in the land titles register in the municipality in which the land is situated.

Title to land can be specifically encumbered by mortgages or charges, or by caveats recording the interests of third parties in the land (such as easements or rights of way).

22.15   Requirements for Transferring Intellectual Property

Title to all forms of intellectual property can be transferred by assignment.

The benefit of a licence to use the intellectual property of a third party may also be assignable, but typically requires the licensor's consent.

Where the intellectual property is the subject of registration (which includes trade marks, registered designs and patents), notice of the assignment must be given to the appropriate registry.

22.16 Requirements for Transferring Business Contracts, Licences and Leases

A business contract governed by Mexican law is only transferable or assignable in accordance with its terms. Assignment of the benefit of a contract does not release the transferor from the burden of the contract without a specific release from the other party to it. For this reason, many business acquisitions involve a formal novation of contracts (in which the buyer steps fully into the seller's place, the seller being released from all further liability) rather than a simple assignment.

Licences and business leases (finance leases, operating leases or hire purchase agreements) operate under the same rules.

In most cases, the consent of the other party to the contract (e.g. a lessor) is required before the contract can be assigned. It is not normally necessary to register or record an assignment of a business contract, although notice must be given to the other party that the contract has been assigned.

22.17 Requirements for Transferring Other Assets

With the exception of real property, assets can generally be transferred through delivery of appropriate invoices.

Assets that are the subject of a charge in favour of a bank or other creditor, or in which title has been retained by a seller under a financial lease or conditional sale agreement, in most circumstances, continue to be encumbered by the rights of the third parties following transfer to a buyer.

22.18 Encumbrances and Third Party Interests

Assets can be subject to many types of third party interests. Interests can arise under contract (e.g. a charge or a mortgage), by operation of law (e.g. a property right or a lien in favour of a statutory authority) or by virtue of specific registration on a public register (e.g. an encumbrance affecting title to land).

A buyer for full value (on open market terms) of an asset generally takes good title to it, unless it has actual or constructive notice of an encumbrance, and unless the seller does not, in fact, have a clear title to that asset.

Certain title registers (particularly in the case of land) can be conclusive evidence of the title of the registered proprietor on which the buyer can rely.

22.19 Minimum Shareholder and Officer Requirements

Private and public companies may be managed by a sole administrator or by a board of directors formed with at least two directors, who may or may not be residents in Mexico.

There must be at least two shareholders in a Mexican stock company (SA), whether a private or public company.

22.20 Non-competition Clauses

Restraint of trade or non-competition covenants given by a seller in the context of a sale of business are generally enforceable, provided that the extent and terms of the covenants are reasonable and do not contravene competition laws. What is reasonable depends upon the circumstances of the case, the nature of the business and the effect which competition could have on the buyer.

Covenants given by employees in employment agreements are customary, but in almost all cases are not enforceable. A blanket prohibition on an employee carrying on his or her actual occupation or exercising his or her skills is likely to be considered unenforceable, as is a restraint which goes beyond a short period following termination of employment.

Agreements in restraint of trade may also fall under the provisions of Mexico's Federal Economic Competition Law, which prohibits any agreement or understanding which has the purpose or effect of substantially lessening competition or which is an exclusionary provision (effectively, a collective boycott). The provisions of the Federal Economic Competition Law are far-reaching and potentially apply in all acquisitions, particularly where the seller and buyer are, or would be but for the acquisition, in competition with each other.

22.21 Environmental Considerations

Mexico has sophisticated laws and regulations for the protection of the environment, which are administered either by federal, state or municipal government authorities and agencies. Substantial penalties can be imposed on businesses which damage the environment and a purchaser of a business or of a property can inherit responsibility for cleaning and rectifying environmental damage.

Mexico is a signatory to a number of international environment treaties. Particularly in the case of the mining, manufacturing and chemical industries, appropriate environmental due diligence investigations are always advisable in the context of an acquisition of either shares or assets.

Warranties in relation to environmental damage and liability should also always be obtained from a seller, unless the buyer's own due diligence has extended to a full and satisfactory environmental audit.

22.22 Employee Superannuation/Pension Plans

The concept of 'superannuation' is not known as such in Mexico. However, according to labour laws, a seniority bonus is paid under similar bases when the employee resigns and has worked for the employer for 15 years or more.

The Social Security Law establishes a retirement fund called the 'Saving Retirement System', under which employers make contributions equal to 2 per cent of the employee's integrated salary in order to support the fund. The integrated salary comprises not only what the employee receives in cash but also benefits, food, housing, premiums, commissions, benefits in kind and any other sum of money or benefit granted to the employee in compensation for his or her work, as determined by that Law. Employers' contributions must be paid through the credit institution where each employee has his or her own account. Employees are entitled to withdraw the amount saved, plus interest, upon retirement.

In addition to the above, the Social Security Law also regulates an additional plan in the event of disability, old age and death, under which employees receive from the Mexican Social Security Institute medical attention and a periodic pension. To support this benefit, the employer, the employee and the government make contributions.

Irrespective of the foregoing, some companies implement private pension plans, in addition to the mandatory ones. Such plans can be structured as desired by the employer, provided that fiscal provisions are met. Usually, the employer makes contributions to support the pension plan, and payments upon the employee's retirement can be made in a lump sum or periodically. Rights actually acquired under a private plan may not be withdrawn by the company.

22.23 Employee Rights

The most important labour legislation in Mexico is the Federal Labour Law. Because Mexico is organized as a federation this law is applicable in the entire country and rules the relationship between employers, employees and unions, as well as the activities of labour authorities. Also important are the Social Security Law, regulating all matters related to social security benefits that employees are entitled to, the Housing Fund Law, which created a fund for the purpose of building homes for employees, and the Retirement Fund Law, which created a retirement fund system for employees.

The Federal Labour Law establishes the minimum benefits that employers must grant to their employees. Above these, employers may grant any benefit agreed with the employee. Any stipulation establishing benefits below those provided by the Law is null and void.

Disputes must be resolved through labour authorities, specifically Conciliation and Arbitration Boards, which are formed by one employees' representative, one employers' representative and one government representative. Although Conciliation and Arbitration Boards are part of the executive power, in fact they have jurisdiction to enforce their own resolutions.

22.24 Compulsory Transfer of Employees

According to Mexican legislation, a buyer of business assets may elect to be responsible for the employees previously associated with that business following its transfer, in which event the 'employer substitution' provisions apply. He or she may also elect to 'cherry pick' employees, leaving the seller to continue to have responsibility for any employees to whom offers are not made by the new owner of the business.

The Federal Labour Law regulates 'employer substitutions'. An employer substitution takes place when employees are transferred from one employer to another. Even though the employees' consent is not required for the transfer, it is established that the new employer will continue granting the same wages, salaries and benefits that were paid by the former employer and that the work will be carried out under the same conditions. It is important to record the transfer by delivering notice of the substitution to the employees or to the union representing them.

During a six month period from the date of substitution, the former employer is jointly liable with the new one for complying with those labour obligations that existed prior to the substitution. Upon the expiration of the period, only the new employer's liability remains.

Employees of a company, the shares of which are acquired by a buyer, continue to have all of the rights previously enjoyed, notwithstanding the change in the ultimate ownership of the company, and the company continues to be liable for employee pay and benefits both before and after the date of acquisition of its shares.

22.25 Tax Deductibility of Acquisition Expenses

Where the buyer is a company or individual not resident or taxable in Mexico, the deductibility of its acquisition expenses is determined by the laws of its home jurisdiction.

Where, however, the buyer is a Mexican taxpayer, acquisition expenses are only deductible to the extent that they are an expense properly incurred in order to gain assessable income. Expenses of a capital nature may be included in the cost base of an asset for the purposes of calculating any subsequent capital gains tax payable on disposal of that asset where the proceeds of sale exceed its indexed cost base. Acquisition expenses of business assets are deductible through depreciation.

22.26 Levies on Acquisition Agreements and Collateral Documents

There is no stamp duty or tax in Mexico.

22.27 Financing Rules and Restrictions

According to the Income Tax Law if a company has intercompany loans that exceed three times the amount of its net worth, interest paid on the excess is not deductible. This is basically the thin capitalization rule in Mexico.

22.28   Exchange Controls and Repatriation of Profits

There are currently no exchange controls in Mexico

Dividends paid to resident or non-resident investors in Mexico by resident companies are not subject to dividend withholding tax.

Mexico imposes withholding taxes on interest paid to non-residents. The withholding rate could go from 4.0 per cent to 4.9 per cent. The latter withholding rate only applies to financial institutions registered with the Mexican Secretariat of Finance.

22.29   Groups of Companies

Subject to the compliance of the applicable statutory requirements, a company incorporated under Mexico's Corporations Law has the option for tax purposes to prepare consolidated accounts (profit and loss account and balance sheet) of the company and each of the entities it controls or has controlled from time to time during its financial year (apportioned if necessary). For these purposes, a company controls another if it holds more than 51 per cent of the voting rights in the controlled company or if it has 'effective' control of it.

The financial year of all companies must run from 1 January to 31 December (the calendar year).

22.30   Responsibility for Liabilities of an Acquired Subsidiary

Shareholders in Mexico are insulated from liability for the debts of a company in which they hold shares, other than in circumstances where a specific joint guarantee, indemnity or other undertaking has been given personally by the shareholders in favour of a creditor.

According to Mexico's Corporations Law, a parent company is not liable for a subsidiary's debt.

22.31   Governing Law of the Contract

Mexican courts will honour a choice of law freely made between parties to a contract. They may apply foreign law to a contract for the acquisition of shares or business assets in Mexico, if so agreed by the parties. However, if the acquisition involves real property, the contract is governed by the law of the jurisdiction where the real property is located.

While a foreign law may govern the agreement and the relationship between the parties, Mexican state or federal law usually deals with other questions such as the effect of a transfer of title to shares or other assets, or the rights of creditors and others. Provisions of foreign law do not apply when they contravene major principles of Mexican law or if they are against public order provisions.

22.32   Dispute Resolution Options

Mexican laws, and the courts, recognize that parties to commercial contracts may wish to resolve disputes other than by litigation. The whole range of arbitration options are therefore available to resolve commercial disputes.

Mexican courts recognize and enforce international arbitration awards in certain cases. Mexico also has arbitration bodies which appoint arbitrators to hear disputes. Arbitration has been used successfully in many cases in Mexico to resolve complex commercial disputes and is gaining in popularity as an effective way of avoiding lengthy and costly litigation.

Parties are free to adopt the arbitration rules of any Mexican or international body in their contracts and the Mexican courts recognize and honour the parties' wishes in this respect. It is not possible, however, to oust the jurisdiction of the Mexican courts in a dispute over which they have jurisdiction, although a court may be bound by a determination of an expert or an arbitrator on questions of fact if the parties have so agreed. In the absence of contractual arbitration rules, the provisions of the Mexican Commerce Code apply, unless otherwise provided in an international treaty to which Mexico is a signatory.

Mexico is signatory to a number of treaties giving recognition to the judgments of superior courts overseas and it is possible in many cases to register a judgment obtained overseas for the purposes of enforcing it in Mexico.

22.33 Other Issues

Mexico is a civil law country and form is as important as substance. In other words, to be valid and enforceable, most commercial business transactions should follow clear and specific legal formalities. For example, in a stock acquisition the certificates covering the shares should be endorsed by the seller and delivered to the buyer and the appropriate entries should be made in the issuer company's stock registry book. Transactions involving the acquisition of assets also need to follow legal formalities, especially when real property is the subject of the transaction. The granting of guarantees also needs to follow legal formalities. For example, mortgages over real property must be executed in a public instrument granted before a notary public and recorded in the Public Registry of Property corresponding to the place where the property is located.

Transactions involving assets other than real property should also follow legal formalities such as appropriate invoicing.

In addition, there are legal formalities to be observed in relation to the tax aspects of all assets and share acquisitions in Mexico.

To conclude, legal formalities should be carefully followed and observed in the case of most of the legal issues arising in business acquisitions, i.e. tax, commercial, labour, patents and trade marks, immigration, customs issues, etc.

23. THE NETHERLANDS

Martika Jonk
CMS Derks Star Busmann N.V.

23.1 Introductory Comments

Dutch law is fundamentally non-discriminatory, and as a general rule, does not contain any nationality requirements or foreign investment restrictions or approvals, except for certain specific industries, such as banking and insurance.

The Netherlands is often used by international groups of companies for setting up holding companies or intermediate holding companies for tax purposes. The main reasons for this are the extensive number of tax treaties into which the Netherlands has entered, the opportunity to obtain advance 'rulings' from the tax authorities and the phenomenon of the so-called 'participation exemption'.

23.2 Corporate Structures

The most commonly used corporate structures for Dutch businesses are the private company with limited liability (BV) and the public limited liability company (NV). A BV can only have registered shares, whereas the NV may also issue bearer shares.

The NV is required to have a minimum issued and paid-up capital of EUR 45,000. The minimum issued and paid-up capital for BV's is EUR 18,000.

At the time of going to press of this book, legislative action to simplify Dutch corporate law with respect to BV's is in preparation, and provides for substantial changes (f.i. abolition of the minimum capital requirement, de-formalization of the rules on capital reduction).

The use of the NV is generally limited to companies that intend to list their securities on the stock exchange or over-the-counter market.

Shares in a BV cannot be transferred freely. A restriction on the transfer of shares must be included in the articles of association. This can be either an offering system, which provides for a right of first refusal for the co-shareholders, or an approval system pursuant to which the transfer requires the prior approval of the shareholders' meeting. A combination of both systems is also possible.

Other structures sometimes used by foreign investors for tax purposes are the Limited Partnership (CV) and the General Partnership (VOF). These structures are not legal entities.

23.3 Letters of Intent and Heads of Agreement

The rules that apply to the formation and interpretation of agreements also apply to binding letters of intent.

International Business Acquisitions, M. Whalley, F.-J. Semler (eds.), Kluwer Law International, London, 2007; ISBN 9789041124838.

The binding effect will be determined not only by what has been written in the document, but also by oral and other forms of communication in so far as they were instrumental for the parties to come to the agreement.

A relevant factor is what the parties could understand from statements made and acts performed by them and by what they could reasonably expect from each other. In that context it may be relevant whether one party can be deemed to be more experienced and/or professional than the other.

The contractual relation of the parties is also governed–other than by the agreement– by law, common practice and the principle of reasonableness and fairness. The latter principle may either have a limiting effect or–under exceptional circumstances–may create additional obligations for the parties. In addition, the courts can also supplement, modify, or set aside (in whole or in part) an agreement on the basis of so called 'unforeseen circumstances'.

The Dutch Supreme Court has gradually widened the scope of the principle of reasonableness and fairness, so that the principle does not only apply to all obligations under an agreement but also to the so called 'pre-contractual phase'.

The Dutch Supreme Court has ruled that parties, when negotiating a contract in the pre-contractual phase, must act according to criteria of reasonableness and fairness. This principle imposes on the parties the duty to take into account the other's reasonable interests. This duty may imply that a party either may not break off negotiations, or that it may not break off without paying the other party's damages and costs. The damages may even consist of the so called 'positive contract interest' (loss of profit which the plaintiff would have made from the contract if concluded). The President of the Court may issue an order in an injunction for parties to continue or resume negotiations.

While drafting a letter of intent or heads of agreement parties should be clear as to what extent they wish to be bound. Whereas an agreement to negotiate an agreement is unenforceable in certain other jurisdictions, under Dutch law parties may be bound to the obligations set out in a letter of intent. Substance prevails over form and it is not the title of the document that determines its (non) binding effect. A simple 'subject to contract' may therefore not suffice to avoid binding effect. An action for specific performance may be available.

Lock-ins and lock-outs are common and in principle enforceable, as are confidentiality undertakings. Please note that in the Netherlands punitive damages do not exist. It is therefore customary to include a penalty provision as an incentive to adhere to confidentiality undertakings.

23.4 Taxes Affecting the Structure and Calculation of the Price

From a tax point of view, there are various differences between the acquisition of shares and the acquisition of assets.

In the case of a share deal, the target company continues with the tax liabilities and book values for tax purposes, as it had prior to the acquisition of its shares. This includes the tax liabilities of the company itself, e.g. for hidden reserves in assets with a book value lower than their fair market value. Furthermore, it may entail extraordinary liabilities for taxes payable by a (former) group company, where the target company had been part of a tax consolidated group (fiscal unity) prior to acquisition. This is the result of the fact that there is a joint liability for certain taxes in the case of tax consolidated companies. This issue is important to take into consideration in a share deal, and should be covered in an appropriate way in the share purchase agreement.

In cases where the target company has tax losses to carry forward, it needs to be examined whether such losses can be used by the target company after its shares have been sold. There are some important restrictions in this respect. In general, if and as long as the target company continues the same line of business without reducing it by 70 per cent or more, the losses in general remain available to be offset against future profits of the target company. This assumes that the activities of the target company do not consist of 90 per cent or more of holding or group finance activities, and that the assets of the target company do not consist of 50 per cent or more of portfolio investments.

In the case of a share deal, the acquirer often needs to pay a higher price, as the selling company usually needs to pay tax on any realized capital gain. On the other hand, in an asset deal the liability issues as described above generally do not come into play. In case of an acquisition of assets, for depreciation purposes, the acquirer usually may apply the price it paid for the assets.

23.5 Extent of Seller's Warranties and Indemnities

The terms representations and warranties are used synonymously, and they are perceived as being the same as a covenant. Non-fulfilment is considered a breach of the warrantor.

Certain representations and warranties (e.g. with respect to title) are implied. The purchaser may expect that the object of the transaction possesses the qualities that are necessary for a normal use thereof and the presence of which he does not have to doubt, as well as those qualities that are necessary for any special use specified in the contract.

Generally the claim period for warranties may range from one to three years (and five to seven years for tax warranties). The content of the representations and warranties are *grosso modo* the same as in Anglo-American practice.

The statute of limitations with respect to payment of damages is generally five years, running from the moment the damage became known.

Provided certain legal conditions are met, one can claim damages, annulment or recession of the purchase agreement. Annulment or recession may also be claimed partially, in which case an adjustment of the purchase price is one of the options.

23.6 Liability for Pre-contractual Representations

The reason for conducting a proper due diligence is in essence that Dutch law entails a duty to investigate. Improper due diligence may preclude a party from invoking nullity on the basis of mistake (*dwaling*). Dutch practice regarding due diligence investigations strongly resembles the Anglo-American practice.

If the agreement does not contain any specific representations and warranties, a buyer can, under certain circumstances, nevertheless raise a claim against the seller when it has been provided with incorrect or incomplete information about the target. Annulment of, or amendment of the conditions of, the agreement such as an adjustment of the purchase price, is possible under certain specific circumstances if the buyer has been given a wrong impression of the target and such impression has been material for the buyer in entering into the transaction. Furthermore, the agreement may be rescinded under certain circumstances or the buyer may claim damages if the target is not in conformity with the buyer, as (agreed upon) requirements.

23.7 Liability for Pre-acquisition Trading and Contracts

The parties may agree that an acquisition is deemed to take effect, economically speaking, at a date other than the completion date. As a result, profits and losses over the relevant period are attributed to the relevant party.

Since parties tend to negotiate on the basis of financial accounts of a certain date, it is customary to agree on a provision that deals with the period between the date of the accounts and the actual transfer of the shares. Generally parties agree on a guarantee issued by the seller that entails that in the interim period no circumstances arise that negatively affect the business/equity.

23.8 Pre-completion Risks

In many cases, completion includes both the execution of the share purchase agreement and the actual transfer of the shares. All risks relating to the period until completion remain the seller's, unless otherwise agreed. Should the parties wish to make a distinction between the execution of the purchase agreement and the transfer date, however, it is important to agree beforehand who will bear the risk during the interim period.

It is customary to include a number of conditions precedent in the share purchase agreement that must be fulfilled prior to the date of the closing.

In addition, parties may agree on certain escape clauses, such as the condition that the agreement is subject to (supervisory) board approval, or subject to financing, or subject to satisfactory due diligence.

23.9 Required Governmental Approvals

There are no requirements to report a proposed merger or acquisition, except when the Dutch Competition Act (see **23.10**) or the Merger Code (see **23.11**) is applicable. In this respect there is no distinction between a domestic or a foreign buyer of a Dutch business.

23.10 Anti-trust and Competition Laws

Merger control

Merger control in the Netherlands is governed by the Dutch Competition Act (*Mededingingswet,* the 'DCA') which entered into force on 1 January 1998. The DCA requires that 'concentrations' of a certain size are notified to the Dutch Competition Authority (*Nederlandse Mededingingsautoriteit,* the 'NMa'). The DCA provisions dealing with merger control are modelled on the European merger regime and are very similar in many aspects. The DCA in principle does not apply to transactions which are caught by the European merger regime. A concentration occurs when:

- Two or more undertakings merge;

- One or more undertakings acquire direct or indirect control of the whole or parts of one or more undertakings; or

- A joint venture is established which performs on a lasting basis all the functions of an autonomous economic entity and which does not give rise to coordination of the competitive behaviour of the parent companies (concentrative joint venture).

Currently, cooperative joint ventures fall outside the bounds of the DCA, however, a pending legislative proposal to amend the DCA will change the rules on cooperative joint ventures and bring these in line with the European merger regime. A cooperative joint venture which performs on a lasting basis all the functions of an autonomous economic entity will then be caught by Dutch merger control.

The NMa's jurisdiction is determined by reference to turnover. A concentration falls within the scope of the DCA if the following tests are satisfied:

- The aggregate combined worldwide turnover of all the undertakings concerned in the previous calendar year exceeds €113,450,000; and

- The individual turnover in the Netherlands of each of at least two of the undertakings concerned was at least €30 million in the previous calendar year.

Special thresholds apply to credit institutions, financial institutions and insurance companies. Foreign to foreign concentrations are caught by the DCA if the thresholds are met regardless of whether the undertakings concerned have a subsidiary in the Netherlands.

A concentration falling within the scope of the DCA cannot be completed before it has been approved by the NMa. It is not required that an agreement is signed or that a controlling interest is acquired for notification to be triggered. A mere intention to do the transaction is sufficient.

As in the European merger regime, there is a two-stage filing procedure. The NMa must decide whether the concentration falls within the scope of the DCA and whether a licence is required within four weeks after the receipt of the notification. The NMa will decide that a licence is required if it has reason to assume that a dominant position could be created or strengthened as a result of the concentration which could impede competition within the Netherlands. If no licence is required, the concentration can be completed. If a licence is required, the parties must formally apply for a licence and provide more detailed information. The second stage of the investigation takes, in principle, 13 weeks as of the date of receipt of the application for a licence. If the NMa fails to act within that period, it is deemed that the licence has been granted. The NMa will refuse to grant a licence if the merger creates or strengthens a dominant position as a result of which competition in the Dutch market or part of it would be significantly impeded.

Appeals of NMa decisions can be made to the specialist court dealing with competition cases, the Rotterdam District Court (*Rechtbank Rotterdam*). Appeal against judgements of the Rotterdam District Court can be made to the Trade and Industry Appeals Tribunal (*College van Beroep voor het bedrijfsleven*).

Anti-competitive agreements

According to Article 6 of the DCA, which mirrors Article 81 of the EC Treaty, agreements, decisions and concerted practices are prohibited if they have as their object or effect the prevention, restriction or distortion of competition on the whole or a part of the Dutch market. The prohibition covers all types of behaviour, horizontal or vertical, irrespective of whether it is based on formal, oral or tacit agreements or concerted practices. As is the case in EC competition law, agreements restricting competition are only prohibited if they have an appreciable effect on competition.

Abuse of dominant position

Article 24 of the DCA prohibits undertakings from abusing their dominant position. Its terms are substantially the same as those of Article 82 of the EC Treaty, except that there is no requirement for a potential effect on trade between EU Member States. According to the explanatory note to this provision, its substantive interpretation and application should follow the decisional practice and case law under Article 82 of the EC Treaty.

23.11   Required Offer Procedures

The main way of obtaining control of a public company is a public offer. There are three types of public offers; a firm offer, which is a public offer to acquire all the share capital of the target at a specified offer price, a partial offer, which is a public offer for no more than 30 per cent of the share capital of the target at a specified offer price and a tender offer, which is a public offer inviting holders of no more than 30 per cent of the share capital of the target to tender shares and state the consideration they would like to receive. A tender offer is always for cash consideration. An offer to purchase shares admitted to trading on a regulated market, as defined in the Financial Supervision Act (*Wet op het financieel toezicht*) ('Supervision Act'), can only be made if an offer document is publicly available.

Public offers are primarily regulated by the Supervision Act and the accompanying orders in council. The Authority for the Financial Markets (*Autoriteit Financiële Markten*, or 'AFM') supervises compliance with the Supervision Act. The Supervision Act includes provisions covering the events and circumstances requiring a public announcement, the information to be supplied to the AFM, consultation requirements in the event of a hostile bid, the contents of the offer document, duration and extension of the offer period, shareholders' meeting of the target company and other conditions applicable to the bid.

In addition, the parties involved in a public bid are subject to insider trading rules, set out in the Supervision Act, and furthermore to general provisions set out in the Civil Code (such as rules on fair and reasonable behaviour within the company, the duties of the managing and supervisory directors, mismanagement proceedings, statutory mergers, squeeze-out proceedings) and regulatory controls of ownership in certain industries (defence and banking).

There is an obligation to inform the AFM when the number of shares held passes thresholds of 5 per cent, 10 per cent, 15 per cent, 20 per cent, 25 per cent, 30 per cent 50 per cent and 75 per cent of the issued share capital pursuant to the Supervision Act.

In relation to labour matters, a quasi-legislative code, the SER Merger Code (*SER Besluit Fusiegedragsregels 2000*), and the Works Council Act (*Wet op de ondernemingsraden*) (WCA) apply. The Merger Committee monitors compliance with the SER Merger Rules.

The Merger Code applies to the acquisition of direct or indirect control (more than 50 per cent) over all or part of the activities of another enterprise, as well as the formation of a co-operation of enterprises (the definition includes joint ventures). The Merger Code must be observed in the event of any 'merger' (as defined in the Code) involving one or more enterprises that are established in the Netherlands and regularly employ 50 employees or more, or belong to a group of enterprises with one or more enterprises established in the Netherlands that in aggregate employ 50 employees or more. If applicable, the trade unions must be consulted.

The Works Council Act requires prior consultation of the Works Council in the event of a change of control of all or part of the relevant enterprise, or if there is the take-over or forfeiting of control over another enterprise, or if a long-term co-operation with another enterprise, including financial participations, is envisaged. No merger can be completed without finishing these consultation proceedings, which may take considerable time.

Collective Bargaining Agreements may also contain specific consultation or notification requirements.

Finally, mention must be made of Directive 2004/25/EG of 21 April 2004 on takeover bids (the 'Takeover Directive'). The Takeover Directive provides for a mandatory public offer in case of acquisition of considerable control, at least 30 per cent, in a public company by an individual buyer or entities acting in concert. The offer must be in respect of all remaining shares, the proposed price must be reasonable, which is, roughly speaking, taken to mean the highest price paid for shares of the target company prior to the public offer. The Takeover Directive does not apply to individuals or entities holding control in a company prior to its implementation.

The debate on a legislative proposal for implementation of the Takeover Directive (*Wetsvoorstel 30419*) was ongoing in the Netherlands at the moment this book went to press. The proposal, which entails substantial changes to Dutch company law, approaches completion and will be implemented in the Supervision Act.

23.12   Continuation of Government Licences

Many types of businesses require a licence to operate their businesses. Such licences may be issued in the name of the legal entity conducting the business, or may be tied to the location where the business is conducted or may be tied to the business activities.

Whether a licence is required is dependent upon the type of business activities that are being conducted. Note that, with respect to environmental issues, the Netherlands has very strict legislation, and violation of an environmental licence may result in severe consequences.

It is important to verify the specific contents of a licence and to verify, in the case of a transfer of a business, whether a licence is transferable and, in the case of a change of control, whether the licence will terminate upon the transfer. Assurances may be obtained by appropriate conditions precedent to the closing.

23.13   Requirements for Transferring Shares

Bearer shares are transferred by surrendering the share certificates. A transfer of registered shares in a BV requires the execution of a notarial deed before a Dutch civil law notary. The notary ensures that the transfer takes place in accordance with approval or pre-emption rights of existing shareholders. The transfer is to be notified to or acknowledged by the company. Generally, the acknowledgement is made by the company in the deed of transfer.

There are special requirements for the transfer of shares in listed companies.

The management of the BV is required to keep a shareholders register stating, inter alia, the names and addresses of the shareholders, the date of acquisition as well as the names and addresses of persons having a right of pledge or usufruct. This register is to be kept by the management board at the offices of the BV in the Netherlands.

23.14   Requirements for Transferring Land and Property Leases

Title to real property must be registered in the Land Register. Conveyance of real property can only take place through execution of a notarial deed and the subsequent registration of such deed in the Land Register. Other rights that need to be notarized and filed with the Land Register include neighbouring rights of adjacent landowners, rights of co-property, attachments and mortgages and conveyance of real property. Rental agreements need not be registered.

23.15   Requirements for Transferring Intellectual Property

In principle, the ownership of all intellectual property rights can be transferred. The different intellectual property acts state specific requirements for transfer of the different rights. Copyrights, trademark rights, design rights and patent rights are transferred in written form by public or private deed. This means that these rights can be transferred by a written agreement. Rights can be transferred partially and in whole or joint ownership and it is also deemed possible to transfer future copyrights.

For trademark rights, design rights and patent rights, an entry in the appropriate public register is required in order for the transfer to be effective on third parties. Since trademark and design rights are subject to legislation that is applicable for the Benelux, a transfer of these rights is only valid if the transfer extends to the entire territory of the Benelux.

The so-called 'moral rights' of an author, which include the paternity right and the right to oppose changes or impairment of the work, cannot be transferred because of the personal nature of these rights. The author can, to a certain extent, waive these rights. Although according to the law, a trade name can only be transferred together with the company that is conducted under the trade name, this restriction is deemed increasingly undesirable and in some case-law the restriction has been set aside.

Instead of transferring intellectual property rights, it is also possible to grant a licence for the use of these rights. There are no prescribed formalities for a licence, which means that a licence can be granted orally. However, for trademark rights, design rights and patent rights, an entry of the licence in the appropriate registers is required in order for the licence to be effective on third parties. It is debatable whether a licence can be granted for a trade name. In case-law, there are several occasions in which a licence for a trade name has been accepted, namely in the case of franchises.

23.16 Requirements for Transferring Business Contracts, Licences and Leases

Licence agreements and lease agreements may, in principle, only be transferred and assigned with the contracting party's approval. Some lease agreements with respect to real estate may be transferred or subleased without the landlord's approval or with the court's approval. There is no registration requirement for the transfer of a contract.

It should be noted in this respect that the Netherlands has very detailed legislation with respect to the lease of real estate.

23.17 Requirements for Transferring Other Assets

The transfer of physical goods can only take place either by putting the goods legally at the buyer's disposal or by a written (private) deed. There are special provisions, similar to those provisions for the transfer of real estate, applicable to certain aircraft and vessels. The transfer of a claim takes place by the execution of a deed of assignment.

23.18 Encumbrances and Third Party Interests

Certain rights attaching to a specific asset remain in place following the transfer of the asset, since, under Dutch law, they may be invoked against a third party. These rights include rights of pledge and mortgage.

Under certain exceptional circumstances the acquirer is protected if he or she has acted in good faith. There is no general register of charges or other liens in the Netherlands. There are, however, certain public registers including those for rights in ships, aircraft and real property.

23.19   Minimum Shareholder and Officer Requirements

There are no minimum shareholder requirements. There are no restrictions on foreign ownership. The articles of association of a company may contain quality requirements for shareholders, but these are rare. Such quality requirements may be that the shareholder should be a Dutch resident or have EU nationality.

Please note, however, that when a company only has one shareholder, the identity of that shareholder must be disclosed in the Trade Register.

Dutch corporate law allows for a two-tier board system. In a two-tier system the company may have two separate boards: a management (executive) board and a supervisory board.

Supervisory board members have no executive powers; they have an advising and supervising function towards the management board. They do not interfere with the day-to-day management.

Both natural persons and legal entities can be members of a management board, whereas, members of the supervisory board must be natural persons. Members of the management board and members of the supervisory board are not required to be Dutch citizens.

Every BV must have a management board. The creation of a supervisory board is optional, except for certain large corporations.

23.20   Non-competition Clauses

Non-competition clauses are not covered by a general prohibition under the DCA (see **23.10**) and therefore are generally enforceable. However, if the duration or scope of a non-competition clause is excessive, a party to such non-competition covenant may try to limit the effects of that covenant before a court. Such a claim could be based on the principle of 'reasonableness and fairness' according to which a contractual clause between parties may not be enforced if, under specific circumstances, that would be manifestly unreasonable. Furthermore, if the buyer and the seller of a business are competitors, an overly restrictive, non-competition covenant might be considered an 'anti-competitive agreement' (see **23.9** and **23.10**).

Non-competition covenants entered into by employees are only enforceable when concluded in writing. The Dutch Civil Code provides that an employee may file a petition with the Cantonal Court to limit the scope of a non-competition clause or declare that clause null and void, if the clause unreasonably restricts the employee's freedom to find a new job.

23.21   Environmental Considerations

Under environmental law, licences to operate a company may be required.

Furthermore, legislation was introduced concerning liability for environmental contaminations. Under such legislation, a property owner may be held liable for contamination that has been caused before its acquisition. In an acquisition of shares, one should therefore be aware that such liability might be carried by the company. There may be a liability with respect to both contamination of premises owned or formerly owned by the company, and contamination of the premises of third parties, if such contamination has been caused by the company.

The owner of a property may be forced to clean up, even when he or she did not cause the pollution. A tenant can only be forced to clean up pollution when he or she is responsible for causing that pollution. Under specific circumstances a tenant may, however, be required to take (quite costly) measures to contain the possible effects of a pollution.

In view of the possibly substantial financial consequences of environmental claims, a purchaser is strongly advised to make a thorough investigation of all environmental matters prior to the purchase.

23.22   Employee Superannuation/Pension Plans

Most Dutch enterprises have pension plans for their employees. If the target company has a pension fund, it may be of interest to know whether the fund is overcapitalized, as under certain conditions the company may claim a distribution of the surplus, although the chances of this happening are decreasing.

Pension contributions are often paid, in whole or in part, by the employer. The amount of the final old age pension is, inter alia, related either to the wage that was payable at retirement or to the average wage received during employment. If the pension is related to the final wage, it sometimes happens that, for example, after a salary increase the funding of the pension falls short and additional payments must consequently be made to the pension fund. A buyer of a company is therefore advised to check any back-service obligations and to request representations and warranties in respect of payments of pension contributions.

Finally, it should be noted that certain liabilities may arise if, as has been decided in case law, certain pension rights must be granted to special categories of employees retrospectively.

There are some types of businesses in which there are regulations in force pursuant to which employees may retire at an earlier age, and for which certain contingencies must be made.

23.23   Employee Rights

Dutch labour law strongly protects the employee's position. Dismissal of an employee requires the prior approval of the court or of a specific governmental agency. It should be noted that an approval for dismissal is not automatically granted. In addition, obligations to pay severance payments may be imposed. This does not apply to terminations for cause. The employment relationship is governed not only by the contents of the employment contract, but also by extensive legislation contained in the Civil Code and, in some instances, by existing collective bargaining agreements. All these rules remain in place on the transfer of relevant assets or shares. Employee participation is well developed in the Netherlands. Enterprises (whether or not a legal entity) that employ 50 employees or more are required to have a Works Council. The Works Council has the right to be consulted in the event of a change of control.

23.24 Compulsory Transfer of Employees

The transfer of shares does not affect the position of the company's employees.

The Netherlands has implemented the Acquired Rights Directive. Therefore, in case of a transfer of an enterprise's assets, in as far as such assets form an 'undertaking', all employees related to those assets are, by operation of law, transferred to the buyer. Transfer of the employees implies the transfer of all rights and obligations relating to the employment relationship, including rights in respect of a non-competition clause.

23.25 Tax Deductibility of Acquisition Expenses

As a general rule, acquisition expenses are tax deductible. However, some important restrictions apply.

In some situations, some or all of the expenses need to be capitalized as part of the consideration paid for the acquired shares or assets. This applies in particular in an acquisition of shares, whereby the shares represent 5 per cent or more of the share capital of the company.

As shares generally cannot be depreciated, the acquisition expenses in relation to an acquisition of shares generally do not lead to tax deduction. An exception applies in case the target company is liquidated; a liquidation loss is, under certain circumstances tax deductible.

In the case of an asset deal, the question of whether acquisition expenses can be deducted at once or whether they need to be capitalized depends on the type of assets acquired and the type of acquisition expenses. In cases where the expenses need to be capitalized, they usually lead to tax deduction by way of depreciation over a number of years.

To the extent the expenses concern interest payments, note that there are certain restrictions as to tax deductibility. Reference is made to para. **23.27**.

23.26 Levies on Acquisition Agreements and Collateral Documents

There is no specific Dutch tax or levy on the concluding or signing of agreements or the transfer of shares or other assets. The only exception is real estate transfer tax which is levied on the transfer of Dutch real estate or shares in a company that qualify as a real estate company. The latter may i.e. be the case if the company has assets that consist of 70 per cent or more of Dutch real estate. Real estate transfer tax is levied at a rate of 6 per cent on the value of the real estate. An exemption with conditions applies in case of a transfer to a related company.

23.27 Financing Rules and Restrictions

Interest expenses are generally deductible for tax purposes. However, there are various rules that deny or limit interest deduction under certain circumstances. Some of the more important restrictions are addressed below, in outline.

Under the thin cap rules, interest is not deductible if a certain debt-to-equity ratio is exceeded. For most cases, the maximum debt-to-equity ratio is 3:1.

Interest may not be deductible if it is paid on a debt to a related party and the funds of the debt have been used for a 'tainted transaction'. The transactions that are tainted are described in the law. They encompass, i.e., the distribution of a dividend, the repayment of share capital, the contribution to share capital of a subsidiary, and the acquisition of shares in a company. On the other hand, an exception to this interest deduction restriction may apply, if the recipient of the interest effectively pays at least 10 per cent profit tax on the interest received.

Furthermore, there are rules that deny or limit interest deduction in case of hybrid financing and in fiscal unity situations.

23.28 Exchange Controls and Repatriation of Profits

The Sanctions Act 1977 includes a prohibition against financial transactions with certain countries and persons (such as terrorists or persons linked with terrorists). These measures aim to prevent persons or organizations mentioned in the Sanctions Regulations from accessing financial assets. In addition to the requirements to freeze the financial assets of certain persons, the measures also include a prohibition against the funding or financial support of countries listed in the Regulations. All names of persons (or legal entities) to which the Sanctions Regulations apply, are set out in the so called 'electronic Combined Targeted Financial Sanctions Lists' (e-CTFSL) published on the web-site of the European Commission.

Dividend distributions by a Dutch company are subject to 15 per cent dividend withholding tax. However, certain important exceptions apply, as a result of which in a large number of situations no (or low) dividend withholding tax is due.

If the receiving shareholder is resident in the EU, no dividend tax needs to be withheld, provided that certain conditions are met. Most importantly, the shareholder must hold 5 per cent or more of the share capital of the dividend paying company.

If the shareholder is resident in a country outside the EU, the dividend withholding tax rate may nevertheless be reduced to e.g. 0 per cent or 5 per cent, in case the shareholder is resident in a country with which the Netherlands has concluded a tax treaty. The Netherlands has concluded tax treaties with approximately 80 countries.

There is no withholding tax on interest or royalty payments by Dutch companies.

23.29 Groups of Companies

Dutch companies are obliged to prepare and file their annual accounts with the Trade Register. The company's size determines which criteria are applicable to the composition of the annual accounts. If a company is an ultimate shareholder of a group of companies, the details of all the other companies belonging to such a group must be included in consolidated annual accounts. A Dutch subsidiary of a foreign parent company may be exempted from the obligations to prepare its own accounts, as long as its accounts have been published in the consolidated accounts of its parent company, and provided such parent company is established in one of the EU countries and certain other conditions have been met. One such condition is that the parent company must have held itself severally liable for the debts of its subsidiary. It is important to note that if a Dutch company has not fulfilled its obligations with respect to the preparation and filing of its annual accounts, the members of the management board may be held personally liable for payment of the company's debts in the event of bankruptcy.

23.30 Responsibility for Liabilities of an Acquired Subsidiary

The main principle of Dutch corporate law is that a shareholder is not liable for the company's debts, except when such a liability has been expressly accepted.

Case law has established, however, that a parent company may be held liable for certain debts of a subsidiary when the parent company has acted unlawfully ('*onrechtmatig*') in respect of certain actions. This may be the case, for example, when the parent company:

- In practice acted as managing director of the subsidiary and this action was considered to be unlawful;

- While acting for the subsidiary, knew or should have known that the subsidiary was not able to fulfil its (financial) obligations;

- Has created an appearance of the creditworthiness of its subsidiary; or

- Has received payments from its subsidiary in the knowledge of the imminent insolvency of that subsidiary.

For a transfer of assets it may be important to verify whether the position of all or certain of the seller's creditors is harmed by the transaction under which the assets are purchased, because, in bankruptcy, the creditors could secure an annulment of the transaction, leaving the buyer without the assets and only a claim against the (possibly insolvent) seller.

23.31 Governing Law of the Contract

A bona fide choice of law is, in general, respected by the Dutch courts. Certain rules of public order, however, apply in any case, whatever the chosen law. Moreover, Dutch corporate law remains applicable with respect to, for example, the transfer of shares and the structure of a Dutch company in general.

23.32 Dispute Resolution Options

Generally, the parties may elect to have disputes resolved by a panel of arbitrators or by other advisers. The Dutch Code of Civil Procedure contains certain provisions regarding arbitration, although it is possible to deviate from these.

The Netherlands is a party to the 1958 New York Convention on the Enforcement of Arbitration Awards under which foreign arbitration awards may be enforceable in the Netherlands in accordance with the rules of that convention.

If arbitration is chosen, the Netherlands Arbitration Institute ('NAI') and its rules are often chosen. Furthermore, the Netherlands is a party to a large number of treaties for the enforcement of foreign judgments.

23.33 Other Issues

Certain interested parties may ask a special court (Enterprise Chamber in Amsterdam) to make an inquiry into the management and affairs of a Dutch company, provided there are reasonable grounds to believe the company is mismanaged. If such an inquiry is made and the court is of the opinion that there may be mismanagement, the court may impose a number of stringent measures. In the past, this procedure has been used, *inter alia,* to prevent the closure of a Dutch branch of an international group of companies. The court may also judge to what extent the statutory requirements regarding the Works Council (see **23.23**) has been complied with.

Special provisions apply to so called 'Large Companies', i.e., companies that have an issued share capital of at least Euro 16 million, that have installed a Work Council and that employ at least 100 employees.

The so called Large Company Regime provides for a compulsory two-tier board system (see **23.19**) consisting of a management board and a supervisory board, whereby the latter body has been granted extensive powers, such as the appointment and dismissal of the management directors. Under recent legislation the Works Council has rights with regard to the appointment of one third of the supervisory board of a Large Company.

24. NORWAY

Thomas Aanmoen Advokatfirmaet Schjødt AS

24.1 Introductory Comments

In general, there are few formal restrictions on acquisitions in Norway. Acquisitions including companies with a large market share may be restricted in accordance with Norwegian and EU competition regulations. Additionally, ownership restrictions apply to acquisitions of financial institutions. There are rules governing voluntary and mandatory offers for listed securities.

24.2 Corporate Structures

The two most common forms of legal entities in Norway are the private limited company (AS) and the public limited company (ASA). Companies listed on the Oslo Stock Exchange are public limited companies (or foreign companies of a similar form).

The minimum share capital for a public limited company is NOK 1 million; the minimum for a private limited company is NOK 100,000.

In addition to the two different forms of limited companies, companies in Norway can also be structured as general partnerships, limited partnerships and similar. Such corporate structures are, however, seldom used in general, and particularly when structuring medium-sized and large undertakings.

24.3 Letters of Intent and Heads of Agreement

Letters of intent and heads of agreements are often entered into by two parties intending to enter into an acquisition agreement. Even though they are practical instruments for setting out the parties' intentions for the acquisition, it is important to emphasize that such documents may be interpreted to be binding, as a whole or in part, between the contract parties. Whether a letter of intent or a head of agreement is binding will need to be determined by interpretation of the document itself and the surrounding circumstances. If the document is not intended to be legally binding, this should be stated expressly in the document.

24.4 Taxes Affecting the Structure and Calculation of the Price

Gains derived from a sale of shares by a personal shareholder are liable to taxation. Correspondingly a loss is deductible from other taxable income. The general income is taxable at a rate of 28 per cent for 2006.

© World Law Group
International Business Acquisitions, M. Whalley, F.-J. Semler (eds.), Kluwer Law International, London, 2007; ISBN 9789041124838.

The taxable gain or loss is equal to the sales price less the cost price of the share. From this capital gain, Norwegian personal shareholders are entitled to deduct a calculated allowance.

A shareholder who is not a Norwegian resident for tax purposes is not taxed on the gains from the sale of shares, unless the shareholder has ceased to be resident in Norway. In such case the shareholder is subject to Norwegian taxation for any potential gains related to the shares owned at the time when the shareholder ceased to be resident, or the foreign shareholder carries on business which is subject to Norwegian taxation, and the shares are considered to be owned in connection with that business.

Corporate shareholders will not be subject to tax in Norway on capital gains related to realization of shares in Norwegian companies, and losses related to such realization are not tax deductible.

A purchase of shares in a Norwegian company results in the investor inheriting all the target's taxation liabilities. An acquisition of shares by a non-resident investor does not normally result in any Norwegian taxation other than taxation paid by the Norwegian target on its profits and any withholding taxes due on dividends received by the buyer. Corporate shareholder tax resident within the EEC area is not liable to Norwegian withholding tax on dividends distributed from a Norwegian company.

There is presently no withholding tax on interest in Norway.

A merger may, in certain circumstances, be carried out tax free, provided that some formal rules for the merger are followed. A merger between a Norwegian company and a foreign company is not considered as a tax-free merger under Norwegian law. Accordingly, the transaction is considered as a sale of the shares in the Norwegian company. As a rule, such transfer of shares is subject to capital gains taxation. However, such transaction may be carried out tax free following acceptance by the Norwegian tax authorities.

For tax purposes, a purchase of assets or of a division of an existing company is usually treated as a sale of the underlying assets, and a capital gains tax charge arises on any gain realized.

The acquisition price must be allocated to the different assets in accordance with the market value of the assets involved. The market value may also be assessed by the tax authorities.

Gains or losses on the sale of assets are treated differently depending on whether the assets belong to different categories. A non-resident acquiring business assets in Norway may however be deemed to have set up a permanent establishment in Norway, and its profits attributable to the Norwegian permanent establishment are then subject to Norwegian taxation.

24.5   Extent of Seller's Warranties and Indemnities

It is customary in Norway, as it is elsewhere, that the seller, in connection with an acquisition, gives the buyer representations, warranties and indemnities relating to the company's affairs, including the accounts, taxes, assets, claims, intellectual property, governmental approvals etc. It is also common that the buyer requires that the seller's parent company warrants the correctness and the enforcement of such warranties.

Sellers, on the other hand, try to limit the scope of such warranties. Such limitations are often achieved by giving the buyer access to carry out a due diligence investigation of the target company and by limiting claims to direct losses only.

24.6 Liability for Pre-contractual Representations

The seller, under Norwegian contractual law, is obliged to give the buyer relevant information about circumstances and conditions relevant for the buyer's judgment of the acquisition target. The seller is, however, not required to give the buyer any information about his or her view of future performance or any other information which is not factual.

If the seller misrepresents information, it may be held responsible for eventual damages resulting from it.

Liability for pre-contractual representations may, depending on the circumstances, be limited by a due diligence investigation carried out by the buyer.

To avoid eventual disagreements with respect to what information the buyer has obtained from the seller before entering into the agreement, it is advisable to explicitly state in the acquisition agreement what information the seller has provided and which surveys the buyer has carried out.

24.7 Liability for Pre-acquisition Trading and Contracts

In the case of a share acquisition, pre-acquisition profit and losses are generally the target company's liability. The buyer, therefore, in a share acquisition, indirectly succeeds to the target company's pre-acquisition rights and obligations. The buyer may however demand that the seller gives a balance sheet guarantee or similar. In this case, the seller may become liable for potential pre-acquisition losses.

In the case of an asset acquisition, the buyer succeeds to the pre-acquisition rights and obligations to the extent he or she agrees with the seller. It is therefore important that the parties in an asset acquisition set out accurate conditions for the pre-acquisition liability.

24.8 Pre-completion Risks

In general, the risk is transferred upon completion of the acquisition. The moment the risk of shares or assets is transferred from the seller to the buyer is, however, subject to agreement between the buyer and the seller. The moment for the transfer of the risk should be explicitly set out in the acquisition agreement.

Where there is a period between signing of the acquisition agreement and completion of the acquisition, the parties should agree to how the seller shall manage the company and/or the assets in the interim period, and agree on consent rights for the buyer, etc.

It is also advisable that the parties explicitly agree to the consequences of an eventual mismanagement of the company or the assets in the interim period.

24.9   Anti-trust and Competition Laws

In Norway, two sets of rules are particularly relevant with respect to mergers and acquisitions: the Norwegian Competition Act and the EC/EEA Merger Control Rules (Regulation 139/2004). The 'one-stop shop' applies, signifying that if the acquisition has community dimension, there is no duty to notify the acquisition to national competition authorities.

According to the Competition Act, the Norwegian Competition Authority (NCA) is entitled to prohibit a merger or an acquisition if the transaction will have an adverse negative effect on the competition in the market. The Competition Act applies to both acquisitions of shares, assets and other relevant transaction structures, and applies when the buyer is acquiring control of one or more undertakings.

There is a duty to notify a concentration to the NCA by way of a standardized notification provided that certain thresholds are met. As from 1 January 2007, new thresholds for triggering duty to notify, applies. If the undertakings concerned have a joint annual turnover above 50 MNOK and each of the undertakings concerned has an annual turnover above 20 MNOK, the thresholds are met.

The NCA may order the submission of a complete notification. Such an order must be issued no later than 15 working days after receiving the standardized notification. The NCA must notify the parties that intervention may take place no later than 25 working days after receipt of a complete notification and, no later than 70 working days after receipt of a complete notification; the NCA must present a reasoned preliminary decision.

The Competition Act's stated purpose is to further competition and thereby contribute to the efficient utilization of society's resources. Special consideration shall be given to the interests of consumers. Since business acquisitions often occur to produce efficiency gains, the criteria for intervention are strict if the parties to the transaction are non-dominant entities.

24.10   Required Offer Procedures

In general, there are no required offer procedures when buying shares in a public limited company. If, however, the buyer is acquiring shares that gives such buyer a more than 40 per cent holding of the shares of a Norwegian company listed company on a Norwegian stock exchange, he or she must offer all shareholders of the target company to purchase their shares on terms not less favourable than offered to any othershareholders in the preceding six month period. These rules are likely to be amended in 2007, with, among other probable changes, the effect that the mandatory offer threshold will be lowered from 40 per cent to 33 per cent and with new offer obligations being triggered at 40 per cent and 50 per cent.

A shareholder who owns more than 90 per cent of a limited company, either public or private, is furthermore entitled to redeem the other shareholders of the company.

Based on the same principle, minority shareholders owning less than 10 per cent of a limited company are entitled to demand redemption from a shareholder owning more than 90 per cent of the shares. The redemption price must be set at the company's pro rata value. The company's value will, if the parties cannot agree, be set by the court of law.

In some companies there may also be required offer procedures in the articles of association.

24.11 Continuation of Government Licenses

There are several fields of business in Norway which require an official license or permit. Among them are banking, insurance and investment banking.

As a general rule, official licenses may not be assigned to any third parties. If the official license is issued to the seller, the buyer must apply for a new official license. If the official license is issued to the target company, and the buyer is buying the shares of the company, the license continues unless there is a change of control clause attached to it.

24.12 Requirements for Transferring Shares

With respect to public limited companies, there are no statutory restrictions on the transfer of shares unless the articles of association state otherwise.

With respect to private limited companies, an acquisition of shares must be permitted by the company's board of directors. The board must make its decision as soon as possible after the acquisition has been notified to the company, and can only deny acceptance if it has an objective reason to do so. Additionally the original shareholders have a pre-emptive right to purchase the shares acquired by the buyer. The articles of association may also contain additional restrictions.

The owner of shares in a public limited company must be registered in the Norwegian Registry of Securities (VPS). A transfer of shares of a public limited company must therefore be notified to the VPS.

The owner of shares in a private limited company must either be registered in a shareholder register kept by the company or in the VPS. All transfer of shares in a private limited company must therefore be notified either to the company or to the VPS.

24.13 Requirements for Transferring Land and Property Leases

Norway has a system of land and property registration under which all interests in land and property must be registered. Originally, every municipality of Norway had a land registry (called 'Grunnboken') where each piece of real property has its own file. This land registry is now centralized in one national register in the City of Hønefoss called 'Statens Kartverk'.

In addition to the ownership of the land or property, all kinds of encumbrances must be registered in the land registry. If the ownership or the encumbrance is not registered, the owner of the right has no protection of that right against a third party which, in good faith, acquires the land or property. Registration of change of ownership in the land registry entails a registration tax of 2.5 per cent of the purchase price.

All registered encumbrances will encumber on the land or property until it is deleted. When purchasing real property, it is of importance not to pay the purchase price before the seller has handed over a deed of conveyance free from encumbrances. If one uses a real estate agent to handle the transaction, the agent is obliged to delete all registered ownership rights and encumbrances before transferring the purchase price to the seller.

There are development plans for the whole territory of Norway, which may be regional or local. The development plans regulate how the land or property within the area of the development plan may be used (e.g. residential settlement, industry, forestry or agriculture). Before purchasing land and property in Norway it is advisable to survey the development plans applying to the area of the land or property.

As a main rule, purchase of land in Norway requires a concession from the local authorities. These concession rules will also apply to property leases agreed for more than ten years.

24.14 Requirements for Transferring Intellectual Property

Intellectual property (IP) rights encompass several different rights (e.g. patents, trade marks, copyright and design rights). All of these rights are assignable, in whole or in part. The original right holder may transfer the rights of ownership in their entirety. However, because of the specific nature of IP rights, it is often more common to license the rights, thus giving the licensor the right of use as specified in the license. A license may be either exclusive or non-exclusive, and the terms and conditions of licenses may vary greatly. Subject to the licensor's consent, the licensee may also sublicense his or her rights to a third party.

Some IP rights, such as patents, trade marks and design rights, are registrable under Norwegian law. Upon transfer of a registered right the Norwegian Patent Office must be notified as it is responsible for the registration of all IP rights in Norway.

With respect to transfers of IP rights from employee to employer, special rules may apply; for example, the employer may need to pay a special compensation to the employee to acquire his or her rights to a patentable invention.

24.15 Requirements for Transferring Business Contracts, Licenses and Leases

If the contract has no provisions regarding transfer, a party who wishes to transfer his or her entitlements and obligations according to the contract must obtain his or her counterpart's permission to do so. If such permission is not given, the transferor remains bound by the contract, irrespective of whether the transferee declares that he or she wishes to undertake the obligations.

There are no general stamp duties applying to all contracts. However, transfer of real property is subject to a document and registration fee, amounting to approximately 2.5 per cent of the consideration.

24.16 Requirements for Transferring Other Assets

Third party interests are relevant also when transferring other assets than contractual ones. Several types of encumbrances exist. In case of such third party interests, the third party's consent to the transfer must be obtained.

24.17 Encumbrances and Third Party Interests

Encumbrances and third party interests in assets or real property may follow from contractual relationships or legislation. In several cases, but not all, public registries may give the necessary information, however, a seller, transferor, assignor or likewise should also guarantee that all encumbrances and other third party interests have been disclosed.

24.18 Minimum Shareholder and Officer Requirements

There are no requirements for the number of shareholders in a company.

A company must have a board of directors of at least three members, although if the company has a share capital of less than NOK 3 million the board may consist of less than three members. The board is elected by the general meeting.

In companies with more than 30 employees, the employees have the right to elect one board member and one observer to the board. If a company has more than 50 employees, the employees have a right to elect one third of the board members, and if the company has more employees than 200, a corporate assembly shall at the outset be put in place.

In general, at least half of the board members must be domiciled in Norway. This rule does not apply to citizens of an EEA country. From 2006 on, and for existing companies from January 2008 on, public limited companies will need to have particularly defined representation from both genders in the board of directors.

24.19 Non-competition Clauses

The Norwegian Competition Act includes a prohibition on anti-competitive agreements or concerted practices. A non-competition clause may potentially fall within such a prohibition if the non-competition clause is not considered to be directly related to and necessary to concentrations.

The NCA has not issued guidelines on how to assess whether non-competition clauses are directly related to and necessary. However, the NCA has stated that the Commission's guidelines will give adequate guidance. Hence, normally, non-competition clauses are assessed in accordance with the Commission's guidelines on restrictions directly related and necessary to concentrations (2005/C 56/03).

The guidelines state that the criteria of direct relation and necessity are objective in nature. Hence, restrictions are not directly related and necessary to the implementation of a concentration simply because the parties regard them as such (clause 11 of the guidelines). Directly related to the implementation signifies that the non-competition clause must be closely linked to the concentration itself. Further, the non-competition clause must also be necessary for the implementation of the agreement. This signifies that in the absence of the non-competition clause the concentration could not be implemented or could only be implemented under considerably more uncertain conditions, at substantially higher cost, over an appreciably longer period or with considerably greater difficulty.

In general, non-competition clauses are justified for a period of up to three years when the concentration includes the transfer of customer loyalty in the form of both goodwill and know-how. When only goodwill is included, they are justified for periods of up to two years.

Further, non-competition clauses do not apply when the transfer is limited to physical assets or to exclusive industrial and commercial property rights. In addition, the geographic scope of a non-competition clause must be limited to the area in which the vendor has offered the relevant products or services before the concentration, and the non-competition clause must remain limited to products and services forming the economic activity of the undertaking transferred.

Non-competition clauses accepted by employees are normally acceptable during the course of, and also for some time after termination of, their employment. There are limitations on the contractual freedom of the parties concerning the length of the latter period, in order to protect the employee. The length of such a period depends, for example, on the employee's position in the undertaking and the size of the remuneration received.

24.20   Environmental Considerations

According to the Norwegian Constitution, the environment shall be utilised in accordance with a long-term and all-round perspective. There are also several more specific legislative provisions securing a proper utilization of the environment. It is advisable to study the applicable environmental legislation before making a business acquisition.

In general, the liability for pollution damages lies with the owner of the polluting devise or operation. The liability is strict. If the company cannot discharge its obligations, the management and board of directors may be held responsible.

Since liability is imposed on the owner, it is of importance to include warranties regarding environmental matters when acquiring a company. This applies notwithstanding whether the buyer has carried out a due diligence investigation of the company.

24.21   Employee Superannuation/Pension Plans

All employees in Norway are members of the Public Pension Fund, and taxes to the fund are deducted from employees' salaries directly by the employer.

Every citizen is entitled to a retirement pension when he or she reaches age 67. In addition, an act regarding mandatory occupational pension came into force 1 January 2006. This pension-act applies to all enterprises that have employees. Many undertakings also have collective pension arrangements concerning early retirement.

24.22 Employee Rights

The relationship between the employee and the employer in the private sector (included municipalities) is regulated by the Workers Protection Act (WPA). The WPA regulates topics such as grounds for dismissal, working hours, working environment and employees' rights during transfers of undertakings.

The WPA is applicable for all employment relationships in the private sector, and is enforceable without any kind of demand for a qualifying employment period.

Legal disputes between employees and employers are settled by the ordinary courts. The proceedings are presided by a professional judge and two lay people—one lay person suggested by the employee and one suggested by the employer.

The relationship between trade unions and employers or employers' organizations is regulated in the Labour Disputes Act. This act regulates, among other things, the employees' right to a collective agreement and collective bargaining. The act also regulates the institution and authority of the Labour Court. The Labour Court handles disputes relating to collective agreements. The parties in the Labour Court are therefore usually trade unions and employers' organizations.

24.23 Compulsory Transfer of Employees

As a member of the EEA, Norway has an obligation to implement the EEC Directive 2001/23 concerning acquisitions of assets. The previous directives were implemented in the WPA in January 1994 and 2002.

According to the WPA, the buyer is obligated to employ the target company's employees on similar terms as before, regardless of whether the buyer is acquiring the company itself or the company's assets. The WPA also states that the acquisition must be discussed with the employees' representatives as early as possible. The representatives are entitled to receive information about and consultation of the transfer's objectives. They are furthermore entitled to receive information about the implication of the transfer for the employees.

If the buyer does not wish to take on all the employees, this must be settled well ahead of the acquisition date. It is important to emphasize that the acquisition itself cannot be reason for a dismissal.

24.24 Tax Deductibility of Acquisition Expenses

Whether the buyer is a company or an individual, non-resident or taxable in Norway, deductibility of acquisition expenses is determined by the laws of its, his or her home jurisdiction.

Generally, expenses incurred in the acquisition of shares are not deductible for tax purposes until the shares are sold.

24.25 Levies on Acquisition Agreements and Collateral Documents

Share transfer tax is not payable on the sale of shares in Norway. Stamp duties may be payable on transfers of assets, and applicable rates vary according to the nature of the transaction involved.

24.26 Financing Rules and Restrictions

Norway has no specific rules regarding thin capitalization related to onshore activity. Accordingly no specific debt–equity ratio is applicable. However, in offshore activity a ratio of 80:20 seems to apply. The relevant acts for private and public companies states that the company shall at all times have 'sound equity' and that steps need to be taken if the equity is less than 50 per cent of the share capital.

There is a general rule in the Norwegian Tax Act stating that provided a Norwegian company's taxable income is reduced because of a relationship to another taxpayer (Norwegian or foreign resident), the income may be assessed by the tax authorities, based on arm's length principles. This 'substance over form' rule also applies in respect to thin capitalization.

The rule applies regardless of how the Norwegian taxpayer formally has handled the amount in his or her books etc. The essential question is whether the loan and the terms of the loan agreement are based on arms length principles.

The result of a potential reclassification is normally that the interests are not considered deductible for tax purposes. Instead, the distribution, wholly or partly, is treated as dividends.

24.27 Exchange Controls and Repatriation of Profits

Foreign investment is generally encouraged. There are no important restrictions on the transfer of currency to and from Norway. Certain reporting requirements exist, however, the most important being that if irregular means of payment (i.e. other than banks) are used, this must be reported to the relevant authorities prior to transferring the payment. Reporting obligations apply, also for various advisors, for large cash transactions and other 'irregular' transactions.

Norwegian resident shareholders are entitled to a tax credit equal to the full amount of tax paid by the company in respect of the dividend. Non-resident shareholders receiving dividends from Norwegian companies are not entitled to such credit. In the absence of an appropriate tax treaty, non-resident shareholders are subject to withholding tax at the rate of 25 per cent. The company is responsible for the withholding tax towards the tax authorities.

24.28 Groups of Companies

Consolidated accounts must be prepared. Certain exceptions exist, and the most important is related to foreign subsidiaries domiciled in an EEA country; providing that the subsidiary is obliged to prepare consolidated accounts for itself and its subsidiaries according to the rules of the jurisdiction to which it belongs. Certain other provisions may also apply in order to fulfil the exemption rule.

24.29 Responsibility for Liabilities of an Acquired Subsidiary

A parent company is not liable for its subsidiaries' debts or other liabilities, unless guarantees or indemnities are granted.

An obligation to pay damages to third parties of the subsidiary may arise if the subsidiary has been unlawfully stripped of its values by the parent company or if management of the subsidiary has been performed negligently.

24.30   Governing Law of the Contract

Choice of law and legal jurisdiction clauses are enforceable. However, for business performed in Norway, certain mandatory legislation and principles of law always apply. An example is the Workers' Protection Act. The order public principle may also, in rare cases, give the courts a possibility to set aside choice of law and legal jurisdiction clauses.

24.31   Dispute Resolution Options

In general, Norwegian courts provide an effective, though perhaps somewhat time-consuming, forum for the resolution of commercial disputes. Large commercial contracts or contracts covering long-term relationships often contain an arbitration clause. Statutory provisions cover all the procedural rules relating to arbitration, unless they have been otherwise decided. Arbitration is less time consuming, although more expensive, than litigation. The arbitration award may not, as a general rule, be appealed, and it is not generally publicly accessible. Dispute settlement by international arbitration is also known, although not very common outside certain particular industries, such as shipping, etc.

The use of other dispute resolution mechanisms of a more informal character is increasing.

25. PERU

José Antonio Payet, Payet Rey Coun

25.1 Introductory Comments

The Peruvian Constitution of 1993 guarantees economic and legal freedom by providing rules to protect and promote national and foreign investment, such as:

- free competition;

- that contracts shall not be modified by any Law;

- freedom to hold and dispose of foreign currency;

- prohibition of discriminatory treatment between foreign and local investors; and

- guarantee of private property.

25.2 Corporate Structures

The General Law of Corporations (GLC), which is the main law in corporate matters, governs the organization of business entities in general.

Local and foreign investors mostly prefer the stock company (*'sociedad anónima'*), which may be compared to the US corporation. The *sociedad anónima* is a legal entity separate and apart of its shareholders that provides limited liability up to the amount of the shareholder's contribution, and where capital is represented by shares.

The GLC permits three types of *sociedades anónimas*: the privately held corporation (*'sociedad anónima cerrada'*), which may have no more than 20 stockholders, may not list its shares on a stock exchange and does not need to have a board; the publicly held corporation (*'sociedad anónima abierta'*), which is one that has made a public offer of its stock or has more than 750 stockholders or has more than 175 shareholders holding individual stakes of more than 0.2 per cent of the shares but not more than 5 per cent of the shares and which together hold more than 35 per cent of the capital; and the 'normal' stock corporation, which is a standard stock corporation that may register its shares on a stock exchange, must have not more than 750 stockholders and must have a board.

In addition, the GLC regulates various other business structures such as limited liability and general partnerships. Foreign investors can also establish a branch to conduct their business in Peru.

© World Law Group
International Business Acquisitions, M. Whalley, F.-J. Semler (eds.), Kluwer Law International, London, 2007; ISBN 9789041124838.

25.3 Letters of Intent and Heads of Agreement

The legal value of letters of intent and heads of agreement depends basically upon their terms. The Peruvian Civil Code provides that a contract is not considered to be formed until the parties are in agreement over all of the contract's elements.

The Code also recognizes the validity of a preliminary contract ('*compromiso de contratar*'). This is a binding agreement under which the parties undertake to execute a contract on a certain future date. Failure to execute the contract on the set date is considered a case of breach and may make the responsible party liable for damages.

Therefore, it is especially important to carefully draft the terms of a letter of intent. If the parties' intent is not to have a binding agreement, this should be stated expressly.

25.4 Taxes Affecting the Structure and Calculation of the Price

The main taxes in Peru are income tax and valued added tax.

Under Peru's Income Tax Law, legal entities domiciled in Peru are subject to income tax on their global income. Non-resident legal entities and branches in Peru are subject to income taxes applicable only to their Peruvian source income. Capital gains obtained by the transfer of shares issued by a company incorporated in Peru are considered Peruvian source income. The main rates are the following:

- Resident individuals: 15 per cent and 30 per cent;

- Resident companies: corporate income flat tax rate of 30 per cent, including branches;

- Non-residents: natural persons not domiciled in Peru are subject, in most cases, to a flat rate of 30 per cent of their income from Peruvian sources; in other cases there are different rates depending the activity or business performed by taxpayers;

- Dividends paid to domiciled physical persons or non-domiciled physical or legal entities are levied with a 4.1 per cent rate.

Valued added tax is levied on individual and legal entities that perform sales of goods (*bienes muebles*), import goods, construction agreements, the first sales of real property made by builders and rendering of services, except those services which are expressly exempt such as transportation of people, airport services, banking, energy and water. The tax is not applicable to sales of shares. The rate is 19 per cent with a tax credit on the same tax paid by a buyer or user of services.

There is also an excise tax assessed on many goods and services.

25.5   Extent of Seller's Warranties and Indemnities

The general principle applicable under the Civil Code is that the seller is responsible for all the latent defects the goods may have at the moment the goods are delivered. However, whatever the buyer is in a condition to know, acting with normal diligence according to his or her personal aptitude and the circumstances, is not considered a latent defect.

In addition, the Civil Code provides that disclaimers and limitations of liability are not valid in contracts of adhesion, unless they are approved by an administrative body.

In consumer transactions there are implied warranties of fitness and safety.

25.6   Liability for Pre-contractual Representations

According to the Peruvian Civil Code, contracts must be negotiated and performed in good faith. This provision therefore establishes a duty to deal in good faith during the negotiations prior to a contract. The breach of this duty may make the responsible party liable for damages caused by the reliance of a party on representations made negligently or in bad faith.

In consumer transactions there is a duty of the suppliers to inform the consumer. Misleading statements or omissions may give rise to liability.

25.7   Liability of Pre-acquisition Trading and Contracts

Where a stock purchase is conducted, the company remains liable for pre-acquisition trading and contracts notwithstanding the change in shareholders. Also, in a merger the resulting corporation is liable for pre-acquisition trading and contracts of the absorbed company.

On the other hand, in an asset purchase there is generally no liability for pre-acquisition trading and contracts of the seller. There are certain exceptions regarding workers' rights and tax liabilites.

25.8   Pre-completion Risks

As established by the Civil Code, the risk of loss of identifiable goods, without guilt of either party, is transferred from the seller to the buyer upon delivery. The risk of loss is transferred to the buyer before delivery if, being able to, the buyer does not receive them at the time designated by the contract.

25.9   Required Governmental Approvals

Almost all activities are open to foreign investment. In general there are no limitations whatsoever on the participation of foreign investors. Also, local and foreign investments are governed by the same conditions. As an exception, foreign investment exceeding 40 per cent of equity is not allowed in TV broadcasting.

Authorization from no other governmental body is required for any foreign investment.

Foreign investment is automatically authorized at the moment it is done, and may be registered at the investment promotion agency (Proinvertion) at the investor's choice. In addition, incertain cash investors may enter into legal stability agreements to protect their investment in Peru.

25.10 Anti-trust and Competition Laws

Anti-trust legislation forbids the abuse of a dominant position in all or in part of the domestic market. It also prohibits all agreements and collusive practices having the effect of impeding, distorting or limiting competition.

In the electricity sector, some purchases are subject to a prior approval. Failure to obtain authorization when required makes the acquisition void.

The National Institute for the Defense of Competition and the Protection of Intellectual Property has the mandate of enforcing legislation related to anti-trust, intellectual property, unfair competition, anti-dumping, aonsumer protection and insolvency.

25.11 Required Offer Procedures

The Securities Market Law establishes a mandatory tender offer requirement for any acquisition of shares giving a direct or indirect stake of more than 25, 50 or 60 per cent in the voring stock corporation the stocks of which are listed on a stock exchange. The offer is subject to equal price and *pro rata* adjudication principles.

No special offer procedures are required for unlisted companies. Nevertheless, privately held companies frequently have provisions in their by-laws giving share-holders a preferential right to acquire the shares before their transfer to a third party. Such provisions must be complied with before making a valid acquisition.

25.12 Continuation of Government Licences

Companies operating in the financial sector, as well as those operating in certain other regulated industries, such as broadcasting, must obtain administrative approval prior to a change of control. Non-compliance with such requirements may make the transaction invalid or jeopardize the company's license.

Also, in certain privatized companies, restrictions on the transfer of shares have been imposed, whereupon acquirers of control must be qualified by the privatization authorities.

In all other cases, a change of control does not affect the licences, authorizations or concessions obtained by the target company.

25.13   Requirements for Transferring Shares

The general rule is the free transfer of shares. However, for limited liability and general partnerships and the closed corporation the shares cannot be transferred freely because the shareholders have a right of preference to acquire the shares before third parties.

On the other hand, the articles of incorporation and by-laws may establish restrictions or limitations on the transfer of shares, except when the company is listed on a stock exchange.

25.14   Requirements for Transferring Land and Property Leases

All transfers of real property should be implemented through a public deed and registered in the Real Estate Registry of The Public Registries in order to exclude third party claims against the transferred assets.

Real property can also be encumbered by mortgages or other charges, which must be registered in the same way as transfers.

Leases may be entered into with a determined or a non-determined term. In the first case this period of time shall not exceed ten years. In addition, rights over real estate may be granted through usufruct or surface rights.

25.15   Requirements for Transferring Intellectual Property

Trade marks, patents, copyrights and other intellectual property rights must be registered before the National Institute for the Defence of the Competence and the Protection of the Intellectual Property (INDECOPI).

Intellectual property is considered a 'good' by the Civil Code and may be freely transferred without prior authorization from INDECOPI. The transfer, as well as licences, should be registered.

Payment of royalties from a subsidiary to its foreign parent corporation is allowed. Parties may freely negotiate the terms and conditions of the agreement.

25.16   Requirements for Transferring Business Contracts, Licences and Leases

The transfer of a business contract is permissible, but requires the authorization of the other party. The authorization may be provided in advance and, in that case, only a notification must be made to make the transfer effective.

Rights (as opposed to obligations) may be transferred without the counterparty's authorization.

25.17   Requirements for Transferring Other Assets

There is no required formality for the transfer of movable assets. Movable assets are transferred by delivery, but the purchase should be carried out in good faith.

Movable assets registered in special registers may only be transferred with an agreement in writing and the transfer must be registered. Registration protects the purchaser against third parties.

Securities may be transferred by book entry (if so represented), by delivery (if in bearer form) and by register of the transfer in the issuer's books (in the case of shares and nominative bonds).

25.18 Encumbrances and Third Party Interests

According to the Civil Code, movable assets may be pledged. The pledge is created by delivery of the assets or the document representing them. The creditor is given a preferential right on the asset with respect to the obligation secured. Pledges need to registered in the public Registry.

Immovable assets (such as real property) and registered movable assets may be subject to mortgages. The mortgage is created by its registration in the Real Estate Register. The mortgage grants to the creditor a preferential right over the relevant asset against rights of third parties with respect to the assets secured.

25.19 Minimum Shareholder and Officer Requirements

The general rule for the General Law of Corporations is that all corporations must be formed with at least two partners or shareholders, which can be either individuals or other corporations, regardless of their nationality. The plurality of partners is not required when the only partner is the Peruvian Government.

Directors, managers and even the chairman of the board may be foreigners. When a board exists, there must be not less than three directors. Directors must be individuals and need not be shareholders. A corporation must have a general manager.

25.20 Non-competition Clauses

These clauses are commonly established in some contracts, such as distribution, concession, sale and franchise agreements. Under these clauses a party undertakes an obligation not to carry out an activity specified in the aggrement.

Because there is no specific legal regulation of these clauses, they must be carefully established, otherwise the constitutional right to work and to choose freely an occupation would be violated. Anti-trust law may also be breached.

25.21 Environmental Considerations

Peru has special legislation to protect the environment which provides that activities which may damage the environment require an environmental impact study before being initiated.

Also, activities that modify the natural state of resources such as water, land, fauna and fiora require a technical opinion of the Ministry of Agriculture before being initiated.

Damage to the environment is subject to administrative, civil and criminal liabilities.

25.22   Employee Superannuation/Pension Plans

All workers must belong to a pension regime. Workers may choose between the Private Pension System (PPS) and the National Pension System (NPS). The PPS operates on a defined contribution basis. Employers must withhold approximately 13 per cent from the employees' salary. 10 per cent is saved in an account with an AFP and the balance is used to pay for AFP fees and insurance. The NPS is operated by the government. Employers must withhold 13 per cent of each workers salary to finance a pension.

Mandatory health insurance must be paid by the employer (9 per cent of income).

25.23   Employee Rights

Workers may be hired for a fixed term or for an indefinite term. Temporary contracts may be executed only for seasonal activities, temporary needs, or some other situations specified in legislation (including new businesses or business expansion). If a fixed term agreement is terminated by the employer before the term expires, or if a worker is fired without just cause defined by law, significant penalties may have to be paid.

Minimum salary is approximately USD 150.00. In addition to salary, workers are entitled to other benefits, including one additional monthly salary in July and one in December ('gratificaciones'), one additional salary as termination benefit ('compensacíen por tiempo de servicios'), and one month paid vacation. In addition a statutory profit sharing regime gives all workers of business with more than 20 workers a participation in the yearly profits of the business. The aggregate percentage varies by economic sector, between 5 per cent (services) to 10 per cent (manufacturing). Contracting of firing employees is subject to administrative approval and certain limitations.

Peru has very detailed labour laws and it is important that legal advice be obtained before executing any labour agreements.

25.24   Compulsory Transfer of Employees

There is no general legal provision for the transfer of employees from one legal entity to another. These individual agreements need to be reached with employees.

Where a company ceases its operations, labour contracts are terminated.

25.25   Tax Deductibility of Acquisition Expenses

In order to establish net income, the law allows a deduction from the gross income of the expenses necessary to generate taxable income or to maintain the business entity's source of income, unless the deduction is expressly excluded or prohibited. In the absence of proof to the contrary, it is presumed that expenses incurred abroad are related to foreign income and are consequently non-deductible items.

Start-up expenses (including expenses caused by an expansion of the business) may be deducted when incurred or carried over and deducted over a period of up to ten years.

25.26 Levies on Acquisition Agreements and Collateral Documents

There is no levy or stamp tax on transfers or mortgages of assets other than fees to be paid to the notary issuing the deed and the Public Registry for registration, when applicable.

25.27 Financing Rules and Restrictions

Local and foreign investors and companies have the same rights and obligations in relation to access to credit and to operating banks and other financial services companies.

Banks are free to establish interest rates and insurance companies are free to establish the conditions attaching to insurance policies. The government is not permitted to own banks or insurance companies.

25.28 Exchange Controls and Repatriation of Profits

The Constitution guarantees the right to hold and dispose of foreign currency.

There have been no exchange controls in Peru since 1991. No government authorization is required for any foreign exchange transaction.

Anti money-laundering legislation requires banks and other entities to report suspect transactions.

25.29 Groups of Companies

An 'economic group' is defined as a group of corporations where one of them has control over the rest, or where control over the corporations that form the group is held by one individual or group of individuals. 'Control' is defined as the capacity to direct the corporation's administration.

No substansive legislation regarding company groups exists in Peru. However, publicly traded companies are required to furnish information on the economic groups they belong to. Also, all financings of related companies are totalled for credit limit purposes under the financial sector legislation.

25.30 Responsibility for Liabilities of an Acquired Subsidiary

A parent corporation is generally not liable for its subsidiary's obligations. Peruvian law does not authorize piercing the corporate veil.

On the other hand, the General Law of Corporations establishes that a company is always responsible for the liabilities of its branch.

25.31 Governing Law of the Contracts

According to the Civil Code, parties are free to elect the jurisdiction and the applicable law of a contract. However, the parties' choice of now may be disregarded if it is against international public order.

25.32 Dispute Resolution Options

Arbitration is possible and strongly recommended. A new General Law of Arbitration was enacted in 1996. Private agreements on arbitration have precedence over the Law, which is applicable only in cases where specific provisions are not included in private arbitration clauses. The courts will enforce an award deriving from such procedure. Peru is also signatory of the arbitration conventions of New York of 1958 and Panama of 1975.

26. THE PHILIPPINES

José Ma. G. Hofilena and Andrew P. Fornier
SyCip Salazar Hernandez & Gatmaitan

26.1 Introductory Comments

Historically, the Philippines has had a closely regulated business climate. While current government policy is to liberalize the business environment and make it more conducive to foreign investment, the extent of permissible foreign participation in certain business activities, such as land holding, mass media, mining, public utilities and retail trade, continue to be limited by law. In these 'nationalized' industries, foreign investments are generally restricted to anywhere from 0 per cent to a maximum of 40 per cent of the capital of Philippine entities engaged in these activities. Failure to comply with the nationalization requirements has serious repercussions, from possible criminal penalties to the dissolution of the business enterprise, including forfeiture of the business's property.

Legislative and administrative enactments, however, have sought to expand the range of opportunities and incentives for foreign investment. These acts include the relaxation of the nationalization requirements, and the liberalization of foreign exchange rules affecting the repatriation of capital and remittance of profits.

Liberalization of the entry of foreign investments is largely embodied in the Foreign Investments Act. As a general rule, foreign investors can now invest up to as much as 100 per cent in a business enterprise unless the activity falls within the Foreign Investments Negative Lists (hereinafter the 'Negative Lists'). The Negative Lists enumerate the activities in which foreign equity participation is restricted. Hence, foreign investors should first consult the Negative Lists to determine the feasibility of an intended acquisition. In addition, legislation has liberalized the banking sector. Under the General Banking Act, foreign banks are allowed to acquire 100 per cent of the voting stock of a single Philippine bank by the year 2007, subject to guidelines issued in accordance with the Foreign Banks Liberalization Act. Foreigners have also recently been allowed to acquire up to 60 per cent of the voting stock of new or existing Philippine financing companies.

Concomitant with these efforts is the government's ongoing privatization programme. By allowing private investors to acquire government-owned or controlled corporations, the government limits its intervention in business to that of governance. The privatization process is open to both local and foreign investors. It is, however, governed by special bidding procedures which are not applicable to ordinary business acquisitions. The restrictions on permissible foreign equity ownership continue to apply, however, depending on the type of entity the government is seeking to privatize.

© World Law Group
International Business Acquisitions, M. Whalley, F.-J. Semler (eds.), Kluwer Law International, London, 2007; ISBN 9789041124838.

26.2 Corporate Structures

Corporations in the Philippines are, as a general rule, limited liability companies and, accordingly, the exposure of stockholders to liabilities to creditors is limited to their shares of stock in the corporation. However, in cases of close corporations, where the stockholders are actively involved in the corporation's management, the stockholders may be held personally liable for tortious acts imputed to the corporation.

Close corporations are corporations where the stockholders are limited to no more than 20, where there are restrictions on the transfer of the shares and where the shares are not offered to the public. However, where two thirds of the voting stock or the voting rights is owned or controlled by another corporation which is not a close corporation, the corporation is not a close corporation.

A publicly held corporation offering its shares to the public may be listed on the Philippine Stock Exchange.

26.3 Letters of Intent and Heads of Agreement

An agreement, whether oral or written, is generally binding on the parties if there is an intention to create legal relationships and obligations, and if there is consideration given for any obligations undertaken by any party.

If the letters of intent are not intended to be binding until a formal contract is executed, this must be expressed in clear terms. Although these documents do not necessarily constitute the final deeds of sale, the parties are bound to honour these agreements, specifically the obligation to enter into negotiations in good faith. To avoid confusion, the agreement must clarify whether, and to what extent, the parties intend to be bound by it.

26.4 Taxes Affecting the Structure and Calculation of the Price

A purchase of shares results in the buyer effectively inheriting, albeit indirectly, the existing tax liabilities of the acquired corporation. Insofar as the government and other third persons are concerned, the corporation continues to have the same juridical personality despite a change in ownership. However, a purchase of the entire assets or business of a going concern may avoid this, as the tax liabilities continue to belong to the seller, subject to liens on the assets, which would remain on such assets.

The sale of the assets of a corporation may be subject to capital gains tax in respect of the sale of capital assets, and value added tax in respect of the sale of assets in the course of a trade or business. The seller may pass on the value added tax to the buyer, thereby increasing the purchase price.

The parties may agree who shall pay the taxes. Moreover, their agreement may require warranties against tax liabilities.

26.5 Extent of Seller's Warranties and Indemnities

The sale of shares and assets is subject to the Civil Code provisions on warranties of a seller. Under the Code, implied warranties consist of the warranty as to the seller's right to sell the shares or assets, a warranty against eviction, and a warranty against any charge or encumbrance not declared or known to the buyer.

Aside from the warranties provided for under Philippine law, the parties may agree on other warranties which the seller may be required to give. These warranties typically include warranties against existing liabilities, claims and other similar contingencies on the shares or assets sold, or to which such shares or assets are exposed. The nature and extent of warranties and indemnities may depend on the parties and on the value and extent of the acquisition.

26.6 Liability for Pre-contractual Representations

Negligent, false or fraudulent misrepresentations may be asserted as grounds to rescind or annul contracts, depending on the nature and extent of the misrepresentations, with a right to recover damages against the party who committed the misrepresentation or fraud. Acquisition contracts often provide for the representations required by the buyer from the seller, with a stipulation for possible liability in case of breach. The parties are not precluded from excluding certain kinds of misrepresentations unless fraud is involved or unless the material misrepresentations induced the other party to enter into the contract.

26.7 Liability for Pre-acquisition Trading and Contracts

The parties normally come to an agreement on which party shoulders the tax liability and other expenses. The commencement of such liability is usually fixed with reference to specific dates such as the date of execution of the final deed of sale.

Sellers are generally liable for any pre-existing contract entered into with third parties unless the requisites of novation are met, in which case the buyer is substituted for the seller. More often, however, the parties resort to assignment of contracts, rights and obligations where, with the requisite notice to, or consent by, the relevant third parties, the buyer assumes the seller's obligations in the contract and the buyer agrees to indemnify the seller for any future breach.

In a share acquisition, pre-acquisition profits may be paid to the seller by way of dividend or may be retained in the company, in which case the buyer inherits the profits.

26.8 Pre-completion Risks

The shares or assets of the corporation to be acquired remain at the seller's risk until ownership is transferred to the buyer, unless the parties agree otherwise. The acquisition agreement usually provides which party bears the risk of loss of assets between signing and completion although, typically, it is the seller who assumes such risks.

26.9 Required Governmental Approvals

Certain types of entities, such as public service corporations or public utilities, require the approval of certain government agencies before any sale or disposition of assets or shares may be considered valid and binding on third parties. In the case of corporations engaged in non-nationalized activities, a resulting increase in the total foreign investment in such corporation may require the corporation to notify, or seek approval from, the Securities and Exchange Commission (SEC) in respect of such increase. Where all or substantially all of the corporation's assets will be sold, the required approval of the board of directors and stockholders must be submitted to the SEC.

26.10   Anti-trust and Competition Laws

The Constitution does not prohibit monopolies outright, but does prohibit unfair competition and illegal combinations in restraint of trade. The Anti-trust Law currently found in the Revised Penal Code (RPC), defines and penalizes three general acts which prevent or manipulate free competition. The RPC has repealed the penal provisions of the old anti-trust law, Act 3247, without abolishing the treble damages provision of the old law. Philippine authorities, however, have rarely enforced these penal provisions to prevent anti-competitive acts.

Having primary jurisdiction over all corporate entities, the SEC is empowered to regulate acquisitions which may result in illegal combinations in restraint of trade and has the statutory authority to conduct relevant investigations or to disapprove of mergers which may result in a restraint of trade.

Specific legislation may likewise provide specially applicable restrictions. Recently, legislation has been enacted supplementing the de-monopolization of certain types of corporate business. The Electric Power Industry Reform Act (EPIRA) contains a provision preventing the ownership of more than 25 per cent of the voting stock of any distribution utility or any of its holding companies by a single entity, unless that corporation is publicly listed in the Philippine Stock Exchange. Violation of this provision is subject to corresponding fines and penalties under the EPIRA.

26.11   Required Offer Procedures

The articles of incorporation of a target corporation may contain restrictions, such as a right of first refusal with respect to the transfer of shares or assets of the corporation. The seller and/or the buyer must comply with these restrictions in order to ensure a valid purchase.

In addition, the Securities Regulation Code also provides that, in the event that an entity intends to acquire a substantial percentage of the equity shares of a public company, the purchaser is required to observe public tender offer requirements in the manner prescribed by the Code.

The sale of all or substantially all the corporation's assets requires approval by the board of directors and by the stockholders owning or representing at least two thirds of the corporation's outstanding capital stock, unless a higher vote is required under the corporation's constitution.

26.12   Continuation of Government Licences

A business may be required to secure business licences and permits from various government agencies and political units, depending on the kind of industry it is involved in. These licences are often non-transferable, thereby requiring the buyer to apply for new franchises, licences and permits unless the licensee's juridical personality is not affected by the acquisition and it is intended that the current licensee is to remain the same.

26.13 Requirements for Transferring Shares

The articles of incorporation or a shareholders' agreement may provide for certain reasonable restrictions in the transfer of shares, which must not be more onerous than a right of first refusal. In order that such restrictions may be valid and binding as against third parties, they must be found in the articles of incorporation, by-laws and in the certificate of stock. Hence, any investor should review these documents to determine the existence of such restrictions and the conditions attaching to them.

Shares may be transferred by endorsement and delivery of the certificates of stock, with an intent to transfer title, unless the articles of incorporation, by-laws and the certificate of stock contain other restrictions or procedures.

26.14 Requirements for Transferring Land and Property Leases

The Philippines has adopted the Torrens system of land registration. In order to bind third parties, any mortgage or lease and any rights, contractual or otherwise, or other encumbrances affecting the land must be noted on the title. Buyers are bound not only by encumbrances and liens found on the title, but also by those of which they have prior knowledge. No conveyance shall affect third parties unless it is registered and a new title is issued in the buyer's name.

Deeds affecting the land must be executed in a public instrument and duly registered in order to bind third parties. However, an unregistered contract remains valid and binding between the contracting parties.

26.15 Requirements for Transferring Intellectual Property

Title to all forms of intellectual property may be transferred by assignment.

Assignment and transfers of intellectual property, whether copyright, patents or trade marks, must be made in writing, acknowledged before a notary public and filed with the proper government agency. Otherwise the assignment does not bind third parties who had no notice of the assignment.

Licences may also be assigned, unless the licence is exclusive and non-transferable. In most cases, however, licensor's consent is necessary.

26.16 Requirements for Transferring Business Contracts, Licences and Leases

A business contract may be assigned or transferred in accordance with its terms. A valid transfer or assignment results in the assumption by the buyer of the seller's obligations under the contract. However, the other contracting party's consent is necessary if the transfer is to bring about a substitution of the person of the debtor.

Regulatory licences and business permits are often non-transferable depending on the specific law or regulation governing them. Hence, the buyer either obtains the prior approval of the transfer from the licensing agency or applies for the issue of a new licence.

A lessee is normally required to obtain the lessor's consent before he or she may assign his or her rights under the lease contract. A lessor of real property however, may generally transfer his or her rights without the lessee's prior approval. The buyer of the land is bound by a registered lease and is also bound by a lease where he or she has knowledge of the lease's existence.

26.17　Requirements for Transferring Other Assets

Assets are generally transferred by delivery, which may be actual or constructive. Assets subject to a charge or encumbrance in favour of third parties, such as creditors, are often transferred subject to such encumbrance or charge. The transfer of the assets may be subject to capital gains and value added taxes.

The sale of a corporation's entire business and assets may also be governed by the Bulk Sales Law. This law requires the seller to deliver to the buyer a sworn written statement of the names and addresses of creditors and the debts due or to become due to them and an inventory of the assets or business to be sold, and requires the payment of valuable consideration. The Bulk Sales Law does not extend to the acquisition of shares of stock of the corporation.

26.18　Encumbrances and Third Party Interests

Assets can be subject to different types of third party interests such as those which arise from contract, by operation of law or by virtue of specific registration on a public register. As a general rule, an innocent purchaser for value generally takes good title to the asset unless it has actual or constructive notice of an encumbrance. There are certain encumbrances which must be registered in order to bind third parties, such as encumbrances on registered land and chattel mortgages on goods.

Land titles can be conclusive evidence of the registered owner's title on which the buyer may rely. Other assets may be subject to certain unregistered interests which the buyer may not be able to uncover. In these cases, warranties from the seller as to clean title are essential.

26.19　Minimum Shareholder and Officer Requirements

There is no minimum nor maximum number of stockholders in a corporation, unless it is organized as a close corporation which must have no more than 20 stockholders. In partly nationalized industries, total foreign equity holding must not exceed the maximum allowed by law or the Constitution.

Corporations must have at least five directors, a majority of whom must be residents. A director must own at least one share which shall stand in his or her name in the corporation's books. In partly nationalized industries, however, the number of foreign directors must be proportional to the allowable foreign equity holding in the corporation. The Corporation Code requires a corporation to have a president who must be a director of the corporation, a treasurer who may or may not be a director, and a secretary who must be a resident Philippine citizen. Any two or more positions, except the positions of president and secretary or president and treasurer, may be held by the same person. The by-laws may provide for other officers of the corporation. In certain industries, such as public utilities, the president and the managing officer must be Philippine citizens.

26.20   Non-competition Clauses

Non-competition covenants given by a seller in the context of a sale of business are generally enforceable, provided the terms and duration of the restraint are reasonable. A restraint for an unreasonable or for an indefinite period is generally struck down as unreasonable and as a violation of the seller's right to pursue a profession or a legitimate business. What is reasonable depends on the circumstances of the case, the extent and duration of the restraint, the nature of the business and the effect which competition could have on the buyer.

A similar covenant given by an employee is also enforceable, although the standards of reasonableness are stricter than in the case of a seller. The measure of reasonableness largely depends on the restriction's effect on an employee's right to employment and a means of livelihood.

26.21   Environmental Considerations

The Philippines is a signatory to international environmental treaties which, among other things, require industries to comply with minimum environmental standards set by law and government agencies. Highly pollutive industries are required to utilize anti-pollution devices.

Projects or ongoing industrial operations generally require a subsisting environmental compliance certificate, which may be transferred to subsequent owners or operators of the project or operation, provided notice is given to the Department of Environment and Natural Resources. Any significant alterations in the project or operation may require application for a new environmental compliance certificate, due to a potential change in the project or operation's environmental impact.

Violations of environment law may have severe repercussions on the business, which range from fines to closure and cessation of business operations. Hence, appropriate environmental due diligence investigations are always advisable. It is also advisable to require the seller to give warranties relating to compliance with environmental standards, liability and damage.

26.22   Employee Superannuation/Pension Plans

Philippine companies typically have employee retirement and pension plans or trusts to which an employer makes periodic contributions. Under the National Internal Revenue Code, an employer establishing or maintaining a pension trust to provide for the payment of reasonable pensions to his or her employees may, under certain conditions, claim, as a deduction from his or her gross income, amounts transferred or paid into such trust during the taxable year.

Where an acquisition is by a purchase of shares, the buyer should evaluate any existing obligation on the part of the company to be acquired to make contributions to an employee retirement or pension plan. However, in a purchase of assets, where employees will be transferring to the buyer, arrangements must be made for the withdrawal of such employees from their existing pension plans and their coverage under new plans.

26.23   Employee Rights

In the acquisition of a business's assets, the buyer is not required to retain the seller's employees. The buyer is not liable for unpaid salaries and benefits, unless it can be shown that the purchase was conducted to evade compliance with labour policies. The buyer is not considered a successor-employer and may choose which of the former employees it wishes to employ.

In the case of an acquisition of shares, it is advisable to conduct due diligence on the seller's employment policies and its legal and contractual obligations as an employer since the buyer assumes the seller's obligations as employer, and the employer–employee relationship continues between the acquired corporation and the employees. There may be accepted employer practices which have evolved into vested rights of the employees and, thus, may not be withdrawn by the buyer at any time without justifiable reasons. The buyer should also be aware of existing retirement benefit plans and the extent of employer participation in the plan. The amount of employer contributions may affect negotiations on the purchase price of the shares or assets.

The buyer must always try to obtain as complete a picture as possible of the seller's labour practices. Existing and potential labour claims and restlessness may have serious repercussions on the viability of the target business or corporation.

26.24   Compulsory Transfer of Employees

As a rule, Philippine law does not require a purchaser of assets to employ all or some of the employees of the company the assets of which are acquired. In a purchase of shares, however, the employer remains the same and notwithstanding the change of ownership, such employer continues to remain liable for the payment of salaries to and benefits of its employees. Accordingly, the purchaser of shares indirectly is required to retain, generally, the acquired company's employees.

26.25   Tax Deductibility of Acquisition Expenses

Domestic companies and resident foreign companies are permitted deductions for all ordinary and necessary expenses paid or incurred during a taxable year in carrying on any trade or business. As a rule, acquisition expenses are not deductible, but are added to the cost of the asset acquired.

26.26 Levies on Acquisition Agreements and Collateral Documents

Documentary stamp taxes are levied on documents evidencing the sale and transfer of shares, assets or business from the seller to the buyer. The tax is imposed regardless of where the contracts were executed as long as properties in the Philippines are affected. The tax is computed on the amount of the sale, in the case of a transfer of real property, and on the par value of the shares, in the case of a transfer of shares.

Since documentary stamp taxes are taxes on the privilege of executing the document, each separate document related to the sale may be subject to tax. Amendments to existing agreements or the execution of additional documents may be subject to a separate tax. To minimize such taxes, it is advisable to keep the documents as complete as possible and as components of only one contract.

26.27 Financing Rules and Restrictions

The Philippine Corporation Code does not prohibit outright a company giving financial assistance to another company for generally any purpose including the purchase of its own or its holding company's shares, or the acquisition of the assets or shares of other companies. However, in the event the lending and borrowing corporations have interlocking directors or if the borrower is a director, trustee or officer of the lending company, certain special requirements may apply in relation to the required corporate approvals for such financing.

26.28 Exchange Controls and Repatriation of Profits

Philippine foreign exchange rules have been liberalized. The proceeds of foreign investments which have been duly registered may be freely repatriated. The foreign exchange required for the purposes of the repatriation and remittance may be freely sourced outside the banking system. However, where the foreign investment has been duly registered with the Central Bank of the Philippines, the foreign currencies may be sourced from the Philippine banking system. The remittance of dividends to non-resident investors is subject to a withholding tax at the rate of 33 per cent for 1999 and 32 per cent from 2000 onwards, which may be reduced on the basis of applicable tax treaties or tax sparing credits in the non-resident foreign corporation's country of domicile.

26.29 Groups of Companies

The Philippine Corporation Code does not require that Philippine companies prepare accounts consolidated with entities they control or have controlled. Such consolidation of accounts, however, may be a requirement for company shares listed on a stock exchange.

26.30 Responsibility for Liabilities of an Acquired Subsidiary

Corporations in the Philippines are limited liability companies. The shareholders's liability for corporate debts is limited to their contributions to its capital stock. Shareholders may nonetheless be liable in some other capacities, for example as sureties or guarantors of the corporate debts. The independence of the subsidiary from the parent corporation may be pierced if the corporate vehicle is used to violate the law or for some illegitimate purpose.

26.31   Governing Law of the Contract

As a general rule, the law of the place of its execution governs the forms and solemnities of the contract. As to the contract's substantive validity, the parties' choice of law is generally respected by Philippine courts subject to proper proof of such foreign law.

26.32   Dispute Resolution Options

Philippine law allows the parties to a contract to agree on the form of dispute resolution, such as, but not limited to, arbitration, to settle disputes arising from the contract. Philippine courts recognize international arbitral awards. Arbitration is advisable to avoid lengthy and costly litigation in the Philippines. Courts may be bound by the determination of experts or arbitrators, although the parties may not oust the jurisdiction of Philippine courts in respect of disputes over which they may have jurisdiction.

Foreign judgments may be enforced in the Philippines with the approval of the courts. The courts, however, are not bound to recognize a foreign judgment should there be fraud or absence of jurisdiction in the proceedings held in the foreign court.

26.33   Other Issues

Philippine law prohibits indirect foreign ownership beyond the maximum limits set by law. The Anti-Dummy Law penalizes the use of 'dummies' to own, control or exercise rights reserved to Philippine nationals or citizens. Penalties range from fines, imprisonment, dissolution of the corporation and forfeiture of corporate assets.

27. PORTUGAL

Manuel P. Barrocas, Barrocas Sarmento Neves

27.1 Introductory Comments

The setting-up of a Portuguese company, the acquisition of a Portuguese company or corporate assets by foreign investors is not generally subject to any statutory restrictions. Exceptions exist, however, in connection with the area of defence and other strategic public sectors.

Portugal does not have a federal system and therefore the law is the same all over the country, with some minor exceptions to administrative regulations in the islands of Madeira and the Azores which are considered to be semi-autonomous. Municipalities do, however, have the power to impose supplementary taxes to the corporate income tax.

There are no currency exchange control regulations and repatriation of profits does not attract additional costs, subject to limited and exceptional restrictions.

27.2 Corporate Structures

As a general rule, a Portuguese company will usually establish or operate as a partnership, a private company or a public company.

The partnership model (either a '*sociedade em nome colectivo*' or a '*sociedade em comandita*') is rarely used due to the unlimited liability of all (or some) of the partners.

The limited liability company is the private company model ('*sociedade por quotas*' or '*Limitada*') and is equivalent to the private limited company or the GmbH under German law. It must have a minimum of two shareholders, a minimum share capital of EUR 5,000, and a minimum par value for each share (or 'quota') of EUR 100.

The public company ('*sociedade anónima*' or 'SA') is equivalent to the public limited company or joint stock corporation—the '*Aktiengesellschaft*' in Germany. It must have at least five shareholders and the minimum legal value of each share is required to be one cent of one Euro. The minimum stock capital requirement is EUR 50,000. There must also be an odd number of board members. Please note, however, that it is possible for a public company to 100 per cent own another (group structure) in which case it would be the only shareholder.

No special rules apply to subsidiaries under Portuguese law. The subsidiary's main characteristic is that it is usually dependent upon another foreign or national company. This dependence can be the result of a mere holding by the foreign or national company in the subsidiary's share capital, as well as any other contractual links that result in its dominance over the subsidiary. In relation to branch offices, the law

© World Law Group
International Business Acquisitions, M. Whalley, F.-J. Semler (eds.), Kluwer Law International, London, 2007; ISBN 9789041124838.

requires that a company with a registered office abroad, having carried out activities in Portugal for more than a year, should formally set up a branch and comply with provisions relating to registration in Portugal. If a foreign company carrying out its activity in Portugal fails to establish a branch, both it and specific officers of the company can still be held liable for acts committed as well as the directors of the foreign company who shall be held jointly liable.

It is therefore clearly necessary and to the advantage of companies intending to carry out their business activities in Portugal for any period longer than one year to permanently establish themselves in one of the various ways permitted by law, generally either a branch or subsidiary. Although a branch may have some advantages when compared to a subsidiary, the applicable laws are generally the same for both. The main differences relate to tax treatment (see **27.4**).

A branch office is required to have a representative whose appointment, powers and function should all be entered in the Trade Register. The branch has no separate legal personality from the foreign parent company and as such the branch's actions and liabilities bind the parent company. They do not, however, bind the respective representatives, except in the circumstances already mentioned above and where personal responsibility is specifically provided for by law. There are no other specific accounting rules, auditing requirements and rules relating to the publication of accounts, with the exception of banking and insurance branches which are subject to special regulation. Whilst not compulsory, it is possible to register the amount of capital engaged in the branch. As previously stated, the Portuguese labour laws, as well as tax laws, apply to the branch's activities and it is generally subject to administrative regulations in force in the country.

27.3   Letters of Intent and Heads of Agreement

Letters of intent are not binding statements under Portuguese law and are considered to be merely a preliminary understanding between parties who intend to enter into a contract.

A binding preliminary agreement arises only where the parties make a formal promise to enter into a final and definitive contract. In the absence of such a promise to enter into a contract, no binding preliminary obligation can arise. In addition, such a promise must generally be expressed in writing.

Heads of agreement form part of the contract and they are therefore relevant in its construction, except where the parties have expressly excluded them as interpretative aids.

27.4   Taxes Affecting the Structure and Calculation of the Price

No taxes apply on the actual acquisition of shares in a company, except for an acquisition that results in the ownership, by an associate, of 75 per cent or more of the shares in a limited private company (*sociedade por quotas,* or the ownership of a company by husband and wife married under community of assets/joint tenants) where that company owns real property. In this case, real property transfer tax (*'Imposto Municipal sobre Transmissões* or 'IMT'') must be paid. The applicable tax rates are 5 per cent for rustic land and 6.5 per cent for building land of the total tax value of the real property held by the company.

This tax applies not only in case of a transfer of shares in the circumstances described above, but also on the tax value of any real property transferred in a sale of a company's fixed assets.

The buyer of a company should take care to ensure that all tax charges and liabilities are included in the agreed purchase price since the company will continue to be responsible for all prior as well as contingent tax liabilities. The same applies to the acquisition of real property, since tax charges and liabilities relating to taxes levied on previous transfers of property (IMT and Stamp duty) and municipal taxes ('*Imposto Municipal Sobre Imóveis*' or 'IMI') constitute a lien in favour of the state.

An important point affecting the decision to set up or acquire a subsidiary or to establish a branch relates to the taxes affecting the activity of both business frameworks. In Portugal, a branch and a subsidiary are subject to the same tax and accounting obligations and their taxable profit and income are computed using the same rules. Currently the general Corporate Income Tax rate is 25 per cent, for both resident companies and non-residents with a permanent establishment in Portugal. The branch does not, however, distribute dividends as it is not considered a separate legal entity from the company operating the branch (parent company). The subsidiary, on the other hand, is required to deduct withholding tax when distributing dividends. A branch structure may therefore avoid withholding tax being paid by the beneficiary of dividends.

The most obvious and possible disadvantage of setting up a branch, ignoring for a moment others such as those relating to commercial strategy and business organization, is the fact that the company controlling the branch is directly involved in and responsible for the business operations concerned. Conversely, the subsidiary is a separate entity and as such responsible for its own liabilities.

Certain additional costs such as public notary fees, stamp duty and registration costs may also be incurred usually with an average cost between 1 per cent and 3 per cent of the purchase price.

An additional stamp duty (0.8 per cent on the tax value of the immovable property) is levied on the price of any real property.

Capital gains resulting from a sale by non-resident entities with shareholding interests or other securities in a Portuguese resident company may be exempt from capital gains tax if certain requirements are met. A 'non-resident entity' is considered to be an entity which does not have a registered seat or actual management within the Portuguese jurisdiction nor does it hold any permanent establishment there to which the capital gains can attach.

Capital gains resulting from the sale of assets located in Portugal by a non-resident entity (buildings, movable property attached to a branch, etc) are subject to capital gains tax at a rate of 25 per cent.

Capital gains resulting from the sale by resident individuals or companies of shares or other securities owned in companies as well as the sale of a company's fixed assets are generally subject to income tax. The exception to this is where the seller is a company that has owned the assets for at least 12 months, which reinvests the respective sale proceeds in other fixed assets or securities issued by Portuguese companies or the Portuguese state in the 12 months preceding the year of the sale, or within 24 months from the date of sale. In this case only 50 per cent of the capital gains computed on the sale will be considered taxable.

Also exempt from tax are the capital gains resulting from the sale by an individual taxpayer (resident or not in Portugal for tax purposes) of shares in a Portuguese public company *(sociedade anónima)* where the shares have been held by the seller for at least one year. If the shares sold were held for less than one year, capital gains will be subject to taxation at a flat rate of 10 per cent (both for resident and non-resident taxpayers).

27.5 Extent of Seller's Warranties and Indemnities

Under Portuguese law, title to goods sold passes from the seller to the buyer (in the absence of a retention of title clause) at the time the sale and purchase contract is entered into, irrespective of the dates of delivery to the buyer or payment of the price to the seller.

There is an implied term or undertaking that the seller owns the item offered for sale and that he has good title to transfer, that the transfer is proper and that the asset will be delivered free from any undisclosed security interest, liens or encumbrances. The protection of a party acting in good faith is expressly provided for in Article 892 of the Portuguese Civil Code. In principle, where a defective title is conveyed the sale is deemed to be null and void, however, the seller is not entitled to invoke the validity of the sale against a buyer in good faith.

Exclusions and modifications to warranties are permitted where expressly agreed between the seller and buyer. Where there is no agreement, the seller may exclude or modify warranties only if unilaterally and expressly stated at the time of contracting in good faith. The right of disclaimer is not permitted under Portuguese law (Civil Code, Art. 809). A contractual provision purporting that the buyer (or any other party) renounces in advance its right to terminate the contract, to demand performance of the seller or to claim damages is null and void.

The buyer is entitled to recover damages from the seller covering the full amount of any loss suffered, whether direct, indirect or consequential, if and to the extent that the loss was incurred as a result of a breach of contract or law by the seller and that the loss would not have arisen but for the seller's act or omission (causal link).

27.6 Liability for Pre-contractual Representations

The legal regime for pre-contractual misrepresentations and liability is governed by Article 227 of the Civil Code under the principle of pre-contractual liability, *culpa in contrahendo*.

Contracting parties during the pre-contractual negotiation stages are required to proceed in a *bona fide* manner under the sanction of being found liable in damages for losses caused to the other party.

The *bona fide* rule implies that a party, in negotiating and entering into a contract, must at all times proceed in good faith, disclosing any defects or any other irregularity which may affect the other party's decision in order to avoid unnecessary expenses incurred in conducting the negotiations or in performing the contract at a later stage.

A breach of this duty, in addition to the innocent party being entitled to recover damages, may result in the agreement being deemed null and void.

27.7 Liability for Pre-acquisition Trading and Contracts

There are no restrictions to entering into what is known as a *'contrato promessa'* which is effectively a promissory agreement to enter into a formal and binding contract at a later stage. This type of contract must be executed in writing if the final proposed contract is also to be executed in writing.

Breach of a promissory contract may give rise to the remedy of specific performance. Where a deposit or other some other amount is paid by one party at the time of signing the promissory contract, the parties are not entitled to specific performance as the payment is treated as the only remedy acting in practice as a form of liquidated damages. This entitles the seller to retain the payment as an indemnity where the buyer breaches the promissory agreement. It also entitles the buyer to claim the return of the promissory contract payment twice over as an indemnity where the breach is committed by the seller. In these circumstances, unless the parties expressly provide that specific performance is allowed as a remedy even though a down payment has been made specific performance will be excluded.

27.8 Pre-completion Risks

Transfer of title under Portuguese law is generally effective simply by virtue of the parties consent through entering into a contract for sale irrespective of the actual transfer or delivery of the goods from seller to buyer. This explains why promissory agreements are commonly used in Portugal. In practice the contract for sale will effect the transfer of title merely as soon as it is executed. Therefore, where parties, before the transfer of title, have not reached agreement on all secondary points but simultaneously need to be bound in order to execute the transaction, then a binding promissory agreement is more appropriate rather than the final contract for sale.

As the title is transferred on entering into the sale contract, the risk of loss after sale but before delivery is assumed by the buyer/new owner. This principle, however, is subject to the following exceptions:

- the goods remain in the seller's possession despite the fact that a contract has been entered into and title has passed to the buyer;

- the seller is in default of its obligation to deliver the asset to the buyer; and

- the contract had been entered into subject to some form of suspensory condition and until that condition is met the risk remains with the buyer, by way of example: a retention of title clause is considered to be a suspensory condition in the transfer of title.

In addition, Portuguese law provides for a number of remedies against hidden defects or non-disclosed liens, charges or liabilities affecting the asset or the company depending upon the circumstances. These remedies allow the buyer to rescind the contract, obtain a court annulment of the sale or a price reduction where the buyer has acted in good faith.

In relation to a share acquisition, the buyer may address this matter by attaching to the agreement a balance sheet and other accounting documents as well as requesting warranties and a tax indemnity against any contingent liability which might affect the company and conditions of sale. Certain aspects of the acquisition are subject to registration either with the Companies Registrar for example, where shares of a private limited company (*sociedade por quotas*) are assigned, although this does not apply to the shares of a public company (*sociedade anónima*) or registration with the Land Registrar where real property is acquired in the context of a sale of company shares. In addition, a buyer may register its right to purchase prior to completion in order to ensure legal priority against any third party who might register a conflicting right or interest in the meantime. This pre-registration procedure is an important precautionary measure for prospective buyers as it is not available in many other foreign jurisdictions.

27.9 Required Governmental Approvals

Foreign investment operations in Portugal are not subject to prior registration with or consent from any regulatory authority. However, there is a requirement to notify the Bank of Portugal of an investment or sale of an investment where the value in question exceeds €250,000 and no Banks have been involved in the transaction. This should be done within ten business days after completion as is for statistical purposes only.

In relation to share acquisitions, where public officials (with reporting obligations) such as notaries, registry officers and others have not assisted with the formalities of the transaction, the parties involved (seller and buyer) must report to the tax authorities the sale/acquisition within 30 days following the sale date.

27.10 Anti-trust and Competition Rules

The control of concentrations between undertakings, in other words the merger, acquisition of control of the whole or parts of another undertaking, largely follows the relevant EU regulations. Prior notification to the '*Autoridade da Concorrência*' (Competition Authority) is required when one the following circumstances arise:

- The transaction gives rise to or strengthens a market share of more than 30 per cent in the whole or in a substantial part of the domestic market of the goods or services in question; or

- All of the companies/entities involved in the concentration operation had a combined turnover in the last trading year which exceeds €150 million (net of taxes directly connected with the business concerned) as long as the turnover directly derived from Portugal by, at least, two of the parties involved exceeds €2 million.

Concentrations of undertakings and operations concerned with these caught by the relevant rules must be notified to the Competition Authority within seven business days after concluding the transaction or, where appropriate, until the date of publication of the advert relating to a public offer of acquisition or exchange or acquisition of a controlling majority.

Included in the concept of a preliminary transaction is any type of binding agreement which has been signed with a view to concluding the concentration (for instance, a shareholders agreement, a promissory contract to buy/sell, etc.)

The concentration of undertakings is viewed as affecting competition and will not be authorized where it creates or strengthens a dominant position the consequence of which is to impede or significantly restrict competition in the whole or in a substantial part of the domestic market. Conversely, a concentration is permitted and likely to be authorized where it does not create or reinforce a dominant position and does not significantly eliminate competition in a substantial part of the respective market.

Factors which will be considered by the Competition Authority in making this determination include, inter alia, market structure and the existence or not of competitors; the positioning and strength of the concentration participants; barriers on entry to that market; the freedom of choice for suppliers and end-users; distribution networks; infrastructure control and access competitors to it; technical and financial development which benefits consumers without restricting competition; amongst others.

Fines and other sanctions may be imposed on concentrations established contrary to a decision of the authorities prohibiting the concentration.

27.11 Requisite Offer Procedures

When the target is a public subscribed company, a compulsory public bid may be necessary. This is governed by a complex system of rules which can briefly be summarized as follows.

A public company of this type (*'sociedade com subscrição pública'*) is also by definition a *sociedade anónima* and includes companies:

- set up through a public subscription offer aimed at persons resident or established in Portugal;

- holding shares or other securities which confer a right of subscription or acquisition of shares which have been the subject of a public subscription offer aimed at persons resident or established in Portugal;

- holding shares or other securities which confer a right of subscription or acquisition of shares which are or have been admitted to trading on regulated stock markets in Portugal;

- holding shares which have been transferred by public offers of acquisition or exchange for consideration in excess of 10 per cent of the share capital aimed at persons resident or established in Portugal;

- resulting from a split or break-up of another public company or which incorporate, by merger, all or part of its assets.

The following circumstances are considered to constitute public offers:

- An offer relating to securities directed or addressed in whole or in part to unidentified or undetermined persons. The undetermined nature of the addressees is not affected by the fact that the offer is effected by multiple standard communications addressed in some instances to persons identified;

- An offer addressed to the generality of the shareholders of a public company even where the respective share capital is made up of nominative shares;

- An offer which, in whole or in part, is preceded or accompanied by the gathering of investment information from the undetermined addresses or promotion which is advertising in nature;

- An offer directed at more than 200 persons.

Under Article 486 of the Companies Code, a company is controlled by another when the latter is in a position to exercise, either directly or through another controlled company or individual, a dominant influence. There is a legal presumption that a company is controlled whenever, directly or indirectly, the dominant company:

- holds a majority shareholding interest in the other company;

- holds more than one half of the voting rights in the other company; and

- is entitled to nominate more than one half of the members of the board of directors or supervisory board.

Only an offer which is made in respect of all of a company's shares or securities conferring a right of subscription or acquisition can be accepted.

The applicable law (Stockmarket Code, Article 20; Companies Code, Article 482) includes a detailed description of the relevant forms of indirect ownership of shares to which these mandatory rules also apply.

27.12 Continuation of Government Licences

As a general rule, there is no need for governmental authorization to carry out business activities in Portugal. However, in relation to certain sectors and industries the operator is required to hold a licence. The requirement to obtain a licence depends on the type of business activity.

As an example, licences are required for the following (regulatory authorities are indicated in brackets):

- banking (the Minister of Finance and the Bank of Portugal);

- insurance (the Minister of Finance and the Portuguese Insurance Institute);

- public and civil works (the Superior Council for Transport and Public Works);

- television and telecommunications (the Portuguese Communications Institute); and

- travel agencies (the Tourism Board).

Licences are normally granted on a temporary basis and are automatically renewed provided the operator files documentation periodically to prove that it continues to meet the requisite legal requirements. In certain circumstances, changes in the company's control and ownership must also be notified to the licensing authority.

In the event of a sale of the business, it may be necessary to apply to the licensor for prior authorization or to apply for a fresh licence in the new buyer's favour.

27.13 Requirements for Transferring Shares

The company's by-laws or articles of association may outline certain restrictions on the transfer of shares, usually in the form of a right of first refusal conferred on the other stockholders. The by-laws may also make the transfer subject to, for example, the company's prior consent or compliance with requirements relating either to the buyer or to the conditions and circumstances in respect of which the transfer can be made to protect the company's interests.

The requirements which legally apply to the transfer of shares depend on the type of shares in question.

The shares of a public company (*sociedade anónima*) can be nominative (or nominal, i.e.: expressly held in the name of someone) or bearer shares: if nominative, the shares must be either deposited with an authorized entity (e.g. a bank) or registered with the company by filing a special form; if bearer, the owner can opt to have the shares deposited in a bank or registered with the company.

The transfer of nominative shares is not complete until the transfer is registered in the proper company books. The transfer declaration must be signed by the seller either on the share certificate itself or on a separate form.

The transfer of bearer shares is effected through the delivery of the share certificates. Where the shares are deposited with a bank or registered with the company the buyer's possession can only be established if the deposit or registration is in the buyer's name in respect of which the correct form must be completed and signed.

The shares in a private limited company (*sociedade por quotas*) may only be transferred by notarial deed. Title must be registered with the Companies Registrar in order to prove ownership.

27.14 Requirements for Transferring Land and Property Leases

Real property ownership is subject to a comprehensive registration system and in Portugal the principle of prior registration before actual transfer or assignment of the title applies. It is therefore advisable to always effect a prior provisional registration of the title before actual completion of the transfer. This is done to avoid third parties from applying to register conflicting rights or interests between the closing date of the acquisition and the buyer submitting its application to register the transfer.

As in most jurisdictions, it is necessary to review the property's registration records to ensure that there no pre-existing liens, encumbrances, mortgages, rights or other similar charges over the property or that these will be released on sale and that the seller is actually entitled to sell.

The constitution and transfer of any interest in real property requires the execution of a notarial deed and further registration with the respective Land Registry. Tenancies or commercial lease agreements must also be executed by notarial deed.

27.15   Requirements for Transferring Intellectual Property

Title to all forms of intellectual property (not including copyright in artistic and similar works, which are subject to certain limitations) can be transferred without restrictions, however, the transfer must be evidenced in writing.

The owner may also grant a licence (whether exclusive or not) to third parties to use the intellectual property provided that the licence agreement is executed in writing. In these circumstances the licensee may also in turn transfer the licence to a third party, subject to obtaining the licensor's written consent.

Except where expressly agreed otherwise, the transfer of a business includes the right to the business name and logo, which cannot be transferred without the business. Title to all forms of intellectual property (trade and service marks, designs and patents, business names and logos) can be registered with the Portuguese Institute of Intellectual Property in which case a transfer must also be registered to be effective *vis-à-vis* third parties.

The licensee of an intellectual property right may also register that licensing agreement if authorized by the owner.

27.16   Requirements for Transferring Business Contracts, Licences and Leases

As a general rule, all business contracts can be assigned to third parties on the condition that the other party has agreed to it prior to or after execution of the contract. Unless the parties have agreed otherwise, the transferor is released from their obligations under the contract once it is transferred.

Certain business contracts allow one party to rescind where there has been a change in control in the other contracting party, although the general rule is that business contracts continue despite this. Whenever the acquisition of a business as a whole occurs, certain contracts included or related to the undertakings (e.g. lease and employment agreements) are also transferred with the business, although the transferor is not usually released from their obligations and liabilities under the contract in the absence of a specific discharge statement from the other party.

The assignment of a contract must be executed in the same form (notarial deed, written form, verbal form) as the underlying contract.

The general rule is that contracts are not subject to a specific form, although there are a number of exceptions, the most important being:

1. Where a notarial deed is legally required, which is the case for the:

    *   creation or transfer of any rights over or interests in real property including a mortgage;

    *   incorporation of a company and any amendment to the articles of association; and

    *   transfer of a business establishment.

2. Where a written document (not notarized) is required such as for the:

    *   execution of lease agreements for residential purposes or the transfer or licensing of intellectual property;

    *   transfer or pledge of shares in a *sociedade por quotas* or execution or assignment of a business lease agreement;

    *   assignment or transfer or any agreement which has previously been executed in writing (even when such format was not legally required but the parties have opted for this);

    *   execution of a promissory agreement where the final agreement is to be executed in a specific form (e.g. by notarial deed);

    *   sale and purchase of a car;

    *   transfer of nominative shares in *sociedade anónima*; and

    *   transfer of registered or deposited shares in a *sociedade anónima*.

27.17 Requirements for Transferring Other Assets

A transfer of assets does not normally require any specific formality and is usually effected by the act of delivery. The major exceptions to this general principle are mentioned in **27.16** above.

27.18 Encumbrances and Third Party Interests

Security interests in movable and real property can take several forms and may be created by law, by contract or by a court decision.

In the case of real property (and a certain other movable assets such as cars, aircraft and vessels which are subject to registration), the most appropriate security is the mortgage ('*hipoteca*') which must be registered with the relevant Charges Registry to take effect. The only exception to this requirement is the creation of liens by operation of law in exceptional circumstances, for example, tax liabilities in favour of the state and certain maritime liens. Liens under Portuguese law may be created by operation of law only, and never by operation of contract: they are not subject to registration to be valid and fully effective.

Taking the latter point into account, the relevant title should be examined (with the Land or Companies Registry) to ascertain not only that the title to property exists and is registered, but also that it is registered in the name of the correct person.

The same applies to *sociedades por quotas* where the title to and pledge over shares are also subject to registration.

As to movable assets in general which, as a rule, are not subject to registration, warranties should be sought from the seller where their value is significant.

27.19   Minimum Shareholder and Office Requirements

A *sociedade por quotas* must have a minimum share capital of EUR 5,000, at least two shareholders with a minimum value of EUR 100 per share and at least one director. It may, however, exceptionally be set up with only one shareholder or, once incorporated, with two or more shareholders, but then reducing to one shareholder subsequently. Please note that in these cases it is compulsory to include in the company's name the words '*Unipessoal*' or '*Sociedade Unipessoal*', which indicates a company having only one shareholder. The company may also need to have a public chartered accountant verify its accounts where the number of employees and the total gross income and assets meet certain legal thresholds.

A *sociedade anónima* must have a minimum share capital of EUR 50,000 and at least five shareholders. If the share capital is less than EUR 200,000 then only one director is required. If the share capital exceeds EUR 200,000 then the board of directors must consist of an odd number of directors and have a supervisory board with one or three members.

The supervision of the company's business activities and accounts must conducted by either a public chartered accountant or a supervisory board composed of three or five members appointed at the company's discretion.

Additionally, companies operating in certain business sectors are required to have specific minimum amounts of share capital, for instance, in the case of companies operating in the financial sector.

27.20   Non-competition Clauses

As a general rule and pursuant to Decree Law No. 18/2003 of 11 June 2003 (the basic competition law statute), any agreement or concerted practice between undertakings which purports to restrict or has as its effect a restriction of trade or competition is forbidden and consequently invalid.

Within the context of a business sale, the seller may include restraint of trade or non-competition covenants, as may be done in the event of termination of a franchise or agency agreement. This issue should, however, be reviewed on case by case basis, as such covenants may only exceptionally be permitted under the relevant competition law provisions.

Non-competition clauses in employment contracts are also permitted against payment of specific compensation to the employee of an amount not exceeding three years remuneration.

27.21 Environmental Considerations

Tortious and criminal penalties are established by law to punish the infringement of environmental laws. Civil liability exists for both vicarious and general liability irrespective of intent or negligence. All of the following must be established in order to proceed with a civil action:

- there must have been a failure to act;

- the act in question (or failure to act) must have been unlawful;

- the act (or failure to act) must be attributable to the party charged with the pollution;

- damage must be shown to have been caused; and

- a causal link must exist between the act (or failure to act) and the damage caused.

Article 41 of the Basic Law on the Environment No. 11/87 of 7 April 1987 provides that: 'There is an obligation to indemnify, irrespective of any fault, whenever someone has caused significant damage to the environment as a result of a particularly dangerous activity, even though he has complied with the law and all applicable technical rules.' Except as provided for in Article 41, all five of the above factors must be established for a civil action to proceed. In addition, only damage which can be shown to be directly caused by the act (or failure to act) in question gives rise to liability and a right to be indemnified.

In relation to criminal liability, there are no other environmental crimes or criminal sanctions in accordance with the principles *nullum crimen sine lege* and *nulla poena sine lege poenali* (in other words, no crime (can be committed), no punishment (can be imposed) without a previous penal law) except those expressly provided for in the law. The penal code provides for the following environmental crimes:

- exposure of people to radioactive substances;

- exposure of goods belonging to others to radioactive substances;

- emissions of toxic or asphyxiating gases;

- contamination or poisoning of water sources;

- the propagation of infectious diseases;

- the introduction of epizootics;

- the deterioration of animal foodstuffs; and

- the deterioration of human foodstuffs and medicines.

The following crimes are also provided for by other legislation:

- forest fires (caused by both intentional and negligent acts);

- illegal hunting of protected animal species;

- crimes against public health; and

- non-compliance with embargoes, conservation orders, etc.

Company directors are not responsible in tort if they acted in performance of their corporate functions. Where this is not the case, the company is liable to third parties without prejudice to its right to make a claim against the director responsible for the infringement.

Company directors who infringe criminal law are personally liable and may be subject to fines although this does not affect the company's duty to indemnify third parties.

27.22   Employee Superannuation/Pension Plans

It is usual for larger companies to have special salary schemes in place such as pension funds for named beneficiaries in accordance with calculation methods provided for by the pension fund rules.

Detailed rules relating to the creation, operation and funding of, and all relevant issues concerning, pension funds have been legally established to provide security and reliability in connection with the funds. Where a company has in place a pension fund, there may be ongoing contribution obligations which a buyer should take care not to overlook.

27.23   Employee Rights

It is not possible in this guide to summarize the legal position governing employment relationships which are often also subject to collective labour agreements. Expert and specific advice should be sought on these issues.

Examples of important employee rights include:

- The right to oppose unfair dismissal and seek either reinstatement or compensation;

- Restricted and exceptional situations where time-limited employment contracts are allowed which include limitations on overtime practice; and

- The right to a Christmas and holiday allowance every year, each equivalent to one month's salary.

27.24   Compulsory Transfer of Employees

On the transfer of an undertaking, its ownership the business or part of the business, when this part constitutes an economic unit, the legal position of the employer in relation to the employment contracts of the employees is transferred to the purchaser including any penalties payable in respect of breaches of statutory employment rights.

During the period of 1 year from the date of transfer the transferor is liable for all obligations which arose or had accrued at the date of transfer.

27.25 Tax Deductibility

The following amounts may, subject to certain limitations, be deducted for tax purposes:

- expenses incurred in the production or acquisition of goods or services;

- charges arising from sale and distribution;

- financial costs;

- assets amortization and depreciation;

- capital losses;

- indemnities in relation to uninsurable risks;

- provisions for:
  - Bad debts resulting from the normal activity of the enterprise, such as receivables in respect of which the debtor has a case pending for execution, bankruptcy or insolvency, disputed receivables and amounts overdue for payment for over six months. In the latter case the annual cumulative amount of the provision (and bad debt relief permitted) is equal to 25 per cent for payments outstanding for periods between six and 12 months, 50 per cent between 12 and 18 months, 75 per cent between 18 and 24 months, and 100 per cent for those outstanding for more than 24 months;
  - Stock devaluation, calculated according to the difference between the acquisition or production cost of inventory recorded in the balance sheet at the end of the financial period and the market value with reference to the same date: any taxable person adopting the permanent inventory system may increase the amount of the provisional expenses by a third;
  - Liabilities and charges arising in connection with court proceedings;
  - Provisions established in accordance with the relevant rules applying to insurance companies and banking institutions; and
  - Provision made by companies engaged in the exploration for, or exploitation of, petroleum for the replacement of petroleum deposits.

It is also possible to deduct for tax purposes, subject to certain limitations and conditions, expenses in connection with social utility arrangements which the company, personnel and their families may have including contributions to pension funds and supplementary social security schemes, as well as gifts made to certain entities, namely those for cultural, charitable or benevolent purposes and associations.

Taxable losses are deductible from taxable profit for a period of up to six tax years from their verification. This rule does not apply if, at the tax year end date (generally 31 December) of the year in which the deduction is applied, there is a substantial change in the social object of the company, the nature of the activity performed, or where a change of at least 50 per cent of the nominal capital or the majority of the voting rights has occurred. In special circumstances the Ministry of Finance may permit, if required, a relaxing of or exception to this restriction.

27.26 Levies on Acquisition Agreements

Notary and registration fees are due when the intervention of the notary or the registrar is required in connection with the transfer of title, as is the case with real property, creation or transfer of any rights over or interests in real property including a mortgage; the incorporation of a company and any amendment to the articles of association; and the transfer of a business establishment.

Stamp duty is levied when the title to real property is transferred.

27.27 Financing Rules and Restrictions

There are no restrictions on shareholder loans (whether provided by resident or non-resident shareholders), the only exception being that the agreed contractual interest rate can be challenged by the relevant Portuguese tax authorities whenever it differs from the prevailing financial market rates (arm's length). The Portuguese tax regime has specific regulations regarding transfer pricing which accepts inter-company loans on the condition that they are made at arms length and on commercial market terms. Tax authorities are entitled to adjust taxable income if this rule is not accomplished.

A loan made by a bank (whether resident or non-resident) to a resident company is subject to stamp tax/duty on the amount of the loan as well as on the interest (rates range between 0.04 per cent and 0.60 per cent depending on the loan period agreed).

There are strict restrictions on a company purchasing or providing the finance to purchase its own shares or the shares of its holding or controlling company.

Payment of interest on loans to a non-resident shareholder is subject to a general 20 per cent withholding tax, without prejudice to lower rates which may apply under any relevant treaty against double taxation. It should be noted, however, that in accordance with EU Directive n. 2003/49/CE, of 5 June, interest paid to a company resident in a EU country is subject to a rate of 10 per cent withholding tax during the first 4 years after the EU Directive's implementation and in the subsequent four years is subject to a rate of 5 per cent withholding tax (the requirements and conditions of the Directive to apply). This Directive and transposing legislation has been in force in Portugal since 1 July 2005.

In relation to capitalization, the indebtedness of a resident taxpayer entity to a non-resident entity, not resident in an EU country, is deemed to be a special relationship and where the amount of the debt is considered excessive (see further below) will not be accepted as a cost. A special relationship is deemed to exist where (1) the non-resident entity holds, directly or indirectly, at least 10 per cent of the resident company's share capital, or (2) the non-resident entity (even without a 10 per cent holding) exercises a *de facto* significant influence over the management of the resident company, or (3) the non-resident entity and the resident company are both under the control of the same holding entity.

The indebtedness of a resident taxpayer to a third party non-resident entity is treated in the same way as the concept referred to above of a special relationship where a guarantee is given to the resident company and with which it has a special relationship. A debt is considered excessive where on any date of the trading year its amount is higher than twice the value of the nominal amount of the shareholding interest held by the non-resident in the resident company's share capital. For this purpose share capital is considered to include not only subscribed and paid up capital, but also all other elements as legally provided for.

The capitalization rules do not apply if the resident taxpayer produces evidence that, having regard to the type of activity, the business sector, the size of the enterprise and other relevant criteria, it would have obtained the same funding/loan, under similar conditions, from an independent entity. This exception does not apply to creditor entities resident in jurisdictions which benefit from clearly more favourable tax regimes and which are included in the 'black-list' as approved by the Ministry of Finance as explained in the following paragraph.

In relation to anti-trust legislation, amounts paid or due by resident companies in Portugal to individuals or entities resident or registered outside of the jurisdiction benefiting from a tax regime which is clearly more favourable than the Portuguese one are not tax deductible, unless the Portuguese resident company proves that the respective transactions were actually made at arms length. A tax regime is considered to be more favourable where (1) the jurisdiction is included in the 'black-list' as established by the Ministry of Finance, or (2) it does not levy income tax in the place where the payee is located or (3), the amount of tax paid there is equal to or less than 60 per cent of the amount of tax payable if the entity was resident in Portugal.

27.28   Exchange Controls and Repatriation of Profits

There are generally no exchange controls in Portugal. Except where a lower rate applies under an international double taxation treaty, repatriation of dividends and payment of interest to non-residents is subject to 20 per cent withholding tax (please see above specific comments on the payment of interest to EU companies).

Dividends paid by a Portuguese subsidiary to its parent company in an EU Member State are subject to the regime of the Parent/Subsidiary EU Directive as implemented in Portugal.

27.29   Group Companies: Tax Issues

Any company having its registered seat and actual management located in Portugal and which controls one or more other companies may opt for the specific group companies' taxation regime. This is computed by using the total individual taxable income for each company within the group applied over the following five years.

A group of company exists when a company directly or indirectly owns at least 90 per cent of the share capital of the subsidiary or subsidiaries forming part of the group so long as this participation also confers 50 per cent or more of the voting rights.

Eligibility for the application of this special tax regime is subject to the fulfilment of several requirements, including:

- all related companies have their registered seat and actual management in Portugal;
- the controlling company must have held its participation in the subsidiary for more than one year;
- the controlling company is not controlled by any other company resident in Portuguese territory.

There are also several circumstances which may exclude a company from the application of the group taxation regime, such as companies which:

- have been inactive for more than one year or that have been dissolved;
- that are subject to formal corporate insolvency or recovery procedures;
- do not fall within to the normal regime of corporation tax;
- have a tax period which differs from the controlling company;
- where the participation requirement (90 per cent) is indirectly obtained through a company that does not fulfil the legal requirement to be included in the group;
- are not capital/corporate entities entities (*'Sociedade Anónima'*, *'Sociedade por Quotas'* or *'Sociedade em Comandita por Acções'*, in other words public or private limited companies).

In general, group taxable income is computed by the controlling company by adding together cumulatively the total sum of the taxable profits and tax losses assessed in the individual tax return for each entity of the group. However, group tax losses computed in a specific tax year are only deductible from the future taxable profits of the group.

Tax losses computed by the group entities before the application of the special tax regime may only be carried forward against the particular company's taxable income.

When the application of the regime ceases, or when a company no longer qualifies for this regime, tax losses computed during the application of the regime may not be carried forward and deducted from future individual company profits.

27.30   Other Relevant Tax Issues

Tax Neutrality Regime

The Portuguese Corporate Income Tax Code establishes a special tax neutrality regime for mergers, company disposals, company acquisition or incorporation by transfer of assets and share capital exchanges. This regime results from the transposing of

EU Directive no. 90/434/CEE, of 23 July 1990. To benefit for the tax neutrality offered, the entities intervening in the operation must be resident in Portugal or in another EU State Member for tax purposes.

Tax losses computed by the merged entity may be offset and deducted against profits computed by the new or incorporated entity over the next six tax years. However, this possibility is subject to authorization from the Ministry of Finance.

General Anti-avoidance Rule

Contracts or acts are deemed ineffective whenever it can be demonstrated that their purpose or intention is the reduction, elimination or temporary deferment of taxation obligations that are due in other contracts or actions of a similar nature having a similar economic effect.

27.31 Responsibility for Liabilities of an Acquired Subsidiary

As a general rule, a company is responsible for its subsidiary's liabilities where the subsidiary is 100 per cent owned by it. Where a company, however, acquires at least 90 per cent of another company's share capital, further special rules apply and must be taken into account. These rules are outside the scope of this guide and specific advice should be sought in this regard.

27.32 Governing Law of the Contract

The obligations of the parties to a commercial contract as well as the contract itself can be governed by any national law which the parties have freely chosen, provided that such national law has some reasonable or commercial connection with the parties or the agreement. Portugal is a signatory to the 1980 Rome Convention on the Law Applicable to Contractual Obligations.

27.33 Dispute Resolution Options

Portuguese law allows the parties to a commercial contract to opt to have their disputes resolved by arbitration, submitting it either to the law or to a judgment under general principles of equity.

Portugal is a signatory to the 1958 New York Convention on the Enforcement of Foreign Arbitral Awards; the 1927 Geneva Convention; and the Washington Convention, dated 18 March 1965, on the settlement of disputes between Contracting States and nationals of other Contracting States in relation to investments. Portuguese courts recognize and enforce international arbitration awards. The Brussels Regulation, Council Regulation (EC) No 44/2001 of 22 December 2000, on jurisdiction and the recognition and enforcement of judgments in civil and commercial matters has been implemented into Portuguese law.

An arbitration award may be enforced by the Portuguese courts if certain legal rules are met in relation to the arbitrators' appointment, the internal rules of arbitration procedure and other matters which in general concern the requirement to ensure the equality of the parties before the arbitrators, amongst others.

Given these requirements, it should be noted that a mediation decision or any other similar ADR statement is not effective and enforceable Portugal before or by the Portuguese Courts.

Certain private entities and bodies have been legally recognized and authorized by the government to deal with disputes under the arbitration rules.

28. SCOTLAND

Kenneth Chrystie
McClure Naismith

28.1 Introductory Comments

Perhaps the most important point to be made in this introduction is to emphasise that within the UK Scotland has its own separate legal system. Its courts are entirely independent from the English courts, its procedures are distinct and in many substantive areas, including property, the law of Scotland differs from that in England. While England is a common law system Scots law is based in civil law.

In contrast to these fundamental differences, however, there is a very high degree of uniformity so far as commercial law is concerned and in this contribution it has been thought appropriate only to highlight points of distinction and difference between the two systems.

The taxation and company law regime referred to at 9.2 basically also applies in Scotland as do the general remarks on the business climate. Significantly, both Scotland and England share the same tax regime.

28.2 Corporate Structures

The position in Scotland is very much the same as in England but there is a separate Registrar of Companies in Scotland and a separate Register of Charges. This is in part necessary because the law of fixed securities and of floating charges in Scotland are quite distinct from those in England. A company that is incorporated in Scotland cannot have its registered office in England, nor vice-versa, and companies in Scotland and England cannot change their nationality by changing their registered tax office from one jurisdiction to another.

Under the Partnership Act 1890, section 4, a partnership in Scotland has a separate persona (in contrast to the position in England), and this leads to a number of important distinctions between the law of partnership in England and Scotland extending to the enforcement of obligations and the extent of partner liabilities. For the purpose of this commentary it is probably sufficient that the underlying difference is noted.

28.3 Letters of Intent and Heads of Agreement

In Scotland a unilateral undertaking in writing will be enforced. No consideration in return for a promise made or undertaking given in a letter of intent or heads of agreement is required to constitute a binding voluntary obligation. There is, however, a very fine line between an undertaking or representation on the one hand, which can

© World Law Group
International Business Acquisitions, M. Whalley, F.-J. Semler (eds.), Kluwer Law International, London, 2007; ISBN 9789041124838.

be enforced, and an expression of intention, on the other hand, which cannot. There is no reason why heads of agreement cannot be enforced if they are sufficiently specific and the general comments in relation to the enforceability of letters of intent and heads of agreement in the second paragraph of paragraph 9.3 of the English commentary apply equally in Scotland, save that (as mentioned above) in Scotland no consideration is required. It is worth bearing in mind that in Scotland documents *in re mercatoria*, i.e. used in the ordinary course of business, may be enforced even if they are informally constituted.

28.4   Taxes Affecting the Structure and Calculation of the Price

The tax regime in Scotland is the same as in the rest of the UK although differences in trust law in Scotland can lead to important tax consequences.

28.5   Extent of Seller's Warranties and Indemnities

While the style of warranties and indemnities relating to property matters differs in Scotland from that in England to reflect the underlying legal system differences, the approach to and the nature and extent of the warranties and indemnities and the limitations outlined in the English commentary also apply in Scotland.

28.6   Liability for Pre-contractual Representations

Pre-contractual misrepresentation can be actionable in Scotland. A distinction is drawn between innocent, negligent and fraudulent misrepresentations. An innocent misrepresentation will allow rescission of the contract to the extent that this is practicable (in many cases it is not) but not damages. A negligent or fraudulent misrepresentation will allow recission of the contract (again to the extent practicable) and the party who has been induced to enter into the contract can sue the other party in respect of any loss or damage he has suffered. Generally, there is no duty of disclosure.

The practice outlined in the English commentary in relation to excluding actions based on pre-contractual misrepresentations is also adopted in Scotland.

28.7   Liability for Pre-acquisition Trading and Contracts

The position is generally as set out in the English commentary. The main differences between the Scottish and English positions in relation to these matters arises by virtue of the fact that on an assignation in Scotland the assignor does not remain liable along with the assignee for the obligations which are assigned.

28.8   Pre-completion Risks

The position is as stated in the English commentary but it should be noted that in Scotland in theory at least the primary remedy is specific implementation (in England specific performance) or, failing that, damages.

28.9   Required Governmental Approvals

28.10   Anti-trust and Competition Law

28.11   Required Offer Procedures

28.12   Continuation of Government Licences

28.13   Requirements for Transferring Shares

In all of these areas the law is essentially the same in Scotland as it is in England.

28.14   Requirements for Transferring Land and Property Leases

Scotland also has a registration system but it is not as comprehensive as that in England and Wales. The law relating to transferring land and leasing in Scotland is entirely distinct from that in England as are the forms of registration and security. There are separate statutory provisions covering floating charges in Scotland and covering the creation of heritable securities.

28.15   Requirements for Transferring Intellectual Property

The position is as in England, although title to intellectual property is transferred by assignation (rather than assignment).

28.16   Requirements for Transferring Business Contracts, Licences and Laws

The position in Scotland is as set out in the English commentary (although, again, the term used in Scotland is an assignation rather than an assignment). An assignation is effected in writing although no particular form of words is necessary. In order to be effective, the assignation must be intimated to the other party to the contract.

As has been noted above, the common law provides that the assignor is released from the burden of the contract once it has been assigned.

28.17   Requirements for Transferring Other Assets

It suffices to note that the common law for transferring moveables in Scotland is distinct from that in England and care should be taken therefore to take appropriate advice in circumstances where Scottish assets are involved. Delivery in some form or another is necessary to pass property. Risk can pass separately from property.

28.18   Encumbrances and Third Party Interests

It is sufficient for present purposes to note that the Scottish systems are similar to but separate and distinct from those in England and appropriate advice should be taken when dealing with Scottish assets which are or may be subject to some form of third party right or interest. Equitable charges are not recognized in Scotland.

28.19   Minimum Shareholder and Officer Requirements

Basically, the terms of the Companies Acts apply, with minor differences, both in England and in Scotland. The differences principally relate to security matters and reflect underlying philosophical differences in the common law. The rules in relation to minimum shareholder and officer requirements for Scottish companies are the same as for English companies.

28.20   Non-competition Clauses

Restraint of trade or non-competition covenants are *prima facie* unenforceable as being contrary to public policy on the basis that they unduly or unreasonably restrain the liberty of a person to practice his trade or profession, or to engage in business. However, such a covenant will be enforced to the extent that it is reasonably required in the circumstances and imposed for the protection of the buyer or employer. The attitude of the courts in Scotland is, in material respects, different from that in England and although English authorities are cited in the Scottish courts, limited regard is paid to them. A contractual restriction must also be clear and specific and is likely to be unenforceable if it is indefinite or insufficiently precise.

A restraint of trade clause is more likely to be upheld in the case of a sale of a company or business, where it is reasonable to protect the purchaser's interests, than in the case of a covenant in an employment contract prohibiting certain activities post-employment.

The Competition Act 1998 applies in Scotland as well as in England and the Office of Fair Trading is similarly active in both jurisdictions.

28.21   Environmental Considerations

The position in Scotland is, broadly speaking, the same as that in England.

28.22   Employee Superannuation/Pension Plans

Whilst the English commentary basically reflects the position in Scotland, trust law differs between Scotland and England and Wales and it should be checked whether an occupational pension scheme is set up under trust in accordance with Scots law or English law and the appropriate law applied.

28.23   Employee Rights

28.24   Compulsory Transfer of Employees

It is perhaps sufficient for the present commentary to point out that the law and formalities of employment contracts are different in England but the end result and the approach outlined in the commentary on England applies generally in Scotland.

28.25   Tax Deductibility of Acquisition Expenses

The commentary on England basically reflects the position in Scotland.

28.26 Levies on Acquisition and Collateral Documents

Whilst the position in Scotland is basically as set out in the English Commentary, it should be noted that there are certain differences in the treatment of leases for stamp duty reserve tax purposes north and south of the border.

28.27 Financing Rules and Restrictions

28.28 Exchange Controls and Repatriation of Profits

28.29 Groups of Companies

28.30 Responsibility for Liabilities of an Acquired Subsidiary

In all of these cases the commentary on England basically reflects the position in Scotland.

28.31 Governing Law of the Contract

Because the Scottish legal system is entirely distinct from that in England and Wales it may be of some importance whether the proper law is stipulated as being that of England or Scotland. Scottish courts will honour any reasonable choice of proper law and, where the application of Scots law is specifically excluded, the Scottish courts will apply the relevant rules of law of the chosen jurisdiction to the exclusion of any corresponding rules of Scots law. The choice of proper law will not necessarily prevail over the requirements of Scots law in such matters as the creation of securities and trust and the chosen foreign law will not be applied if the application of the foreign rule of law would be incompatible with public policy or if the choice of law is made to evade the mandatory requirements of a statute designed to protect Scottish contracting parties.

28.32 Dispute Resolution Option

Although the bodies that deal with dispute resolution are different in Scotland the whole range of options set out in the commentary on England are also available in Scotland. The UNCITRAL Model Law on International Commercial Arbitration has applied in Scotland since 1990 and all international arbitrations conducted in Scotland are governed by the UNCITRAL Model Law.

29. SINGAPORE

Gerald Singham & Angelyn Koh Rodyk & Davidson

29.1   Introductory Comments

The legal system in Singapore is founded upon and derived substantively from the common law of England. As such, case law from common law jurisdictions throughout the world, especially the Commonwealth, is well regarded. Coupled with parliamentary legislation and other regulatory mechanisms, the common law system in Singapore adds to the infrastructural stability of a progressive, newly industrialized economy.

Singapore has always encouraged foreign investments; in fact, the backbone of her economy is very much the strength of multinationals. Thus, restrictions on foreign acquisitions of Singaporean companies and assets are fairly minimal. Instead, there are substantial investment incentives offered by the government through statutory and regulatory concessions, exemptions and rebates.

Singapore has no foreign exchange control nor minimum equity content rules. Incorporation and ownership of companies wholly by foreigners is not restricted except in areas such as banking and finance, newspaper publishing or broadcasting (i.e. in economically or politically sensitive areas).

The important statutes, regulations, and codes governing mergers and acquisitions in Singapore are the Companies Act, the Securities and Futures Act, the Singapore Code on Takeovers and Mergers issued by the Monetary Authority of Singapore (the 'Code') and the Listing Manual of the Singapore Exchange (the 'LM'). The Code and the LM however, apply only to listed public companies and unlisted public companies with 50 or more shareholders.

29.2   Corporate Structures

Most companies are non-listed companies which may be private or public. A private company limited by shares has members numbering from two to 50. Above 50, the company must be a public company. Companies limited by guarantee are usually charities or public bodies, and these are rare.

Non-corporate structures include (1) businesses, which are either sole proprietorships or partnerships comprising of 2–20 partners (except for partnerships engaged in professional practice), and (2) the limited liability partnership ('LLP'), a new business vehicle which was introduced in Singapore with effect from 11 April 2005. The LLP combines the flexibility of partnership operations together with the benefit of limited liability. The partners of an LLP will not be held personally liable for the LLP's business

© World Law Group
International Business Acquisitions, M. Whalley, F.-J. Semler (eds.), Kluwer Law International, London, 2007; ISBN 9789041124838.

debts. In addition, a partner of an LLP is only personally liable for debts resulting from his own wrongful act or omission and not those of any other partner of the LLP.

29.3   Letters of Intent and Heads of Agreement

Letters of intent and heads of agreement are preliminary documents encapsulating the good faith generated during initial negotiations so as to facilitate progress in later negotiations. They may involve setting down markers for the proposed agreement. Lock-out provisions and confidentiality may also be included and may be binding on the negotiations.

Legally, letters of intent or heads of agreement may or may not, at the option of the parties, be binding on the sale and acquisition. To exclude any residual contractual effect that may follow after intense negotiations, it may be expedient to include a 'subject to contract' clause. The courts are of the view that a document containing the clause 'subject to contract' will, prima facie not constitute a binding obligation unless there are exceptional circumstances that show otherwise. However, it is advisable not to place sole reliance on such a clause as its meaning has not been conclusively established by the courts, rather, specific provisions for the non-binding effect of the agreement ought to be incorporated within it.

29.4   Taxes Affecting the Structure and Calculation of the Price

When a takeover is made by the acquisition of shares, the buyer bears the target's tax liabilities. This is to be contrasted with a takeover made through an acquisition of assets, where the buyer is spared any tax burden.

The tax rate payable by companies incorporated in Singapore is 20 per cent for the Year of Assessment 2005 onwards. Dividends paid by Singaporean companies to non-resident shareholders are subject to a withholding tax of 22 per cent, subject to the terms of specific double taxation agreements.

There are numerous tax incentives offered by the Singapore Government under the incentives legislation and the Income Tax Act to encourage foreign companies to invest in Singapore.

29.5   Extent of Seller's Warranties and Indemnities

The negotiations leading towards an agreement between the seller and the buyer decide the extent to which warranties and indemnities will be included in the eventual sale and purchase contract.

Seller's warranties usually include representations that the company's latest accounts are true and accurate, that it is not engaged in litigation, that its book debts will be realized in full and that it has good title to all its properties.

The areas in which the target's activities may be warranted to be as they have been represented are numerous and really depend on the relative positions of the contracting parties, the degree of scrutiny permitted and the extent to which facts relating to the seller's business can be easily verified.

Any undisclosed tax liabilities not provided for in the target company's accounts may be indemnified to protect the buyer against the seller. Also, such protection may be available in case of the denial of future tax reliefs or benefits (e.g. carrying forward tax losses).

Collateral provided by the target's parent or related companies in the form of guarantees, as well as a retention of a portion of the purchase price, should also be resorted to as a buffer for the warranties and indemnities.

29.6 Liability for Pre-contractual Representations

As in other common law jurisdictions, the actionability of innocent, negligent or fraudulent misrepresentations is dependent upon both case law and statutory provisions. Generally, an action for damages lies against breaches of pre-contractual representations made negligently or fraudulently, and even if made innocently. However, it is usually in instances when fraud is involved that the buyer may rescind the contract, in addition to claiming damages.

The practical effect of the law in the area of pre-contractual misstatements and misrepresentations is that the seller often tries to circumvent it by incorporating exclusion clauses in the agreement to eliminate the effect of any such misrepresentations. However, judicial pronouncements tend to strike down such exclusions in appropriate cases.

29.7 Liability for Pre-acquisition Trading and Contracts

Any pre-acquisition activity for which the buyer may become liable because of a retrospective or backdating clause should be reflected in the seller's accounting and taxation records. The intending buyer should raise this with the seller.

The seller remains contractually bound by all contracts in which it participated even after completion, unless it is able to procure novation and release from them. Usually, post-completion assignments of contracts are undertaken with the buyer giving the appropriate indemnities and warranties to the seller.

29.8 Pre-completion Risks

Parties to a sale and purchase agreement of shares or assets are free to decide on the allocation of risk between themselves.

In a sale of assets, the question of risk allocation must be addressed from the moment of agreement until completion. Typically, the seller underwrites the risk of loss of assets by mutually agreed insurance until completion. Naturally, post-completion risks rest with the buyer, unless agreed otherwise in the contract.

In an acquisition of shares, the seller often warrants that no change of an adverse or material nature has affected the business since the signing of the agreement and, if this warranty is breached, the buyer can rescind.

29.9 Required Governmental Approvals

Foreign ownership is restricted in the acquisition of certain assets and investments in Singapore. In relation to the acquisition of shares in companies operating in the financial, securities or media industries, specific laws regulate the obtaining of prior approval from governmental authorities.

Such approval may be required when there are changes in company shareholding, issued share capital levels or variations in voting shares, or when control of the company shifts.

Restrictions are also imposed on foreign persons or companies wanting to acquire residential property: they must obtain the prior approval of the Controller of Residential Property or seek an exemption from the Minister of Law.

29.10 Anti-trust and Competition Laws

Anti-competition Law was introduced in Singapore with the recently enacted Competition Act 2004. The Act applies to all commercial and economic activities by the private sector in all areas except where expressly excluded, and has retrospective effect when the relevant provisions of the Act come into force (i.e. it will apply to all existing agreements and conduct).

There are three core prohibitions under this Act, namely:

(1) Agreements (including both legally enforceable and non enforceable agreements and 'gentlemen's agreements'), decisions and concerted practices (such as where there is informal cooperation without any formal agreement or decision) which have as their object or effect the prevention, restriction or distortion of competition.

(2) The abuse of a market player's dominant position in a manner which is anti-competitive and which works against longer term economic efficiencies.

(3) Mergers and acquisitions which result or which will result in a substantial lessening of competition.

The first and second prohibitions will come into effect on 1 January 2006. Significantly, both prohibitions do not apply with regard to (a) undertakings entrusted with the operation of services of a general economic interest or having the character of a revenue producing monopoly in so far as the prohibition in question would obstruct the performance, in law or in fact, of the particular tasks assigned to that undertaking; and (b) goods and services sectors regulated by other sector specific competition law or code of practice (i.e. the telecommunications; media; electricity and gas; and armed security services sectors).

Certain activities are also excluded from the operation of both these two prohibitions, and they are (i) the supply of ordinary letter and postcard services; (ii) the supply of piped potable water; (iii) the supply of wastewater management services; (iv) the supply of scheduled bus services; (v) the supply of rail services; (vi) cargo terminal operations; and (vii) clearing house activities.

In addition, vertical agreements (arrangements between businesses at different levels of the production chain) are excluded from the operation of the first prohibition. However, there is a claw back provision to this exclusion and the Minister may order certain vertical agreements to be subject to the first prohibition.

The third prohibition relating to mergers and acquisitions will come into effect in 2007. It must be noted that this prohibition does not apply to any merger or acquisition approved under any written law, or under any code of practice issued under any written law relating to competition (e.g. the Code of Practice for Competition in the Provision of Telecommunication Services, which applies to the telecommunications sector), or to any of the activities (i) to (vii) stated above.

29.11 Required Offer Procedures

Offer procedures do not apply to acquisition of shares in private companies. However, for unlisted public companies, specific provisions of the Companies Act and the Singapore Code on Takeovers and Mergers require the buyer of shares to make a compulsory takeover bid once his or her shareholding exceeds a certain 'trigger' limit.

29.12 Continuation of Government Licences

Government permission, in the form of a licence, is required before businesses in certain industries can be carried on. The granting of such licences is controlled by regulations which are promulgated through legislation, and which create offences for non-compliance.

The industries affected are lucrative or potentially politically sensitive ones (e.g. insurance, banking and broadcasting).

Unconditional licences are rare; instead, numerous conditions are typically attached. The buyer should ensure that the licence is not revoked and that it continues despite changes to the ownership of the business. If assets are acquired as opposed to shares, the non-transferability of licences needs to be addressed.

29.13 Requirements for Transferring Shares

The right of existing shareholders to pre-empt the transfer of shares to the buyer is a restriction commonly found in a company's articles of association. Similar restrictions may also be found in a shareholders' agreement. Such restrictions must be addressed by the buyer before embarking on the acquisition proper.

Provided there is nothing to the contrary either in the articles or in any shareholders' agreement, the transfer may take place using a stamped share transfer form which is registered upon approval by the company's board of directors. Once the transfer is complete, the buyer's name is inserted on the company's register of members.

29.14 Requirements for Transferring Land and Property Leases

Singapore's land registration system is based upon the Torrens system in Australia. As such, title once registered is indefeasible. Any interest affecting the title which is registrable must be registered or risk being relegated to lesser priority, unless it has been earlier caveated. Specific encumbrances on the land such as mortgages and charges, after execution on prescribed forms and due stamping, must be lodged with the Singapore Land Authority, as must transactions such as transfers of real property.

Legislation regulating these areas should be observed; for example, non-compliance with stamping requirements may lead to the documents being inadmissible in a Singapore court.

29.15 Requirements for Transferring Intellectual Property

Intellectual property in the form of copyrights, trade marks, patents, registered designs and layout-designs of integrated circuits can be assigned.

In Singapore, the Intellectual Property Office of Singapore regulates the registrability of intellectual property. Any assignment or transfer of registered intellectual property must be notified to the Intellectual Property Office of Singapore.

There is also accompanying legislation which may impose other requirements for transferring intellectual property, which should be reviewed.

29.16 Requirements for Transferring Business Contracts, Licences and Leases

As with any contract, the general principles of contract law operate so that the benefits and burdens of a business contract can only be assigned or transferred according to its terms. It often happens that an assignor remains beset with the burdens of the contract despite having assigned the contract to the assignee because the other party to the contract has not yet released the assignor from those burdens. In order to avoid this situation, a specific release should be sought.

In practice, it is recommended that a formal novation of the contract be entered into rather than a mere assignment.

The same would apply to licences and leases.

29.17 Requirements for Transferring Other Assets

Generally, chattels can be transferred by delivery *simpliciter*. This is also provided for in specific legislation such as the Sales of Goods Act, a UK Act which has been re-enacted in Singapore.

An encumbrance on the title of such assets follows the transfer unless specifically redeemed, but a *bona fide* purchaser for value without notice of that encumbrance takes the asset free of it. In addition, the common law principle that a transferor cannot transfer a better title than he or she actually has applies.

29.18 Encumbrances and Third Party Interests

In the acquisition of assets, it is pertinent to ascertain the extent to which third party interests encumber the title of the assets. These encumbrances may arise contractually (e.g. a hire purchase agreement), by circumstances in accordance with the law (e.g. a vendor's lien), or by registration in a public registry.

In cases of doubt, for example if the buyer is not a *bona fide* purchaser for value without notice and suspects that the seller has an encumbered title or if the registries cannot prove absolute title, the buyer should obtain specific warranties of good title from the seller.

29.19   Minimum Shareholder and Officer Requirements

A company must have at least one director 'ordinarily resident in Singapore' (i.e. a Singapore Citizen, a Singapore Permanent Resident, or a person who has been issued an Employment Pass/Approval-In-Principle letter or a Dependant Pass).

In a private company, the number of shareholders must number between two (if natural persons) and 50. Once the membership exceeds 50, the private company is statutorily required to convert to a public company.

29.20   Non-competition Clauses

Covenants restraining trade or competition procured by a buyer from a seller of a business are generally enforceable by courts of law provided they are reasonable in extent and nature. The doctrine of severance is sometimes applied judicially to excise any unreasonable or unconscionable terms from the whole agreement so that the rest can stand legitimately.

The test of reasonableness is dependent on the circumstances of the case, the industry in which the business operates and the relative market positions of the buyer *vis-à-vis* the seller.

Employees giving covenants for the employer's benefit are usually protected by the courts' stricter regard for such clauses in the context of employment agreements: only covenants which are clearly reasonable can be enforced. Any covenant that deprives an employee of his or her livelihood or prevents him or her from exercising his or her skills is usually construed as unreasonable.

29.21   Environmental Considerations

The Ministry of the Environment and Water Resources is responsible for the regulation of considerations relating to the environment. Stiff sanctions and penalties can be imposed on errant companies that pollute the environment, for example the confiscation by the government of vehicles involved in the act of environmental damage.

Generally, however, Singapore's environmental laws are nascent, which can be attributed to the fact that the exploitation of natural resources on the island republic is scarce. It is important, therefore, that, if a full environmental audit is not carried out, the buyer procures indemnities for any environmental damage that may have occurred prior to acquisition and for which the target company remains liable.

29.22 Employee Superannuation/Pension Plans

Many of the huge economic entities in Singapore, such as multinational corporations and government-linked companies (whether privatized or not), as well as many larger companies, have comprehensive superannuation and pension plans on behalf of their employees.

The Central Provident Fund set up by the government also brings with it a whole host of complex rules and regulations which effectively ensures that Singaporean employees receive contributions from their employers and also contribute a certain portion of their salaries towards this retirement fund.

If the acquisition is of assets, the buyer may want to bring over key employees of the target business; this would mean that previous superannuation schemes must be replaced by new ones. The same applies when the target company belongs to a group, whether the acquisition is by assets or shares. Also, appropriate adjustments to Central Provident Fund contributions must be made.

29.23 Employee Rights

Rights of employees and their relationships with their employer are regulated by the Employment Act or by contract if the Act is not applicable. There is also other legislation affecting this area of the law relating to industrial relations.

When contemplating a share acquisition of a target company, it may be prudent for the buyer to ask the seller to indemnify it against any outstanding damages claims for unfair dismissal or redundancy payments.

29.24 Compulsory Transfer of Employees

It has been provided statutorily that when there is a change of employer (i.e. if a trade, business or undertaking is transferred from one person to another), the employee's period of employment prior to the time of the transfer counts as a period of employment with the transferee, and the transfer must not break the continuity of the period of employment.

Based on the above, it seems that the buyer of business assets from a target company becomes compulsorily responsible to the extent that the continuity of the period of employment cannot be broken.

There are no statutory provisions for the compulsory transfer of employees.

29.25 Tax Deductibility of Acquisition Expenses

For a non-resident or non-taxable foreign buyer, the question of the tax deductibility of acquisition expenses must be determined according to the laws of the foreign jurisdiction.

For the Singaporean taxpayer, the Income Tax Act provides that tax deductibility only applies to expenditure wholly and exclusively incurred in the production of income.

As expenses incurred in the acquisition of shares or business assets are for the acquisition of capital or capital assets, it follows from the Act that acquisition expenses are not tax deductible.

29.26   Levies on Acquisition Agreements and Collateral Documents

Stamp duty is generally imposed on transactions (e.g. agreements and collateral documents) in relation to the acquisition of assets only. In respect of the acquisition of shares, the agreement for sale and purchase is not chargeable with stamp duty as such: instead, *ad valorem* stamp duty is imposed on the share transfer form. The rate of stamp duty chargeable is 0.2 per cent based on the higher of consideration paid and the market value of the shares.

Where the acquisition of shares is facilitated by a share-for-share exchange between the buyer company and the seller target company, Section 15 of the Stamp Duties Act provides for exemption from stamp duty in certain circumstances.

The impact of the recently introduced goods and services tax, currently at a rate of 5 per cent, must be considered, if not as a first concern, then as a secondary issue.

29.27   Financing Rules and Restrictions

Singapore has no minimum equity content regulations. Borrowings are virtually unrestricted and unlimited.

Tax paid on income usually accounts for any additional tax to be paid by the company on dividends.

Company law in Singapore prohibits the target company from providing financial assistance for the purpose of or in connection with the acquisition of shares in the target company. Any arrangements of a financial nature tending to assist such a purchase (e.g. the giving of collateral) are deemed to be financial assistance.

29.28   Exchange Controls and Repatriation of Profits

Singapore has no foreign exchange controls. However, there is a general policy to prevent the 'internationalization' of the Singapore dollar.

Taxation on repatriated profits is determined by Singapore's own tax legislation together with a well-established network of double taxation treaties.

29.29   Groups of Companies

Under the Companies Act, all locally incorporated holding companies are required to prepare consolidated accounts (i.e. year end financial statements for all of the companies in the group). However, where a holding company is at the end of its financial year itself a wholly owned subsidiary of another corporation incorporated in Singapore, consolidated accounts are not required.

29.30   Responsibility for Liabilities of an Acquired Subsidiary

The concept of limited liability is entrenched in most private companies in Singapore and elsewhere in other common law jurisdictions. Shareholders are immune from any further liabilities beyond the value of any of their unpaid shares. However, where separate guarantees, indemnities or warranties are given for the company, these remain valid against the contracting shareholder.

If the contracting shareholder is the parent corporate shareholder, the specific liabilities of the acquired subsidiary remain the parent's responsibility. Warranties and indemnities included in the sale and acquisition contract for a holding company (as opposed to a subsidiary) must be made to extend expressly to every subsidiary, whether wholly or partly owned.

29.31 Governing Law of the Contract

Choice-of-law clauses freely entered into between parties to a contract are generally enforceable by the Singapore courts, barring any exceptional circumstances (e.g. on grounds of public policy).

29.32 Dispute Resolution Options

The use of other means of resolving, disputes besides traditional courtroom litigation is constructively encouraged in Singapore, often with assistance from the courts themselves (e.g. in court dispute resolution and settlement conferences).

The Singapore International Arbitration Centre caters to a broad spectrum of international commercial arbitration needs. Selected arbitrators mutually agreed between the parties are appointed to hear disputes.

The International Arbitration Act makes provision for the conduct of conciliation proceedings as well as international commercial arbitrations based on the UNCITRAL Model Law. The Act also gives effect to the New York Convention on the Recognition and Enforcement of Foreign Arbitral Awards.

29.33 Other Issues

For target companies with key expatriate employees or with sizable foreign staff, immigration rules and policies are of relevance to the intending buyer. Generally, immigration policies in Singapore are encouraging to foreign investors and should pose no great problem to the employer.

30. SOUTH AFRICA

Project co-ordinator: Colin Allkin, Mallinicks Inc.

30.1 Introductory Comments

While South Africa is regarded by foreign investors as an emerging market, it is a hybrid of third world and first world countries which has proved to be a very attractive destination to many investors from various parts of the world. In addition to the usual investment opportunities, privatization of state-owned industries provides huge opportunities for foreign investors prepared to do their homework and this process is underway.

South Africa is the gateway to sub-Saharan Africa and provides the headquarters and infrastructure for foreign investors interested in doing business in sub-Saharan Africa. The South African currency, the Rand, has stabilized markedly against other major currencies in the recent past. The legal, banking, accounting, stock exchange and regulatory environments are distinctly First World and provide foreign investors with the confidence needed to make significant investments.

Whilst foreign loans usually introduced in support of equity investments are still subject to the exchange control regulations, these regulations are being phased out gradually and a fair rate of interest is always permitted to be repatriated in addition to the investor's capital.

The legal environment is particularly secure and encourages investment in South Africa.

30.2 Corporate Structures

Although there are nine provinces within South Africa, the Companies Act No. 61 of 1973, as amended, is applicable to all companies (both public and private) registered in South Africa. Most investment in South Africa is introduced by the foreign investor incorporating a South African company as opposed to registering a branch of its own company there, although the latter method is also permitted. The tax advantages for this latter course no longer exist.

If the foreign company wishes to acquire control of a company listed on the stock exchange, then it should be aware that acquisition of 35 per cent of the shares in that company, in terms of the takeover regulations in force, obliges it to extend the same offer to all the minority shareholders of the company.

The stock exchange has its own rules and regulations governing the conduct of those companies listed on it. Significant numbers of listed South African companies have been the subject of takeovers by foreign investors in recent years. Most recently

© World Law Group
International Business Acquisitions, M. Whalley, F.-J. Semler (eds.), Kluwer Law International, London, 2007; ISBN 9789041124838.

Barclays Bank plc acquired a majority stake in ABSA Bank. The stock exchange has a number of unique categories to enable companies at their start up stage to raise capital by listing their shares.

Many investments by foreigners are undertaken by way of joint ventures with South African partners, which can be structured to suit the participants' tax profiles.

There are other vehicles available through which foreign investors may invest, but these, such as close corporations (a simplified type of corporation) and investment trusts, are usually inappropriate for foreign investors.

30.3   Letters of Intent and Heads of Agreement

Letters of intent and heads of agreement are usually the prior documents to final agreements. They have been incorporated into practice through the influence of foreign jurisdictions over the last decade. Their colloquial interpretation is that letters of intent mean 'we are going out (dating)', heads of agreement mean 'we are engaged', and the final agreement means 'we are married'. There may, however, be clauses contained in letters of intent or heads of agreement, such as secrecy and restraint clauses, which are binding upon the parties notwithstanding the fact that no final and definitive agreement is ever concluded and the breach of those clauses may give rise to litigation.

30.4   Taxes Affecting the Structure and Calculation of the Price

The following taxes should be taken into account when buying a South African business (rates are given as at January 2006):

- Company tax (normal tax), imposed on taxable income (29 per cent in respect of years of assessment commencing on or after 1 April 2005);

- Small business corporations (a specifically defined concept) (10 per cent on amounts from ZAR 35,001 to ZAR 250,000);

- Trusts (excluding special trusts) (40 per cent);

- Secondary tax on companies (STC), triggered by dividend declaration, and imposed on companies declaring dividends (12.5 per cent);

- Royalty withholding tax (RWT), a final tax imposed on royalties derived by non-residents (12 per cent);

- Branch profits tax, imposed on the taxable income of a branch (34 per cent in respect of years of assessment commencing on or after 1 April 2005);

- Value-Added Tax (VAT), imposed on a supplier of goods and services (14 per cent), a registered vendor incurring input VAT may claim a credit;

- Personal income tax on taxable income of individuals and special trusts (maximum progressive rate: 40 per cent on taxable income of ZAR 300,001 or above);

- Stamp duty, imposed on the transfer of marketable securities (0.25 per cent); and

- Transfer duties (see section 26).

South Africa applies a residence based system of taxation, having changed from a source-based system for years of assessment commencing on or after 1 January 2001. Consequently, residents are taxed on their worldwide income, subject to certain exclusions. Foreign taxes on that income are generally allowed as a credit against South African tax payable. Non-residents are subject to normal tax on receipts and accruals derived or deemed to be derived from a South African source.

Capital Gains Tax has been introduced for assets disposed of on or after 1 October 2001. A portion of a person's taxable capital gain for a year of assessment is included in his taxable income and is subject to normal tax resulting in the following effective tax rates:

- Individuals/Special trusts–10 per cent;

- Companies–14.5 per cent;

- Small business corporations–5 per cent to 14.5 per cent;

- Trusts–20 per cent.

A non-resident may either purchase the target company's share capital or the business directly from the target company.

30.5 Extent of Seller's Warranties and Indemnities

The extent of the seller's warranties and indemnities are a matter for determination between the negotiating parties. These warranties are generally much more extensive when a private company, rather than a public listed company, is being acquired. In the latter instance the seller may only be prepared to offer the buyer an opportunity to undertake extensive due diligence with limited warranties relating to the extent of liabilities only.

Where the buyer is not satisfied with the financial position of the target company or the financial strength of the seller giving the warranties, the target company's business can be acquired rather than its shares.

30.6 Liability for Pre-contractual Representations

A party who has been induced to enter into a contract by misrepresentation is entitled to rescind the contract provided the misrepresentation was material and was intended to induce the party to enter into it. If the misrepresentation was fraudulent or negligent, the aggrieved party may also be entitled to damages.

Acquisition agreements typically contain a provision stating that no party is bound by any representation or warranty not recorded in writing in the agreement.

30.7   Liability for Pre-acquisition Trading and Contracts

An acquisition agreement may have a retrospective effective date in terms of which the buyer may bear the loss or be entitled to the profits of the business with effect from the retrospective effective date.

After completion of the transaction, the seller remains liable in respect of the contracts to which it was a party, unless the acquisition agreement contains a provision in terms of which the buyer agrees to step into the seller's shoes under the contracts and release the seller from all further liability under them (i.e. there is a novation of the contracts). This can only take place if the other party to any contract with the seller agrees to release the seller from the contract provisions and to enter into a contract directly with the buyer. Alternatively, instead of contracts being novated, they may be assigned and the buyer may undertake to the seller to perform all the seller's obligations under the contract and to indemnify the seller accordingly. In most cases an assignment also requires the consent of the other party to the contract. The terms, and nature, of the contract should be studied to determine whether an assignment is permissible.

In the case of a business acquisition, provided the advertising provisions of the Insolvency Act are carefully followed, the buyer can be put in the position where the new company it forms to acquire the business bears no responsibility for the debts of the target company from which the business has been acquired.

30.8   Pre-completion Risks

As a general rule, the risk in property passes to the buyer as soon as a sale agreement is concluded, regardless of whether ownership has yet passed to the buyer or even whether the buyer has taken delivery.

The parties may by agreement vary the incidence of the risk and, in a business acquisition agreement, it is common to have a provision stating that the risk and profit in the business will pass to the buyer against completion of the transaction. The seller therefore retains the risk between the date of signature of the agreement and the date of completion and must maintain insurance of the assets until completion of the transaction.

A share acquisition agreement usually also provides that the risk in and benefit to the shares passes on completion of the transaction. The agreement also typically contains a provision warranting the state of the business as appears from a set of warranted accounts. If there is a material deviation as at closing, the buyer has the right to claim against the seller, rescind the agreement or adjust the purchase price in accordance with a formula determined by reference to the warranted accounts.

30.9   Required Governmental Approvals

A non-resident party does not require prior approval of the Exchange Control Department of the South African Reserve Bank for the acquisition of shares in a South African company. However, the share certificates for the acquired shares must be endorsed 'non-resident' by a commercial bank (who acts as a registered agent of the South African Reserve Bank or 'authorized dealer'). The agent of the South African Reserve

Bank will not endorse the share certificates 'non-resident' before they have been presented with documentary proof that the purchase price for the shares has been paid with imported funds.

If a non-resident takes cession of shareholders' loan accounts in addition to the shares acquired, the Reserve Bank's prior approval must be obtained. Such prior approval must be obtained before a South African company can accept a loan from a non-resident and before payment is made.

Any new loan agreement made by a non-resident to a resident will also require exchange control approval. If a non-resident seeks South African funding for an acquisition, it will have to match the amount of local borrowings with foreign capital. Agreements for the payment of royalties, management and administration fees and other regular payments also require exchange control approval.

A foreign company must register as an external company in South Africa once it has established a place of business or acquired immovable property in South Africa.

30.10   Anti-trust Competition Laws

In the competition law domain, the Competition Act of 1998 is the governing statute. The Act recognizes that the South African economy is characterized by unusually high levels of product market concentration and applies to all economic activity within, or having an effect within, the Republic of South Africa.

The Act prohibits anti-competitive practices and regulates mergers and acquisitions with respect to their likely impact on competition. It prohibits any agreement between competitors and any agreement between a supplier and a customer if such agreement is likely to have the effect of substantially preventing or lessening competition in the market, unless a party to the agreement can prove that any technological, efficiency or other competitive gain resulting from it outweighs that effect. The Act also prohibits outright price fixing, collusive tendering, market division and minimum resale price maintenance. In the case of dominant firms, which are defined as having at least 45 per cent of a market or having market power, it prohibits abuse of their dominant position.

In the context of an acquisition, the most important aspect is merger control. The Competition Commission, and independent body, must be notified within certain time periods, of any acquisition of control by one person over another, whether by means of an amalgamation, acquisition of shareholding, interest, assets or otherwise, where the combined annual South African turnover or South African assets of the merging entities are valued at or above certain thresholds. The Commission must consider the proposed merger before it either approves or prohibits it. The Commission must initially determine whether the merger is likely to substantially prevent or lessen competition by assessing various factors. If it is likely to substantially prevent or lessen competition, then the Commission must determine whether the merger can be justified on the basis that it is likely to result in a technological, efficiency or other pro-competitive gain which will be greater than, and offset, the prevention or lessening of competition that may result or is likely to result from the merger. Thereafter the Commission must consider whether the merger can be justified on substantial public interest grounds. This final enquiry entitles the Commissioner to prohibit a merger which would otherwise not be considered anti-competitive.

A proper and careful analysis of the relevant market(s) affected by the acquisition is essential if substantial penalties for non-compliance with the Act are to be avoided.

30.11   Required Offer Procedures

Where the target company is a public company, whether or not listed on the Johannesburg Securities Exchange or a statutory corporation, the provisions of the Securities Regulation Code of the Companies Act apply. The Code also applies where the target company is a private company with more than ten shareholders and where the shareholders' interests valued at the offer price and the shareholders' loan capital exceeds ZAR 5 million. It is important to note that if 35 per cent of the issued shares in a listed company are acquired, the offeror is required to extend the same offer to all other shareholders.

The Code operates principally to ensure fair and equal treatment of all holders of relevant shares in relation to the transaction and provides an orderly framework within which the transaction is to be conducted.

If the target is a listed company or a subsidiary of a listed company or its assets, the provisions of Section 9 of the Johannesburg Securities Exchange Listings Requirements must be complied with. Section 9 categorizes transactions by a listed company and stipulates the requirements for announcements, circulars and shareholder approval for each category of transaction. Where the consideration to be paid in terms of the transaction divided by the aggregate market value of all of the equity securities of the listed company is 30 per cent or more, the target company's shareholders must approve the transaction in general meeting.

30.12   Continuation of Government Licences

Certain businesses require licences to operate, for example banking, insurance, asset management, life assurance, pension and provident fund administration, gaming and telecommunication businesses. In addition to these licences, which are regulated at a national level by Statutes of Parliament, licences may also be required under provincial or local authority legislation. Licences should be reviewed to determine the conditions attaching to them and whether they are revocable in the event of a change of majority shareholding in the licence holder or are deemed to be assigned in other circumstances, which may occur when a business or share acquisition takes place.

Licences are generally not transferable and the buyer must apply for a licence in its own name. It is important to note that in South Africa regard is also had to affirmative action criteria in the granting of licences to applicants (e.g. the grant of gaming and telecommunications licences), and in those cases foreign investors require the right partners.

30.13   Requirements for Transferring Shares

There may be restrictions on the transfer of shares contained in a private company's articles of association or in a shareholders agreement, if there is one. These documents should be reviewed prior to conclusion of the transaction in order to ensure that there are no restrictions which preclude the transfer of shares from taking place or, if there are any such restrictions and in particular pre-emptive provisions, that these are removed or waived.

Shares are transferable by a written share transfer form in accordance with the formalities prescribed in the company's articles of association and the Companies Act provisions. The share transfer form must be stamped with the stamp duty payable on the transfer of shares (0.25 per cent of the consideration).

Subject to compliance with any formalities prescribed by the company's articles and the Companies Act provisions, the transfer of shares is perfected by inserting the buyer's name in the company's register of shareholders.

The foregoing remarks apply to shares in private companies. The articles of association of public companies do not restrict the transferability of shares, which is usually regulated by the controlling shareholders in a pooling agreement.

30.14   Requirements for Transferring Land and Property Leases

South Africa has a well developed system for the registration of title to land including interests held under lease for periods in excess of ten years. All land registrations and mortgages thereon are a matter of public record. The land registration system is managed and administered by the state and transfer of rights to immovable property is effected by specialist conveyancers to be found within the attorney profession. The transfer of title to land is effected by conveyancers on compliance with legislative requirements in relation to the transfer of land and subject to the payment of transfer duty or value added tax, depending on the tax status of the seller and the nature of the property, i.e. residential or commercial. (See section **26**).

30.15   Requirements for Transferring Intellectual Property

Title to all forms of intellectual property can be transferred by assignment.

In the cases of patents, design registrations, trade mark registrations and copyrights, an assignment must be reduced to writing and signed by the assignor. In the cases of patents, design registrations and trade mark registrations, an assignment must be recorded on the relevant register in order for the assignee to be able to enforce the relevant rights against third parties.

It is possible to assign the copyright in a future work.

30.16   Requirements for Transferring Business Contracts, Licences and Leases

A business contract is only transferable or assignable in accordance with its terms. It is possible to assign both the benefits and the obligations of a business contract, usually with the specific consent of the other party to the contract.

The transfer (or novation) of a contract can also only take place with the specific consent of the other party to the contract. A novation releases the seller from the contract and places the buyer in the seller's place under the contract.

The same rules apply to licences and business leases. A business acquisition agreement typically contains a provision making the agreement subject to all third parties to contracts entered into with the seller consenting to the assignment of these contracts to the buyer or, alternatively, conditional upon these third parties consenting to the release of the seller from the contracts and identical contracts being entered into with the buyer.

A business acquisition agreement may contain a provision ceding the debtors of the business to the buyer. No other formalities are required in order to give effect to this cession. Avoiding the transfer of debtors with the business does, however, require compliance with certain formalities under the Insolvency Act.

30.17 Requirements for Transferring Other Assets

Assets which are the subject of hire purchase agreements, instalment sale agreements or financial leases can only be transferred with the permission of the financier thereof (i.e. the bank or finance house which financed the transaction).

In the absence of a contract to the contrary, ownership of unencumbered assets passes on delivery, whilst risk passes on sale. However, where physical assets such as stock in trade are sold, these rules may be overturned unless the advertising provisions of the Insolvency Act are carefully followed.

30.18 Encumbrances and Third Party Interests

Title to land can specifically be mortgaged and generally no preferential right is afforded to any creditor in the absence of such mortgage (exceptions are the rights of local authorities in respect of the recovery of taxes and some specific liens at common law afforded to e.g. a building contractor in respect of improvements to the land). Title cannot pass without dealing with any mortgages which may be registered over the property, and payment of outstanding local authority taxes and confirmation by the Revenue Services that the seller's tax affairs are in order.

Movable assets may be pledged, as can book debts. In addition, special notarial bonds may be registered over particular movable assets. The security afforded by registration of mortgages over immovable property on the one hand, and notarial bonds over movable assets on the other, can be very different and care must be taken in distinguishing the nature and extent of such security.

The interests of third parties in the land by way of lease for a duration greater than ten years or other limited rights and interests (e.g. rights of way, life rights of occupation and many others) can be recorded by way of registration of such limited rights against title to the land.

30.19 Minimum Shareholder and Officer Requirements

A private company is required to have one director and a public officer to whom the company's office and other regulatory authorities may send notices requiring documents to be filed. A private company requires at least one shareholder and not more than 50. A public company must have at least two directors and not less than seven shareholders and, if the public company is listed on the stock exchange, then there are minimum shareholder requirements which depend upon the area of activity.

30.20 Non-competition Clauses

Contracts in restraint of trade are generally enforceable in South African law. However, there are circumstances where they are held to be unenforceable. The criterion in assessing the enforceability or otherwise of restraint of trade clauses is that of reasonableness. Certain factors are taken into consideration in determining reasonableness.

The basic test is that a restraint is held to be unreasonable if it prevents one party, after the termination of contractual relations, from practising freely in the commercial and professional world without a protectable interest on behalf of the restrainor being served thereby. One cannot therefore contract out of competition. Although there is no crystallized category of protectable interests, trade secrets and trade connections have been held to be protectable interests.

Further factors impacting on reasonableness are geographical area of restraint and the period of restraint. To the extent that restraints are held to be unreasonable on these bases, the court has a discretion to modify such restraints to render them reasonable. In addition, a clause in a restraint of trade which stipulates that the restraint is reasonable does not make it so and the court determines reasonableness at its discretion.

It is, however, important to realize that the reasonableness or otherwise of restraints depends to a large extent on the nature of the industry/business involved. Accordingly each case must be taken on its own merits.

30.21 Environmental Considerations

Environment matters are primarily regulated by the National Environmental Management Act. The Act co-ordinates and harmonizes the policies, plans, programmes and decisions of the various national departments entrusted with powers and duties directed at the achievement, promotion and protection of a sustainable environment. In terms of the Act, substantial penalties can be imposed on businesses which damage the environment and a buyer of a business or of a property can inherit responsibility for rectifying environmental damage. It has become compulsory for a variety of categories of development to be accompanied by an Environmental Impact Assessment Study before development can proceed. In the areas of mining, manufacturing and chemical industries, appropriate environmental due diligence investigations are vital. Accordingly, before acquiring a significant industrial or commercial site, environmental due diligence exercises are frequently undertaken.

30.22 Employee Superannuation/Pension Plans

Employee retirement schemes in South Africa can be broadly categorized into defined benefit and defined contribution schemes. The buyer should obtain full details of the target company's pension fund. This can be obtained from the seller (preferable) or the Registrar of Pension Funds. The fund's rules should be obtained, as well as the last actuarial valuation report and the last set of financial accounts.

Where the seller's fund is in deficit, or where it is underfunded (particularly defined benefit funds), the buyer must ensure that the acquisition agreement and the purchase price take full cognisance of the deficit.

The buyer should also determine whether there are any unfunded liabilities in the pension fund of the target company and whether there are enhanced pension benefits that have, or shall, accrue at some future time. The seller may have a large group of employees who are not on any pension or provident fund and this could be a potential future liability for the buyer.

If the fund is a defined benefit fund, a company may have an ongoing obligation to make contributions to the fund to ensure that it will have sufficient assets available to meet its expected obligations for the benefit of retiring employees. If the fund is underfunded, this should be taken into account in the purchase price.

Where the acquisition is of the target company's assets and the employees are to be transferred with the business, arrangements may have to be made to transfer the provident pension fund or retirement scheme. The fund's rules should be checked to see whether there is a mechanism for transfer and, if so, the necessary arrangements for transfer must be made in accordance with those rules and the applicable legislation.

Where the funds' rules do provide for transfer, it should be ascertained whether the timing of the transfer (which is subject to the approval of the Board of Trustees of the Pension Fund as well as the Registrar of Pension Schemes) has any financial implications for the buyer (the value of the fund may vary between the time of transfer and the date of approval).

30.23 Employee Rights

Of paramount importance in any employer–employee relationship is the Labour Relations Act (LRA) and, more specifically, the Code of Good Practice, containing guidelines on fair labour practice in the workplace. This Act supersedes any other Act in South Africa other than the Constitution where these conflict with fair labour relations.

Any contract of employment entered into merely provides a structure for the formal relationship between the parties and sets out the practical issues as the rights and obligations of employers and employees are guaranteed by legislation. It is possible to contract out of the LRA and the Basic Conditions of Employment Act by forming collective agreements, which are agreements between unions and employers/employer organizations. One can only contract out of these Acts to the extent that the benefits provided for in the collective agreements are better than those provided for in the Acts.

Although the LRA represents a codification of existing common law, the Labour Court still has persuasive power in the awards that it makes.

The LRA deals with all issues relating to fair labour practice including collective bargaining, dismissals based on operational requirements and the severance packages to be paid in such a case, and how and when it is possible to dismiss an employee. Any disputes relating to unfairness in the workplace, including dismissals, are referred to the Council for Conciliation, Mediation and Arbitration (CCMA), the first step of which referral involves an attempt to conciliate the relationship between the parties. Thereafter matters are either referred to arbitration or to the Labour Court.

Two new acts have been added to the spread of legislation affecting employment in South Africa. These are the Employment Equities Act and the Skills Development Act.

The purpose of the Employment Equity Act is twofold. Firstly, it is to achieve equity in the workplace by promoting equal opportunity and fair treatment by the elimination of unfair discrimination; and secondly, to provide for the compulsory implementation of affirmative action measures in the workplace. Affirmative action does not institute compulsory quota systems as was the case in the USA; the Act prefers to place the emphasis on removal of barriers to employment for people from designated groups. These designated groups are Blacks, Indians, Coloureds, women, and people with disabilities. Designated employers include all companies that employ 50 or more employees, organs of state and municipalities. Monitoring of these Acts is internal—employees can report non-compliance and any defaulting companies will attract compliance orders which lead ultimately to payment of fines.

As far as the Skills Development Act is concerned, its focus is to address skills shortages in South Africa by introducing in-house training with an emphasis on sectorally relevant training and grading. Compulsory levies equal to 1 per cent of the payroll of companies will be enforced. The Act affects all companies and organs of State.

30.24 Compulsory Transfer of Employees

The LRA provides for automatic transfer of employment contracts in the case of transfers of businesses, if such businesses are transferred as a going concern. It also provides for automatic transfer of employment contracts in instances where the company or business is insolvent or is wound up. In the first case (transfer of business) the employment contract is transferred with all its benefits including the continuity of service. In an insolvent situation, it is merely the contract of employment which is transferred (*viz.* the right to continued employment) without necessarily transferring all the benefits.

Both the LRA and the Basic Conditions of Employment Act recognize the continuity of service in such transfers.

30.25 Tax Deductibility of Acquisition Expenses

The target's ancestry and financial history could affect the choice between shares or business acquisition. If questionable, the buyer will be more inclined to acquire the assets. All things being equal, the acquisition of assets (the business of the target) is typically preferable (for the purchaser) to the acquisition of the target company (shares in the target). Tax allowances are available on certain assets, but may trigger recoupments for the seller. This choice is thus often set in an adversarial context and may affect pricing.

A significant difference in the income tax treatment of each alternative is the deductibility of finance costs. South African tax law requires that expenses must be incurred in the production of 'income' to be deductible. 'Income' is defined to exclude dividends. Therefore, interest incurred in the financing of the acquisition of the target itself (shares in the target) is not deductible in the hands of the buyer if the acquisition will only produce dividend income. Such expenses, however, are deductible if the business is acquired, since business income generally qualifies as 'income' for normal tax purposes.

Legal fees and other professional costs incurred in the acquisition of a business (or a company) are normally regarded as a capital expense, and are thus not deductible.

30.26 Levies on Acquisition Agreements and Collateral Documents

Transfer duties are imposed on a sliding scale dependent on the value of the property acquired where the acquisition is by a natural person and at a flat rate of 10 per cent in the case of acquisitions by corporate entities. Transfer duty may be recoverable in certain instances where the buyer is registered for VAT purposes (see **section 4**) and is not applicable where VAT forms a portion of the purchase price i.e. when the seller is disposing of his property as a vatable supply. Leases are subject to stamp duty on a sliding scale dependent on the lease duration and the full total rent payable. Stamp duty is charged on mortgages at the rate of 0.2 per cent.

30.27 Financing Rules and Restrictions

The presence of distributable reserves in the target serves as a disincentive to purchase its shares, or leads to a depreciation of the purchase price. Upon distribution, such reserves are subject to STC payable on the net dividend.

The purchase price for shares is not an income tax deductible expense in the hands of the buyer (unless the buyer is a dealer in shares) and will form part of the base cost of such assets for capital gains tax ('CGT') purposes. However, the purchase price paid for the target company's assets could be deducted over time for tax purposes insofar as it is allocated to depreciable assets. Most notably, wear and tear allowances can be claimed on the acquisition costs of manufacturing equipment and other trade assets. Land, trade marks and goodwill are not depreciable for income tax purposes. Due to abuse in the past, tax allowances on the acquisition costs of intellectual property is severely curtailed.

If the target company is registered for VAT purposes, the transfer costs of business assets (including land) may be less than the transfer cost of shares since the transaction may be zero-rated for VAT purposes. For zero-rating to apply, both parties need to be registered for VAT and the assets sold must be capable of independent operation.

The vehicle used for the purchase is also relevant for the transaction. The buyer may make the purchase:

- directly;

- through a domestic subsidiary;

- through a partnership with a domestic partner; or

- through a domestically authorized trust.

Direct investment by a non-resident, whether with a local partner will typically constitute a permanent establishment for the non-resident in South Africa. If it is a company, it must register as an external company if it has a place of business in South Africa. Taxable income that can be attributed to the permanent establishment is taxed in South Africa, but related expenses are deductible. A degree of isolation from South African income tax liability can be achieved by the use of a domestic subsidiary.

If domestic finance is used, the finance costs relating to the purchase of shares are typically income tax deductible. Finance costs related to the purchase price of business assets are deductible.

The non-resident buyer is not free to structure his or her domestic investment vehicle at any debt–equity ratio. The tax authorities may intervene if the amount of foreign debt to equity is considered excessive. As a general guideline, a debt–equity ratio not exceeding 3:1 is acceptable.

The South African tax authorities also apply transfer pricing provisions based on New Zealand precedents and OECD guidelines.

30.28 Exchange Controls and Repatriation of Profits

In terms of South Africa's Exchange Control Regulations, no South African company or resident may acquire foreign assets or incur foreign liabilities without exchange control approval. The controls are administered by the South African Reserve Bank through its authorized agents who are dealers in foreign exchange (commercial and merchant bankers).

Exchange control restrictions in South Africa are being relaxed steadily, but there are certain restrictions which still apply and which have relevance to a share or business acquisition.

If shareholders' loan accounts are acquired together with shares as part of a share acquisition transaction, exchange control approval is required for the acquisition of the shareholders' loan accounts. No South African company may accept loans from offshore without approval of the South African Reserve Bank.

South African companies, the shares of which are owned as to 75 per cent or more, directly or indirectly, by non-residents, have a restricted ability to borrow locally in South Africa without the approval of the South African Reserve Bank. Local borrowings by non-resident controlled companies are restricted to ensure adequate capitalization from abroad and to prevent excessive gearing. Wholly foreign-owned companies may borrow up to 100 per cent of their total shareholders' funds/ investment as specified below.

To encourage local participation in enterprises, the basic 100 per cent is increased depending upon the percentage of local shareholding. The equivalent of the percentage of shareholder's funds that may be borrowed locally is calculated in terms of the following formula:

100 per cent + [(South African participation/non-resident participation) × 100 per cent]

The Exchange Control Regulations also require that the new share certificates issued to a foreign buyer be endorsed as 'non-resident'. This endorsement may be effected by any authorized dealer in foreign exchange which is typically a commercial bank. The buyer cannot be entered in the company's share register as the buyer of the shares until this endorsement has been effected.

Dividends paid to non-resident shareholders are not generally restricted by exchange control. Where the company has local borrowings, the remittance of dividends is only permitted where it can be shown that the remittance will not result in the company becoming over-borrowed locally in terms of the local borrowings formula above. Under company law provisions, any payment made to any shareholder is subject to liquidity and solvency criteria.

30.29 Groups of Companies

A company incorporated under the Companies Act is required to prepare consolidated annual financial statements of the company and its subsidiaries consisting of a consolidated balance sheet, consolidated income statement and consolidated cash flow statement of the company and its subsidiaries. The annual financial statements must be prepared as consolidated accounts unless the directors of the company are of the opinion that the required information about the state of affairs, business and profit or loss of the company and its subsidiaries would be presented more effectively and meaningfully by preparing group annual financial statements consisting of:

- More than one set of consolidated annual financial statements, that is to say one set dealing with the company and one group of subsidiaries, and one or more sets dealing with other groups of subsidiaries; or

- Separate annual financial statements dealing with each of the subsidiaries; or

- Statements annexed to the company's own financial statements expanding the information therein contained about the subsidiaries, or any combination of these forms.

The financial year end of a holding company and of its subsidiaries must coincide. The legislation, however, contemplates that there may be an exception where the subsidiaries' financial year does not end with that of the holding company in the case where the subsidiary is incorporated outside South Africa, and by the relevant foreign law its financial year must end on a particular date which differs from that on which the holding company's financial year ends.

30.30 Responsibility for Liabilities of an Acquired Subsidiary

There is no liability on the part of a holding company or its directors or shareholders for a subsidiary company's debts. However, the provisions of Section 424 of the Companies Act should be borne in mind at all times, since that section allows the court to hold anybody responsible for a company's debts if that person was engaged in the management of the company and its affairs were conducted 'recklessly or with intent to defraud'. The courts, in the rare cases which come before it, are enforcing this section strictly and are increasingly requiring company directors to discharge their obligations in a responsible way.

30.31 Governing Law of the Contract

Where contracts are concluded in South Africa, a number of universal connecting factors, for example, domicile, habitual residence, nationality, place and where the property is situated (situs), place where the court is sitting, place where the transaction takes place, place of performance, place where the delict was committed, intention of the parties, law of the jurisdiction which has the 'closest and most real connection' with the case, determines which law will apply to the contract. If one of these connecting factors is linked to South Africa, the contract will be interpreted, in the absence of provisions to the contrary in the contract, in accordance with South African law. Accordingly, if it is intended to have the law of another country govern such a contract, the contract should say so, but determining the law which governs the contract does not necessarily determine which court will have jurisdiction to hear any dispute and this should be regulated in the agreement. There are instances where foreign investors prefer to have what they perceive to be a neutral court or other forum determining their dispute. The South African courts are, however, known for their accessibility and reliability.

30.32 Dispute Resolution Options

Recourse to alternative dispute resolution mechanisms, rather than the formal procedure in the courts, is becoming increasingly important in South Africa. Parties wishing to so resolve their disputes may do so through various bodies by agreement. This usually shortens proceedings considerably and sometimes a non-adversarial approach is adopted.

In labour matters, unfair dismissals are always referred first to conciliation and thereafter, possibly to arbitration, or to trial at the Labour Court. For this a permanent body, the Council for Conciliation, Mediation and Arbitration, has been established. Only certain disputes are referred to the Labour Court.

Bodies such as the Arbitration Foundation of South Africa provide a managed arbitration in the sense of providing a set of rules and a list of arbitrators and managing other aspects of the arbitration. Several other bodies provide mediators and mediation services in South Africa. South Africa has an Arbitration Act, the rules of which are usually followed if parties agree to an arbitration in terms of the Act.

Similarly to other countries, South Africa is a signatory to several treaties which provide for enforcement of civil judgments in foreign jurisdictions and vice versa.

30.33   Other Issues

The Companies Act is set to undergo a complete overhaul during 2006 and 2007. In a policy document issued by the Department of Trade and Industry it was indicated that, *inter alia*, the following changes can be expected: the establishment of a single form of corporate entity for businesses of all sizes; the development of new mechanisms to protect creditors and other stakeholders in companies, probably through the intro-duction of a solvency and liquidity based test for distributions to shareholders; and a possible re-drafting of section 38 which prohibits companies providing financial assis-tance for the purchase of their shares to allow a relaxation of the rules for BEE transac-tions. There have also been developments in Securities regulation in South Africa. The Security Services Act came into effect at the beginning of February 2005. This Act consolidates and amends the laws relating to the regulation and control of exchanges and securities trading, the regulation and control of central securities depositories and the custody and administration of securities, and the prohibition of insider trading. The Act also provides for the licensing of clearing houses and the approval of nominees. The Act has repealed the Stock Exchanges Control Act, the Financial Markets Control Act, the Custody and Administration of Securities Act and the Insider Trading Act.

Black Economic Empowerment in South Africa

Having achieved political parity in the mid-nineties, the South African government's focus has now been to address the economic disparity along racial lines which still exists in South Africa today. The process of Black Economic Empowerment ('BEE') is central to achieving this aim.

Regulatory Framework

The overarching legislation in this regard is the Broad-Based Black Economic Empowerment Act, 53 of 2003 ('the BEE Act'). This Act establishes a legislative framework for the promotion of BEE and, inter alia, allows the Minister of Trade & Industry to issue codes of good practice from time to time and to publish various sector transformation charters.

Since 2004, there have been a number of private sector initiatives, notably the various transformation charters aimed at providing a BEE framework for specific sectors within the South African economy in order to assist companies within that particular sector to self-regulate in respect of BEE compliance. The Minister of Trade & Indus-try has now issued the second phase of its Codes of Good Practice. Whilst these Codes are still in draft format and therefore not 'law' until they have been gazetted, they nevertheless provide a concrete framework for a generally applicable BEE regulatory framework.

What is BEE?

BEE can be viewed as having three separate but linked contexts. The first of these is direct empowerment; the objective being the promotion of ownership and control by black persons over the South African economy. In this regard, the key criteria are ownership and management.

The second aspect of the government's approach to BEE relates primarily to the promotion of human resource development. In this regard, the key criteria are the transfer of skills and employment equity across the workplace.

The final element of the government's approach to BEE is referred to as 'indirect empowerment'. Indirect empowerment is an evaluation of a range of criteria applying to a business, such as the level of procurement sourced from businesses which are BEE compliant as well as enterprise development through investment in and joint ventures with BEE compliant businesses.

Who are the beneficiaries of BEE?

According to the Codes, the beneficiaries are black persons. A 'black person' is defined as an African, Coloured or Indian South African citizen who:

- is a citizen of the Republic of South Africa by birth or by descent; or

- is a citizen of the Republic of South Africa by naturalization, completed prior to the coming into effect of the Constitution of the Republic of South Africa Act of 1993; or

- became a citizen of the Republic of South Africa by naturalization after the coming into effect of the Constitution of the Republic of South Africa Act, 1993, but who, but for the apartheid policy that had been in place prior to that date, would have been entitled to acquire citizenship by naturalization prior to that date.

Who must comply with BEE?

The BEE Act obliges organs of state and the public sector, through the application of the Codes of Good Practice to assess prospective applicants or contractors for BEE compliance when considering the award of state tenders or contracts and the granting of licences, etc. Private entities are encouraged, but not legally obliged, to do so, however, it is important to note that businesses dealing with organs of state and public entities who are being tested for BEE compliance, will themselves have little choice but to impose the Codes upon their own suppliers, thus triggering a domino effect which leaves very few businesses outside of the ambit of BEE regulation. In addition, all companies must have regard to various pre-existing legislation relating to empowerment which may impact their business and which may, in itself, include certain provisions relating to the attainment of empowerment objectives which are made prerequisites for the granting of licences, etc.

How is BEE measured?

A company's BEE compliance is measured by a generic BEE scorecard which takes into account the various criteria referenced above. The overall weighted average score obtained then categorizes a business in accordance with its level of contribution to BEE. Furthermore, in terms of the Codes, the only reliable evidence of any business' BEE compliance will be a Verification Certificate issued by an accredited verification agency.

BEE has gone through many stages of development over the past decade and is still in a relatively high state of flux. Companies intending to do business in South Africa will be well advised to seek the appropriate advice on this issue.

31. SPAIN

Raimon Segura—Cuatrecasas

31.1 Introductory Comments

Spain has witnessed a remarkable growth in cross-border acquisitions over the last fifteen years, encouraged by the establishment in Spain of multinational companies, by companies merging to become more competitive, by the re-structuring of family businesses and by the privatization of a significant number of companies.

Traditionally, a company purchase contract was as brief as any other purchase contract. Most of the issues are regulated in the Civil Code and need not be addressed in the contract unless the parties wish to modify the Civil Code provisions, which they are allowed to do with regard to most aspects of the contract. Nowadays, cross-border acquisitions are embodied in lengthy and detailed contracts, because of the influence of the Anglo-American forms, and the need to increase the protection of the parties (especially the buyer) regarding issues of misrepresentation, inaccurate information, time limits to bring an action when an evaluation of the company reveals that its value is considerably lower than the price paid for it, warranties, etc.

31.2 Corporate Structures

Most businesses in Spain are organized in the form of a corporation, as either a '*sociedad anónima*' (SA) or a '*sociedad de responsabilidad limitada*' (SRL or SL). For small or medium-sized companies, and when there are a limited number of partners, the most suitable vehicle is an SL, since the regulations governing SLs are more flexible than those applied to SAs and have fewer formal requirements. Listed companies must be SAs.

In the majority of cases, the buyer acquires the target company by purchasing its shares rather than its assets, unless the buyer is interested in only some of the business's assets or intends to avoid full liability for the target company's existing obligations.

31.3 Letters of Intent and Heads of Agreement

To secure cover against damages sustained when negotiating the acquisition of a company, it is advisable to sign heads of agreement at an early stage, as otherwise it is very difficult to obtain restitution from a court on the basis of pre-contractual liability.

To this end, parties are free to enter into any type of contract or agreement, whether oral or written, and to introduce clauses to regulate their legal relationship. However, the contract is enforceable only when the subject-matter of the obligation and the payment are defined precisely. Thus, in a letter of intent, only the clauses containing a precise obligation are enforceable; for example, a share purchase option, an exclusive right to negotiate during a certain period or the obligation not to disclose confidential information.

Careful drafting is necessary when the contract is not intended to create binding obligations on the parties.

31.4   Taxes Affecting the Structure and Calculation of the Price

Revenues, earnings and capital gains obtained or generated in Spain are subject to taxation, either through personal income tax (up to 43 per cent) or corporate tax (at a maximum fixed rate of 32.5 per cent for the accounting period 2007 and at a maximum fixed rate of 30 per cent for next accounting periods).

According to Spanish law, non-resident legal persons are obliged to pay taxes on income obtained in Spanish territory and on assets and rights that are located or can be exercised in Spanish territory.

The profit taxed through the Corporate Tax Act comprises net revenue (revenue obtained, less deductible expenses), capital gains and acquisitions without payment. Transactions between related parties must be at market price, which must be provable.

Losses can be carried forward for up to fifteen successive years. Besides the criteria established by tax treaties signed by Spain, Spanish tax legislation provides a partici-pation exemption system under certain circumstances and a credit system for taxes paid abroad on profits received from non-resident companies.

Natural persons or legal entities, which are non-resident in Spain but subject to taxation there, must appoint a tax representative with legal domicile in Spain and must notify the administration of this appointment.

31.5   Extent of Seller's Warranties and Indemnities

This issue requires careful negotiation and drafting, since the protection afforded by the law alone may be insufficient if the information given to the buyer is revealed to be inaccurate after closing. Thus, buyers usually seek to include further protections in the acquisition agreement and sellers often try to limit their exposure to liability. The parties are free to determine the extent of the warranties and indemnities to be given by the seller to allow the buyer to bring an action for damages caused by any breach or inaccuracy of any representation or warranty.

In general, it is advisable to include a provision stating that the seller is liable for any hidden defects or claims from a third party that reduce the value of the business or any of the items sold, or which make it impossible to carry on the business under normal conditions, specifying the items considered essential for the business.

In the absence of specific provisions, if payment is made for the transfer of a group of assets comprised in a business, the seller may only be liable for claims relating to the whole or a substantial part of those assets or the business, but not for each one of the items individually. Therefore, it is advisable to clarify whether the seller guarantees each item being transferred or only items above a certain amount or, alternatively, whether the guarantee covers only the whole of the business and not each of its parts.

In addition to establishing the extent of the seller's warranties and indemnities, it is advisable to extend the period during which the buyer is entitled to claim for any hidden defects. Otherwise, it must bring the action within six months of delivery of the item sold or, if the court applies the shorter term applicable to commercial sales, within 30 days.

31.6   Liability for Pre-Contractual Representations

Under Spanish law, any exclusion of liability for damages caused by fraud is null and void. Therefore, an exclusion of liability for any inaccuracy or misleading statement in the information provided to the buyer will not be upheld if the seller was aware of it and if the buyer would not have entered into the contract had the information provided by the seller been correct.

However, liability for damages caused by negligence can be excluded. Therefore, if the contract provides for an exclusion of liability for the information given by the seller, it can rely on the exculpatory clause and avoid liability in the event that the information provided while negotiating the contract, or the contract itself, contains an error (for example, in accounting, in the information provided regarding the company's prospects or in the description of the business).

31.7   Liability for Pre-Acquisition Trading and Contracts

In a share-purchase agreement, the buyer also acquires any liabilities and debts for which the acquired company is responsible from the date the transfer takes place, as the company's personality is separate from that of its shareholders. For the same reason, and unless the contracts provide otherwise, no novation or assignment of the contracts to which the acquired company is a party is needed. Notwithstanding that, changes of control clauses are common, for instance, in distribution and financing agreements.

The situation differs if the buyer, instead of purchasing the target company's shares, acquires all or part of its assets and liabilities, as in this case the target company retains everything that has not been transferred to the buyer. For example, contracts must be individually assigned to the buyer and it is necessary to obtain acceptance of the assignment from the other party to the contract.

It is therefore advisable to obtain the other party's consent prior to the sale or to include it as a condition precedent to payment of the full price. Concerning the liabilities that may arise for the buyer, it is important to note that, even if it is acquiring only specific assets and liabilities of the target company, it could be held liable for the target company's employee and tax debts, as heir or successor of the business activity.

31.8   Pre-Completion Risks

In a purchase agreement, the seller bears the risk of the loss of the assets sold until it delivers them to the buyer. If prior to delivery the assets are lost, the buyer is exonerated from its obligations under the contract.

However, the legal regime is not sufficient to secure the buyer's position in a share acquisition or in the event of the partial loss of assets. The contract should contain provisions making payment conditional upon delivery of the business, as detailed in the information and terms of the contract.

31.9   Required Governmental Approvals

The European Community Treaty proclaims the free movement of capital. The Treaty recognizes also the Member States' powers to lay down procedures for the declaration of capital movements for purposes of administrative or statistical information or to take measures that are justified on grounds of public policy or public security. These two aspects are the purpose of Royal Decree 664, of 23 April 1999, on foreign investments.

According to Royal Decree 664/1999, foreign investments in Spain may be carried out in the following categories: (i) participation in Spanish companies; (ii) establishment of branches and increase of the funds allocated to them; (iii) subscription and acquisition of negotiable securities representing loan stock issued by Spanish residents; (iv) participation in investment funds registered with the National Stock Market Commission (*Comisión Nacional del Mercado de Valores*); (v) acquisition of real estate located in Spain; and (vi) constitution, execution or participation in contracts for silent partnerships, foundations, economic interest groupings, cooperative societies and community of property.

The regime provides for a general 'ex post' declaration system, which abolishes any requirements for prior clearance and permission. However, if the foreign investor is a resident of a tax haven, the investor will normally have to make a prior declaration in addition to the 'ex post' declaration that is obligatory for every investment.

The 'ex post' declaration shall be made by the non-resident investor. However, the following particular rules apply:

- If it is an investment in securities, it must be declared by the investment service corporations, the lending institutions or other finance companies indicated in the Stock Market Law 24/1988.

- If it is an investment in unlisted securities, it must be declared either by the depository (if the unlisted securities are deposited or registered) or by the Spanish company in which the investment is made (if such unlisted securities are registered shares).

- If it is an operation in Spanish investment funds, it must be declared by the management company.

The procedure for making the declaration is to file a completed form with the Foreign Investment Registry of the Ministry of Industry, Tourism and Commerce within one month from the date the investment is made. In certain cases, it is also necessary every year to produce an annual report and file it with the Foreign Investment Registry.

31.10 Anti-Trust and Competition Laws

The acquisition of full or joint control over a Spanish undertaking or the creation of a joint venture in Spain may be governed by national or EC competition rules and regulations governing concentrations, depending on whether the parties to the transaction meet certain revenue and market share thresholds.

In this regard, EC law may apply if the parties to the transaction (typically the buyer and the acquired business, or both parents in the case of a joint venture) have a combined worldwide annual turnover of more than EUR 2.5 billion and each have annual Community-wide turnover of more than EUR 100 million (subject to meeting certain additional thresholds in individual Member States).

If the EC thresholds are not met, then the transaction may be notifiable in Spain. In that regard, the operation will need to be notified to the Spanish competition authorities if the parties have combined annual turnover in Spain of more than EUR 240 million and each of the two parties have annual turnover in Spain of more than EUR 60 million, or if the transaction would result in the acquisition or an increase of a market share of 25 per cent or more in any market in Spain. Although note that changes are expected in 2007 that may affect the precise level of these thresholds.

Should the transaction be notifiable to the EC or Spanish competition authorities, then it may not be implemented without approval. Both regimes provide for an initial investigative period of around one month, although this may be significantly extended if the transaction gives rise to competitive issues.

31.11 Required Offer Procedures

Spanish takeover regulations are only applicable to listed companies. A foreign investor acquiring shares in a non-listed company does not need to comply with any statutory law on takeovers.

Even though Spanish law does not contain any takeover provisions for non-listed companies, the target company's articles of association may contain specific rules that need to be complied with for the acquisition to be valid and enforceable. For example, they could require a full offer to be made for all shares, in order to acquire shares above a certain percentage of the share capital. In practice, it is rare to find this kind of provision or other anti-takeover devices.

Nowadays (December 2006), a takeover bid is the prescribed way to achieve a significant shareholding in, or control of, a company with shares listed in Spain. A mandatory bid is triggered when an entity intends to acquire shares in a company listed in Spain (or instruments that would give direct or indirect rights to subscribe or acquire such shares), which represent a significant shareholding in the target company, or intends to appoint a significant number of directors to the company's board. However, the takeover rules contained in the Spanish Market Securities Act 24/1998 are being amended in order to implement the EU takeover bid directive. The main changes to the Spanish takeover bid regime (which are expected to come into force in August 2007) are the following:

- '*A posteriori*' takeover bid system. The obligation to launch a takeover bid will arise only following the acquisition of a controlling position. This implies a significant change from the existing regulation on takeovers. Currently, a mandatory offer obligation arises when there is the intention to acquire a significant stake in a listed company. The takeover bid is the route for acquiring a controlling position ('*a priori*' takeover bid system) and not the consequence of having achieved it ('*a posteriori*' takeover bid system). It is important to highlight that voluntary '*a priori*' takeover bids will continue to exist under the new regime.

- Complete takeover bid system. Mandatory takeover bids will be made only for 100 percent of the capital. The thresholds that trigger the obligation to launch a mandatory takeover bid are the acquisition of 30 per cent of the voting rights of the target company or the acquisition of a smaller state that entities the offeror to appoint the majority of the members of the Board of Directors. Existing mandatory partial bids will be eliminated, although an offeror can voluntarily launch a partial bid.

- Squeeze-out and sell-out. For the first time in Spain, the new regime introduces 'squeeze-out' rights (which will enable successful bidders to buy out minority interests) and 'sell-out' rights (which will enable residual minority shareholders to compel a successful bidder to buy them out).

31.12 Continuation of Government Licenses

In general, administrative licenses do not need to be renewed. For example, the opening license required to start a company, an establishment or shop, and any industrial permit, continues in force.

However, to perform certain activities (for example, telecommunications, banking, pharmacy, energy), it is necessary to obtain specific licenses that are subject to the owner complying with statutory requirements. A change of control in a company in any of these sectors must be reported and the buyer must obtain a new license (or obtain an authorization for the change of ownership).

31.13 Requirements for Transferring Shares

Transfers of shares may be subject to the restrictions imposed by the law or, in the case of registered shares, by the company's shareholders (through covenants between the shareholders, which may or may not be incorporated into the company's articles of association; however, if the covenant has not been incorporated, the transfer is valid and enforceable, regardless of any breach of covenant). Pre-emption rights are commonly included in the articles of association of SA companies with registered shares. SL units (*'participaciones'*) are always subject to restrictions on transfer.

Local advice should be sought, as a transfer contrary to mandatory law is null and void, and a transfer of registered shares contrary to any restrictions in the articles of association may be rejected by the company, with the result that the transferee is not acknowledged as a shareholder.

Transfers of units (*'participaciones'*) in an SL must be made by a public document authorized by a notary public and notified in writing to the company's directors, who enter the transfer in the company's register of members.

Transfers of registered shares represented by shares certificates in an SA do not need to be made through a public document, but it is common practice, and it is advisable to do so, to provide verification of the transfer.

31.14 Requirements for Transferring Land and Property Leases

Transfers of rights in real property that can be registered at the Land Registry must be made by a public deed and registered at the Land Registry to be valid and legally enforceable against third parties. These transfers are subject to transfer tax (in 2007, at a rate of 6 per cent or 7 per cent in several regions in Spain), unless they are subject to and not exempt from value add tax (VAT). The buyer is liable for paying the transfer tax.

The seller should retain part of the price to pay the value added property tax ('*plusvalía*'), a local tax on the increase in the property's value from the price paid when the property was originally acquired. Even if the contract provides that the buyer will pay the '*plusvalía*', the seller, as the last owner of the real property, is liable for its payment, but without prejudice to its right to be reimbursed by the buyer.

31.15 Requirements for Transferring Intellectual Property

Industrial and intellectual property rights are only transferred if expressly included in an assets acquisition agreement. However, pursuant to Article 47 of the Spanish Trademark Law, the transfer of an undertaking as a whole entails the transfer of the undertaking's trademarks, unless agreed otherwise or unless it is clear from the circumstances of the case.

It is also important to distinguish the requirements for transferring industrial property rights (patents, utility models, designs, trademarks, plant varieties rights) from the requirements for transferring intellectual property rights (copyright).

As regards industrial property rights, the assignment of the licenses held by the seller requires the licensors' consent. However, licenses that have been granted by the seller as licensor are transferred without the consent of the licensee or licensees. To be effective *vis-à-vis* third parties, the transfer must be filed at the Spanish Trademark and Patent Office.

The assignment of licenses for intellectual property rights (copyright) held by the seller requires the author's consent (the owner of intellectual property rights), except in the case of transfer of an undertaking. Pursuant to Articles 49 and 50 of the Spanish Intellectual Property Code, no consent shall be necessary where the transfer of intellectual property rights (exclusive or non-exclusive) occurs because of the change in ownership of the undertaking. As intellectual property rights do not have to be registered to be valid, it is not necessary to register the transfer of the license contract.

31.16 Requirements for Transferring Business Contracts, Licenses and Leases

The assignment of contracts with third parties requires, in general, the express acceptance of the transferor (the seller), the transferee (the buyer) and the third party. This rule applies to supply and maintenance agreements, distribution agreements, etc. However, certain types of contracts (such as employment contracts and insurance policies) are automatically assigned, to protect the continuity of these contracts and the business organization. Lease agreements for business premises may be assigned without the landlord's consent, unless the contract provides otherwise. However, in the case of assignment, the landlord has a right to increase the rent by 20 per cent.

Accounts receivable must be transferred expressly (giving details of each account receivable) and debtors must be informed of the transfer, so that debtors cannot extinguish their debts by paying the seller. However, the debtors' acceptance of the assignment is not required. A debtor who pays the seller before being notified of the transfer will have made a valid payment.

The seller is only released by its creditors if each agrees to the assignment.

31.17 Requirements for Transferring Other Assets

Non-registrable movable goods (i.e., movable items that cannot be registered at the Registry) do not need a public deed to be transferred. It is sufficient that the goods are made available to the buyer. However, in practice, when transferring a set of assets making up a business, a transfer by public deed is advisable.

The regime applicable to the transfer of a negotiable instrument depends on the type of negotiable instrument. For example, a bearer negotiable instrument can be validly transferred upon delivery to the buyer; a registered instrument must be renewed by the issuer; and bills of exchange must be endorsed.

31.18 Encumbrances and Third Party Interests

Encumbrances, pledges and any other third-party rights in the shares of a company must be established by a public document and, except in the case of bearer shares, notified to the directors of the company, which will register the encumbrance in the company's Register of Nominative Shares (or, in the case of an SL, in the Register of Members).

31.19 Minimum Shareholder and Officer Requirements

SA and SL companies may have a single shareholder, whether a natural person or a legal entity, and whether through incorporation or as a result of the concentration of all shares of the company into the hands of the single shareholder. The sole shareholder status must be referred to in company correspondence, documentation, order forms, invoices and advertisements, and a declaration to this effect must be registered at the Commercial Registry. If the declaration of the company's status is not filed at the Commercial Registry within six months from the date the company acquires sole shareholder status, the shareholder is jointly and severally liable for company debts incurred during the period it is under a sole shareholder.

As regards the management body of SA and SL companies, under Spanish law there are a number of different possibilities: (i) sole director; (ii) joint directors; (iii) joint and several directors; and (iv) board of directors. Directors do not need to be Spanish residents or citizens. However, if non-resident, individuals must hold a foreigner identification number (NIE) and entities must hold a tax identification number (NIF).

If there is a board of directors, it must have at least three members, and a chairman and secretary must be appointed. The secretary of the board does not need to be a director. Under Spanish law, the chairman has no special powers. The board of directors may appoint one or more managing directors, among its members, and delegate to them all the faculties that may be delegated under the law and the by-laws. The appointment of managing directors often facilitates the daily operation of the company. The scope of the managing director's authority is standard and non-derogable, and any limitations imposed on the delegated authority will not be effective *vis-à-vis* third parties. General powers of attorney may be granted to certain executives, regardless of whether they are members of the board.

31.20 Non-competition Clauses

Under Spanish competition law, any agreement, decision or collective practice that has the object or effect or is capable of having the effect of impeding, restricting or distorting competition in all or part of the domestic market is null and void, unless it comes under an exemption provided by the law.

Covenants given by employees in this regard are valid and enforceable, as long as the employer can prove it has a valid commercial and industrial interest, the employees are adequately compensated for the restriction that such covenant implies, and the obligation does not last longer than two years.

As regards non-competition clauses between companies, the Spanish competition authorities adhere strictly to the EC rules. As such, non-competition clauses will only be considered valid if necessary to protect legitimate rights (for example, good-will) and are for a limited duration. Thus, in the case of an acquisition, a non-compete on the seller may be considered justified for a period of two years (in exceptional cases, three years), and in the case of a joint venture, a non-compete may be considered justified for the life of the joint venture.

31.21 Environmental Considerations

Until 1985, Spain had no comprehensive set of regulations protecting the environment. This has changed dramatically, and standards of conduct and liability for damage to the environment are regulated by general legislation and by different statutes that apply to specific areas of activity. The legislator aims to protect the elements of nature (water, air and soil) with general statutes that refer to the polluting of each of the elements.

In addition to these rules and any others applicable to the particular type of investment activity, the autonomous community and the county where the business is located will have local rules that must be complied with.

In general, environmental law imposes joint and several liabilities on everybody participating in the chain (producer or manufacturer, wholesaler, transporter, seller) for infringing the applicable regulations. The parties cannot be excluded from the liability imposed by the law; they are liable if the law so provides. A contract is not a valid reason to exclude liability, although the party who is compelled to pay has a right to be reimbursed by the other party according to the provisions of the contract.

31.22 Employee Superannuation/Pension Plans

The state guarantees persons covered by the scope of social security, and their families and dependants, health care, disability, unemployment, pension and death benefits.

Social security contributions are based on a percentage of the salary (a total of 36.95 per cent in 2005), determined by the government each year, and which must be paid by employers (30.6 per cent) and employees (6.35 per cent). However, employers are responsible not only for the payment of their allocated contributions, but also for their employees' contributions, which must be deducted from the salary and paid to social security. Non-payment to social security can result in administrative sanctions and surcharges. The company's liability for social security payments elapses after a four-year period from the date the payment is due. It is advisable to check whether the target has paid all social security debts relating to that period, as, according to Spanish law, the buyer will be jointly and severally liable for them. Pension plans cannot be a substitute for social security contributions. Pension plans are voluntary and private, and the employer's obligations, if any, are stipulated by the contract or applicable collective agreements. If the seller has assumed any obligations under a pension plan, employees will have acquired a right to the additional compensation provided for by the plan and the buyer is obliged to continue with the same or a similar scheme.

31.23 Employee Rights

Spanish labour law has tended to be protective. Besides the law, it is necessary to consider collective agreements, which are agreements adopted by the worker's representatives and the management to govern working conditions and productivity.

Foreign workers' rights are equal to Spanish workers' rights. Notwithstanding this, foreign workers not belonging to EU Member States must obtain residence and work permits prior to engaging in any paid labour or professional activity in Spain.

On acquiring a business, as a result of the automatic transfer of all labour contracts to the buyer, it succeeds the seller as employer and employees continue working under the same conditions, subject to certain notification requirements. Employees are compelled to abide by the transfer, as they cannot oppose the succession unless fraud or a criminal offence is committed during the transfer.

When acquiring a company's shares, the employment contracts continue to be the company's responsibility and should be respected. If the buyer intends to make redundancies or transfer personnel from the target company to other companies within the group, this should be negotiated prior to closing, in order to include the necessary clauses in the contract of sale, particularly, the redundancy mechanism and the cost of redundancies, as reducing personnel can result in high costs (in general, redundancy payments amount to 45 days' pay for each year worked at the company, to a maximum of 42 months' salary).

31.24 Compulsory Transfer of Employees

Employees cannot oppose the change in ownership of the business or the target company and are compelled to abide by it, unless fraud or a criminal offence was committed during the transfer. Employees continue to work under the same conditions as before.

Both the transferor and the transferee must inform the workers' legal representatives of their respective concerned employees, or inform the employees directly if they do not have representatives, of the following: (i) planned date of the transfer, (ii) reasons for the transfer, (iii) legal, financial and social consequences of the transfer for the employees, and (iv) measures foreseen regarding the employees.

Unless otherwise provided in their employment contracts, according to the Royal Decree governing senior managers' employment relationship, senior managers are entitled to claim for the indemnified termination of their contracts if there is a substantial modification in the company's ownership that involves a change in the governing bodies of the company or in its main business. According to such regulations, unless otherwise agreed in the contract, in such circumstances and as long as the senior manager announces the termination within three months from such changes, he or she would be entitled to severance pay equal to seven days' cash salary per year of service, to a maximum of six months' salary.

In the case of an acquisition of business assets, the buyer can also be held to have succeeded the seller as employer, if the transferred assets constitute an autonomous production unit that maintains its identity as a set of means organized for carrying out an essential or ancillary business activity. If the buyer intends to make any redundancies or transfer personnel from the target company to any other companies within the group, this must be negotiated prior to closing, and the agreement must include the necessary provisions, particularly the redundancy mechanism and the allocation of the cost of redundancies, as this can be very high (see 31.23).

31.25 Tax Deductibility of Acquisition Expenses

The deductibility of acquisition expenses incurred by a non-resident in Spain is determined by the laws of its own domestic jurisdiction. However, if these expenses are re-charged to the Spanish company, the Spanish tax authorities may consider the expenses related to the parent–subsidiary relationship (e.g. custodial or management expenses) as non-deductible expenses.

31.26 Levies on Acquisition Agreements and Collateral Documents

According to Spanish law, taxes are levied on:

- the transfer of property rights ('transfer tax');
- corporate operations ('capital tax'); and
- legal documentation for transactions with a notarial, commercial or administrative character, showing a quantity or item that can be valued ('stamp tax').

These three different taxable situations must be co-ordinated with VAT. Operations carried out by businessmen and professionals in the course of their activities, as well as the delivery of goods or the rendering of services, are subject to VAT. The transfer of property rights between individuals (not businessmen and professionals) against payment is subject to transfer tax instead of VAT. The tax rate applicable under this tax to the transfer of real property is 6 per cent (7 per cent in several regions).

The creation of rights of guarantee and sureties is charged at 1 per cent of the secured value. The transfer of shares, quoted or not, is an important exception; it is exempt from VAT and transfer tax. Nevertheless, these transfers are deemed taxable at the transfer tax rate of 6 per cent (7 per cent in several regions), if:

- they represent the capital stock or the net worth of entities owning real property located in Spain, the value of which amounts to 50 per cent or more of their total assets; and

- the buyer acquires a controlling equity share in the entity, or once he has achieved such control acquires an additional participation.

Stamp tax is levied at a rate of 0.5 per cent (1 per cent in most regions of Spain), calculated on the value of the consideration included in any notarized contract that can be registered in a public registry (such as the Commercial Registry or Land Registry), provided the contracts are not subject to transfer tax. Stamp tax normally applies when the relevant transaction is subject to VAT.

31.27 Financing Rules and Restrictions

Spanish tax law recognizes the concept of thin capitalization in relation to finance from foreign-related entities. Thus, when the direct or indirect debt of a corporation resident in Spain with a non-resident parent company exceeds three times its net equity, the interest paid on such excess is treated as a dividend for tax purposes. The thin-capitalization rule does not apply to loans granted by companies resident in an EU country.

The Corporation Law also prohibits an SA from granting any kind of financial assistance for the purchase of its own shares or the shares of its holding company. The only exception is for loans granted by the company to its employees for that purpose.

31.28 Exchange Controls and Repatriation of Profits

The holders of direct foreign investment that do not require authorization, or which have been authorized, have the right to transfer abroad, without limit:

- capital invested and capital gains, if any, derived from any disposals; and

- profit and dividends legally distributed, including any proceeds from the sale of subscription rights.

In general, the application and the amount of withholding tax depend on the relevant double-taxation agreement between Spain and the state where the shareholder is domiciled. Payments of dividends to parent companies resident in an EU country are exempt from withholding tax under the Parent-Subsidiary Directive, provided that several requirements are met (basically the parent company must have held at least 20 per cent -15 per cent from January 2007 to December 2008 and 10 per cent from January 2009, of the Spanish subsidiary's shares for more than one year).

Double taxation agreements usually provide for a 10 per cent-15 per cent withholding tax on dividends. If there is no applicable treaty, the withholding tax amounts to

18 per cent. With some exceptions, non-resident entities directly owning real property in Spain are subject to a special yearly tax, equivalent to 3 per cent of the property value listed in the land records (cadastral value).

31.29   Groups of Companies

Companies in a group that are allowed and have elected to be taxed under the tax-consolidated system are jointly and severally liable for the tax debts of the companies in the group. In addition, if there is a group from a labour law perspective, there might be joint and several liabilities for employee debts incurred by any company in the group.

Companies are considered to form a group when decisions are taken in unison. In particular, it is presumed that decisions are taken in unison when a company (the parent company) holds shares in another company (the subsidiary company) and (i) has the majority of the voting rights in the subsidiary company; or (ii) has the right to appoint or remove a majority of the members of the governing body of the subsidiary company; or (iii) may hold, pursuant to an agreement with other shareholders, a majority of the voting rights; or (iv) has appointed solely as a result of the exercise of its voting rights the majority of the members of the governing body of the subsidiary company, who have held office during the two previous financial years and up to the time the consolidated accounts are drawn up. For these purposes, the voting rights held through any subsidiary company, as well as those of any person acting in his/her own name but on behalf of the parent company or of another subsidiary company, or those held jointly with any other person, must be added to those of the parent company.

It is also presumed that there is a decision-making unit when one or several companies are managed on a unified basis. In particular, when the majority of the members of the governing body of the subsidiary company are members of the governing body, or executives, of the parent company or of any of its subsidiaries.

A parent company must prepare consolidated annual accounts and a management report (notwithstanding the obligation imposed on every company in the group to prepare its own annual accounts and management report), unless it falls under any of the following exceptions:

1. Over two consecutive years, the aggregated annual accounts of the companies in the group do not exceed two of the following limits:

    *   Assets below EUR 9,495,991;

    *   Net annual turnover below EUR 18,991,982;

    *   Average number of employees below 250.

2. The parent company subject to Spanish law is controlled by another EU company, under certain conditions.

As mentioned above, groups are entitled to be taxed on a consolidated basis, whereby the group (taxpayer) is taxed on the profit obtained by all the companies in the group, on fulfilment of certain requirements (i.e., all the companies in the group for which the application is made must be Spanish corporations domiciled in Spain and the parent company must hold at least 75 per cent of the consolidated subsidiary companies). Groups are not obliged to be taxed on a consolidated basis; whether it is advisable to choose this particular regime depends on the particular circumstances of the case.

31.30   Responsibility for Liabilities of an Acquired Subsidiary

In general, companies are not liable for the debts of companies in the same group. However, care should be taken with regard to labour liabilities (if the group presents consolidated accounts) and tax debts (if the group is taxed under the tax-consolidation system), as there could be responsibility for the group's debts in this case. Moreover, companies owned by a single owner must have this fact declared and registered (see **25.19**). Otherwise, the single owner is jointly liable for the company's debts.

31.31   Governing Law of the Contract

Under the 1980 Rome Convention, parties are free to choose the law applicable to the contract. Spanish courts are to recognize the election of the parties, irrespective of the domicile or nationality of the parties involved. However, any provision of the contract that is contrary to Spanish mandatory law will not be enforceable when all elements of the transaction are located in Spain.

If the parties have not agreed on any applicable law, it is presumed that Spanish law shall govern the contracts for sale of real estate located in Spain. To register real property rights, it is required that the contract for sale of real property be documented in a public deed, authorized before a notary public and registered at the Land Registry upon payment of applicable taxes.

Note also that, before Spanish Courts, the party pleading the application of foreign law must prove that it is in force, as well as its content, existence and interpretation. The Spanish Supreme Court has admitted that proof of foreign law is given if the party submits a public document, certified by a public authority (i.e., consul) and accompanied by the legal opinion of two jurists from the foreign country. Spain is also party to the European Convention on information on foreign laws, made in London on 7 June 1968.

31.32   Dispute Resolution Options

In international transactions, parties are free to submit disputes to the courts of a foreign state, unless Spanish courts are exclusively competent (for example, trademarks, companies' registration, real estate and property rights). It is presumed that the parties' choice grants exclusive jurisdiction over the foreign courts. However, if the parties have not chosen a particular venue, any company domiciled in Spain could be sued before Spanish courts. The courts of first instance are competent to recognize and enforce foreign judgments in accordance with either Regulation 44/2001 and the applicable international treaties or with the domestic law provisions in the Spanish Civil Procedure Act 1881 related to the recognition of foreign judgments.

Regarding arbitration, since the enactment of Arbitration Act 60/2003, Spain has become a highly advisable place for conducting arbitration. With this modern law,

Spain has brought in line with the principles of the 1985 Uncitral Model Law on Commercial Arbitration, and with developed international practices of commercial arbitration in other countries. The law favours arbitration, reduces formal requirements, gives flexibility to arbitration and promotes Spain as a proper venue for arbitration. Spain is party to the 1958 New York Convention and the 1961 Geneva Convention on the recognition and enforcement of arbitral awards.

31.33   Other Issues

Enforcement of Public Deeds

Obligations in public deeds to pay sums of money would allow the creditor to apply for direct enforcement in summary proceedings under Spanish Procedural Law. Public deeds meet the requirements established in Article 4.3 of Regulation 805/2004 and would therefore permit the creditor to enforce the public deed in any European Member State (except Denmark). Therefore, it is advisable to formalize the purchase in a public deed granted before a notary or a stockbroker.

Legal Costs

In Spain, statutory criteria determine the person liable for the costs of legal proceedings and for attorneys' fees. Under these criteria, the legal costs in the first instance shall be borne by the party whose claims are totally dismissed, unless the court decides that the case entailed serious doubts of fact or law. If the losing party is ordered to pay legal costs, he or she cannot be compelled to pay the costs incurred by attorneys, experts and civil servants who are not paid by tariff, an amount that exceeds one-third of the total value in dispute for each party. This limitation does not apply if the losing party is declared to have proceeded with the action recklessly. If the claim is partially upheld, each party pays for the costs it instigated and half of the common costs, unless the court declares that the party acted recklessly in the proceedings.

32. SWEDEN

Åke J. Fors, in collaboration with Jamie Stanbury and Karl Broomé Setterwalls

32.1 Introductory Comments

Since the early 1980's, the Swedish economic and political environment has undergone a series of important changes which have substantially improved the investment climate.

Some of the most significant changes through extensive deregulation and privatization, including the abolition of currency exchange controls, elimination of restrictions on foreign acquisition of Swedish companies and the elimination of clauses in corporate by-laws that limited foreign stock ownership, as well as a major tax reform in 1991 which reduced the corporate tax rate to only 28 per cent. Furthermore, Sweden joined the EU in 1995, but is not a member of the EMU.

32.2 Corporate Structures

The most significant type of corporate structure in Sweden is the limited liability company ('*Aktiebolag*' (AB)), which is established and regulated through the Swedish Companies Act ('*aktiebolagslagen*', SFS 2005:551). There are two forms of limited liability companies: the public limited liability company (minimum share capital SEK 500,000) and the private limited liability company (minimum share capital SEK 100,000). The term 'company' for the purposes of this guide refers to a Swedish limited liability company.

All shares in a limited liability company must carry voting rights, although different classes of shares with different voting rights may be issued. No share may be issued with more than ten times the voting rights of another.

Only shares in public limited liability companies may be offered to the public and listed at a stock exchange. On 2 October 2006 the Nordic List was introduced at the OMX exchange in Stockholm, Copenhagen and Helsinki (OMX Nordic Exchange). Swedish, Danish and Finnish companies are now presented on one comprehensive list with common listing requirements. Companies are presented in segments based on market value—divided into three segments: Large Cap, Mid Cap and Small Cap—and in sectors according to industry affiliation. As of January 1, 2007, also Icelandic companies have become a part of the Nordic List. There is also First North which is an alternative marketplace for small growth companies. First North is a part of OMX Nordic Exchange.

Other authorized marketplaces are the Nordic Growth Market (NGM) and *Aktietorget*. In addition there are some non-authorized marketplaces where unofficial trading takes place, such as *Nya Marknaden* and Nordic OTC.

International Business Acquisitions, M. Whalley, F.-J. Semler (eds.), Kluwer Law International, London, 2007; ISBN 9789041124838.

There are also other corporate forms, such as trading partnerships ('*Handelsbolag*' (HB)), limited partnerships ('*Kommanditbolag*' (KB)), simple partnerships, foundations and corporate societies. However, these forms are not described further.

32.3   Letters of Intent and Heads of Agreement

Generally, a letter of intent is only considered to have a moral effect in negotiations and is therefore not legally binding under Swedish law. However, although the heading indicates that there are no actual legal obligations associated with such a document, the substance of the document and/or other circumstances may mean that legally an obligation is inferred. For that reason, if the document is not meant to be legally binding, this should be expressly stated.

According to Swedish case law and doctrine, any negotiating party preventing a final agreement by negligence (i.e. breaking off negotiations) may be liable for damages (*culpa in contrahendo*). Even though a letter of intent is not legally binding, it may constitute an obligation to take future steps necessary for a final agreement. While such a document is based on loyalty, it often leads to firmer obligations towards negotiating parties.

32.4   Taxes Affecting the Structure and Calculation of the Price

A share acquisition of a Swedish target company does not result in any changes in the target's tax liabilities since the legal entity is constant. A foreign company is liable for taxation in Sweden for income from real property business in Sweden and income from a business conducted out of a permanent place of business in Sweden. All income, excluding profit made from business related shares, is, in a limited liability company, taxed as business income, for which the tax rate is a fiat 28 per cent. Profits from a Swedish branch of a foreign country are thus subject to corporate tax of 28 per cent. Profits from business related shares are not taxable, and as consequence, losses from business related shares are not deductible.

Dividends paid by Swedish limited liability companies to foreign shareholders are subject to a 30 per cent withholding tax. This percentage is, however, normally reduced or waived under double taxation treaties. The reduction is either effectuated direct at the time for payment or afterwards, after application for repayment.

A Swedish company is tax exempt with regards to dividends from a subsidiary if the shares are considered to be held for business purposes. For shares to be considered 'held for business purposes,' the subsidiary's shares must not be listed on any stock exchange or, if the subsidiary's shares are listed, then at least 10 per cent of the voting power has to have been held by the recipient of the dividends for a period of no less than twelve months. Even if the 10 per cent threshold is not met, the dividends can be tax exempt if it can be shown that the shares in question are held for business purposes. An example of where this could be possible is the situation where a producer of pulp owns shares in the shipping company which transports the producer's products.

32.5   Extent of Seller's Warranties and Indemnities

The extent to which warranties and indemnities are required is dependent on the size of the acquisition and the risks connected to it. It is nevertheless customary for the seller to provide warranties for, *inter alia*, the accuracy of annual and interim reports, title to assets, taxation, intellectual property rights, and employee matters.

In addition to warranties, it is advisable to conduct due diligence investigations in respect of the target company. The use and legal significance of such investigations must be considered in the light of the Swedish Sale of Goods Act ('*köplagen*', SFS 1990:931).

According to the Act, goods should conform to the buyer's justified expectations. A deviation from those expectations gives the buyer a right to claim compensation or even to rescind the agreement. The buyer may not claim defects that he or she should have noticed at the time of the acquisition.

Furthermore, if warranties or limitations of liability or more specifically the effect of such clauses, are held to be unreasonable and unjust, they may be mitigated or set aside in accordance with Section 36 of the Contracts Act ('*avtalslagen*', SFS 1915:218).

32.6   Liability for Pre-contractual Representations

As mentioned in **32.3**, a negligent negotiating party may be liable for damages (*culpa in contrahendo*).

A seller is also held liable for information regarding the goods that it gave when entering the contract or in the marketing of goods, if this marketing was deemed to of had an influence on the contract. The seller may also be held liable for information provided by a party active at an earlier stage of distribution (including a manufacturer) or for the account of the seller unless the seller was not aware of this information being given.

Note that the seller may be held liable even if the incorrectness of the information was unknown to the seller or even if the seller could not have known it.

The liability for pre-contractual representations may, depending on the circumstances, be limited by due diligence investigations carried out by the buyer. This is rather unusual however.

32.7   Liability for Pre-acquisition Trading and Contracts

In a share acquisition, the target company retains all rights and obligations under pre-acquisition contracts throughout the transaction since there is no change of contracting party. On the other hand, when assets are acquired the seller is not released from its contractual liabilities unless consent is given by the buyer.

Concerning pre-acquisition dealing, insider dealing is an offence in Sweden under the Market Abuse Penal Act ('*lag om straff för marknadsmissbruk vid handel med finansiella instrument*', SFS 2005:377). The Market Abuse Penal Act prohibits certain dealings in securities on the securities market by anyone who possesses information which is significant regarding the price of such securities and which has not been made public. It also prohibits improper influence on share prices and unauthorized disclosure of inside information which may materially influence the price of financial instruments.

There is also the Reporting Duty for Certain Holdings of Financial Instruments Act (*'lag om anmälningsskyldighet för vissa innehav av finansiella instrument'*, SFS 2000:1087) which states that persons who are in an insider position in a listed company must report their shareholdings, and any changes in such shareholdings, to the Swedish Financial Supervisory Authority (*'Finansinspektionen'*). The Authority maintains an insider registry in respect of such reports and the registry is a public document. The reporting duty encompasses legal entities which are owned indirectly by the person subject to a reporting duty through another closely affiliated person or legal entity.

A company which has issued securities on the securities market or whose shares are subject to trade on a securities market within the EEA must keep records of all persons who, due to employment, are in possession of insider information concerning the company. Furthermore, there is an all inclusive ban for corporate insiders to trade thirty days before the publication of an interim report. Notwithstanding these provisions, shares may be sold in compliance with the terms of a public offer.

The infringement of these provisions is subject to sanctions by fine or up to four years' imprisonment (depending on the seriousness of the offence) as well as the forfeiture of any gains due to insider knowledge. Also under certain circumstances (e.g. fraud), insider dealing may constitute an offence under the Swedish Penal Code (*'brottsbalken'*).

32.8   Pre-completion Risks

Swedish regulation of the passing of risk is subject to vast contractual freedom for the parties to agree upon the specifics for the transaction in question. In the absence of contractual stipulations, Section 13 of the Sale of Goods Act states that the risk passes to the buyer when the goods are delivered in accordance with the contract. The Act is applicable to shares and other personal property as well. The passing of risk in real property transactions is regulated in the Swedish Real Property Code (*'jordabalken'*).

Detailed provisions should be included in the transaction documentation with respect to seller actions during the pre-closing period, including insurance requirements.

32.9   Governmental Approval

With regards to banking, insurance, securities, and credit market companies the law requires that an acquisition resulting in a qualified holding in such a company be notified in advance to the Financial Supervisory Authority. The Authority will allow the acquisition provided it cannot be assumed that the buyer will obstruct a sound development of the target company's activities.

See also **32.10**.

32.10   Anti-trust and Competition Law

The Competition Act ('*konkurrenslagen*', SFS 1993:20) requires acquisitions which meet certain requirements to be notified to the Competition Authority ('*Konkurrensverket*'). The requirements are that:

- the target company conducts business in Sweden;

- together, the companies have an annual turnover exceeding SEK 4,000 million;

- at least two of the companies concerned has an annual turnover in Sweden exceeding SEK 100 million alone.

Within 25 working days of the notification the Competition Authority must decide whether to continue with an in depth special investigation. During this period the parties to the transaction must not take any action to proceed with the acquisition. When assessing the notifications, the Authority examines whether the acquisition will affect the relevant market in a way which will create or strengthen a dominant position or restrain competition.

If the Competition Authority finds that the acquisition will have these effects it may request the Stockholm City Court to prohibit the acquisition or, with regard to acquisitions that have been effectuated on a stock exchange or on another market regulated by a recognized authority, they can order the acquired assets to be dispersed. Such a request must be made within three months of the notification. The Authority may also request the Stockholm City Court to prohibit the parties from proceeding with the acquisition.

In practice, it is more common that the parties and the Authority negotiate a solution where the parties promise to carry out structural changes in order to mitigate the acquisition's anti-competitive effects.

Note that an acquisition of a major Swedish company could constitute a concentration with a Community dimension, according to the EC Merger Regulation (Council Regulation (EC) No 139/2004). This regulation is exclusive (i.e. it excludes application of the Swedish Competition Act).

32.11   Required Offer Procedures

When an offer to acquire shares is directed to the public, a prospectus shall be drafted and submitted to the Financial Supervisory Authority unless (a) the offer only targets qualified investors, (b) the offer targets less than a hundred persons or legal entities, who are not qualified investors, in a state within the EEA, (c) the offer concerns the acquisition of securities up to an amount of at least 50,000 Euro per investor, (d) each security is worth at least 50,000 Euro, or (e) the total amount which is being paid by the investors during a period of twelve months do not exceed 1 million Euro.

Through the Act on Public Offers for the Acquisition of Shares ('*lag om offentliga uppköpserbjudanden på aktiemarknaden*', SFS 2006:451) Sweden has implemented the Directive 2004/25/EC. In addition the Swedish Industry and Commerce Stock

Exchange Committee ('*Näringslivets Börskommitté*' (NBK)) has issued Rules Concerning Public Offers for the Acquisition of Shares. The purpose of the rules is to ensure the non-discriminatory and equal treatment of shareholders in the target company in various respects. These rules are binding upon all companies listed on the Nordic List, the Nordic Growth Market (NGM), and *Aktietorget*. The Act on Public Offers for the Acquisition of Shares stipulates that a public offer may only be made by a company which has committed itself to adhere to the rules issued by NBK. When a public offer is made the offeror has to notify the Financial Supervisory Authority. Furthermore the offeror is required to draw up and make public an offer document containing the information necessary to enable the holders of the offeree company's shares to reach a properly informed decision on the bid. As soon as the offer has been made public the offeror and the offeree also have to inform their employees of the offer. If an offeror, as a result of the acquisition, holds securities in the offeree representing at least 30 per cent of the voting rights in that company the offeror is required to make a bid on the remaining shares.

In addition, where a person or a legal entity owns more than 90 per cent of the shares in another Swedish company, the Companies Act allows the compulsory acquisition of the minority shareholding. Under these circumstances, minority shareholders are entitled to require the majority owner to acquire their shares. This right is also available where the majority shareholder is a foreign natural or legal person.

32.12   Continuation of Government Licenses

The operation of banking, insurance, securities, and credit market businesses requires a license from the Financial Supervisory Authority. The assignment of shares in such companies requires, under certain circumstances, the Authority's approval (see **32.9**).

Licenses related to environmental matters are, in general, transferable with the business operation to which they are connected. If the business operation will change in scope or character, a new license is required. There exists no legal obligation to notify the transfer to the relevant supervisory authority, but it is advisable to do so.

32.13   Requirements for Transferring Shares

Restrictions and requirements for transferring shares may be found in the target company's articles of association, or in shareholders' agreements. There exist no statutory requirements or restrictions in this respect.

32.14   Requirements for Transferring Land and Property Leases

The general regulations governing real property transactions and leases are contained in the Land Law Code ('*jordabalken*').

Sales agreements on real property must be concluded in writing, but there is no need for acknowledgement or notarization. In addition to the sales contract, which generally contains the terms of the transaction, the parties normally draft a bill of sale, which contains the date for taking possession. The bill of sale's purpose is to ensure for the seller that the completion of the transfer is dependent on the payment of the purchase price. Note that the following formal requirements apply to both of these documents.

As stated, the contract must be in writing. It must be signed by both the seller and the buyer. The contract must contain a declaration that the seller conveys the land unit to the other party. Furthermore, the document must refer to the name of the unit and contain information on the purchase price. As far as witnesses are concerned this is not in itself a formal requirement, but the registration procedure may be delayed in its absence. If the seller is married, his or her spouse shall accept the transaction in writing.

A site-lease ('*tomträtt*') is a right between title and tenancy. Site-lease holders have a right to use the property, often owned by a municipality. The concept is equivalent to a tenancy of land and the holder of the site-lease pays an annual fee ('*tomträttsavgäld*') to the property owner. The holder essentially has the same legal status as a property owner. The main difference is that the holder has no right to transfer the actual property, merely his or her site-lease right. Although the right is considered to be personal, legally it is to a substantial degree treated as ownership of property. The leaseholder has the power to sell, give away and dispose of the right to any person or entity. He or she can also mortgage, sublease and agree an easement of the right. The requirements described above in relation to the transfer of real property apply to the transfer of site-leases.

32.15   Requirements for Transfer of Intellectual Property

The seller can, in principle, assign any intellectual property right in his or her possession. However, with respect to copyrights, it should be noted that an author's moral rights cannot be assigned. Moreover, assignments of licenses often require the licensor's permission. Trademarks connected to a business are presumed to be included in an assignment of that business.

In order to be able to enforce patents, trademarks and patterns against intellectual property rights infringements, it is necessary to notify all assignments to the Swedish Patent and Registration Office ('*Patent- och registreringsverket*').

32.16   Requirements for Transferring Business Contracts, Licenses and Leases

A contract can only be transferred in accordance with the contract terms. When a contract is transferred in connection to an asset acquisition it is mandatory to obtain the third party's consent in order to release the seller from his or her liabilities. On the other hand, rights and accrued claims may, as a principle, be transferred without the debtor's consent while the debtor is not entitled to unilaterally transfer his or her obligations.

With reference to assignments of real property it is important to note that tenants and leaseholders are provided extensive legal protection. An assignor of real property is also obliged to include a provision in the assignment contract regarding the rights of tenants and leaseholders.

32.17   Requirements for Transferring Other Assets

There are relatively few requirements under Swedish law regarding the transfer of assets. See further **32.16**.

32.18   Encumbrances and Third Party Interests

Assets may be subject to encumbrances and third party interests. Certain situations, such as a sale of property reducing the assets available for the satisfaction of creditors or a double sale of an asset, are dealt with under property law. Under general rules it is also possible to assign one's rights, but not one's obligations, under a contract. As a general principle the assignee of such rights acquires the same position as the original contracting party had.

32.19   Minimum Shareholder and Officer Requirements

There exists no requirement for the number of shareholders in a Swedish limited liability company. For a company to be listed at any of the authorized marketplaces specific requirements apply though. They concern, *inter alia*, the number of shareholders and the percentage of shares and votes owned by the general public. The requirements vary depending upon which marketplace the shares are listed on.

Public limited liability companies must have a board of directors consisting of at least three members. Private limited liability companies are permitted to have only one or two board members, provided that at least one deputy director is elected. Only public limited liability companies are required to have a managing director.

The managing director and at least half of the board members must be residents of the EEA. It is possible to apply for exemption from this requirement.

Where a limited liability company or a corporate society has more than 25 employees, the employees are entitled to nominate two representatives to the board of directors. If the company is active in several lines of business and employs more than 1,000 employees, the employees are entitled to nominate three representatives. But the number of employee representatives must not exceed the number of board members elected by the shareholders.

32.20   Non-competition Clauses

Non-competition clauses are in principle legal and binding under Swedish law. However, they restrict competition and therefore may infringe Section 6 of the Competition Act.

As concerns acquisitions which meet the requirements to be notified to the Competition Authority (see further **32.10**), the following are examples of the Authority's practice in relation to scrutinizing non-competition clauses as an integrated part of the notification procedure.

The Authority has in earlier decisions accepted a time period of three years in cases where the acquisition covered both goodwill and know-how, where the buyer had pre-acquisition know-how corresponding to the transferred know-how. However, in cases where the buyer lacked such know-how, a time period of five years has been accepted. As concerns acquisitions that only cover goodwill, the Authority has accepted a time period of two years for a non-competition clause.

With particular reference to former employees and members of the management who are the subjects of a non-competition clause, Section 38 of the Contracts Act may be used to reduce the scope of the clause.

32.21   Environmental Considerations

New comprehensive environmental legislation was introduced on 1 January 1999, developed in accordance with the 'polluter pays' principle. The liability remains until the problems have been removed regardless of whether the operations have been discontinued prior to the acquisition. So, the target company's environmental liabilities are effectively transferred to the buyer. These liabilities can be far-reaching and include a duty to decontaminate polluted property, works and buildings.

The liability rests with the company alone. Only where members of the management or employees have committed criminal acts do they have a personal liability.

By transferring the assets instead of the shares, the primary liability is avoided. This does not exclude all liability. Particularly in acquisitions relating to industrial and other environmentally hazardous operations, it is advisable to conduct an environmental due diligence investigation.

Considering the magnitude of potential costs and damages involved, it is very important to ensure that the buyer obtains adequate and effective environmental warranties and indemnities from the seller.

32.22   Employee Superannuation/Pension plans

The Swedish social security system is based on the general pension (*'allmän pension'*) scheme, where a certain percentage of all earnings become pension rights (*'pensionsrätter'*), which ultimately becomes the income pension (*'inkomstpension'*) or premium pension (*'premiepension'*). The premium pension is placed in funds. There is also a third part of the general pension, the guaranteed pension (*'garantipension'*), which forms a basic security for those who have little or no income. Furthermore, persons born between 1938 and 1953 get a part of their income pensions calculated according to the old system; these plans are called the fiat rate basic pension scheme (*'allmän folkpension'* (AFP)) and the earnings-related pension scheme (*'allmän tilläggspension'* (ATP)). Social security coverage also provides for survivor and disability benefits, workers' compensation, medical care, and parental benefits. The social security contribution rates amount to 32.28 per cent (increased to 32.42 per cent for income year for tax purposes 2007) of the employees' gross salaries and are paid by the employer.

Further coverage for employees comes through agreements reached during collective bargaining or by separate agreement between the employer and employees. Such schemes are the ITP system, which provides compulsory coverage for salaried employees, and the *Avtalspension* SAF-LO scheme, which provides coverage for blue-collar workers in the private sector.

The work injury compensation system consists of a combination of social security, workers' compensation ('*arbetsskadeförsäkring*' (LAF)), and collective bargaining agreements. In the private sector the policy is called '*trygghetsförsäkring*' (TFA). Most workers are covered by both social security and LAF. Under these systems compensation is paid for lost income, medical costs, survivor benefits, and funeral grants. TFA covers most union members and many other workers and the scheme provides, in addition to the above, benefits for pain and suffering, disability or deformity, alimony, and inconvenience.

For salaried employees there are no statutory provisions for severance payments in Sweden. Collective agreements, however, often provide termination indemnities for employees aged 40 or over with at least ten years' service.

According to the Vacation Act, employees are entitled to 25 days' holiday per year. Some collective agreements provide improvements over this statutory requirement.

Employers have the possibility of engaging in more extensive pension plans for their employees than required by law or collective agreements. In principle the alternatives are:

- service pension;

- deposits on a specified account for pensions;

- allocation to superannuation funds; and

- cash payments after retirement.

The right to make tax deductions arises only to an amount regarded as a reasonable pension in relation to the salary. Both quality and quantity requirements must be fulfilled. Quality is in respect to the design of the pension plan. The quantity measure limits the deductible amount. This deduction should not exceed the allowed amount according to the general pension plan as determined between the main organizations on the labour market.

32.23 Employee Rights

Swedish labour legislation primarily covers the rights of union activity, settlement of disputes through the Labour Court ('*Arbetsdomstolen*'), working environment and safety, industrial democracy measures, and prohibition of discrimination by sex, sexual orientation, race, and national origin. The labour market is heavily organized and the overall rate of unionization is 78 per cent of the working population. Union membership is fairly evenly distributed among employees in private, local government, and state employment.

Agreements to perform work fall into two categories: employment work agreements and contract work agreements. Labour law is concerned with employment work. There is very little legislation concerning contract work.

The employment relationship regarding individual employment law is not covered by any legislation of general range; instead, a number of matters of a specific nature have been regulated separately. Freedom of contract prevails, but a large number of important principles have been laid down by the Labour Court, and labour market customs also play an important role. Regulation in collective agreements is of major importance, much greater than that of individual employment agreements, which have little individual content and mainly refer to the applicable collective agreement.

The collective agreement can encompass any matter subject to collective bargaining and is legally binding upon the parties and all members of the parties. It could also be industry wide and thus bind on all individual members and member-organizations on both sides.

The Act on Employee Participation in Decision-Making ('*Medbestämmandelagen*' (MBL)) was passed in 1976, and gave unions the right to be consulted on a wide range of issues that could affect employees (e.g. major investments, changes in the corporate organization, sale of the company or some of its activities, use of subcontractors, appointment of managers, or implementation of new technologies or processes). Employers are obliged to provide information and consult with labour representatives before making a final decision. However, employees have no formal veto power on management decisions. Disputes under the Act are settled by the Labour Court.

As mentioned at **32.19**, employees under certain circumstances are entitled to nominate two or three representatives to the board of directors.

Employment protection is extensive. The Employment Protection Act ('*Lag om anställningsskydd*', SFS 1982:80) is probably the single most important piece of labour legislation. It completely outlaws at-will termination and replaces it by a just cause requirement.

Legal disputes involving labour issues are settled by the Labour Court. Cases brought to the Labour Court involve claims of wrongful dismissal, breaches of union–employer contracts, discrimination, and illegal wildcat strikes. The court hears about 400 cases annually.

32.24 Compulsory Transfer of Employees

Through EU Directive 77/187/EEC (this directive has since been amended and clarified through the Directives 98/50/EC and 2001/23/23/EC), which has been implemented into Swedish labour law, the employee's rights must be protected in the event of a change of employer. All employee rights according to Swedish legislation have thereby been extended into the transfer of ownership of companies, businesses, or parts of businesses.

As in a situation of transfer of shares, there is no actual change in employer but the employment agreement remains the same and is not affected by the transfer. A transfer of assets is not treated as a 'just cause for dismissal' as required by the Employment Protection Act for termination of employment. Both present and future employers have a duty to negotiate with unions by the use of collective agreements with the company prior to a transfer.

An employee has the right to agree to be transferred with the transaction, leave his or her employment, or remain with the former employer.

32.25 Tax Deductibility of Acquisition Expenses

Where the buyer is a company that is not taxable in Sweden, this question is determined by the regulations in his or her home jurisdiction.

Under Swedish tax legislation, costs and expenses directly connected with an specific acquisition (e.g. costs for due diligence investigations and contract negotiations) are not directly tax deductible but are instead added to the total acquisition cost and are thereby reflected when the loss of profit is later realized (e.g. if the purchased company is later resold). However, certain other costs and expenses usually caused by an acquisition but not directly related to the specific acquisition such as costs for tax restructuring, tax advice, and financing are directly deductible.

32.26 Levies on Acquisition Agreements and Collateral Documents

There are no levies on acquisition agreements, with the exception of transfers of real property which bear a stamp duty of 3 per cent for companies and 1.5 per cent for individuals. Real property, vessels and aircraft do not become encumbered until the property owner pledges a mortgage deed as collateral; such mortgage deeds are obtained after registration with the relevant register and are subject to stamp duty. Stamp duty on the mortgaged amount is 2 per cent on real property, 1 per cent for aircraft and 0.4 per cent for vessels.

32.27 Financing Rules and Restrictions

A limited liability company must enter into voluntary liquidation should the company's capital be less than half of the registered share capital.

Tax deductions are allowed for running expenses (i.e. the cost of acquiring and preserving proceeds). Please note that there are certain limitations to the deductibility of deficits. These limitations are divided into two groups, firstly when the tax-paying company is not the entity being directly affected by the actual loss, and secondly when the tax-paying company attempts to profit from a loss by trading the loss.

Central in the Swedish company legislation are the restrictions given though the loan prohibition rules. These rules are constructed to protect the company's creditors. As a principal rule, a company may not grant a loan to a shareholder or any closely related natural or legal persons. There are however some exceptions. For example, a company may grant a loan to another company within the same group of affiliated companies also a loan may be granted if the loan is intended exclusively for the borrower's operations and the company provides the loan for purely commercial reasons. Regarding the granting of loans for the acquisition of shares, a company may not grant an advance, provide loans, or provide security for loans so that the debtor or any natural or legal person connected thereto shall acquire shares in the company or any parent company of the same group.

The rules regarding Swedish companies purchasing and owning their own shares have been changed in recent years so that, if specific criteria are met, Swedish companies are allowed to purchase their own shares. However, Swedish companies may still not give loans for the purpose of buying the shares in the company, except for certain loans to employees. The legislation differentiates between Swedish listed and unlisted companies. Swedish listed companies can, if certain criteria are met, purchase their own shares up to a limit of 10 per cent of the total number of shares after a decision taken at a shareholders' meeting. Own shares bought in accordance with this legislation by unlisted companies have to be sold or redeemed within six months of the purchase or else the shares are disqualified and the share capital reduced accordingly.

Value transfers from the company may take place only in the purpose of distribution of profits, acquisition of the company's own shares, reduction of the share capital, or statutory reserve for payment to the shareholders and certain gifts for charitable purposes. Following the principle of corporate benefit, value transfers from the company may not take place where, after the transfer, there is insufficient coverage for the company's restricted equity. Moreover, the company may effect a value transfer only provided that it is justified taking in consideration e.g. the demands with respect to size of shareholder's equity which are imposed by the nature, scope, and risks associated with the operations.

32.28 Exchange Controls and Repatriation of Profits

There are no restrictions applicable to transfers of funds from Sweden to foreign countries, with the exception of transfers to certain countries which are subject to international economic sanctions.

Profits from a Swedish branch may be repatriated without taxation (see **32.4**).

32.29 Groups of Companies

According to the Companies Act, a group of companies exists where a company (the parent company) holds the majority of votes in another company (the subsidiary). A supplementary definition holds that a group of companies exists where a company, by virtue of its holding of shares or parts, or by virtue of the articles of association or agreement, has a controlling influence in another company.

The parent company must each financial year prepare a consolidated account, consisting of a consolidated income statement and a consolidated balance sheet.

If a limited liability company owns more than 90 per cent of the shares in a subsidiary, the Companies Act authorizes the compulsory acquisition of the remaining shares. This applies both at the request of a majority and a minority of the shareholders.

32.30   Responsibility for Liabilities of an Acquired Subsidiary

The Companies Act does not contain any rules on the parent company's liability for its subsidiaries. In principle, the subsidiaries are separate legal entities and are liable for their own obligations. There are, nevertheless, some tendencies in practice and jurisprudence towards a 'lifting of the corporate veil'. This is an area of law still under development, and is beyond the scope of this guide.

The parent company is, however, liable as a shareholder if it wilfully or by gross negligence, by being an accessory to a contravention of the Companies Act, the laws regarding the annual report or the articles of association, causes damage to the company, a shareholder or any other person.

32.31   Governing Law of a Contract

Under Swedish private international law, the parties to a contract are free to determine which law shall govern a contract. This general principle may be set aside where the effect of applying a foreign law is in violation of Swedish *ordre public*. Moreover, Swedish courts generally do not enforce the public laws of other countries.

Sweden has ratified the Rome Convention on the Law Applicable to Contractual Obligations and Swedish courts normally adhere to its principles also in relation to parties which are not nationals of a party to the convention.

32.32   Dispute Resolution Options

Swedish law recognizes that the parties to a contract can agree to settle their disputes in arbitration proceedings, in Sweden or in another country. It is still unusual to refer disputes to mediation. Sweden has ratified both the New York Convention and the Geneva Convention of 1927 on the Execution of Foreign Arbitral Awards and thus foreign arbitral awards may be enforced in Sweden to full extent. The procedure for enforcement is laid down in the Arbitration Act (*'lag om skiljeförfarande'*, SFS 1999:116). Applications for recognition and enforcement are made to the Svea Court of Appeals in Stockholm.

Sweden does not have any uniform legislation regarding the recognition and enforcement of foreign judgments. Whether a foreign judgment is recognized and enforced in Sweden varies depending on the subject-matter and on which country has rendered the judgment. If the parties to an agreement enter into a prorogation agreement with respect to a court in a foreign country, a Swedish court in general, respects this choice, and considers itself unable to exercise jurisdiction.

33. SWITZERLAND

Max Albers-Schönberg / Matthias Leemann CMS von Erlach Henrici

33.1 Introductory Comments

Switzerland is a federal republic consisting of 26 states (Cantons). Most areas of substantive law which are relevant for business acquisitions (e.g. the laws on contracts, companies, accounting, property, etc) are governed by federal legislation.

Nevertheless, the Cantons have retained far-reaching legislative and administrative powers in various areas, including tax matters. In addition to the taxes collected by the federal government, the Cantons have the power to levy their own taxes on income and net worth at rates which vary considerably from Canton to Canton and even amongst the municipalities. Following the rejection by Switzerland of the Agreement on the EEA in the national referendum held on 6 December 1992, various pieces of national legislation were passed by the Swiss Parliament to adapt Swiss law to EU law in certain areas.

33.2 Corporate Structures

Corporate structures are governed by federal law.

The target of an acquisition of shares in Switzerland is usually a stock corporation ('*société anonyme*'). Other business entities provided by Swiss law include limited partnerships with shares ('*sociétés en commandite par actions*'), limited liability companies ('*sociétés à responsabilité limitée*') and co-operative corporations ('*sociétés coopératives*'). Furthermore, Swiss law provides three types of partnerships: the simple partnership ('*société simple*'), the general partnership ('*société en nom collectif*') and the limited partnership ('*société en commandite*'). Partnerships do not have a separate legal personality, but it is possible to contract with partnerships.

The shares of Swiss stock companies can be listed on the Swiss Stock Exchange. Special accounting and reporting rules apply to stock companies which are so listed.

33.3 Letters of Intent and Heads of Agreement

The fact of two parties opening negotiations creates a quasi legal relationship which imposes the obligation for these parties to act in good faith. Such an understanding can be entered into orally or in writing, or even by mere actions implying an intention to do so.

© World Law Group
International Business Acquisitions, M. Whalley, F.-J. Semler (eds.), Kluwer Law International, London, 2007; ISBN 9789041124838.

There is also an increasing tendency in Switzerland to conclude formal letters of intent. Such agreements may comprise a number of concrete obligations, including:

- a covenant not to negotiate with third parties;

- an obligation to grant to the other party access to material documentation and possibly to inspect the company's books;

- a commitment to keep the negotiations in confidence and not to disclose any information exchanged in the course of the negotiations;

- an undertaking to return all materials obtained by the other party in case of failure of the negotiations;

- the parties' right to terminate the negotiations at any time.

The legal significance of letters of intent depends on their contents and the individual facts.

Depending on the circumstances, some of these obligations may be considered to be already included in the generally recognized legal duty to act in good faith.

While an informal agreement to negotiate or a letter of intent cannot impose an obligation actually to conclude the contract at issue, such agreement may, depending on the circumstances, still result in damage claims for non-compliance with the obligations set out in it.

33.4   Taxes Affecting the Structure and Calculation of the Price

General

The acquisition of an enterprise, through the purchase of assets or shares, involves a large number of complex tax issues, the examination of which is beyond the scope of this guide. Appropriate tax advice should therefore in any event be obtained to avoid unexpected problems.

Asset Acquisition

If securities are purchased in an asset acquisition, the federal transfer stamp tax is levied on the transfer of the securities if a domestic securities dealer is involved in the sale either as a party or as an intermediary.

If a transfer of real property is involved, special cantonal/communal transfer taxes are levied. The capital gain realized upon the sale of the real property is, in principle, subject to the ordinary federal and cantonal/communal income tax. However, certain Cantons levy a special cantonal/municipal real estate capital gains tax[1] instead of the ordinary income tax, which takes into account the holding period (i.e. a shorter holding period results in a higher real estate capital gains tax). In most Cantons a statutory lien exists on the real property to secure both the real estate transfer tax and the cantonal/communal real estate capital gains tax (but not the federal and the cantonal/communal income tax).

It is strongly advisable to include in the asset purchase agreement specific provisions dealing with the tax consequences regarding each type of assets to be transferred.

Share Acquisition

Careful consideration should be given to the tax consequences resulting for the buyer and the seller in a share deal.

A share acquisition does neither trigger income taxes on the level of the company acquired (the book values remain unchanged, i.e. there is in particular no step-up in basis available) nor on the level of the acquirer. As a general rule, individuals holding the shares in their private wealth ('*Privatvermögen*') will—subject to certain exceptions[2]— realize a tax neutral capital gain (or loss) upon the sale of the shares. Any capital gain realized by any other seller is, in principle, subject to income taxes. However, capital gains realized by corporations are subject to the participation exemption scheme and, thus, factually tax exempt provided (i) the minimum holding period of one year is met and (ii) at least 20 per cent of the total shares in the target company are sold.

In case of a real estate company, some Cantons do tax the transfer of the economic ownership regarding the real estate situated in the Canton in question like a transfer of the real property itself. In these Cantons, a rather complex special set of rules applies which could involve cantonal/communal real estate capital gains taxes and cantonal/communal real estate transfer tax issues, the description of which is beyond the scope of this guide.

The buyer is usually burdened with a deferred tax liability on the level of the target company which will materialize if and to the extent hidden reserves are effectively realized (e.g. in the event of a sale of an asset having a low book value for a higher price or in case of liquidation of the target company). An individual shareholder holding the shares in his private wealth is, in addition, burdened with a deferred income tax liability (difference between nominal value and fair market value of the shares). Such income tax liability will materialize upon dividend distributions made by the target company and in the event of the liquidation of the target company.

The federal transfer stamp tax is levied on the transfer of the shares if a domestic security dealer is involved in the sale either as a party or as an intermediary.

33.5 Extent of Seller's Warranties and Indemnities

The Swiss statutory sales law does not cover all possible situations that might be involved with business acquisitions, especially with those carried out in the form of a share purchase. It is therefore strongly advised to include in the purchase agreement a comprehensive set of rules regarding the warranties and indemnities to be given by the seller or, under certain circumstances, the buyer. Such warranties should cover a variety of areas (including title situation, corporate existence, financial statements, business activity since effective dates of financial statements, taxes and duties, material contracts, employee matters, permits, licences, environmental matters, litigation, insurance, real estate, IP, etc).

Support of these warranties by appropriate guarantees from the seller's parent company should in any event be considered.

33.6 Liability for Pre-contractual Representations

Negligent and fraudulent misrepresentations made by one party may give the other party the right to annul the contract based on material error and to claim damages. Deceptive warranties may, under certain circumstances, also result in a subsequent reduction of the purchase price. It is advisable to lay down all representations and promises in formal warranty clauses. Such clauses should specifically address and regulate the consequences that will result from a breach of such warranties (e.g. claims for damages, annulment of the contract, reduction of the purchase price, including relevant calculation methods, etc).

33.7 Liability for Pre-acquisition Trading and Contracts

Asset Acquisition

As a general rule, contracts cannot be transferred as a whole to a third party, but the transfer would have to be carried out by way of an assignment of rights and assumption of debts under the contract. Rights under the contract may be assigned without the obligor's consent unless the contract itself or the legal nature of the claim prohibits such assignment. The assumption of debts under a contract will only release the contracting party (debtor) if the creditor of such claim consents.

The Swiss Merger Law, which came into effect in July 2004, provides for a new institute of *transfer of assets and liabilities* ('*Vermögensübertragung*'). The transfer of assets and liabilities allows a company registered in the Commercial Register to transfer all or part of its assets and liabilities to another legal entity by universal succession (i.e. without the need to transfer single items), upon entry of the transfer in the Commercial Register. The transferor remains jointly and severally liable for the liabilities transferred for a period of three years. While the leading Swiss legal doctrine suggests that contracts may also be transferred without the obligee's consent based on such transfer of assets and liabilities under the Swiss Merger Law, the Swiss Federal Supreme Court has not yet decided on this issue.

Usually, a reference date ('*Stichtag*') is stipulated, stating the date upon which the benefits and risks under the contract shall pass from the seller to the buyer.

Share Acquisition

In a share acquisition, existing business contracts remain—subject to potential change-of-control-rights—unchanged because the party to such contracts is the target company as a legal entity and shareholders are, as a general rule, not liable for the company's debts.

33.8 Pre-completion Risks

As mentioned above, the Swiss statutory sales law does not contain sufficiently detailed rules governing the transfer of benefits and risks in business acquisitions.

A business acquisition agreement should therefore contain specific provisions as to which party will take the risk involved with events occurring after signing but prior to completion of the agreement.

In a share acquisition, the seller is usually requested to give a warranty to the effect that there will be no material change to the business after the signing date possibly combined with a clause providing for a reduction of the purchase price in the event a pre-completion risk materializes.

33.9 Required Governmental Approvals

Investments made by non-resident aliens are not subject to a general authorization requirement, but are limited in certain areas.

In accordance with a federal law restricting foreign investment in Swiss real property ('*Lex Friedrich*'), the purchase of real property, or shares of a company owning such property, by non-resident individuals, foreign companies or Swiss companies controlled by non-residents may be subject to government approval. The acquisition of an enterprise owning Swiss real property by a foreign buyer may therefore involve proceedings to obtain government approval. Restrictions apply, however, in particular to the acquisition of residential real estate, but not to commercial real estate ('*Betriebsstätte-Grundstücke*', i.e. properties which are used as business premises).

In a number of professions and trades a licence is required (see **33.12**). Some licences are reserved to Swiss residents and corporations registered in Switzerland.

33.10 Anti-trust and Competition Laws

The Swiss Law on Cartels enacted in 1995 adapted to a substantial degree rules which are similar to substantive EU competition law and it aimed at establishing the basis for a stronger competition policy. Under the Swiss Law on Cartels, the Swiss Competition Commission is competent to forbid unlawful restrictions on competition, such as unlawful agreements and unlawful practices of undertakings having a dominant position. It also provides for a preventive merger control: if the turnover of the companies involved exceeds certain thresholds, or one of the companies dominates its market, the Competition Commission must be notified of the merger before its consummation. The Commission may prohibit the merger or impose conditions and obligations on the parties if it is deemed to have a negative impact on competition.

On 1 April 2004, the revised Law on Cartels came into force and, among other things, provided the Swiss Competition Commission with sharper tools: while previously sanctions could only be imposed in case of a repeated breach of the Law on Cartels, the Competition Commission may now impose substantial fines (of up to 10 per cent of the total turnover realized by the undertaking in Switzerland during the last three financial years) without prior warning for certain first-time infringements, such as hard-core cartels, certain vertical restraints and abuse of a dominant market position.

33.11 Required Offer Procedures

Public offers for listed shares are subject to the Law on Stock Exchanges and Securities Trade. A buyer acquiring, directly or indirectly, more than one third of a corporation's voting rights must offer to buy all of its listed shares.

However, a potential target company can raise the marginal value to 49 per cent ('opting-up') or even exempt itself from these takeover rules ('opting-out') by provision in its articles of association. The purchase price to be paid for the remaining shares shall be at least the stock exchange price and may not be less than 75 per cent of the highest price paid by the offeror for the target company's shares during the last 12 months prior to the public offer.

There are no takeover rules for private companies or for asset purchases.

33.12 Continuation of Government Licences

With respect to a number of industries, a licence is required and sometimes only granted or upheld if the business operator is a Swiss resident or a Swiss company not controlled by non-residents. Industries in which a licence is needed include banking, insurance, air traffic, job placement, broadcasting, cinemas and motion picture distribution.

In many cases, government licences are not transferable. In a business acquisition, therefore, new licences may have to be obtained by the buyer in its own name.

In a share acquisition, the change in ownership or control of the licensee (target company) may, with respect to certain industries (e.g. banking) involve the need to obtain a new government licence.

33.13 Requirements for Transferring Shares

Swiss stock companies may issue registered or bearer shares.

Restrictions on the transfer of registered shares may be contained in the company's articles of association or in shareholders' agreements. With a private company, the company's right to reject a transfer is legally limited to a number of reasons. Where a company is listed on a Swiss stock exchange, a transfer may only be rejected if the buyer of the shares would exceed the ownership percentage limits provided in the articles. Registered shares of private corporations are transferred by delivery and endorsement of the share certificate and the transfer is (if so provided for in the articles) subject to consent by the board of directors. If shares of a public company are acquired, the voting rights are suspended until such consent is granted, while the financial rights (dividend claims, etc) are transferred with the endorsement.

Bearer shares are transferred by delivery of physical or legal possession. According to government plans to amend the law on stock corporations, bearer shares shall be abolished in the future.

The transferability of the shares and the seller's authority and ability to transfer the shares should be covered by adequate warranty provisions.

33.14 Requirements for Transferring Land and Property Leases

Switzerland maintains a sophisticated land registration system governed by federal law which covers most of the Swiss territory.

Title to land, mortgages, options and pre-emptions, easements and other charges on land are registered in the Land Register. Registration of these rights in the Register is generally exclusive, in the sense that no rights with respect to land exist except those properly recorded in the Register. Third parties acting in good faith may rely on the transcripts from the Land Register as being conclusive regarding the titles, mortgages or any other rights existing with respect to such property.

Formal requirements make it necessary that a transfer of title to or creation of a mortgage on land be made by way of a public deed and subsequent registration in the Land Register. In case of a transfer of assets and liabilities under the Swiss Merger Law (see **33.7**), the transfer of land takes place by way of universal succession upon registration of such transfer in the Commercial Register. In this exceptional case, the subsequent registration in the Land Register is merely of declaratory nature.

The transfer of land to a non-resident may be subject to government approvals under the *Lex Friedrich* (see **33.9**). Special restrictions apply to the sale of agricultural property.

33.15 Requirements for Transferring Intellectual Property

Formal requirements apply regarding the transfer of patents and trade marks, whereas copyrights, industrial designs and models, plant varieties and topographics of semiconductor chips may be transferred without formal requirements. Registration of the transfer into the respective federal register (which exist with respect to all of the mentioned rights except the copyright) is not a condition precedent thereto but the only means to make the transfer effective *vis-à-vis* third parties. In case of a transfer of assets and liabilities under the Swiss Merger Law (see **33.7**), such intellectual property rights transfer by way of universal succession.

In a share acquisition, no rights need be transferred. Therefore, while the owner of the shares changes, the acquired company continues to be the owner of the rights. Licence agreements may, however, contain provisions which are relevant in the case of a sale of the licensee.

33.16 Requirements for Transferring Business Contracts, Licences and Leases

As a general rule, the transfer of a contract to a third party and the release of the contracting party of its obligations thereunder, is only possible with the other contracting party's consent.

Based on a transfer of assets and liabilities under the Swiss Merger Law, contracts may be transferred without such consent, but the seller remains liable for a limited time (see **33.7**).

In view of this, a formal novation of the contracts (whereby the purchaser assumes all rights and obligations and the seller is released from its obligations) should be adopted in the case of complex business contracts.

Special provisions apply to employment contracts and lease agreements: a tenant needs his or her landlord's written consent to transfer the lease agreement, but this consent may not be withheld unreasonably. In case of a sale of real property, the lease agreements relating to such property automatically pass to the buyer and new owner of the object by operation of law. With respect to employment contracts, see **32.24**.

33.17 Requirements for Transferring Other Assets

Title to movable assets (chattels) is transferred by conveying possession ('*Besitz*'). Transfer of possession can be effected either by physical delivery or (if the goods are physically maintained with third parties) by way of a contract. As a general rule, rights in chattels acquired by a party on the assumption made in good faith that no other third party rights exist thereon take priority over any such third party rights.

Receivables can be transferred by way of simple assignment in writing unless otherwise specifically stipulated in the underlying contract from which the receivables originate. Notification to and consent by the debtor is not a precondition to the validity of the assignment. However, prior to notification of the assignment, the debtor of the claims assigned may validly discharge the claims by making payment to the assignor. Appropriate stipulations should be included in the business purchase agreement regarding notification to the debtor.

In case of a transfer of assets and liabilities under the Swiss Merger Law (see **33.7**), both receivables and title to movable assets (chattels) transfer by way of universal succession upon entry of the transfer in the Commercial Register.

33.18 Encumbrances and Third Party Interests

Assets can be subject to a variety of third party interests. With regard to land, as a general rule, third party interests (such as mortgages or easements) do not come into existence unless they are properly recorded in the Land Register. For those parts of Switzerland which are covered by the Federal Land Register, extracts from the Land Register can be relied upon by the buyer of a real property as conclusive evidence regarding the title and mortgage situation. For those areas not covered by the Federal Land Register, further inquiries will be necessary.

Pledges on chattels do not come into existence as long as the assets are left within the pledger's exclusive possession. Therefore, a buyer of movable property acting in good faith generally acquires unencumbered title to the assets.

Chattels in which the seller has retained title remain encumbered with such title if the title is recorded in a special register ('*Eigentumsvorbehaltsregister*'). There are a number of liens which come into existence by operation of law (including the repairer's lien, the lessor's right of retention, certain statutory liens on land to cover the real property gains tax, etc).

In order to protect the buyer, warranties from the seller as to clear title and the absence of statutory liens are essential.

33.19   Minimum Shareholder and Officer Requirements

Stock companies must have at least three shareholders and at least one director.

A reduction to less than three shareholders after establishment of the company is tolerated, but any of the company's creditors may require an increase of the number of shareholders to the legal minimum.

If the stock company has more than one director, the majority of the board of directors must consist of Swiss, EU or EFTA citizens domiciled in Switzerland. Exemptions from this board nationality requirement may be granted by the authorities for holding companies if the majority of the enterprises held by the holding companies are located outside Switzerland.

If there is only one director, he or she must be a Swiss, EU or EFTA citizen domiciled in Switzerland. However, the mentioned majority requirement is expected to be abolished at the beginning of 2008.

If there are several classes of shares in respect of voting or pecuniary rights, the articles of association must ensure that each class of shares is represented by at least one representative in the board of directors.

33.20   Non-competition Clauses

A seller may agree with the buyer not to compete with the buyer (in relation to the business sold) for a certain period of time. Such agreement is enforceable provided that it is reasonably limited in terms of place, time and subject and may be secured by a conventional penalty (liquidated damages). However, a judge may reduce excessive non-competition clauses or penalties at his or her discretion.

33.21 Environmental Considerations

Switzerland's legislation protecting the environment is covered by a variety of federal laws, such as the Environmental Protection Statute, the Water Pollution Statute and the Civil Code. The owner of an industrial plant is subject to a non-fault liability for any pollution caused by such plant and may be obliged to modify polluting structures in order to meet legal standards. Future owners and occupiers may also become liable for contamination already present at the real estate when they acquire it.

A full environmental audit should thus always be carried out by the buyer. Acquisition due diligence may involve the appointment of environmental consultants to consider documentary information, to carry out site visits or to undertake further investigation. Due to the serious potential effects of environmental issues, it is important to ascertain such problems at an early stage, also to enable negotiation on the price. In addition, comprehensive warranties with respect to environmental liability and damage should always be obtained from the seller.

33.22 Employee Superannuation/Pension Plans

The Swiss mandatory social security system is based on two 'pillars':

- the government Old-Age, Survivors and Disability Insurance; and

- occupational pension plans: in addition to the state insurance, employers are required to contribute to pension plans managed by separate entities under government supervision.

Employers are not liable for losses of the pension foundation unless they are members of the foundation council, the liability of which resembles that of the directors of a stock company. Moreover, the employer must contribute to the employees' unemployment and accident insurances. Usually, the employer also takes out a voluntary health insurance policy in favour of his or her employees in order to cover his or her obligation to pay the wage for a limited time during an employee's sick leave.

Employees who have served at least 20 years and are at least 50 years old are generally entitled to a special severance compensation upon termination of the employment relationship. Unless otherwise agreed by written agreement, standard employment contracts or collective contracts, the severance compensation should not be less than an amount equal to the employee's wages for two months and may not exceed an amount equal to the employee's wages for eight months. The severance compensation is reduced by the amount of benefits received by the employee from personal welfare institutions if and to the extent these benefits have directly or indirectly been funded by the employer.

33.23 Employee Rights

Four sources of law may be relevant for determining the rights and duties under an employment relationship:

- the individual specific employment contract;

- collective employment contracts concluded between employers and unions;

- standard employment contracts decreed by the federal or a cantonal government agency for certain branches; and

- the provisions of the Swiss Code of Obligations (CO) and the Federal Labour Law.

33.24 Compulsory Transfer of Employees

In an asset acquisition, if the seller transfers the whole or part of the business to the buyer, the employment contracts related to the business so transferred automatically pass to the buyer by operation of law with all rights and duties. The seller and the buyer remain jointly and severally liable for the due performance of the employment contract until the expiration of its term or the date upon which such contract can be validly terminated in accordance with its terms. In order to protect the seller, appropriate warranties should be obtained from the buyer as to its due performance of the employment agreements so assumed.

It needs to be mentioned in this context, however that the employee has the right to refuse such transfer. In order to enable the employee to take a well-informed decision in this respect, the employer has a duty to inform. Accordingly, if an employer transfers a business or a part thereof to a third party, the employees' representatives or, if there are none, the employees, shall be informed in good time prior to the transfer of the reason for the transfer as well as its legal, economic and social consequences for the employees. In case of non-compliance with these requirements, the employees' representatives may request the court to prohibit the entry of the transfer of assets and liabilities, or another transaction under the Swiss Merger Law (such as a merger), in the Commercial Register.

The simultaneous termination of employment relationships of a certain minimum number of employees is considered a mass dismissal. An employer planning such a dismissal is required first to consult with the employees' representatives and then to report the dismissal and the results of the consultation to the public employment agency. However, neither the employees' representatives nor the public authorities are able to prevent the mass dismissal or to impose any additional duties upon the employer.

33.25 Tax Deductibility of Acquisition Expenses

If the buyer is an individual or a company not resident in Switzerland, the deductibility of the acquisition expenses is governed by the tax laws of the buyer's home jurisdiction.

If the buyer is a Swiss taxpayer, as a general rule the acquisition costs are deductible to the extent they are justified business expenses (i.e. to the extent they represent a decrease in assets and thus need not to be activated as part of the acquired assets). Appropriate tax advice should be obtained regarding these issues.

33.26 Levies on Acquisition Agreements and Collateral Documents

In an asset acquisition, stamp duty payable on the sale of securities is levied if taxable securities (such as bonds, shares, fund units, etc) form part of the assets purchased and if the purchase is effected and if one of the contracting parties or the person or company serving as intermediary to the transaction is considered a domestic securities dealer.

In a share acquisition, the stamp duty is levied on the shares sold provided the person or company serving as intermediary to the transaction is considered a domestic securities dealer.

Except for public notary fees, which are payable if the agreements are concluded by way of public deeds, and the fees which are payable to land or other registers to effect the transfer of the property concerned (such as land), no significant duties are imposed on the acquisition agreements.

33.27 Financing Rules and Restrictions

The Federal Tax Law and all the cantonal Tax Laws contain certain debt to equity limits which must be observed in order to ensure the deductibility of interest payments made by the company. Interest payments made on the debt portion exceeding the admissible ratio are denied for deduction.

Loans granted to a Swiss company by related enterprises need to be structured on an arm's length basis. Interest payments made by a Swiss company to a related entity need to be made in compliance with guidelines issued by the Federal Tax Administration. Interest payments made at rates exceeding the admissible rates may be treated as constructive dividends for corporate income and Swiss withholding tax purposes.

The issue of new share capital and payments to the company's paid-in surplus are subject to stamp duty of 1 per cent. No stamp duty is payable if the consideration paid to the stock company is below CHF 1,000,000. If such amount has not been reached upon the formation of the stock company, the unused balance is exempt from stamp duty in the event of a subsequent increase of capital. The repurchase by the company of a substantial portion of its own shares is, under certain circumstances, treated as partial liquidation for tax purposes and thus triggers Swiss withholding tax at the corporate level and may constitute taxable income to the Swiss resident shareholders. As of 1 January 1998, however, revised Swiss federal corporate legislation came into effect which grants a more favourable tax treatment of the redemption of shares.

33.28 Exchange Controls and Repatriation of Profits

There are no general restrictions on the transfer of money from Switzerland to a foreign country. However, governmental sanctions are imposed at present on certain countries (including Liberia, Myanmar, Sudan, Zimbabwe, Ivory Coast, Democratic Republic of Congo and Yugoslavia) as well as persons and organizations with links to Osama Bin Laden, the 'Al-Qaeda' group or the Taliban.

Dividend payments made by Swiss companies are subject to 35 per cent withholding tax which is to be deducted by the company from the gross amount of the dividend declared. In relation to Swiss taxpayers, the 35 per cent withholding tax is a collection device only. Swiss taxpayers can obtain a tax credit for such tax against their income taxes. Non-resident recipients of the dividend may be entitled to obtain a reduction or a refund of the 35 per cent withholding tax in accordance with applicable international tax treaties.

There is, in general, no withholding tax on interest payments made by Swiss companies on loans. Withholding tax is, however, deducted from interest payments made by banks or finance companies on interest-bearing accounts or other accounts of a similar nature ('*Kundenguthaben*').

33.29   Groups of Companies

Swiss stock companies must prepare consolidated financial statements if they control one or more other companies by way of a majority of votes or any other means.

Exemptions are granted for groups of companies not exceeding certain thresholds concerning assets, revenues and employees provided they are not listed on a Swiss stock exchange and do not have bonds outstanding. Moreover, shareholders whose combined holdings represent at least 10 per cent of the capital stock may request consolidated financial statements.

33.30   Responsibility for Liabilities of an Acquired Subsidiary

It is a fundamental rule of Swiss company law that the shareholders of a company are, in the absence of specific guarantees given by the shareholders, not liable for the company's debts. In a decision rendered by the Federal Supreme Court, however, a parent company was held to be liable for the debts of one of its subsidiary companies on the grounds that it acted *vis-à-vis* third parties in a way that led them to believe that the parent company would support the subsidiary and be liable for its debts. Careful consideration must be given to the issue of a shareholders' potential liability.

33.31   Governing Law of the Contract

The choice of law made by the parties in the share or business purchase agreement is recognized if it has been agreed upon explicitly or becomes clearly evident from the circumstances. It would, depending on the wording of the clause, be limited to the share or business purchase agreement itself. The substantive law applicable to special issues, such as the requirements for the transfer of title to goods, may be subject to different substantive laws (i.e. *lex fori*) and only a limited or even no choice of law may be possible.

33.32   Dispute Resolution Options

A choice of forum is generally accepted by Swiss courts. The parties may also agree on arbitration proceedings to resolve disputes arising in connection with the contract. Switzerland is well-known for its longstanding tradition of international arbitration and offers a sophisticated system of arbitration rules and services. The Swiss Private International Law Statute codifies, among other things, a set of rules dealing with international arbitration. Switzerland is also a party to the New York Convention on the Enforcement and Recognition of Foreign International Arbitration Awards.

Foreign decisions are generally recognized and enforceable in Switzerland provided that certain constitutional standards have been observed by the foreign judicial authorities. Such standards are usually set out in bilateral or multilateral treaties such as the Lugano Convention (to which Switzerland has been a party since 1992). If no such treaty exists with a country, the recognition rules contained in the Private International Law Statute are applicable.

33.33   Other Issues

In principle, foreign individuals wishing to take up residence and to work in Switzerland need a government permit.

Companies wishing to employ foreign (non-Swiss) employees or executives to stay in Switzerland therefore must obtain a residence and work permit. These permits are governed by a quota system and are issued, depending on the circumstances, either by the federal government or the cantonal government where the company or the foreign individual is domiciled. There are various types of permits available including annual residence and work permits (Permits B), permanent residence permits (Permits C), temporary residence permits and cross-border permits. In granting the permits, the authorities do have a relatively wide discretion allowing them to take into account the facts and circumstances of the individual case.

Special rules apply to EU nationals: the Agreement on the Free Movement of Persons between Switzerland and the EU allows nationals from the EU countries access to the Swiss labour market as well as the right to settle. Such persons must, however, find employment in Switzerland or be able to finance their own living expenses. Certain restrictions (such as quotas) continue to apply during transition periods until 2007 (for nationals of the old EU member states) respectively 2011 (for nationals of the new EU member states). EU nationals of the old member states do not need a residence permit for a stay of up to three months; in case of longer stays they must submit an application to the cantonal authorities. EU nationals of the new member states need a residence and work permit from the first day of work in Switzerland.

The Swiss parliament has enacted certain amendments to the Swiss law on stock corporations which are expected to come into force at the beginning of 2008. Accordingly, a single shareholder will be able to incorporate a Swiss stock corporation. In addition, the requirement that the majority of directors must consist of Swiss, EU or EFTA citizens domiciled in Switzerland will be abolished. In addition, directors will no longer be required to be shareholders of the company.

At a later stage a general revision of the law on stock corporations is planned to take place which aims at improving corporate governance and will introduce new rules on capital structures as well as accounting and reporting requirements; in addition, the provisions governing annual general meetings will be updated.

34. TAIWAN

Paiff Huang
Chun-yih Cheng
Feng-chun Yen
Formosa Transnational

34.1 Introductory Comments

In Taiwan, excepting those industries involving significant public interest such as the postal service, power and gas supply and radio and television broadcasting, among others, most companies have traditionally been owned by private groups and have operated in the domestic market. Following economic developments in the past decade in Taiwan, many groups, through formal or informal reform, have successfully expanded their international operations.

More and more companies believe that they must be further transformed into multinational companies to keep up with the pace of the quickly changing business environment created by the economic and social changes in Taiwan.

Taiwan has always had an attractive business climate, and is seeking to develop into an Asia-Pacific Regional Operation Centre, vigorously encouraged and supported by the Taiwanese Government. Mergers and acquisitions are the common and quick measures for helping companies to expand their scale of businesses. An accurate assessment of the target company is a crucial and indispensable factor for a successful transaction. Professional advice, therefore, is essential for a correct and wise decision on the transaction.

The past few years have seen a dramatic change in the legal framework of Taiwan's business and commercial law. The Financial Institutions Merger Law was enacted in 2000, in an effort to encourage business combination and strengthen the competitive advantage of Taiwanese financial service industries, followed by the Financial Holding Company Law of 2001 and the Merger and Acquisition Law of 2002. Accordingly, the Fair Trade Law, Securities and Exchange Law and the Company Law have all undergone significant amendments so as to incorporate the new legal requirements.

The legal overhaul has sparked quite a few high-profile and interesting cases, notably in the financial sector. In brief, Taiwanese companies are now far more aggressive in expanding their business activities through mergers and acquisitions.

34.2 Corporate Structures

There are four types of companies under the Taiwanese Company Law: an unlimited company, a limited company, an unlimited company with limited liability shareholders

International Business Acquisitions, M. Whalley, F.-J. Semler (eds.), Kluwer Law International, London, 2007; ISBN 9789041124838.

and a company limited by shares. The target of an acquisition can be any of these companies, public or private.

Pursuant to the Company Law, the Board of Directors is elected by shareholders, and is accountable for the performance of the company, while the supervisor(s) serves in the capacity of monitoring the functioning of Directors. The management is retained by the Board and is in charge of the daily business operation.

34.3   Letters of Intent and Heads of Agreement

An agreement is binding if it appears either from the document itself or from the circumstances that there is a meeting of minds with intentions from both sides to create legal relationships and if there is consideration given for any promises and undertakings given by either party.

If it is intended that letters or heads of agreement should not be binding on the parties until the exchange of further formal contracts, clear words should be used to that effect. A formal agreement should have more specific provisions inserted to clarify whether, and to what extent, it is intended to be binding.

The parties to a merger/acquisition often enter into a letter of intent at the initial stage of the negotiations. Although the letter of intent may cover essential terms and conditions of the transaction, thus would be considered a contract in substance pursuant to the Civil Code, the practice is that counsels would, in order to avoid any potential controversies, prepare the letter of intent with a statement that the letter of intent would not be binding upon the parties. The same practice applies to heads of agreement.

34.4   Taxes Affecting the Structure and Calculation of the Price

The purchase of shares results in the buyer assuming all the target company's obligations and liabilities, including taxation liability, while a purchase of assets avoids this problem. However, the buyer of the assets still needs to check if there is any security charged on the assets to be acquired. The seller's appropriate warranties or taxation indemnities may protect the buyer to a degree from any unforeseen liabilities of the target in the former case.

The transfer of shares in the target is subject to securities transaction tax. The buyer is required to withhold 0.3 per cent of the purchase price as the tax and pay that amount to the tax authority. The tax rate may be changed by the authority from time to time and will be announced before a new rate is enforced.

The purchase of land or buildings is subject to both land value increment tax and deed tax. Land value increment tax is borne by the seller; the deed tax is borne by the buyer.

The structure of a transaction, including the consideration to be paid and the business operation after the transaction, will affect the tax liability of the participating companies. Parties contemplating a merger/acquisition/spin-off should look to the Merger and Acquisition Law and other relevant laws and regulations to see if they can make use of the various taxation deferrals and exemptions.

34.5   Extent of Seller's Warranties and Indemnities

Generally speaking, in either a purchase of shares or of assets, the buyer requests the seller to give full warranties and indemnities relating to the accounts of the financial and business status of the company to be acquired, valid title to the assets, taxation, litigation, contracts, intellectual property rights and employment and environmental issues, etc.

It is advisable that warranties and indemnities from a seller be supported by a joint and several guarantee issued by its parent or related company, or by the previous chairman and directors of the target company. It is preferable that any such guarantee be secured by mortgages or pledges on the guarantor's assets.

34.6   Liability for Pre-contractual Representations

Before an agreement is made either orally or in writing, there is no liability for representations made by the parties to the transaction. If a contract is rescinded because of a pre-contractual representation which is false, the party making the representation is liable to the other party for any losses (including the cost of preparation and negotiation of the contract and any opportunity costs).

34.7   Liability for Pre-acquisition Trading Contracts

In an asset purchase agreement the buyer may, for accounting and taxation purposes, request the seller to bear the loss, debts or other liabilities incurred before the effective date of the acquisition agreement. Most contracts are assigned to the buyer. The terms and conditions of the assignment are one of the considerations of the acquisition.

In a share acquisition, pre-acquisition profits may be paid to the seller by way of dividend. If it is retained in the company, the buyer inherits those profits. If accepted by the seller, the seller may, following closing, be liable to the buyer in respect of contracts to which the target company was a party. However, the target company remains the direct debtor to the creditor.

34.8   Pre-completion Risks

A typical business acquisition agreement provides that the seller shall bear the risk of loss of, or damage to, the target company's assets during the period of time between the execution of the agreement and closing.

Similarly, in a share acquisition the risks are borne by the seller. The seller warrants that there has been no material adverse change to the business since a specific date and, if there is, the buyer has a right to rescind the agreement and request damages, if any.

34.9   Required Governmental Approvals

According to the Statute for Investment by Foreign Nationals, an acquisition of shares in a Taiwanese company by a foreign individual or a foreign company must be approved by the Investment Commission under the Ministry of Economic Affairs (IC). A company in which foreign shareholders have invested with the IC's approval is called an FIA company. The 'Negative List' in Taiwan specifies those companies the shares of which may not be acquired by foreign interests. In some cases the prohibition on foreign acquisition is absolute, but where inclusion in the list is by decree of the executive branch of the government, the government can give consent to such an acquisition.

A purchase of land or buildings by foreign individuals or companies is subject to a special approval from the local government. There are some restrictions in Taiwanese land law on foreign individuals or companies purchasing real property located in Taiwan.

34.10 Anti-trust and Competition Laws

The Fair Trade Law covers anti-trust and unfair competition. In an acquisition, the most important aspect is merger control. The Fair Trade Law abandoned the prior approval requirements in 2002 in an effort to relieve firms of procedural hurdles and to offer a more flexible and efficient time frame when planning for acquisitions. The amendment to the Fair Trade Law of 2002 requires firms planning an acquisition to file a merger notification with the Fair Trade Commission (FTC). Once the FTC receives complete filing documents, a waiting period of thirty days begins to run, which may be early terminated or extended to another 30 days by the FTC as it deems necessary. If the FTC does not object to the merger within the waiting period, the parties may proceed to consummate the merger.

34.11 Required Offer Procedures

According to the Company Law, any shareholder may freely sell his or her shares to any party at any time after the company's incorporation, except the company's promoters, who may only sell their shares after one year following incorporation. Therefore, any shareholder in a target company may accept an offer by a foreign party for the shares.

A company may do any of the following acts with the consent of a resolution adopted by a majority of shareholders present at a shareholders' meeting which represents two-thirds or more of the total number of issued shares:

- Enter into, amend, or terminate any contract for lease of the company's business as a whole, or entrust the operation of the business to, or permanently operate the business jointly with, others;

- Transfer the whole or any essential part of its business or assets; or

- Accept the transfer of another's whole business or assets, which has a significant bearing on the company's business operations.

However, if a company is listed, its shares can only be bought in a stock market or through certain particular procedures subject to relevant government regulations.

Any public tender offer to purchase the securities of a public company bypassing the centralized securities exchange market or the over-the-counter market may be conducted only after it has been reported to the Securities and Futures Bureau and publicly announced, except under the following circumstances:

- The number of securities proposed for public tender offer by the offeror plus the total number of securities of the public company already obtained by the offeror and its affiliates do not exceed five percent of the total number of voting shares issued by the public company;

- The securities purchased by the offeror through the public tender offer are securities of a company of which the offeror holds more than 50 percent of the issued voting shares; or

- Other circumstances in conformity with the regulations prescribed by Securities and Futures Bureau.

34.12 Continuation of Government Licenses

According to the Company Law, a company which has not duly registered and obtained proper licenses from the competent authority cannot perform any business activity. Any change of the registered business must be approved by competent authorities.

Certain industries may need to obtain special licenses from specific authorities. Requirements for granting such licenses vary depending upon the nature of the industry concerned.

34.13 Requirements for Transferring Shares

Unless otherwise provided for in the Company Law, the freedom to transfer shares cannot be prevented by the company's articles of incorporation under the Company Law.

Shares are transferable by an assignment, purchase or share transfer agreement together with the surrender of the share certificates, which must be duly endorsed by the seller. The buyer's name must be registered in the company's shareholders registry. Otherwise, the company continues to treat the seller as the valid shareholder of the company.

34.14 Requirements for Transferring Land and Property Leases

A foreign company duly recognized and registered in accordance with the Company Law may purchase land or buildings with the special approval of a local government for the normal operation of its business. A foreign individual may purchase land or buildings only for residential purposes.

Title to land or buildings can be specifically encumbered by mortgages or charges, or by caveats recording the interests of third parties in the land or buildings.

34.15 Requirements for Transferring Intellectual Property

All intellectual property rights can be transferred by assignment. However, the assignment of registered intellectual property rights should be registered with the relevant authorities accordingly.

34.16   Requirements for Transferring Business Contracts, Licenses and Leases

A business contract or a lease is a private contract between the parties concerned and is usually transferable. However, the other party to the contract or lease must be duly informed of the transfer. Whether a license is transferable is a matter for the relevant laws and regulations under which it has been issued.

34.17   Requirements for Transferring Other Assets

All assets other than shares, real property, goodwill, intellectual property, trading debtors and the benefits of contracts can be transferred by delivery. Assets that are the subject of a charge in favour of a bank or other creditors, or in which title has been retained by a trade supplier or a seller under a purchase or conditional sale agreement, continue to be encumbered by the rights of the third parties.

Pursuant to Article 25 of the Merger and Acquisition Law, the transfer of all rights and obligations pertaining to any properties acquired from the dissolved company by the surviving company or the newly incorporated company shall become operative on and after the closing date specified for the merger/consolidation provided, however, that any acquisition, hypothecation, loss or change of any right under other applicable laws shall be registered before its disposition is permitted.

34.18   Encumbrances and Third Party Interests

Assets can be subject to a third party interest, which usually arises from a mortgage or pledge contract. A buyer generally obtains the full title of the assets from the seller, unless the seller does not, in fact, have a clear title to them. Nevertheless, if the purchased assets are subject to a mortgage or pledge, the buyer is liable for the mortgage or the pledge even it has obtained full title to the assets.

Normally, title–registered land, buildings and shares are conclusive evidence of the owner's title on which the buyer can rely, but certain assets may carry the risk of being subject to unregistered or unascertainable interests which a buyer will not discover. Therefore, warranties from the seller concerning clear title are required in certain situations.

34.19   Minimum Shareholder and Officer Requirements

In the case of merger/consolidation between two independent companies limited by shares or between a company limited by shares and a limited company, the surviving or the newly incorporated company shall be limited to a company organized in the form of a company limited by shares.

A company limited by shares shall be organized by two or more individual shareholders or one government or corporate shareholder. The Board must be comprised of a minimum of three Directors.

34.20 Non-competition Clauses

Restraint of trade or non-competition clauses in an acquisition agreement are enforceable, provided that the extent and terms of the restriction are reasonable. The criteria for the determination of 'reasonableness' should take into account the nature of the business as well as the effect and the impact on the restricted party.

Non-competition clauses in an employment agreement can also be enforceable if they are reasonable. A prohibition after termination of employment of an employee using his or her professional and occupational expertise or exercising his or her skills is considered unreasonable and a violation of the Constitutional Law.

Nevertheless, a clause in an employment contract prohibiting an employee from working in a company engaged in the same line of business as that of the previous company is considered to be enforceable if the period is not more than two years.

34.21 Environmental Considerations

Under the Environment Protection Law and related regulations, substantial penalties may be imposed on businesses which damage the environment. The buyer of a business or property is required to inherit the responsibility for rectifying any environmental damage caused by the seller.

It is advisable to obtain appropriate warranties regarding environmental damage and liability from the seller. Nevertheless, the buyer or the target company must assume direct liability to the relevant authorities even when the buyer has obtained such warranties.

34.22 Employee Superannuation/Pension Plans

Under the Labour Standards Law, most companies in Taiwan have Pension plans. Employees' pension payments are calculated with reference to their final salary and years of service.

Pension contributions must be set aside from the employee's salary in accordance with the Income Tax Law and deposited with a financial organization designated by the relevant authorities.

A company must deposit pension contributions in proportion to the employees' total salary and ensure that the fund will always have sufficient assets available to meet its expected obligations to provide benefits for retiring employees. If the buyer is to retain all or some of the employees, it must consider and check whether the fund contributed by the target company complies with the relevant law and regulations.

In the past, many Taiwanese workers often failed to secure their pension upon retirement, since the majority of small-and-mid-sized companies do not survive long enough to enable employees to be eligible for a retirement pension. In this regard, the pension system has undergone significant reform, which led to the promulgation of the Labour Pension Law of 2005.

The new pension scheme is a defined contribution plan, under which the employer is obligated to contribute 6 per cent of the employee's wage and deposit into the employee's individual portable pension account. However, it is not mandatory for workers to convert their retirement benefits accrued under the former pension system into the new system.

An alternative is available for companies with 200 or more employees, which can opt for annuity insurance instead of contribution pension plan.

It is also stipulated that, in a merger/acquisition scenario, the acquiring company shall assume all outstanding pension obligations of the target company.

34.23   Employee Rights

The relationship between an employer and an employee is subject to the Labour Standards Law, its Enforcement Rules and related regulations, which set forth the minimum standards of working conditions. An employer's obligations to provide a safe working environment and to purchase labour and health insurance for employees is compulsorily required by amongst others, the Factory Law, the Labour Insurance Law, the National Health Insurance Law and strictly enforced by the authority without any exception.

In a merger/acquisition scenario, the prior service years of the employees who accept the employment offered by the surviving company, newly incorporated company or the transferee company will be recognized as part of their total service with the new employer.

34.24   Compulsory Transfer of Employees

There is no law compulsorily to make a buyer of business assets take over all employment agreements. The buyer may, at its sole discretion, select the employees it needs and leave the seller to continue to have responsibility for the remainder of the employees.

Employees of a company, the shares of which are acquired by a buyer, are entitled to all rights previously enjoyed, and the company must meet all its liabilities for wages and benefits for its employees occurring both before and after the date of acquisition of its shares.

However, pursuant to Article 16 of the Merger and Acquisition Law, the surviving company, newly incorporated company or transferee company shall no later than thirty days before the closing date of the merger serve a written notice expressly describing employment terms and conditions to the employees who the existing and new employers have agreed to employ by the new employer after the merger/consolidation.

Any staying employee, upon receiving such notice, must notify his decision whether to accept the offer in writing to the new employer within ten days. The absence of such notification of the employee shall be deemed as consent to accept the offer.

34.25 Tax Deductibility of Acquisition Expenses

Where a buyer is a Taiwanese taxpayer, acquisition expenses are deductible to the extent that they are incurred for the ongoing operation of the business. Expenses of a capital nature may be included in the cost base of an asset for the purpose of calculating any subsequent capital gains tax payable on disposal of that asset where the proceeds of sale exceed its costs base.

Further, the expenses incurred from the merger/consolidation and acquisition of a company may be equally amortized over ten years, pursuant to Article 36 of the Merger and Acquisition Law.

34.26 Levies on Acquisition Agreements and Collateral Documents

Stamp duty is levied in relation to the sale of movable and immovable property. Securities transaction tax is levied on the acquisition of shares. Land increment value tax and deed tax is levied on the transfer of land and buildings.

However, in an asset or share acquisition carried out pursuant to Articles 27 through 29 of the Merger and Acquisition Law, if the acquiring party uses voting shares as the consideration to pay the company so merged/consolidated and acquired and such shares is at a value not less than sixty-five percent of the total consideration, or a company is carrying on merger/consolidation and/or division, any and all deeds and certificates so created are exempt from stamp tax. In addition, the title of real estate so acquired is exempt from deed tax.

34.27 Financing Rules and Restrictions

A buyer may raise funds from any financial organization or any third party, either a company or an individual, for the acquisition transaction. The interest expenses arising therefrom are deductible. Except in certain limited cases as otherwise authorized by the law, a company is not allowed to buy back its own shares. It is also prohibited from facilitating any funds to any individual or to another company without a business relationship.

If the result of merger/consolidation, acquisition and/or division will put a company in violation of the credit limit as permitted by relevant banking laws, the original credit limit will still be made available until the expiration date of the term of credit agreement.

34.28 Exchange Control and Repatriation of Profits

Under Foreign Exchange Transaction Law, any legally registered company, enterprise or group and any resident individual over age 20 bearing a Taiwanese Alien Resident Certificate may, without prior approval of the relevant authorities, remit up to an amount specified by the Central Bank of Taiwan each year. According to a decree issued by the Central Bank of Taiwan, the current quota is USD 50 million or its equivalent in other foreign currency for a company, enterprise or group, and USD 5 million for a resident individual. There is no limitation on remittance of funds into or out of Taiwan for an acquisition carried out with the IC's approval.

International Business Acquisitions

Dividends paid to non-resident investors in Taiwanese companies are subject to dividend withholding tax. The tax rate for dividends distributed by an FLA company is 20 per cent of the payment. The tax rate for dividends paid by a non–FLA company to non-resident individuals is 30 per cent (25 per cent for non-resident companies). The dividends can be repatriated freely.

34.29   Groups of Companies

In June 1997, Taiwan added and promulgated a new chapter to the Company Law, comprising provisions governing 'affiliates'.

The term 'affiliated enterprises' as used in this new law refers to companies which are independent in existence but are interrelated in either of the following manners:

- companies having a controlling and subordinate relation between them; or

- companies which have invested in each other.

Controlling and Subordinate Companies

Companies in any of the following situations are considered to have a controlling and subordinate relation:

- One company holds a majority of the total number of the outstanding voting shares or the total amount of the other company's capital stock;

- One company has direct or indirect control over the management of the personnel and financial or business operations of the other company;

- A majority of executive shareholders or directors in one company are contemporaneously acting as executive shareholders or directors in the other company; and

- A majority of the total number of outstanding voting shares or the total amount of the capital stock of one company and the other company are held by the same shareholders.

Once a company is defined as a controlling company, it is liable for damages suffered by the subordinate company if it has caused the subordinate to conduct any business which is contrary to normal business practice or not profitable, but fails to adequately compensate the subordinate at the end of the relevant business year. In the event that the controlling company fails to compensate the subordinate, the subordinate's creditors or the shareholders who hold 1 per cent or more of the total number of the outstanding voting shares or of the total amount of the capital stock of the subordinate may exercise, in their own names, the rights of the subordinate company to claim payment of the compensation from the controlling company to the subordinate.

Mutually Invested Companies

Where two companies have invested in each other to the extent that one third or more of the total number of the voting shares or the total amount of the capital stock of both companies is held or contributed by each other, these two companies are defined as mutually invested companies.

Where both companies hold half or more of the total number of the voting shares or of the total amount of the equity capital of each other, or have direct or indirect control over the management of the personnel and financial or business operations of each other, they are deemed to have the status of a controlling company as well as a subordinate company to each other.

Subject to the condition that the fact of mutual investment is known to both companies, the voting power exercisable by either investing company in the invested company must not exceed one third of the total number of the outstanding voting shares or of the total amount of equity capital of the invested company, provided that the voting power associated with the dividend shares distributed from capitalization of surplus earnings or excess legal reserve shall remain exercisable.

In addition, the new Law also requires that a company which holds one third or more of the total number of voting shares or of the total amount of capital stock of another company must give written notice to the other company within one month from the date that interest arises. In the event that any of the following changes occur later in the particulars contained in the notice previously given, a further notice must be given within five days from the date of occurrence of such change where its holding of voting shares or equity capital of another company:

- becomes less than one third of the total number of the voting shares or the total amount of the capital stock of that other company;

- exceeds one half of the total number of the voting shares or the total amount of the capital stock of that other company; or

- as described in the preceding item has been reduced again to a level below one half of the total number of the voting shares or the total amount of the capital stock of that other company.

The notified company must, within five days after its receipt of the notice given under either of the situations mentioned above, post a public notice stating the name of the notifying company, the number of shares held, and the amount of capital contribution made by the notifying company.

In the event that the responsible person of a company fails to give any notice or to make any public notice, he or she will be fined an amount of not less than NTD 6,000 but not more than NTD 30,000. In addition, the competent authority shall order the violator to post a notice or the public notice within a given time limit. If the violator again fails to do so after expiry of the given time limit, the competent authority may fix another time limit for the violator to post the notice and impose an additional fine of an amount not less than NTD 9,000 but not more than NTD 60,000 for each occurrence of non-compliance by the violator until the notification requirement is duly complied with.

The new Law also requires that a subordinate company the shares of which have been issued to the public must, at the end of each business year, prepare and submit a report regarding the relationship between itself and its controlling company indicating the legal acts, funds flow and profit and loss status between the two companies. A controlling company the shares of which have been issued to the public also, at the end of each business year, prepare for submission a consolidated business report and consolidated financial statements of the affiliated enterprises involved.

The rules for preparation of the reports and statements are prescribed by the Taiwan Securities and Futures Bureau.

34.30   Responsibility for Liabilities of an Acquired Subsidiary

Under the Taiwanese laws, a parent company and an acquired subsidiary are considered separate legal entities. The law does not require a parent company to be responsible for the liabilities of an acquired subsidiary unless otherwise undertaken.

34.31   Governing Law of the Contract

A choice-of-law clause in an acquisition agreement is accepted and enforced by Taiwanese courts. However, Taiwanese laws and regulations govern the effect of a transfer of title to shares or other assets even if the governing law of the acquisition agreement is not Taiwanese.

34.32   Dispute Resolution Options

The parties to a contract may wish to resolve disputes other than by litigation. Arbitration and mediation options are therefore provided for in the contract. Parties are free to adopt the arbitration rules of any international body in their contracts.

Though Taiwan is not a signatory party to any international convention, Taiwanese courts recognize and enforce international arbitration awards under certain conditions. The Taiwan Arbitration Association offers the service of arbitration for any dispute. It conducts arbitration proceedings in accordance with the Taiwan Arbitration Law.

35. UNITED STATES OF AMERICA

David N. Kay Drinker Biddle Gardnercarton

35.1 Introductory Comments

As the largest 'host country' for foreign investment in the world, the USA has consistently endorsed a policy to encourage foreign investment, both directly and indirectly through corporations, limited liability companies, limited partnerships, buy-out funds and other investment vehicles. Except for national security reasons, the USA has imposed few restrictions on sellers or buyers in the context of sales of, or investments in, businesses owned by US or foreign shareholders. There are, however, certain requirements of securities laws, anti-trust law and other regulations that a foreign buyer must comply with in conducting mergers or acquisitions of US corporations.

The USA has adopted a federal system in which both federal and state laws affect the acquisition of US businesses. It is essential, therefore, for a foreign buyer to realize that it is the state laws and regulations, rather than federal laws that govern the major aspects of acquisitions. Although state laws relating to foreign investment tend to be uniform, it is always prudent and preferable to seek specific advice on the law of the state which is closely connected with contemplated mergers and acquisitions.

The USA has a sophisticated and complex legal regime to regulate foreign investments in general and acquisitions in particular. A seasoned understanding of governmental economic regulations and restrictions may not only facilitate the merger or acquisition, but should also help foreign businesses avoid negative consequences resulting from failure to comply with laws and regulations. Foreign businesses, therefore, are strongly encouraged to seek early legal advice in connection with an acquisition involving US corporations and US assets. The following is no substitute for reviewing original source materials and consulting competent local counsel.

35.2 Corporate Structures

Corporations and other forms of business entities are governed by state laws, and each individual state enacts its own corporate laws. As some states have adopted the Model Business Corporation Act and others follow the Delaware General Corporation Law, there are certain variations between state corporation laws which merit specific attention.

Foreigners will most likely acquire shares of a corporation, or form a corporation under the laws of one of the US states to acquire assets, because this form of operation is favoured by most large enterprises and is usually preferred by the foreign investor. A corporation can be either closely held or publicly held, with publicly held corporations usually having their stocks listed on one of the major exchanges or over-the-counter. The limited liability company is another form of business entity which has

© World Law Group
International Business Acquisitions, M. Whalley, F.-J. Semler (eds.), Kluwer Law International, London, 2007; ISBN 9789041124838.

now been adopted by all but a few US states. A limited liability company combines the organizational flexibility and pass-through tax treatment of a partnership with the limited liability protection of a corporation.

General and limited partnerships are convenient targets for an acquisition because foreign buyers can contract with one partner of a general partnership to bind all other partners, and with a limited partnership to bind limited partners, up to the amount of capital contributions. Additionally, the shares or assets of a joint venture can be acquired by a foreign business.

35.3   Letters of Intent and Heads of Agreement

Letters of intent are often prepared to express the parties' intention to enter into a business transaction and to outline the transaction's basic terms and conditions. Such letters can be binding on the parties, but are typically non-binding and subject to the parties entering into definitive agreements addressing the substance of the transaction described in the letter of intent. It is important that, if the letter of intent is intended to be non-binding, it should very clearly state this intention.

Portions of the letter of intent, however, are often purposely made binding, such as confidentiality and 'no-shop' provisions or break-up fees if the transaction is not consummated.

35.4   Taxes Affecting the Structure and Calculation of the Price

In general, upon the acquisition of a target company's stock, the target continues to be liable for all of its prior tax obligations, including liabilities for unpaid taxes of any consolidated group of which the target had been a member prior to the purchase. As a result, in the case of a stock acquisition, appropriate warranties or indemnities from the target's former stockholders should be included in the acquisition contract to protect the buyer from any unforeseen tax liabilities of the target.

Purchasing assets instead of stock can avoid this problem altogether, and usually also results in a favourable step up in the assets' tax basis. Upon the sale of the US business, the sale of assets renders the foreign owner (or its US subsidiary) subject to US tax on any gain or loss resulting from the sale. The sale of a US subsidiary's stock by a foreign parent company generally does not result in a US tax liability, although any gain or loss may be required to be recognized with respect to such stock if the US company owns or has owned within five years of the disposition substantial direct or indirect interests in US real property.

In general, a non-resident operating a US business, directly or through an entity treated for US tax purposes as a partnership, is subject to US tax on income (both US and foreign) attributable to such operations. In addition, a 'branch profits tax' is imposed upon foreign corporations operating in the US to the extent the foreign corporation repatriates earnings from its US operations. A non-resident operating a US business through a US subsidiary, on the other hand, generally is not subject to US tax, unless such a non-resident also conducts business in the US directly or if the US subsidiary acts as an agent of its parent. However, dividends and interest paid by the US subsidiary to its parent are subject to US withholding tax. Even though use of a US subsidiary may thus shield the foreign parent from US taxation, the US tax laws require extensive reporting by the subsidiary concerning its foreign parent company and all related entities regarding the non-US taxable operations, business assets and income.

35.5 Extent of Seller's Warranties and Indemnities

Although the nature and extent of representations, warranties and indemnities vary, the parties make representations and warranties and give indemnities in almost every acquisition agreement. Typical warranties and indemnities given by a seller include capitalization and share ownership of the seller, authorization, accounts receivable, taxation, title to tangible and intangible assets, litigation and compliance with the law, labour and employee issues and environmental law. It is also common for a seller to give warranties as to the business's financial condition and, if publicly held, the accuracy and completeness of documents filed with relevant authorities.

Whether warranties will survive the closing depends on the nature of the company acquired and the structure of the transaction. While a buyer seldom requires the seller of a publicly held company to give warranties surviving the closing, it is common for the seller of a closely held company to give warranties surviving the closing and allow the buyer to retain the rights to set-off for breach of warranty. Acquisition agreements typically contain express and detailed indemnification provisions for the benefit of both buyer and seller against inaccuracies in the representations and warranties that are contained in the acquisition agreement and related documents. Indemnification provisions are often the most seriously negotiated provisions of any acquisition agreement. Issues to be considered include the indemnifying parties' identity, the indemnification obligation's post-closing term, the 'cap', if any, on the amount of the indemnification obligation, and other matters such as 'floors' (i.e. the minimum claim amount that can be asserted) and 'deductibles' (i.e. the minimum claim amount for which no obligation to indemnity exists).

35.6 Liability for Pre-contractual Representations

Inaccurate representations or warranties, whether made knowingly, recklessly, negligently or otherwise during the course of negotiation of merger and acquisition transactions, can serve as the basis for various kinds of actions, including actions for monetary damages, rescission or injunctive relief. In addition, under US securities laws, any sale of a security, such as the common or other capital stock of a corporation, carries with it an obligation on the seller's part neither to make any untrue statements of 'material' fact, nor to have omitted to state any material fact necessary to make the statements which have been made not misleading. Sellers of securities may not legally disclaim this responsibility. Sellers of a corporation's assets are generally not subject to such high disclosure requirements, but may still be liable for any false, misleading or inaccurate representations or warranties that they do make. Buyers may also be subject to similar legal obligations if, for example, any part of the purchase price paid to a seller consists of the buyer's capital stock, warrants or promissory notes (which are also securities under US law).

Typically, acquisition agreements expressly disclaim that either party has made any representation or warranty to the other party that is not set forth in writing in the acquisition agreement or other agreements or documents referred to in the acquisition agreement. Although such disclaimers may not always be effective, it is prudent for all parties to an acquisition transaction to assure themselves that any representation, warranty or other statement of fact or covenant upon which they are relying in large or small part is embodied in the acquisition agreement or related documents.

35.7 Liability for Pre-acquisition Trading and Contracts

Generally, in an acquisition by a buyer of a seller's assets, liabilities and business, the buyer only has responsibility for profits, losses, contracts and liabilities actually incurred after the completion (the 'closing') of the sale. In some cases, however, such as liabilities for so-called 'product liability' claims, certain environmental claims, tax claims (of previously unpaid taxes or taxes of affiliates in a consolidated group of companies), employees' claims and other situations, a buyer is held responsible to third parties for liabilities incurred prior to the completion of the sale. Buyers typically demand indemnification from the seller against any such pre-sale liabilities and may require that funds be escrowed to ensure that the indemnification provisions will adequately protect the buyer.

If a buyer and a seller both desire that the buyer assume responsibility for pre-sale obligations, losses or profits, it is possible to so state in the acquisition agreement. Unless novations are entered into with respect to pre-existing obligations to third parties (which is rarely the case), the seller remains responsible for such obligations (subject to any indemnity the seller has received from the buyer). Pre-acquisition profits and losses can sometimes be transferred to the buyer both for financial reporting and tax purposes through this structuring method. In a sale of shares, the obligations of the company whose shares are being transferred remain with that company and are usually unaffected, at least in any direct way, by the sale. However, the corporation's contracts, agreements and leases should be reviewed for 'change in control' or other 'consents' which may be required in connection with the transfer of ownership. Pre-acquisition profits or losses can be distributed to the selling person by way of dividends or purchase price adjustments in both asset and shares sales.

35.8 Pre-completion Risks

A business or share acquisition agreement typically provides that the seller retains the risk of loss between signing and closing, and that the buyer is not required to close the acquisition if the condition of the assets or the company's financial condition has materially deteriorated between signing and closing.

35.9 Required Governmental Approvals

Section 7a of the Clayton Act requires that mergers and acquisitions meeting certain size thresholds must be reported, prior to closing, to the two US anti-trust enforcement agencies, the Department of Justice and the Federal Trade Commission. If this section applies to the acquisition, both the buyer and the seller must file a form and supporting documentation on such topics as market share, sales and strategies. Completing such a filing (called a 'Hart Scott Rodino' filing) can be quite burdensome.

The initial waiting period under this law is 30 days from the date of filing. Early termination of the waiting period may be requested and is routinely granted only when it is determined that the transaction is not likely to have anti-competitive consequences. If the government takes no action within the 30-day waiting period, the transaction is automatically cleared but, unlike EU law, this does not preclude the government from challenging the merger at a later date. In certain transactions, either the Department of Justice or the Federal Trade Commission will ask for further information in a 'second request'. Such a request extends the waiting period until all the information requested in it has been submitted, after which time the government has 20 days to decide whether to challenge the transaction.

The 'Exon-Florio' provisions of the Omnibus Trade and Competitiveness Act 1988 provide the US government with a mechanism to respond to foreign acquisitions. Under these provisions, the inter-agency Committee on Foreign Investments in the USA (CFIUS) has 30 days if it is notified of a transaction to decide whether to conduct a formal 45-day investigation. Following a formal investigation, the US President has 15 days to decide whether to take action based on the CFIUS recommendation. Through this process, the Exon-Florio provisions grant the President the authority to suspend or prohibit an acquisition of a US firm by a foreign person if the President determines that it will impair, or threaten to impair, the US's national security. The President has rarely exercised this power to block a transaction.

35.10　Anti-trust and Competition Laws

The Sherman Act, the Clayton Act and the Federal Trade Commission Act constitute the basis for federal anti-trust law, which imposes criminal as well as civil liability on any anti-competitive acts or agreement in restraint of foreign or domestic trade or commerce. While most states have their own anti-trust laws which are applicable to acts taking place within that jurisdiction, the provisions of such state laws are generally similar to those of the federal laws. The Department of Justice and the Federal Trade Commission are charged with enforcing federal legislation which covers anti-competitive practices. In addition, private parties are also entitled to bring civil actions to enforce the anti-trust laws.

In the context of mergers and acquisitions, the US anti-trust laws prohibit any acquisition that has the effect of substantially lessening competition or creating a monopoly. As discussed in **35.9**, certain mergers and reorganizations must be reported to the Federal Trade Commission and the Department of Justice before they can be effected.

Although the US has no special rules prohibiting acquisitions by foreigners, and the anti-trust and competition laws treat foreign and US companies equally, an international acquisition can be derailed if the federal government concludes that the acquisition has the effect of substantially lessening competition. While some defences, such as foreign sovereign immunity and the act of state doctrine, are available to foreigners, the prospective buyer ought to conduct careful and comprehensive market research regarding the competitive element of the acquisition and familiarize itself with reporting requirements in order to avoid punishment for non-compliance with anti-trust and competition laws.

Certain regulated industries, such as broadcasting or air transport, are subject to rules that limit foreign ownership. It is not possible to list all of these, but in general they relate to industries where limited public resources (such as radio frequencies) are utilized. In one of these industries any foreign ownership may be subject to approval by a federal agency.

35.11   Required Offer Procedures

The required offer procedures vary from state to state, although certain provisions are commonly found in most state corporation laws. If a target in a proposed acquisition is publicly traded, and the buyer proposes to acquire the target company's shares through a tender offer, state laws generally require that all shareholders be treated substantially the same in connection with the tender offer. In addition, federal and state securities laws impose complicated procedures for conducting a tender offer.

If the buyer is an 'interested shareholder' (usually a party owning 15 per cent or more of the target corporation's stock which has been acquired without the target corporation's board approval), most state laws prohibit a 'squeeze-out' merger between the interested shareholder and the target corporation for three years after the transaction which resulted in the interested shareholder becoming a shareholder. A number of exemptions apply to this prohibition, and each proposed transaction must be examined carefully to determine whether such exemptions apply. In addition, a number of publicly held companies have so-called 'shareholder rights' or 'poison pill' plans which restrict the buyer's ability to acquire the target company on a non-negotiated basis.

35.12   Continuation of Government Licences

There are licensing requirements under both federal and state laws applicable to certain industries. Licences and permits are required for the import and export of goods, telecommunications, wire communications, pollutant discharges and hazardous waste disposal, etc. Often, export and import licences and other licences and permits need to be replaced or transferred prior to consummating the transaction to avoid interruption of business operations.

35.13   Requirements for Transferring Shares

The transfer of securities is subject to a complex body of federal and state securities law regulations. Restrictions on transfers of shares may also be found in a company's charter documents or, if there is one, in a shareholders' agreement.

Shares are transferable by endorsement or by means of a simple written transfer form, which must include tax stamps in a minority of states. Bearer shares are not permitted in the US, and the buyer's name must therefore be inserted in the company's stock transfer register.

35.14 Requirements for Transferring Land and Property Leases

The purchase of any interest in real property requires, among other things, the execution of a deed, which may or may not contain warranties as to the title of the land and other real property, the payment of transfer taxes (to the extent required in the jurisdiction where the property is located), the registration or recording of the transfer of title in the land with the appropriate local agencies, and often title insurance insuring title in the property. Many of these requirements can vary considerably from jurisdiction to jurisdiction depending upon local law, custom and usage.

Title to land can be specifically encumbered by mortgages or liens, or by other interests of third parties in the land (such as easements or rights of way). Such encumbrances are recorded with the appropriate agency, and will often appear in surveys made by a licensed surveyor. Considerable negotiation sometimes occurs in respect of removal of mortgages, liens or other interests which will transfer with the property.

Warranties as to the physical condition of land or improvements are typically not contained in the deed or instrument of conveyance, but rather in the purchase agreement or other document.

35.15 Requirements for Transferring Intellectual Property

The buyer and the seller should negotiate an appropriate non-disclosure agreement to the extent that the seller's proprietary, confidential or trade secret information or technology will be reviewed and evaluated by the buyer prior to entering into a definitive agreement. The buyer should attempt to avoid the need for any such agreement. If this cannot be avoided, however, the buyer should negotiate a nondisclosure agreement which is very specific in content and limited to a short time period. When necessary, the seller should attempt to negotiate a broad nondisclosure agreement in terms of coverage and time period and require the return of all documentation and copies thereof, if any, which are reviewed by the potential buyer if the transaction is not consummated.

The buyer should identify all proprietary rights and assets to be acquired, including any patents, patent applications, patent disclosures and inventions, trade marks, service marks, trade dress, copyrighted works and copyright registrations and applications, trade secrets, licences for any of the foregoing with third parties, distribution agreements, franchise agreements, manufacturing agreements, software development or licence agreements, and employee and consultant agreements.

All of these agreements should be reviewed to determine whether the seller's rights and obligations thereunder are freely assignable to the buyer, or whether in some circumstances a third party's consent is required for assignment. The seller should determine whether any change of control restrictions exist in such agreements with respect to the transfer of any intellectual property assets. The buyer should perform an ownership verification of all proprietary rights assets that it expects to receive, including whether any security interests have been recorded against registered trade marks, service marks, copyrighted works or patents at the appropriate registry, whether the patents and trademark registrations have been maintained and to ensure that the chain of title is complete to the Seller. Any intellectual property litigation (both defensive and offensive) as well as the strength and scope of key intellectual property should be reviewed.

If the transaction is an asset purchase, at closing the seller should assign to the buyer all rights, title and interest in the intellectual property assets made a part of the transaction. Post-closing, the buyer should record the assignment of all registered patents and trade marks with the US Patent and Trade Mark Office, and record the assignment of all registered copyrights with the US Copyright Office.

35.16   Requirements for Transferring Business Contracts, Licences and Leases

A contract governed by the laws of a US state is generally assignable if the contract is silent regarding assignability, unless the contract is one for personal services. Personal service contracts (such as executive employment contracts) or contracts prohibiting assignment are generally only transferable or assignable as specifically allowed under the contract terms. Assignment of the benefit of a contract generally does not release the transferor from accrued obligations under that contract without a specific release from the other party to the contract. For this reason, the seller usually attempts to receive a formal release from the third party, in which the buyer steps into the seller's place, with the seller being released from all further liability. The more likely result is that the third party will permit the assignment but without releasing the seller from secondary lia- bility under the agreement. It is not normally necessary to register or record an assign- ment of a business contract (other than assignments of a registered patent or trade mark or certain real estate assignments) and usually notice must be given to the other party that the contract has been assigned.

35.17   Requirements for Transferring Other Assets

With the exception of real property and certain specific intangible assets such as good- will, intellectual property and contract rights, assets can generally be transferred by delivery, together with:

- a bill of sale specifying the assets being transferred (in the case of tangible personal property);

- an assignment (in the case of contracts and certain other intangible rights);

- an endorsement or stock power (in the case of certain instruments, such as promissory notes or stock certificates); or

- an endorsed title (in the case of certain vehicles or machinery).

Assets that are subject to a creditor's lien, or in which title has been retained by a third party under a conditional sale agreement, generally continue to be encumbered by the rights of the third parties following transfer to a buyer. These liens generally must be of public record (or otherwise properly disclosed) in order to be enforceable against a *bona fide* buyer.

35.18   Encumbrances and Third Party Interests

An owner's property may be encumbered by liens and other interests of third parties created by contract or by common or statutory law such as the Uniform Commercial Code (UCC). Statutory liens and other interests may arise under federal or state law and include tax liens and liens in respect of environmental remediation costs, among other things. Common law and statutory liens of mechanics, warehousemen and the like are found in many states.

Generally, public registries of title to personal property do not exist, except as to certain classes of property such as boats and ships, aircraft, patents, trade marks and service marks, and copyrights. Nonetheless, as far as most types of personal property are concerned, security interests are 'perfected' under the UCC by the making of a filing in the appropriate state or local office. Title and other interests in real property are recorded in public offices. It is prudent for a buyer to conduct a UCC search of the public records to determine the existence of liens against the assets to be purchased.

Buyers of personal property generally take the property subject to a perfected security interest that is in existence at the time of the transfer, whether or not the buyer had knowledge of the security interest. Further, some states still have 'bulk sales' laws, which (in general) apply to sales of a majority of a business's assets and impose notice and other obligations on the buyer and the seller. Failure to comply with bulk sales laws may render the sale ineffective as to, or make the buyer liable in damages to, the seller's creditors. A number of states have repealed their bulk sales laws.

35.19   Minimum Shareholder and Officer Requirements

Some jurisdictions require a minimum of three directors, while other jurisdictions require that a corporation's board of directors consists of one or more members. Most state corporation statutes require that every corporation name one or more officers. The minimum number of shareholders in a company is one.

Most states have no minimum capital requirements for corporations.

35.20   Non-competition Clauses

A covenant not to compete given by a seller in connection with the sale of a business, and especially its goodwill, will very likely be enforced in the US if the territorial scope, duration and manner of restriction are reasonable. Under the reasonableness test, courts look into the facts of each case, the nature of the business and the effect of the restriction to determine whether the restriction is necessary to protect the buyer.

Courts also generally enforce a covenant not to compete given by an employee in an employment agreement, provided the restriction is reasonable. However, because of the unequal bargaining position between an employer and an employee, US courts have adopted a stricter test for reasonableness in post-employment restriction cases than in sale of business cases. Several states have also enacted legislation either to invalidate covenants in all or certain circumstances or to codify the rule of reason in regulating the use of restrictive covenants. Normally, the validity of a covenant not to compete in an employment contract is determined on an enquiry of whether the restriction is greater than necessary to protect the employer, whether the restriction is oppressive to the employee, and whether the restriction is injurious to the general public. The consideration received by the employee in exchange for the non-compete obligation can also affect retirement arrangements since, if an individual violates the non-competition agreement, his or her retirement plan payments may be adversely affected by the employer.

Non-compete covenants must comply with anti-trust and competition laws. Courts do not enforce agreements in restraint of trade if they will have the effect of substantially lessening competition or creating a monopoly.

35.21   Environmental Considerations

The US environmental laws are extensive and complex. Environmental policy, and the implementing laws and regulations, may be developed and enforced by federal, state, regional and local governments. Administrative agencies, particularly at the federal and state level, also play an essential role.

The principal US environmental laws are organized around the appropriate environmental element. Hence, the Clean Air Act regulates emissions of pollutants from industrial operations into the atmosphere; the Clean Water Act addresses discharges of contaminants into US waterways; the Resource Conservation and Recovery Act imposes broad obligations on companies that generate, transport and dispose of hazardous waste; and the Comprehensive Environmental Response, Compensation and Liability Act (CERCLA or 'Superfund') regulates the cleaning of contaminated waste sites and imposes liability for unpermitted releases of hazardous substances.

At the federal level, the US Environmental Protection Agency is given wide-ranging authority to enforce these laws. This is accomplished primarily though permit programmes that impose limits of pollutant discharges into the air and water and ensure the proper design and operation of waste disposal facilities. CERCLA's clean-up requirements are enforced through the statute's pervasive liability provisions which impose far-reaching liability on past and present site owners and waste generators and transporters regardless of whether such parties were responsible for any spills or releases into the environment.

Many companies are affected by the broad liability and substantial remediation costs imposed by Superfund given that liability is so closely tied to property ownership and operation. Consequently, it is a common business practice to conduct environmental assessments of property prior to purchase in order to avoid the strict, joint and several liability imposed by CERCLA and similar statutes. For the same reason, environmental warranties and indemnification provisions are critical aspects of corporate acquisitions to ensure that these considerable environmental liabilities are properly allocated among buyers and sellers. Environmental assessments are also commonly required by landing institutions to ensure that real property has not been impaired by contaminants.

The pre-acquisition environmental assessments are also important tools for evaluating the compliance status of a business enterprise with its various environmental permitting obligations. Determining the state of a company's compliance with these requirements is important, as failure to comply may result in the imposition of civil penalties and criminal liability as well as affecting the operations of a facility.

35.22   Employee Superannuation/Pension Plans

There are basically two different types of pension plans in the US: defined contribution plans and defined benefit plans. Examples of defined contribution plans include 401(k) plans, profit-sharing plans and ESOPs (employee stock ownership plans). A defined contribution plan provides each employee with an individual account and each employee's retirement benefit will generally be equal to the total of contributions made during the employee's working life to that account plus any applicable earnings or losses on these contributions. Instead of expressing each employee's retirement benefit in an individual account, a defined benefit plan provides each employee with a specified monthly retirement benefit beginning at each employee's normal retirement age. The amount of this retirement benefit is typically based on a predetermined formula (such as a specific dollar amount times the employee's years of employment with the employer or a specified percentage of the employee's average compensation during the employee's final years of employment with the employer).

US employers are not required to offer any pension benefits to their employees. However, if an employer chooses to offer a pension or other employee benefit plan (such as health benefits or profit sharing), there are very complex and sophisticated rules that each plan must satisfy.

The Employee Retirement Income Security Act (ERISA) provides certain minimum standards that a pension plan and the individuals responsible for operating it must satisfy. In addition, ERISA requires each employer sponsoring a pension plan to file certain information with the Internal Revenue Service (the government agency responsible for enforcing the Code) and with the Department of Labour (the government entity responsible for enforcing ERISA). ERISA also requires that each employer provide employees participating in a pension plan with certain information about their benefits and rights under the plan. Employers should be aware that failure to provide ERISA-required information to the appropriate government agency or to a participating employee can result in significant penalties against the employer (perhaps as much as USD 1,000 per day). ERISA also imposes a requirement that defined benefit plans obtain insurance with respect to the benefits promised under the plan. Finally, ERISA provides (through the federal pre-emption rules) the exclusive means through which employees can enforce their rights to any benefits promised under a pension plan. Failure to comply with ERISA can result in loss of tax deductibility for the employer's cost of the plan.

Certain liabilities related to ERISA plans may exist, such as unfunded pension plan liabilities, and an investigation of potential pension plan liabilities should be undertaken by a buyer. Additionally, arrangements for the termination or continuation of the ERISA plans need to be made in connection with the acquisition.

Defined contribution and defined benefit plans are required to benefit broadly the employees of an employer in order to obtain favourable tax treatment. However, a separate set of benefit plans also may have been established to compensate executives, officers and directors of a company. Although these arrangements typically are unfunded and do not offer the same favourable tax treatment as broadly based plans, a specified event, such as an acquisition or other change in control, may cause these benefits to become fully funded and taxable. The funding requirements for these plans need to be addressed in connection with restructurings, recapitalizations and acquisitions.

35.23   Employee Rights

The employment relationship under US law is highly regulated by a complex and sometimes duplicative system of statutes, administrative regulations and judicial precedent at the federal, state and local level. The scope of regulation extends to all aspects of employment including hiring decisions, wage payment, overtime, compensation, collective bargaining, employee discipline and workplace safety. Civil rights legislation at the federal and state level prohibits discrimination in employment based upon age (40 and over) (mandatory retirement at any age is also prohibited), race, gender, colour, national origin, religion and disability. Most of the major components of the regulatory process are applicable to employers of as few as 15 employees.

The collective bargaining process for labour unions is regulated at the federal level by the National Labour Relations Act which establishes procedures under which employees can freely choose their own representatives for the purposes of collective bargaining through the secret ballot election process and protects employees from adverse action when they exercise their preference for or against union representation. Unions that are lawfully recognized are entitled to serve as the employees' exclusive bargaining representative in the appropriate bargaining unit and employers under those circumstances are obligated to bargain exclusively with the union over wages, hours and other terms and conditions of employment. Strikes in the private sector are permitted unless the right to strike has been waived contractually.

35.24   Compulsory Transfer of Employees

Under the traditional US rule, in the absence of a contractual arrangement to the contrary, the employment relationship is regarded as 'at-will' and may be terminated with or without advance notice and with or without reason. In recent years two categories of exceptions to this doctrine have emerged: implied contract exceptions and public policy exceptions. The public policy exception protects an at-will employee who has been discharged for acts that conform to or which further clearly expressed public policy and prevents an employer from taking adverse action against employees because they have exercised their statutory rights. The implied contract theory imposes limitations on an employer's power to terminate an employee or otherwise modify the employment relationship based upon statements or 'promises' implied from personnel manuals, policy statements or other promises of job security. Some states have attempted to enact legislation requiring payment of severance benefits to employees who are terminated in connection with a merger or acquisition. Federal courts, in at least one instance, have found such legislation to be inconsistent under federal law and invalid.

35.25   Tax Deductibility of Acquisition Expenses

If the buyer is not resident in or otherwise subject to tax in the US, the deductibility of its acquisition expenses is determined under the laws of such jurisdictions in which the buyer is subject to tax.

Where, however, the buyer is a US taxpayer, expenses incurred in connection with the acquisition of capital assets, such as stock of a US company or business assets, are generally not deductible. Instead, such expenses are included in the cost basis of such stock or assets. To the extent the acquired assets can be depreciated or amortized for US tax purposes, such acquisition expenses may thereby be recovered rateably over the period of such depreciation or amortization. Upon the acquisition of assets constituting a business, US tax laws require a joint reporting by the buyer and the seller of the allocation of the purchase price among the various assets acquired, and the acquisition expenses incurred by the buyer are allocated in accordance with the rules for allocating the purchase price.

35.26   Levies on Acquisition Agreements and Collateral Documents

Stamp duty is generally not applicable to business and share acquisitions, but transfer taxes are often assessed on the transfer of certain specific assets such as real estate. In addition, some states impose transfer taxes on the transfer of other personal property (usually tangible). However, there may be exceptions for isolated, occasional or bulk transfers. In addition, state practices differ on whether these transfer taxes are imposed on the seller or the buyer.

Another matter for early determination is the identity of the purchasing entity. Transfer tax exceptions for intra-group transfers may not be available, depending on the form of the transaction. Therefore, to avoid transfer tax on a subsequent intragroup transaction, it may be important to finalize the intended structure before the acquisition.

35.27   Financing Rules and Restrictions

US tax rules include 'earnings stripping' rules which have the effect of denying a deduction to US companies under certain circumstances for all or a portion of the interest paid to certain types of parent companies, including foreign parent companies able to claim complete or partial exemption from US tax with respect to such interest payments under any applicable tax treaty. In addition, debts of US companies owed to parent companies may be re-characterized for tax purposes as equity under US common law if certain factors are present.

Factors tending to indicate equity status include the existence of variable rates of return based upon the debtor's profitability and the debtor's thin capitalization, although all facts and circumstances are considered.

The tax laws also contain 'anti-conduit' rules designed to prevent application of treaty benefits to payments from US companies to foreign owners or lenders through a third party under circumstances in which the ultimate beneficiary of such payments would not be entitled to the favourable treaty rates.

35.28 Exchange Controls and Repatriation of Profits

Unlike many other countries, the US has no exchange controls to restrict or limit the fiow of foreign capital into or out of the country. Foreign investors can freely repatriate any loss, income and share capital to their home country.

The US imposes a 30 per cent withholding tax on dividends, interest, royalties and service fees paid to foreigners. The US has entered into treaties with some countries that will reduce the fiat 30 per cent withholding rate on dividends, interest, royalties and service fees earned in the US.

35.29 Groups of Companies

An affiliated group of US corporations may (but is not required to) file a consolidated corporate income tax return. In general, companies are part of an affiliated group if a US common parent company owns at least 80 per cent of the total voting power and of the total value of the stock of at least one other corporation in the group, and at least 80 per cent of the total voting power and of the total value of the stock of each other corporation in the group is owned by one or more other members of the group. In the event the group elects to file a consolidated return, inter-company transactions are generally eliminated or deferred and the group reports income or loss earned by the group as a whole. Once a consolidated group elects to file the tax returns on a consolidated basis, it may not cease doing so in subsequent years without the US tax authorities' consent. Even if a consolidated group does not file a consolidated return, however, losses from inter-company transactions are disallowed or deferred and inter-company dividends can generally be excluded from income.

Although filing consolidated returns is optional for tax purposes, non-tax accounting rules typically require commonly controlled groups to report profits and losses and prepare balance sheets on a consolidated basis.

35.30 Responsibility for Liabilities of an Acquired Subsidiary

Traditionally, shareholders in the US have been insulated from liability for the debts of a company in which they hold shares, other than in circumstances where a specific guarantee, indemnity or other undertaking has been given in favour of a creditor and other than in circumstances where the subsidiary is so undercapitalized or the formalities of corporate governance are so ignored so as to permit the piercing of the corporate veil by a creditor. Certain environmental liabilities, in particular those commonly referred to as environmental 'Superfund' liabilities, are also sometimes imposed on the shareholders.

35.31 Governing Law of the Contract

Courts in the US enforce the choice of law made by the contracting parties, provided the law chosen has reasonable connections with the underlying transactions or the parties. Generally, the choice of law of the buyer's jurisdiction and the law of the place that has commercial connections with the transaction will satisfy the requirement. It is essential to note that the law chosen by the contracting parties only governs the agreement, the relationship between the contracting parties and the dispute resolution. US law, especially state law, governs issues such as transfer of assets and third party interests.

35.32 Dispute Resolution Options

In recognition of the high cost and general disruption resulting from litigation, the US has provided a wide range of alternative dispute resolution procedures to minimize the disruption and expense associated with commercial disputes.

Arbitration in the US is governed either by the Federal Arbitration Act or by state arbitration acts. The parties are at liberty to prescribe the rules of procedure to follow in arbitration and arbitrators choose the rules where the parties fail to agree. While arbitration can be conducted in the US, it is not unusual for parties to make provisions in international agreements to conduct the arbitration on neutral soil. As a signatory to the New York Convention on the Recognition and Enforcement of Foreign Arbitral Awards, US courts enforce a foreign arbitration awards provided that the court has personal jurisdiction over the party and none of the grounds for refusal or deferral exist.

The 'mini-trial' has been favourably accepted as an alternative dispute resolution. The hearing for the case attended by a lawyer, senior executives for both parties and an independent adviser facilitates a settlement based on a realistic evaluation of each party's case.

Mediation is another viable alternative dispute resolution technique, but has not gained in popularity for resolution of major disputes because of laws that allow the parties to use a compromise offer against each other in court after the mediation has failed.

US courts will enforce foreign judgments on the basis of treaties or international conventions to which the USA is a signatory. In the absence of treaties and conventions, the Uniform Foreign Money Judgment Recognition Act, which has been adopted by several states, provides for the recognition and enforcement of foreign judgments which grant or deny the recovery of a sum of money and which fulfil certain conditions.

36. EUROPEAN UNION—SOCIETAS EUROPAEA

Dirk Jannott
CMS Hasche Sigle, Düsseldorf

36.1 Introduction

More than four decades passed between the birth of the idea of a European public
limited (leerstelle) liability company and the actual formation of the first such company.
The enabling legislation was set out in Council Regulation (EC) No. 2157/2001 on
the Statute for a European company dated 8 October 2001 (SE Regulation) which
came into force on 8 October 2004 (Official Journal L294/1). While the SE
Regulation sets out the legal framework for the company structure, it is supplemented
by a Directive regarding the involvement of employees in the SE (Council Directive
2001/86/EC of 8 October 2001, Official Journal L294/22—SE Directive). The SE
Regulation is directly applicable law and merely allows the Member States certain
options and implementation rights. The SE Directive, however, is an order to the
Member States to transpose the provisions of the Directive into national law.

36.2 The New Legal Form

The SE is a new legal form which exists in parallel to all of the corporate forms existing
in each of the Member States. It is a separate legal person and has a subscribed capital of
at least EUR 120,000 divided into shares; its name must include the letters 'SE'. Where
Member States require a greater subscribed capital for companies carrying on certain
types of activity these requirements shall apply to SEs with registered office in that
Member State (Article 4 SE Regulation). An SE is domiciled in the Member State
where its head office is located and is registered with the appropriate commercial
register for that Member State. Although an SE is subject to and governed by the
SE Regulation which applies Community-wide, it is also subject to the national law of
the Member State in which it is domiciled, including the national law implementing
the SE Regulation and SE Directive and the national corporate law. As a result the basic
requirements for an SE are the same in each Member State, but much of the detail is
determined by local law—meaning the SE cannot be seen as a Europe-wide uniform
legal form.

36.3 The Possible Applications

The SE offers special advantages, particularly at a supranational level. It enables for the
first time cross-border mergers of companies within the EU even before the transposition of the Directive on cross-border mergers of limited liability companies (2005/
56/EC of 26 October 2005—Official Journal L310/1), which is to be done by 15
December 2007. If companies want to merge as equal partners, the SE is a neutral legal
form which even makes it possible for the domicile of the new merged company to be

© World Law Group
International Business Acquisitions, M. Whalley, F.-J. Semler (eds.), Kluwer Law International, London,
2007; ISBN 9789041124838.

located in a third Member State. For groups engaged in business throughout Europe it offers the possibility to harmonize both the legal form of all group companies and their management structures and also offers numerous possibilities to restructure, for example, cross-border relocation of registered office and cross-border merger of affiliates or of all subsidiaries into the holding company. The SE is also interesting for cross-border joint ventures and holding companies, and, perhaps most significantly, as an acquisition vehicle.

36.4   Means of Formation

There are five different ways to form an SE (Articles 2, 3 SE Regulation), although each alternative reflects the basic requirement that there is a cross-border or international element. Firstly, existing public companies (stock corporations) can merge to form an SE, provided that at least two of the merging companies come from different Member States. Secondly, companies, both stock corporations and limited liability companies, can form a holding SE, provided that at least two of the promoting companies are from different Member States or have had a subsidiary or branch in another Member State for at least two years. Thirdly, under the same conditions of internationality, a subsidiary SE may be formed as a joint venture company. Fourthly, an existing stock corporation can convert itself into an SE if it has had a subsidiary in another Member State for at least two years. Fifthly and finally, an SE can itself form subsidiaries as SEs.

In order to form an SE by way of merger, to form a holding SE or to transform an existing company into an SE, the respective founding companies have to draw up a proposal which is similar to the proposal required for national mergers of public limited liability companies and which has to be approved by the Shareholders' Meetings of the founding companies. If an SE is formed as a subsidiary SE or as the subsidiary of an SE, this is achieved by way of cash contribution or contribution-in-kind in accordance with national corporate law. In every case the SE comes into existence when it is registered in the national commercial register in the country of its registered office, notice of which must be given in the Official Journal of the European Union.

36.5   Management Bodies; Employee Involvement

SEs can be structured according to what is known as the 'two-tier system,' which implements the 'separation principle' by dividing responsibility between the Management Board and the Supervisory Board. In some countries (for example Germany), this is the only structure provided for stock corporations.

An alternative model for corporate governance can be seen in the so called 'board system'—which is often referred to as a 'one-tier system'. In English and American companies, authority is traditionally split between the Shareholders' Meeting and the Board of Directors with the Board being a uniform administrative organ with combined management and supervisory functions. The Board of Directors is headed by the Chairman of the Board, who may also be the Chief Executive Officer (CEO). Other countries like France allow stock corporations to choose between 'one-tier' and 'two-tier' structures. The European legislator, recognising that no single system predominates within the EU, has left it open to the Shareholders' Meeting of the SE to decide whether to implement a two-tier system with a Supervisory Board and a Management Board or a one-tier system with a unified Administrative Board (Article 38 (b) SE Regulation). In some Member States the Administrative Board can appoint external Managing Directors.

Some Member States have extensive rules regarding employee co-determination which do not apply to SEs. Instead, the SE Directive and the respective national laws provide for a concept of negotiations and agreement between the management and the employees regarding the implementation of co-determination. Should an agreement not be reached, the employees are protected by standard rules that provide for a certain level of co-determination subject to the existing level of co-determination in the founding companies. It is not possible to elaborate on this subject in the context of the present chapter. It should be noted, however, that due attention is to be paid to these questions when an SE is formed, merged or relocated.

36.6 Cross-Border Relocation of Registered Office

Cross-border relocation of a corporate's registered office while maintaining corporate identity is possible through an SE (Article 8 SE Regulation). A cross-border relocation of domicile takes place on the basis of a transfer proposal drawn up by the management of the SE which, in addition to other formal requirements, must contain the proposed new registered office, the proposed statutes of the company, the implications on employee involvement, a timetable for the transfer and any rights provided for the protection of shareholders and/or creditors. In addition to the transfer proposal, the management of the SE must draw up a transfer report which—similar to a merger report—is supposed to enable its readers to subject the transfer to a plausibility review.

The statutes of the SE must be amended to reflect the transfer of registered office, and this amendment will require a resolution of the Shareholders' Meeting of the SE passed with the requisite majority. If a shareholder objects to the transfer and the objection is recorded in the minutes, the SE is required to make an offer to acquire the shares of the objecting shareholder for a reasonable cash payment. The SE may also be required to provide security to its creditors, if the creditors can show that payment of their claims will be put at risk by the transfer.

The transfer of the registered office becomes effective when the SE is registered in the Member State where it establishes its new registered office. This registration is subject to the precondition that the commercial register of the current Member State of the registered office has issued a certificate stating that all formalities relating to the transfer have been observed.

36.7 Tax Treatment

The SE Regulation expressly does not cover taxation. An SE is treated for tax purposes like any other stock corporation in the country of its domicile. Given that the establishment of an SE is *per se* a cross-border event, consideration should be given to the respective relevant tax treaties on the avoidance of double taxation and the provisions of foreign transaction tax law.

In addition, the Merger Directive as of 17 February 2005 (2005/19 EC, official Journal L58/19) now provides for a guideline for Member States that the means of formation of an SE may, under several preconditions and as a general rule, be effected tax neutral.

It is more significant that the tax laws are only now in the process of being adapted to this new corporate creature. It is difficult to make statements on the tax regime of cross-border transactions in all of the Member States. However, a general tendency is found to tax hidden reserves in the country where these reserves have been built up.

37. EUROPEAN UNION—EU MERGER CONTROL

Martijn van de Hel
CMS Derks Star Busmann, Brussels★

37.1 Introduction

Two aspects of business acquisitions are to be assessed under EU competition law. The effect of acquisitions on the market structure are dealt with in the framework of the EU Merger Control Regulation 139/2004 (hereinafter: the 'Regulation'), the Notices and Guidelines explaining the Regulation, the European Commission's decisions and the judgements of the Court of First Instance and the Court of Justice of the EC. The effects of additional restrictions on market behaviour agreed upon between the parties are dealt with under Article 81(1) of the EC Treaty (hereinafter: 'EC'), which contains a general prohibition on anti-competitive agreements capable of affecting trade between Member States.

The acquisition of control of a target business (by purchasing shares or assets) usually constitutes a 'concentration' within the meaning of the Regulation. The following is an explanation of this Regulation.

37.2 Background

The EU merger control regime has a long history. Since the early seventies, regulators acknowledged that Articles 81 and 82 EC, which deal with anti-competitive agreements and abuses of dominant positions respectively, do not provide an adequate basis for remedying the structural changes to markets, which may be caused by large-scale mergers and takeovers. Article 81 EC, for example, is only applicable to the acquisition of a minority shareholding or the creation of a joint venture (it could serve as an instrument for influencing the conduct of the companies in question) and Article 82 EC was applied to takeovers only where the aim of the takeover was to drive remaining competitors off the market.

As the creation of a common merger control regime meant that Member States would have to give up sovereignty in this field, it took more than 15 years to agree on the text of the old Regulation 4064/89, which was finally adopted on 21 December 1989 and came into effect in 1990. It proved an immediate success, as it provided for a clear procedure for assessing mergers, acquisitions and certain joint ventures with fixed deadlines for reaching decisions. Since 1990, the Commission has dealt with more than 3,000 transactions.

As of 1 May 2004, the Regulation has replaced Regulation 4064/89 introducing a new substantive test as well as significant procedural changes.

★ Chapter revised by Martijn van de Hel, EU Competition lawyer Brussels.

© World Law Group
International Business Acquisitions, M. Whalley, F.-J. Semler (eds.), Kluwer Law International, London, 2007; ISBN 9789041124838.

37.3   Scope of the Regulation

The Regulation is applicable to all 'concentrations' with a 'Community dimension'. A 'concentration' arises in three different situations where:

- One undertaking acquires (joint or sale) control over another undertaking;

- Two previously independent undertakings merge; or

- A so-called 'full function joint venture' is created (see below).

A concentration has a Community dimension if either the conditions of the basic turnover test or of the alternative turnover test are met. According to the basic test, a Community dimension arises if:

- The combined aggregate world-wide turnover of the parties is more than EUR 5 billion; and

- The turnover in the EU of each of at least two parties is more than EUR 250 million; and

- The parties each do not achieve more than two thirds of their turnover in one and the same Member State (the so-called 'two-thirds rule').

According to the alternative test, a Community dimension also arises if:

- The combined aggregate worldwide turnover of all the parties is more than EUR 2.5 billion;

- In each of at least three Member States, the combined aggregate turnover of all the parties is more than EUR 100 million;

- In each of at least three Member States included for the purpose of the previous bullet point, the aggregate turnover of each of at least two of the parties is more than EUR 25 million; and

- The aggregate Community-wide turnover of each of at least two of the parties is more than EUR 100 million;

Under the alternative test, the two-thirds rule is also applicable. Note that, in case of takeovers, only the group turnover of the acquiring party and the turnover of the 'target company' have to be taken into account. In case of the creation of a joint venture the entire group turnover of both the parents is taken into account. Where an acquisition is being made by a joint venture company, the Commission will look at the substance and economic reality of the transaction to decide whether the joint venture as a 'full-function' entity (see below) is to be regarded as making the acquisition or whether the acquisition is actually being made by the parent companies through the joint venture entity. There are special rules for calculating the turnover of banks and insurance companies. Further guidance on the calculation of turnover can be found in the Commission's Notice on the calculation of turnover and the Notice on the concept of undertakings concerned. These notices will be replaced by a consolidated jurisdictional notice in 2007.

37.4   Joint Ventures

If a joint venture qualifies as a full-function joint venture it is dealt with under the Regulation. To be qualified as 'full-function', a joint venture must bring about a lasting change in the structure of the parent companies. This is the case where the joint venture operates on a market, performing the same functions as the ones normally carried out by other companies operating on the same market. The joint venture must have a separate management dedicated to its day-to-day operations and must have access to sufficient resources including finance, staff and assets, in order to conduct its business activities on a lasting basis.

A joint venture is not full-function if it only takes over one specific function within the parent companies' business activities without access to the market. This is the case, for example, for joint ventures limited to R&D or production. Such joint ventures are auxiliary to their parent companies' business activities. This is also the case where a joint venture is primarily limited to the distribution or sales of its parent companies' products and, therefore, acts principally as a sales agency. Whether a non full-function joint venture is in compliance with EU competition law has to be assessed under Article 81 EC. Further guidance on these issues can be found in the Commission's Notice on the concept of concentration, the Notice on the concept of full-function joint ventures (both to be replaced by the aforementioned consolidated jurisdictional notice) and the Guidelines on the applicability of Article 81 EC to horizontal co-operation agreements.

The creation of a joint venture bears the risk of possible coordination of competitive behaviour between the parent companies. Coordination of behaviour between companies may infringe Article 81 EC. The problem of coordination is however dealt with within the framework of the Regulation, within one and the same procedure and without any changes regarding the time limits. To the extent that the creation of a joint venture leads to the coordination of its parents, such coordination is appraised in accordance with the criteria of Article 81 EC. If such coordination infringes Article 81(1) EC, the Commission will assess whether the coordination is exempted under Article 81(3) EC. This will be the case if the following four criteria are met:

- The transaction brings about economic advantages for the parties; and
- Consumers receive a fair share of the benefits; and
- There are no indispensable restrictions; and
- There is no substantial elimination of competition.

37.5   One Stop Shop and Referral

The Regulation provides for a one-stop shop. If a concentration has a Community dimension, the Commission has exclusive competence to review it. Transactions that fall below the turnover thresholds of the Regulation will be subject to relevant national merger control rules. If a transaction threatens to significantly affect competition in a distinct market within a Member State, the Commission may refer the whole or part of the case relating to the distinct market concerned to the national competition authority. By contrast, one or more Member States may request the Commission to examine a concentration that does not have a Community dimension but affects trade between Member States and threatens to affect competition within the territory of the Member State. Moreover, prior to the notification and upon the parties' request, the Commission may examine a transaction, when it is to be reviewed by the national competition authorities of at least three Member States, and no Member State has expressed its disagreement. Further guidance can be found in the Commission's Notice on Case Referral in respect of concentrations.

37.6 Procedure

A proposed concentration must be notified prior to implementation. Unless the Commission grants derogation, the transaction may not be put into effect before notification and until the final decision is adopted. The Regulation permits a transaction to be notified prior to the conclusion of a binding agreement, provided that the parties intend to enter the agreement in good faith. The Commission then launches the first stage (Phase I) of the investigation. Within 25 working days, it must make a decision. The 25-day working period is extended to 35 working days in case of a referral request of a Member State or in case parties submit remedies (see below). If the Commission requests further information, this period may be suspended until the required information has been provided in full. If the Commission decides that the concentration does not fall within the scope of the Regulation or does not raise competition concerns, it gives the green light and parties may implement the transaction.

However, if the Commission considers that the concentration 'raises serious doubts as to its compatibility with the common market', it will launch a second stage (Phase II), in-depth investigation. The Commission must complete its investigation within 90 working days, although this period may be extended under various circumstances (e.g. in case remedies have been offered) and can last up to 125 working days. This period may also be suspended if the Commission requests further information. If the Commission, during the Phase II investigation, comes to the conclusion that the concentration is not compatible with the common market, it can prohibit the concentration or approve it conditionally. Further guidance on time limits et cetera can be found in the Implementing Regulation 802/2004 and in the best practice guidelines on the conduct of EC merger control proceedings.

37.7 Substantive Test

A concentration, which significantly impedes effective competition in the common market, or a substantial part of it, in particular as a result of the creation or strengthening of a dominant position, will be prohibited by the Commission. Previously (before May 2004), the test was solely focused on the existence of (joint or sole) market dominance. It was often criticized as being too limited in scope, as was shown by the Airtours case.

This case led to the conclusion that in the absence of joint dominance, non-coordinated or unilateral effects (a strategic collusion between competitors without coordination) from a merger (in oligopolistic markets) were not caught by the old Regulation. After the Boeing/McDonnell Douglas decision and especially the prohibition of the merger between GE and Honeywell, it was furthermore concluded that there was a discrepancy between the dominance test of the EU and the 'substantial lessening of competition' test in the US including the lack of recognition of efficiencies in the EU.

With the new substantive test, the Commission intends to capture all mergers, including mergers in oligopolistic markets without sole or joint dominance but with market power concerns due to unilateral (non-collusive) effects. The Commission has also adopted the view that efficiency claims form an integral part of the competitive assessment. In case the efficiencies generated by the transaction are likely to enhance the ability and incentive of the parties to act pro-competitively for the benefit of consumers, thereby counteracting the adverse effect on competition which the transaction might otherwise have, the Commission may decide that there are no grounds for declaring the transaction incompatible with the common market.

Further guidance on mergers and efficiencies can be found in the Commission's Guidelines on the assessment of horizontal mergers. In the course of 2007, the Commission is expected to issue guidelines on the assessment of non-horizontal mergers.

37.8 Remedies

In cases where a transaction is likely to significantly impede effective competition in the common market, the parties can offer commitments (remedies), which would meet the Commission's concerns, such as the divestiture of assets or changes to existing contracts. For example, as one of the conditions for clearing the Air France and KLM merger, both parties committed themselves to surrendering 94 single take-off and landing slots. Another example can be found in the acquisition of Gillette by Procter & Gamble, in which the Commission demanded that Procter & Gamble divested its battery toothbrush business. Further guidance on remedies can be found in the Commission's Notice on remedies and in the best practice guidelines on divesture commitments, both of which will be reviewed by the Commission in the course of 2007.

37.9 Ancillary Restraints

Contractual obligations capable of restricting the parties' market behaviour, such as non-competition clauses, must be assessed under Article 81(1) EC. If such obligations are directly related and necessary to guarantee the successful conclusion of a concentration, these obligations may be qualified as 'ancillary restraints'. Ancillary restraints are automatically covered by the decision declaring the concentration compatible with the common market. In its Notice on ancillary restrictions, the Commission has set out a number of obligations, which it considers acceptable in view of Article 81(1) EC.

Non-competition clauses are justified for periods of up to three years, when the transfer of the business includes goodwill and know-how, and for a period of up to two years when it includes only goodwill. However, these are not absolute rules; they do not preclude a prohibition of a longer duration in particular circumstances where, e.g. the parties can demonstrate that customer loyalty will persist for a period longer than two years or that the economic life cycle of the products concerned is longer than three years and should be taken into account.

The geographic scope of a non-competition clause must be limited to the area where the seller had established the products or services before the transfer. A non-competition clause must be limited to those products and services that form the economic activity of the undertaking transferred.

The Commission's Notice may also be used for guidance when assessing transactions not caught by the Regulation, e.g. when the turnover thresholds are not met. If clauses in a takeover contract are more restrictive than the 'ancillary restraints' accepted by the Commission, these clauses may be caught by Article 81(1) EC and, consequently, be null and void.

Furthermore, the EU competition rules may be applicable to (temporary) purchase and supply contracts between the buyer and the seller. The Commission recognizes that, in many cases, the buyer of a business entity will need to procure goods or services from the seller for a transitional period. In principle, purchase and supply agreements concluded for that purpose should not contain exclusivity clauses, and must be limited to the period necessary for the replacement of the relationship of dependency by autonomy in the market. Purchase or supply obligations aimed at guaranteeing the (fixed) quantities previously supplied can be justified for a transitional period of up to five years. Obligations providing for unlimited quantities, exclusivity or conferring preferred-supplier or preferred-purchaser status, are not necessary to the implementation of the concentration.

37.10 Judicial Review and Standard of Proof

Commission decisions by which a transaction is approved or prohibited can be challenged before the Court of First Instance. A further appeal can be made to the Court of Justice of the EC. The European Courts, and in particular the Court of First Instance, play a decisive role in reviewing Commission decisions and shaping the Commission's practice.

In 2002, the Commission suffered a trilogy of defeats in the landmark merger cases of Schneider/Legrand, Airtours/First Choice and Tetra Laval/Sidel. In Schneider, the Court of First Instance annulled the Commission's decision on the grounds that there had been serious infringements of the parties' rights of defence. In Airtours, the Court of First Instance annulled the Commission's prohibition decision on the basis that the Commission had failed to prove the essential elements of its theory of joint dominance. In Tetra Laval, the Court of First Instance ruled that the Commission had failed to prove its case to the 'requisite legal standard' and condemned the decision for being 'vitiated by a series of errors of assessment as to factors fundamental to any assessment of whether a collective dominant position might be created'.

In 2005, the Court of Justice criticized the Commission's economic basis for prohibiting the merger between Tetra Laval and Sidel. Although the Commission has a margin of discretion with regard to economic matters that does not mean that the European

Courts must refrain from reviewing the Commission's interpretation of information of an economic nature. Such a review is all the more necessary in case a prospective analysis is required when examining a planned merger with possible conglomerate effects. In the GE/Honeywell case, the Court of First Instance reiterated these conclusions. The decision of the Commission in GE/Honeywell was nevertheless upheld, despite the fact that the Commission had made a number of errors in its assessment of the merger.

Chapter 3

DUE DILIGENCE

'Due diligence' has become a term of art, signifying as it does the responsibility of the buyer or of its advisers diligently to examine all aspects of the target and its business in order to satisfy itself that all is as it has been represented. The expression is derived from the USA's Securities and Exchange Commisions's requirements on its market participants in securities transactions to ensure that they have available all proper and sufficient information for investors. It has been adopted and used more widely as a generic term for the process by which any buyer or investor will satisfy itself that all is as it seems with a proposed target of an investment or acquisition.

The buyer faces four basic risks in an acquisition of another business.

First, and in view of the almost worldwide principle of *caveat emptor* (let the buyer beware), the title of the seller to the shares or assets of the target must be established, along with its ability to sell them free of restrictions (which could be imposed by government licences, joint venture or shareholder agreements, Financing Security or customer contracts).

Secondly, an acquisition rarely involves only an investment in a profit-making enterprise. Its purpose is usually to gain access to a new market, the broadening of a business base (by vertical or horizontal integration), the acquisition of otherwise unavailable technology or intellectual property, or the strengthening of a competitive position. In this case, the buyer's risk is failing to achieve its internal objectives from the acquisition. To give a simple example, a buyer may wish the target to become the distributor of its products in the target's territory. The target may, however, be bound by an existing contract with a competitor which restricts the target's rights to distribute the buyer's products.

Thirdly, the buyer must be sure of the target's ability to continue to carry on its business after the acquisition. This risk is most real in the case of an assets acquisition, where the legal entity which operates the business will change, necessitating the novation or assignment (or renewal) of business contracts, and the obtaining of fresh operating licences and consents. But a share acquisition often presents similar risks, if regulatory authorities have the power to cancel or withhold business licences, or if material suppliers or customers have the right to terminate contracts, on a change of control.

International Business Acquisitions, M. Whalley, F.-J. Semler (eds.), Kluwer Law International, London, 2007; ISBN 9789041124838.

Fourthly, the buyer must be confident of its ability to integrate, and then to manage and control, the target within its own group, and to preserve the target's goodwill. The risk here is that existing employees of the target will be unwilling to comply with the buyer's management style or methods, or customers or essential suppliers (including financiers) will be reluctant to continue to support the business under its new owners.

The specific function of legal due diligence in the context of an acquisition of shares or assets is therefore to:

- confirm that the target has good title to its material assets;
- confirm the existence of tangible and intangible assets and rights;
- confirm that the target has all necessary licences to carry on its business;
- confirm that the target is in compliance with applicable laws;
- identify actual and threatened material actions, claims and disputes;
- identify unusual or onerous terms in material contracts;
- confirm that material contracts are properly executed and enforceable; and
- ensure that the change of control, or change in ownership of assets, will not have a material adverse effect on the business.

For example, while the major legal issues checklist in Chapter 2 may ask whether government consents are required for carrying on the target's type of business, due diligence will determine whether the target does, in fact, have those consents for its particular business, and whether it has complied with any conditions attaching to them.

Warranties and Indemnities v Due Diligence

It is often thought that the warranties and indemnities requested by a buyer from a seller are a substitute for due diligence or, conversely, that a buyer should not expect warranties where an opportunity is given to the buyer and its advisers to conduct full due diligence. Acquisition warranties and due diligence are not, however, mutually exclusive.

While there is a certain interdependence between warranties and the due diligence process, they serve different, but complementary, purposes. The aim of due diligence is to identify and quantify risk; warranties and indemnities, on the other hand, seek to allocate the responsibility for risks, which are often unidentified, to either the buyer or the seller. Due diligence is therefore a pro-active process of identifying and measuring risk. Warranties constitute the buyer's protection, in a reactive way, against its expectations not being met in the future as a result of the representations of the seller not being accurate. Indemnities also identify specific known risks which are as yet unquantifiable, and which are considered to be the responsibility of the seller.

In a sense, therefore, the purpose of due diligence is to establish known or identifiable facts to assist the buyer with its decision to buy, and to determine the price at which it is prepared to do so. To the extent that there are still questions unanswered, this then leads to:

- warranties, in relation to statements or representations made by the seller which are unprovable or unidentifiable but which give essential comfort to the buyer (the damages suffered by the buyer as a result of any warranty being untrue then being recoverable from the seller); and

- indemnities, in relation to matters discovered to be real and present risks, the implications and costs of which cannot be immediately quantified but where the costs or damages, when ascertained, are considered to be the responsibility of the seller.

While more intrusive, the due diligence process can therefore be in the best interests of both buyer and seller, as it gives each party an opportunity to apportion risk and responsibility with the benefit of full information. It can also, in extreme cases, lead to the abandonment of a transaction if it discloses matters which are unacceptable to the buyer. This is often a better result than the transaction proceeding with both parties becoming locked into protracted and expensive warranty claims and litigation.

There is therefore still a place for warranties even where the buyer has been given the opportunity to perform a full due diligence examination of the target. Effective due diligence often, in fact, identifies issues that call for specific warranties from the seller, thereby making the warranties more focused and relevant. The extent of the warranties, however, and the extent to which a buyer and its advisers are given access to the target's business in order to perform due diligence, are always a matter for negotiation.

In many cases, effective due diligence may have to substitute for warranties. The seller may be unable or reluctant to give warranties, or may not have the financial resources required to meet any claims. Common examples are sales by venture capital and private equity investors who do not have sufficient knowledge of the business, or are reluctant, to give warranties, and receivers or liquidators who cannot accept warranty liabilities. Avoiding future warranty disputes is also particularly important when the seller is continuing in the business, for example where the buyer is acquiring shares from owner managers who will continue to work for the business after the sale.

In such cases, effective due diligence or reliance on warranty insurance are often the buyer's only protection.

Warranties and the due diligence process should both be regarded as valuable tools for the buyer in ensuring an effective transfer of the business into its ownership. Full and proper disclosure by the seller against warranties, and thorough due diligence enquiries by the buyer, also make subsequent disputes and warranty claims less likely.

The Risks of Due Diligence

It must be recognized, however, that the due diligence process carries with it certain risks for the buyer and its advisers, for the seller and for the target:

- the seller may be disclosing trade or scientific secrets or confidential information to an existing or potential competitor—secrecy or confidentiality agreements are usually essential, and a two stage process (with commercially sensitive information held back until the last minute) is often essential;

- the seller may inadvertently extend its liability for representations made to the buyer, particularly where the buyer has unrestricted access to the target's officers and employees, and it may not be possible to exclude these representations under contract;

- the seller may weaken its negotiating position by exposing problems in the target business to the buyer (e.g. the existence of employee or customer dissatisfaction);

- the due diligence process can add to employee unease and uncertainty, with a potentially serious impact on employee morale;

- for the buyer and the seller, confidentiality is more difficult to maintain if due diligence is carried out, as many more people become aware of the buyer's interest in the target; this could have serious implications if the seller, the buyer or the target is a listed company and if the acquisition is price sensitive;

- failure to maintain confidentiality can also lead to other buyers becoming aware that the target is 'in play' and can encourage competing offers;

- in some jurisdictions, personal liability may attach to the directors of a company who issue a formal document (e.g. a prospectus, an information memorandum or a circular to shareholders) based on due diligence carried out at their request or under their direction;

- the buyer's advisers (principally lawyers and accountants) who perform the due diligence enquiries on its behalf are usually liable if their enquiries are carried out negligently or carelessly, or if they fail to draw to their client's attention a material matter discovered by them;

- the buyer may be prevented (or 'estopped') from relying on representations or warranties, notwithstanding specific provisions in the purchase agreement to the contrary, if it has full knowledge of a matter before the exchange of contracts as a result of its due diligence enquiries, but chooses to proceed;

- unless the seller is well prepared, the time and effort required to assemble information for due diligence and respond to a buyer's requests for further information can substantially delay the transaction;

- dealing with due diligence enquiries effectively requires dedicated management resources, which can be a significant distraction from the day-to-day demands of the target's business;

- the results of a due diligence exercise will only be as good as the information made available—incomplete material can give a mistaken impression of the health of a business, but a seller will usually refuse to give a broad warranty that all relevant material has been disclosed, leaving the buyer at risk of the unknown: effective questioning is essential.

Due diligence can therefore be a two-edged sword, and advisers should consider its implications carefully, and advise their client accordingly, before proceeding.

Protection for the Seller and the Buyer

The buyer and seller can guard against some of these risks in different ways. For the seller's part, it can ensure that it is well prepared for the due diligence process, identifying a closed group of executives charged with managing the process efficiently and ensuring that all of the basic information is available in a physical or electronic data room in good time. That also has the advantage of heading off the need to respond to the buyer's own question list. The seller should also put in place effective confidentiality and non-disclosure arrangements.

For the buyer, it can guard against wasting time and professional fees by requesting a lock-out or exclusive dealing agreement from the seller, so that it has exclusive access to the seller and the due diligence material for sufficient time to be able to reach an agreement, while excluding other potential buyers from having any contact with the seller. It can also request a break fee, which the seller would be required to pay to the buyer to cover the buyer's costs if the transaction does not proceed because the seller withdraws or receives a higher offer, particularly in cases where the buyer is considered to be a 'white knight' who has been invited to bid by the seller.

The Risks of Failing to Make Proper Enquiry

It would be a foolish buyer, however, who elects to dispense with due diligence, and rely only on warranties. The risks associated with such a strategy, for both buyer and seller, include:

1. the buyer being held to have constructive notice or knowledge of a matter (e.g. something noted on a public register), which in some jurisdictions could bar a warranty claim;

2. as noted above, the potential failure of a warranty claim (in relation to something coming to light only after closing) as a result of:
   - the seller not having the resources to meet the claim;
   - the claim being statute barred;
   - the claim being barred by protection clauses in the sales contract relating, for example, to the time for bringing claims or limits to the size of claims (either minimum or maximum); or
   - inadequate warranty provisions, which fail to extend to the particular circumstances which are the subject of the claim;

3. the seller's silence or non-disclosure may be actionable under relevant legislation as misleading or deceptive conduct (e.g. section 47 of the UK Financial Services and Markets Act makes it an offence dishonestly to conceal any material facts in the context of a sale of shares or other investments);

4. failure to identify particular issues which could have justified the buyer in insisting on indemnities from the seller or a retention from, or reduction in, the purchase price;

5. the buyer (or its directors) leaving itself open to criticism later if an acquisition fails, or if the price paid is judged to have been excessive in the light of facts which subsequently come to light; and

6. a breakdown in the relationship between the buyer and seller, particularly if they are both still shareholders in the target or have other relationships, if adverse information was withheld or not discovered before the sale.

The Checklist

The questions to be asked during a due diligence examination vary from country to country. This chapter provides the reader with a checklist designed to serve as a starting point for a detailed examination of the target's business and assets in virtually any jurisdiction. However:

*   the extent to which the seller will permit due diligence;
*   the matters to be examined;
*   their relative importance within the jurisdiction;
*   the implications of making either inadequate or excessive enquiries;
*   how and by whom particular subjects are investigated; and
*   the cost and other factors;

will necessarily vary from jurisdiction to jurisdiction and acquisition to acquisition, depending upon the nature of the target or the buyer's priorities. Accordingly, the scope and nature of any due diligence enquiry should always be considered only after obtaining the advice and assistance of local counsel.

The due diligence process can be costly and time consuming. Its scope depends on the purpose of the acquisition and the nature of the target's business. It is therefore important for a buyer and its advisers to discuss and refine the due diligence checklist, so that all advisers are aware of the buyer's purpose and priorities, sometimes referred to as the 'deal drivers'. For the same reason, it is important that the buyer's advisers have an understanding of the buyer's and the target's industries. Their report should always be prefaced with a description of their understanding of those priorities and a description of the target's business and market, demonstrating that they understood the buyer's needs when carrying out their enquiries.

The matters identified under a number of headings below should therefore be viewed only as sign-posts to guide the enquirer. They will usually lead on to further enquiries, depending upon the initial responses and specific local factors. This checklist should therefore be regarded only as a starting point for the buyer's enquiries, and not as exhaustive.

The checklist is also not intended to instruct the reader on the evaluation of the material obtained once the initial enquiries have been made. The evaluation process is always determined by the specific circumstances and the prevailing laws of the relevant jurisdiction. For example, a property title certificate may, in some jurisdictions, be conclusive of absolute title, while in others it is necessary to enquire further about unregistered interests or encumbrances to which the property may be subject.

Where a group is being acquired, the due diligence process must be applied not only to the target, but also to each of its subsidiaries.

Shares v Assets

While the checklist has been designed for use in connection with an acquisition of either shares or assets, some aspects of it will assume greater or lesser importance according to the nature of the transaction.

For example, the share capital structure of a target is of central importance in the context of a share acquisition, but of much less importance when the company concerned is selling its business. Similarly, taxation is a leading issue in a share purchase, where a buyer will be inheriting all of the target's taxation liabilities, but may have only peripheral importance in the context of an assets or business acquisition.

Prospectus Due Diligence

It should be emphasized that the following checklist is offered for use only in the context of an acquisition. It is not appropriate for a due diligence exercise carried out in the context of a flotation or capital raising prospectus. In that case, the due diligence process has as its main purpose:

- the verification of statements made by the company or its promoters;

- the identification of any matters which should be drawn to the attention of investors if the company or its promoters are to satisfy statutory disclosure tests.

Prospectus due diligence must therefore focus on commercial and business issues in addition to the purely legal issues identified below, and is significantly more wide-ranging.

Other Issues

The due diligence checklist does not remove the need to advise generally on the acquisition. Ancillary questions often arise (in addition to those already included in the major legal issues checklist in Chapter 2), for example whether a buyer may be able to rely upon audit or other reports provided to it in the course of its enquiries.

More important is the need for comprehensive commercial due diligence, usually carried out by the buyer itself and its key executives, to examine the target's business history, its projections for the future and its key and critical strengths, weaknesses, opportunities and threats. This handbook, and the due diligence checklist that follows, assumes that this process is already well under way, or has been completed, giving the buyer the confidence to instruct, and bear the often considerable costs of, outside advisers to complete its investigations.

Specialist advice may also be required from other professions in the course of the due diligence process. This often includes advice from:

- investigating accountants (examination of accounts and business plans, verification of audit procedures, analysis of taxation computations);

- surveyors (property and structural surveys);

- environmental engineers/surveyors (environmental impact statements, environmental audits);

- actuaries (pension fund valuations and funding obligations);

- specialist engineers (e.g. marine, mining, construction);

- intellectual property specialists (particularly where technical patents underpin the value of the business, for example in biotechnology)

- insurance brokers (adequacy of insurance cover); and

- valuers.

Inevitably, the scope and quality of due diligence in any specific case will vary with the size and risk elements of the transaction, the quality and reputation of the target and its owners, and the attitude of the client for whom the due diligence is to be performed. Huge acquisitions by clients with substantial resources generally warrant and receive exhaustive due diligence—particularly if the target is a troubled company or is not well known to the buyer. Small acquisitions are much less likely to justify the expense and accompanying risks of a full scale due diligence process.

As a consequence, the lawyer should be prepared to assist the client in prioritising the due diligence task in order to make it commensurate with the size and nature of the transaction, while keeping significant risk to a minimum. An effective lawyer will also play a central role in managing the entire due diligence process and coordinating the activities of all professional advisers.

Many lawyers often also assume a role as commercial, as well as legal, advisers. The distinction between commercial and legal due diligence is often unclear, as questions will also be raised about the business and its products or services, its strengths and weaknesses, and its competitive advantages and disadvantages. Lawyers must therefore be prepared to familiarize themselves with their client's business, and the industry in which their client and the target business operate, in order to ensure that they make effective, and comprehensive, enquiries. The professional adviser can then be confident that the due diligence process will identify:

- the significant issues which are truly 'deal breakers';

- the issues which will affect the buyer's assessment of the business's value, and hence the price it is willing to pay;

- any requirement that the acquisition be structured in a specific way, for example to preserve intellectual property rights, to avoid onerous contracts or taxation penalties, or to gain a taxation advantage; and

- the need for specific contract terms or warranties, which may introduce conditions precedent, protect the buyer from future claims or put the risk of non-performance of the business back onto the seller.

The due diligence process must be thoroughly integrated with the preparation of the acquisition documentation and the whole process of negotiation with the seller. Effective communication between the buyer and its advisers, particularly where different teams are involved in separate aspects of the due diligence process, is essential.

DUE DILIGENCE CHECKLIST

1   Incorporation and Constitution

1.1   Certificate of incorporation/registration or extract from the commercial register.
1.2   Certificates evidencing any change of name or change of status.★
1.3   Current constitution, articles of association or by-laws.★

2   Share Capital

2.1   Authorized and issued share capital together with details of all shares issued subject to special rights.★
2.2   Voting rights attaching to shares of different classes.★
2.3   Details of debt securities having rights of conversion into equity.★
2.4   Details of all increases and decreases of capital and any redemption, buy-back, merger, consolidation or splitting of capital and any alterations of the rights attaching to shares.
2.5   Details of any placement of shares or convertible debt securities within the last three years, including copies of any placing and associated underwriting agreements.
2.6   List of all current shareholders of each class, and details of:★
     2.6.1   shares held on trust for a third person, if known;
     2.6.2   all transfers of shares from the establishment of the target up to the present.
2.7   Requirements for calling and holding shareholders' meetings.
2.8   Agreements creating any option or encumbrance over issued shares, or any rights in respect of the shares (e.g. as to dividends or voting).
2.9   Agreements, if any, between shareholders.
2.10   Amount of any treasury stock held by the target, or shares allotted but not yet issued.
2.11   Details of any options, warrants or other rights granted by the target over un-issued share capital.

2.12   Confirmation that all issued shares have been fully paid up, or details of any amount unpaid on issued share capital.
2.13   Dividend history, including details of any declared but unpaid dividend, together with details of tax credits attaching to dividends or advance tax payments paid by or credited to the company.
2.14   Details of any dividend reinvestment plan.
2.15   Location of principal share registry and details of share registers maintained in any other jurisdiction.*

3   Administration

3.1   Statutory books and registers.
3.2   Names and addresses of directors, secretary, chief executive officer and any other officers.*
3.3   Address of registered/principal office.
3.4   Powers of attorney granted by the target and not registered in any public register.
3.5   Requirements for calling and holding directors' meetings.
3.6   Records or minutes of shareholders' or stockholders' meetings.
3.7   Records or minutes of all meetings of the board of directors or supervisory board, and all committees of either, within the last three years.*
3.8   By-laws, rules of procedure and statements of practice or policy of the board of directors or supervisory board (e.g. policy in relation to directors' share transactions, remuneration committee guidelines).*
3.9   Organization chart of the target.
3.10   Group structure chart of any group of which the target is a member.
3.11   Management information systems.

4   Restrictions on Sale of Assets or Transfer of Shares

4.1   Internal requirements for shareholders' or directors' resolutions or approvals in relation to the sale or purchase of shares or assets.*
4.2   Announcements, circulars or shareholders' resolutions required by the listing rules of any relevant securities or stock exchange.
4.3   Statutory requirements for shareholders' or directors' resolutions or approvals for the sale or purchase of shares or assets.*
4.4   Statutory or contractual pre-emption (or 'take (tag) along' or 'piggy-back') rights in favour of other shareholders in relation to either the transfer or the issue of shares.
4.5   Any contracts or agreements which impose a duty to obtain approval from any third party for any change of ownership or the sale of major assets.

5   Restrictions Under Public Law

5.1   Examination of the relevant market(s) to determine anti-trust or competition law implications: the buyer, the seller and the target.
5.2   Nationality of the buyer, the seller and the target for the purposes of the application of foreign investment restrictions.
5.3   Identification of any special or policy-sensitive businesses or assets requiring special government consents (e.g. media, telecommunications, defence, nuclear power or nuclear research, high technology).*

6   Other Restrictions on Transfer

6.1   Restrictions under family law, (e.g. joint matrimonial property).*
6.2   Restrictions arising from guardianship or incapacity (minors, mental illness).*
6.3   Restrictions under the law of succession (inheritance laws, validity of wills, administration of estates, powers of executors or trustees to deal with estate assets).
6.4   Appointment and powers of any receiver or liquidator selling shares or assets.

7   International Aspects

7.1   Registration or operation of the target in other jurisdictions.
7.2   Application of foreign laws in connection with the target (e.g. foreign laws applying to real property, foreign tax or duty laws).
7.3   Liability of buyer under domestic or foreign laws.
7.4   Requirements for visas or residence permits for new owners/managers.

8   The Business

8.1   General description of the target's business.
8.2   Joint-venture, co-operation, profit-sharing or partnership agreements entered into by the target.★
8.3   Contracts between the target and any directors or shareholders, directors' or shareholders' associates or companies in which directors or shareholders or their associates have a material interest.
8.4   Contracts with associated or group companies.
8.5   Consultancy agreements (including agreements with associated companies).
8.6   Contracts with commercial agents, contract dealers or distributors (or under which the target itself acts in that capacity).★
8.7   Agreements with principal clients and suppliers.
8.8   Details of all outstanding tenders or quotations submitted by or to the target.
8.9   Details of the ten largest customers of the business and principal suppliers.
8.10   General terms and conditions of trading (suppliers and customers), and their conformity with current laws.
8.11   Agreements restricting competition, especially agreements which restrict or exclude the target's rights to do business in certain areas, with certain customers, or at certain prices.
8.12   Competition law internal compliance procedures.
8.13   Internal procedures to ensure compliance with the laws under which the target carries on, or is licensed to carry on, its business.
8.14   Contracts granting any trade credit, excluding any customary extension of the terms of payment.
8.15   Statutory or contractual warranties granted by the target.
8.16   Other material agreements or obligations outside the ordinary course of business.
8.17   Outstanding obligations of the target under any agreement for the purchase or sale of shares or assets.
8.18   Details of any contracts which may be terminated as a result of the purchase of the target or the business.
8.19   Details of any obligations which will arise as a result of the purchase of the target or the business (e.g. employee rights).
8.20   Obligations towards public agencies.★
8.21   Effect of transaction on public or private funding (e.g. special rate loan agreements, lease agreements with community or state-owned agencies, regional development grants).

9   Intellectual Property

9.1   Details of all trading names and logos used by the target in connection with its products or services.
9.2   Details of all intellectual property, registered, registrable or unregistered, with details of all applications pending, including:
       9.2.1   patents;
       9.2.2   registered designs;
       9.2.3   trade marks;
       9.2.4   copyright;
       9.2.5   business names;

9.2.6   domain names;
9.2.7   trading or service names;
9.2.8   logos;
9.2.9   licence agreements;
9.2.10 royalty agreements;
9.2.11 confidentiality agreements.

9.3   Details (including expiry dates) of intellectual property rights registered, applied for or claimed in other jurisdictions.

9.4   Licence agreements, development agreements, and other agreements relating to the protection or use of intellectual property.

9.5   Terms of employment agreements, or supplier or sub-contractor agreements, dealing with intellectual property rights.

9.6   Software required by the target for its business:

9.6.1   software developed in-house: applicability of work for hire doctrine in the respective jurisdiction and in all jurisdictions where software is used:
9.6.1.1   payments due to employees;
9.6.1.2   residual rights of employees?

9.6.2   software commissioned by the target: terms of licence to use or evidence of ownership:
9.6.2.1   scope of licence (e.g. site licence, target licence or multi-user licence);
9.6.2.2   exclusivity (assessment of risk that competitors may obtain software);
9.6.2.3   availability of source code;
9.6.2.4   assignability of warranties;

9.6.3   software licensed by third parties, including standard software:
9.6.3.1   is licence expressly transferable?
9.6.3.2   if not, are transfer restrictions enforceable under anti-trust law?
9.6.3.3   do transfer restrictions apply on a transfer of shares (as opposed to asset sale)?

9.6.4   maintenance contracts:
9.6.4.1   is maintenance needed or is documentation sufficient?
9.6.4.2   are rights of modification granted?
9.6.4.3   term of maintenance agreements?
9.6.4.4   risk of unreasonable remuneration claims upon termination?

9.7   Details of all computer hardware used by the target, including relevant installation, supply and maintenance agreements.

9.8   Internal procedures to ensure compliance with third party intellectual property rights.

9.9   Procedures for data security (anti-virus and firewalls) and disaster recovery.

10   Environmental/Safety

10.1   Environmental compliance procedures and manuals.

10.2   Details of any claims made or examinations or enquiries pending or threatened against the target arising out of any pollution of the environment.

10.3   Details of any contamination of any land, water or air occurring at any time caused by the target.

10.4   Copies of all consents, permits, licences and other authorities held by or issued to the target including:*
10.4.1   planning and use approvals;
10.4.2   approvals concerning the erection of buildings, their occupation and use;
10.4.3   licences granted by environmental or pollution control authorities.

10.5 Confirmation that the target has complied with all conditions attaching to consents, permits, licences or other authorities relating to the environment.
10.6 Liability for subsisting or residual pollution.
10.7 Existing or potential liability under environment liability statutes.★
10.8 Claims made or threatened in respect of nuisances, including noise pollution.
10.9 Details of any treatment plant into which sanitary or industrial wastes are discharged.
10.10 Procedures for health and safety of employees in the workplace.★
10.11 Environmental assessments, surveys or reports.

11 Real Property

11.1 Details of all real property: freehold, leasehold or held under tenancy or licence.
11.2 In respect of each property:★
  11.2.1 title details (including lease agreements);
  11.2.2 address and description;
  11.2.3 use/zoning classification;
  11.2.4 mortgages, charges or other encumbrances (including crystallisation provisions);
  11.2.5 where tenanted, full details of tenancy;
  11.2.6 structural or site surveys;
  11.2.7 development agreements;
  11.2.8 building contracts;
  11.2.9 terms attaching to rents payable or receivable;
  11.2.10 details of, and title to, immovable fittings and fixtures;
  11.2.11 other agreements affecting the property.
11.3 Entries in public land registers.★
11.4 Third party interests registered or unregistered.
11.5 Restitution or compensation claims made or in progress.
11.6 Hereditary building rights, lease, tenancy or licence agreements.
11.7 Contracts for the purchase or sale of any interest in real property (including any options held or granted by the target in respect of any real property).
11.8 Agreements to create any tenancy or lease or to terminate any tenancy or lease.
11.9 Building licences or permits and any use restrictions relating to the target's property.
11.10 Details of any default notice received from any third party.★
11.11 Details of any enforcement or compulsory acquisition notices received from any statutory authority.
11.12 Details of any third party (landlord or other) consents required for transfer.★
11.13 Contingent liabilities under leases assigned to third parties.

12 Other Assets

12.1 Interests in shares or convertible securities of other companies.
12.2 Options held by the target to acquire any other shares or assets.
12.3 Material contracts for the purchase of goods or capital assets.
12.4 Details of all lease (finance or operating), hire purchase, instalment purchase or rental agreements relating to the assets of the business.
12.5 The target's assets register.
12.6 Conditions or restrictions relating to the use of assets.
12.7 Liens, charges or encumbrances over assets (including retention of title by suppliers).
12.8 Recent sales of assets at an undervalue or by way of preference which could be avoided under any laws relating to insolvency or creditors' rights.

13   Insurance

13.1   Details of all insurance held by the target, including:
      13.1.1   errors and omissions;
      13.1.2   fire, theft and accident;
      13.1.3   workers' compensation;
      13.1.4   performance or completion risk;
      13.1.5   environmental damage;
      13.1.6   freight and transport;
      13.1.7   export credit insurance;
      13.1.8   employer's liability;
      13.1.9   directors' and officers'
      13.1.10 fidelity;
      13.1.11 occupier's and public liability;
      13.1.12 product liability;
      13.1.13 professional indemnity;
      13.1.14 advertiser liability;
      13.1.15 defamation;
      13.1.16 buildings, plant and contents;
      13.1.17 business disruption;
      13.1.18 warranty liability.
13.2   Details of the target's insurance brokers.
13.3   Confirmation that:
      13.3.1   all premiums have been paid and there are no notices from any insurer to cancel or avoid a policy;
      13.3.2   the insurance coverage is adequate for the target's present operations.
13.4   Risks uninsured, under-insurance, breaches of the conditions of any insurance contract, notices of termination by the insurer of liability or any notice of increase of premiums.★
13.5   Details of all claims made under the target's insurance policies over the last three years or presently contemplated.★

14   Finances and Taxation

14.1   Annual financial statements of the target (balance sheet, profit and loss statement, statement of source and application of funds, cash flow statement) with reports of directors and auditors for the target's last three financial years or since incorporation, if less.★
14.2   Last audit report for the target.
14.3   Correspondence with auditors and auditors' working papers.
14.4   Taxation returns and computations for the target's last three financial years, and details of any tax rulings binding on or affecting the target.★
14.5   Details of open or outstanding tax assessments or claims.
14.6   Monthly management accounts from the last audited accounts date to the present.★
14.7   Budgets, projections and business plans.
14.8   Details of contingent liabilities and guarantees.
14.9   Bank account details and authorized signatories.
14.10   Cash management procedures.
14.11   Copies of all current financing documents including:
      14.11.1 facility agreements;
      14.11.2 loan agreements;
      14.11.3 bill facilities;
      14.11.4 overdraft facilities;
      14.11.5 debt instruments or trust deeds;

14.11.6   interest rate or currency swap or hedge
agreements or arrangements;

14.11.7   material finance and operating leases;

14.11.8   extended trade credit granted to or by the
target.

14.12   Details of all securities given or granted by the target including:

14.12.1   charges;

14.12.2   mortgages;

14.12.3   guarantees;

14.12.4   comfort letters;

14.12.5   warranties and indemnities;

14.12.6   performance bonds;

14.12.7   covenants and negative pledges;

14.12.8   priority and subordination agreements.

14.13   Factoring agreements.

14.14   Details of the terms attaching to all debt securities currently in issue.

14.15   Name and address of the target's accountant and auditor (including authority to release information).

14.16   Amounts due to and from associated companies.

14.17   Agreements for granting loans to the target by any officer or shareholder or by any enterprise or person associated with the target or an officer or a shareholder.

14.18   Agreements for granting loans by the target to any officer or shareholder or to any enterprise or person associated with the target or an officer or a shareholder.

14.19   Tax reference and all relevant registration details (turnover tax, income or corporation tax, value added tax, employee taxation, social security or national health schemes).

14.20   Details of any transactions within the last six years which could have adverse taxation consequences, for example:

14.20.1   transfers of assets to shareholders, directors or associates at an undervalue;

14.20.2   transactions other than in the ordinary course of business;

14.20.3   transactions with associated companies abroad;

14.20.4   value shifting transactions.

15   Personnel, Labour

15.1   Details of all employees and directors (including non-executive directors) including age, date of employment, job description, notice period and salary and benefits, including bonuses, pension benefits and other non-cash benefits.

15.2   Employment or consultancy agreements with members of the board of directors/ supervisory board and all senior executives.★

15.3   Agreements granting profit-sharing or performance-related remuneration or bonuses.

15.4   Standard form employment agreement for employees.★

15.5   Employee handbooks and policy manuals.

15.6   Obligations in respect of social insurance benefits and occupational training (e.g. health, accident, life insurance, national pension contributions, compulsory training and development programmes) including any voluntary schemes.★

15.7   Obligations in respect of annual leave, illness, maternity leave, long service or sabbatical leave.

15.8   Agreements between the target and unions and identification of all recognized or proposed union affiliations.★

15.9   Details of regional or national collective awards or agreements binding on the target.★

15.10   Membership of professional associations.

15.11   Share or stock option or purchase plans or share award or bonus plans implemented or announced.

15.12   Agreements containing restrictive covenants or confidentiality obligations binding on employees.

15.13 Redundancy/retrenchment compensation policies or agreements.

15.14 Details of any agreement to increase salaries or benefits implemented, announced or proposed, or of any recent benefits conferred or announced on a non-contractual or *ex gratia* basis.

15.15 Formal or informal policy for reviews of employee remuneration.

15.16 Details of any dispute, actual or threatened, between the target and any employee applicant for employment, ex-employee or union.★

15.17 Details of any redundancy programme implemented, announced or proposed.

16 Pensions and Superannuation

16.1 Details of all existing or proposed pension schemes and arrangements providing for retirement, death or *ex gratia* pension benefits.

16.2 Details of all scheme documents including the current trust deed and rules, any amendments to the deed and rules, all deeds relating to the removal, addition or substitution of trustees, the principal employer or participating employees, all trustees' resolutions, the explanatory booklet given to eligible employees and scheme members and copies of all announcements to members.

16.3 The latest actuarial report or valuation for each scheme and details of any additional advice received in relation to the scheme since the date of the last valuation.

16.4 The latest accounts for each scheme and the trustees' annual report.

16.5 Insurance policies relating to each scheme.

16.6 A list of all members of each scheme together with their date of birth, current salary, length of service with the company and scheme entry date.

16.7 Details of any early retirement, accelerated, special or enhanced benefits paid in excess of standard entitlements or pursuant to the exercise of a discretion by the scheme trustees or administrators.

16.8 Any certificates evidencing the approved or taxation status of the scheme, together with any notices issued by any statutory or regulatory authority.

16.9 Contributions currently payable by the target, each participating employer and the members, and details of any provision made by, or claim notified to, the target for any underfunding.

16.10 Names and addresses of present trustees of the scheme and the name, address and telephone number of the scheme's actuary.

16.11 Details of any disputes or potential disputes or claims in relation to the scheme either with members, trustees, actuaries or statutory (taxation or otherwise) authorities.

17 Litigation and Other Risks

17.1 Confirmation that the target is not in receivership and no petition has been presented or resolution proposed for winding up the target.

17.2 Details of all actual, pending or threatened actions to which the target is or will be a party (civil law, labour law, administrative law and arbitration proceedings).★

17.3 Details of all criminal proceedings and proceedings arising as a result of administrative or regulatory breaches or offences involving the target or, if connected with the target's business, its directors or employees.

17.4 Infringements of anti-trust law or any notice or other request received by the target from any regulatory body administering anti-trust or competition laws.

17.5 Details of any actual or alleged infringement by:

17.5.1 the target of the intellectual property rights of any third party;

17.5.2 any third party of the intellectual property rights of the target.

17.6 Details of all product liability actions, pending or settled, or product recalls of products still offered by the target, together with any related insurance claims.

17.7 Circumstances known to management which might give rise to litigation.

18   Government/Regulatory

18.1   Details of all government or semi-governmental licences or permits, certificates, authorisations, registrations, concessions or exemptions held by the target.

18.2   Confirmation that the target holds all licences required for the conduct of its business.

18.3   Confirmation that all licences held are in force and no notice of revocation has been given, and that they will not be revoked or affected by the transfer of the target to the buyer.★

19   Other Matters

19.1   Facts or events which will or may have a material adverse effect on the business.

19.2   Investments proposed, implemented or completed.

19.3   Press releases of the target and its associated companies for the last three years.★

19.4   Copies of all notices or reports fled with any relevant securities or stock exchange within the last three years.★

19.5   Procedures for quality protection and quality control including details of any ISO or equivalent standard held.★

19.6   Registration and compliance with data protection or privacy laws.

End Notes

1.2   Germany: the extract from the Commercial Register will also disclose this information.

1.3   USA: also proof of good standing.

2.1   Mexico: plus copy of issued and outstanding share certificates.
        Portugal: special rights attaching to shares will be disclosed by the notarial deed authorising the share issue and the certificate of incorporation.

2.2   Germany: generally only if an *Aktiengesellschaft* (joint stock corporation).

2.3   Portugal: only listed corporations may issue convertible securities.

2.5   Brazil: five-year period preferable.

2.6   Australia, UK: companies do not have power to request details of shares held on trust except in the case of substantial shareholdings in public companies.
        Switzerland: bearer shares not subject to registration.
        Portugal: bearer shares not subject to registration and trusts are not registrable unless the trust is an *usufruto*.

2.15   USA: plus transfer agent.
        Portugal: note also national register of company names.

3.2   USA: plus agent for service of process.
        Portugal: Portuguese companies do not have a statutory secretary.

3.7   Brazil: five-year period preferable.

3.8   Germany: plus rules of procedure for the (optional) advisory board *(Beirat)* if relevant.

4.1   Japan: *kabushiki kaisha*: approval of the board of directors; *yugen kaisha*: approval of a meeting of shareholders.

4.3   Netherlands: even in the absence of a specific statutory requirement, it is generally accepted that the approval of shareholders is required for the transfer of an enterprise as a whole.

5.3   Cf. sections 9, 10 and 12 in Chapter 2 (major legal issues).
        Switzerland: note restrictions under *Lex Friedrich* if target holds Swiss real property.

6.1   Germany: joint marital property, disposition of entire property.
        The Netherlands, Mexico and Portugal: disposal or encumbrance of joint matrimonial property requires consent of both spouses.
        Switzerland: Articles 227, paras' 2 and 653, Swiss Civil Code.

6.2   Germany: contracts by minors or mentally disabled require court approval.

8.2   Portugal: registration of ACE (Complementary Group of Companies) or EEIG (European Economic Interest Grouping) with companies' registrar.

8.6 Italy: plus social security contributions in respect of agents.

8.20 Germany: *Treuhandanstalt* (public trust fund), often stipulates contract penalties to secure promises to invest and job guarantees.
Mexico: commitments imposed on the target by the Foreign Investments Commission.
Netherlands: plus any obligation to repay 'WIR-premiums'.

10.4 Italy: plus details of any amnesties granted or applied for in connection with the erection of buildings.

10.7 Germany: *Umwelthaftungsgesetz.*

10.10 Portugal: plus compliance with compulsory workers' compensation insurance arrangements.

11.2 USA: title insurance is customary and should be reviewed.

11.3 Germany: *Grundbuch.* Switzerland: *Grundbuch.*

11.10 USA: an estoppel certificate should be obtained from each landlord at closing confirming that company is not in default, etc.

11.12 Switzerland: BewG (*Lex Friedrich*).

13.4 Germany: any deviation from the standard insurance model for industry (Article 4, Section 2, *Allgemeine Haftpflichtbedingungen*).

13.5 Brazil: five-year period preferable.

14.1 Brazil: five-year period preferable.

14.4 Brazil and Mexico: five-year period preferable. Italy: plus details of any taxation amnesties applied for or granted. Portugal: plus certificates of good standing for taxation and social security purposes.

14.6 Germany: plus monthly 'BAB'.

15.2 Portugal: plus service agreements (*contrato de comissao de servico*).

15.4 Italy: plus any arrangements for part-time, probationary or trial labour.

15.6 Switzerland: *Bundesgesetz über die Alters- und Hinterlassenenversicherung* (AHV), *Bundesgesetz über die Unfallversicherung* (UVG), *Bundesgesetz über die berufliche Vorsorge* (BVG), *Bundesgesetz über die Arbeitslosenversicherung* (AVIG).

15.8 The Netherlands: plus minutes of works council meetings.

15.9 Germany: plus agreements with workers' council (*Betriebsvereinbarung*). Switzerland: *Gesamtarbeitsverträge.*

15.16 Italy: plus claims filed in connection with redundancy funds legislation (*Cassa Integrazione Guadagni*).

17.2 Mexico: plus federal or *amparo* legislation. Switzerland: plus extract from the debt collections register (*Betreibungsregister*).

18.3 Taiwan: plus samples of the registered chops (seals) of the target and of each of the directors and supervisors and details of their location.

19.3 Brazil: five-year period preferable.

19.4 Brazil: five-year period preferable.

19.5 Brazil: plus copies of licences, permits or registration certificates issued by the competent authority in relation to the products manufactured or distributed by the target.

INDEX